THE CARNEGIE COUNCIL ON POLICY STUDIES IN HIGHER EDUCATION

A Summary of Reports and Recommendations

THE CARNEGIE COUNCIL ON POLICY STUDIES IN HIGHER EDUCATION

A Summary of Reports and Recommendations

Jossey-Bass Publishers

San Francisco • Washington • London • 1980

THE CARNEGIE COUNCIL ON POLICY STUDIES IN HIGHER EDUCATION
A Summary of Reports and Recommendations
The Carnegie Council on Policy Studies in Higher Education

Copyright © by: The Carnegie Foundation
for the Advancement of Teaching

Jossey-Bass Inc., Publishers
433 California Street
San Francisco, California 94104

Jossey-Bass Limited
28 Banner Street
London EC1Y 8QE

Copies of this report are available from Jossey-Bass, San Francisco,
for the United States and Possessions, and for Canada,
Australia, New Zealand, and Japan.
Copies for the rest of the world are available
from Jossey-Bass, London.

Library of Congress Cataloging in Publication Data

The Carnegie Council on Policy Studies in Higher Education.

Includes index.
1.   Higher education and state—United States—
Addresses, essays, lectures.
LC173.C365   1980   378.73   80-7999
ISBN 0-87589-474-7

Manufactured in the United States of America

JACKET DESIGN BY WILLI BAUM

FIRST EDITION

Code 8030

Contents

Foreword

One of the deliberate practices of the Carnegie Council on Policy Studies in Higher Education, and also of the Carnegie Commission on Higher Education, was to issue reports and analyses on various topics when they were of greatest interest and importance. Its findings and recommendations, therefore, became available over a sustained period of time, and in a sequential way, rather than all at once when the work was completed. One consequence of this strategy has been that it is difficult for anyone with an interest in the work of the Council to review its entire effort without access to all of the individual reports. This summary report is intended to overcome that difficulty.

As the title for the volume makes clear, the emphasis will be on the work of the Carnegie Council on Policy Studies in Higher Education, which began in 1974 and concluded its work in January 1980. During that time, the Council issued 15 policy reports and 38 sponsored research and technical reports. Digests of all of these publications are included in this summary report.

Because the termination of the Carnegie Council also marked the conclusion of a dozen years of independent studies of higher education policy that began with the creation of The Carnegie Commission on Higher Education in 1967, our summary report also contains certain information about the work of both the Commission and the Council. Part One, for example, reviews the objectives, strategies, and achievement of both efforts.

The substantive work of the Carnegie Commission on Higher Education is not summarized in this volume, however. Summaries of the Commission's policy reports may be found in *A Digest of Reports of the Carnegie Commission on Higher Education* (McGraw-Hill, 1974), and summaries of sponsored research are available in *Sponsored Research of the Carnegie Commission on Higher Education* (McGraw-Hill, 1975).

In offering the summaries included in this volume, the Council would suggest that two cautions are in order:

1. Because the digests offer only highlights of the full works they represent, readers are encouraged to refer to the original documents before attempting detailed analysis of the information and conclusions reported in the summaries.
2. Because policies of the Council and the Commission may have changed slightly during the period in which they were active, readers should also review all recommendations and conclusions on any given subject before reporting them as final policy of the Council.

Compilation of the summaries included in this report was an enormous task, accomplished only with the cooperation of the many authors and members of our staff who had either written or contributed to the development of the original work. We wish to express our appreciation to all of them for their assistance. The major responsibility for summarizing the reports and working with members of the staff in the preparation of the final manuscript was assumed efficiently, with good judgment, and with the benefit of a detailed knowledge of the work of the Commission and Council by Scott Christopher Wren, who devoted virtually full time to the project in the closing year of the Council's work. We also wish to thank Nancy Blumenstock, Marian Gade, Sean Cotter, Verne Stadtman, and Claudia White for their contributions to the editing and final preparation of the manuscript.

CLARK KERR
Chairman
Carnegie Council on Policy Studies
in Higher Education

THE CARNEGIE COUNCIL ON POLICY STUDIES IN HIGHER EDUCATION

A Summary of Reports and Recommendations

Part One

Charting Higher Education Policy

The Carnegie Policy Series, 1967–1979: Concerns, Approaches, Reconsiderations, Results
By Clark Kerr

The comments that follow are my own reflections on the work of the Carnegie Commission on Higher Education (1967-1973) and the Carnegie Council on Policy Studies in Higher Education (1974-1979). They do not necessarily reflect the views of any other member of the Commission or the Council, although they do draw upon discussion in both bodies and on comments by their individual members.

Concerns

The Carnegie Commission and the Carnegie Council concentrated their attention in six areas:[1]

- *Social justice.* The provision of equal opportunity for talent to be discovered and advanced is a central function of higher education. It was of urgent national importance in the middle 1960s at the time of the civil rights revolt. It will continue to be an urgent matter for at least the duration of this century as minority youth rises to 25 to 30 percent of all youth.
- *Provision of high skills and new knowledge.* A rough balance in the labor market of supply and demand for high skills is essential to the effective operation of society. The Carnegie policy series was concerned with the overall balance of high skills, but particularly, given the period in which it was developed, with surplus facilities for training Ph.D.'s and a deficit of facilities for preparing health care personnel (with a warning in the later years of a potential oversupply of new medical schools). At all times, there was a conviction of the need for adequate and steady support for basic research.
- *Effectiveness, quality, and integrity of academic programs.* In this area, attention was concentrated on basic skills, broad learning experiences, library resources, the role of the performing and creative arts, the place of the new electronic technology, the integration of education with work and service, and the integrity of academic life. Concern was directed toward maintaining diversity among pro-

---

[1]For a series of notes on the history of the Carnegie policy series, see Alan Pifer, "Report of the President," in the *Annual Report of The Carnegie Foundation for the Advancement of Teaching* for the year ending June 30, 1979, and for the year ending June 30, 1970. Brief reviews also appear in the *Annual Reports* for the years 1971 through 1978 (New York: Carnegie Foundation for the Advancement of Teaching).

grams and institutions, partly so as to provide a wide variety of academic opportunities as new kinds of students entered higher education.

- *Adequacy of governance.* The policy reports under this heading were directed to the preservation of the independence of institutions of higher education; to the role of the faculty in governance, including through collective bargaining; to the influence of students and the appropriate channels for its expression; and to the need for effective administrative leadership and the conditions that make it possible.
- *Resources available to higher education.* Attention was directed both toward the human resources of faculty and students, including their changing numbers, characteristics, attitudes, and interests; and toward the financial resources provided from federal, state, and private sources. A special concern was that resources be distributed in such a fashion as to increase the fairness of competition between public and private institutions of higher education.
- *Purposes and the performances of institutions of higher education.* This concern was evident throughout most of the reports of both the Commission and the Council. The main purposes, throughout, were identified as: (1) the education of the individual student and the provision of a constructive environment for developmental growth; (2) advancing human capability in society at large through finding and training talent, developing new ideas, and enhancing understanding; (3) educational justice for the postsecondary age group; (4) pure learning—by supporting intellectual and artistic creativity; and (5) evaluation of society for self-renewal through individual thought and persuasion. The most serious failures of performance during the period of the policy series were found to be (1) the decline of funding for basic research, (2) the inadequate although improving provision of equality of opportunity, and (3) excesses in the methods used by some students and faculty members to criticize the surrounding society. In judging the performance of higher education, we also looked at what happened to individual students as a result of attending college, and at the outcomes or effects of higher education as seen in the attitudes, career choices, lifestyles, and incomes of college graduates.

Attachment A sets forth the policy reports that were devoted, in whole or in large part, to each of these areas of concern. The three areas of greatest concentration were (1) provision of social justice, which reflected both the needs of the times and the intense personal concern of several members of the Commission and later of the Council; (2) financial resources, which involved both the current needs of higher education and the origin of the Commission in an early proposal that the thrust of its effort be directed solely to the subject of financing higher education; and (3) academic programs and content, which constitute the central activity of higher education at all times and in all places.

The earlier reports of the Carnegie series were more heavily directed at reform, which was more possible in a period of growth. The later reports were devoted more toward the maintenance of effort and of contributions, which by then was more in doubt. There was a clear shift in emphasis from new directions in the Golden Age to preservation of long-term values in the Age of Survival.

The sponsored research reports by individual authors have generally concentrated on the same areas of concern as have the policy reports of the Commission and Council, as indicated in Attachment B. There were much fewer such reports under the auspices of the Council, primarily because real resources available to the Council were about one-half those of the Commission.

Approaches

The central goal of the Commission and the Council was to be effective in making public policy toward higher education and private policy within higher education, and effective in increasing understanding of higher education. The Commission, in particular, as it started its operation, spent a great deal of time discussing how to be effective, drawing on the experience of other study groups inside and outside of the area of higher education. The challenge was to be effective while (1) not actually being able to make decisions; (2) not being on the inside of policy-making agencies situated to give direct advice and constantly urge implementation of recommendations; and (3) not being governmental in origin, which might at least have implied endorsement by public authority. Some of the early guidelines and some of the experience accumulated over the years are summarized below.

Be independent and have integrity. The Commission and the Council spoke about higher education from an informed and friendly point of view but did not speak for it. Neither ever acted as a business agent. As a consequence, both the Commission and the Council occasionally took positions quite contrary to those of important organized segments of higher education. The first report, *Quality and Equality,* was a dramatic case. It went against the "united front" of all of higher education—a "united front" forged with great effort. Both the Commission and the Council on occasion made recommendations that they knew in advance would raise opposition. But they did not publicly identify this opposition as such in advance or seek to mollify it—acting instead as though they were innocent of it. They thus dealt with some otherwise "untouchable" topics. A consequence of this general approach was that the reports of the Commission and the Council gained a credibility outside higher education that was quite substantial. A Southern governor (then Governor of Georgia) at a meeting of the Council of Southern Governors once said, and it gained the assent of the other governors, that "the only voice of higher education that we trust is Carnegie." This was an exaggeration, but the sense of public trust was important.

The attitude of the sponsoring organization is important to the opportunity to be independent. The Carnegie Foundation for the Advancement of Teaching at all times and in all ways supported the independence of the Commission and the Council, sometimes in the face of insistent criticism.

Be oriented toward the national welfare first and the welfare of all of higher education second. The reports gained credence, in part, because they were aimed at the advancement of American society through higher education and not the other way around. They also related to the welfare of all institutions of higher education, public and private, two-year and four-year. The effort was to support appropriate roles for each of the segments of higher education and not to advance the cause of one segment against another.

Move ahead of historical events. Neither the Commission nor the Council was inclined just to endorse the status quo. The status quo was not satisfactory and, in any event, was in flux. The conscious effort was to study and to make recommendations about current problems that lacked solutions, and to identify oncoming problems that would need solutions later. The effort was to be somewhat out in front of history but not so far as to be irrelevant to current and approaching concerns. This meant devoting attention to the next few years, but never more than about the next twenty. The most effective reports, generally, were those subject to early action. This mitigated against pie-in-the-sky proposals.

Take time to build a consensus. It was always assumed that reports would be less effective, that the audience or audiences would pay less attention to them, in the absence of internal agreement. The first report, *Quality and Equality,* was discussed at nine separate meetings ending in the "summit session" in Chapel Hill in November 1968. This was a very controversial report, but no member of the Commission later deserted it, even in the face of intense institutional and personal pressure. Most reports were discussed at a minimum of three sessions, and all members participated in the discussion of every report. A final draft was always circulated for detailed suggestions. No member was ever personally urged to sign a report. This was a matter of individual judgment. Signing a report did not mean full agreement with every recommendation or every phrasing in the text. It meant general agreement, and acknowledgment that all points of view had been heard and considered, and that the position of the group as a whole was a reasonable one. There were no dissents and only one abstention in the course of 36 reports. Consensus, of course, only works when the members of the group have similar general goals and compatible approaches to the discussion of problems, and are not committed to the discipline of an outside organization or to using the group as a basis for personal advancement. It also only works when time is available to build personal relations, to create a common fund of knowledge, and to share and react to individual views.

Pay attention to the comments of all members. To begin with, they were mostly helpful—every draft was substantially improved by the comments of the members; and, beyond that, attendance at meetings would only hold up if each member felt a sense of effective participation. Attendance over the course of the 33 meetings of the Commission and the 33 meetings of the Council was phenomenal. Absences seldom numbered more than two or three. Having meetings in interesting and varied places was not only helpful in sustaining attendance but made possible contacts with representatives of local universities and colleges and offered opportunities to hear their concerns and points of view.

The heavy emphasis placed on the views of members, however, was difficult for the staff. Draft after draft was dissected, analyzed, and revised. This not only took staff time and effort but added the frustration of having to accept criticism time after time, to give up cherished positions and phrasings, to submit to new or changed policy positions from meeting to meeting, and then, in the end, to see 19 or 15 other people sign the report. This was very hard for some short-term staff members to take.

Base reports on careful research. It was important to have a solid base of fact, and, when possible, to provide new information. Reports educate as well as recommend. The "Carnegie Shelf" of publications was often looked upon as standing behind the policy reports of the Commission and Council. Careful research lends credibility to reports and affects the whole effort. Congresswoman Edith Green, for example, relied on Carnegie data that was specially supplied at her request when arguing for a legislative proposal that was in complete opposition to the position of the Commission. She said she considered the Commission to be the most reliable and useful source of data she could find. There was one major error, however. It was made in the base for calculating the level of tuition paid in comparison with the policy recommended *(Higher Education: Who Pays? Who Benefits? Who Should Pay?)* and this was later corrected *(Tuition: A Supplemental Statement).*

Concentrate reports on a specific topic or a related series of topics. The alternative to issuing a series of specific reports was one conglomerate report at the end of our work, which was the standard practice in previous reports on higher education. The topic-by-topic approach not only helped us to target audiences, but also made possible an earlier and recurring sense of accomplishment by the Commission and Council members and by the staff, the imposition of intermediate deadlines for completion of work and for publication, the facilitation of topic-by-topic followup, the building along the way of a reputation for issuing useful reports, and the opportunity to imprint more messages in total than would have been possible if many of the messages were lost in the complexity of a single report.

Have an audience in mind for each report in advance. This was a corollary of the last guideline, but it also meant trying to target a report mainly on the federal government, on state governments, on individual institutions, or on other selected audiences, such as the Supreme Court of the United States in the case of *Selective Admissions in Higher Education.* This affected both how the report was written and the followup efforts on its behalf. An illustration of the lack of an audience was the report *Continuity and Discontinuity,* which dealt with relations between secondary and tertiary education—these are two separate worlds, and there are almost no agencies or individuals seeking to draw them together. The failure of that report to gain much attention helped to make the point (though this was, of course, little consolation) that nobody was there to pay attention, and that a great and costly gap existed between the two worlds. One report, *Federal Reorganization,* had an audience, but it opposed formation of a separate Department of Education to which the President of the United States was already committed. Preferably, not only should an audience exist, but it should be potentially both able and willing to act.

Make specific recommendations. This was the suggestion of James Conant, former President of Harvard, who had led a prior study of the American high school for the Carnegie Corporation of New York.[2] He advised that it was better to make a specific recommendation with which people could agree or disagree but at least debate, than to put forward essentially meaningless generalizations about principles or directions of movement or need for further study. Both the Commission and the Council followed this advice throughout. It was not easy. It would have been easier, given the 19 members of the Commission and the 15 members of the Council, to have agreed on more generalized recommendations. It took discipline within the group, a sense of responsibility by individual members, a large measure of good will and sometimes a degree of courage among the members, and always extra time and effort to be specific. Recommendations should be precise and operational in nature. There also should not be too many of them. There was no effort to invent distant and indistinct Utopias.

Have a good title or a tersely worded theme. We discovered over time how important a title was or, in lieu of a title, some quotable phrase that carried the theme. *Less Time, More Options* as a title carried the theme of the report, as did *More than Survival;* and a widely quoted phrase about general education being a disaster area carried our major theme in *Missions of the College Curriculum.* Most readers remember little if anything about a report very long after they have first read or leafed through it. It is the title or the summarizing phrase that often constitutes the remembered message. So it is im-

---

[2]The series included *The American High School Today: A First Report to Interested Citizens* (New York: McGraw-Hill, 1959); *The Child, the Parent, and the State* (New York: McGraw-Hill, 1960); *Recommendations for Education in the Junior High School Years* (Educational Testing Service, 1960); and *Slums and Suburbs* (New York: McGraw-Hill, 1961).

portant to have in mind what that one most important message might be. Controversy and strong statements helped to draw attention to major themes.

Time the issuance of reports carefully. Several reports were timed to come just in advance of decision-making by branches of the federal government, and gained in effectiveness as a consequence. The report on *Higher Education and the Nation's Health* is a good example. It was published just as legislation was being proposed that became the Health Manpower Act of 1971. The report *Dissent and Disruption,* on the other hand, was not as effective as it could have been because it came out after student unrest had suddenly disappeared in 1970 and also because it appeared after the issuance of the Scranton Report, with its similar philosophical approach to operational recommendations *(The Report of The President's Commission on Campus Unrest.* Washington, D.C.: U.S. Government Printing Office, 1970). William W. Scranton, Chairman of the President's Commission, and Kenneth Keniston, a principal staff member, were both members of the Carnegie Commission. The on-going discussion within the Carnegie Commission served as an advance opportunity to discuss the same subject matter as was contained in the Scranton Report. *Faculty Bargaining in Public Higher Education* also lacked effectiveness because it came out at a time of little activity on the bargaining front and followed a great flow of literature on the subject. It also contained contradictory views between the two essays it included and the Council's policy recommendations.

Followup. This meant getting press attention, which often was quite extensive, and getting reports into the hands of people who could act. We were careful at all times to act within the confines of federal laws relating to nonprofit foundations. We found out, however, how crucial it was, with the growing importance of legislative aides and their improved competence, to make contact with them. A carefully developed mailing list was essential. Generally we sent all of our reports to heads of institutions of higher education, and then to selected government officials depending on the nature of the report. We came to realize the essential roles in public policy played by some reporters, by some powerful legislators, by some well-situated staff members in the White House and in governors' offices, and by some top leaders of higher education. Followup began with advance consultation with persons engaged in making policy. But there was much less consultation of this kind than would have been desirable if more time and staff had been directed to individual reports, or if there had been fewer reports. Consultation should relate to problems to be encountered rather than to specific recommendations to be advanced, since consultation on the latter can compromise the independence of the recommending body.

Reconsiderations

In retrospect, both the Commission and the Council had these tendencies:

1. To overestimate the willingness of institutions of higher education and the federal government to entertain and undertake reforms such as:
    *   Introduction of the Doctor of Arts degree *(Less Time, More Options)*
    *   Introduction of the three-year degree, although much use has been made of time-variable degrees, as was also recommended *(Less Time, More Options)*
    *   Utilization of facilities on a year-round basis *(More Effective Use of Resources)*
    *   Creation of Learning Pavilions *(The Campus and the City* and *Toward a Learning Society)*

- The introduction of an urban-grant program paralleling the earlier land-grant approach *(The Campus and the City)*
- The establishment of "middle colleges" *(Continuity and Discontinuity)*
- The integration of the new electronic technology into academic life *(The Fourth Revolution)*
- The creation of a "two-years-in-the-bank" program to provide opportunities for all youths to draw on reserved funds for education, apprenticeship programs, and other ways of preparing for productive lives
- The preparation of Academic Codes of Conduct by colleges and universities *(Reform on Campus* and *Dissent and Disruption)*
- The drastic revision of federal student loan programs and establishment of a National Student Loan Bank *(Quality and Equality* and *Next Steps for the 1980s in Student Financial Aid)*

Some of these suggestions may still be followed. The least likely is the three-year degree, which runs up against both the decline in the level of prior preparation by students entering college and the desire of colleges to maintain, not decrease, enrollment levels.

2.   To have too high expectations, such as expectations for:
- Future enrollment levels, with too little appreciation of the difficulties of drawing additional students from the lower half of the income range even with greatly expanded student aid programs, and too late an understanding of the degree and duration of the decline in the fertility rate *(New Students and New Places* and *More than Survival)*
- Faculty salary levels, which were expected to keep up with the rising cost of living but have failed to do so, as colleges, faced with high inflation and increasing costs of supplies such as fuel, have had to save money by reducing real levels of salaries *(More Effective Use of Resources)*
- Rising real resources expended per student, as happened in the 1960s but did not in the 1970s, to make possible higher-quality programs and to offset the lack of productivity increases in higher education *(More Effective Use of Resources)*.

3.   To underestimate certain forces in American society and in higher education:
- The unwillingness of the middle class to support adequate financial aid for low-income groups without sharing in the subsidies made available
- The impact of hedonism on the willingness of families to sustain the support level of their children in college
- The degree of deterioration of the American high school and of the qualifications of students entering college
- The intensity of the competition between the public and private segments of higher education in some states and at the national level, and even among some public categories of institutions
- The difficulties of overcoming, at the level of higher education, the prior handicaps of many students due to the circumstances of family, community, social class, and early schooling backgrounds
- The reluctance of the federal government to step in and correct clear deficiencies in its programs, particularly in the student loan program and in support for basic research
- The willingness of some institutions of higher education to allow their programs and products to deteriorate in order to survive

●   The rapidity with which demands for equality of opportunity would be replaced by demands for equality of results.

At the same time, however, our high expectations have been fulfilled in the good support given by many states to their systems of higher education, in the ability to adjust and the resiliency of most institutions of higher education in the face of new circumstances, in the responsiveness of women and upper-income blacks to the new opportunities opened up to them, in the return to normalcy of higher education after the shocks of the student revolt of 1968-1970 and of the OPEC crisis of rising costs, in the capacity of the labor market to absorb vast new numbers of young persons including college graduates, in the recovery of public opinion in its comparative support of higher education among the totality of American institutions after the decline at the time of the student revolts, and in other areas.

The overall mistakes of judgment were to be too optimistic about the future, too charitable about the attitudes and performances of some groups of individuals, and too convinced that all problems have reasonable and possible solutions. Yet the Commission and the Council both retained their fundamental beliefs in the long-run values of academic life and in the rising needs of society for better training, better research, better service to society. The convictions of their members, if anything, were intensified.

Results

Results are inherently difficult to estimate when making recommendations. What happened that otherwise would not have happened, or would have happened but at another time or in another way? What that otherwise might have happened did not happen? And was the impact, if any, good or bad? Some reports had little impact. We found the biggest obstacle to gaining results was the inability to make adequate contact with faculty opinion, and much policy is still made by faculties. Numbers were our problem; generally, the fewer the decision-making units, the more effective the reports. There is one federal government; there are 50 states; there are 3,000 institutions of higher education; there are half a million faculty members.

It is particularly difficult for a group to evaluate the results of its own efforts; this is better done, if done at all, by others. (Attachment C sets forth a few evaluations by others of the value of the Carnegie policy series on higher education.) However, it is possible to suggest some categories that might be examined:

1. *Public policy results proximate in time and content.* For example, the Health Manpower Act of 1971 became law after the report on *Higher Education and the Nation's Health* was issued, and included support for an increase by about 50 percent in the number of first-year places in medical schools, for Area Health Education Centers, and for other suggestions, much as recommended. The Higher Education Amendments of 1972 were passed after release of our *Quality and Equality* and included provisions for Basic Educational Opportunity Grants, the Fund for the Improvement of Postsecondary Education, and other programs, roughly as recommended. Shortly after release of a Council report on youth late in 1979, the Administration recommended to Congress a $2-billion increase in expenditures on youth, including $1 billion in funds for secondary schools. These recommendations largely paralleled those in our report *(Giving Youth a Better Chance)*.

2. *Public policy results dispersed in time and in content.* For example, the report on

Open Door Colleges was often cited in state planning documents, and community colleges spread across the nation generally in the form recommended. The report about the colleges founded for blacks, *From Isolation to Mainstream,* which called these colleges a national asset, was widely used by them and their supporters at a time when others were calling them an anachronism in a period of integration. The report on *Selective Admissions in Higher Education* took a position, as did two or three other separately prepared reports, that was subsequently paralleled by the majority position of the Supreme Court in the *Bakke* case.

3. *Introduction of new practices by institutions.* For example, the "stop-out" (a phrase coined by the Commission) spread rapidly and almost universally; time-variable degree programs were extended widely; and the Doctor of Arts degree was adopted by about 40 institutions—all recommended in *Less Time, More Options.* Carnegie proposals may have helped both to call attention to these possibilities and to place a "Good Housekeeping Seal of Approval" on the efforts of those who already wanted to act in these directions.

4. *Early alerts to new problems.* For example, attention was called to the inadequacies of existing student loan programs, beginning with *Quality and Equality* and in a series of subsequent reports. The "reluctant attenders" *(More Effective Use of Resources* and *Reform on Campus)* were identified as a problem at the time of the Vietnam war, and their presence foreshadowed the decline in attendance of majority males after the war was over. One of our reports alerted the nation to unfair practices on campus that were spreading in the face of the selective shortage of students in the late 1970s *(Fair Practices on Campus).* Another outlined the possible impacts of the demographic depression on the internal life of the campus *(Three Thousand Futures).*

5. *Presentation of different points of view.* For example, we urged the view that student unrest in the late 1960s was mainly the result of public policy and especially of the Vietnam war, and not of institutional failures within higher education as the national administration was then contending, and that most students were quite satisfied with their college experience *(Dissent and Disruption* and *Reform on Campus).* The council presented the view that the troubles within higher education in the early 1970s due to restricted finances and to decline in some enrollments were not the end of the world for higher education *(More than Survival),* and that the 1970s were a better decade for higher education than commonly assumed *(Three Thousand Futures).*

6. *Contributions to broader understanding and broader perspectives.* For example, many campus administrators know mostly about their own campuses, and many Carnegie reports informed them as to how their situation related to that of others. Most of higher education concentrates on its own students and not on the problems of youth in general *(Giving Youth a Better Chance).* Most of higher education is concentrated on the immediate moment and a short time horizon ahead, and *More than Survival* and *Three Thousand Futures* sought to extend that horizon.

7. *Extension of the framework for the study of higher education.* For example, we invited scholars from several disciplines (economics, sociology, political science, history) to study higher education, in addition to those drawn from the subject-matter schools and departments of education. Several foreign scholars were also invited to look at American higher education, and American problems and solutions were examined in the international context, as in the area of youth policy (see the publications listed under International Perspectives in Attachment B.)

A network of teachers and scholars who have been associated with the Commission and Council as members, staff, authors, and consultants has emerged and, along with the "Carnegie Shelf" of publications, they have changed teaching and research, as in the case of a new course in American higher education at Harvard that makes extensive use of the Carnegie publications.

8. *Presentation of portraits at moments of time.* The policy reports and the sponsored research studies together provided a wealth of data on higher education in the United States in the important period of the late 1960s and the 1970s. Several special studies gave snapshots of critical aspects of the changes as they were taking place.[3] Especially valuable were the Carnegie surveys of faculty and students in 1969 and 1975-76, which provided information about shifts in attitudes and practices on campuses during the late 1960s and early 1970s.

9. *Provision of new information.* Many policy reports and sponsored research studies provided new information or new ways of looking at old information. Perhaps worthy of special note is the Carnegie Classification of Institutions of Higher Education, now widely used and being perpetuated by the American Council on Education, which is taking it over and will keep it up to date [*A Classification of Institutions of Higher Education* (1973); and *A Classification of Institutions of Higher Education, Revised Edition* (1976)].

10. *Creating a running commentary on developments within higher education.* This commentary sought to rely upon competently analyzed facts, to discuss problems in constructive ways, to avoid apocalyptic judgments, to give a sense of assurance that what was being done was worth doing and had a future, to reaffirm basic academic values, to state that higher education was not just a helpless victim of forces beyond its control, to set a civil tone for argument, to hold out some hopes and set forth many possibilities for action, and to fortify the sense of purpose of higher education. In providing this running commentary, the Commission and the Council helped to set the agenda for discussion within and outside of higher education, and to supply facts, ideas, and analyses for this discussion.

The Commission and the Council ended, as they began, with the belief that an independent, but basically supportive, study of higher education could make contributions to the welfare of higher education and of society; and perhaps also, at least to a modified degree, with the belief that it is better to err—if err one must—on the side of optimism, charitable faith in others, and the availability of at least partial solutions than to err in the direction of pessimism, cynicism, and defeat; and with the belief that a counterbalance was helpful, under the circumstances of the times, to the dominant atmosphere of gloom, criticism, and anticipatory acceptance of failure. Both the Commission and the Council believed that, while higher education needed major reforms, it had many past achievements to its credit and many contributions still to be made in the future; that it was increasingly indispensable to the advancement of the welfare of society. They also acted on the belief that "Nothing great was ever achieved without enthusiasm" (Emerson).

---

[3]These included Blackburn et al., *Changing Practices in Undergraduate Education* (1976); Cartter, *The Ph.D. and the Academic Labor Market* (1976); Cheit, *The New Depression in Higher Education* (1971); Glenny, Shea, Ruyle, and Freschi, *Presidents Confront Reality* (1976); Gross and Grambsch, *Changes in University Organization, 1964-1971* (1974); Hodgkinson, *Institutions in Transition* (1971); Ladd, *Change in Educational Policy* (1970); Ladd and Lipset, *The Divided Academy* (1975); Ladd and Lipset, *Professors, Unions, and American Higher Education* (1973); Riesman and Stadtman, Eds., *Academic Transformation* (1973); Stadtman, *Academic Adaptations* (forthcoming); Trow, *Aspects of American Higher Education, 1969-1975* (1977); and Trow, Ed., *Teachers and Students* (1975).

Attachment A

Carnegie Policy Reports Relating to Major Areas of Concern

The chart on the following pages lists the policy reports of the Carnegie Commission and the Carnegie Council and indicates which areas of major concern each one dealt with.

Social Justice

High Skills & New Knowledge

Effectiveness, Quality & Integrity of Academic Programs

Adequacy of Governance

Human Resources

Financial Resources

Purposes & performance

Carnegie Commission Reports

Quality and Equality, Dec. 1968

A Chance to Learn, March 1970

The Open-Door Colleges, June 1970

Higher Education and the Nation's Health, Oct. 1970

Less Time, More Options, Jan. 1971

From Isolation to Mainstream, Feb. 1971

The Capitol and the Campus, April 1971

Dissent and Disruption, June 1971

New Students and New Places, Oct. 1971

Institutional Aid, Feb. 1972

The Fourth Revolution, June 1972

The More Effective Use of Resources, June 1972

Reform on Campus, June 1972

The Campus and the City, Dec. 1972

College Graduates and Jobs, April 1973

Governance of Higher Education, April 1973

The Purposes and the Performances of Higher Education in the United States, June 1973

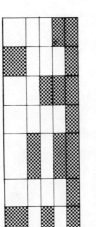

Higher Education: Who Pays? Who Benefits? Who Should Pay?,
   June 1973

Continuity and Discontinuity, Aug. 1973

Opportunities for Women in Higher Education, Sept. 1973

Toward a Learning Society, Oct. 1973

Priorities for Action, Oct. 1973

Carnegie Council Reports

The Federal Role in Postsecondary Education, April 1975

More Than Survival, April 1975

Low or No Tuition, May 1975

Making Affirmative Action Work in Higher Education, Aug. 1975

The States and Higher Education, May 1976

Progress and Problems in Medical and Dental Education, Sept. 1976

Federal Reorganization, April 1977

Faculty Bargaining in Public Higher Education, May 1977

Selective Admissions in Higher Education, Oct. 1977

The States and Private Higher Education, Dec. 1977

Missions of the College Curriculum, Dec. 1977

Next Steps for the 1980s in Student Financial Aid, March 1979

Fair Practices in Higher Education, April 1979

Giving Youth a Better Chance, Nov. 1979

Three Thousand Futures, Jan. 1980

Carnegie-Sponsored Research and Technical Reports Relating to Major Areas of Concern

Historical Perspectives

Centers of Learning: Britain, France, Germany, United States
Joseph Ben-David

American Learned Societies in Transition: The Impact of Dissent and Recession
Harland G. Bloland and Sue M. Bloland

The Useful Arts and the Liberal Tradition
Earl F. Cheit

The American College and American Culture: Socialization as a Function of Higher Education
Oscar Handlin and Mary F. Handlin

Challenges Past, Challenges Present: An Analysis of American Higher Education Since 1930
David D. Henry

Content and Context: Essays on College Education
Edited by Carl Kaysen

Education and Politics at Harvard
Seymour Martin Lipset and David Riesman

Curriculum: A History of the American Undergraduate Course of Study Since 1636
Frederick Rudolph

The Academic Melting Pot: Catholics and Jews in American Higher Education
Stephen Steinberg

The Beginning of the Future: A Historical Approach to Graduate Education in the Arts and Sciences
Richard J. Storr

The Academic System in American Society
Alain Touraine

The Home of Science: The Role of the University
Dael Wolfle

International Perspectives

Any Person, Any Study: An Essay on American Higher Education
    Eric Ashby

American Higher Education: Directions Old and New
    Joseph Ben-David

Centers of Learning: Britain, France, Germany, United States
    Joseph Ben-David

Expanding the International Dimension of Higher Education
    Barbara B. Burn

Higher Education in Nine Countries: A Comparative Study of Colleges and Universities Abroad
    Barbara B. Burn

Education and Youth Employment in the Federal Republic of Germany
    Klaus von Dohnanyi

Youth Education and Unemployment Problems: An International Perspective
    Margaret S. Gordon with a chapter by Martin Trow

Education and Youth Employment in Belgium
    Henri Janne

Education and Youth Employment in Japan
    Hidetoshi Kato

Observations on the Relations Between Education and Work in the People's Republic of China: Report of a Study Group, 1978.
    Clark Kerr, Chairman

Education and Youth Employment in Poland
    Barbara Liberska

Education and Youth Employment in Great Britain
    Stuart Maclure

Education and Youth Employment in Less Developed Countries: Mexico and South Asia
    Alberto Hernández Medina, Carlos Muñoz Izquierdo, and Manzoor Ahmed

An Owl Before Dusk
    Michio Nagai

Education and Youth Employment in Sweden and Denmark
    Gösta Rehn and K. Helveg Petersen

Bridges to Understanding: International Programs of American Colleges and Universities
    Irwin T. Sanders and Jennifer C. Ward

The Academic System in American Society
    Alain Touraine

Educational Leaves for Employees: European Experience for American Consideration
    Konrad von Moltke and Norbert Schneevoigt

Social Justice

Where Colleges Are and Who Attends: Effects of Accessibility on College Attendance
C. Arnold Anderson, Mary Jean Bowman, and Vincent Tinto

Escape from the Doll's House: Women in Graduate and Professional School Education
Saul D. Feldman

Youth Education and Unemployment Problems: An International Perspective
Margaret S. Gordon with a chapter by Martin Trow

Credit for College: Public Policy for Student Loans
Robert W. Hartman

Women and the Power to Change
Edited by Florence Howe

Antibias Regulation of Universities: Faculty Problems and Their Solutions
Richard A. Lester

The Pursuit of Fairness in Admissions to Higher Education*
Winton H. Manning

The Status of Selective Admissions*
Warren W. Willingham, Hunter M. Breland, and Associates

High Skills and New Knowledge

American Learned Societies in Transition: The Impact of Dissent and Recession
Harland G. Bloland and Sue M. Bloland

Trends and Projections of Physicians in the United States
Mark S. Blumberg

Ph.D.'s and the Academic Labor Market
Allan M. Cartter

The Useful Arts and the Liberal Tradition
Earl F. Cheit

Black Elite: The New Market for Highly Educated Black Americans
Richard B. Freeman

Higher Education and the Labor Market
Edited by Margaret S. Gordon

Education for the Professions of Medicine, Law, Theology, and Social Welfare
Everett C. Hughes et al.

Graduate and Professional Education, 1980: A Survey of Institutional Plans
Lewis B. Mayhew

Area Health Education Centers: The Pioneering Years, 1972-1978
Charles E. Odegaard

The Nonprofit Research Institute: Its Origin, Operation, Problems, and Prospects
Harold Orlans

*Originally published as part of the volume entitled *Selective Admissions in Higher Education.*

New Directions in Legal Education
    Herbert L. Packer and Thomas Ehrlich

Demand and Supply in United States Higher Education
    Roy Radner and Leonard S. Miller

Professional Education: Some New Directions
    Edgar H. Schein

The Beginning of the Future: A Historical Approach to Graduate Education in the Arts and Sciences
    Richard J. Storr

The Home of Science: The Role of the University
    Dael Wolfle

Effectiveness, Quality, and Integrity of Academic Programs

The Invisible Colleges: A Profile of Small, Private Colleges with Limited Resources
    Alexander W. Astin and Calvin B. T. Lee

Changing Practices in Undergraduate Education
    Robert Blackburn, Ellen Armstrong, Clifton Conrad, James Didham, and Thomas McKune

Between Two Worlds: A Profile of Negro Higher Education
    Frank Bowles and Frank A. Decosta

A Degree for College Teachers: The Doctor of Arts
    Paul L. Dressel and Mary Magdala Thompson

Colleges of the Forgotten Americans: A Profile of State Colleges and Regional Universities
    E. Alden Dunham

From Backwater to Mainstream: A Profile of Catholic Higher Education
    Andrew M. Greeley

Flying a Learning Center: Design and Costs of an Off-campus Space for Learning
    Thomas J. Karwin

Content and Context: Essays on College Education
    Edited by Carl Kaysen

Models and Mavericks: A Profile of Private Liberal Arts Colleges
    Morris T. Keeton

Change in Educational Policy: Self Studies in Selected Colleges and Universities
    Dwight R. Ladd

The Emerging Technology: Instructional Uses of the Computer in Higher Education
    Roger E. Levien

Breaking the Access Barriers: A Profile of Two-Year Colleges
    Leland Medsker and Dale Tillery

The Rise of the Arts on the American Campus
    Jack Morrison

The Demise of Diversity? A Comparative Profile of Eight Types of Institutions
    C. Robert Pace

Education and Evangelism: A Profile of Protestant Colleges
    C. Robert Pace

Computers and the Learning Process in Higher Education
    John G. Rockart and Michael S. Scott Morton

The Academic Degree Structures: Innovative Approaches–Principles of Reform in Degree Structures in the United States
    Stephen H. Spurr

Academic Adaptations: Higher Education Prepares for the 1980s and 1990s
    Verne A. Stadtman

Educational Leaves for Employees: European Experience for American Consideration
    Konrad von Moltke and Norbert Schneevoigt

Adequacy of Governance

Leadership and Ambiguity: The American College President
    Michael D. Cohen and James G. March

State Officials and Higher Education: A Survey of the Opinions and Expectations of Policy Makers in Nine States
    Heinz Eulau and Harold Quinley

Legislative Issues in Faculty Collective Bargaining*
    David E. Feller and Matthew W. Finkin

Faculty Bargaining: Change and Conflict
    Joseph W. Garbarino

State Experience in Collective Bargaining*
    Joseph W. Garbarino

Presidents Confront Reality: From Edifice Complex to University Without Walls
    Lyman A. Glenny, John R. Shea, Janet H. Ruyle, and Kathryn H. Freschi

Changes in University Organization, 1964-1971
    Edward Gross and Paul V. Grambsch

Professors, Unions, and American Higher Education
    Everett Carll Ladd, Jr., and Seymour Martin Lipset

Managing Multicampus Systems: Effective Administration in an Unsteady State
    Eugene C. Lee and Frank M. Bowen

The Multicampus University: A Study of Academic Governance
    Eugene C. Lee and Frank M. Bowen

The University as an Organization
    Edited by James A. Perkins

May 1970: The Campus Aftermath of Cambodia and Kent State
    Richard E. Peterson and John A. Bilorusky

*Originally published as part of the volume entitled *Faculty Bargaining in Public Higher Education.*

Academic Transformation: Seventeen Institutions under Pressure
    Edited by David Riesman and Verne A. Stadtman

Human Resources

Political Ideologies of Graduate Students: Crystallization, Consistency, and Contextual Effects
    Margaret A. Fay and Jeff A. Weintraub

U.S. Faculty After the Boom: Demographic Projections to 2000
    Luiz Fernandez

Presidents Confront Reality: From Edifice Complex to University without Walls
    Lyman A. Glenny, John R. Shea, Janet H. Ruyle, and Kathryn H. Freschi

Institutions in Transition: A Profile of Change in Higher Education
    Harold L. Hodgkinson

Enrollment and Cost Effects of Financial Aid Plans for Higher Education
    Joseph Hurd

Market Conditions and Tenure for Ph.D.'s in U.S. Higher Education: Results from the 1975 Carnegie Faculty Survey and Comparison with Results from the 1973 ACE Survey
    Charlotte V. Kuh

The Divided Academy: Professors and Politics
    Everett Carll Ladd, Jr., and Seymour Martin Lipset

Professors, Unions, and American Higher Education
    Everett Carll Ladd, Jr., and Seymour Martin Lipset

When Dreams and Heroes Died: A Portrait of Today's College Student
    Arthur Levine

American College and University Enrollment Trends in 1971
    Richard E. Peterson

Demand and Supply in U.S. Higher Education
    Roy Radner and Leonard Miller

Market Conditions and Tenure in U.S. Higher Education 1955-1973
    Roy Radner and Charlotte V. Kuh

Preserving a Lost Generation: Policies to Assure a Steady Flow of Young Scholars Until the Year 2000
    Roy Radner and Charlotte V. Kuh

On Higher Education
    David Riesman

Field Disaggregated Analysis and Projections of Graduate Enrollment and Higher Degree Production
    Christoph von Rothkirch

Education for Employment: Knowledge for Action
    National Academy of Education Task Force on Education and Employment; Clark Kerr, Chairman

Academic Adaptations: Higher Education Prepares for the 1980s and 1990s
    Verne A. Stadtman

Mental Ability and Higher Educational Attainment in the 20th Century
    Paul Taubman and Terence Wales

Aspects of American Higher Education, 1969-1975
    Martin Trow

Teachers and Students: Aspects of American Higher Education
    Edited by Martin Trow

Financial Resources

Costs of Higher Education: An Inquiry into the Educational Expenditures of American Colleges and Universities
    Howard R. Bowen

Efficiency in Liberal Education: A Study of Comparative Institutional Costs for Different Ways of Organizing Teaching-Learning in a Liberal Arts College
    Howard R. Bowen and Gordon K. Douglass

The Finance of Higher Education
    Howard R. Bowen

The Economics of the Major Private Universities
    William G. Bowen

Foundations and Higher Education: Grant Making from Golden Years Through Steady State
    Earl F. Cheit and Theodore E. Lobman

The New Depression in Higher Education: A Study of Financial Conditions at 41 Colleges and Universities
    Earl F. Cheit

The New Depression in Higher Education: Two Years Later
    Earl F. Cheit

Financing Medical Education: An Analysis of Alternative Policies and Mechanisms
    Rashi Fein and Gerald I. Weber

The Venture Capital of Higher Education: The Private and Public Sources of Discretionary Funds
    Martin Kramer

Papers on Efficiency in the Management of Higher Education
    Alexander M. Mood et al.

Resource Use in Higher Education: Trends in Outputs and Inputs 1930-1967
    June A. O'Neill

Sources of Funds to Colleges and Universities
    June A. O'Neill

Alternative Methods of Federal Funding for Higher Education
    Ronald A. Wolk

Purposes and Performance of Institutions of Higher Education

Investment in Learning: The Individual and Social Value of American Higher Education
    Howard R. Bowen

Expanding the International Dimension of Higher Education
    Barbara A. Burn

Estimating the Returns to Education: A Disaggregated Approach
    Richard S. Eckaus

Vocational Education and Training: Impact on Youth
    John T. Grasso and John R. Shea

The American College and American Culture: Socialization as a Function of Higher Education
    Oscar Handlin and Mary F. Handlin

Education, Income, and Human Behavior
    Edited by F. Thomas Juster

Content and Context: Essays on College Education
    Edited by Carl Kaysen

The Future of Higher Education: Some Speculations and Suggestions
    Alexander M. Mood

The University and the City: Eight Cases of Involvement
    George Nash et al.

Recent Alumni and Higher Education: A Survey of College Graduates
    Joe L. Spaeth and Andrew M. Greeley

Higher Education and Earnings: College as an Investment and a Screening Device
    Paul Taubman and Terence Wales

A Degree and What Else?: Correlates and Consequences of a College Education
    Stephen B. Withey et al.

Reference

The Great American Degree Machine: An Economic Analysis of the Human Resource Output of Higher Education
    Douglas L. Adkins

A Statistical Portrait of Higher Education
    Seymour E. Harris

Inventory of Current Research on Higher Education, 1968
    Dale M. Heckman and Warren Bryan Martin

An Inventory of Academic Innovation and Reform
    Ann M. Heiss

Handbook on Undergraduate Curriculum
    Arthur Levine

A Classification of Institutions of Higher Education

A Classification of Institutions of Higher Education, Revised Edition

Attachment C

Evaluations of the Carnegie Commission on Higher Education

There have been several major reviews of the work of the Carnegie Commission, as well as numerous articles about it. Two short evaluations of the work of its successor the Carnegie Council have appeared, but on the whole the Council's policy reports and sponsored research reports await retrospective evaluation, since it has only recently (December 31, 1979) ceased operation. The three major reviews and a number of the articles (chosen for their variety of viewpoints) excerpted here provide some indication of outside reactions to the approaches and impact of the Carnegie policy series.

Major Reviews

A Fresh Look at Higher Education: European Implications of the Carnegie Commission Reports. By Jack Embling. Amsterdam, The Netherlands: Elsevier, 1974.

Mr. Embling has been a senior administrator with the British Ministry of Education/Department of Education and Science and has been active in education at the international level, serving as the United Kingdom's representative on the Education and Science Committees of the OECD and UNESCO for ten years. This volume is an extended essay that presents those elements of the Carnegie Commission's policy reports of direct interest to European readers and suggests what their relevance is to the situation in European countries, particularly Britain.

> The Carnegie Commission adopted a different strategy [than traditional review bodies] by producing, at irregular intervals, reports on specific aspects or problems of higher education. None of the subjects was or is self-contained—aid to students is linked to equality of opportunity, to institutional independence, to economic use of resources, to teaching methods and so on. The strategy adopted by the Commission has therefore had two results. First, their recommendations in successive reports are cumulative and evolving, partly because of the pressure of external events, partly because of developments in the Commission's own thinking; some of the proposals in earlier reports are modified in later ones—which may be disconcerting to the casual reader. Secondly and more deliberately, it amounts to a strategy of gradual penetration with continual reiteration of ideas and recommendations and, hopefully, stronger and stronger impact resulting from greater familiarity and increasing acceptance on the part of the public and interested parties . . . .
>
> The procedure adopted by the Commission of meeting in different places, making themselves accessible to interested parties of all kinds and gleaning information at first hand; their periodic reports which while

aimed primarily at influencing opinion at critical moments, at the same time gave them the chance of testing opinion and learning from it; above all perhaps the simplicity of their reporting and the directness of their recommendations—all these are an immense advance on a similar inquiry in any country and cannot fail to have an impact .

It is not the purpose of this book however to make a general assessment of the work of the Carnegie Commission. It is unlikely that any foreigner could do this for the Commission are truly American, concerned above all with the problems and the future of their own system. They laboured under a strong sense of crisis arising from an extraordinary range of developments—political unrest, financial depression, demographic decline, the painful adjustment to "universal access", labour market uncertainties, the pressing expectations of women and minorities and perhaps above all the loss of confidence in higher education not only among the general public but in the universities and colleges themselves. It is difficult for any outsider to judge whether this gloomy picture is a true image of the present state of higher education in the United States or whether the Commission were unduly pessimistic. If they were, this would in itself be an indication of their very strong commitment to the "virtue" of higher education, its fundamental value and its power.

The Carnegie Commission on Higher Education: A Critical Analysis of the Reports and Recommendations. By Lewis B. Mayhew. San Francisco: Jossey-Bass, 1973.

Mr. Mayhew is Professor of Education at Stanford University and writes from the perspective of a professional in higher education. Each of the chapters in his volume is designed to summarize one of the Commission reports (including sponsored research) and additionally to criticize the reports in the light of generally available knowledge about higher education and to suggest implications for individual institutions, or the entire profession. As to the overall approach of the Commission, Mr. Mayhew notes that

> The Carnegie Commission however has adopted the posture that higher education is a very large, complicated enterprise that can be moved only slowly and with some consensus on the part of the various elements of leadership. Thus most of the Carnegie Commission reports and policy statements are only critical to a degree and generally reflect optimism that some changes can be made. It is as though members of the Commission have agreed not to alienate purposely or to antagonize any major element in higher education in the hope of gaining support for the principal directions of change that the Commission advocates . . . .
>
> The long-term significance of the Carnegie Commission on Higher Education will be dependent in large part on the degree to which the Commission has accurately sensed the direction of educational thinking and has been able to link its recommendations to social tendencies. Influence is thus likely to derive from shaping and giving focus to powerful although sometimes latent social tendencies rather than from creating completely new goals or foci. . . .
>
> In total, the work of the Carnegie Commission on Higher Education must be judged highly successful. The research studies and reports are technically competent and focus on perplexing matters central to higher education. The level of writing and editing is consistently superior to that of most educational writing. The chairman of the Commission has devoted himself assiduously to the dissemination of Commission findings. Virtually

all of the policy recommendations and studies are sophisticated and tuned to prevailing knowledge about higher education. The Commission has avoided dramatic but naive recommendations. The documents will not, therefore, satisfy extreme reformers, but it is possible that a substantial number of Commission recommendations will become operative elements of public policy. The work of the Commission is so nearly definitive that another Commission of similar magnitude is probably not in order for at least another generation.

The College Student and Higher Education Policy: What Stake and What Purpose? By Scott C. Wren. New York: Carnegie Foundation for the Advancement of Teaching, 1975.

Mr. Wren was active as an undergraduate student in student affairs within the University of California and in educational innovations as Director of the Experimental College on the Davis campus. This report, written primarily for student readers, analyzes the major themes of the Carnegie Commission of particular importance and concern to college students.

> I have not attempted to provide my own critique of the Commission's work, but rather have meant this to be a straightforward, resource document for students—leaving the value judgments for each individual to make. Students, like any other group, have a wide range of concerns and there is no one point of view that will be acceptable to all. The Commission's proposals represent one of a number of viewpoints on quite a few issues. I am sure that it is viewed as a very liberal outfit by some, and by others as a mouthpiece for the powers that be. Other groups have strongly held alternative positions on issues discussed herein. The whole question of tuition is a good example. Most student groups disagreed with the Commission's recommendations for moderately increased tuition, arguing that higher education should be a right and therefore ought to be free for every individual.
>
> Thus the main function of this report should be to contribute to an expanded student knowledge base, not only with regard to the Carnegie Commission's specific proposals, but in terms of identifying some of the major educational issues of the times. It is essential, if students are to play an active role in the development and improvement of higher education, to make sure they have full access to the best information available on the problems, resources, and alternatives for meeting present and future educational needs.
>
> But these caveats are not meant to imply that most of the Commission's recommendations are outdated or represent a narrow point of view. Hardly the case; I find myself in agreement with many of its proposals and with others as far as they go. A proposal may be quite helpful on one campus; yet on another the same proposal might be completely innocuous or simply irrelevant. But that is just the point; such things will depend on the nature of your campus. There is no "ideal" in this respect as the types of college campuses should and do vary considerably. So you will have to adapt anything you read in this report to your local conditions.

Articles

A number of observers have evaluated specific parts of the Commission and Council work or have commented upon their impact in journal articles, chapters of books, and book reviews.

Harold L. Enarson, president of a major state university, noted in a review of the Commission's final report, ". . . the Commission is pragmatic to the core. Start with the system, the changing needs of our times, the visible problems that plague us, and then propose steps and solutions at the edge of the possible. All this is a distinct public service. It builds on present strengths. It stimulates our latent idealism for educational change. It presents us with an impressive body of recommendations for an equally impressive catalog of problems.

"It is no small thing to give voice to the best *emerging thought* among the best minds of the land . . . . It is the great triumph of the Commission that it gave us a new agenda."[1]

Eric Ashby, Master of Clare College, Cambridge, a member of the Carnegie Commission and author of one of its commentaries from abroad on United States higher education, wrote the article from which the following extracts are taken in 1971, after the Commission had published nine of its reports and 21 monographs. Thus, it is in the nature of a progress report rather than a final evaluation of work completed.

"The Commission's first concern has been to urge that the inequalities suffered by the present generation should not become the legacy of succeeding generations." But providing access to higher education for all must be accompanied by protection of "the thin stream of intellectual excellence upon which, in the long run, the nation depends for innovation and change. Reconciliation of the autonomous and popular functions of higher education remains a formidable problem for which the Commission still has to find a solution."

Ashby noted that Commission reports were "setting out not just logistics, but a comprehensive philosophy for American higher education." At the time he wrote, "It has yet to be ascertained whether this gigantic mound of evidence can be refined into clear and simple principles for the reform of higher education. There are, in my view, grounds for optimism that the principles will emerge . . . ." However, "Even if no synthesis were to be attempted, the material assembled and published . . . constitutes the most thorough analysis of a nation's higher education which has ever been made. And even if the synthesis . . . fails to lead to reforms in American higher education, it would remain the most massive and courageous effort to plan the future for American youth that any group of men have ever attempted. Many of the Commission's reports and monographs have a relevance far beyond the United States."[2]

After the Commission completed its work in 1973, Ashby wrote another evaluation, this time in response to criticisms that the Commission had not been sufficiently philosophical in its approach to higher education, that it had dealt too much with means and too little with ends. Ashby wrote:

> Five feet of shelf space on my bookshelves; some 80 publications, including 21 reports; that is the visible and physical achievement of the Carnegie Commission on Higher Education. But what does its political and philosophical achievement amount to? Between 1967 and 1973 the Commission subjected American universities and colleges to a more meticulous analysis than any other educational system has ever received.

[1] Enarson, Harold L. "Book review of *Priorities for Action: Final Report of the Carnegie Commission on Higher Education." Journal of Higher Education,* 1974, *45* (4), 311-312.

[2] Ashby, Eric. "The Great Reappraisal." In W. R. Niblett and R. F. Butts (Eds.), *Universities Facing the Future: An International Perspective.* San Francisco: Jossey-Bass, 1972.

Analysis, yes. But what about synthesis? These are the questions which have to be asked, now that the final report of the commission is published.

. . . undoubtedly the Commission concerned itself with means more than with ends, with priorities—as the final report makes explicitly clear— more than with purposes. Reams of print about how to expand the system and how to pay for the expansion; hardly a pamphletful of print about what the system is for.

The reports convey an air of bland consensus. There are two reasons for this. For one thing, the style of an American commission (so unlike an English one) does not permit the spirited note of dissent, the lively minority report, the clever clash of contention, to appear in print.

For another thing, most of the issues tackled in the reports are not contentious anyway. Everyone wants equality of opportunity in education. Everyone wants more diversity. Everyone wants quality to be sustained and options to be maximized. The controversies notorious for elevating the adrenalin level of academics have for the most part been studiously eschewed . . . .

For the reports of the Commission are not philosophical treatises nor were they intended to be. They are frankly political documents. There are lots of things wrong with American higher education, but you cannot put them right by highfalutin' rhetoric, nor by utopian scenarios, nor by doing anything except the dull and pedestrian job of taking institutions as you find them and resigning yourself to the exasperating constraints of the democratic process, working to make these institutions a little more efficient, a little more just, a little more humane.

None of this is heady stuff. You will read the reports of the Commission in vain if you seek the soaring eloquence of Newman or the pungent passion of Flexner, or the bizarre iconoclasm of Ivan Illich.

But congressmen in Washington and representatives in state capitals do not care for eloquence or passion, and as for iconoclasm, they detest it. They want simple homely recipes, acceptable to their voters, for improving the American way of life, and they will not listen to anything else.

It is just these simple recipes which the Commission has given them. The Commission's message, it is true, is entombed in (at a rough guess) some 12 million words which, if Donald McDonald's financial estimate is correct, cost 50 cents a word. But in my view it has been an investment immensely worthwhile. For higher education in America is going to grow in pretty much the shape it has already assumed. Even $6-million worth of Carnegie Commission could not alter its shape or make it into a different creature.

But what the Commission could do, and realized it could do, and has, I think, done, is first, to understand the anatomy and physiology of higher education and second, to prescribe a diet and regimen for it which will in the short run (and nobody knows about the long run) improve its health.[3]

Another British observer, W. Roy Niblett, contributed "A View From Abroad." Niblett, the only holder of a chair in higher education in a British university, criticized the Commission for its emphasis upon the performance of higher education rather than its purposes or content: ". . . it does not inquire into what is meant by quality with a rigor equal to that with which it pursues its inquiries into the quantitative. . . The commissioners re-

[3]Ashby, Eric. "The Carnegie Commission's Snarling Critics: Rebuttal." *Chronicle of Higher Education,* November 5, 1973, p. 10.

main weakest on the philosophical side, strongest on the sociological and in their common sense and grip on the actual." He had special commendation for the sponsored reports of the Commission: "The series of sponsored studies they commissioned is a whole library of literature on higher education, some of which will be conspicuous for a long time. The reports themselves might perhaps be best used for plotting a wise course out of the harbor rather than for setting a clear direction for the long voyage ahead. But then, as the commissioners might retort, it may take 30 years to get out of the harbor."[4]

The 1972 volume in the series *Current Issues in Higher Education* contained several articles about the Carnegie Commission. In "A Reaction to the Commission Recommendations," Richard C. Richardson, Jr., a community college president, noted:

> Any attempt to be objective about the work of the Commission must recognize its significant contributions as well as the constructive influence of the magnitude and visibility of this work during a period of great uncertainty in higher education.
>
> There are also aspects of Commission work which cause me serious concern. Evident throughout are attempts to compromise serious differences of opinion through choice of recommendations and through qualifying these recommendations. While I recognize the practical necessity of such action when dealing with widely divergent interests and concerns, the results often unsuccessfully seek to chart bold new directions while at the same time preserving all of the established practices. Perhaps the greatest problem of this aspect of the effort, in addition to the confusion it causes about what the recommendations actually mean, is the appearance of consensus about issues when none, in fact, actually exists.[5]

Paul C. Reinert, president of a metropolitan Catholic university, stated in his essay in *The Expanded Campus*, ". . . I support the bulk of their recommendations." However, he did say he had a "fundamental dispute with the general stance of the Commission," arising from conflict between the Commission's concern with equality of opportunity and its commitment to diversity among institutions and kinds of education. "It seems to me The Commission is willing to sacrifice the second of these priorities in order to guarantee the first. . . . the Commission wants to make sure that our system of higher education is an effective instrument for social change but in doing so seems willing to let that system lose one of its essential, intrinsic characteristics—its pluralism and diversity."[6]

In the same volume Alan Wolfe, a sociologist, expressed a belief that the work of the Commission suffered from great problems, not so much because of "the actual content of the reports" as "the assumptions underlying them." He thought that the

> most significant. . . problem facing the Commission is its failure to be theoretical, to place things in their political context, to examine causes,

[4]Niblett, W. Roy. "A View From Abroad." *Change,* 1973, *5* (9), 38-44.

[5]Richardson, Richard C. "A Reaction to the Commission Recommendations." In D. W. Vermilye (Ed.), *The Expanded Campus: Current Issues in Higher Education, 1972.* San Francisco: Jossey-Bass, 1972.

[6]Reinert, Paul C. "Pluralism and Diversity in Higher Education." In D. W. Vermilye (Ed.), *The Expanded Campus: Current Issues in Higher Education, 1972.* San Francisco: Jossey-Bass, 1972.

to be historical—in short, to comprehensively analyze what is wrong with higher education. The Commission accepts the present political and economic system as a given and only seeks to tamper with its least essential operations. It never questions whether corporate capitalism will permit a humane educational system and it never examines the reasons for the enormous problems which exist. . . . Given the close corporate connections and ruling-class ties of the Commissioners, it is no wonder they never lay the blame for the problems with capitalism itself or go into great detail about who is responsible for the system's failures. But so long as this bias is present, the issues discussed will only be tangential ones and the remedies suggested will only be temporary.[7]

The sociologist Norman Birnbaum, like Wolfe, criticized the Carnegie Commission for not sufficiently understanding the social context in which higher education functions. He noted that the Commission likened "the educational revolution to the democratic and industrial revolutions that preceded it. But upon examination, this revolution seems to be no more and no less than a considerable growth in formal education. . . . The Commission does not insist upon the analogy to a revolution, nor could it plausibly do so. The burden of its entire analysis is that a nation's education largely depends on its economic and political trends. . . . The Commission, however, overlooks the tension between the economic and political functions of education in a democracy. . . . The two aims are not entirely compatible; political justice and the unlimited growth of American capitalism may be in conflict."

Birnbaum concludes, "I have been unremittingly critical of the commission—but its reports were written to stimulate discussion, and perhaps it can account this response a measure of success. . . . It would be ridiculous to deem the enterprise not worthwhile. The research studies alone constitute a very valuable library on American higher education. The recommendations, flawed as they are from my perspective, do convey major concern for fundamental issues, among them justice, quality, and autonomy in higher education."[8]

George Bonham, publicist and journalist, commended the Commission: "Its work will long be admired for the sheer organizing genius inherent in its prolific output, much of it accomplished with astonishing quality." However, "The great virtue of the Carnegie Commission, which will be largely overlooked, is that it successfully spanned a six-year period of unprecedented debacles, and it maneuvered about these shoals with commendable adroitness. It acted out of higher motives now largely absent from the higher education scene; . . . the Commission's contribution to the general good cannot be overestimated, for between it and most other national initiatives there stands little else."[9]

The most publicized critique of the work of the Carnegie Commission's work was that of the supporter of traditional liberal education, Donald McDonald. He argued that the Commission

decided to do a strictly social science job on higher education—they climbed all over it, counting, measuring, describing, gauging, and projecting enrollment trends, demographic patterns, financing practices,

[7]Wolfe, Alan. "The Carnegie Commission: Voice of the Establishment." In D. W. Vermilye (Ed.), *The Expanded Campus: Current Issues in Higher Education, 1972.* San Francisco: Jossey-Bass, 1972.
[8]Birnbaum, Norman. "The Politics of the Future." *Change,* 1973, *5* (9), 28-32, 34-37.
[9]Bonham, George, "Editorial." *Change,* 1973, *5* (9), 7-8.

student and alumni attitudes, governance procedures, and community relations. In short the Commission spent most of its energy and attention on the arrangements and circumstances of higher education rather than on the education itself. . . . My own major criticism of *The Purposes and the Performance of Higher Education in the United States,* as, indeed, of the Commission's study in general, is that it reveals no coherent theory of the nature of knowledge and higher education. This leads the Commission into at least three serious errors: the confusing of the effects of higher education with its purpose; the grossly oversimplified, and thus misleading, way in which it presents the "contending philosophical views" about education; and the intellectually and operationally unsatisfying way in which it tries to deal with the relationship between the institutions of higher education and society.[10]

A study of blue-ribbon commissions was undertaken by Stanford University, and the results were published by researchers David Longanecker and Patrick Klein. They found that several national commissions' reports lacked impact because of having to compromise to get consensus from their members, thus diluting recommendations to the lowest common denominator. They noted that the Carnegie Commission avoided this fate and suggested two reasons: "First, the membership of the Carnegie Commission was far more homogeneous than that of Filer. And second, the Commission insisted that members reach a true consensus on every major issue. That is, there had to be unanimous agreement on the best alternatives available; they were not satisfied with a majoritarian approach that produced compromise solutions. Because there were really no unreconcilable interests, the process of arriving at a consensus did not dilute the power of the Carnegie prescriptions." They also noted that "only Carnegie Commission reports can be shown to have changed the law," citing Basic Educational Opportunity Grants, the Fund for the Improvement of Postsecondary Education, the Health Manpower Act, and state 1202 commissions. Finally, the authors attempted to account for Carnegie's success, stressing its uniqueness:

> When it arrived on the scene, nothing like it had existed for over two decades. It was well financed, independent of its endowing foundation, and comprised some of the most prestigious figures in higher education. Its program was ambitious. . . . Moreover, the sheer volume, the broad scope, and the overall excellent quality of its research must be largely responsible for its considerable influence on public policy makers and leaders of higher education. It will be some time before another group can match the resources, prestige, and opportunity that Carnegie had in the late 1960s.
>
> One factor in Carnegie's success applies to certain other reports as well. From the outset, Carnegie's intent and strategy were to influence public policy makers. This public effort had two components. First, the Commission tried to secure as much public visibility as possible. . . . But the Commission leadership also was astute in attracting news coverage and in maintaining open lines of communication with the press, holding news conferences throughout the country and making sure that the efforts of the Commission did not go unheralded. . . . Second, Commission members

---

[10]McDonald, Donald. "A Six Million Dollar Misunderstanding." *The Center Magazine,* September/October, 1973.

and staff, including its exceptionally competent chairman, were not reluctant to lobby for their recommendations. They viewed this as a necessary step in bringing each report to its logical conclusion.[11]

Alan Pifer, who headed the foundation sponsoring the work of the Carnegie Commission and Council, came to some conclusions about the Commission's achievements
and impact in 1972. He noted that:

> The most remarkable thing about the Commission, to me, has been its
> capacity to take under review the entire, vast, diffuse enterprise of Amer-
> ican higher education in virtually all of its multifold aspects—aspects as
> varied as functions, structure, governance, relationship to other institu-
> tions and levels of education, demand and access, expenditure, effective
> use of resources, technology, and reform. Conceptually, this has been a
> remarkable feat. The Commission has described and analyzed higher edu-
> cation as this has never been done before and in the process has con-
> tributed enormously to the literature on this subject.
>   I have also been impressed by the general temper of the Commis-
> sion's work, which, it seems to me, has been dispassionate, objective, fair-
> minded, factually based, and imbued with a sense of pragmatic realism.
> Carrying out its study in a period when higher education itself has been
> in a state of turmoil and the object of more public concern than ever be-
> fore in its history, the Commission might easily have joined the chorus
> of emotional critics or die-hard defenders of the academic enterprise.
> But it has resisted these temptations.
>   I have also been pleased by the wide press coverage many of the
> Commission's reports have received and by evidence that they are being
> carefully studied by public officials concerned with higher education,
> by college and university trustees, by presidents and by other adminis-
> trative officers. Little evidence has come to my attention that faculty
> members or students are reading the reports or have much interest in
> them, but I hope I am wrong about this. . . .
>   Lastly, there is the question of the Commission's impact. Some of
> the Commission's recommendations have already been widely influential
> and have clearly affected the development of both public and private
> policies. Other recommendations have provoked extensive discussion
> and debate. The research by specialists and observers that the Commission
> has sponsored, and the work of its own chairman and staff have unques-
> tionably increased the available knowledge about higher education sub-
> stantially. Impact of this kind will be even greater before the Commission
> concludes its work.[12]

More recently, Pifer replied to the many critics who thought the Commission was
too little concerned with the content of the curriculum: " . . . the Commission's work
directly reflected the assignment given to it by the Foundation. In a way the Commission

[11]Longanecker, David A. and Klein, Patrick F. "Why Commissions Miss the Mark." *Change,* 1977,
9 (10), 42-45, 62.

[12]Pifer, Alan. "The Nature and Origins of the Carnegie Commission on Higher Education." Based on
a speech delivered to the Pennsylvania Association of Colleges and Universities, October 16, 1972.

(Reprinted, Carnegie Commission on Higher Education, 1972.)

was a victim of its own output, which was so prodigious it created the impression that the Commission's terms of reference were as broad as higher education itself. Neglect of the curriculum was therefore bound to seem like a failing, although in actuality the Commission had never been asked and had never intended to tackle this subject."

"On balance, the reports issued by the Council have tended to be somewhat longer and more heavily researched than those of the Commission. . . . " However, "It is probably too early to judge the Council's overall record of accomplishment, although clearly several of its reports have been highly influential, and its youth report . . . may well, over time, have a considerable impact on national policy."[13]

As the work of the Council drew to a close, but prior to issuance of its final report, Malcolm Scully, an experienced reporter of the higher education establishment in the United States, attempted an appraisal of the effectiveness of the Commission and Council: "In terms of policy, the Commission and the Council were most successful in influencing the federal government, somewhat less successful with state governments, and least successful with individual campuses. In terms of philosophy, they embody the predominant liberal view that the United States can and should move toward universal access to higher education while maintaining the quality of its advanced institutions. . . . While the Commission and the Council rarely issued reports on broad philosophical questions, they both were concerned primarily with preserving quality while increasing equality, and their recommendations reflect that concern."[14]

When the final report of the Council appeared early in 1980, George Bonham, editor of *Change* magazine, wrote that the Council had "capped and terminated a remarkable record of public service." The shelf of studies produced by the Commission and Council " . . . represents an accumulation of knowledge and projections about the American academy that can only be termed a national treasure. Few other private efforts have applied such intelligence and social thought to a single facet of American life." He noted that the report *Three Thousand Futures* was considerably more optimistic about the future of higher education in the United States than some other predictions, and commented that

> It is better to be bullish, with a wary eye on the realities, than to be overcome by a sense of impending doom. . . . Whatever the outcomes of the two decades ahead, academic professionals will no doubt require qualities of flexibility and imagination that were relatively unnecessary in the growth period just ended. And a sense of optimism will be necessary. America's colleges and universities are better equipped to summon these initiatives because of the work and publications of the Carnegie Commission and Carnegie Council. Whether the Council's projections of future outcomes turn out to be consonant with events is less important than its unique force as an independent and distinguished center of thought that defined the turf and identified priorities.[15]

[13]Pifer, Alan. *Annual Report of The Carnegie Foundation for the Advancement of Teaching, 1978-79.* New York, 1979.

[14]Scully, Malcolm. "After 13 Years, the 'Clark Kerr Era' Draws to a Close." *Chronicle of Higher Education,* February 11, 1980, 5-6.

[15]Bonham, George. "Editorial." *Change.* 1980, *12* (2), 12-13.

Part Two

Policy Reports

The Federal Role in Postsecondary Education:

Unfinished Business, 1975–1980

March 1975

The states have played the major role in the financing of higher education in the past, and they should continue to provide basic institutional support to public colleges and universities in the future. But the principle that the federal government should play an important role in the financial support of postsecondary education also has become firmly established, and there is substantial agreement on the broad purposes for which the federal government should assume special responsibility. These are:

1. To promote equality of opportunity in postsecondary education.
2. To promote scholarship and the advancement of knowledge through support of graduate education and research.
3. To attain a nationwide balance of opportunities to benefit from postsecondary education and from the advancement of knowledge.

In this report we make a number of suggestions as to how the performance of the federal government in these areas can be improved between now and 1980.

Recent Changes in Federal Funding

Between the mid-1950s and about 1967-68 federal funds flowed to colleges and universities in rapidly increasing amounts. However, in terms of constant dollars and as a percentage of the Gross National Product (GNP), federal funds received by institutions of higher education tended to level off after 1967-68 (see Figure 1) as the rate of inflation accelerated.

The same statement cannot be made, however, about total federal expenditures related to postsecondary education, which have risen steadily and substantially in current dollars—reflecting primarily the constant increases in student aid expenditures shown in Figure 2. Such expenditures are not recorded as revenue that comes to institutions from the federal government.

As the number of veterans receiving educational benefits continues to decline as Vietnam War veterans grow older, total expenditures on veterans' educational benefits, at least in terms of constant dollars, will also decrease. We suggest that this decrease be accompanied by an increase in expenditures on other student aid programs.

The present federal share of total public support for postsecondary education is 44.4 percent. Because of inflation, because federal taxes are more progressive than those

Figure 1. Federal appropriations relating to higher education, 1964-65 to 1974-75, and current-fund revenue of institutions of higher education from federal sources, 1953-54 to 1971-72

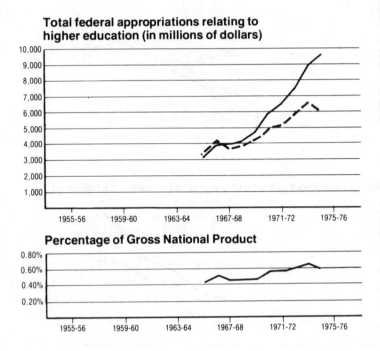

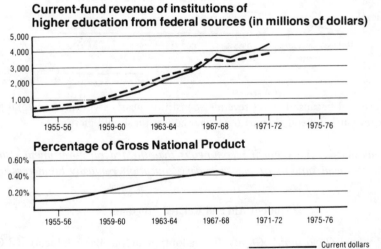

Figure 2. Federal appropriations for selected student aid programs, in current dollars and constant (1967) dollars, 1964-65 to 1974-75

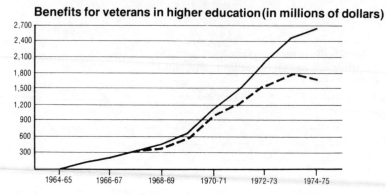

Benefits for veterans in higher education(in millions of dollars)

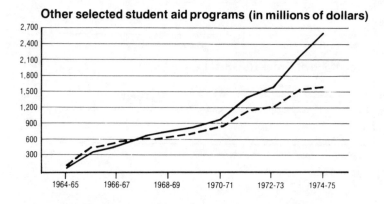

Other selected student aid programs (in millions of dollars)

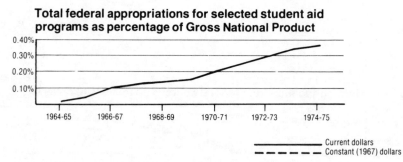

Total federal appropriations for selected student aid programs as percentage of Gross National Product

—————— Current dollars
— — — — — Constant (1967) dollars

of the states, and because federal revenues constitute nearly two-thirds of total governmental tax revenues, federal support for higher education should increase.

Recommendation 1: *The Council recommends that the federal government's share of total public financial support of postsecondary education gradually be increased to 50 percent.*

Student Aid and Related Programs

Basic Educational Opportunity Grants. The adoption of the Basic Educational Opportunity Grant (BEOG) program in the Educational Amendments of 1972 was a major step toward a policy of federal aid to higher education designed primarily to encourage equality of opportunity.[1] Unlike student aid programs adopted before 1972, the grants are awarded directly to students and are based on need.

Ideally, the BEOG program would have the following advantages:

- Encourage free student choice of institution and field of study.
- By emphasizing aid to students rather than aid to institutions, encourage diversity and preserve institutional autonomy and integrity.
- Assist both public and private institutions.
- As an integral part of its contribution to equality of opportunity, ensure a relatively large flow of student aid funds to states and areas that have low per-capita incomes, and to institutions that enroll large proportions of low-income students.

In practice, however, the program has fallen far short of achieving these objectives. Its major weaknesses are:

1. Despite recent liberalizing modifications, the eligibility conditions continue to be very restrictive. As a general principle, a student from a family in the lowest income quartile should receive the maximum grant, about one-half of the maximum grant should be the average received by a student in the second lowest quartile, and some grants should be made under unusual circumstances to students from families in the lower part of the upper half of the income range. The upper boundary of family income in the first quartile in 1974 was about $7,600, the upper boundary of the second lowest quartile was about $12,900, and the upper boundary of the third quartile was about $19,400. But the BEOG program essentially uses the federal poverty line standard for computing discretionary family income, and very little aid is received by students from families with incomes of more than about $9,000.

Recommendation 2: *The eligibility conditions for Basic Educational Opportunity Grants should gradually be liberalized, but only as appropriations increase sufficiently to permit such liberalization without penalizing students in the family income range in which students are currently eligible.*

2. The provision that grants may not exceed 50 percent of the student's cost of attendance is inconsistent with the program's major objectives—to ensure equality of opportunity. This limitation discriminates against students from low-income families who attend relatively low-cost public institutions and students from lower-middle-income families who attend public community colleges.

   The BEOG program should provide only for students' noninstructional costs for the following reasons:

   a. Frequently the only feasible option for low-income students is attendance at a nearby low-cost public college. Their financial need is primarily for non-instructional costs, but the 50 percent limitation typically means that they will by no means be fully covered.

---

[1]For revised recommendations on student aid, see summary of *Next Steps for the 1980s in Student Financial Aid.*

    b.   Noninstructional costs vary little from state to state, whereas tuition and required fees vary widely.

    c.   State policies already subsidize instructional costs either through subsidization of educational costs at public institutions or through scholarship programs to private institutions (frequently in the form of tuition grants).

    d.   Restructuring the BEOG program to provide for noninstructional costs and restructuring other student grant programs—especially the State Student Incentive Grant (SSIG) program—to provide for tuition would create a clear-cut division of function between the BEOG and other student grant programs.

Recommendation 3: *The Basic Educational Opportunity Grant program should gradually be restructured to cover 100 percent of noninstructional costs for students eligible for the maximum grant ($1,600) and lower percentages for students entitled to reduced grants on the basis of their families' contributions. Student aid designed to help students meet instructional costs should be shifted to other programs.*

3.   The funds appropriated for the BEOG program have been seriously inadequate. When the BEOG program was enacted it was intended to be an entitlement program, comparable to veterans' educational benefits or social security, but it cannot function in this way without full funding.

Recommendation 4: *Appropriations for the Basic Educational Opportunity Grant program should be increased over the next several years so that funds will be adequate to ensure that the program meets its objectives and gradually becomes an entitlement program. We estimate that this will require about $2,230 million in constant (1974) dollars by 1979-80.*

Supplemental Educational Opportunity Grant Program. The BEOG program clearly conforms more satisfactorily to the principles that we endorse for federal student aid than does the Supplemental Educational Opportunity Grant (SEOG) program. In particular, the BEOG program is more consistent with the principles of freedom of student choice among institutions and of uniform treatment of all students from comparable family income groups. The Panel on Student Financial Need Analysis (appointed by the College Entrance Examination Board [CEEB]) found that the amount of SEOG aid allocated by individual institutions did not tend to vary with family need.

    The provision of the Educational Amendments of 1972 that no BEOG payments can be made unless the appropriation for SEOG grants amounts to at least $130 million should be removed. We also urge removal of similar requirements relating to the funding of the College Work-Study (CWS) and National Direct Student Loan (NDSL) programs.

    Although the SEOG program should be phased out and replaced by the SSIG program, there is a case for a residual SEOG program, partly because some states may not be induced to take full advantage of the increased grants from the federal government that we recommend for the SSIG program.

Recommendation 5: *The Council recommends the partial phasing out of the Supplemental Educational Opportunity Grant program, along with a major increase in the relative role of the State Student Incentive Grant program. The State Educational Opportunity Grant program should be restructured to cover only instructional costs and to meet more effectively the needs of low- and middle-income students attending moderate- and* *higher priced institutions. Funds available for the program should gradually be reduced from the present $240 million.*

State Student Incentive Grant Program. The Carnegie Council urges adequate funding of the SSIG program for three important reasons.

1. State governments should provide financial aid to private as well as public institutions, and aid to private institutions should take the form of state tuition grant programs.
2. The primary responsibility for planning the future development of higher education should remain with the states, and federal aid should be provided in a form that will involve minimal interference with this traditional state role.
3. In general, the percentage of state personal income expended on higher education varies inversely with the proportion of total state enrollment in private colleges and universities. The SSIG program would induce all the states to increase spending on scholarship programs, while at the same time encouraging states with strong private sectors to use this means of assisting private institutions to compete with public institutions.

If BEOG grants are restructured to cover noninstructional costs, the state undergraduate scholarship programs should be limited to aid for instructional costs. Federal provisions should also recognize that state aid should be available for students attending both public and private institutions. In addition, federal provisions should require that, in order to qualify for matching funds, states should provide scholarships for students attending out-of-state institutions.

Finally, federal matching funds should be made available for increases in state appropriations for scholarship programs from 1969-70 on. This would adjust for the inequality among states that already were spending large sums in 1972-73, the year for which increases in state appropriations would be matched by federal funds.

Recommendation 6: *The funds saved through partially phasing out the Supplemental Educational Opportunity Grant program should be transferred to the State Student Incentive Grant program, and total appropriations for the latter program should be gradually increased, so that combined federal-state expenditures will be adequate to meet the need of low-income and lower-middle-income students for tuition grants by 1979-80. This would require an estimated federal appropriation of about $470 million in constant (1974) dollars by 1979-80.*

Recommendation 7: *The criteria for state scholarship programs to be eligible for federal matching funds should be augmented to provide that (1) state programs should be designed to cover tuition and required fees up to a maximum of $1,500, but not any portion of noninstructional costs; (2) tuition grants should be available for students attending both public and private institutions; (3) students should be permitted to qualify for tuition grants to attend colleges and universities in other states; and (4) federal matching funds should be available for all increases in state expenditures on eligible scholarship programs from 1969-70 on.*

Tuition Equalization Grants. Rising costs and financial stringency have created a very difficult situation for private colleges and universities. They have had to raise tuition sharply to meet accelerated increases in costs. Although the widening tuition gap between private and public institutions (from 4.1 to 1 in 1961-62 to 5.0 to 1 in 1974-75) is probably not the sole reason for sagging enrollment in private institutions, it is widely believed to be a primary one.

Private colleges and universities have played a distinctive role in the development of American higher education and contribute greatly to diversity and flexibility within our system. Their existence provides a strong incentive for public institutions to maintain comparable standards of quality and helps strengthen academic freedom in the public sector. Finally, to the extent that there are social benefits from public subsidization of higher education, the benefits accrue in private, as well as in public, institutions. Therefore, the federal government should take decisive steps to assist the states in their efforts to preserve private institutions. The preferable way is through "Tuition Equalization Grants," which would be provided for students attending private institutions and would equal a certain proportion of the education subsidy per student at a public college or university. They should not equal the entire public subsidy because that practice could create pressures for tuition increases in at least some private institutions.

Equalization grants should be available to all students attending private institutions without a needs test. Low- and lower-middle-income students could also qualify for supplementary tuition grants under the SSIG program.

(It was decided, however, not to include the following recommendation in subsequent Council reports.)

Recommendation 8: *Federal matching funds should be provided for one-half of the cost of a state tuition equalization grants program, which would provide an average tuition grant of about $750 for all undergraduate students attending private colleges and universities. The actual amount of the grant would be set by the states and would represent about one-half of the average educational subsidy per undergraduate FTE (full-time equivalent) student in public four-year colleges and universities in each state. The estimated cost of the federal share is about $675 million in constant (1974) dollars in 1979-80.*

College Work-Study Program. The College Work-Study (CWS) program is a particularly successful form of student aid. But there is impressive evidence that many more students could be employed under the program if appropriations were larger and made at a time when public service employment is being increased. Work-study programs should not be extended, however, to include jobs in private employment, because it would be difficult to prevent employers from replacing nonsubsidized jobs with subsidized ones.

The relationship of the CWS program to other student assistance programs should be carefully reexamined. For example, the tendency of institutions to give more able students relatively more grant aid, as compared with work-study or loans, is regrettable. In contrast, students from low-income families are relatively likely to experience educational disadvantages initially and should receive relatively large amounts of grant aid in the lower-division years. Upper-division students and lower-division students who are educationally well prepared are the ones who should be encouraged first to take part in the work-study program.

Consideration also should be given to a gradual elimination of family income eligibility standards for the CWS program. This would be a particularly appropriate way of making student aid available to students from middle-income families who are now almost entirely excluded from most aid programs.

Recommendation 9: *The annual appropriations for the College Work-Study program should be increased from the $300 million made available in 1974-75 to at least $500 million in 1975-76. Additional increases should be seriously considered in subsequent years if experience indicates that more funds can be advantageously used. We estimate a need for approximately $700 million in constant (1974) dollars by 1979-80.*

Family income eligibility conditions under the College Work-Study program should gradually be eliminated, but only as appropriations increase sufficiently to permit such liberalization without penalizing students in the family income range now eligible for College Work-Study jobs. Colleges should also be encouraged to structure student aid "packages" to provide relatively more grant aid to lower-division students and relatively more work-study assistance to upper-division and graduate students.

In addition, the allocation formula should be revised so that each participating institution receives the same percentage of panel-approved funding as every other.

Student loan programs. We do not subscribe to the view that students capture all or most of the benefits of higher education, but we believe that there are substantial social benefits from higher education that justify substantial public support. Nevertheless, a well-designed loan program is an essential part of a comprehensive student aid program, to enable needy students to supplement the limited aid that can be received in an equitable grant program and to enable students who do not come from needy families to borrow.

No aspect of student assistance is in greater need of major legislative restructuring than provisions relating to student loans. The main weaknesses of the Guaranteed Student Loan (GSL) program are:

1. The inequality of opportunity in a program in which lenders are likely to be influenced by the credit standing of a student's family
2. The necessity for special allocations from the federal government when the interest rate rises above 7 percent
3. The difficulty of ensuring student access to loans in a tight money market
4. The lack of incentive for banks and other lenders to use adequate collection procedures when loans are guaranteed by the federal government
5. A fundamental question as to whether interest subsidies, as opposed to deferral of interest during periods of enrollment, are appropriate
6. The disadvantages of a short repayment period—difficult to avoid when banks predominate among lenders—in view of income and expenditures during the life cycle.

The National Direct Student Loan (NDSL) program presents serious problems in treating different students equitably if it is to exist side by side with the GSL program. Its 3 percent interest rate was appropriate in the late 1950s when the program was adopted, but does it make sense today for some students to be eligible for 3 percent loans while others have to pay well over 7 percent?

Minor improvements will not remove all of these weaknesses in existing programs. Instead, we strongly support a program along the lines of the National Student Loan Bank recommended by the Carnegie Commission, which provides that:

1. The federal government should charter a National Student Loan Bank, a nonprofit private corporation to be financed by the sale of government-guaranteed securities. The bank would be self-sustaining, except for administrative costs and

the cost of cancellations of interest and principal, which would be met out of federal funds.

2. The bank would make loans in amounts not to exceed $2,500 per year up to a total of $6,000 for undergraduate studies and $10,000 for graduate studies.

3. Borrowers would be required to repay loans by paying at least three-quarters of 1 percent of income a year for each $1,000 borrowed until the total loan and accrued interest was repaid. This level of repayment would permit the average income earner to repay his loan in approximately 20 years.

4. Provisions relating to initial repayments after completion of studies and after service in military or national service programs would resemble those in existing legislation. There would also be provision for deferral of payment during any periods of exceptionally low income.

5. The bank would be authorized to enter into an agreement with the Department of the Treasury under which the Internal Revenue Service would undertake all collections.

6. The interest rate charged the student would be set at a level that is adequate to permit the bank to obtain the funds and to cover cost of cancellation upon the death of the borrower.

7. There would be no needs test.

8. There would be no cancellation of indebtedness for entering a particular profession. Any remaining indebtedness would be cancelled upon the death of the borrower or at the end of 30 years from the date of the first payment.

There may be serious obstacles in the path of early adoption of this type of program, but we believe that its many advantages over existing provisions will attract increasing support.

Recommendation 10: *The Council recommends that careful consideration be given to the development of a National Student Loan Bank and to the gradual phasing out of existing federal student loan programs. The possibility of converting the Student Loan Marketing Association into a National Student Loan Bank should be carefully considered.*

Recommendation 11: *Federal legislation relating to the Guaranteed Student Loan program should be amended to discontinue eligibility for participation of students enrolled in postsecondary institutions in states lacking a state-guaranteed loan program after a specified date, for example, July 1, 1978.*

Part-time students. Although provisions of federal legislation relating to the various student aid programs generally allow aid to part-time students on a prorated basis, administrative regulations, notably in the case of the BEOG program, have limited aid to full-time students.

Recommendation 12: *Provisions restricting access to student aid to full-time students should gradually be removed to permit part-time students to be eligible for aid on a prorated basis under all federal student aid programs.*

Cost-of-education supplements. Provision for cost-of-education supplements for colleges and universities enrolling students awarded federal grants were included in Title IV of the Education Amendments of 1972, but these provisions have never been funded. We stress the importance of achieving adequate funding as rapidly as possible. The supplements are appropriate as an instrument of federal financing because they encourage equality of opportunity, for which the federal government has a special responsibility. They are also appropriate because, in contrast with capitation payments, they do not tend to duplicate the types of institutional support provided by state governments and therefore are not likely to induce states to withdraw support. Moreover:

1. Institutions of postsecondary education continue to be faced with financial difficulties that are likely to become more serious as enrollment growth slows down and, in the 1980s, levels off.
2. Cost-of-education supplements aid both private and public institutions in an even-handed manner.
3. Open-access places cannot be successfully implemented without special educational programs to assist students who enter college with inferior preparation. Cost-of-education supplements would play a particularly important role in providing financing for such programs.

Recommendation 13: *Funds should be provided for the cost-of-education supplements adopted under the Educational Amendments of 1972, with annual appropriations gradually rising to about $800 million in constant 1974 dollars by 1979-80.*

Other programs. Five additional federal programs have been quite successful in attaining their objectives and merit continued support.

Recommendation 14: *The Council recommends gradually raising appropriations for: (a) special programs for disadvantaged students, (b) aid to developing institutions, (c) support for cooperative education, (d) ACTION (Peace Corps/Vista), (e) the Fund for the Improvement of Postsecondary Education (FIPSE).*

Improved coordination. Because federal legislation relating to student aid has developed in a piecemeal manner, there are serious inconsistencies among programs. These should be eliminated.

Recommendation 15: *The Council recommends the revision of federal legislation relating to student aid programs to provide for a single set of family income eligibility conditions under all federal student aid programs and also under state scholarship programs receiving matching federal funds through the State Student Incentive Grant program. Federal and state agencies should also cooperate in the development of a single application form.*

Coordinated congressional consideration of appropriations relating to postsecondary education is hampered by the fact that a number of different subcommittees in both the House and the Senate are involved in determining appropriations.

Recommendation 16: *Congressional procedures relating to appropriations should require meetings of the chairmen of all subcommittees concerned with any aspect of postsecondary education before appropriations relating to postsecondary education are finally determined.*

Federal Support of Vocational Education

The immensely important federal role in support of vocational education tends to be ignored. Of the $3 billion total federal expenditures for vocational education in 1973, 28 percent, or $843 million, was expended on postsecondary education programs. The steady expansion in expenditures and enrollments (1.3 million in 1973) has been accompanied by a steady growth in the variety of occupations for which training has been provided.

Recommendation 17: *At a minimum, federal appropriations for vocational education should be steadily increased to meet the needs of postsecondary students. We estimate a need for about $190 million in constant (1974) dollars by 1979-80.*

However, there is also a serious need for more imaginative approaches to vocational education and for more flexible ways of combining education and work experience. As these innovations are developed, the case for more pronounced expansion of vocational education funds may be strengthened.

In the meantime, the Fund for the Improvement of Postsecondary Education (FIPSE) should provide financing for innovative experiments in new ways of combining education and work experience, and the fund's appropriations should be augmented to meet this need.

Recommendation 18: *There is a critical need, in federally sponsored research and data-gathering programs, for more adequate data on both secondary and postsecondary occupational education in all types of institutions offering occupational programs, as well as for much more extensive data on job outcomes for students completing the program.*

Federal Support of Research and Graduate Education

Research. The unique combination of circumstances that was responsible for an increase in total research and development expenditures from 1 to 3 percent of the GNP between 1952 and 1964 is not likely to be repeated in the foreseeable future. However, the critical problems that are clearly emerging in relation to world shortages of energy, raw materials, and foods are creating new needs for research that were not foreseen a decade ago. Thus, we may well be approaching a period in which the case for increasing the proportion of GNP spent on research and development activities is becoming stronger. The complexity of the problems of readjustment facing our society—especially the problems associated with maintaining a reasonable balance between population growth and increased use of resources—calls for steady advances in the social, as well as in the natural, sciences.

Recommendation 19: *Federal funding for research and development activities in colleges and universities should rise at least along with real Gross National Product, and an increased share of those funds should be allocated for research in the social sciences and humanities.*

Graduate education. The cutback in the number of federal fellowships and traineeships has been much too sharp and has been overly influenced by the decline in academic demand for Ph.D. and other doctorates.

The demand for new Ph.D.'s may amount to about 20,000 a year in the early 1980s. In 1970, there were approximately 30,000 Ph.D.'s awarded, and about one-half of these, or 15,000, took jobs in government and industry, while the other half accepted academic jobs. Assuming an annual average growth rate of real GNP of 3.5 percent from 1970 to 1980, and assuming also that the demand for new Ph.D.'s rises with real GNP, the demand for Ph.D.'s in government and industry would rise to about 21,000 by 1980. This estimate can readily be criticized as very rough, but it should suffice for our purposes, because we are seeking to provide a rationale for the number of fellowships and traineeships that should be provided by the federal government. We favor a program of support for the ablest doctoral candidates, on a competitive basis, and we do not believe that such support should be provided for more than about one-fourth of all doctoral candidates.

Federal policy on support of graduate education should not be designed to provide fellowships or traineeships continuously throughout the years of preparation for the doctorate. Rather, it should be assumed that, in most cases, fellows will serve as teaching or research assistants during part of this period.

Needs tests cannot appropriately be used in aid programs for graduate students, because these students are nearly all aged 22 and over and frequently no longer expect support from their parents.

Recommendation 20: *The Council recommends three groups of fellowships and traineeships:*

1.   Merit fellowships available for a two-year period, to be awarded through nationwide competition on the basis of academic excellence, to 5,000 beginning graduate students who are planning to undertake a doctoral program each year.

2.   Predoctoral fellowships available for a two-year period on the basis of demonstrated academic ability for 5,000 graduate students advanced to candidacy for the Ph.D., the Doctor of Arts, or other doctoral degrees.

3.   Traineeships for a total of about 2,000 graduate students at any one time in a limited number of newly developing fields requiring special encouragement.

Recommendation 21: *Fellowships would provide $3,500 annually and would be accompanied by cost-of-education supplements to institutions in the amount of $2,000 for each fellow in the first two years of postbaccalaureate study and of $5,000 for each predoctoral fellow who has been advanced to candidacy for a doctoral degree. Traineeships would also provide $3,500 per full-time graduate student and would be incorporated in training grants providing institutional funds for development of the selected programs.*

The estimated cost of our recommended program of federal support for graduate education would be about $180 million in constant (1974) dollars by 1979-80.

Research libraries. Research and graduate education of high quality require access to large research libraries. Financial stringency and exceptionally rapid increases in costs of library materials have resulted in sharp cutbacks in the funds available to many leading university libraries in recent years in terms of constant dollars.

The case for some degree of federal support of large research libraries is precisely parallel to the case for federal support of research and graduate education, as the states cannot capture all the benefits from their support of such libraries.

Recommendation 22: *The Council recommends a new program of federal support for research libraries, with an initial appropriation of $10 million.*

Conclusion

There are still some eternal purposes, such as equality and progress, to be served by higher education despite current restraints on the availability of funds. The federal government already has made great contributions, particularly in the post-World War II period, to the advancement of these purposes. Further contributions still need to be made and can be achieved at modest, or even no, additional cost in percentage of the GNP.

More Than Survival:

Prospects for Higher Education in a Period of Uncertainty
April 1975

Higher education in the United States is experiencing the greatest overall and long-run rate of decline in its growth patterns in all of its history. It now stands in the fifth broad phase of its development in relation to growth and is facing a sixth. The phases are:

1.   1636-1870 Slow growth
2.   1870-1880 Fast acceleration of growth
3.   1880-1960 Rapid growth
4.   1960-1970 Fast acceleration of growth
5.   1970-1985 Fast deceleration of growth
6.   1985-2000 Slow growth or no growth.

The decline of growth patterns is basically the result of demographic factors, but also of changing national and individual priorities and of shifting demands for college graduates in the labor market.

The consequences of all this is that discourse regarding higher education is couched in terms of survival. For some institutions survival is a crucial issue. But for all of higher education, the challenge is to do more than survive. Much remains to be done both by individual institutions and by public policy to assure universal access to higher education, to enlarge the creative capacity of our society, and to keep institutions vital. The central theme of this report, therefore, is "More than Survival." Great public purposes remain to be served.

Initial Responses to Reduced Growth

We see at least two phases in the future: (1) a period of downward adjustments in growth rates to the early 1980s and (2) a subsequent period of comparative stability of enrollments to 2000. Much of the current anxiety is caused by uncertainty as to when and where the decline of growth rates may end.

Some observers predict that the effects of this period will be wholly beneficial, but these predictions contrast sharply with the responses to reduced growth made by

This volume was originally published as a commentary of the Carnegie Foundation for the Advancement of Teaching.

those who directly confront its early effects. Instead of a more secure community, a Council-sponsored study finds disappointment, conflict, fears of rigidity, and, increasingly, concern about the ability of some institutions to survive. Our own prediction is for a relatively soft landing, not a hard crash. On most campuses the immediate prospect is not one of failure, but of difficult adjustments. These adjustments are likely to be particularly severe for new entrants into the faculty labor market as the demand for new doctoral faculty declines precipitously in the mid-1970s, reaching zero in the mid-1980s.

Adjustment Problems

Because of the decline in growth, problems that might otherwise have been bypassed must now be solved. And because the means to solve or bypass both old and new problems are diminished, an atmosphere of suspicion and conflict has been created. Some of the conflict is caused by attempts to avoid financial rigidity by changing tenure rules, tightening employment practices, and revising budget policies. College administrators predict more centralization of authority; an increase in the number of students per faculty member; and a decline in the quality of programs, students, and, to a lesser extent, faculty.

Most of higher education today faces a declining rate of growth that is not of its own planning and occurs in a short period of time, in an unfavorable economic context, and (some believe) hard on the heels of two decades of underfinanced growth for certain types of institutions. Colleges and universities also are victims of inflation and of the policies used to fight it. And no one claims that universal access is being fully funded.

But beyond these considerations lies the psychology of the total context. The psychology of the growth years was one of expanding opportunity for individuals, even if some institutions were stable in size. Now that psychology has fundamentally changed. When no doors are open, a sense of claustrophobia sets in—and that is a morbid dread for all institutions. Higher education is in the throes of one of its greatest periods of transition.

Past Growth

The present situation is, in part, the product of periods of remarkable expansion. By every relevant measure—students enrolled, campuses built, professors employed, degrees earned, or money spent—the growth has been phenomenal.

The expansion of education in the United States was propelled primarily by three forces. One was the national commitment to expand access to higher education, a goal that was set more than a century ago and has become, in recent years, a dominant factor in public policy. The second was a growing belief that the nation's welfare depends on higher education, not only because expanded enrollment serves social justice and provides an educated citizenry, but also because a capacity for advanced study and research helps the nation meet important needs. A third force has been an increase in the service functions of higher education in many areas—service to agriculture, industry, and the professions; student activities; cultural programs for the community; and adult education, among others.

Since 1970, evidence has been accumulating that higher education is no longer a substantial growth segment of American society. A turning point in college enrollment patterns occurred in 1969, when enrollment rates of young males reached a peak and enrollment rates of young women began to level off.

At least four factors have been significant in the recent decline in enrollment rates among those of traditional college age: (1) the abolition of the draft, (2) the sharply rising costs of college attendance associated with accelerated inflation rates and accompanying increases in tuition and other college charges, (3) changes in the job market for college graduates, and (4) liberalization of college rules to permit students to defer admissions and "stop out" in the midst of college careers. The fact that the sharpest contrast between the pronounced rise in enrollment rates in the 1960s and the decline since 1969 is found among young males suggests that the change in the draft situation is a major influence. Another significant factor has been a leveling off of (and even a slight decline in) the high school graduate rate since the late 1960s. Some institutions are being affected already; even more are concerned for their futures. The direction and rate of change in basic conditions are the overwhelming preoccupations of higher education.

Enrollment Projections, 1975-2000

The level of college enrollment is of crucial concern to many colleges and universities. Enrollments generate income in the form of tuition or subsidies and affect public interest in higher education. Our projections suggest three phases of change in enrollments between now and the year 2000: (1) a slowing rate of enrollment growth; (2) a leveling of enrollment and, perhaps, an absolute decline by the early 1980s; (3) slow growth again after 1995. These Council estimates anticipate a slower rate of declining growth than do most other projections, although they can hardly be called bullish.

Any projection of enrollment must recognize that there are extraordinary uncertainties in the future of higher education. Foremost among these is the state of the economy, but even with reasonable price stability and economic growth, labor market changes could have great effects on enrollments, especially on graduate enrollments, which are particularly volatile. Other uncertainties include possible changes in lifestyles of the young and the impact of a volunteer army.

Changes in the high school graduation rate and the birthrate could be factors. Benefits to veterans will be declining. To offset enrollment decreases caused by such factors, colleges will seek to tap many new pools of potential students: high school seniors, high school graduates who are now nonattenders, college dropouts, potential transfer students from two-year colleges, and adults. Their chances of success are as yet uncertain.

Forecasts for Institutions: A Diversity of Outlooks

The major uncertainty, however, is public policy toward student aid, institutional aid, graduate education, and research. In our base-line projections of enrollment we have assumed no major shifts in public policy, but subsequently we urge that changes be made, and the changes we suggest would significantly alter the projections in this section (see Figure 1).

In 1973, a total of 7.1 million students (full-time equivalent [FTE] basis) were enrolled in over 2,800 institutions of higher education in the United States. This figure is distributed among the six groups of institutions in these percentages:

Universities	33.4%
Comprehensive colleges and universities	33.1
Highly selective liberal arts colleges	2.7
Less highly selective liberal arts colleges	6.9
Public community colleges	22.5
Private two-year colleges	1.4

The projected enrollment in 1985 creates an intricate series of possibilities. We have looked at this uncertain future from six points of view that yield six forecasts:

Forecast 1: Status Quo of Shares. Assumes that each category keeps its 1973 share of students—and that many institutions will be fighting to hold this "share of the market."

Forecast 2: Share Trends of 1963-1973. Assumes that the trends in shares of the period 1963 to 1973 will continue. (The changes were substantial—and many institutions are looking, either with fear or with hope, at the developments of the past decade as indicators for the future.)

Forecast 3: Share Trends of 1968-1973: Assumes that trends in shares of the period 1968-1973 will continue. Since the number and magnitude of factors causing these enrollment shifts were anything but uniform between 1963 and 1973, the effects of more recent changes might be given even greater emphasis with a forecast based on the last five years rather than on the entire ten-year period.

Forecast 4: Four Factors that May Affect Future Enrollment Shares. Assumes that four of the most important factors now at work will continue their differential influences. These are continuing effects of population changes, the market for teachers, increased interest in part-time nondegree credit study, and public policy toward support of private institutions.

Forecast 5: Ability to Make Selective Adjustments. Evaluates the ability of individual institutions to make selective adjustments based on size, location (urban), competitive status, reputation, age, decisions of 1960s, graduate enrollments, health professions, financial conditions, and management attitudes.

Forecast 6: Comprehensive View. Evaluates factors and judgments in forecasts 1 through 5.

On the basis of Forecast 6, we end up with two broad categories of institutions: (1) institutions which, on the average, are likely to do relatively well with their enrollments and institutional health—the public community colleges, the universities, and the more highly selective liberal arts colleges; and (2) institutions which, on the average, are likely to do relatively less well, given the same amount of effort, with their enrollments and institutional health—the comprehensive colleges and universities (particularly the private ones), the less highly selective liberal arts colleges, and the two-year private colleges.

What Institutions Can Do

If and when effective adjustments are made to the new condition of American higher education, they will have been made, in large part, through the efforts of individual institutions, not an abstraction called "higher education." Among the institutional actions we believe to be necessary are analysis and strategic planning to attain flexibility in operations and program offerings; more sophisticated cost-cutting and management; a measure of institutional specialization; and new methods of operating in increasingly competitive markets.

We wish to stress in advance the need for institutions to act on their own behalf: (1) public policy may not develop as favorably as we recommend; (2) even if it does so, there will be some delay; (3) in any event, the prospective enrollments may be at considerably lower levels than we project; (4) even under favorable public policy and enrollment results, most institutions will still be under some pressures; (5) institutions have an obligation to do their best to adapt to the new circumstances and not to depend on public authorities alone to bail them out—in fact, good faith institutional effort is a prior requirement for favorable public response; and (6) in the course of competition, some actions are desirable as a basis for success, even if not needed for institutional survival, and should be undertaken as a matter of course regardless of changes in the external environment.

Strategy: Analysis of Situation and Planned Flexibility

Those institutions facing declining growth, no growth, or actual decline may profit from developing an overall strategy for the new condition, one that projects, realistically, several years into the future and directly questions generally accepted (but often not precisely formulated or heretofore tested) wisdom about the environment of the college (or system), its strengths, weaknesses, and role.

Recommendation 1: *That institutional leaders prepare analyses of their institutions to determine, as accurately as possible, the present situation and the factors shaping the future course. These analyses should be used to inform their colleagues and constituents, and should be part of a larger effort designed to create attitudes receptive to and conditions conducive to change.*

Inflexibility is a major concern of nearly all institutions and systems. Reduction of income growth has already forced cuts and attention to budgeting practices that diminish internal sources of flexibility. Reallocation is the main source of flexibility when income growth ends. But reallocation in a no-growth situation raises issues of centralized planning and authority that are little understood and sometimes feared. Internally, colleges and universities generally are not well suited to the type of decision making required. They developed in a decentralized form and are not organized to express the overall objectives of the campus. Successful reallocation involves peer review and participation, and this is difficult to accomplish. To facilitate adapting existing resources to new needs, we suggest that guidelines for reallocation be developed by boards of trustees and regents.

This type of planning is essential when growth is declining, and it should proceed from a basic reexamination of institutional identity and mission. Program review should shift the burden of defending the status quo to departments. We also suggest:

- Withdrawing funds (perhaps to 3 percent annually) from existing campus programs in their entirety for a self-renewal fund to be directed to new or expanded programs
- The provision of greater incentive for effective use of resources by altering budgetary procedures to induce cost-saving change, giving special attention to the possibilities of permitting departments and schools to carry over from year to year significant proportions of unspent balances in their budgets, and of permitting them to return a portion of the budgetary savings resulting from innovation or investment in more efficient equipment.

We suggest joint public and private approaches for relieving the problems of dwindling growth. Joint efforts to share capacity should be undertaken, and these are likely to be most successful if the initiative comes from the institutions themselves.

Declining growth means declining demand for new faculty and rising fears about the inflexibility of existing faculty and programs. We suggest careful planning in the replacement of faculty in order to avoid rigidity, and thoughtful control over recruitment and promotion. We do not suggest rigid tenure quotas. Instead, we believe that institutions can obtain needed flexibility through such procedures as the following:

- Recapturing for central campus assignment positions vacated through retirement, resignation, or death (but not through denial of tenure status)
- Hiring temporary and part-time members
- Specifying that tenure does not necessarily apply only to an original assignment of specialized field and location
- Making increased use of joint appointments by more than one department
- Seeking persons with subject matter flexibility, and encouraging field shifts through retraining and use of leaves for study
- Providing opportunities for early retirement on a full- or part-time basis.

Recommendation 2: *Each institution, if it has not already done so, should develop an overall strategy for flexibility in the use of funds, assignment of faculty, and utilization of space, and effective processes to make the necessary decisions.*

The prospects for higher education are for more than survival, but both strategic institutional planning and supportive public policy are required to produce the desired results. We emphasize two main points regarding institutional strategies. First, they can make a difference. The responses of institutions will do better in striking a balance between survival and excellence than some critics of higher education are inclined to suggest.

Second, the possibilities for the future that lie in public policy should not lull anyone into the belief that salvation lies there alone. The survival of institutions of higher education and, beyond that, their vitality in a dynamic state depends both on public policy and on what each institution does.

What Public Policy Can Do

There is a significant public stake in the new condition of higher education, because most institutions will be affected, the survival of some institutions is in question, and the ability of all institutions to respond to the new condition depends not only on their own initiatives but also on public policy. The problem is national because enrollment rates, in particular, can be substantially influenced by national public policy.

The complex and varied state and national policy issues can be grouped as follows: (1) providing for universal access; (2) full funding by 1980, achieving universal access by 2000; (3) contributing to the health of the private sector; (4) supporting research capacity; (5) improving teaching in the schools; and (6) retaining conditions that encourage self-help and local initiative.

Universal Access

We define universal access as a condition where (1) all college-age persons are financially able to attend college if they wish to do so, and (2) there are places for them. We do not expect that universal access will lead to universal attendance but, rather, will result in a situation where, by the year 2000, the rate of attendance of 18-24 year olds will be 36 percent as against the current 24 percent (and 42 percent versus 31 percent for 18-21 year olds). This would involve an initial rise by one half in the attendance of young persons from families in the lower half of the income range. The actual results of such a policy are uncertain and should be kept under constant study with new projections as experience warrants them (see Figure 1).

Figure 1. Transition to universal access by the year 2000 compared with base-line and constant 1973 projections, total and full-time equivalent enrollments

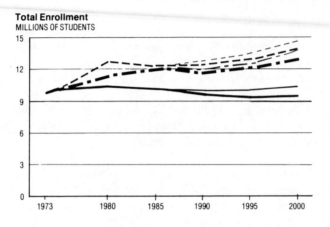

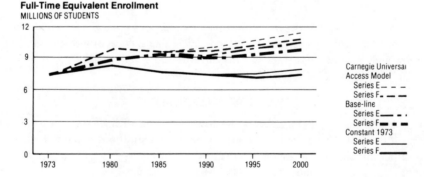

Note: Series E uses population estimates from Census Bureau Series E data, which assume a fertility rate of 2.1. Series F uses population estimates from Census Bureau Series F data, which assume a fertility rate of 1.8.

Recommendation 3: *Public policy should make possible universal access to higher education by the year 2000 for all those who wish to attend, beginning with full funding of existing student access programs by 1980.*

Full Funding by 1980, Universal Access by 2000

In *The Federal Role in Postsecondary Education,* the Council made a number of recommendations that must be adopted if our goal of universal access is to be achieved. (See summary of *Next Steps for the 1980s in Student Financial Aid* for revised recommendations.) The most important of these are as follows:

1. Full funding of the Basic Educational Opportunity Grants (BEOG) and Cost-of-Education Supplements programs by 1980.
2. The BEOG program should gradually be restructured so that the maximum grant equals 100 percent of a student's noninstructional costs.
3. Funds appropriated for the Supplemental Educational Opportunity Grants program should be reduced somewhat, and the amounts should be reallocated to the State Student Incentive Grants program.
4. A new program of federal matching funds for a federal-state Tuition Equalization Grants program should be adopted.

The estimated cost of these increased public expenditures for student aid and educational subsidies is shown in Table 1 and Figure 2. Substantial as the increases are, total public expenditures for these purposes would decline as a percentage of real Gross National Product (GNP). We assume that the real GNP will grow at 3.5 percent per year and enrollment at only 1 percent a year (with costs per student rising, in real terms, 1.5 percent a year).

Our major conclusion is that universal access can be achieved in the United States for all young persons who wish to attend college or university at a reduced percentage of the GNP (after 1980) in terms of public funds (see Table 1) and also in terms of the total expenditures of institutions of higher education from all sources of funds, both public and private (see Table 2).

Table 1. Public expenditures for undergraduate student aid and institutional support for undergraduates, actual, fiscal year 1975, and projected, 1980 and 2000 on the basis of Carnegie Council recommendations, in millions of constant (1974) dollars)

Sources of funds and types of support	1975 actual	Total 1980 Base-line projection	Total 2000 Base-line projection	Total 2000 Universal access projection	Increase over 1975 (rounded) 1980 Base-line projection	Increase over 1975 (rounded) 2000 Base-line projection	Increase over 1975 (rounded) 2000 Universal access projection
Federal government	$ 5,470	$ 6,610	$ 7,350	$ 8,850	$1,140	$ 1,880	$ 3,380
Student aid	5,470	5,840	6,490	7,650	370	1,020	2,180
Cost-of-education supplements	0	770	860	1,200	770	860	1,200
State and local governments	9,110	12,010	17,500	20,270	2,900	8,840	11,160
Student aid	440	1,260	1,400	1,610	820	960	1,170
Institutional support	8,670	10,750	16,100	18,660	2,080	7,430	9,990
Total	$14,580	$18,620	$24,850	$29,120	$4,040	$10,270	$14,540
Percent of GNP	0.97	1.04	0.70	0.82			

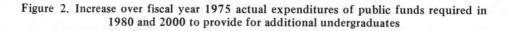

Figure 2. Increase over fiscal year 1975 actual expenditures of public funds required in 1980 and 2000 to provide for additional undergraduates

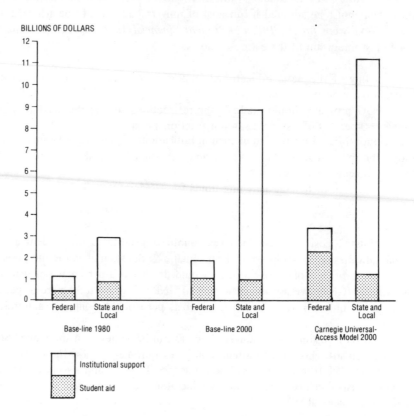

Table 2. Current-funds expenditures of institutions of higher education, estimated, fiscal year 1975, and projected, 2000 (in millions of constant dollars)

		2000		
		Constant enroll-ment rate projection	Base-line projection	Universal access projection
Type of expenditure	*1975*			
Total current-funds expenditures[a]	$30,100	46,400	$56,500	$60,600
Educational and general	25,200	39,300	48,400	51,900
Educational	21,100	29,700	48,700	42,200
Research and related activities	4,100	9,700	9,700	9,700
Auxiliary enterprises	3,300	3,300	4,300	4,900
Major public services	1,600	3,800	3,800	3,800
Percent of GNP	2.1	1.4	1.7	1.8

[a]Does not include expenditures for construction from current funds.

Health of Private Sector

A growing cost-income gap is putting serious pressure on private institutions. Because of a record level of inflation, a large tuition differential between private and public institutions, and a decrease in the level of enrollment in some cases, many private institutions are now operating with costs increasingly out of proportion to income.

We do not recommend "bailing out" all private institutions in financial difficulty, nor do we recommend policies that will shield them from indirect forces. We believe, rather, that (1) each state should provide for the existence of an adequate number of open-access/low-tuition institutions within commuting distance of most citizens, and that (2) beyond this basic provision it should rely on competition for the survival and progress of individual institutions within reasonable financial parameters and fair rules of the game. The private sector should be able to compete mainly on merit. If the policies for funding universal access were adopted, the ability of the private sector to compete would be considerably strengthened, but more than this is needed.

Recommendation 4: *Each state should develop an explicit overall policy toward its private sector under the new conditions of higher education.*

Now that growth is declining, it is important to develop a plan directly for the private sector, taking into account its relationship to the public sector. In states that do not have such a policy, which is most of them, the governor may wish to appoint a special commission to recommend the key elements of such policy as it relates to the special circumstances of each state. Such a policy might include the concept of what percentage of private enrollments are essential to retain the diversity of higher education.

Research Capacity

The United States relies more than any other nation on its universities for its basic research, and its universities have performed at the highest level of competitive competence. The nation also depends on its universities for the advanced training of the scientists who participate in both basic and applied research, whether in higher education, government, or industry. As problems multiply and as their interrelationships intensify, more—not less—research is required. We are particularly disturbed by the implications for the future of recent drastic cutbacks in support of graduate students. We are also disturbed by the declining quality of some university research libraries. Research support should be both more steady and more certain than it has been. It should be attached over the long run to the level of the real GNP and rise with it, or possibly even faster.

Recommendation 5: *The United States should develop a new, long-run policy toward research capacity in its universities.*

Teaching Capacity

We have a surplus of teachers in some areas, but we have a deficit of teaching in many schools, in preschool programs, for dual-language students, and for handicapped students. Many institutions are, understandably, cutting back on their teacher-training activities but may be cutting back too far. Public policies that provide more teachers and related facilities in carefully selected areas can greatly advantage many American youths.

Self-Help and Local Initiative

Steady-state pressures produce two important changes in the governance of institutions of higher learning that affect both their autonomy and the local power of initiative: (1) authority becomes increasingly centralized and (2) additional governing structures and review procedures are created. The main consequence of these changes is that the criteria by which education and its processes are judged are increasingly fashioned by decision makers removed from the campus but who have the power to enforce their judgments.

It is important, first, that the states exercise restraint in the application of their potentially great powers and, to this end, should be prepared to agree with institutions of higher education on the outer boundaries of state control; and second, that coordinating agencies should serve, in part, as a buffer and communicator, protecting the institutions, when necessary, from undue legislative, executive, or public interference in carrying on their educational functions.

To assist institutional coordination, states should provide a data base adequate to help institutions project their enrollments; should require all public and private institutions receiving state aid to undertake reexamination of their missions and develop long-range academic and fiscal plans; and should define the proper parameters for the state coordinative and regulatory role.

Conclusion

Higher education is now having its first sustained experience with deceleration of growth, and it comes right after a period of sharp acceleration of growth. Higher education stands today at a turning point in its history.

The central purpose of our several public policy suggestions is not to aid institutions as such but rather to employ more fully the enormous facilities of higher education, developed over more than three centuries, to achieve greater social justice, to respond to the pluralism of a nation that is a mosaic of religions and cultures, to enlarge the capacity of society to solve pressing problems, and to respond to the special needs of youth so that their welfare and subsequent contributions to society may be improved.

Low or No Tuition:
The Feasibility of a National Policy for the First
Two Years of College
May 1975

The concept of "two years of free access" to higher education in the United States has a long history, dating back to some of the first public junior colleges that were established in the early years of the present century. Also, most state universities and land-grant colleges have had a long tradition of very low or no tuition, from which some of them have departed only in recent years.

Another factor in the growing support for two years of free public education beyond high school has been technological development, which has increased the demand for employees with paraprofessional training in several fields. Increasingly, many high school graduates have not been well equipped to meet the changing occupational requirements they face as adults.

Supporters of two years of low or no tuition also have in mind more general considerations relating to opportunity in postsecondary education. Many lower-division students are uncertain about their probability of succeeding at and, sometimes, even of their motivation or taste for advanced study. They should be given maximum opportunity to try out their chances for successful achievement in the first two years, with a minimal financial burden.

Policies of low or no tuition in the first two years of higher education also have great appeal to those who are concerned with encouraging educational opportunities for adults. For many adults, and especially for married women, student aid under existing policies is not likely to be available, but low or no tuition might mean all the difference in making the option to enroll feasible.

It is important to keep in mind, however, that low tuition policies do not necessarily enable young people from low-income families to enroll in nearby colleges. The problem of meeting subsistence costs and of incidental educational expenses, such as the cost of books, may make it impossible for them to attend in spite of low tuition and easy admissions policies. Thus, low-income youth are likely to need student aid even when low-cost colleges are accessible.

There is, of course, one significant school of thought that opposes the entire concept of low tuition in public higher education. Adherents to this position argue that tuition should be raised to cover total educational costs, so that public subsidies can be more effectively targeted to needy students, and public and private institutions can compete for students and resources on a more even basis. While we appreciate these arguments, we nevertheless believe that implementation of such a policy would force many young people to borrow heavily to achieve their degrees. This would represent a sudden and unfair shift away from the traditional pattern in which the parental generation has financed the education of the college generation.

The difficulties of maintaining low tuition have been exacerbated in the last few years by inflation, which has frequently made it impossible for institutions to meet rising costs without substantial tuition increases. These increases, in both public and private institutions, have played a role in stimulating renewed interest in a possible federal government policy to assist the states in maintaining low tuition in public post-secondary education.

This report is concerned primarily with two questions:

1. What is the likelihood of concerted state action toward low or no tuition in the first two years of college?
2. Should the federal government become directly involved in encouraging low or no tuition policies in the first two years of postsecondary education through a new program of grants either to institutions or to states?

After a careful study of interstate variations in tuition charges in public institutions, we conclude that:

1. Achievement of a national pattern of low or no tuition in the first two years of college through state action alone is improbable, in view of the trend toward rising tuition in public colleges and universities in many states and the growing emphasis on scholarship programs as a means of alleviating the effects of the rising tuition gap between public and private institutions.
2. Achievement of such a pattern through federal action would be very difficult, given the widely differing circumstances among the 50 states.
3. Tuition policy, for this and other reasons, is better subject to state and institutional action, as it has been historically, than to action by the federal government.
4. The federal government, in any event, should give its highest priority to those programs to which it is already committed and which are inadequately funded, and, in some cases, inadequately developed.

Public Two-Year Colleges

A relatively modest objective of proponents of low or no tuition in the first two years of postsecondary education might be to implement such a policy in public two-year colleges. Average tuition and required fees are almost invariably lower in these institutions than in public four-year institutions and much lower than in private colleges. The overall U.S. average tuition in public two-year colleges was $252 in 1972-73. One-sixth of the institutions had zero tuition, and another 65 percent had tuition and required fees of less than $400, while the proportion with tuition and required fees of $400 or more was less than one-fifth of the total. Thus, the cost per full-time equivalent (FTE) student of moving toward very low or no tuition would be much less in two-year public colleges. Moreover, there is widespread acceptance of the idea that public two-year colleges should pursue open-door policies with respect to both tuition and standards of admission.

To develop a proposal to implement a national policy of low or no tuition in public two-year colleges, it is necessary to analyze substantial variations from state to state. Our own analysis of several factors associated with such variations yielded some interesting results:

1. There was no consistent relationship between tuition charges and the percentage of revenue derived from local sources.
2. Tuition levels tended to rise with increasing per capita personal income among the states, but the relationship was not altogether consistent.
3. Tuition and fees tended to vary positively with the percentage of total state enrollment in private institutions (see Figure 1).

Figure 1. Average tuition and required fees in public colleges and universities, by percentage of total state enrollment in private institutions

Two-year colleges, 1972-73

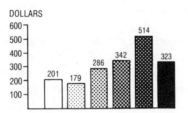

Comprehensive universities and colleges, 1973-74

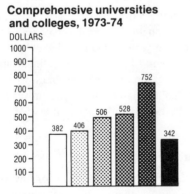

Universities, 1973-74

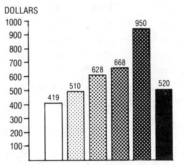

PERCENTAGE IN PRIVATE INSTITUTIONS

0-9   10-19   20-29   30-39   40-49   50 or more

4. There were also regional variations in tuition and fees that tended to be clearly related to percentages of enrollment in private institutions.

There were two main reasons for these last two relationships:

- There is a strong tradition of low tuition in states in which public institutions have been historically dominant.

●   In states with large private enrollments, private institutions have exerted pressure on state government to raise public tuitions.

The probabilities that states might be induced to move toward a nationwide policy of low or no tuition in public two-year colleges in the absence of some type of federal subsidy designed to induce tuition reductions do not appear to be very high. In the great majority of states, tuition and fees at public two-year colleges have been rising, and without federal assistance it is unlikely that they will reverse this trend in the face of costs that can be expected to continue to rise.

Public Four-Year Institutions

Many of the arguments supporting a policy of low or no tuition in public two-year colleges also support a policy of low or no tuition for lower-division students in public four-year institutions—for example, the uncertainty of many students about their probabilities of success in higher education during the first two years, or easing the path of adults desiring to attend.

On the other hand, most private institutions probably would view a move toward a national policy of low or no tuition in the first two years of *all* public higher education with greater alarm than a move confined to public two-year colleges. This is because most private institutions compete more directly with public four-year institutions. Thus, it is likely that a policy of low or no tuition in the first two years of all public higher education would be difficult to implement in the absence of substantially increased aid to private institutions.

In 1973-74 tuition and required fees at public universities averaged $576, and the great majority of these institutions had charges ranging from $400 to $700. Interstate variations are pronounced and reflect some of the same influences that were identified for the two-year colleges, particularly the proportion of total state enrollment in private institutions (See Figure 1). Tuition and required fees tend to be somewhat lower in public comprehensive universities and colleges (state colleges) than in public universities, but the differences are not very pronounced and the factors influencing interstate variations are very similar to those of public universities.

Private Institutions

The problem of implementing a national policy of low or no tuition for lower-division students in private institutions is much more complex than is the case in public institutions, in that tuitions are substantially higher. Average tuition and required fees in private colleges and universities were estimated at $2,095 in 1973-74 by the U.S. National Center for Education Statistics.

Alternative Formulas for Federal Aid to the States

Since it seems highly likely that federal financial support would be needed to bring about a nationwide move toward low or no tuition, several federal aid provisions can be suggested for such a program.

First of all, we would suggest that any federal aid designed to induce lower tuition should flow to the states rather than to individual institutions of higher education. Decisions relating to tuition in public higher education have rested with the states, or have involved some combination of decision making between state and local authorities or boards of trustees. We believe that the intrusion of the federal government into this decision-making process through aid to institutions that would be conditional on lower tuition charges or on maintaining them at existing or lower levels would be undesirable. It could easily lead to greater federal involvement in monitoring costs in higher education—a development that would widely be regarded as a threat to institutional autonomy.

The concerns of colleges and universities about federal monitoring or costs are not rooted in an irresponsible attitude toward their expenditures. The real fear is that federal monitoring could threaten diversity and flexibility, leading perhaps to a deadly uniformity in programs.

Second, because of the substantial variations in average tuition and fees charged from state to state, federal aid should not take the form of reimbursing states for all or any particular share of the cost of reducing tuition. Such an approach would penalize the states in which tuition charges are now zero or very low and reward states in which charges are now high.

This leaves two other types of formulas under which federal aid might be granted for this purpose: (1) capitation payments to states based on FTE enrollment or (2) federal grants-in-aid to states based on formulas that consider such factors as the number of high school graduates, the number of persons aged 18 to 24, and an appropriate measure of state expenditure effort. Either capitation payments or federal grants-in-aid could be made conditional on reducing tuition and fees.

Capitation Payments

During the debates preceding the enactment of the Education Amendments of 1972, capitation payments to institutions of higher education—that is, so many dollars per FTE student—became highly controversial. The Carnegie Commission opposed them for several reasons, but most importantly, for our present purposes, because they would involve the federal government in supporting higher education in the same manner that has traditionally been used by the states. This could lead to efforts by the states to induce the federal government to assume a steadily rising proportion of total support.

Capitation payments to states for the specific purpose of inducing tuition reductions would not involve the same dangers as across-the-board institutional payments for several reasons: (1) they would flow to states rather than to institutions and would be conditional on tuition reductions and possibly other policy changes, and (2) they could be adopted only for a temporary period while such changes were being carried out, although on this basis, of course, the states and local jurisdictions would ultimately have to bear the total cost of tuition reductions.

However, in analyzing the probable effects of capitation grants, we are led to the somewhat paradoxical result that states with the highest tuition charges would be least likely to participate in the program. This is probably an inevitable result of the need for even-handed federal treatment of the states in a situation in which states and local districts have widely differing tuition policies. In other words, the higher average charges in a state, the larger the amounts per FTE student that would have to be raised from state or local sources, and the more likely would be a decision on the part of the state not to participate in the tuition-reduction program.

Grants-in-Aid

Some advocates of low tuition in public higher education believe that the survival of private institutions is in jeopardy and that decisive moves should be made to strengthen their financial position. However, they tend to oppose any move to improve the relative position of private institutions by reducing the tuition gap, arguing that private institutions should, instead, receive increased public subsidies. A federal program of grants-in-aid to the states might be designed to accomplish three major objectives.

1.   Lowering tuition in the first two years of public higher education, and perhaps providing capitation grants to private colleges equivalent in dollar amount to tuition reductions in comparable public institutions
2.   Pursuing policies designed to ensure that a certain proportion, say one-third, of all student places conformed to open-access criteria
3.   For states that ranked below the average for the nation on the basis of an objective measure of state expenditure effort, adopting a financial plan that would induce those states to increase the proportion of personal income spent on post-secondary education.

However, we have seen that states with relatively high tuition levels in public higher education also tend to be states that fall below the national average on measures of expenditure effort, and that these tend to be states with comparatively high proportions of enrollment in private higher education. Thus, some of these states would probably not participate in the federal program because of the problems they would face in financing both the required tuition reductions and the required increases in state expenditure effort.

Conclusion

The prospects for state action to lower tuition in the first two years of public higher education *without federal assistance* are not promising. Although federal government assistance designed to induce tuition reductions would be influential, there is no magic formula that would achieve a uniform national policy and at the same time maintain equitable treatment of the states and preserve their historical role in decisions about tuition and related financing matters.

Our analysis suggests the desirability of further exploration of federal grants-in-aid to the states, but tends to underscore advantages of funding existing cost-of-education supplement provisions of the Education Amendments of 1972 as a means of aiding both public and private institutions.

Making Affirmative Action Work in Higher Education:

An Analysis of Institutional and Federal Policies with Recommendations
August 1975

Nondiscrimination in employment, promotion, and pay is a high national priority in higher education, as in other segments of American society. However, the historical record of many institutions of higher education in employing, promoting, and paying women and members of minority groups has been grossly inadequate in this regard.

Sustantial progress has recently been made, but affirmative action is needed to overcome the residue of a past record of discrimination, which was partially purposive and partially inadvertent. It will be necessary until a better record of nondiscrimination has been established—until there is no discrimination on the basis of sex, race, or ethnic origin, and discrimination only on the basis of ability and contribution to institutional needs. Affirmative action does not mean entitlements to proportional representation. It means actions to eliminate discrimination: creation of more adequate pools of talent, active searches for talent wherever it exists, revision of policies and practices that permit or abet discrimination, development of expectations for a staff whose composition does not reflect the impacts of discrimination, provision of judicial processes to hear complaints, and decision making without improper regard for sex, race, or ethnic origin.

We are now in a transition period between past deficiencies of major proportions and future achievement of true equality of opportunity. There are at least two tragedies involved in this transition period:

- That it should be necessary at all. Higher education, in keeping with its own principles of finding and rewarding merit wherever it might exist, should have been searching more actively long ago for merit among women and minorities.
- That it should take place in the 1970s and beyond. The 1960s saw a doubling of faculty members. The 1980s may even see a slight decline. The effort at redress of past errors comes 10 years too late to be easily effective.

Theme Number One: *Colleges and universities are increasingly assuming and should continue to assume the initiative in securing equality of opportunity in higher education.*

A great individual and organized institutional effort has been mobilized with federal prodding. The next stage calls for more action by higher education itself and less by government. This does not mean that a federal presence should not be maintained for some time to come. It should be, but its role should be increasingly supplemental.

This assumes (1) that institutions now making progress will continue to do so and (2) that the number of institutions that do not follow a progressive course will be relatively small.

As they assume,primary responsibility, institutions should be sure they:

- Have a carefully developed affirmative action plan and the administrative and advisory mechanisms to make it work
- Make annual public reports on progress
- Actively recruit women and minorities into the pool of names considered for openings
- "Select the most qualified candidate" as federal policy now requires, regardless of race, sex, or ethnic origin
- Provide fair procedures for processing complaints.

Theme Number Two: *The supply aspects of the equality of opportunity effort are now generally more important than the demand aspects.*

Demand for faculty members encourages an increase in the supply of new Ph.D.'s. But there are also other steps needed to increase supply, such as better financial support for low-income students in college and for graduate studies. The supply gap for women is smaller than it is for minorities and is easier to fill, because the problems of origins in low-income families and of other sources of deprivation are less universal.

Theme Number Three: *A better distribution of women and minorities among institutions and among fields of specialization and ranks is badly needed, even though there appears to be no overall demand gap.*

Theme Number Four: *Efforts at "fine-tuning" by the federal government can lead to ludicrous results and can be counterproductive.*

We recognize the strong desires of those who wish to eliminate every potential pocket of discrimination on campus, however small, and to give a chance to every disadvantaged group, however miniscule its contribution to a pool of qualified persons. Unfortunately, the smaller the pocket and the smaller the pool, the smaller the chance of drawing someone from the pool to place in the pocket in the name of parity. The federal government should allow institutions of higher education to exercise their best judgments in individual cases; to concentrate more on fair processes than on statistical projections.

Theme Number Five: *Goals, broadly defined as to academic units included and groups covered, and timetables should be continued during the current transition period as part of the federal affirmative action program.*

We define a goal as the object to which effort or ambition is directed. Goals are not quotas. Quota means the part or share of a total that belongs, is given, or is due to one.

We define timetable as a statistical forecast of the expected date by which a goal might be met, or of when a nondiscriminatory result might be obtained. Meeting such forecasts should be viewed not as a certainty but as a probability within fairly wide margins of error. There are two reasons for this "probability approach": (1) the data on which the forecasts are based are often inadequate and always out of date and (2) the competition among institutions for scarce personnel may make the supply situation quite erratic.

Theme Number Six: *The federal affirmative action program is confused, even chaotic, and should be brought quickly into closer conformance with good governmental practices.*

Theme Number Seven: *Compliance should rest on persuasion in the vast majority of cases, and on punishment that fits the crime for the small minority.*

We favor maximum use of internal grievance procedures to settle individual cases. This will avoid overburdening the courts and federal agencies.

We favor a series of penalties to fit the nature and degree of noncompliance. As a first step, simply declaring an institution out of compliance, and nothing more, would set powerful internal and external forces at work to bring about corrections. The atomic bomb of total withdrawal of contract funds should be reserved for serious cases of noncompliance.

Women and Minorities on Faculties—Recent Changes

During the rapid enrollment growth of the 1960s, women lost relative ground on faculties of four-year colleges and universities, except at the instructor level (see Table 1). This reflects, in part, the heavy emphasis on childbearing and childrearing immediately after World War II. Fewer women prepared for entry to the academic labor market. Under the impact of affirmative action, the women's movement, and other forces that encouraged more women to seek Ph.D.'s, this trend has been reversed in the early 1970s. Increases in the proportion of women among faculty members have continued at the instructor level, but they have also occurred at a significant rate at the assistant professor level, where, by 1974-75, the percentage of women was well above the level of the early 1960s. The trend has also been reversed at the associate and full professor levels, but the proportions of women at these levels had not reached those of 1959-60 by the 1974-75 academic year.

Table 1. Women as a percentage of faculty members in four-year colleges and universities, by rank, 1959-60 to 1974-75

Faculty rank	NEA data[a]			NCES data[a]	
	1959-60	*1965-66*	*1971-72*	*1972-73*	*1974-75*
All ranks	19.1%	18.4%	19.0%	20.6%	22.0%
Professor	9.9	8.7	8.6	9.4	9.4
Associate professor	17.5	15.1	14.6	15.8	16.2
Assistant professor	21.7	19.4	20.7	23.1	26.3
Instructor and other	29.3	32.5	39.4	43.5	47.6

[a]National Education Association and National Center for Educational Statistics data.

The familiar pattern of relatively small percentages of women in universities, intermediate proportions in other four-year institutions, and largest proportions in two-year colleges has not been altered by the gains of recent years (see Table 2). Moreover, except in two-year colleges, recent gains have been largely confined to the instructor and assistant professor level. This is to be expected, because most hiring is done at those levels, and it takes time for changes in sex ratios to be reflected at high levels.

Table 2. Women as a percentage of full-time faculty members, by rank and type of institution, 1972-73 and 1974-75

Type of institution and rank	1972-73	1974-75
All institutions	22.3%	24.1%
Professors	9.8	10.3
Associate professors	16.3	16.9
Assistant professors	23.8	27.1
Instructors and other	38.0	39.4
Universities	16.4	18.5
Professors	6.3	6.3
Associate professors	12.5	13.3
Assistant professors	19.8	23.9
Instructors and other	44.4	46.4
Other four-year institutions	23.4	25.0
Professors	12.5	12.9
Associate professors	18.1	18.7
Assistant professors	25.1	28.1
Instructors and other	43.1	45.5
Two-year institutions	32.9	33.3
Professors	22.1	24.8
Associate professors	25.0	24.9
Assistant professors	31.9	34.4
Instructors and other	35.9	34.9

Minority groups have been much more sparsely represented on faculties than have women, and data relating to them are considerably less adequate.

Degree Recipients

Data on recipients of master's and doctor's degrees play an important role in federal guidelines for the determination of "availability pools" in affirmative action programs. Following a drop after 1930 and slow gains from 1950 to 1970, the proportion of women recipients of doctoral degrees rose rapidly from 1970 to 1973 (see Table 3).

Table 3. Women as a percentage of total recipients of doctoral degrees, selected years, 1900 to 1973

1900	5.8%
1910	9.9
1920	15.1
1930	15.1
1940	13.0
1950	5.7
1960	10.5
1970	13.3
1973	18.0

Note: The actual peak in the relative representation of women among recipients was during World War II, but this reflected the drop in male recipients during those years.

Information about the proportion of minority group members among doctorate recipients has been available only in very recent years, and the deficiency of information is still very serious. Although minority groups form a very small proportion of doctorate recipients, they have recently been increasing in number.

How do pools of qualified women and minorities compare with their "utilization"? Majority women have probably received 16 to 17 percent of all doctor's degrees awarded to majority U.S. citizens, on the average, between 1968 and 1973. This can be compared with the proportion of majority women (about 18 percent in 1974-75) among ladder faculty members to have Ph.D.'s). On an aggregative national basis, therefore, it might be said that majority women are not underutilized on faculties of four-year colleges and universities.

Even so, if majority women are ever to reach a proportion of professional faculty members in four-year colleges and universities corresponding to their percentage of majority persons in the labor force—currently about 38 percent—their representation among recipients of doctor's degrees will have to increase by a very large amount. We may characterize the difference between these figures (19 percent of doctor's degrees in 1973 and 38 percent of the labor force) as the overall "supply gap" in relation to the employment of majority women in professional ranks in four-year institutions.

The situation for minorities is also most serious on the supply side, although data for precise comparisons are insufficient. Increasing the supply of doctorate recipients among women and minorities calls for a concentrated national effort, especially among minority groups, whose members often have relatively poor preparation and difficulties financing prolonged graduate or professional education.

Recommendation 1: *All institutions of higher education with doctoral and professional programs should include within their affirmative action plans a "supply plan," that is, a plan designed to provide maximum opportunities for women and minorities to participate on a basis of equal opportunity in graduate and professional education.*

The plan should ensure not only that there is no discrimination on the basis of race, national origin, or sex in admission to graduate and professional schools, or in the administration of financial aid, but also that positive efforts are made to recruit women and minorities along with majority male students, and that special programs are developed to improve, when needed, the preparation of women, minorities, and other persons who have been underprivileged in their prior education for graduate and professional education.

Special emphasis should be placed by high schools and other appropriate community agencies on the development of improved career and financial guidance, especially for young people from low-income families, who are less likely to receive informed guidance from parents and friends than those from more affluent families. Young women capable of aspiring to traditionally male careers need encouragement and guidance at an early stage.

The federal government has a special responsibility to maintain stable financial support of graduate education. The Council's recent recommendation for 20,000 graduate fellowships and 2,000 traineeships should be promptly implemented.

Recommendation 2: *Graduate and professional schools should review their policies, where this has not been done, in order to revise any rules that discriminate against students on the basis of sex, marital status, or family responsibilities. Policies should include (1) rules permitting part-time study to accommodate men or women whose family* *circumstances necessitate part-time study, (2) policies permitting a moderate extension of the time period for completion of requirements for advanced and professional degrees for such students, (3) eligibility for fellowships for such part-time students, (4) no discrimination on the basis of race, sex, or marital status in appointing teaching or research assistants or in awarding fellowships, (5) no antinepotism rules in connection with these appointments or awards, and (6) opportunities for persons entering graduate school after some years away from higher education to overcome special deficiencies in preparation, as in mathematics.*

Recommendation 3: *The Council recommends that federal agencies—in particular, the National Center for Education Statistics, the National Research Council/National Academy of Sciences, and the Equal Employment Opportunity Commission—improve their programs for collecting and promptly publishing data on the sexual and racial or selected ethnic characteristics of degree recipients and academic employees. There is a special need for breakdowns by sex within particular racial and ethnic groups.*

In addition, the Office for Civil Rights should assume the responsibility of making these data available to colleges and universities as soon as possible.

Academic Policies Under the Impact of Affirmative Action

Virtually all campuses are now affected in one way or another by federal government laws and regulations requiring nondiscrimination in the admission of students and in the hiring and promotion of academic and nonacademic employees. The federal responsibility for enforcement of affirmative action in education has been delegated by the Department of Labor to the Department of Health, Education and Welfare (HEW), within which the Office for Civil Rights (OCR) is the responsible agency. A university or college need not submit its affirmative action plan to OCR for approval unless it becomes subject to a compliance review, either under routine enforcement of the executive order or as the result of the filing of a complaint.

Recommendation 4: *The primary and long-term responsibility for affirmative action in higher education should be assumed by colleges and universities themselves. They should take the initiative in developing effective affirmative action policies without waiting to be coerced in that direction by federal or state agencies. Federal and state policy should be supplemental to institutional efforts and for only such period of time as it is essential.*

Among institutions, research universities need to take their affirmative action responsibilities especially seriously, because they have traditionally had few women or minorities on their faculties, and they are particularly subject to federal government interference if they do not comply with federal affirmative action requirements.

Effective pursuit of affirmative action policies requires not just the adoption of an adequate plan but also procedures that ensure the involvement of decision makers at all levels of the institution in furtherance of the objectives—the board of trustees, the administration, the academic senate, faculty members in individual schools and departments, and all others involved in the selection and promotion of academic and nonacademic employees.

An annual report providing data on changes in the sexual and racial composition of employment should be published.

Recommendation 5: *The Council recommends that primary responsibility for implementation of affirmative action policies be clearly assigned to a top official who reports* *directly to the president ŏr chief campus officer. Reporting to this top official there should usually be, especially on larger campuses, a full-time affirmative action officer, with a staff appropriate to the size of the campus.*

Affirmative Action Committees

In most of the institutions with affirmative action plans, a special committee plays a role in the affirmative action program and works closely with the affirmative action officer.

The functions of committees vary but usually include one or more of the following: (1) review of affirmative action plans, including goals and timetables; (2) review of progress in achieving affirmative action goals; (3) review of departmental recruitment, selection, and promotion procedures; and (4) much less frequently, serving as an appeal body in grievance cases.

Affirmative action committees are important and should be given meaningful and clear responsibilities relating to the monitoring of recruitment, selection, and promotion procedures, and of progress toward the advancement of affirmative action goals.

Recruitment

Recruitment for faculty positions traditionally has tended to be carried on in a confidential manner. A major purpose of affirmative action plans has been to break down these confidential, and often exclusive, patterns of recruitment.

Federal guidelines for the enforcement of affirmative action are explicit about methods of broadening recruitment procedures, and the affirmative action plans of colleges and universities have clearly been influenced by these provisions and by consultation with relevant federal officials.

All departments should be required to submit their recruitment plans for administrative review and also for scrutiny by the appropriate affirmative action committee, if one exists. Recruitment plans should be reviewed annually, well before the recruitment process begins. Whenever feasible, departmental search committees should include women and minority members.

Selection

Traditionally, departments have been required to submit documents justifying a recommendation for the appointment of a particular candidate for a faculty position, but typically they have not been required to provide evidence that candidates were considered in a strictly nondiscriminatory manner. In fact, information relating to rejected candidates has not usually been required by campus administrators. In contrast, affirmative action plans require departments to maintain records relating to all candidates who are considered in the selection process.

We believe that departments should be required to submit evidence indicating that women and minority candidates have been seriously considered, and the reasons for selection of the preferred candidate should be carefully stated, along with documentation indicating the relative qualifications of the recommended and rejected candidates.

In addition to the normal administrative review procedure, all recommendations for appointment should be reviewed by the top administrative official in charge of affirmative action. This review should be in addition to, and should not replace, review by the faculty committees that have traditionally been involved in the review process.

Promotion

Affirmative action policies and procedures should call for careful documentation of departmental recommendations on promotions that indicates that strictly nondiscriminatory policies were followed. These recommendations should also be reviewed by the top affirmative action official. Experience in promotions should be periodically reviewed by appropriate affirmative action committees.

Salary Analyses

In public institutions of higher education with formal salary structures, women in regular faculty ranks normally receive compensation appropriate to their step and rank. Thus, overt salary discrimination is not likely to arise, but a charge of failure to grant a merit increase or promotion because of sexual or racial discrimination may be accompanied by a charge of unequal pay, because the higher step or rank would involve higher pay.

Private institutions with less formal salary structures face a more difficult task than do other institutions in eliminating salary discrimination, because a more thorough-going analysis of relationships between sexual or racial differences in compensation and qualifications of the individuals involved is likely to be required.

Recommendation 6: *The affirmative action plans of institutions of higher education should include carefully framed provisions ensuring strict observance of nondiscriminatory procedures in recruitment, selection, and promotions, and providing for analysis of salary differentials.*

The mere inclusion of appropriate provisions will not ensure nondiscrimination unless there are adequate requirements for administrative review, including review by affirmative action officials, of recruitment plans, selection procedures, and promotion procedures.

Where affirmative action committees have been appointed, such committees should periodically review departmental procedures and experience in recruitment, selection, and promotions.

Part-Time Appointments

There frequently has been no provision for part-time faculty appointments except in lecturer or other nonladder faculty positions, or when faculty members were partly on research or administrative appointments. These policies have seriously impaired opportunities for women, and sometimes for men, with family responsibilities to obtain regular faculty appointments and promotions.

Recommendation 7: *Part-time appointments should be permitted in regular faculty ranks for persons whose sole employment commitment is to the college or university, and not elsewhere. Under appropriate conditions, these appointments may lead to tenure on a part-time basis.*

Policies relating to promotions should allow for a moderate extension of the usual period for qualification for promotion for persons who have been granted leaves of absence or who have been employed part time because of family responsibilities.

Lecturers and Nonfaculty Academic Employees

Qualified women and minority group members are sometimes permanently classified in lectureships and nonfaculty research positions, with little prospect of appointment to regular faculty positions or of acquiring tenure. Frequently, antinepotism policies have prevented the appointment of married women holding such positions to the faculty.

Recommendation 8: *As part of their affirmative action policies, colleges and universities should systematically review the status of lecturers and nonfaculty academic employees on their campuses. The purposes of such reviews should be (1) to identify and reclassify individuals who are qualified for regular faculty positions and (2) to ensure that lecturers and nonfaculty academic employees are covered by fringe benefits (on a prorated basis if they are part time) and are compensated on the basis of equitable salary structures.*

Recommendation 9: *Employment of near relatives within the same department should be permitted, provided they are not in a supervisory subordinate relationship and that neither is involved in an employment decision concerning the other.*

Opportunities in Administration

An especially important aspect of affirmative action policies is the encouragement of opportunities for women and minorities to rise in the administrative hierarchy. In academic administration, deans and top administrators are typically selected from among persons who have served ably as department chairmen, or, in some cases, as directors of research institutes or other special units. Thus, it is important to provide opportunities for women and minorities to serve as chairpersons or directors.

Recommendation 10: *Institutions of higher education should emphasize policies and procedures that will provide opportunities for women and minorities to serve in administrative positions.*

Goals and Timetables

At the heart of the controversy over federal affirmative action regulations are the requirements for the development of goals and timetables in affirmative action plans. Goals and timetables require that an employer make special efforts to recruit, employ, and promote women and minorities in order to overcome the effects of past discrimination.

Federal regulations and guidelines distinguish between goals and quotas. Yet a legitimate fear exists that in actual administration, at the campus level or by federal agencies or both, goals and quotas might be regarded as the same thing.

A related issue in hiring is how the term *most qualified* should be interpreted. *Most qualified* may be determined on strictly academic grounds—knowledge of the subject and ability to teach it and add to it. It may additionally be judged on grounds of overall contributions, including the ability to serve as models and mentors to women and minority students, and finally it may be considered loosely as being whatever is most suitable in meeting established goals. We clearly favor the second interpretation, namely, consideration of overall contributions.

One source of major misunderstanding is the implication that the goals of affirmative action will not be achieved until women and members of minority groups are represented in the same proportions as in the total labor force. There is nothing in the federal guidelines that implies any such result. The guidelines refer to recent recipients of appropriate degrees.

We believe that the federal government should continue, at least for the immediate future, to require the development of goals and timetables, but there is a need for careful reconsideration of whether rigid application of ratios of pools of qualified persons to existing representation, department by department, yields the most desirable results. Where very few women or minorities have doctor's degrees in a field of study, this method can indicate no need for women or minorities, or need for only a fraction of a person, in many cases.

"Availability Pools" Versus
"Pools of Qualified Persons"

The use of the word *availability* is misleading. A measure of the relative representation of women or minority groups among doctorate recipients during the most recent five-year period actually tells us little about how many qualified persons may be available for particular job offers. Some may be employed in academic jobs or in government or industry in which they are quite satisfied and which they could not be induced to leave except on the basis of an especially attractive offer. Thus, actual availability pools are not susceptible to measurement.

What is being measured would be more appropriately described if the term *pools of qualified persons* were used instead of *availability pools.* Even this term is not wholly satisfactory, because not all persons in these pools are equally qualified. But it is less misleading than *availability pools,* because it does not imply that all persons in the pools are available or that persons not in these particular pools of recent doctoral recipients are not available.

Recommendation 11: *Goals and timetables should be included in affirmative action plans of colleges and universities. Analyses of current employment patterns of pools of qualified persons should be undertaken for each department, but decisions as to whether goals should be formulated for individual departments, or, as would more usually be appropriate, for groups of related departments or schools, or for the entire campus, should be made only after careful study of the probable overall results for all units and for the campus as a whole. Whatever the decision, the performance of each department in contributing to the achievement of goals and timetables should be subject to periodic review by the campus administration.*

Goals and timetables, as well as strictly nondiscriminatory policies, should relate to appointments to instructor and assistant professor positions. For promotions to tenured ranks, strictly nondiscriminatory policies should be followed, and the experience with promotions in each department should be periodically reviewed to ensure that such policies have been followed. A search for outside candidates for tenured appointments will be appropriate in many situations.

Recommendation 12: *Timetables should be set for periods not exceeding five to ten years. The institution should make a good faith effort to achieve its goals for additions of women and minorities to the faculty during that period.*

Recommendation 13: *The Department of Labor—in consultation with the Department of Health, Education, and Welfare—should develop a special supplement, or set of interpretations, to Revised Order No. 4 that will be especially appropriate for higher education.*

This document should embody the following principles: (1) goals and timetables, as well as strictly nondiscriminatory policies, should relate to entry-level academic appointments (instructor and assistant professor in the case of faculty appointments) and should be based on data relating to degrees awarded in the most recent five-year period; (2) institutions should be free to formulate goals and timetables for groups of depart-

ments, or schools and colleges or for the campus as a whole, rather than for individual departments, when they deem it appropriate; (3) proportions of women and minorities among faculty members should not be regarded as adequate if unduly concentrated in certain schools or departments; (4) timetables should not exceed five to ten years, and institutions should be expected to make a good faith effort to achieve projected additions of women and minorities in that period— not necessarily to achieve "parity"; (5) appointments and promotions to tenured positions should be made on the basis of strictly nondiscriminatory procedures, and institutions should be expected to provide evidence that experience with such appointments and promotions in each department is periodically reviewed by the administration to ensure that nondiscriminatory procedures have been followed; (6) the existing eight requirements relating to local labor market conditions in Para. 60-2.11 should be interpreted as relevant only to nonacademic employment and not to most academic positions; and (7) any provision that women or minority candidates should not be required to have higher qualifications than those of the "least qualified incumbent" should be declared inapplicable to academic employment.

Regulations and guidelines of the Department of Health, Education, and Welfare relating to enforcement of the executive order should be revised to reflect the provisions of the special supplement or set of interpretations to Revised Order No. 4.

Data requirements should be revised to reflect the modified provisions. Institutions should be expected to compile annually and keep available detailed data—on a departmental basis for each racial and selected ethnic group and for each job classification—on utilization, pools of qualified persons (based on data supplied by the Office for Civil Rights), recruitment, selection, promotions, salaries, and separations. Separate data should not be required on placement/assignment, tenure, transfer (reassignment), fringe benefits, or training, because (1) they would overlap with other required data or (2) are not particularly relevant to academic employment or (3) in the case of fringe benefits, are usually uniform for large groups of employees and do not need to be provided on a detailed departmental basis.

Recommendation 14: *The special supplement to Revised Order No. 4 and accompanying changes in Department of Health, Education, and Welfare regulations should give explicit recognition to the need for increasing the supply of qualified women and minorities by requiring institutions involved in doctoral and professional education to include a supply plan, along the lines of our Recommendation 1. The regulations should also give explicit recognition to an institution's progress from year to year in adding women and minorities to faculties.*

Recommendation 15: *When an institution can demonstrate that its proportions of women and minorities among faculty members and other academic employees approximate pools of qualified persons and are well distributed throughout the institution, it should be exempted from requirements calling for continuous reassessment of goals and timetables and from detailed reporting requirements relating to academic employment. It should, however, be required to continue to pursue nondiscriminatory policies and to maintain relevant records that will be available on request. Any evidence of a significant diminution in proportions of women and minorities would call for a new compliance review.*

An appropriate proportion is likely to be achieved sooner for majority women than for minorities, and thus the relaxation of requirements might relate first to majority women.

Deficiencies in the Administration of Federal Programs

Observers of federal affirmative action tend to agree on the inadequacy of the staff of the Office for Civil Rights (OCR) and also of the Equal Opportunity Employment Commission (EEOC) and the Office of Federal Contract Compliance (OFCC). In relation to higher education, the most frequently expressed criticisms concern preparation of the OCR staff to deal with the intricate problems and difficulties of interpretation of nondiscrimination and affirmative action in faculty employment. They also relate to the seriously inadequate size of the staff when viewed against the large number of colleges and universities affected by the provisions.

Recommendation 16: *The Council recommends that the Department of Health, Education, and Welfare give special emphasis to the development within the Office for Civil Rights of an adequate and highly qualified staff that is knowledgeable about the special characteristics of academic employment. This staff should be largely centered in the Washington office, and negotiations relating to academic employment in institutions of higher education that hire in a national market should be conducted by officials of the Washington office, rather than by regional officials. A larger staff will be needed in the transitional period than will be required after institutions have made substantial progress in implementing affirmative action.*

One persistent criticism of OCR's administration of affirmative action relates to the long delays in processing of compliance reviews and complaints, the tiny proportion of cases in which affirmative action plans have received final approval, and the resulting involvement of institutions in negotiations over periods of several years. Campus administrations also complain that too many federal agencies are involved in the enforcement of antidiscrimination and that a campus may be involved simultaneously with several federal or state agencies, sometimes relating to the same issues or the same complaints.

Recommendation 17: *The Department of Labor should continue to delegate responsibility for enforcement of affirmative action requirements in higher education to the Department of Health, Education, and Welfare (HEW). The Department of Labor's involvement should be confined to (1) final approval of regulations and guidelines developed by HEW within the general framework of Department of Labor regulations, (2) periodic review by the Department of Labor of HEW's policies and performance in relation to enforcement vis-à-vis higher education, and (3) occasional modification of the Department of Labor's general policies and requirements on the basis of such reviews or other indications of needs for changes. The Secretary of Health, Education, and Welfare should have final authority to approve affirmative action plans and to impose sanctions on institutions.*

Recommendation 18: *All the federal agencies involved in nondiscrimination and affirmative action matters in higher education should cooperate in developing coordinated guidelines. Along with the development of these coordinated guidelines, requirements for the provision of data should be unified and simplified. Wherever possible, federal agencies should develop procedures for sharing data instead of requiring separate reporting to each agency.*

Recommendation 19: *The Council recommends the concentration of authority for pro-*

cessing complaints relating to discrimination in employment in higher education with the Equal Employment Opportunity Commission (EEOC), along with such additions to the commission's staff as may be necessary to process such complaints. The Office for Civil Rights should continue to refer all individual complaints to EEOC and should also refer class complaints to EEOC except in special circumstances in which they are closely associated with compliance investigations.

It is also recommended that Title VII of the Civil Rights Act of 1974 be amended to authorize the EEOC to issue cease and desist orders, along the lines of the provisions of H.R. 1746 (1971).

The Equal Employment Opportunity Coordinating Council (EEOCC) should play a much more decisive role than it now does in coordinating federal agency involvement in cases relating to higher education. Procedures should be developed for ensuring that a complaint would not be processed by two or more agencies simultaneously but would be referred to a single agency.

The Secretary of Health, Education, and Welfare should be invited to attend EEOC meetings whenever problems under his jurisdiction are discussed.

Recommendation 20: *Title IX of the Education Amendments of 1972 should be amended to make it clear that the title does not make specific provision for nondiscrimination in employment, but respects the employment provisions of Title VII of the Civil Rights Act and of the executive order.*

Equal Pay Issues

Complaints of employment discrimination brought before EEOC frequently involve allegations of unequal pay, along with other types of discrimination, and complaints on unequal pay are often filed both with the Wage and Hour Administration and the EEOC, where sex-based discrimination is involved. Complaints of discrimination in pay may also be filed with OCR.

Recommendation 21: *Because complaints filed with the Equal Employment Opportunity Commission (EEOC) charging salary discrimination usually also involve allegations of other types of employment discrimination that cannot clearly be separated from salary discrimination. EEOC should have jurisdiction over such complaints, but should refer any special analyses that need to be conducted to the Wage and Hour Administration.*

The Office for Civil Rights should refer salary analyses conducted in connection with affirmative action compliance procedures to the Wage and Hour Administration (WHA) of the Department of Labor. The staff of WHA should be increased to include persons familiar with academic salary relationships and with salary relationships in professional and managerial employment generally.

In view of the financial stringency faced by many public and private institutions of higher education, obtaining funds for affirmative action expenditures is difficult. The federal government, in imposing affirmative action obligations on colleges and universities, should provide some financial support to assist institutions in carrying out these obligations.

Recommendation 22: *Since federal policies permit inclusion of a small portion of the costs of affirmative action programs as indirect costs, Congress should supplement federal* *agencies' research budgets to reflect these new indirect costs. Congress should also consider appropriating funds to meet a fraction of the cost of record-keeping and administration associated with affirmative action.*

State governments and private donors should be receptive to requests from colleges and universities for special budgetary allocations or private gifts to aid in meeting the costs of affirmative action programs.

A number of the recommendations could be made more detailed if a special task force made up of persons drawn from higher education and from women's and minority groups were appointed to provide advice on the revision of regulations, guidelines, and data requirements we have recommended. One of the problems with the development of federal affirmative action policies is that there has been too little consultation with appropriate and knowledgeable groups in the formulation of policies and regulations.

Recommendation 23: *The Secretary of Labor, the Secretary of Health, Education, and Welfare, and the chairman of the Equal Employment Opportunity Commission should act jointly to appoint a special task force, including persons drawn from institutions of higher education, women's groups, and minority groups, to advise them on the revision of regulations, guidelines, and data requirements recommended in this report.*

Confidentiality of Personnel Records

The confidentiality of personnel records is especially important to faculty members and administrators, because confidential evaluations by faculty members of a candidate for appointment or promotion play an important role in the selection and promotion process. If a faculty member becomes fearful that his confidential evaluation may fall into the hands of a government official or a court, he is likely to become reluctant to express himself frankly.

On the other hand, a complainant may have great difficulty in proving discrimination without access to his or her confidential personnel records and those of other candidates who were considered for the same appointment or promotion. The difficult problem of weighing the rights of complainants against the rights of institutions is increasingly becoming an issue in which court decisions will play the crucial role. But legal experts tend, on the whole, to believe that it will not be possible for universities to refuse access to confidential files in the face of the conflicting rights of complainants to have records made available to federal and state agencies and the courts.

Grievances and Enforcement Procedures

OCR's failure to issue show-cause orders and to go beyond mere delays in allocation of federal funds to campuses may be related to the severity of the penalty involved in actual withholding of contracts or, in extreme cases, debarment from future contracts. The development of more even-handed sanctions, not as a replacement for withholding of federal contracts and grant funds, but as a more generally applicable type of penalty, might make for more effective enforcement.

Recommendation 24: *A special supplement or set of interpretations under the executive order should be developed to provide for a more flexible set of sanctions for noncompliance with affirmative action enforcement requirements in higher education. The* provisions for withholding of federal-contract funds should be retained for use in cases in which milder sanctions have failed to have any effect. There should be strict requirements for "show-cause" orders and the holding of hearings before any sanction is imposed.

The Secretaries of Labor and of Health, Education, and Welfare should take joint action to appoint a special advisory committee, including legal and constitutional experts, to draw up specific recommendations for appropriate penalties.

Internal Grievance Procedures

Many colleges and universities have long had grievance procedures for members of the academic senate, in the form of a right of appeal to a standing or special ad hoc faculty committee. These procedures apply primarily to cases involving dismissal of faculty members with tenure or of nontenured faculty members before the expiration of their current contracts. And in recent years, under the impact of actual or potential unionization, and under the impact of civil rights pressures, grievance procedures have been developed for nonacademic employees in a good many institutions.

Increasingly, the right of appeal under an internal grievance procedure has come to be recognized as an essential aspect of adequate personnel policies. In the context of affirmative action in higher education, effective internal grievance procedures should greatly reduce the number of complaints that are filed with state or federal agencies or that wind up in court.

Where collective bargaining enters the scene, the important question is whether a provision for binding arbitration should be included in the collective bargaining agreement. It is our view that arbitration deserves careful consideration as one means of solving disputes locally and quickly. Arbitration procedures must, of course, meet standards of due process, and decisions cannot be contrary to law. Appeal to the courts should be possible where violation of due process is claimed, but the courts should otherwise defer to the arbitration process. Use of private arbitration can greatly reduce resort to the courts.

Recommendation 25: *The Council recommends that all institutions of higher education develop one or more sets of grievance procedures that will be available to all of its employees, or to academic and nonacademic employees separately. In the development of grievance procedures, institutions should consult with all concerned groups on the campus. All grievance procedures should provide for hearings in which normal principles of due process are observed.*

Recommendation 26: *The coordinated federal regulations that we have recommended should include a requirement that all institutions of higher education develop internal grievance procedures for all employees, if they do not already have them. At least for the present, however, the federal government should not attempt to stipulate the precise form those grievance procedures should take, except to require that generally accepted standards of due process be observed.*

Federal agencies empowered to investigate complaints should encourage complainants to exhaust internal remedies before formally filing a complaint with the federal agency, where grievance procedures are deemed to be adequate and equitable. This may require changes in federal legislation, especially Title VII of the Civil Rights Act.

For all the reasons given above, we have one final recommendation:

Recommendation 27: *The federal government, no later than 1980, should undertake a comprehensive review of affirmative action requirements and of mechanisms of enforcement to determine what, if any, requirements and mechanisms are still needed and in what segments of higher education. The presumption should be in favor of disengagement as soon as reasonably possible, at first perhaps for certain types of institutions and for majority women, because of the probability that the supply of qualified majority women will increase relatively rapidly and parity will be achieved more quickly for them than for minorities.*

The States and Higher Education:
A Proud Past and a Vital Future
May 1976

This report concerns the interrelations between the states and higher education at a time when higher education is experiencing continuing but reduced growth. This phase lies between the enormous expansion of the "golden age" of the late 1950s and the early and middle 1960s, and the "steady state" that looms ahead for the 1980s and most of the 1990s.

Commentary—A Proud Past and a Vital Future

Higher education can look back on a past that includes many accomplishments and ahead to a future that can continue a long record of vitality.

1. The United States, with its tripartite method of support from state, federal, and private sources, has developed a system of higher education that compares favorably with other systems on an international basis.
2. Higher education has gone through a period of great expansion, and there are now some excess facilities as measured by the current level of effective demand. We find, however, no record of general mismanagement; quite the contrary, the present surplus resulted, in large measure, from our success in meeting the demands for more teachers and faculty members in the 1960s.
3. Much remains to be done. Many states still rank low in their provisions of student places, in support of their public institutions of higher education, and in provision of aid to their private institutions. Also, some states recently have reduced their real levels of support in general and for research universities in particular.

    Overcoming these deficiencies and deficits will be costly. The costs can be met, however, probably over the remainder of this century, without any increase, and possibly even with a small decrease, in the percentage of the Gross National Product (GNP) spent on higher education.

4. Many states are in financial difficulty resulting, in part, from (a) impact on their resources of the recession and then a depression during the first half of the 1970s;

This volume was originally published as a commentary of the Carnegie Foundation for the Advancement of Teaching.

(b) the long-term rising costs of health, welfare, and other social programs; and (c) the impact of fast-rising wage, salary, and fringe benefit costs in the public sector.

The current crisis, however, will not necessarily continue indefinitely:

- The depression is lifting, and this increases revenues and reduces welfare costs.
- Rises in social welfare benefits and state personnel costs may have reached something of a plateau.
- Enrollments in primary and secondary education, whose expenditures are somewhat competitive with those of higher education, are stabilizing.
- The federal government has taken over some welfare costs and may take over more; funds from revenue sharing may increase.

We recognize that the states may incur some new costs and that tax cuts are more and more appealing politically. We also recognize that some states have serious problems of fiscal capacity, while others are in considerably more favorable positions.

The situation among the states is both very dynamic and very complex. On balance, however, many, and perhaps most, states may have improved capacity to support higher education in the near future.

Five Concerns

Dynamism. The preservation of dynamism is mostly up to the institutions themselves, but the states can help by (1) providing state funds to support innovations; (2) encouraging institutions, in the course of budgeting, to set aside 1 to 3 percent of existing funds each year for use in new endeavors; (3) preserving the private sector of higher education, which, compared to the public sector, historically has been more innovative and responsive to change; (4) encouraging, with financial support, the introduction of new technology in instruction; (5) avoiding undue rigidity in state formulas for financial support; and (6) halting the spread of more and more detailed controls.

Parochialism. An increasing tendency to advance the "new parochialism" concerns us. It shows up in many ways, including (1) higher and higher out-of-state tuition charges; (2) restriction of state scholarships to use at in-state institutions; (3) quotas on the number of out-of-state students admitted; (4) federal graduate fellowships distributed to individual institutions rather than to students who can take them where they choose; (5) pressures to distribute federal research funds on the basis of geography rather than on merit alone; (6) the reduction of exchange provisions for students and faculty going or coming from abroad; and (7) setting professional examinations so as to favor locally trained persons.

We oppose these tendencies and instead favor freedom of choice for students and scholars that, to the maximum extent possible, is unimpeded by geographical boundaries. But solutions are not easy to find. They rely on self-denial of parochial tendencies by the states, on regional compacts, on careful attention by the federal government to its own direct programs, and on federal encouragement of interstate mobility in its joint programs with the states. We particularly urge the federal government to require the states to allow some reasonable portability of grants under the State Student Incentive Grant program.

Preservation of the private sector. It is in the interest of the states to assist in the preservation of the private sector, since it (1) has special contributions to make; (2) reduces the burdens on state funds; (3) increases the competitive pressure on public institutions for effective performance; and (4) suggests free market standards for salaries and teaching loads.

Assistance should be given to private institutions in such ways that:

- The public institutions are not neglected. This means caring first for the basic needs of public institutions. Support for private institutions should be gradually increased so that the additional fiscal burden in any one year is moderate.
- The private institutions remain private. A "peril point" is reached when an average of one-half as much state subsidy, on a per student basis, is given to private institutions as is given to comparable public colleges and universities to support institutional costs.
- The private institutions remain competitive with each other and with public institutions in the student market. This favors support on an enrollment basis, not on a lump sum or "bail-out" basis.
- Private institutions get funds on as assured a long-term basis as possible. Otherwise they can be held "on the string" by political forces.

The basic role for the future should be: The states should make the best possible use they can of all higher education resources, both public and private.

Coordination and control. We regret the tendency toward centralization of authority over higher education because:

- It reduces the influence and sense of responsibility of students, faculty members, campus administrators, and members of campus governing boards—all persons who know the most about their institution and are most directly involved in its operations.
- This concentration seems to have had no measurable direct impact on policies or practices.
- The governance processes worsen, becoming more costly, cumbersome, time-consuming, and frustrating.

This is not to say that higher education should not have restraints, but it is already subject to many restraints, particularly by the student market and by state budgetary controls. The best restraint is competition, and it is partly for this reason that we strongly support continuation of the private sector to provide competition with the public sector.

These restraints, however, are not fully adequate as mechanisms for long-range planning because they respond more to immediate considerations. Consequently, we strongly favor a mechanism for preparing long-range plans to inform and improve decisions made at all levels. Advisory councils are the best mechanisms for preparing such plans because they are not committed to operating decisions and can be selected specifically for this purpose. Their success relies solely on the quality of their plans and their reputations for independence and integrity. What is needed is good information, careful analysis of it, and thoughtful judgments about policy so that those with final authority can make better decisions if they wish.

We place reliance, then, on an effective market, an effective budget-making mechanism, and an effective plan—and not on detailed regulation. More specific comments follow.

- Within multicampus and consolidated systems, we favor lay boards, with substantial delegated powers, at the campus level. This provides better opportunities for lay board members, students, and faculty to work together. Campus diversity is best preserved in the long run if separate boards help to define and protect it.
- We believe it is unwise to have no planning mechanism at the state level. Higher education can benefit from plans that take the long-range view into consideration. The entire system should be evaluated in depth periodically in ways that market, budget, and legislative mechanisms cannot do.
- If a state goes beyond an advisory mechanism, which we do not recommend, it is better to develop a consolidated board than a regulatory agency. The trend toward more regulation should and can be reversed. The use of a consolidated board means that basic decisions are made inside higher education and that it has a spokesman to the state instead of one from the state, as is the case with regulatory agencies. We do not in any case favor a regulatory agency with its own final authority. In practice, staffs of such agencies tend more often than not to come from outside higher education. They create another level of bureaucracy between higher education and state authority, and thus serve to duplicate the work that other state agencies perform.
- Consolidated boards, however, present some inherent difficulties. Operating boards are not usually very successful at planning, require especially excellent administration to be effective, and, in the long run, may yield to pressures to homogenize functions among institutions and to move costs upward.
- Private institutions can relate to higher education more effectively through an advisory mechanism than through a consolidated board or regulatory agency.
- Decisions about coordination should continue to be quite various; what works well in one place may not be satisfactory in another.
- We regret that much of the struggle over coordination is based on power considerations alone and not on which method of coordination will produce the best results.

The burden of proving that something can be done more effectively through centralization and regulation should be borne by the advocates of such policies.

Institutional independence. The independence of colleges and universities has been eroding rapidly, not just through centralization, but also through other mechanisms of control. Guerilla warfare takes place across the nation over what belongs to the institution and what belongs to the state. We believe that all states should follow the example of the state of Washington and seek to draw up a "treaty" openly and on the basis of long-run considerations. (Some suggested guidelines are set forth in Section E of the supplement to this report.)

In many states, the governor is now the dominant figure in higher education. We consider this to be an unwise long-term development. We suggest, as a check and balance, that governing boards be structured so that, first of all, governors are not members of them, and second, that appointments to these boards be recommended through appropriate screening mechanisms and be subject to some form of legislative approval.

Roles of State, Federal, and Private Support

Three great shifts have occurred in patterns of support for higher education since 1929-30 (see Figure 1). We take 1929-30 as our base since it was the last year before the major impacts of the Great Depression were felt by the nation. There has been:

- *A vast increase in total costs and in educational costs of institutions.* Total costs, including subsistence costs of students, have risen (in terms of constant 1967 dollars) from about $1.6 billion to over $25 billion—a 15-fold increase, while educational costs of institutions increased 23 times over.
- *A shift from private toward public sources of financial support.* The private share of total costs dropped from 79 to 41 percent, and the public share rose from 21 to 59 percent, while the shift in educational costs of institutions was from 58 percent private and 42 percent public to 32 percent private and 68 percent public.

    In 1929-30 the educational costs of public institutions were met about one-fifth from private sources, and the percentage remains about the same today. The big change has been in the financing of private institutions. In our base year, private institutions received only 4 percent of their support from public sources, but today 37 percent of their support—a ninefold increase—is from public sources.
- *A shift of public support from state and local toward federal sources.* In 1929-30 the federal government provided 9 percent of governmental appropriations, while today its share has risen to 45 percent.

Figure 1. Changes in public and private shares of costs of higher education, including educational costs of institutions and subsistence costs of students, 1929-30 to 1973-74 (in constant 1967 dollars)[a]

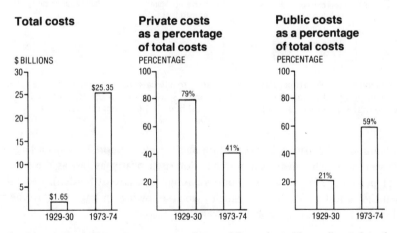

[a]Estimated tuition and subsistence expenses met from public student aid are allocated to the public share; includes total research funds.

Characteristics of Support

Comparative composition of support. If support is divided among three categories—support for institutions, support for research projects, and support for student aid—the three major sources of financing are seen to have different interests. The states (and localities) concentrate heavily on support of institutions, the federal government on student assistance and research projects, and private sources on student subsistence, and, to a lesser extent, on support of institutions (see Figure 2).

This distribution reflects two developments since 1929-30. The first is the enormous increase in funds for research at the universities, mostly from the federal government. The second is the vastly augmented public support of students from lower-income families as the nation has moved from selective to mass to universal access to higher education. Once again, the federal government has been the main source of the additional funds.

Figure 2. Shares of financial support for (1) educational costs of institutions, (2) research, and (3) student subsistence from federal, state and local, and private sources, 1974-75[a]

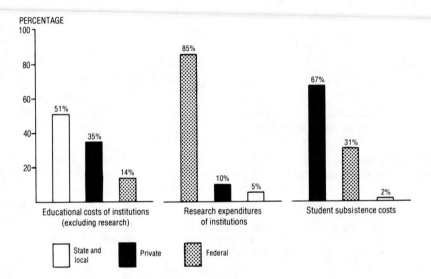

[a]Tuition income of institutions has been adjusted to allocate to public sources the estimated proportion of tuition paid from public student aid funds. Similarly, the proportion of student subsistence paid from public sources (including federal Veterans' benefits) has been estimated.

Constancy and volatility of support. State and private support have been largely enrollment-driven, although private support has not risen nearly as fast as the state share in terms of percentage of personal income (a rough measure of burden). Federal support has risen the fastest of all. It is also highly volatile, owing, in large part, to the fact that federal support is essentially problem-driven.

Shifting burden of support. If enrollment as a factor is excluded and support per student is viewed independently, we see that the net cost to the family has actually gone down in constant dollars by about 9 percent since 1929-30.

For the state taxpayer, the burden per student has risen, however, by more than three times over, and even more than that for the taxpayer at the federal level. The family is comparatively better off, and the taxpayer is comparatively worse off. (See Figures 3 and 4.)

Figure 3. Tuition and subsistence expenditures of students and their families as a percentage of total personal income, 1929-30 to 1974-75 (biennial to 1973-74)[a]

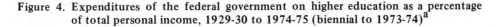

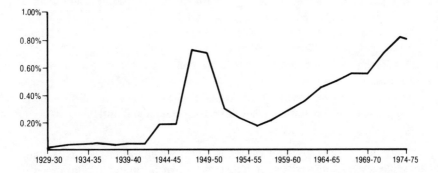

●●●●●●●● Tuition and subsistence expenditures
────── Tuition expenditures

[a]Estimated student aid allocated to tuition and subsistence expenditures has been deducted, including student aid from all public and private sources.

Figure 4. Expenditures of the federal government on higher education as a percentage of total personal income, 1929-30 to 1974-75 (biennial to 1973-74)[a]

[a]Includes revenue of institutions from the federal government plus student aid allocated directly to students under the Basic Educational Opportunity Grant, veterans' benefits, and social security benefits programs.

Future Prospects

The next 40 to 50 years will not duplicate the changes of the past 40 or 45 years. If they did, by the year 2015 or 2020 the educational costs of higher education would be over $400 billion, or five times the present budget (1967 dollars) for national defense. It is more likely that:

● Total costs and educational costs of institutions will rise in accordance with rising enrollments and rising costs per student, which tend to rise in the long run 2 or 2.5 percentage points per year faster than the general cost of living.

- Some shift from private toward public sources of funds will continue to take place, but at a reduced rate.
- Absolute increases will occur in both federal and state funds in terms of constant dollars, but the current balance of federal versus state and local support will not be shifted drastically.
- The current major emphases of state, federal, and private support will be maintained.
- The high volatility in components of federal support will continue.
- There will be some modest further shift of burdens from families to taxpayers.
- All of this assumes that the economy will continue to recover; that the GNP per capita will continue to grow; that the fiscal position of the states will not continue to deteriorate; and that the total social demand for higher education will continue at about the current rate.

Surpluses, Deficits, and Special Accomplishments

Surplus capacity is inevitable in a period of suddenly reduced expectations and realizations after a time of vast expansion. Surplus capacity now exists nationally in teacher training and production of Ph.D.'s, and there is at least a potential surplus of health science centers and law schools. The existence of surpluses has been caused by:

- The momentum of more than doubling enrollments in the 1960s led to some overshooting of actual needs.
- The sudden decline in the birthrate reduced the need for teachers.
- The slowdown in the percentage of the college-age cohort enrolling in college further reduced the expected need for teachers.
- Some institutional aspirations for Ph.D. programs and medical schools in the 1960s and early 1970s were excessive.
- The declining population of many rural areas shifted the locations of need for student places.
- Enthusiasm at the federal level greatly added to the impetus toward certain surpluses. The greatest source of surpluses has been federal initiative.

Only one of the causes for surpluses—excessive ambition—can be laid at the doors of the colleges and universities, and that cause can be placed at the doors of a small minority of 3,000 institutions of higher education.

But even where surplus capacity exists, in the case of doctorate production, strong caution is in order. There remain serious deficiencies in the supply of women and minorities with Ph.D.'s. The drastic cutbacks that have occurred in federal fellowships are disastrous in relation to these deficiencies.

It is also important to recognize that, when we speak of a surplus in Ph.D. output, we are referring primarily to the fact that too many doctorate-granting institutions were developed during the rapid expansion period of the 1960s. We are not recommending wholesale cutbacks in Ph.D. programs of institutions with long-established and high-quality doctoral programs.

We find deficits in four special areas, which are essential to correct:

1.   *Open-access places.* Enough places now exist to take care of all students except in

the category of open-access places—defined as ones with low or no tuition that are open to all high school graduates.

2. *State scholarship programs.* The states have made impressive progress in developing student aid programs in recent years, yet the variations in amounts made available under these programs are very wide. Our estimates suggest that the state share of a fully-funded tuition aid program would be about $135 per full-time equivalent (FTE) student, and only three states provided more than this average in 1975-76.

3. *Area health education centers.* Eleven states have demonstrated less than adequate progress in developing such centers.

4. *Health science centers.* Three metropolitan areas are inadequately served.

The existence of surpluses and deficits should not obscure the fact that much has been done very well. We have developed listings of the states at the top of several scales of accomplishment, which include access, research, quality, public support, and planning.

Diversity of Structures

Support for institutions of higher education is divided between state and local governments at 43 percent, the federal government at 25 percent, and private sources at 32 percent.

State support is heavily concentrated on public institutions, while federal support is spread more or less evenly over both public and private institutions, and private support is comparatively more concentrated on private institutions. Consequently, when one is talking about the states, attention is directed more heavily toward the public sector of higher education. The states are best viewed, however, not collectively, in our tripartite support structure, but rather one at a time. When viewed in detail, each seems to constitute a separate case. It is important to understand this diversity for these reasons:

- It is essential to an understanding of higher education in the United States, where diversity is greater than in any other nation.
- It is helpful in understanding the great pluralism of American society.
- It explains why it is difficult to generalize about the states and make recommendations that apply equally to all of them.
- It explains why the federal government could not easily take over higher education and make it into a single national system.

The one simple statement about the states and higher education that is true is that no simple statement about them is true.

Diversity of Support

State support for higher education follows no conforming patterns. Variations are the dominant theme in "effort" as measured by the percentage of state personal income spent by state and local governments on higher education and in "concern" as measured by expenditures per FTE student in public institutions.

The competitive position of higher education as against other types of state expenditures is another way of looking at comparative support. The average percentage of state appropriations spent on higher education is about 15 percent of revenues, but the range is enormous.

Generally, the position of public research universities has deteriorated within the totality of state-supported higher education. The relative decline in support per FTE student in research universities is a source of concern for the long run, even though federal research and development funds have greatly expanded, because these universities, among the public institutions, are the major sources for the training of persons at the highest levels of professional skill and for research.

Finally, the states not only determine their own direct support of higher education, but they also either determine or influence the tuition charged to students. Here again, patterns vary.

Diversity of Relations to the Private Sector

The private sector is an essential but diminishing part of higher education in the United States. In 1929-30 it provided more than half of all student places, but by 1975 this proportion had fallen to 22 percent. The decline is not due to a reduction of absolute numbers, which have quadrupled since 1929-30, but is, rather, the consequence of the great rise in public enrollment. However, about one-quarter of private institutions have recently been found to be in serious fiscal distress, and the tuition gap between public and private institutions is substantial.

Almost one-half of the states now give direct support to private institutions. Combining general aid to private institutions and aid to students attending them, about two-thirds of all states have programs of support.

The basic issue over state support for private institutions is no longer so much whether it should be undertaken at all, but, rather, how it should be supplied and to what degree.

Diversity of Coordination and Regulation

Coordination, regulation, and consolidation of higher education have been increasing rapidly at the state level. In 1940, 33 states had no coordinating, planning, or consolidating mechanisms covering the entire public sector; today, none are without them.

Many forces have encouraged the growth of coordination and regulation beyond the campus level.

- Much more money is now spent and many more students are accommodated in higher education. Public interest, as a result, has been strengthened.
- More intercampus rivalry exists.
- Federal aid and interests have been added to state aid and interests.
- Governors and legislatures now have larger and more competent staffs intent on exercising authority.

Alternatives

As centralization progresses, three central issues arise:

- Campus governance. There are three clear-cut possibilities for four-year institutions: (1) that each campus have its own board (5 states); (2) that each segment have its own board (8 states); and (3) that all campuses and segments be covered by a single board (22 states).
- Coordination of all public institutions. There are four alternatives in current practice: (1) no coordination (9 states); (2) coordination by a consolidated board (13 states); (3) coordination by an advisory council (9 states); and (4) coordination by a regulatory agency (19 states).

- Association of the private sector with public policy formation. There are five patterns: (1) no state planning mechanism in which the private sector participates (1 state); (2) consolidated boards (8 states); (3) advisory coordinating councils (8 states); (4) regulatory coordinating boards (18 states); and (5) state 1202 commissions (15 states).

As centralization has progressed, the states have adopted widely varying mechanisms for campus governance, coordination of public institutions, and associating the private sector with public policy formation.

It cannot yet be shown that any one approach is superior to any other one in its impact, as there is no known quantifiable consequence for actual operating results that can be associated with one or another approach to centralization of authority.

We observe, however, that the best state plans for higher education seem to derive from advisory and regulatory mechanisms, and least of all from consolidated boards, and that the quality of the plan is the most important factor in coordination.

The course of movement, in summary, has been in one direction: toward centralization of planning, coordination, and control. But the specific paths followed have been many, and the differential operating practices have apparently been largely related to the paths pursued.

The States and Higher Education: Supplement

Issued in June 1976, this supplement contains technical information for persons who wish to obtain a more detailed understanding of some of the findings reported in the basic document.

It includes statistical tables, information on state funds for innovation (1960-1975), a list of methods by which states can assist private institutions, a list of actual and potential state controls over private institutions, proposals to define areas of institutional independence and state control, and a list of state 1202 commissions and their relations with other state boards. The supplement also describes patterns of (1) campus governance of senior institutions, (2) state coordination, and (3) association of the private sector with public policy. Finally, it contains organizational charts of public higher education in eight states.

Progress and Problems in Medical and Dental Education:
Federal Support Versus Federal Control
September 1976

Three Warnings and Five Urgent Recommendations

According to an official statement in the spring of 1970 there was a shortage of 50,000 physicians in the United States. Then, between 1970 and the end of 1975, the total number of active physicians and osteopaths rose from about 323,000 to an estimated 378,000, or by about 55,000.

Whether this increase represents an end to the shortage is subject to debate, but one aspect of this situation has received little attention. In the face of rapid increases in the supply of physicians graduating from existing institutions, we are in serious danger of developing too many medical schools. The chief reason for new medical schools now is to achieve a more adequate geographic distribution of schools. Efforts also should be made to increase the proportion of physicians who are engaged in primary care.

But we favor creating incentives to attract health professionals to underserved areas and to encourage training programs for primary care physicians, rather than imposing rigid federal controls on medical and dental education to achieve these goals. Such controls would involve unwarranted interference with academic decisions of the schools and a degree of federal control over the allocation of health manpower that goes far beyond interference in any other field.

First Warning: *We are in serious danger of developing too many new medical schools, and decisive steps need to be taken by both federal and state governments to stop this trend.*

We recommend only one new medical school in a community that now has no existing or developing school—Wilmington, Delaware. We also see a need for one new dental school in Arizona.

Second Warning: *There is a critical danger that concern over geographic maldistribution of health manpower and overspecialization in medicine will lead to excessive and unwieldy federal controls rather than to policies emphasizing incentives to effect the required changes.*

In the last few decades, we have become too dependent on an inflow of foreign medical graduates (FMGs) in meeting our physician supply problems. In view of the rapid increase that is now taking place in the number of U.S. medical graduates, a continued heavy inflow of FMGs could greatly exacerbate the dimensions of a possible future surplus. Our projections, which assume a gradual decline in the inflow of FMGs, indicate that the ratio of physicians to population will reach an unprecedented level by the mid-1980s (see Figure 1).

The issue of the supply of dentists has not been debated as vigorously as the question of physician supply. There has been less evidence of a shortage of dentists and almost no influx of foreign-trained dentists.

Third Warning: *The time has come to cease relying on foreign medical graduates to meet the need for physicians in the United States. The number of U.S. medical graduates is now increasing so rapidly that we can expect ample future increases in supply from existing medical schools.*

University health science centers are a national resource. They provide substantial social benefits (e.g., in combating disease) over and above the pecuniary benefits that flow to their graduates. In addition, physicians and, to a lesser extent, dentists are highly mobile geographically. A majority of physicians do not practice in the states in which they received their M.D. degrees. Thus, although many states have an excellent record of support, which has increased substantially in recent years, the record is very uneven and there is no clear-cut relationship between a state's investment in medical and dental education and its supply of physicians and dentists. This means that the federal government has an important responsibility for the national supply of physicians and dentists.

Urgent recommendation 1: *The nation has a vital stake in maintaining high standards of health among its residents. In recognition of the social benefits flowing from medical and dental education, the federal government should pursue a stable policy of financial support of university health science centers. It should provide a basic floor of support for these centers, which can be supplemented by support from state governments and private sources.*

The problem of geographic maldistribution of health manpower is serious. Particularly deficient in manpower are states with low per capita income, rural areas generally, and inner-city areas. The most affluent portions of cities and suburban areas tend to be adequately supplied and are sometimes oversupplied.

Geographic maldistribution of health manpower can be substantially alleviated by policies that create stronger incentives for health professionals to practice in underserved areas. These policies include: (1) expansion of the National Health Service Corps (NHSC) and the associated NHSC scholarship program; (2) improved financing of medical care, including financial incentives for practicing in underserved areas; (3) changes in reimbursement policies under such programs as Medicare and Medicaid, which now encourage subspecialization and do not provide adequately for primary care; (4) continued development and expansion of area health education centers (AHECs); and (5) continued development and expansion of physician's assistant, nurse-practitioner, and dental auxiliary programs.

Urgent recommendation 2: *The geographic disparities in the supply of health manpower will be overcome only with great difficulty and through a combination of policies that provide positive incentives for physicians, dentists, and other health professionals to*

Figure 1. Active physicians[a] and dentists per 100,000 population, actual,
1930 to 1970, and projected, 1975 to 1990

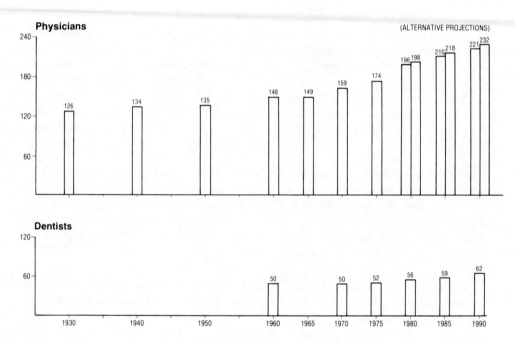

[a]Includes doctors of osteopathy from 1960 on.

*practice in underserved areas. There should be more effective coordination among exist-
ing federal programs and greater emphasis on federal-state cooperation in overcoming
geographic maldistribution.*

The trend toward excessive specialization in the medical profession has led to an
excessive supply of specialists, especially of surgeons, and a deficiency of primary care
physicians. This problem is also of growing concern in dentistry.

In the last few years, however, the proportion of first-year medical residents entering primary care training has increased impressively. A combination of factors, including federal capitation payments for residents in primary care training, is probably responsible.

Urgent recommendation 3: *The federal government should continue to provide incentives for both students and schools to emphasize primary care training, rather than establish complex federal controls.*

The research capabilities of university health science centers cannot be maintained in the face of stop-and-go federal support.

Urgent recommendation 4: *The federal government should pursue a stable and consistent policy of support of research in the health sciences, increasing its allocations for this purpose along with the rise in real Gross National Product. Federal allocations should cover full research costs and should encourage increased emphasis on ways of achieving greater efficiency in the training of health manpower and in the delivery of health care.*

Finally, we believe that there must be greatly increased emphasis on health education in our society. There is much evidence that the comparatively high mortality rates for American males from middle age onwards are associated with unwise diets, excessive smoking, use of alcohol and drugs, and accidents.

Urgent recommendation 5: *In the light of accumulating evidence that mortality rates in the United States are excessively high chiefly because of unwise personal habits and high accident rates, major emphasis should be placed in the coming years on the development of more effective programs of health education. Health professionals also need to be trained to place greater emphasis on educating patients to play a more active role in their own care and treatment.*

The 1971 Legislation

Building on earlier enactments that had provided support primarily for research and for construction of new schools, the Comprehensive Health Manpower Act of 1971 included provisions for capitation grants to health-professions schools designed to encourage expansion and acceleration of education programs. It also included special-project grants to induce various types of innovation and reform.

The appropriations to implement the provisions of the 1971 legislation have fallen short of authorization and of the intent of the law. In terms of 1967 dollars, the capitation payments rose to a peak of about $1,475 in fiscal 1973 and fell back to about $930 in fiscal 1976. Full implementation of the provisions of the 1971 legislation would have provided payments well above $2,500 per student in current dollars.

The 1971 legislation was intended to be effective for three years and thus would have expired June 30, 1974, had it not been continued over several years while Congress debated amendments. We think it would be advisable to continue the present legislation for a year after the effective date of any new legislation, because the schools need assurance of a continued flow of funds during the interim period while administrative guidelines are being established.

Detailed recommendation 1: *The Council recommends extending the provisions of existing health manpower legislation for a year after the effective date of revised legislation in order to avoid a disruption of the flow of federal support funds to university health science centers.*

Shortages or Impending Surpluses?

In 1970 the Carnegie Commission recommended that the number of entrant places in medical should be increased from 11,300 in 1970 to 16,400 by 1978. In fact, this figure was exceeded in 1978 by over 200 places.

What happens in the future will depend on whether national health insurance legislation is enacted and whether that legislation is sufficiently comprehensive to bring about another sharp increase in the demand for medical care.

We have developed projections that indicate a supply of 491,000 to 510,000 physicians by 1985, arriving at physician/population ratios ranging from 210 to 218 per 100,000 population. Physician/population ratios rising above 200 per 100,000 population are very high in relation to previous American experience, yet they do not necessarily imply impending surpluses. In fact, there is no precise way of determining the optimum physician/population ratio, and the adequacy of any given ratio can be adversely affected by forces leading to an increase in demand, or favorably altered by other forces leading to an increase in the productivity of physicians.

Our low projection for 1985 implies about one active physician for every 477 persons. Yet it is not clear that this implies a serious problem of surplus supply. A surplus probably would not manifest itself in unemployment among these highly trained professionals, but rather in some decline relative to other professions in their average incomes and average hours of work, both of which have been exceedingly high.

Increasing the likelihood of an overall surplus, however, is the currently rapid increase in the number of physicians' assistants and nurse-practitioners.

An increase in the aggregate supply of physicians would probably ease shortages in underserved areas, although it is unlikely that an increase in supply alone, in the absence of other measures, would greatly alleviate this problem. The adequacy of any given physician/population ratio also cannot properly be interpreted without a consideration of what proportion of physicians are engaged in primary care.

Finally, as long as there is an appreciable flow of FMGs, we cannot be indifferent to the need to ensure that the increase in the number of U.S. graduates does not suffer a reversal. And we would reiterate the Carnegie Commission's statement that "looking toward the future, the U.S. should become a net exporter of medical manpower, as part of the effort to raise the quality of medical education and medical care in underdeveloped countries."

The Supply of Primary Care Physicians

Between 1931 and 1963, the number of general practitioners fell from 112,000 to 73,000, or from 72 to 28 percent of all physicians. But it is useful to distinguish between physicians (including specialists) who are engaged in primary care and those who treat patients primarily on a referral basis. Using this classification, we find that, as the total number of physicians increased sharply between 1963 and 1970, the proportion engaged in primary practice declined from about 55 to 44 percent.

A more sensitive measure of recent and current changes is the distribution of first-year residencies by field of specialization. The proportion of first-year residents choosing primary care types of residencies rose from 37.5 percent in 1970 to 43.8 percent in 1973. Although it is important not to exaggerate the extent of the change and to recognize that some first-year residents start their specialization in later years, a substantial change does appear to be underway.

Is There a Shortage of Dentists?

The gap between the effective demand for dental care and the need that would exist if the entire population received adequate dental care apparently has been wider than in the case of physicians. This is because a very substantial proportion of the population does not receive the regular dental care that is necessary for proper maintenance of healthy teeth. The regional differences in the ratio of dentists to population are similar to those for physicians.

There is little question that private health insurance coverage for dental care will continue to spread, and a number of national health insurance proposals call for a gradual coverage of dental care. Thus, per capita demand for dental services is likely to rise. However, a continued rise in the productivity of the average dentist may be a moderating force. The use of dental assistants is quite common, and employment of dental hygienists and dental laboratory technologists has been growing rapidly.

The number of first-year dental students has not increased as sharply as that of medical students, but it increased 26 percent from 1970-71 to 1975-76. The number of dental schools has also been increasing. In 1975-76 there were 59 schools, compared with 53 in 1970.

Finally, the growth of specialization in dentistry has not, until recently, been a matter of serious concern. The scope for proliferation of specialties is relatively narrow. Even so, the proportion of specialists among dentists rose from 3.6 percent in 1955 to 10.4 percent in 1973 and is becoming a matter of growing concern in dental education.

Federal Capitation Payments and Related Policies

Federal support of medical and dental education should represent a stable proportion of the costs of education per student, with the remaining costs to be met by other public and private sources, including tuition.

In 1972-73, the average annual net cost of education in medicine (excluding income received from research and patient care) was $9,700, with a range of $5,150 to $14,150. Net costs of education in other health professions were lower, ranging from $3,050 for schools of pharmacy to $7,400 for dental schools.

Basic Principles

Capitation payments amounting to one-third of net educational costs per full-time student would represent an appropriate contribution by the federal government to the costs of education in the health professions. Approximately one-sixth of net educational costs per student should be available to the schools on minimal conditions—maintenance of enrollment and expenditures from nonfederal sources should be the only important conditions. These payments would be regarded as the federal government's basic subsidy in recognition of the social benefits flowing from maintenance of high quality medical and dental education. Additional payments, amounting to one-sixth of educational costs per student, would be provided in the form of bonuses designed to achieve specific objectives.

Detailed recommendation 2: *To implement Urgent Recommendation 1, basic capitation payments amounting to one-sixth of net educational costs per full-time M.D. and D.D.S. candidate, as determined by an appropriate official body, should be provided each year to medical and dental schools. These payments should be subject only to reasonable conditions requiring maintenance of enrollment and of expenditures from nonfederal sources.*

Capitation Payback Proposals

It has been proposed that medical and dental students repay capitation payments made to their schools on behalf of their education, but obligations would be reduced for physicians practicing in underserved areas. We do not favor capitation payback provisions as an approach to the problem of geographic maldistribution of physicians and dentists for the following reasons:

1. Basic capitation payments should be regarded as a contribution to be made on a continuous basis by the federal government. They should not be regarded as payments on behalf of individual students, giving rise to an obligation for repayment by those students.
2. Commitments on the part of students to practice in underserved areas would be exceedingly difficult for the schools to enforce and would impose compulsory obligations on health-professions students not paralleled by obligations on students training for other occupations.
3. The acceptance by a student of special types of student aid that must be repaid if the student does not practice in an underserved area following graduation is a preferable way of encouraging more graduates in the health professions to practice in such areas.

Enrolling National Health Service Corps Scholarship Holders

Opposition to the capitation payback proposals led to proposals that health science schools be required to reserve some of their student places for holders of National Health Service Corps (NHSC) scholarships as a condition for receiving capitation payments. (These scholarships carry an obligation for a certain period of service in the corps.) Although this proposal is less objectionable than capitation payback provisions, it is contrary to the principle that capitation payments should be made in recognition of the social benefits of health science education. In addition, there is no assurance that NHSC scholarship holders will be evenly distributed among applicants to particular schools, among geographic regions, or among students of various ability levels.

A preferable approach is to provide a bonus amounting to one-sixth of net educational costs to a school for each NHSC scholarship holder admitted. This would provide a strong incentive to a school to attract such applicants, without imposing mandatory requirements.

Enrollment Expansion?

The 1971 legislation required increases in first-year enrollment as a condition of capitation payments, but the sharp increase in the size of first-year medical school classes in the first half of the 1970s tends to remove the need for such provisions, except in special cases.

The situation of dental schools is somewhat different. Their expansion has been less pronounced, and the likelihood of a continued substantial increase in the demand for dental services, in relation to the probable increase in the supply of dentists, is quite high. We suggest bonuses that would provide an incentive for expansion of schools with small entering classes but would not compel it.

Acceleration of Medical and Dental Education

The Carnegie Commission strongly recommended acceleration of M.D. candidate education. The Commission included dental education in its recommendations for acceleration, but with less emphasis, because the total duration of predental and dental education has tended to be much less prolonged than that of medical education.

The momentum toward a three-year M.D. program grew in the early 1970s, but three-year programs do not appear to have become more prevalent since 1973-74. Optional three-year programs continue to be more prevalent than regular three-year programs.

Medical education continues to be very prolonged, and dental education is getting longer. Opportunities for students to pursue a three-year program should continue to be available.

Detailed recommendation 3: *Additional capitation payments, designed to increase federal capitation support to about one-third of net educational costs per student, should be designed to overcome geographic maldistribution of health manpower, increase enrollment in uneconomically small schools, and encourage acceleration of medical education. Schools should therefore qualify for payments amounting to one-sixth of net educational costs for each M.D. or D.D.S. candidate holding an National Health Service Corps scholarship; for each first-year student enrolled in a small school over and above the previous year's enrollment until first-year enrollment reaches 100; and for each recipient of an M.D. or D.D.S. degree who has graduated under a three-year program. Total capitation payments to any school based on M.D. or D.D.S. candidate enrollment should not exceed one-third of net educational costs per full-time student.*

Physician's Assistants and Dental Auxiliary Personnel

Programs for training physician's assistants were comparatively new and very few at the beginning of the 1970s but have expanded substantially since then. The growth of these programs can be explained to a considerable degree by federal government support, and their future growth would be jeopardized if that support were withdrawn. The 1971 health manpower legislation provided for capitation payments of $1,000 to medical and dental schools for each student in a physician's assistant or dental therapist training program. Current legislative proposals provide instead for special-project grants or contracts to support such programs. We believe that special-project grants are desirable for developing new programs, but that ongoing programs should be assured of capitation payments.

Detailed recommendation 4: *Schools should be eligible for capitation payments of $1,000 for each student enrolled in a physician's assistant, nurse-practitioner, or dental auxiliary program.*

Graduate Medical Education

The 1971 health manpower legislation included provisions for capitation payments of $3,000 for each trainee in a graduate training program in primary care (as well as in dentistry). It has been proposed that Congress go much further toward imposing a detailed and extensive set of controls on medical residency programs. But changes in the desired direction are under way and should continue to be encouraged by policies that emphasize incentives rather than compulsion.

Detailed recommendation 5: *Special-project grants to encourage the development of family practice and primary dental care training programs should be continued, and capitation grants of $3,000 for each resident in a primary care training program (family practice, primary internal medicine, primary pediatrics, primary obstetrics and gyne-cology, and primary dentistry) over and above the number in such training programs in the preceding year should be provided.*

    Congress should give serious consideration to the recommendations of the Institute of Medicine of the National Academy of Sciences for changes in reimbursement policies under Medicare and Medicaid, but strict federal controls on residencies should be avoided.

Foreign Medical Graduates

There is a reasonable probability that the inflow of foreign medical graduates (FMGs) will decline as the supply of U.S. medical graduates increases. Nevertheless, certain changes in policy are needed to limit the inflow of FMGs, especially those with inferior qualifications.

Detailed recommendation 6: *Foreign medical graduates should be required to meet the same standards as U.S. medical graduates for admission to residency programs, and im-migration legislation and regulations should be amended to remove preferential immi-gration status for physicians.*

Standards for State Licenses

Model standards for state licensure of physicians and dentists have long been needed to bring about greater uniformity in licensing requirements among the states.

Detailed recommendation 7: *The Secretary of Health, Education, and Welfare should be charged with the responsibility of developing national standards for state licensing of physicians and dentists, and state licensing agencies should enforce licensing requirements for all foreign medical graduates employed within each state.*

Special-Project Grants

In view of the indications that we are developing too many medical schools, we are opposed to start-up grants or other types of grants to support the development of new medical schools with special objectives. We place major emphasis on capitation payments to provide basic federal support to medical and dental schools and to induce desired policy changes. But there are certain purposes for which special-project grants are appropriate.

Detailed recommendation 8: *Provision should be made for special-project grants for (1) development of new programs for training physician's assistants, nurse-practitioners, and dental auxiliaries, (2) development of new programs for training in family medicine and primary dental care, (3) educational assistance for individuals from disadvantaged back-grounds, (4) educational assistance or special educational programs for U.S. citizens who have been enrolled in foreign medical schools, (5) development of area health education centers, and (6) curriculum innovation and reform. At the discretion of the Secretary of*

Health, Education, and Welfare, some of the special-project grants should be awarded to state governments on a matching fund basis.

Tuition Controls

Among legislative proposals that have been considered by Congress is a provision requiring the Secretary of HEW to establish criteria for determining allowable increases in tuition and other educational costs. In view of the role the states play in determining the tuition policy of their public medical and dental schools, and their increasing role in providing funds for private medical and dental schools, the intrusion of the federal government into tuition decisions is questionable.

Detailed recommendation 9: *Federal government involvement in determining allowable tuition increases of medical and dental schools should be avoided.*

The National Health Service Corps and Student Assistance

Geographic maldistribution of health manpower can be overcome only by a combination of policies, including expansion of the NHSC and related scholarship programs. There are several reasons for this:

1. The needs of underserved areas are unlikely to be adequately met, despite other policies, by the movement of private practitioners into those areas.
2. Geographic allocation of NHSC personnel can be shifted in accordance with changing needs in a manner that would not be feasible for private practitioners.
3. NHSC employment provides valuable initial professional experience.
4. Members of NHSC may elect to practice in communities in which they have served.

Establishment of the Corps

The NHSC was established under provisions of the Emergency Health Personnel Act of 1970 to improve the delivery of health services to underserved communities and areas. Appropriations for the corps have been modest, amounting to about $12 to $14 million in the last few years. The corps has grown slowly. From an initial placement of 20 health professionals in 16 communities, the corps had expanded by 1975 to include 551 professionals serving communities in 40 states.

Health manpower legislative proposals before Congress in 1976 provided for authorizations of substantially increased funding, and the services of an expanded corps unquestionably would be utilized.

NHSC Scholarships

The NHSC scholarship program is designed to strengthen recruitment to the corps and, under current legislative proposals, would be by far the most important grant program for health-professions students. Each participant would receive an annual scholarship during each year of training. The scholarship would include tuition, other educational expenses, and a stipend for living expenses. In return, the recipient would be obligated to serve as a commissioned officer in the Public Health Service or as a civilian member of the NHSC following completion of his or her academic training. Recipients would give one year of service for each year during which he or she had received the scholarship.

Failure to complete all or any part of the period of required service would entail an obligation to repay scholarship funds plus interest to the federal government within three years. Failure to complete an academic program would entail a similar obligation.

We strongly support the proposed expansion of both the NHSC and the NHSC scholarship program, but we are not convinced that proposals for doubling or tripling repayment provisions are essential to achieving compliance with the commitment to serve in underserved areas. We also believe that a two-year service commitment might be preferable to the four-year commitment that would be required for a student who received a NHSC scholarship for four years. Excessive requirements and penalties could seriously deter voluntary enlistment in the program.

Other Student Assistance

Current proposals involve significant changes in existing student aid provisions. One bill would phase out the scholarship program for needy students, while another includes a modest provision for scholarships to students of exceptional financial need in their first year of postbaccalaureate study.

A case can be made for a modest scholarship program, with emphasis on, but not limited to, first-year students, encouraging enrollment of students from disadvantaged backgrounds without forcing them into the NHSC scholarship program.

The Carnegie Council pointed out serious inadequacies and inequities in existing federal loan programs in *The Federal Role in Postsecondary Education.* (For revised recommendations on student loans, see summary of *Next Steps for the 1980s in Student Financial Aid.*) We have recommended that existing loan programs be phased out and replaced by a National Student Loan Bank. Because of the relatively heavy reliance of medical and dental students on loans as a means of financing, the establishment of such a bank would be especially advantageous for them.

Detailed recommendation 10: *The Council recommends expanded federal financial support for the National Health Service Corps (NHSC) and the associated NHSC scholarship program, along the lines of current legislative proposals. In addition to the NHSC scholarship program, the Council recommends a scholarship program for medical and dental students of exceptional financial need, with major emphasis on, but not limited to, first-year students.*

The Council recommends that Congress give serious consideration to the establishment of a National Student Loan Bank to replace existing student loan programs, as recommended in its report. The Federal Role in Postsecondary Education.

New Medical and Dental Schools

Great caution should be exercised in supporting the establishment of any new medical schools, as there has been a rapid increase in the size of entering medical school classes since the late 1960s.

How Many New Medical Schools?

The Carnegie Commission suggested that there should be a university health science center in every metropolitan area with a population of 350,000 or more, except for those areas that could benefit from centers existing in other geographically convenient communities. It identified nine areas in which new medical schools should be established. Since 1970, medical schools, or clinical branches of existing medical schools, have been established in seven of these areas, and an area health education center has been established in an eighth. However, new medical schools are being developed in 13 communities in which the Commission did not recommend a new school. An important factor in the establishment of five of these schools was the enactment of the Veterans Administration

Medical School Assistance and Health Manpower Training Act of 1972, which authorized (1) a program of Veterans Administration (VA) assistance to states for the establishment of new medical schools, (2) a program of grants to medical schools that have maintained affiliations with the VA, and (3) a program of grants to affiliated institutions to assist in the coordination, improvement, and expansion of allied health education.

We seriously question whether most of the developing schools should be established. We also question whether the VA should have been given authority to provide funds for new medical schools independently of the Health Resources Administration in the U.S. Public Health Service, the agency within the federal government responsible for administering most of the aid to university health science centers.

How Many New Dental Schools?

Like medical schools, dental schools should have adequate geographical distribution, even though new dental schools may not be needed to accelerate an increase in dental school enrollment.

Detailed recommendation 11: *On grounds of adequate geographic distribution, the Council recommends the development of a new medical school in Wilmington, Delaware. Authority for the Veterans Administration to provide funds for new medical schools should be repealed by Congress, and all decisions relating to start-up funds and construction funds from federal sources should be centralized with the Secretary of Health, Education, and Welfare.*

Among developing medical education programs, the Council believes that special consideration should be given to programs in Atlanta, Georgia, and Window Rock, Arizona, that are designed to encourage members of minority groups to train for the medical profession.

The Council recommends the development of a new dental school in Arizona, preferably in Tucson. Apart from Arizona, states that lack a dental school should seek arrangements with neighboring states under the auspices of regional higher education boards to provide dental education for their residents, if they are not already involved in such arrangements.

Congress should authorize the Secretary of Health, Education, and Welfare to make a determination, after consultation with appropriate advisory bodies, to withhold federal funds, including capitation payments, from developing medical and dental schools deemed to be excessive.

Area Health Education Centers

The formation of area health education centers (AHECs) has been one of the most encouraging and impressive developments under the 1971 legislation. (For an evaluation of the 11 federally funded AHEC programs, see summary of *Area Health Education Centers: The Pioneering Years, 1972-1978,* by C. Odegaard.) As recommended by the Carnegie Commission, an AHEC would perform all of the functions of a university health science center except for the basic education of M.D. and D.D.S. candidates. Centers would be located in both the ghetto areas of large cities and in communities located some distance from a university health science center—the communities to be chosen to provide a well-distributed geographic network of centers. Each center would be affiliated with a university health science center, which would supervise its educational programs.

The primary purpose of AHECs is to improve the quality of health care. But they can also play a significant role in the effort to overcome geographic maldistribution of health manpower. The experience with AHECs is too recent to yield hard statistical data on this point, but there is a good deal of anecdotal evidence indicating that development of a high-quality residency program in a community hospital has been of substantial assistance in attracting physicians to communities suffering from shortages.

Since 1971, two basic types of AHECs have emerged, the Carnegie model consortium and (much more common) the community-based consortium. The basic distinction between them is the relationship or lack of it with a university health science center. Because clinical training programs are the central core of a fully developed AHEC program, we consider affiliation with a university health science center essential.

Each of the AHEC programs has its own distinctive characteristics, but all give emphasis to decentralized health manpower training, in many cases with particular reference to M.D. candidates and physician residency training. AHECs are especially suitable for the development of primary care residency programs, which can be conducted effectively in community hospitals. AHEC programs are also well adapted to the training of physician's assistants, nurse-practitioners, and dental auxiliary personnel. Progress toward decentralization of medical and dental clinical training to date strongly suggests the desirability of a more explicit federal-state partnership in the support of AHECs. A portion of the federal funds for AHECs should be allocated to states that are prepared to come up with matching funds and that are developing state plans for AHECs.

Location

Thirty-three states have AHECs, clinical training centers, or area health education systems under the supervision of a university health science center. Only in about four of these states is there comprehensive coverage of all parts of the state.

We have listed about 70 additional suggested centers and have also suggested the conversion of existing community-based consortiums into fully developed centers that are affiliated with a university health science center. With adequate financial support, they could become full-fledged AHECs. Meanwhile, we by no means intend to downgrade their activities in continuing education and health education, to which we attach great importance.

The Carnegie Commissions's suggestions for the location of AHECs did not specifically include many large cities, because it was assumed that decentralized health education programs would develop under the auspices of the university health science centers that exist in large cities. Thus far, relatively few AHECs have been developed in inner-city areas, where there is a vital need for them.

We do not believe that every university health science center should necessarily become involved to an equal degree in developing clinical training centers remote from its central teaching facility. Some medical schools will continue to be especially noted for their research programs, and this is as it should be. Although every university health science center should become more concerned with efforts to improve the quality of health care in its area than has been traditional, these efforts can take a variety of forms, and federal policy should not be directed toward imposing a single model on all schools. Therefore we oppose provisions making capitation payments conditional on conducting a certain proportion of a school's clinical training at sites remote from its main teaching facility.

Detailed recommendation 12: *The Council strongly supports the continued development of area health education centers along the lines of current legislative proposals and recommends that the Secretary of Health, Education, and Welfare be given authority* *to use some of the federal funds for matching grants to states that are seeking to develop Area Health Education Centers (AHECs).*

Final authority for approval of allocation of federal funds for the development of AHECs or area health education systems should be centralized with the Secretary of Health, Education, and Welfare.

State Support of Medical and Dental Education

Although there continue to be wide variations among the states in their expenditures on medical and dental education, impressive progress has been made in many states. State expenditures on medical education increased from $253 per $1,000,000 personal income in 1965-1967 to $470 in 1973-74, while they ranged from $1,647 per $1,000,000 personal income in Vermont to a very small amount in Delaware. As one would expect, states with predominantly public medical schools spend more on medical education than states in which a substantial percentage of enrollment is in private medical schools. In this respect, financing of medical schools parallels state financing of higher education in general. (See summary of *The States and Higher Education.*)

In recent years, there have been strong pressures within states to provide support for private medical schools. These pressures were particularly intense toward the end of the 1960s, when many private medical schools were experiencing severe financial problems. In many states provision of capitation payments for private medical schools was clearly more economical than financing the expansion of public medical school capacity that might be needed if the private schools were closed.

The number of states that provide support for private dental schools is much smaller than for medical schools generally, partly reflecting the absence in many states of private dental schools or any dental school at all. Many dental schools are very small, with entering classes well below 100 in size, and some of these are private schools that would have difficulty expanding, even with the help of federal subsidies, unless they received some support from state sources.

Detailed recommendation 14: *The Council recommends that the states that have no programs of financial support for private medical and dental schools take immediate steps toward adoption of such programs.*

A Classification of Institutions of Higher Education:

Revised Edition

December 1976

The Carnegie Commission's classification of institutions of higher education, first published in 1973, has been used increasingly for research and analysis concerning higher education by many organizations and individuals. Developed several years in advance of publication for use in the Commission's work, it was based on 1970 data. Since 1970, new institutions have appeared, old institutions have disappeared, and many institutions have changed in ways that require that they be reclassified.

The Carnegie Council therefore revised the classification using 1976 data. The Carnegie staff minimized changes in the classification scheme itself so that the continuity of categories for purposes of research concerned with changes over time would not be disturbed.

On net balance, 237 institutions—144 in the public sector and 93 in the private sector—were added to the family of institutions of higher education between 1970 and 1976. In neither sector, however, was the increase explained primarily by establishment of new institutions. In the public sector, the most important single cause was a separate listing of branch campuses that had existed in 1970, but had not been separately listed by the National Center for Education Statistics (NCES) in that year. There were also approximately 10 institutions that had shifted from private to public control. This left 68 public institutions (mainly two-year colleges) that opened between 1970 and 1976; during the same period, 23 closed, leaving a net gain of 45.

In the private sector, the increase in the number of institutions was explained quite differently. Only 35 private colleges opened between 1970 and 1976, while 85 closed, for a net loss of 50. Meanwhile, however, no less than 202 private institutions that had been in existence for some time—often 50 years or more—acquired eligibility for listing by NCES between 1970 and 1976. A number of institutions lost their eligibility for listing during the same period. The classification includes all institutions listed in the NCES's *Education Directory: Colleges and Universities, 1976-77.* It divides institutions into 6 main categories and a number of subcategories, or 19 categories in all, as follows:

1. Doctorate-Granting Institutions

1.1 Research Universities I. The 50 leading universities in terms of federal financial support of academic science in at least two of the three academic years 1972-73, 1973-74, and 1974-75, provided they awarded at least 50 Ph.D.'s (plus M.D.'s if a medical school was on the same campus) in 1973-74. Rockefeller University was included because of the high quality of its research and doctoral training, even though it did not meet these criteria.

1.2 Research Universities II. These universities were on the list of the 100 leading institutions in terms of federal financial support in at least two out of the above three years and awarded at least 50 Ph.D.'s (plus M.D.'s if a medical school was on the same campus) in 1973-74. At least 25 of these degrees must have been Ph.D.'s. Alternatively, the institution was among the leading 60 institutions in terms of the total number of Ph.D.'s awarded during the years from 1965-66 to 1975-76. In addition, a few institutions that did not quite meet these criteria, but that have graduate programs of high quality and with impressive promise for future development, have been included in this category.

1.3 Doctorate-Granting Universities I. These institutions awarded 40 or more Ph.D.'s in at least five fields in 1973-74 (plus M.D.'s if on the same campus) or received at least $3 million in total federal support in either 1973-74 or 1974-75. No institution is included that granted less than 20 Ph.D.'s (plus M.D.'s if on the same campus) in at least five fields regardless of the amount of federal financial support it received.

1.4 Doctorate-Granting Universities II. These institutions awarded at least 20 Ph.D.'s in 1973-74 without regard to field, or 10 Ph.D.'s in at least three fields. In addition, a few doctorage-granting institutions that may be expected to increase the number of Ph.D.'s awarded within a few years are included.

2. Comprehensive Universities and Colleges

2.1 Comprehensive Universities and Colleges I. This group includes institutions that offered a liberal arts program as well as several other programs, such as engineering and business administration. Many of them offered master's degrees, but all lacked a doctoral program or had an extremely limited doctoral program. All institutions in this group had at least two professional or occupational programs and enrolled at least 2,000 students in 1976. If an institution's enrollment was smaller than this, it was not considered very comprehensive.

2.2 Comprehensive Universities and Colleges II. This list includes state colleges and private colleges that offered a liberal arts program and at least one professional or occupational program, such as teacher training or nursing. Many of the institutions in this group are former teachers colleges that have broadened their programs to include a liberal arts curriculum. In general, private institutions with less than 1,500 students and public institutions with less than 1,000 students in 1976 were not included even though they offered a selection of programs, because with such small enrollments they were not regarded as comprehensive. Such institutions are classified as liberal arts colleges. The enrollment differentiation between private and public institutions was made because public colleges with small enrollments are usually new institutions that can be expected to grow rapidly. However, some predominantly teachers colleges, especially in sparsely populated states, have been losing enrollment in recent years, and in such cases we have continued to classify them in the 2.2 group, even when their enrollment has fallen below the usual minimum.

3. Liberal Arts Colleges

3.1 Liberal Arts Colleges I. These colleges scored 1030 or more on a selectivity index developed by Alexander W. Astin or were included among the 200 leading baccalaureate-granting institutions in terms of numbers of their graduates receiving Ph.D.'s at 40 leading doctorate-granting institutions from 1920 to 1966.

3.2 Liberal Arts Colleges II. These institutions include all the liberal arts colleges that did not meet our criteria for inclusion in the first group of liberal arts colleges. Again, the distinction between "liberal arts" and "comprehensive" is not clear-cut for some of the larger colleges in this group and is necessarily partly a matter of judgment.

4. Two-Year Colleges and Institutes

5. Professional Schools and Other Specialized Institutions

5.1 Theological seminaries, bible colleges, and other institutions offering degrees in religion. In general, only those institutions that do not have a liberal arts program as well as a religious program of instruction are included in this category. Colleges that combine liberal arts and religious instruction are generally classified in one of our two liberal arts categories. However, if the liberal arts program appears to be very minor, and the primary purpose of the institution is to train members of the clergy, an institution is classified in this category. Like the distinction between a comprehensive institution and a liberal arts college, this distinction is not always clear-cut and requires judgment.
5.2 Medical schools and medical centers. This category includes only those that are listed as separate campuses in the NCES directory. In some instances, the medical center includes other health professional schools, for example, dentistry, pharmacy, or nursing.
5.3 Other separate health professional schools.
5.4 Schools of engineering and technology. Technical institutes are included only if they award a bachelor's degree and if their program is limited exclusively or almost exclusively to technical fields of study.
5.5 Schools of business and management. Business schools are included only if they award a bachelor's or higher degree and if their program is limited exclusively or almost exclusively to a business curriculum.
5.6 Schools of art, music, and design.
5.7 Schools of law.
5.8 Teachers colleges.
5.9 Other specialized institutions. Includes graduate centers, maritime academies, military institutes (that do not have a liberal arts program), and miscellaneous institutions.

6. Institutions for Nontraditional Study

In recent years, a number of institutions oriented to nontraditional study have been established, usually without a campus in the conventional sense. A separate category has been created for these institutions.

Federal Reorganization:
Education and Scholarship
April 1977

The Council offered several observations and proposals for administrative reorganization of educational programs within the federal government at a time when that subject was under consideration by federal decision makers.

We did not consider postsecondary education to have been neglected within the Department of Health, Education, and Welfare (HEW). On the contrary, postsecondary education generally is well treated. Our concern is, rather, that the federal government might well improve its organizational structure with benefit to public service.

The very process of reorganization has a disturbing influence and careful calculation must be made whether the short-term costs of disturbance outweigh the long-term advantages. We do not believe that our suggestions constitute the only possible solution. We present them as one approach that warrants consideration along with other alternatives, including no action at all.

A reorganization of the federal government in the areas of education and support for scholarship might serve the following purposes:

- Give greater visibility and a higher level of administrative attention to education and the pursuit of knowledge that is more nearly commensurate with their contribution to national growth and welfare
- Provide better coordination of policies and programs across federal agencies
- Relieve the heavy burdens now placed on HEW.

To accomplish these purposes, we suggest the following possibilities:

1. *Establish the position of Undersecretary (or Secretary) of Education, Research, and Advanced Studies within HEW.* This would substantially raise the level of attention to education. We suggest more important duties for this position than are now carried by any comparable post in the federal government. In particular, such a position would combine an interest in education with a concern for the advancement of knowledge—a natural and productive combination. It would reflect the rise of the federal government as the main source of support for basic research and the by now very influential position of the federal government in the development of higher education.

We are doubtful of the need to create a new cabinet-level department of education. Such a department (a) would be a comparatively small department within the federal hierarchy; (b) would exist in any event in an area of relative program stability due to little or no enrollment growth, as compared with rapidly expanding federal interest and expenditures in other areas; (c) might imply that the federal government was assuming basic responsibility for education when it should continue to rest with the states; and (d) might tend to give more attention to primary and secondary education at the expense of higher education.

The first corollary of the proposal to establish an undersecretary position would be to raise the status of the top administrators of the present four major operating divisions (bureaus) of the Office of Education (school systems, occupational and adult education, education for the handicapped, postsecondary education). If this is done, some combination of bureaus might be in order, as well as some reassignment of the organizational locations of the Office of Indian Education, the Fund for the Improvement of Postsecondary Education, and the National Center for Education Statistics. In any event, transfer of Head Start from the Division of Human Development into the education area may be in order.

The second corollary is that the undersecretary would assume the duties of the Commissioner of Education. This would eliminate the confusion, duplication of effort, and rivalry between the present positions of assistant secretary and commissioner. Whatever else happens, this unnecessary and unclear duality of supervisors should be eradicated.

2.   *Make the Undersecretary (or Secretary) of Education, Research, and Advanced Studies the chairperson of three coordinating councils.* These councils would consider overall federal policy in specific areas and submit annual reports on developments and recommendations for future changes.

    a.   Council on Educational Programs. Well over 300 programs in postsecondary education alone exist in at least 25 federal agencies. No adequate mechanism exists for the exchange of information among them, let alone examination of duplications and inconsistencies.

    b.   Council of Institutes of Research and Advanced Studies. No mechanism exists for joint consideration of the total support by the federal government of advances in basic knowledge. The overall flow of funds and support for graduate students would be among the concerns of this council, as would be the contributions of new knowledge to the national welfare.

    c.   Council on Student Aid. Student aid is scattered in several agencies, and no method exists to view it in its entirety or to coordinate it with state efforts.

3.   *Simplify the Department of Health, Education, and Welfare,* which now spends more money than any other federal department and has the second largest total personnel. Two alternatives are possible:

    a.   One alternative is to transfer income maintenance programs to the Department of Labor, making it a Department of Labor and Human Resources, concentrating its attention on work. HEW might then become a Department of Health, Education, and Science, with concentration on growth through better health, higher skills, and greater knowledge.

    b.   Health is increasingly a federal responsibility, and health programs could be transferred to a new Department of Health, making the present HEW a Department of Education and Welfare. We suggest that this possibility be deferred until a clearer view is available of the future shape of the national health care program.

Our current preference between these two alternatives is for (a). Struggling with the policy, fiscal, and administrative complexities of both health care and income maintenance places a very heavy burden on the Secretary of HEW. Also, we believe that there is a natural connection between work and income mainten-ance, as well as one between health, education, and science. In addition, because of the close connection between adequate training and productive employment, federal programs concerned with on-the-job training and with training and place-ment for the underemployed should be located in the Department of Labor.

These inherent connections, if reflected in a new administrative structure, could give greater coherence to federal policy and administration.

Faculty Bargaining in Public Higher Education

May 1977

Collective bargaining by faculty members in higher education is largely a development of only the past decade, but it is already well established.

- Twenty-four states have laws that authorize employees of public institutions of postsecondary education to organize and bargain collectively.
- About 25 percent of the nation's full-time faculty are now included in some form of collective organization on about 30 percent of the campuses.
- In recent years, faculty opinion has moved strongly toward greater acceptance of collective bargaining and use of the strike and greater militancy in defending faculty interests.

No major circumstances ahead are likely to change greatly this growing acceptance of collective bargaining.

The Council endorsed the view of the Carnegie Commission that "state laws, where they do not now permit it, should provide faculty members in public institutions the opportunity of obtaining collective bargaining rights." This was not to recommend, however, that faculty members should necessarily and in all circumstances exercise such rights; nor should they be penalized if they do not choose to bargain collectively. They should give the most careful consideration to the impacts of collective bargaining on:

1. Existing formal and informal arrangements for faculty exercise of influence over academic matters
2. The inclination of students to organize in response
3. Managerial authority and attitudes—its authority may increase and its attitudes become more opposed to the faculty
4. Campus autonomy, public control over higher education, and public attitudes toward higher education
5. Intercampus and interinstitutional uniformity of policies and practice and tendencies toward centralization, formalization, and rigidification
6. The respective positions of influence of senior and junior faculty members and of nonfaculty personnel.

This report of the Council appeared in a volume that also included two essays: "State Experience in Collective Bargaining," by Joseph W. Garbarino, and "Legislative Issues in Faculty Bargaining," by David Feller and Matthew Finkin. These essays are summarized in Part Three of this book.

By now there is enough experience with collective bargaining in higher education to indicate the centrality of three issues that could significantly determine the impact of bargaining on the values, traditions, and relationships of higher education. These issues are the election unit, the scope of bargaining, and the designation of employer.

The Election Unit

We wish to distinguish as clearly as we can between the election unit and the bargaining unit. The bargaining unit that negotiates and signs the contract can be, and often is, much larger than the election unit. Two separate issues are involved: (1) the principle of "unions of their own choosing"—best determined by smaller, more homogeneous units of employees that can express most precisely the "consent of the governed"; and (2) the power politics of achieving effective bargaining levels and alliances on both the employer's and the union's sides. We are concerned here with the first of these issues. To follow the principle of free choice generally leads to smaller, more homogeneous election units. Power considerations, however, frequently lead to larger, more hetero-geneous and comprehensive bargaining units.

However, most current state statutes make no attempt to limit, through articulation of explicit membership characteristics, the occupational character or geographic scope of the election unit organization, and the trend of policy via rule-making by state public employee relations boards also has been in the direction of larger, more heteregeneous election units. Such arrangements are a potential threat to the status and influence of faculty on matters of academic governance, and an actual threat to the principle of self-determination and autonomy of individual campus or institutional units. In contrast, law and administrative policy should provide for and recognize election unit organizations comprising individuals with common, homogeneous professional and occupational interests, traditions, attitudes, and needs.

Our view is that the election unit should be limited to faculty members on an individual campus, which we see as the natural constituency for determining consent. We say "faculty members" because they constitute the colleagues in the collegial governance of academic life, and we say "an individual campus" because that is both the historical orientation of faculty members and the face-to-face community to which they belong. To put it another way, we do not believe that nonfaculty personnel should be able to determine a vote that makes faculty members subject to exclusive representation by a union against their majority will; nor do we believe that votes on other campuses should bind an unwilling campus into such exclusive representation.

The Scope of Bargaining

Currently, most statutes authorizing collective bargaining in higher education and other sectors of public employment impose limits on the scope of bargaining by using, nearly verbatim, the traditional industrial language focusing on "wages, hours, and terms and conditions of employment." There are many practical difficulties in trying to use traditional coverage language in the basic law to demarcate which issues fall clearly within or beyond the boundary of matters mandatorily subject to bargaining in higher education.

Special legislation, administrative rulings, or other actions should safeguard the intellectual missions of higher education, particularly where nonfaculty personnel are included, where students become part of the bargaining process, or where more than one campus is involved, especially when the campuses are diverse in history and functions. The problem is complicated and cannot be solved by reference to management rights alone. In addition to bargaining rights in higher education, there are also academic, professional, or collegial rights that must be protected. Specifically, we believe that collective bargaining should not be permitted to determine:

1.   The selection and conduct of research by individual faculty members
2.   The content of courses and methods of teaching by individual faculty members or the development of programs of study
3.   The selection and promotion to tenure of individual faculty members
4.   The determination of individual student grades and the awarding of individual degrees
5.   The selection of individual academic leadership.

The scope of bargaining in higher education should be limited by legislation, administrative rulings, or practice to issues that bear directly upon "wages, hours, and terms and conditions of employment"—essentially items that have a monetary dimension. Those matters that traditionally constitute the essence of academic freedom and autonomy should be specifically excluded.

The Employer

Authorities on the functioning of collective bargaining in the private sector have traditionally argued that the party to a negotiation functioning as employer must be in a position to deliver the resources required to carry out the negotiated agreement. With the introduction of collective bargaining in the public sector, this principle of traditional labor-management relations has led political chief executives—particularly governors—to seek authority for and equip themselves with specialized staffs to act as the employer in labor negotiations. But higher education does not fit the standard rules. In industry, the employer has the resources; in state government, the governor has the resources. In higher education, the resources come from several different places. Who, then, should be the employer where there are diverse sources of funds and the institution is state supported but not state operated?

The inability of educational authorities to deliver the full resources required to carry out a negotiated agreement without recourse to supplemental consultations and ultimate approval by such political authorities as the governor and state legislature introduces weaknesses and uncertainty into all negotiations conducted on this basis that may call into question the seriousness, usefulness, or validity of the collective bargaining process.

In some instances, representatives of the governor, notwithstanding provisions of the law, substitute for educational authorities in negotiating contracts with faculty. This practice has some appeal, but it invites direct and unacceptable intervention by political authority in institutional management and academic affairs.

The preferable model is one in which the institution's leader and his board are responsible for presenting, defending, lobbying for, and ultimately living with appropriations made available by the legislature and governor for the conduct of higher education, including the payment of wages and salaries agreed upon through a bargaining process.

If incremental appropriations are not sufficient to cover the cost of an agreed-upon contract, the institutional leadership is obligated to find resources elsewhere, either through retrenchment or through tuition or other revenue increases. To make this approach workable, the board needs to have control over such matters as tuition levels and internal transfer of funds. Our preferred model will work best where the institutions of higher education have substantial autonomy. It will apply least well, and is not a viable alternative, where centralized state authority is already well established.

In defining or designating an authority or agent to assume the responsibilities of the employer in collective bargaining proceedings, state enabling legislation should strive to safeguard the tradition of maximum institutional autonomy, leadership, and control in the management of academic programs and all resources that are involved in their provision. State enabling legislation should designate the governing board of each individual institution, or "systems" group of consolidated institutions, to serve as the employer for its sphere in collective bargaining proceedings, allowing it to designate its bargaining representatives—normally the president. In addition, collective bargaining should reinforce the unencumbered authority of the designated employer to manage such financial resources as political authorities may appropriate to fulfill the employers' obligations under negotiated settlements with higher education employees. Our specific preferences are as follows:

1. That the governing board be established as the employer.
2. If the governor is to be directly involved, that there be two-tier bargaining, with money matters bargained with the governor and nonmoney matters with the board, or three-tier bargaining in multicampus systems, with some local nonmoney matters bargained at the campus level.
3. If the governor negotiates the total agreement, that he exercise restraint in accepting or asserting as bargainable items those matters that do not affect the budget of the state, as most governors thus far have done.
4. In the case of both (2) and (3) above, that the budget requests of the state be divided between the basic budget and additive personnel costs, with the additive personnel costs subject to bargaining by the union and the basic budget subject to handling by the board with the governor and legislature. In any event, the governor, functioning as employer, should consult closely with the executive leaders of higher education.
5. In the case of (1) above, some items may need to be left open until the state budget has been adopted. The union should, of course, be free to assist the board to obtain the state funds necessary to fund the agreement. We note that, even when the governor negotiates an agreement, it cannot take effect until the legislature has appropriated the money. Completion of the contract should be subject, as is often the case, to the availability of financial resources.

Any system of arrangements can be made to work, but we are concerned with what system has the best chance of working well in the long run. This involves, among other things, protecting academic influence over academic matters and safeguarding essential institutional independence from government domination.

Selective Admissions in Higher Education:
Public Policy and Academic Policy
October 1977

In this report, we place great emphasis on equality of opportunity, which involves a strong concern for finding and developing potential talent and thus less emphasis upon simply rewarding already developed talent.

We stress consideration for the contributions a student can make to the education of his or her fellow students and prospectively to society after graduation rather than consideration alone for the preexisting academic merit of the student as measured by grades and test scores.

We emphasize consideration for the individual rather than for groups in their entirety, but we urge consideration of special characteristics that have derived from the home and social environment from which the individual comes—specifically, from experience with educational disadvantage or social discrimination and knowledge of a minority culture.

We have sought a "golden mean" balance of these considerations, avoiding the polar positions of a totally meritocratic approach or strict egalitarianism. We draw on several American ideals rather than on any one alone.

We distinguish three different situations:

1. Nonselective admissions at the undergraduate level. All high school graduates and sometimes all persons over 18 years old are accepted.
2. Selective admissions at all levels of higher education, with policies that range from highly to moderately selective.
3. Selective admissions to the graduate and professional schools that, in addition to (2), control or strongly influence entrance to a profession, as in entrance to medicine and law through attendance at accredited medical and law schools.

In this report, we are particularly concerned with the third situation. The question before us is: What approach to admissions should be followed by these schools? We are specifically concerned with public and academic policy governing such admissions, and how the two may best be reconciled if their requirements diverge.

This report of the Council appeared in a volume that also included two essays: "The Pursuit of Fairness in Admissions," by Winton H. Manning, and "The Status of Selective Admissions," by Warren W. Willingham and Hunter M. Breland. These essays are summarized in Part Three of this book.

Public Policy

The public has a clear interest in access to higher education. It begins with the creation of places for students, and all of our states have established and supported public institutions of higher education. Many of these places (40 percent) are open on a nonselective basis. Society also has a special interest in assuring that selective places be filled on the basis of fair and reasonable institutional policies and procedures and that no one is subject to discrimination on the basis of race, sex, religion, or ethnic origin.

The public has additional interests in the case of gatekeeper schools that largely determine the composition of the professions and thus affect the professional services available to society. These schools should make every effort to admit and to graduate persons who will meet the needs of the public for service, and these needs are both quite diverse and subject to change. Individuals within each identifiable group of people should have a fair chance to rise to positions of leadership. And when groups that have suffered discrimination are heavily underrepresented in the privileged roles resulting from selectivity in higher education, there are grounds for making special efforts to find, prepare, and admit qualified individuals from such groups. However, it is individual talent that should be recognized and given a chance to advance in accordance with the effort that accompanied it. Members of all groups must know that advancement is possible but not guaranteed.

Academic Policy

For institutions with selective admissions, the composition of their student bodies is of great importance. This composition is determined, first of all, by those who apply to them, and second, by those who are admitted and then actually enroll.

The United States prides itself on the diversity of its colleges, and since this diversity depends on the diversity of the composition of their student bodies, colleges have historically had very substantial autonomy in setting their own admissions policies. Restraints on institutional autonomy should be imposed, therefore, only when a substantial public interest cannot be served in other ways.

The admissions policies of American colleges are almost infinite in number and take into consideration, among other things, prior scholastic grades and rank in class; test scores; special interests and abilities; and special identities and personal characteristics. In addition, student contributions to the diversity of the student body, to a campus tradition, and potentially to a particular profession may be considered.

1. Grades and tests, looked at together, are more predictive of subsequent academic performance than grades alone or tests alone.
2. Grades are less helpful than they once were because of grade inflation; so also are letters of personal recommendation because they no longer can be as confidential as they once were.
3. Grades and test scores are useful but usually not sufficient as a sole basis for action. They best determine those applicants who are likely to distinguish themselves academically and those likely to fail. They are not, however, suited for fine tuning, and such application constitutes a misuse of these evaluations.
4. Colleges often use their admissions policies to build academic and social communities. Thus, choosing a student body is not just judging a foot race based upon so-called objective credentials.
5. Professional schools have often been too little concerned with providing professionals who will offer a balanced set of services to society.

6.   Too many favors have been given by too many institutions to those with special influence.

7.   Admission is often different at the graduate level than at the undergraduate. There is more of an academic record to review, and the academic standards to be met are usually at a higher level, particularly for the Ph.D. degree. Consequently, it is reasonable that past academic performance should weigh more heavily.

8.   The gatekeeper schools are distinctive in at least three major respects: (a) they must be much more careful not to admit students who lack the ability to practice the relevant profession with competence and integrity; (b) they must be much more conscious of the desirability of supplying graduates who will meet the varied needs of the public; and (c) their graduates face uniform tests after graduation, and the results of these tests are added up as a way of rating the individual schools. These schools may have a quite legitimate interest in special persons with special characteristics that relate directly to potential service with a profession.

The challenges are to apply public policy without undue interference with academic judgment and concerns, and for institutions to satisfy public policy without loss of academic standards.

Recommendations for Public and Academic Policy

We make nine specific recommendations for policy affecting admissions to selective schools at both the undergraduate and graduate levels.

1.   These schools should adhere to a policy of affirmative action in educational practices:
      a.   No policies or practices should discriminate against members of groups subject to discrimination.
      b.   Special efforts should be made to recruit members of these groups.
      c.   Compensatory education should be available to such persons when there is reason to believe that undeveloped potential can be realized by providing it.
      d.   Special financial assistance and counseling should be provided when needed.
      e.   Goals may be set against which progress can be measured.

2.   Race or background in a non-English language home should be considered in individual cases where it (a) reflects prior adverse social discrimination, (b) contributes to prior educational disadvantage, (c) involves direct knowledge of special cultural patterns and experiences, or (d) indicates, along with other evidence, the probability of subsequent provision of specially needed services to society.
      The first and second of these considerations are based on the principles of equality of treatment and equality of opportunity, the third on institutional interest in diversity in the student community, and the fourth on the needs of society for service.
      We emphasize racial experience, not race per se, and experience in a non-English language home, not heritage or surname per se. Thus, we say *in individual cases.* Race or other minority status should be only one of several dimensions considered as aspects of prior disadvantage or adverse discrimination; as one of several indicators of prospective contributions to the diversity and quality of the academic experience for other students; and as one of several intimations of intention to serve society in neglected areas. Thus, individuals from the majority group

may also warrant special consideration, depending upon the circumstances of their background.

3. No student should be admitted who cannot meet the general academic standards set for all students. These standards should be set at the minimum level at which there is a reasonable chance of success of completing the course work without reduction in academic or professional standards. The pool of applicants from which specific selections can be made is almost certainly larger than the pool now receiving individual consideration by many schools.

4. No numerical quota for any component should be set, but goals should be established that may change over time.

5. Financial aid should be provided to students from low-income families to attract them in sufficient numbers into the pool of applicants.

6. All applicants should be processed through the same set of procedures to assure that they are looked at together and not separately, and that each person is being evaluated on his or her own merits.

7. The faculty should participate actively in the admission process and take responsibility for the decisions. In the absence of fully objective criteria, application of professional judgment is the best available approach.

8. Schools should be given maximum latitude in exercising their judgments about the admission of individual students. We note that such autonomy for higher education is a basic principle, but its acceptance in practice can be reinforced by institutions through concern for professional integrity and attention to the needs of society. We suggest the following:

   a. The governing board, as the bearer of the public trust, should set general admissions policies with faculty, student, and administrative advice.

   b. Statements of policies and procedures should be made available to the public.

9. The judgment of courts, legislatures, or government officials should not replace professional judgment except when clearly required by the public interest. Rigid and simplistic formulas externally imposed should, in any event, be avoided.

Conclusion

We hope that race and other minority status will be much less of a distinguishing feature of American society in the future as we overcome the consequences of past discrimination. We hope the current period of transition will not last beyond the end of the current century—less than one generation. In the meantime, in making selective admissions to institutions of higher education, consideration of special characteristics that often derive from such backgrounds is a major means for American society to become more just and more integrated.

The States and Private Higher Education:

Problems and Policies in a New Era
December 1977

This report seeks to present the situation as it now exists, to evaluate the programs under-taken to date, and to make recommendations for future action. It is based in part on the results of a study specifically designed to assess the impact of existing state policies toward private higher education on enrollments, finances, autonomy, academic freedom, and other conditions or private institutions. Technical supplements to the report present data from this study.

General Considerations

1. The private sector enrolls just over one-fifth of all students in higher education, offers a diversity of institutions for student choice, and includes a substantial proportion of high-quality academic programs. It also saves the taxpayers about $5 billion a year (net)—the estimated cost to states of absorbing its enrollments in public institutions.

2. In the late 1960s and early 1970s, this sector went through a difficult time. The current stability of the sector as a whole is due partly to self-help efforts by private institutions and partly to increasing state and federal government responsiveness to the new needs of the private sector for financial support. (See Figure 1.)

    There is no acute general crisis calling for drastic immediate increases in public support to perpetuate private higher education. There are, however, contin-uing reasons for substantial concern over the long run.

3. More public assistance will be necessary in the future. In addition to other factors contributing to the prospective economic problems of private institutions, the age cohort of 18-21 year olds, which has traditionally supplied much of the enroll-ment in private colleges, will decline from its peak level by about 25 percent by 1995. American society, however, will need the enrollment capacity of the private sector when the size of this age cohort again increases after 1995.

4. We value the private sector for (a) its independence of governance; (b) its diversity; (c) its long-standing traditions that are so meaningful to its students and alumni; (d) its devotion to liberal learning; (e) its standards of academic freedom; (f) its attention to and attraction for individual students; (g) its contribution of a high proportion of the institutions with the academically ablest students and faculty; (h) its contributions to cultural life; and (i) its provision of wide access for students by income group and minority status.

Figure 1. Sources of public support of public and private institutions of higher education, per full-time equivalent student, 1976-1977

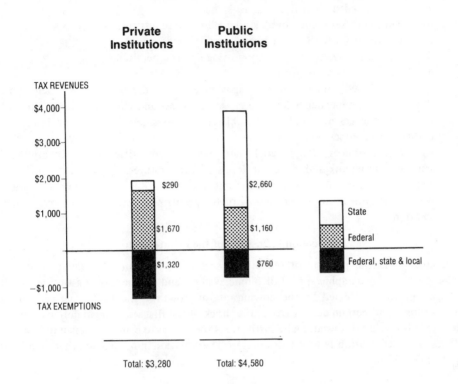

5. The question is not whether more assistance will be needed and given—most states and the federal government are already committed to some support for the private sector—but how it will be given and in what amounts.
6. The private sector should be supported in ways that will (a) be effective; (b) preserve its independence; (c) encourage balanced competition between private institutions and between them and public institutions; and (d) avoid "bailing out" individual institutions on the brink of failure, for this will discourage competition.
7. Any policy aimed at such preservation should observe guidelines that ensure (a) maximum self-help; (b) more state support, but gradual movement in increasing that support; (c) the federal government provides adequate student aid; (d) state programs are tailored to local conditions and traditions; and (e) public policy involves choices of what is best in the long-term public interest and not necessarily what responds to the immediate interest of distressed institutions.
8. Basic to any choice of one type of state aid over another is the impact the program is likely to have—on the institution, on the student, and on society. Important considerations are the program's impact on (a) institutional independence; (b) equality of opportunity, including choice of institution, whether in-state or out-of-state; (c) the degree of competition among private institutions and with public institutions; (d) maintenance of institutional diversity; (e) certainty of receipt of funds based on broad public support; and (f) public institutions and their acceptance of the approach.

9.   Considering these tests and experience to date, our general order of preference among the major alternative programs for state support is as follows:
     a.   Need-based student financial assistance
     b.   Tuition-offset grants for all students in private institutions
     c.   Contracts for services (such as operating a medical school)
     d.   Categorical grants (such as supporting library operations)
     e.   Direct grants to institutions.

   Need-based student financial assistance is placed first because it helps both the cause of independence and the causes of access and choice; creates a program that both the general public and public institutions can support; and intensifies constructive competition.

   Circumstances in individual states will indicate different combinations of assistance programs and different levels of expenditures. There are 50 different states, and there may well be 50 different state policies. Recognition of this variety is essential both to an understanding of the problems and to prescriptions for their solutions.

The Economic Position of the Private Sector

The general financial position of the private sector has been most affected by the increasing size and geographic spread of public systems and by the growing tuition gap. It is beginning to be affected by the slowing rate of growth in the 18-21 year age cohort and its subsequent certain decline. After the shock of the first widespread deficits and the dire predictions that followed, many institutions took steps to bring budgets into balance. Others exercised caution lest deficits develop. The situation improved and then stabilized by the mid-1970s.

Enrollment Trends

Enrollments in private higher education have long been a declining proportion of total enrollments but have increased steadily, albeit comparatively slowly, in absolute terms. The most important forces at work have been these:

*   Increases in both public and private enrollments have slowed down, even though they have continued as the rate of growth of the 18-21-year age cohort has declined.
*   Public enrollments were strongly affected by a sharp reduction in the enrollment of veterans from 1975 to 1976.
*   Among the states, private enrollments have tended to rise most where total enrollments have risen most, and vice versa.
*   Among the states, increased enrollment competition from the public sector has had the greatest impact where private enrollments were a relatively high proportion to begin with. This has been especially true in states in which private institutions draw most of their students from within the state.
*   State aid to private institutions has not fully shielded them, thus far, from loss of enrollments where there has been a quickly expanding public sector.

It is misleading to overgeneralize about the private sector, but some points of special interest are:

*   The comparative stability of the more academically elite sector
*   The great volatility of enrollments in the less selective liberal arts colleges

- The favorable enrollments in institutions responsive to the interests of adult and vocationally oriented students
- The extreme importance to individual institutions of gaining accreditation status (in order to be eligible for government-funded student aid programs)
- The disadvantages of being heavily concentrated on teacher training
- The disadvantages of being very small, very rural, or very new; of being small, female, and Roman Catholic; and of being located in certain geographic regions.

Tuition Gap

Private and public tuitions have, in recent years, generally kept pace with each other in terms of percentage increases; public tuition has risen faster, but the private sector started from a much higher base. The dollar gap, as a consequence, has roughly doubled in the past decade. The general burden of all tuition, however, has remained about the same, because tuition costs have risen more or less parallel with the rise in per capita disposable personal income. The total cost of tuition and room and board, however, has risen less rapidly than personal income, and thus the real burden on families and students has gone down, not up. (See Figure 2.)

Figure 2. Comparative increases of tuition, tuition and room and board, room and board, Consumer Price Index, and per capita disposable personal income, 1970-71 to 1975-76, for four-year colleges other than universities

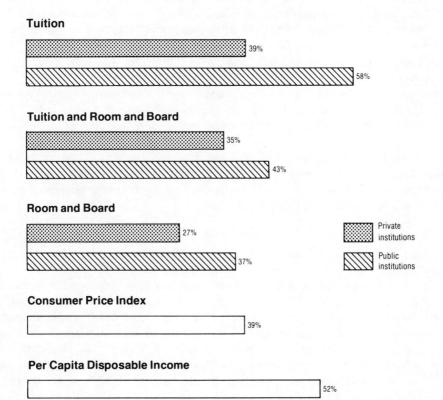

Tuition
39%
58%

Tuition and Room and Board
35%
43%

Room and Board
27%
37%

Private institutions

Public institutions

Consumer Price Index
39%

Per Capita Disposable Income
52%

Tuitions at individual institutions—especially if their students tend to be state residents—are affected less by the general gap between public and private tuitions than by the gap within their state for comparable types of institutions. These gaps vary from $130 to $2,500.

Financial Status

Enrollment is a major factor in the financial well-being of the private sector. Almost two-thirds of the four-year institutions derive at least 70 percent of their unrestricted educational and general revenue from tuition and fees. In light of their dependence on tuition income, the uneven behavior of enrollment in the private sector is a matter of considerable concern. While total full-time equivalent (FTE) enrollment in all private institutions increased 3.9 percent from 1970 to 1975, undergraduate FTE enrollment declined slightly, and in a number of states total FTE enrollment also declined. The overall increase masked what was happening to individual institutions. Both total and undergraduate enrollments were declining in many private institutions, with less selective liberal arts colleges most severely affected and universities the least.

As a group, the less selective liberal arts colleges have little endowment income and, outside of tuition revenue, are heavily dependent on private gifts. Comprehensive universities and colleges also have relatively little endowment income and are more dependent on tuition than are other types of private institutions. But they are less likely to be in a weak financial position, probably because many of them have maintained enrollments through broadening their programs and attracting adult students.

A significant proportion of more selective liberal arts colleges are in a weak financial position. As a group, relatively selective liberal arts colleges receive comparatively more of their income from endowments than do other groups of institutions, but institutional data reveal that they vary markedly in the size of their endowment funds relative to FTE enrollments.

Universities are not in a uniformly sound financial position either. Relatively few of the selected private institutions in our survey could be classified as weak, but there is an enormous variation among universities in the size of their endowments in relation to enrollment.

Most private institutions have responded to their present circumstances in two main ways: by trying to improve revenue and by trying to reduce costs or otherwise use resources more effectively. It would be remiss to leave the impression, however, that private institutions have done all they can.

Vulnerability

The private sector can be divided into the less vulnerable and more vulnerable institutions. The less vulnerable category includes institutions with one or more of the following characteristics: high quality, strong religious orientation, long traditions and loyal alumni support, distinctive academic programs, special clienteles, or attractive locations. The more vulnerable category includes colleges that have concentrated heavily on teachers' education; some of the urban comprehensive colleges and universities that have little but higher tuition to distinguish them from their public counterparts; and very small liberal arts colleges with restricted programs, often located in rural and depopulating areas.

In states with a comparatively large private sector, the public sector usually has developed relatively recently on a large-scale basis and with higher-quality institutions. The new public institutions in such states are now giving real competition for the first time—and when overall growth no longer reduces the competitive impact.

States with few or none of the more vulnerable institutions may be able to preserve their private sectors through comparatively modest programs of support. A state with many of the more vulnerable institutions faces a much more difficult situation, particularly if it also has a number of less vulnerable institutions. The amount of support necessary to preserve all of the more vulnerable institutions may be much more than enough for the less vulnerable ones; furthermore, that amount of support—which may approach 100 percent of the support for similar public institutions—may threaten the independence of the private sector as a whole.

In some states, formula aid alone may not be enough; some system of differential and individualized treatment may also be necessary.

Outlook

Although there is no evidence that a large number of private institutions are about to disappear, about one-fourth may be in distress, and many others face an insecure and uncertain future. Among the reasons:

1. The tuition gap in current dollars between public and private institutions will probably continue to rise.
2. The size of the college-age cohort will decline.
3. Competition based on low tuition costs may become more aggressive as public institutions also feel the impact of declining growth rates.
4. Many institutions have already engaged in extensive cost-cutting, which will diminish their ability to absorb further inflation or loss of enrollments.
5. Reserves in the form of current and endowment fund balances are low for many institutions, and some are already heavily in debt.
6. The growth of collective bargaining in higher education may well be a greater threat to the financial stability of private than of public institutions, because the former cannot depend on increased state appropriations to cover higher faculty salaries.
7. First-generation college attenders may be more likely to attend certain private institutions that are local or religiously oriented or vocationally concentrated than second-and-third-generation attenders, who are likely to consider more institutions.

State Programs Now in Place

In 1975-76, 40 state governments combined spent more than $500 million on private institutions and their students. About 60 percent of this expenditure was used for financial aid to students. Somewhat less than 20 percent took the form of comprehensive formula grants for general institutional support; and somewhat more than 20 percent was used for specific educational programs, institutions, or purposes. The total expenditures amounted to about $275 per FTE student, compared to about $2,500 per FTE student in public institutions—a ratio of 1 to 9.1.

The four general forms of assistance are: financial aid to students, general support grants to institutions, support for specific programs or purposes, and indirect assistance.

Characteristics of Student Aid Programs

The periods of rapid growth of need-based student aid programs affecting students in private institutions were 1968-72, when there was widespread concern over the financial difficulties of many private institutions, and 1974-76, when the federal State Student Incentive Grant (SSIG) program stimulated a number of states to adopt student aid programs in order to receive federal matching funds.

In total, the states have, within a short period of time, set in motion a substantial number of programs to aid private higher education. By 1976-77, only nine states had no programs at all. One of these has no private institutions, and the other eight have small numbers of private institutions—62 in all. Thus the states have shown themselves willing and even eager to support private higher education when the situation warranted it.

Impacts of State Programs

1. State aid is more likely to be given in states with proportionately large private enrollments, but also in states where private enrollments consist more heavily of in-state students.
2. Institutional operating accounts over the years do not seem to have been substantially affected in states with substantial aid programs, as compared to states without such programs.
3. In states with substantial programs as compared to those without, the percentage of undergraduates receiving grants or scholarships is about 20 percentage points higher; more aid is in the form of grants and less in the form of loans or work-study, and more goes to students from higher income families. State aid to date has done more for students (and their families) than for institutions.
4. The year 1970-71 was very difficult; the next three years were better; the last three years have seen deterioration again. Inflation levels are the main cause of this pattern, but changes in enrollment have also contributed.
5. Student aid deficits of institutions have risen, even with much more federal and state student aid available. Deficits rose by about 50 percent from 1970-71 to 1975-76 both in states with substantial aid programs and in those without such programs. The rise in institutional deficits reflects efforts to offset rising tuition and to compete for special categories of students.
6. The number of institutions in a clearly deteriorating condition is small, but it appears to be somewhat larger in states that lack substantial programs of aid to private higher education.

Perceptions of State Programs

The Council's survey of presidential (and financial officer) attitudes toward state programs show that they found the programs particularly helpful in increasing revenues for general purposes (75 percent of respondents) and in slowing down the rate of increase in undergraduate tuition (60 percent); in improving their competitive position vis-à-vis public institutions (70 percent); and in recruiting students more successfully (70 percent). Their most general concern for the future is about the prospective level of enrollment (75 percent).

Special Concerns About Public Policy

Many complex aspects of public policies toward private higher education remain unresolved, and policies vary greatly among the 50 states. Among the considerations that must be kept in mind in suggesting changes are (1) equality of opportunity among students from different income groups, (2) the impact of aid to the private sector on the well-being of the public sector, and (3) relationships between federal and state policies.

Impacts on Income Groups

Methods of state support of private institutions have differential impacts on income groups. The Council, as its first choice, supports need-based grants to students at both private and public institutions. This approach will be of greater benefit to lower- than to higher-income students. Students from lower-income groups go disproportionately to public institutions, sometimes out of necessity rather than choice. State aid, largely to meet tuition rather than living costs, should parallel federal policy (which favors lower-income students) so that lower-income students will have a better chance not only to attend college but also to choose a private institution if they wish to do so.

Proposals have been made to allow a tax deduction for payment of tuition before calculating taxable income, or a tax credit taken from the amount of tax otherwise owed. Both approaches, and particularly the second, would be regressive—aiding the rich much more than the poor—and would have negative impacts on public revenues. They also are inefficient for relieving the burden of high tuition in private institutions, because the bulk of the tax credits would benefit the far more numerous families whose children attend public institutions.

Impacts on Public Institutions

In the legislative process so far, neither education nor appropriations committees work in terms of consolidated budgets for all of higher education. Thus, the introduction of support for private institutions appears to establish one more claimant for state funds rather than to carve off a share of the funds already earmarked for higher education alone.

Nevertheless, support for private institutions could injure public institutions. Forms of support that set the public and private segments against each other should be avoided. Whatever the program adopted, fair treatment of the public and private sectors must be assured.

We oppose raising tuition at public institutions solely to aid private institutions by closing the tuition gap. In other reports we have favored low or no tuition for public community colleges (on the grounds of easing access) and a tuition level of about one-third of educational costs (primarily on the grounds of clear private benefits resulting from the education that warrant a private contribution) at public four-year institutions.

Portability

About 36 percent of all students in private institutions attend out-of-state colleges, but there are great variations among states. The opportunity for students to exercise choice outside as well as inside of their states of residence is of substantial importance.

The national interest lies on the side of portability of assistance to students. It can be accomplished by interstate cooperation—most readily by individual states simply providing reciprocity with other states that also make their aid portable—or by federal action.

Coordination and Planning

From the point of view of student, parents, and employers, it is the totality of higher education resources—public and private—of the state that is important; yet, too often, they are approached as though they were parts of two separate worlds.

For example, one of the greatest impacts on the private sector has been the expansion of the public sector. Consequently, we believe that public policy should require advance consideration of the impact of a new location, new program, or expanded program at an old location by a public institution on nearby private institutions (and vice versa) before a final decision is made. One way to insure such consideration is to make the private segment a participant in all planning processes, as most states now do, although sometimes quite ineffectively.

Complementary Federal Programs

We reaffirm the following recommendations made in *The Federal Role in Postsecondary Education* (for revised student aid recommendations see summary of *Next Steps for the 1980s in Student Financial Aid*).

1.   For lower-division students with full need, Basic Educational Opportunity Grants (BEOGs) should cover 90 percent of noninstructional costs, and the maximum amount should be increased to the $1,800 provided by the 1976 amendments as soon as possible. For upper-division students, who can more easily combine study and part-time work, we favor a maximum grant amounting to 75 percent of non-instructional costs. In other words, we favor a self-help feature but recommend only a modest self-help requirement in the BEOG program at present, pending more vigorous national policies to improve employment opportunities for youth.

2.   Adoption of a federal program mandating portability of State Student Incentive Grants (SSIGs) seems unlikely. We therefore believe that a provision creating a strong financial incentive for portability would be more effective. Federal funds should provide 75 percent of the cost of state scholarships or grants for students enrolled in institutions in other states, compared with the present 50 percent matching formula.

     To ensure increased coordination between federal and state student aid programs, all states should require applicants for state student aid grants to apply for a BEOG.

     The Council's earlier recommendation that federal matching funds should be available for all increases in state appropriations for eligible scholarship programs from 1969-70 on has not received the attention it deserves. The present provision limiting matching funds to increases from 1972-73 on is seriously unfair to states that have had major student aid programs for many years and are spending far larger amounts on student aid than most other states.

Finally, in connection with federal policies, we oppose proposals that the federal government take over primary responsibility for aiding students in private higher education by adding a special tuition allowance on top of regular BEOG awards.

Broad Alternatives

We have a "nonsystem" of higher education in the United States that is characterized by a "double mix": public and private institutions; and state, federal, and private financial support. We could elect instead:

1.   A "national system," with support only from the federal government. This, however, would reduce local initiative, interest, and competition and would be less reflective of regional variations and differing cultural patterns.

2.   A "state only" system, with all public support from the state governments. Some interests, however, are better handled at the federal level, and a "state only" system would lead to undue parochialism.

3.   A "national marketplace" system with vouchers available to students to take any-

where they wish to attend and with no support of institutions as such. This would, in effect, make all institutions private. It would let the market control most or all decisions and thus largely deny public interest in supporting certain services whether or not they draw current consumer demand.

4.   A "public only" system with all private institutions absorbed into state systems. This would clearly reduce the competition and diversity among institutions.

The "double mix" system best serves the United States in the current period. We favor movement, however, toward the "national marketplace" approach through (a) greater portability of student grants among states and (b) a more even-handed approach to competition between the public and private sectors. In a limited way, we favor movement toward a "public only" system by having state planning mechanisms look at the totality of higher education—public and private institutions alike. These two directions of movement would allow more effective competition in terms of quality of service in those areas responsive to consumer demand and more integration in those areas subject to public policy. We urge moderation, however, in moving toward each of these possibilities. If state support of private institutions were to reach the 50 percent level, we would consider that to be a clear peril point beyond which an institution depends more upon state sources than upon private sources for support.

Recommendations

Recommendation 1: *In the broad public interest, the private sector of higher education should be preserved and strengthened in ways that will protect the traditional autonomy of private institutions.*

Recommendation 2: *Private institutions should utilize self-help to the maximum possible extent and should minimize their dependency on government. To this end, private institutions should continue to seek increased revenues from private sources, improve administration, reduce costs, develop new programs, seek out new clienteles, and plan ahead in order to improve their economic situations.*

Recommendation 3: *Even with the most conscientious self-help, the long-run position of the private sector is uncertain and insecure. Consequently, more intensive public support of and encouragement for private higher education will be necessary.*

Recommendation 4: *The federal government should (a) complete the development of its Basic Educational Opportunity Grant (BEOG) program, (b) expand the State Student Incentive Grant (SSIG) program very substantially, and (c) encourage the portability of state grants to students under the SSIG program through a more favorable federal matching formula for students enrolling away from their home states. The BEOG program should become the major vehicle for providing assistance to needy students to meet noninstructional costs, and the SSIG program should help provide for instructional costs. In both programs, there should be an expectation of student self-help—in the BEOG programs, through a maximum grant amounting to 90 percent of noninstructional costs for lower-division students and to 75 percent for upper-division students, and in the SSIG program, through a maximum tuition grant that is below full tuition costs.*

Recommendation 5: *In the national interest, the federal government has a special* *responsibility to support research universities—both public and private—through (a) increasing appropriations for research along with increases in the Gross National Product, (b) restoring funds for graduate fellowships to an adequate level (including funding the new program of minority group fellowships), and (c) providing support for research libraries.*

Recommendation 6: *State governments should act vigorously in developing long-range policies for private higher education, if they have not done so already (in the context of the total plan for higher education), but funding should be increased only gradually as needs become clearly apparent.*

Recommendation 7: *Financial aid to students should be the primary (though not necessarily the exclusive) vehicle for the channeling of state funds to private institutions.*

Recommendation 8: *Need-based tuition grants should be the mainstay of state programs of student aid. Such grants should also be provided for students attending public institutions.*

Recommendation 9: *Need-based student aid programs should:*

- *Provide grants for all students in the lower half of the income range and probably also for some in the lower levels of the upper half of the income range. Grants should be of sufficient magnitude to give students genuine, rather than illusory, choice.*
- *Provide for instructional and noninstructional costs of students separately (where there is any existing provision for noninstructional costs, as in some of the state programs), pending revision of the federal BEOG program to provide adequately for noninstructional costs. After that, state grants should cover only instructional costs.*
- *Provide for a maximum tuition grant of approximately $1,500, the present maximum under the federal SSIG program, although some states may wish to set a somewhat higher maximum. But state policies should allow for significant self-help from students in the form of part-time work or borrowing. Moreover, private institutions with above average tuition charges tend to have institutional student aid funds that are used to supplement student aid from public funds. As tuition levels rise in the future, the $1,500 maximum should be adjusted upward.*

Recommendation 10: *As supplemental forms of aid, to be included where appropriate in a rounded package, the Council recommends:*

- *Contracts with private institutions for educational and other services*
- *Categorical grants for selected programs, such as library activities*
- *Awards for construction, renovation, and purchases of major equipment.*

Recommendation 11: *The Council urges the states to provide funds in modest amounts to both public and private institutions to encourage innovation and experimentation in academic programs. Such funds would augment those provided by the federal Fund for the Improvement of Postsecondary Education (FIPSE).*

Recommendation 12: *Grants for direct institutional support should be provided only where there are adequate protections for autonomy and quality.*

Recommendation 13: *State policies should contemplate special measures, as necessary, (1) to make it possible for selected private institutions to shift to public support (where their contributions as private institutions are not unique); (2) to assist private institutions with weak financial prospects or inadequate academic programs (or both) to merge with other institutions or to phase out their operations in an orderly fashion; and (3) to strengthen marginal institutions whose continued existence is deemed important through temporary support of planned programs for expansion, revision of academic programs, or improvement of physical facilities. State policies should not, however, contemplate "bailing out" all weak private institutions.*

Recommendation 14: *State aid to private institutions should not reach such levels and take such forms that they become more public than private in their operations. We suggest that a state subsidy amounting to about 50 percent of the educational subsidy per student in a comparable public institution may be a reasonable maximum.*

Recommendation 15: *Aid to private institutions should not be given in such ways and in such amounts as to cause significant disadvantage to public institutions.*

Recommendation 16: *Tuition levels in public institutions should be set on their own merits and not specifically to aid private institutions.*

Recommendation 17: *The Council is opposed to either tax credits or tax deductions to offset tuition costs, but we strongly support the continuation of tax exemption for private gifts to institutions of higher education.*

Recommendation 18: *To the maximum possible extent, state programs of student aid should be neutral in their effects on the interstate flow of students. That is, they should neither encourage nor discourage interstate mobility. In addition to proposing a more favorable federal formula for portable grants under the SSIG program, the Council recommends that the Education Commission of the States encourage interstate agreements for student financial aid reciprocity. Residents of one state choosing to attend institutions in another state should be eligible for financial aid from their own state if the receiving state also provides for grant portability. The Council recognizes that some states are characterized by net out-migration of students, while others experience net in-migration—a consideration that strengthens the case for a special federal incentive for portability through SSIGs.*

Recommendation 19: *Private colleges and universities should be exempt from property, sales, and other state and local taxes on the same basis as public institutions. If public institutions do not have to pay certain taxes, neither, under similar circumstances, should private institutions. (Where payments in lieu of taxes are made for special services such as fire protection, public and private institutions should be treated alike.)*

Recommendation 20: *Coordinating councils, governors, and legislatures should insist that, in decisions relating to the expansion of public institutions or their programs, the effects on private institutions should be taken into account. Similarly, private institutions should consult with their public counterparts on plans for program change.*

Recommendation 21: *Private colleges and universities should be fully represented in all state coordinating mechanisms.*

Missions of the College Curriculum:
A Contemporary Review with Suggestions
December 1977

This commentary is concerned with the undergraduate curriculum, which we define as the body of courses that present the knowledge, principles, values, and skills that are the intended consequences of the formal education offered by a college. We have undertaken this effort for three reasons:

- Higher education has gone through a period of considerable change in its curricula over the past decade.
- Changes of substantial significance to curricular development are taking place in the composition and capacities of student bodies.
- A period of no growth for higher education but of fundamental social changes lies ahead.

Orientation

The history of the college can be divided into three eras. The first, from 1636 to about 1870, was marked by a more or less standard curriculum that was liberal in the sense that it concentrated on the cultural heritage of western civilization.

The second era, between 1870 and the 1960s, was characterized by attention to production of new knowledge and of what later came to be called the human capital, which would apply the new knowledge and new technology that sprang from it. The theme was investment for the sake of increase in the Gross National Product (GNP) and in personal incomes.

The curriculum of today strongly reflects these two earlier eras. It seems also to be responding to a new consumerism. Greater consumer sovereignty results in more time allowed for electives, more courses presented in the arts, more courses created for non-majors, more chances for students to stop in and stop out, and more opportunities for part-time students and adults in extension courses to pick and choose individual courses.

There is another, and not entirely unrelated, theme in this third era: the shift from elite to mass education and now to universal access to higher education. The students are more varied in their origins and destinations and, on the average, less prepared. This calls for more varied programs and options and more compensatory education.

This volume was originally published as a commentary of the Carnegie Foundation for the Advancement of Teaching.

Components of the Curriculum

Undergraduate enrollments in majors are approximately as follows:

Area	Percentage
Professional	58%
Social sciences	11[a]
Humanities	5
Biological sciences	7
Physical sciences	4[a]
Arts	6
Other or no major	8

[a]These figures are different from those in the published report owing to correction of a computational error. Figures do not add to 100 because of rounding.

Overall, the professions have been growing, as have the biological sciences within the sciences. The professional schools, which are usually more autonomous within institutions of higher education, are now dominant among academic departments in undergraduate enrollments. In terms of the curriculum, students now divide their time almost equally between general education, major requirements, and electives.

We offer a few observations. First, the curriculum is important, but it is not the most important aspect of undergraduate education. The most important is the quality of the faculty.

Second, no studies show that one undergraduate curriculum is clearly better than another. Curricular preferences rest on judgments, not proof.

Third, the most marked characteristic of American higher education, and of its curriculum, is diversity. Diversity is advantageous in that it enables many colleges to accommodate heterogeneous student bodies and serve a broader portion of society. Diversity also enables colleges and universities to pursue self-determined missions and to conduct themselves in accordance with self-determined philosophies. But diversity obscures the question of whether or not there should be some common characteristics of the education all colleges offer to their students. It also leaves colleges without generally recognized reference points in the quest for quality.

Fourth, the most important impact on the curriculum from both internal and external forces is steady accretion. In the long run, the additive impact of the selection of individual faculty members largely determines the content of the catalog. Thus the larger the faculty, the more courses and the greater the fractionalization of knowledge.

Although it is easy to identify the main components of the undergraduate curriculum, it is nearly impossible to generalize about their use in institutions of higher education. Different institutions give different weight to each component. To correct this situation, we suggest that consideration be given to the development of an analytical transcript that classifies courses taken by students in terms of their type and purpose.

Two choices seem open to us. One is to follow the direction of current trends and restructure American higher education as a totally open system with a common beginning, many places to stop in and out, but with almost no provision for either learning experiences common to all students in the college or for institutional goals short of whatever ultimate aim each person draws as an individual. The other choice is to reassert the value of undergraduate education, not only as preparation for the student embarking on a career or advanced education but also as something that makes a positive, intended difference in the lives of those who are exposed to it and, through them, in society as well.

The Mission of Undergraduate Education

Both students and faculty members seem to be quite content with the status quo on their campuses generally (see Figure 1). There must be few areas of American life where contentment now reigns so supreme. Despite the consensus and the satisfaction, we see opportunities for improvement.

Figure 1. Undergraduate and faculty satisfaction in five types of institutions of higher education

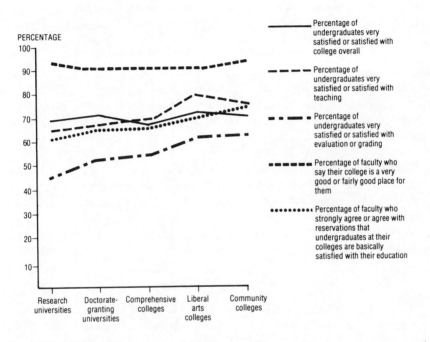

First, there is a lack of overall concern for the curriculum. Faculty members pay attention to their individual courses, departments to their majors, and students to their choice of electives; but few persons pay attention to the other three components and to the overall enterprise. Yet a comprehensive view of the total curriculum is needed. The student is a whole entity, not just a collection of separate parts, and society as a whole is more than just a series of disconnected sectors.

The most important way to start curricular review is to consider the mission of the institution. What is needed is a concise series of statements that:

1. Guide the academic leadership of a college in determining what educational programs are appropriate for accommodation in the institution's curriculum
2. Provide students with information about the institution's intentions so that they can compare them with their own interests and needs
3. Provide the college's governing board, accrediting agencies, and others having a legitimate reason to evaluate the performance of the college with the criteria by which the institution chooses, at least in curricular matters, to be governed.

The result should be a statement that takes into account not only what the intended consequences of an institution's educational efforts should be but also its traditions and resources. Because situations change, the statement should allow for future amendment and be subject to periodic review. Perhaps most important of all, it should be made in clear language that avoids the sales rhetoric often encountered in the introductions to college catalogs and recruiting brochures.

Although the development of the mission statement is properly the work of a college's academic leaders, its influence will be felt throughout the institution and will ultimately need the weight and authority that can be given to it only by those legally entrusted and morally bound to exercise the responsibilities for the long-run welfare of the colleges. We therefore believe that the final definitions of the broad educational missions of colleges should be officially adopted by the colleges' governing boards.

General Education: An Idea in Distress

General education is now a disaster area. It represents the accretions of history more than a thoughtful concern for current needs. It is a mediating influence that, through institutionwide requirements, ensures that all students obtain some knowledge of the ideas and culture that were once the theme of liberal arts colleges. It does so by providing learning that:

1. Builds skills for advanced studies and lifelong learning
2. Distributes time available for learning in such a way as to expose students to the mainstreams of thought and interpretation—humanities, science, social science, and the arts
3. Integrates learning in ways that cultivate the student's broad understanding and ability to think about large and complex subjects.

Advanced Learning Skills

Advanced learning skills are being neglected. Each institution should have a clear idea of what minimum level it will require in English language and mathematical skills and has an obligation to make this clear to high schools. In addition, institutions might suggest certain skill subjects that could also be taught at high schools and establish criteria for recognizing completion of such instruction as satisfying college requirements.

We note that statistical skills have become more important in many occupations and for comprehension by the citizen of current developments, and that skill in using library sources is becoming more and more essential. Both these skills are frequently ignored, and introduction of such subjects, preferably in high school, but in any event early in undergraduate college years, is urgently needed.

We recognize that foreign languages help to expand one's understanding of other cultures and of one's native tongue, but we do not believe that it is essential to require all students to study them to meet general education requirements.

Physical education and nutrition are sufficiently important to individual welfare that their inclusion as required studies could be justified, at least in high school. In college, we particularly favor emphasizing physical education activities that students can cultivate as individuals and use throughout their lifetimes.

Distribution

Breadth or distribution requirements are too often either met by the introductory course intended for persons who plan to major in the field or have become so free and unlimited in their definitions that they are, in effect, an expansion of electives.

One way to improve the part of general education that is drawn from the subject fields is to develop for each one an introductory course for nonmajors that is devoted to the history, concerns, and methods of inquiry used in the field.

It is tempting to suggest that, in instances where it is impossible for subject fields to design high-quality introductory courses, students should be permitted to take a specified number of any regular courses within the subject field instead. The difficulty with this policy is that it effectively excuses the faculty from responsibility for general education and endorses the dubious proposition that any two or three unspecified courses in a subject field adequately introduce students, particularly nonmajors, to a field.

There is one omission among courses designed along the lines of "modes of thought" or "ways of knowing," such as the social and natural sciences and the humanities, which deserves special attention—the arts. Viewed not only for their own sake but also as a means of experiencing and communicating reality, the arts are often overlooked, but they have a legitimate place among other subject fields in any education that claims to be human in its orientation and truly broad in its dimension. Ideally, all students not only should have an opportunity to learn how artists perceive the world and translate their perceptions into visual representations and performance, but should also participate in the arts.

Fragmentation that may be justifiable in free electives is difficult to defend in general education, which, of all components of the curriculum, should most clearly reflect institutional objectives. In the general education component of the undergraduate curriculum, definition and coherence should take priority over diversity. For that reason, we believe students should be confronted with somewhat fewer requirements for distribution and more opportunities for integration.

Integrative Learning Experience

Integrative courses are aimed at cultivating abilities to think about broad, general subjects rather than highly specialized topics. They can take many forms.

1. *Special requirements such as the study of world culture or western civilization.* Presumably, American institutions' requirements are imposed as a guarantee that all persons who graduate from college have an understanding of state and national political philosophy and governmental operations. Perhaps basic requirements of this type should be met at the high school level, where much larger percentages of young Americans could be exposed.

2. *Central subjects.* It is difficult to identify very many courses or subjects that are so useful that they deserve to be studied by all students. Only history, in its broadest scope (including physical, social, and intellectual history), and not restricted to any one specific civilization, may deserve a central role in general education, since no other single discipline has its built-in orienting and integrating potential.

3. *Integrating themes.* We would advocate more opportunities for students to use instruction obtained from several departments and organized around significant themes and problems (often a series of courses put together in an additive way), such as "Man and the Environment" or "East Asian Civilization." These are what the Carnegie Commission previously described and recommended as "broad learning experiences."

Other integrative methods involve core courses and programs and interdisciplinary programs. In addition to thematic learning experiences developed by institutions, students might be given opportunities to construct such programs of their own.

All such ideas should be encouraged. Interdisciplinary programs are so admirably suited to the needs of general education, particularly at upper-division levels, that any effort to overcome the difficulties involved in offering them is worthwhile. A substantial part of the solution is for the college to acknowledge the difficulties involved and to provide special incentives and rewards for individual faculty members who are willing to confront them. For example, colleges should temporarily lighten course loads to free a faculty member's time for developing integrative courses and should take these activities into account in the promotion process.

The erosion of general education is even more severe than its share of the curricula might indicate, for in many cases it is poorly defined and so diluted with options that it has no recognizable substance of its own. The concept continues to have a place in American higher education. But if colleges cannot define what they intend to accomplish in general education, or how it will benefit their students, or they cannot deliver it effectively, then they should seriously consider eliminating it entirely. They should not, however, use their incapacity to define their programs to require students to fill out their graduation requirements with additional electives. Instead, they should question the necessity of requiring students to spend the additional time in college.

General education is that part of the undergraduate curriculum that permits a college or university, as an institution, to make a unique contribution to the education of students, and it should be under the institution's control. No other effort to define the quality and character of education is as important as this one.

Timing of General Education

Most institutions expect their students to complete general education requirements within their freshman and sophomore years. We would encourage, instead, that colleges keep general education as free of time restraints as possible. However, there are logistical reasons for suggesting that the components of general education have time priority in the following order: (1) advanced learning skills, (2) distribution, and (3) integrated learning experiences.

First priority is assigned to advanced learning skills because they must be acquired if further academic progress is to be made. Second priority is assigned to distribution requirements because many students will use them to sample subjects from which they might choose majors. Integrative courses could be concentrated at the end or distributed throughout an undergraduate career.

The Major—A Success Story?

The major is generally well handled by professional schools and departments because they have a clear interest in its effective management. Majors are not, however, an unqualified success. We note three major weaknesses:

1. They are too oppressive, because they take too much of a student's time. Although the formal major requirements of a college may demand no more than one-third of a student's time, many students use substantial parts of their electives to intensify specialization. This is a misuse of the principle of electives.
2. They are too narrow and specialized.
3. They lead to the neglect of courses that are designed for nonmajors.

Typically, majors take up more of a student's time in upper-division than in lower-division studies. However, some time during the last two years of college should always be available for general education and electives outside the subject field of the major. For this reason students should not spend 100 percent of their time in the major in any one college year.

Ideally, the undergraduate major should be designed primarily for students who do not intend to pursue graduate studies, but it will be difficult for colleges to resist student pressures to provide majors as introductions to graduate work. There is apparently a void in the higher education spectrum that needs to be filled by institutions with an undergraduate curriculum that is mainly for undergraduates who do not intend to pursue graduate studies.

To keep the major in perspective as one part and not the totality of undergraduate education, colleges should move in the following directions:

1. Limit the total number of hours that may be invested in the major without extending the number of hours that must be completed for graduation.
2. Encourage departments to develop more courses for nonmajors.
3. Encourage development of two major options in each department: one for students planning to attend graduate school and one for those who are not.
4. Provide more opportunities for students to take double majors, minors, interdisciplinary majors, and self-created majors.

Electives—Abundant for What Purpose?

While electives enable students to sample widely the intellectual offerings of a college, they are also subject to misuse. Some students who are confronted with many choices seek out those that appear to be the least demanding and promise the highest grades. Others may make random choices that have no discernible relationship to their main interests or to the rest of their studies.

But the willingness of colleges to allow the size of the elective component to respond so easily to demand suggests that there may be a substantial part of the time colleges define as necessary for the completion of undergraduate education that no one knows specifically what to do with.

The abundance of electives in the undergraduate curriculum might be more defensible if colleges made the function of such options more explicit, prepared guidelines for their use, and took steps to assure that the intended functions were not ignored or diminished in practice. That does not now appear to be the case. Undergraduates are using electives to increase the depth of their studies within major departments. Of greater concern is the possibility that departments themselves may increasingly assume that their undergraduates will use electives for specialization and will plan the contents of the major on that assumption.

If the proportion of the curriculum devoted to electives continues to increase without efforts by colleges to define their function and offer guidance to students on their appropriate use, perhaps students should be given the opportunity to elect not to include them in their undergraduate education at all.

In general, when the number of electives available to students is clearly out of balance with other components in the undergraduate curriculum, we would prefer some reduction in the number of electives and an increase in the content and options available in general education.

Basic Skills—Where Does College Begin?

There is general indecision about where the schools' responsibilities for teaching elementary skills ends and where colleges' responsibilities for teaching advanced skills begins. Overcoming this indecision is a joint responsibility of state boards of education and state college and university systems. State boards of education have an obligation to make clear what the minimum standards of graduation from high school will be. State systems of higher education should be able to identify the proficiency levels in reading, writing, and mathematics a student needs to begin a college career and the subjects on which a college curriculum builds and to which every entering student should have had some exposure.

Indecision about the levels of preparation that are appropriate for college entrance is aggravated by the fact that student skills, on the average, have been declining for several years. Every effort should be made throughout the schools to make an early diagnosis of learning difficulties and to correct deficiencies in elementary skills as soon as possible after they are discovered. For the student who reaches college without such skills, even the best of remedial education programs may be too little and too late. We therefore urge all states to take such measures as may be needed to ensure that elementary and high school students acquire proficiencies consistent with their abilities and grade levels in reading, computation, and written English.

We also favor the use of tests of competence as supplements to the currently prevailing methods of measuring students' educational progress. A major benefit of performance indicators and other components of tests is that they force educators and evaluators to define more explicitly what a person should be able to do as a result of the school experience. If such tests are given frequently throughout the school years, they will assist teachers in early identification of students who need special attention.

But because neither the standards met by high schools nor the entrance requirements of colleges are uniform, it is inevitable that some students will graduate from high school without the basic skills and knowledge that many colleges consider necessary for entering freshmen. To meet the needs of these students, colleges and universities may offer compensatory education. But we concur in the recommendation of the Carnegie Commission that "every student accepted into a program requiring compensatory education receive the necessary commitment of resources to allow his engagement in an appropriate level of work by the end of no more than two years." We would also suggest that, where credit is given for compensatory education, it should be counted toward meeting graduation requirements other than those for general education or the major.

Finally, colleges should be concerned not only with providing compensatory education in the elementary skills but also with helping students who wish to improve the more advanced skills they have. For this purpose a number of institutions have created skill development centers, usually provided as a student service.

Undergraduate Education and the World of Work

By 1975, 95 percent of American undergraduates considered training and skills for an occupation to be either essential or fairly important goals of their college education. Two possible consequences of this interest would distort the purposes of the college curriculum. One is that students may become so single-minded in their studies aimed toward specific jobs that they become overspecialized and perhaps inflexible. The other is that students and employers alike might overemphasize the importance of degrees and other certification for employment. The result of this emphasis is that the level of credentials required for the positions that are available spirals upward beyond the actual demands of the work to be performed. Any discussion of the relationship between education and the world of work must go beyond specific job preparation and manpower needs of the moment. It is more important that students match their skills and competences with a thorough understanding of work as a characteristically human enterprise.

In the past, students have voluntarily adjusted to labor market demands with remarkable speed. Their ability to adjust might be even greater if they had available to them better information about career opportunities. Attempts to link the educational process with career guidance in colleges and universities are likely to encounter resistance from some faculty members and officials who fear that education is in danger of becoming overly career oriented. At institutions with sound educational policies, such fears are unfounded. There is perhaps a greater danger to the integrity of undergraduate education when the linkage between learning and work is de facto but unrecognized than there is when it is placed in proper perspective.

Undergraduates typically acquire the knowledge and skills they hope to use in employment in their major studies. But there is not always a close correlation between one's major and one's ultimate career. Colleges might, however, improve the employment prospects of students by offering, in addition to departmental majors, interdisciplinary majors determined by broad areas of occupational and professional endeavor. If such majors were more extensively available, concentrations offered by single departments could become, more frankly and perhaps more effectively, what many of them are now—preparation for advanced education or for narrowly defined occupations and professions.

Students should have options to take joint majors and major-minor concentrations that permit them to concentrate on subjects of special interest to them and at the same time to increase their potential value to employers. The principle to be observed is not that every student should be encouraged to acquire a specialized marketable skill before graduation from college but that no student should be involuntarily penalized in the job market for studying a subject of great personal interest but of no obvious demand by employers.

Finally, we believe that work experience can be very valuable to all students in relating their educational activities to the actual world of work. Many institutions have developed programs alternating periods of work with study or combining them concurrently in relevant fields. We believe that many institutions that do not now do so should give serious consideration to the development of cooperative work-study programs, apprenticeships, and internships as part of their undergraduate curricula.

Values and the Academic Tradition

American higher education has intrinsic potentials for exerting wholesome nonreligious influences on students' values fully in keeping with the highest intellectual traditions. At the center of college and university value systems is truth, sought not only as an end in itself, but also because it leads to other truths and because it can be used as the basis for making choices among a range of ideas, policies, and day-to-day decisions.

Related to the academic community's esteem for truth is its reverence for intellectual freedom and its tolerance for ideas that may threaten one's own beliefs or even welfare. Another set of values integral to the academic enterprise involves rewarding persons on the basis of the merit of their work above any other consideration. Related to these values are concepts that one should be rewarded only for work one performs, that the rules for grading and faculty evaluations should be clear and even-handedly applied, and that procedures for evaluation and determining rewards do not disadvantage specific learners or groups of learners.

We believe that the ideals of the academic tradition provide a reasonable basis for an influence worthy of being generated by our nation's colleges. But if colleges are to assume a major role in the value development of undergraduates, they need to be more vigorous than ever before in articulating the ideals of the academic tradition and on insisting that those ideals be honored to the fullest extent possible by all members of the college community.

We would urge the American Association of University Professors, which has been relatively successful in defining the rights and privileges of faculty members, to renew efforts of its members to develop an academic code of ethics. Such a code would be an essential first step in generating faculty awareness of their responsibilities to their profession and to the influence of their own attitudes and conduct on the values of their students.

We also urge individual colleges and universities to adopt some basic principles that will be observed relative to the rights and responsibilities of faculty, students, administrators, staff, and trustees in matters involving the educational process and requirements of the search for truth. It is essential that such statements of rights and responsibilities be accompanied by the development of fair and effective procedures for handling charges of violations.

Implementing Curricular Policy and Change

To effect curricular change, it is generally better to proceed constantly and quietly rather than all at once in a publicized effort. Resistance to reform efforts is to be expected, and institutions should try to liberate progressive forces by giving them a chance, whether as individuals or small groups, to experiment prior to review rather than allowing review committees to condemn in advance.

Some institutions might experiment with separate administrative units for general education. Such units can give general education more coherence, can develop instruction exclusively for meeting its objectives, can encourage interdisciplinary programs, and can evaluate general education on its own terms. One way to overcome resistance by discipline-oriented faculty members would be to centralize the budgeting and financing of all general education programs in this unit, which would have authority to approve any new general education courses given in a department, allocate funding to the departments for these courses, and periodically review all departmental general education courses and programs.

Initiating such procedures may be quite difficult on established campuses that have not already moved in this direction. To achieve it, the central administration must assess each department's educational program and recapture the departmental funds that are utilized for general education instruction.

Creating the position of a dean for undergraduate education where such positions do not now exist could provide a center of educational administration for setting standards and encouraging innovation. Such officers may be particularly essential as a counterbalance to the sometimes unwarranted influence graduate divisions exercise over the undergraduate curriculum.

Finally, there is a need for alternatives to the research-oriented Ph.D. as the degree for college teachers. Whether the alternative is the doctor of arts degree recommended by the Carnegie Commission or some other degree granted for the same purpose, it should be more widely available as the standard degree for persons desiring careers primarily as college teachers.

Conclusion

Since it is impossible for any college or university to expose its students to all available knowledge, perhaps the basic objectives of the curriculum will be to provide students with skills for lifelong learning. In general, colleges should seek to provide:

- Certain learning experiences that all students in a college have in common
- Opportunities for a student to become familiar with at least one subject in depth
- Programs that make students aware of the concerns, methods, and history of several broad fields of learning
- Instruction and experiences that develop students' awareness of their own physical and mental capacities, convictions, and values and beliefs
- Programs and environments that help students cultivate tolerance for ideas that are different from their own.

It is from such concepts as these, rather than from attempts to package and disseminate the world's available knowledge, that academic planners must now receive guidance in determining the components of the curriculum.

We believe that the major tasks ahead are few but important. They are (1) to formulate more clearly the advanced learning skills necessary in college and provide better training in them; (2) to give more attention and use greater ingenuity in improving distribution requirements; (3) to make integrative courses a more central feature of intellectual activity; (4) to assist the primary and secondary schools in teaching basic skills and providing compensatory training in them, when necessary, at the college level; (5) to bridge the gap between thought and action and create more opportunities for students to understand the world of work; (6) to clarify and apply more precisely the essential moral principles of academic life for the sake of the integrity of campus life and for the contribution that can be made to the skills of citizenship; and (7) to assert the corporate interests of the academic community in the quality of the curriculum in its totality as well as in its component parts.

By performing these tasks, our colleges and universities can reassume initiatives and roles of leadership that may have been lost in an era of accommodation and reaction to rapid growth and change. They can assume a more active role in the development of national character and play an even more vital part in the life and learning of their undergraduates.

Next Steps for the 1980s in Student Financial Aid:

A Fourth Alternative
March 1979

Part One: Making Better Use of Existing Resources

When this report was released in 1979, Congress was expected to review the structure of the student aid system in the United States. Three alternatives seemed to be under consideration:

1. Simply extending existing legislation with no, or only minor, changes
2. Expanding the middle-income thrust of legislation that carried aid programs in larger amounts and to higher levels of family income to students whose families were in the upper half of the income range
3. Adding cost of education tax credits to the nation's student aid programs.

We propose a fourth alternative that has the following components:

1. No increase in the total amount spent on student aid. More money for the Basic Educational Opportunity Grant (BEOG), College Work Study (CWS), and State Student Incentive Grants (SSIG) programs, partially offset by less money for loan programs. We propose elimination of Social Security benefits and food stamps for students, on the grounds that our program will make them unnecessary. These reductions should be calculated against the increase in the Office of Education package. The SSIG program we propose would cost the states substantial additional funds. When this is taken into account, the total amount spent on student aid by the federal and state governments together will remain roughly what it is now in constant dollars, assuming all the states take full advantage of federal matching funds (see Figure 1).

2. A redistribution of funds to aid low-income students (our first priority) and enhance students' choice (our second priority) in selecting an institution. The latter will help create fairer competition between institutions (our third priority) based to a greater degree than at present on considerations of the value of their academic programs.

3. Better coordination of federal and state programs, with greater incentive for increased state expenditures. The federal government should be primarily concerned with the subsistence costs of attending college, and the states with adjustments

Figure 1. Estimated expenditures under existing federal and state student aid programs, 1979-80, and under Carnegie Council recommendations, 1982-83 (in millions of constant—1979—dollars, excluding veterans' educational benefits)[a]

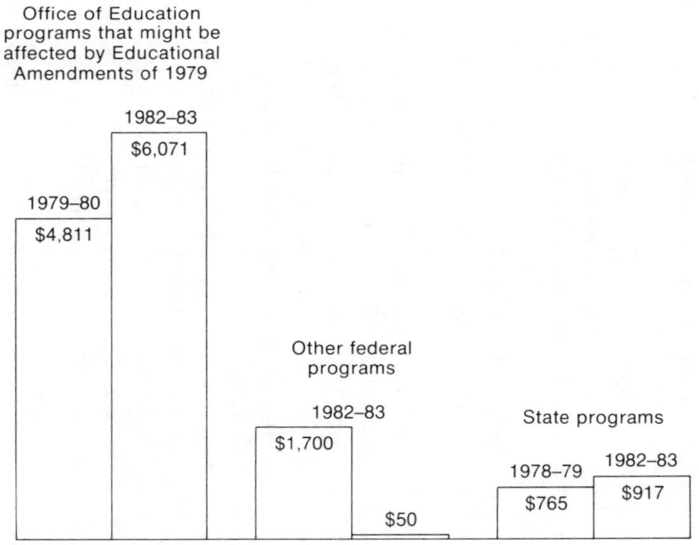

Office of Education programs that might be affected by Educational Amendments of 1979

1982-83 $6,071
1979-80 $4,811

Other federal programs
1982-83 $1,700
$50

State programs
1978-79 $765
1982-83 $917

Suggested changes to 1982-83

Office of Education programs that might be affected by Educational Amendments of 1979

Basic Grants	
Regular program	+$685
Special 10 percent override	+ 324
Supplementary Educational Opportunity Grants	0
College Work-Study program	+ 350
Guaranteed Student Loan program	+ 660
National Direct Student Loan program	− 329
State Student Incentive Grant program	+ 840
National Student Loan Bank	+ 50
Total	+ 1,260

Other federal programs

Social security benefits	− 1,550
Food stamp program	− 100
Total	− 1,650

State programs | + 152

Grand Total | − 238

[a]Estimates are based on projected 1979-80 enrollment (by family income and cost of institutions); actual enrollment in 1982-83 is likely to differ little in total numbers from that in 1979-80.

required by their many different combinations of public and private institutions and of tuition policies among public institutions.

4.   Changes that will add to the integrity of the programs by lower default rates on loans, by less tendency to manufacture independent status for students artificially, and by the requirement of explicit self-help as a basis for aid; and changes that will add to the simplicity and flexibility of the programs by eliminating a need requirement for loans and by adding a 10 percent adjustment to BEOGs to simplify the rules for the distribution of the funds available and to meet individual needs more precisely. We also suggest that consideration be given to a "bank account" approach to student aid so that students could draw only portions of it without exhausting their accounts and becoming no longer eligible. This would encourage students to plan any withdrawals from their accounts more carefully.

We see the following specific opportunities for improvement within the context of political and economic realities:

- The introduction of an explicit self-help component (through earnings but also through borrowing) by the students themselves.
- A loan system that makes loans more easily and widely available and at much less risk of heavy default rates.
- Additional assurances of equality of opportunity for all young persons to obtain a college education if they wish. This has been and continues to be our first priority.
- A greater range of choice for students and potential students.

A self-help requirement. The basic building block of student financial support should be a substantial self-help component. We say this for the following reasons:

- Family income is no longer a sufficient indication of need, both because of the high and increasing proportion of students listing themselves as independent and because aid is now given to students whose families are in the upper half of the income range and who would go to college whether public aid were available or not. Family income levels distinguish students less and less by degree of real need for available student aid funds.
- Self-help, in any event, is intrinsically a better indication of both a student's need for support and of his or her determination to secure a higher education.
- An explicit self-help component is an important aspect of developing in students a sense of responsibility for their own advancement and of encouraging a more acutely sensed necessity for prudent use of time and money.

We also propose that the greater part of the normal self-help expectation be allocated to noninstructional costs through the BEOG program and the remainder to tuition through the SSIG program.

Recommendation 1: *Students should normally be expected to contribute significantly from their own earnings toward college expenses, as a condition of eligibility for student aid. An earnings expectation should gradually be imposed in the Basic Educational Opportunity Grant program and by 1982-83 should amount to $600 for lower-division students and to $1,000 for upper-division students, and a modest additional contribution* *of $250 should be required in the State Student Incentive Grant program. A student should be permitted to meet the self-help expectation wholly or partially through borrowing as an alternative form of self-help.*

Expanding the role of the College Work-Study program. We suggest a major expansion of the CWS program. It will help students meet the self-help component, and it also helps institutions meet their costs of operation.

We also believe that there is a strong case for gradual elimination of the family income eligibility conditions in the CWS program. Such a policy, in our view, would be greatly preferable to any extension of grant aid to students from upper-middle- or upper-income families or to tuition tax credits as a way of helping the families of such students. It would also be consistent with the desirability of eliminating social distinctions between students from low-income and high-income families.

Recommendation 2: *The annual appropriation for the College Work-Study program should gradually be increased to $900 million (in constant 1979 dollars) by 1982-83. Family income eligibility conditions should gradually be removed from the program, but preference in awarding employment opportunities under the program should be given to students, especially women and minorities, who have difficulty in finding jobs in the private employment market.*

Meeting the problems of the independent student. A self-help requirement would also help to resolve the policy problems posed by the increase in student aid applicants seeking independent status. Much of the concern about this trend arises over the possibility that, when their children are granted independent status, parents who could afford to contribute to their children's educational expenses are being relieved of their financial responsibilities. In fact, available data do not suggest that this type of abuse of student aid is widespread; independent students are more likely to be from lower-income families than are dependent students. But the possibility of such abuse exists, and increasing advantage may be taken of it.

In particular, the probability of abuse may increase as a result of a change brought about by the Middle-Income Student Assistance Act of 1978, under which the "family size offset" for an independent student without dependents was raised from $1,100 to $3,400. This means that $3,400 of such a student's income would be disregarded in determining eligibility for a BEOG and that almost every independent student without dependents could qualify for the maximum BEOG. Under these conditions, the temptation to seek independent status in order to avoid a parental contribution would be very great. It is undoubtedly a desirable provision for some groups of independent students, such as divorced or separated women, but its invitation to abuse on the part of students who would otherwise be assisted by their parents is a serious problem.

We also believe that existing rules for determining independent status are difficult to enforce and are intrusive in their concern with intrafamily relationships.

Recommendation 3: *The self-help expectation should normally be applicable to independent as well as to dependent students, and the recently pronounced legislative increase in the "family size offset" for independent students without dependents should be reconsidered by Congress. More objective criteria for determining independent status should be developed—criteria that would take into account the applicant's age, whether* *he or she has dependents, whether he or she is an orphan, and the number of years during which he or she has been self-supporting. The more difficult cases of applicants who do not meet such criteria should be handled by student aid officers. Independent students with dependents should be subject to the same parental contribution schedule as parents of dependent students (with adjustments to meet unusual circumstances), and should not ordinarily receive student aid for their dependents.*

Equitable provision for noninstructional costs. Equitable provision for noninstructional costs should be the first responsibility of a need-based student aid program. Noninstructional costs include basic subsistence expenses and the costs of such essential items as books, supplies, and transportation. Meeting these costs is far more difficult for students from lower-income and disadvantaged families than it is for young people from more affluent families.

Moreover, noninstructional costs vary much less from college to college and from one part of the country to another than do tuition and required fees. Thus they are appropriate for coverage by federal student aid programs. Provision for tuition is more appropriately a responsibility of the federal-state SSIG program, because tuition in public higher education—and thus the tuition gap between public and private institutions in a given state—is determined at the state level.

Recommendation 4: *Student assistance under the Basic Educational Opportunity Grant program should be designed to cover noninstructional costs of needy students.*

Reconciling subsistence needs and self-help expectations. If the BEOG program is to provide adequately for noninstructional costs and incorporate a self-help expectation, the size of the maximum grant should be increased gradually over the years from 1979-80 to 1982-83.

Future adjustments in the BEOG ceiling to meet rising costs will be needed from time to time, but should be left to congressional determination.

Recommendation 5: *The maximum award in the Basic Educational Opportunity Grant program should be increased gradually to $2,400 by 1982-83. This would mean that the maximum grant in practice would normally be $1,800 for lower-division and $1,400 for upper-division students, after taking account of the self-help expectation.*

Providing for exceptional cases. Although a self-help expectation is a reasonable requirement of a student aid program, some students will have unusual difficulty in meeting it. We therefore propose that Congress appropriate an additional sum for the BEOG program to meet the needs of students in unusual circumstances or for whom the earnings expectation would create difficulties.

Availability of such discretionary funds would facilitate uniform treatment for the more usual student applicant under simplified rules. It would also facilitate accommodation of the genuinely needy independent student without opening the door to abuse by students seeking independent status for the purpose of relieving their parents of expected contributions.

Recommendation 6: *Congress should allocate, over and above the sum needed to meet normal expected costs of the Basic Educational Opportunities Grant program, an additional 10 percent for discretionary use in the administration of the program at the* campus level, including waiver or modification of the self-help expectation for students whose employment opportunities are impaired by residence in inner city or rural areas, disabilities, the need for a heavy course load, exceptional family circumstances, or college entrance at an unusually early age.

Removing the 50-percent-of-cost limitation. If our proposal for a self-help expectation under the BEOG program is adopted, one important reason for the existing limitation of a student's grant to no more than 50 percent of the student's total educational costs is removed. Part of the rationale for the 50-percent-of-cost limitation has been that students attending low-cost commuter institutions should not have their full costs of attendance subsidized by the general public.

This limitation has tended to discriminate against low-income students whose most feasible option is attendance at a low-cost commuter institution, and yet its retention has been vigorously supported by some representatives of private institutions, for fear that low-income students would be even more likely to attend low-cost public institutions if their full costs could be covered by a BEOG. However, the impact of our BEOG recommendations should be considered in conjunction with our recommendations for expansion of the SSIG program. If our recommendations relating to SSIG are adopted, not only will the competitive position of private institutions in states now lacking adequate state scholarship programs be greatly improved, but so will the capacity of lower-income students to attend private institutions.

Under our formula, the self-help component would result in a maximum BEOG award equal to about 70 percent of full cost for lower-division students and about 55 percent for upper-division students at a comparatively low-cost institution.

Recommendation 7: *The present limitation of a Basic Educational Opportunity Grant to 50 percent of a student's total educational costs should be removed, since our recommendations for a self-help expectation in the Basic Educational Opportunity Grant program, together with our recommendations for substantial expansion of the State Student Incentive Grant program, remove the rationale for retention of the limitation.*

Preventing erosion of need-based student aid. With the adoption of the Middle-Income Student Assistance Act of 1978, a major step was taken to extend student grants to the children of upper-middle-income families. This movement need go no farther, and, in particular, we oppose adoption of tuition tax credits for the families of college students.

The evidence that young people from middle-income families have been discouraged from college attendance by rising costs is unconvincing. Only among young white males has there been a drop in attendance rates. This decline affects all income groups and is probably chiefly attributable to the removal of the draft.

Congress was wise to prefer helping upper-middle-income families by liberalizing student aid rather than by adopting tuition tax credits. The approach of Congress preserves the principle of need-based student aid; tuition tax credits do not. We also oppose tuition tax credits because:

1. They would be very costly to the U.S. Treasury and would provide such nominal relief to individual families that the pressure to increase the amounts of the credits, once adopted, would be very strong.
2. The temptation for colleges and universities to raise their tuition by the amount

of the tax credit would be very great, thereby nullifying the relief and rendering the aid to families self-defeating.

3. Tuition tax credits are not an effective way to help private institutions compete for students. They would not reduce the tuition gap between public and private colleges, and the bulk of the benefits (if any) would go to the far more numerous families whose children enroll in public institutions.

Recommendation 8: *The movement to provide aid to students from middle-income families should go no further. Any additional changes in this direction would seriously erode the need-based character of student aid. In particular, we strongly oppose adoption of tuition tax credits for the families of college students as a regressive and self-defeating form of parental relief. The central purpose of student aid programs should continue to be the encouragement of equality of opportunity.*

Need for a uniform parental contribution schedule. The liberalization of the BEOG parental contribution schedule adopted under the provisions of the Middle-Income Student Assistance Act has created a situation in which the need for a uniform parental contribution schedule is imperative. The expected parental contribution under the BEOG schedule is higher than the contribution expected under the College Scholarship Service/American College Testing (CSS/ACT) schedule for families with incomes up to $18,000. For higher family income, however, the contribution under the CSS/ACT schedule not only is larger but increases more sharply because it calls for progressively higher proportional contributions from families as income rises, whereas the BEOG schedule calls for a flat contribution rate of 10.5 percent.

There will be pressure from parents, students, and student aid officers to shift from the CSS/ACT to the new BEOG schedule in connection with federal campus-based student aid and state scholarship programs. This would be a major mistake, for the new schedule is so liberal in the upper-income ranges that its widespread use would virtually do away with the concept of need in federally supported student grant programs.

We advocate instead adoption of the CSS/ACT schedule as the standard for all federally supported student aid programs. If the CSS/ACT schedule does become the standard for these programs, however, it is imperative that several complexities (such as graduated allowances for accumulating savings for retirement) be removed from the schedule and that the application form be greatly simplified.

Recommendation 9: *A simplified CSS/ACT parental contribution schedule should be adopted by the federal government to apply to federal student grant programs and to federal matching of state funds under the State Student Incentive Grant program, after minor adjustments to preserve eligibility for Basic Educational Opportunity Grants for students from families in the $22,000 to $25,000 income range.*

Limiting the duration of student aid. The BEOG program, as well as other student aid programs, can be abused by students who may receive aid but do not complete course requirements and then re-enroll.

Recommendation 10: *Eligibility for Basic Educational Opportunity Grants and other types of federally assisted student aid should be limited to two years at a two-year college and four years at a four-year college (on a full-time equivalent basis) and to students making normal progress toward a degree.*

The State Student Incentive Grant program. The federal-state SSIG program should be the primary means of providing tuition assistance for needy students. To this end, we recommend a large increase in federal appropriations for the program in line with our earlier recommendations. (See summaries of *The Federal Role in Postsecondary Education* and *The States and Private Higher Education.*) There are several important reasons why tuition assistance can best be provided by a federal-state program.

1. Tuition policy in public higher education is determined at the state level, and thus it is at that level that the size of the tuition gap between private and public institutions of higher education is also determined.
2. Adequate federal matching grants will provide a powerful incentive for increases in state appropriations for scholarship programs in the many states in which such appropriations are seriously inadequate. Although the SSIG program has demonstrated its effectiveness in inducing states to adopt programs of student aid where they were previously nonexistent, it has been much less effective—chiefly because of small federal appropriations—in inducing such states to provide funds large enough to provide for needy students.
3. In the absence of special federal assistance, state scholarship programs are likely to discourage interstate movement of students and thus are likely to lead to excessive provincialism in higher education.

In addition to proposing a major increase in federal expenditures for the SSIG program, we recommend the following changes in federal provisions:

1. Federal matching funds, which now cover one half of state grants up to a maximum of $1,500, should be modified to cover one half of state grants (for tuition and required fees only) up to a maximum of $1,500 over and above the first $250 of tuition, which should normally be met from the student's earnings or other forms of self-help.
2. In order to induce states to make tuition grants portable, we recommend that the federal government pay 75 percent of the cost of those tuition grants that are used by a student to enroll in a state other than his or her state of residence.
3. We recommend moving the matching date back to 1969-70 for those states that had eligible state scholarship programs at that time.
4. We also recommend that the CSS/ACT parental contribution schedule should apply to federal matching in the SSIG program.

Even if a uniform parental contribution schedule is in effect for both federal student aid and a state scholarship program, state aid will inevitably be available for students from upper-middle-income families and from some upper-income families under the coordinated federal-state policies that we propose. This is because a large proportion of parents will meet all or most of their expected contribution in connection with non-instructional costs and will not be expected to make a contribution of appreciable size in connection with the state scholarship program.

Our recommendations relating to the maximum tuition grant imply that many students, especially those seeking to attend relatively high-cost institutions, will have to borrow to meet their full tuition costs unless they can earn more than the normal earnings expectation, receive aid from the college's own funds or from their parents, or succeed in finding the money in some other way. We do not regard this as undesirable, especially in view of the fact that institutions with high tuition tend to have more student aid funds of their own, and a public policy designed to provide tuition grants that would match tuition costs at such institutions would be highly questionable.

Recommendation 11: *Total appropriations for the federal share of the State Student Incentive Grant program should be increased to $917 million by 1982-83, so that total federal-state funds for need-based undergraduate state scholarship programs would be large enough to provide tuition assistance to all needy undergraduates.*

Federal provisions should also be amended to (1) provide matching funds for grants to meet tuition expenses in excess of $250 up to a maximum of $1,500—the $250 being a self-help expectation for the student—or a total tuition of $1,750; (2) increase the federal matching formula to 75 percent of the cost of grants awarded to students attending institutions in other states (limited to states that reciprocate, if the state prefers); (3) provide for matching increases in state appropriations from 1969-70 on; and (4) limit federal matching to amounts of student aid indicated when the CSS/ACT parental contribution schedule is used.

The Supplemental Educational Opportunity Grant program. Although Congress specified in 1972 that Supplemental Educational Opportunity Grants (SEOGs) should be awarded to students "of exceptional financial need," it is not clear that the program has conformed to that purpose.

With a uniform self-help expectation and a greatly expanded SSIG program, the SEOG program can serve a more clear-cut purpose in providing student aid officers with funds that can be allocated to students who have exceptional need for grant assistance, either because of unusual family circumstances or because of special difficulties in meeting the self-help requirement. Its role would be analogous to that of the special 10 percent augmentation of BEOG funds, but whereas these BEOG funds would be allocated for meeting noninstructional costs, SEOG funds would cover unusual needs for meeting tuition costs.

Recommendation 12: *The Supplemental Educational Opportunity Grant program should be continued at approximately its 1979-80 level of funding, but assistance under the program should be designed for students who have difficulty in meeting tuition costs because of unusual family circumstances, difficulty in meeting the self-help requirement, or other special problems.*

An equitable and accessible loan program. We find serious inequities and deficiencies in existing student loan programs that can be corrected only by replacing them with a more unified and carefully structured program. (For a description of the weaknesses of the Guaranteed Student Loan [GSL] and National Direct Student Loan [NDSL] programs and the Council's specific provisions for chartering a National Student Loan Bank, see summary of *The Federal Role in Postsecondary Education.*)

Although loans should never become the major source of student financing, especially for undergraduates, an equitable and accessible loan program should be available as a supplement to other forms of student assistance, especially for upper-division students, and as an indispensable source of support for graduate and professional students.

We propose, once again, the creation of a National Student Loan Bank. This bank would be largely self-sufficient. It would make loans available toward meeting college costs to students without any proof of their being needy, with repayment over an extended period of time. Under the Council's proposal, loans would be used mainly under these three circumstances: a student could work but prefers not to do so; parents could pay but either do not wish to do so or the student does not wish to call upon them to do so; or the student wants to attend a higher-cost institution. Loans would not be a question of necessity; they would, rather, add to the range of choices available.

No student would be permitted to borrow more than $500 in the first semester of his or her freshmen year. We propose this limit not only because we think an appropriate combination of student grants, parental contributions, and student earnings should prevent any need for substantial borrowing by beginning students, but also because such a limit would discourage abuse of student loans by certain unscrupulous institutions that entice students to enroll with the aid of loans and by some student borrowers who are not serious about higher education.

Recommendation 13: *Congress should give careful consideration to phasing out the National Direct Student Loan and Guaranteed Student Loan programs and replacing them by a National Student Loan Bank. The possibility of changes in the provisions governing the Student Loan Marketing Association to transform it into an institution resembling the proposed National Student Loan Bank may well facilitate such a move.*

Provision for part-time students (including adults). One of the striking developments of the last decade or so has been a pronounced increase in part-time enrollment, especially among persons who are older than the traditional age of college attendance. Most of these part-time students are employed and no longer dependent on their parents. Relatively few of them apply for student aid, but those who do must be enrolled at least half time and are usually eligible for aid only on a prorated basis—that is, a half-time student would be eligible for only one half of the aid available to a full-time student. This implies a larger earnings expectation for part-time students that is clearly justified in most situations.

Increasingly, tuition costs of adult employed students are paid by their employers under "out-service" training programs. Such employer expenditures are tax-exempt, but only if the program of study is job-related. In the United States, in contrast with the situation in some European countries that have developed paid educational leave programs, employer-financed training programs of this type are often confined to white-collar employees who are in line for promotion to supervisorial positions. We believe that there is a case for gradual development of a more general paid educational leave program that would be designed to encourage lifelong patterns of learning.

Recommendation 14: *Student aid should be available for part-time students on a prorated basis, provided they are enrolled for at least half-time study. In exceptional cases, where, for example, employment opportunities are impaired, the individual is handicapped, or an enrolled parent is responsible for childcare, aid should be granted to students enrolled for less than half time at the discretion of the student aid officer, taking advantage of the Basic Educational Opportunity Grant override and Supplemental Educational Opportunity Grant funds.*

Future development of student aid policies for adult and part-time college students should be carefully considered in relation to the need to encourage a more general program of paid educational leave.

Simplification. One common complaint about student aid relates to the complexity of procedures and of federal regulations. Our recommendations aim at the development of relatively uniform and objective policies for handling most student aid applicants, leaving decisions relating to students in exceptional circumstances to the discretion of student aid officers. Student aid officers are almost universally conscientious and are usually in a better position to assess a student's special needs than federal officials.

Recommendation 15: *Federal rules and regulations relating to student aid are in need of simplification, which could be accomplished by adopting our proposals, which call for more uniform and objective policies relating to most student aid applicants, leaving decisions relating to the more complex and difficult cases to student aid officers. The Office of Education should also encourage adequate training and upgrading of student aid officers.*

Increasing emphasis on student aid packaging. The Office of Education has tended to administer individual student aid programs without much consideration of their inter-relationships or of the need to devote more attention to the student aid package. A policy encouraging packaging would contribute a great deal to an improved, accessible student loan program that also would be coherently linked to all other student aid pro-grams. It would also contribute to bringing about a more equitable and structured re-lationship between state and federal student aid programs.

Recommendation 16: *The Office of Education should develop policies and procedures that encourage equitable and consistent student aid packages for all students, rather than treating each student aid program as a separate entity.*

Social security benefits for students. The case for special social security benefits to college students aged 18 to 21 who are children of deceased, disabled, or retired workers provided valuable benefits when it was adopted in 1965, but is now much weaker because most of the students who receive such benefits can qualify, on the basis of family income, for BEOGs and other types of student aid.

Recommendation 17: *The Council recommends the elimination of social security benefits for college students aged 18 to 21 who are children of deceased, disabled, or retired workers.*

Food stamps for college students. If our proposal to meet the subsistence costs of needy students through the BEOG program is adopted, there would no longer be a case for food stamp benefits for college students.

Recommendation 18: *The Council recommends that college students no longer be eligible for food stamps.*

Part Two: The Current System in Operation

This section is primarily descriptive, presenting data and discussing rationales for the various parts and characteristics of the student aid system. It focuses on the growth of student aid funds, need analysis, packaging student aid, recipients of aid, the impact of student aid on enrollments and institutions, and the changing burden of financing higher education.

Part Three: Opportunities For Improvement

Employment has always been a major source of financing for students whose parents could not meet their college expenses. The growth in student grants and loans has, however, greatly reduced reliance on earnings. On the one hand, student aid officers are in a position to provide grants to reduce employment burdens that would exceed the maximum commitment of the student's time that would be desirable in terms of the student's academic load. On the other hand, by using CWS funds, the student aid officer often can provide jobs to students who cannot otherwise find them. Earnings are generally regarded as a resource to be considered in the student aid packaging process, but the amount of expected student earnings is very inconsistent from college to college. A consensus on the role of student earnings and loans in financing college expenses would help to avoid the unfairness that may result from these wide variations in institutional policies. This would require establishing a standard student earnings expectation. Council Recommendations 1 through 7 suggest workable ground rules for a standard meeting these conditions.

Strengthening the Need-Based System

For taxpayers to assume parental costs would add at least $10 billion to public expenditures. There is no reason to think that additional expenditures in this amount have the priority, urgency, and popular support such a policy would call for.

If parents must continue to finance a sizeable share of the educational expenses of their children, there is no good alternative to distributing student financial assistance inversely according to ability to pay. This means assessing costs of attendance and available family resources, calculating need as the difference, and awarding aid to cover the gap between the two.

No one seriously proposes completely doing away with these elements of a need-based system. But several developments have reduced the emphasis of need in awarding aid:

- Relaxed means tests, such that fewer and fewer families are expected to pay full costs
- Proposals for general tax relief for families with college students
- Elimination of income tests of eligibility for student loan interest subsidies
- Criteria for establishing independent student status, under which children of upper-middle- and upper-income families can sometimes qualify for as much aid as children of lower-income parents.

So far, the trend toward less emphasis on differences in family resources in the awarding of aid has not been at the expense of students from lower-income families. The increased eligibility of middle- and upper-income students for aid has been on top of the recognized eligibility of lower-income students, but it is hard to deny that the claims of lower-income and upper-middle-income students are now approaching a point of direct competition. In 1979-80, typical students from families with $25,000 in income will be eligible for BEOGs. In the CSS/ACT system, the income level at which parental contributions are deemed to cover expenses at a public four-year college has risen from $15,750 in 1972-73 to $27,250 in 1978-79. Certainly, the trend toward including students from families with higher and higher incomes among those eligible for aid should now stop.

Expanding Student Choice

For a decade, much of the public policy debate concerning student aid has contrasted the objectives of equal access and choice. More often than not the objective of access has been understood to be the goal of assuring a place in a low-cost college for every student seeking to enroll and enough money to meet the minimum expenses of attending such an institution. Choice, on the other hand, has tended to mean the lowering of financial obstacles to choosing a residential or high-tuition institution, usually private, but often also an out-of-state public institution charging high tuition and fees to nonresidents.

In a system of higher education characterized by large differences in tuition and fees between institutions, achieving both perfect equality of access and perfect equality of choice is illusory. It is far more useful to think of access and choice not as preemptive values but as goals that must be brought into balance.

In these terms, choice is of concern to public policy because the higher education system as a whole can be most effective only if there are mechanisms for matching students of differing educational needs and institutions with differing programs. If unequal costs of attendance impede this matching, student aid can play a role in reducing their impact.

Recent developments have affected the amount of student aid funds available to meet high tuition levels both positively and negatively. On the positive side, there has been rapid growth in the state grant funds, often with the avowed intention of helping to close the tuition gap. Another positive factor is the rapid growth of institutional aid funds set aside from unrestricted revenues (including tuition revenues). And BEOGs, although regarded as an access program, have provided a floor of support that has made it considerably easier for at least the less-selective private colleges to build aid packages and to extend recruitment efforts among low-income and minority students.

On the negative side, student aid officers at public institutions have increased competition for federal campus-based student aid. This competition, together with inflation, has meant that, despite rising federal appropriations, many private colleges have less aid in constant dollars to award from these sources than they had in the early 1970s.

In the early 1970s, most aid was distributed through the student aid officer's packaging process. Aid funds were unevenly matched with aggregate need from institution to institution, but the packaging process uniformly had the effect of treating one dollar of student need as having an equal prima facie claim to aid as any other, whether subsistence costs or tuition costs represented the greater part of a student's budget.

This situation has changed. A larger proportion of total costs at most public institutions represents subsistence than at private institutions. Thus, the advent of the BEOG program also can be seen as making aid to attend a public institution or to meet subsistence costs relatively more predictable, reliable, and simple to obtain than aid to meet tuition costs—at least those of most private institutions. This situation constricts choice, even though the BEOG program has helped private institutions stretch their discretionary aid resources and appears to have helped recruitment at the less selective private institutions.

Council Recommendations 11 through 13 would increase student aid resources for choice and also the predictability of aid for choice independently of the availability of discretionary institutional funds through the student aid officer.

Under our proposals, however, there would not be an attempt to make the choice between a low- and a high-tuition institution neutral in determining financial obligations. Parents would be expected to pay more toward an expensive education if they could. Students would be expected to increase their self-help contribution through additional earnings or loan obligations or both.

The additional burdens of attending a high-tuition institution would, however, be certain and manageable in size and form. Thus families could fairly weigh educational alternatives without excluding high-tuition colleges on the basis of cost alone, and institutions could engage in fair and productive educational competition.

Improving the Student Loan System

The leading cause of criticism of the Guaranteed Student Loan (GSL) program is its very high default rates. The rate of defaults over the life of the program is perhaps 13.5 percent. The default rate on loans currently coming due for repayment is lower—perhaps as low as 10 percent. Such rates are still unacceptable, and new approaches to the problem should be considered.

Students have often been unable to find willing lenders, and lenders have been discouraged about participation in the programs both by the inherent difficulties of managing a portfolio of student loans and by changing regulations. Moreover, student aid officers have been unsure whether student loans could be counted on as part of individual aid packages. There have also been rapid increases in the interest subsidy costs of the GSL program.

Regulations of student, lender, and aid officer conduct are extraordinarily detailed. These regulations have been thought necessary to forestall the proliferation of abuse. A series of very complicated and expensive record-keeping systems have been built, only to fail in providing critical information when it will do the most good.

It seems clear that further tinkering with the program is unlikely to solve the problems encountered. The solutions adopted have generally led to further problems and also to increased costs of administration.

The following principles are fundamental:

1. Access to loans must be assured.
2. It must be possible to coordinate eligibility for loans with other aid.
3. Borrowers must be put in a position such that they can and will repay their loans.

These principles do not necessarily require that commercial lenders have no role in making student loans, nor do they require that new sources of loan capital be tapped. But the first principle does mean that commercial lenders should not have to ration loan funds. The amount of the loan a student receives should be determined by student aid officers according to the ground rules for coordination of aid from all sources. This means that government credit would almost certainly have to play a larger role than at present, and incentives to involve the regular capital sources of commercial lenders a lesser role. It also means that an adequate system for assuring repayment, as required by the third principle, should not rest, if it ever could, on ordinary collection efforts by originating commercial lenders.

Council Recommendation 13 proposes that the federal government charter a new National Student Loan Bank, a nonprofit private corporation to be financed by the sale of governmentally guaranteed securities. Operating in a context of adequate and coordinated grant programs and in the absence of interest subsidies tending to induce unnecessary borrowing, the total volume of loan demand could be much less than under present ground rules. A National Student Loan Bank would also make clear where a student could turn to be assured of getting funds.

The nature of a student's repayment obligation and its implications would change also. A student could no longer expect to enjoy heavily subsidized interest rates. Interest at rates slightly higher than Federal Treasury long-term borrowing costs (to cover the bank's cost of money) would be compounded until the borrower's studies and any period of military or volunteer service were completed. The student, therefore, would not be tempted to borrow more than necessary for the sake of interest subsidy benefits. The borrower would be put in the position of knowing that repayment of necessary debt would be manageable, since repayment could be over a much longer period—on average, 20 years—and annual installments would be geared to current income. But there would be no prospect of evading the stipulated obligations once undertaken.

The Internal Revenue Service (IRS) has traditionally opposed use of its tax collection mechanisms to administer social programs in the way proposed for the National Student Loan Bank, but student loans are unique in requiring a commitment of federal credit without collateral other than the incomes student borrowers will eventually earn and the IRS will monitor.

Aiding Adult, Part-time, and Independent Students

A growing proportion of total enrollments consists of adults, part-time students, and independent students whose parents are determined to have no obligation to provide them with financial support. Financial considerations are an important motive for many decisions in favor of part-time enrollment. Such a decision can represent an individual solution to the basic problem student aid programs address—how to find enough money to live and attend college—since part-time enrollment permits commitment of more time to employment and higher earnings than full-time students can usually achieve.

The simplest situation for which general rules need to be developed is that of part-time students, although the degree of aid should not always be proportional to their reduced course loads. Their subsistence costs are indistinguishable from those of full-time students. Their earning opportunities, however, are generally greater. Putting these characteristics together suggests that an appropriate general rule would be to expect a larger earnings contribution from such students. For example, as a standard minimum, this additional earnings expectation for half-time students might be set at half of standard noninstructional costs ($1,200). Students enrolled more than half-time but less than full-time would be treated similarly, but with prorated adjustments. Students whose enrollment is less than half-time would ordinarily not need a grant toward noninstructional costs, for these are students with sufficient time to commit to fully self-supporting employment.

General rules for independent students are far more difficult to devise. It is probably desirable to regard a student's having a spouse or child as conclusive evidence of independence. There might well be an exception, however, in the case of students of traditional college age (under 22). Younger students, even with family responsibilities, should be treated by the aid system just as though they were single dependent students. This is perhaps the only way to make the aid system's treatment of young students a neutral factor in decisions to form families.

Older students who are determined to be independent because they have family responsibilities of their own may be wage earners, homemakers, or both. Their academic commitments may require relinquishing these roles to differing degrees and with varying consequences for their ability to finance educational expenses. However, public student aid programs should neither meet the subsistence needs of such students' dependents nor compensate for all the opportunity costs of being a student. A reasonable rule for student aid benefits to independent students with family responsibilities would be to add to the standard earnings contribution a specially assessed family contribution, in lieu of an otherwise expected parental contribution. This family contribution would be calculated only after subtracting the earnings expectation from total family income, so as to avoid assessing it twice. The sum of the earnings and the family contributions would then be compared to the cost of attendance to find need.

There is no easy way to determine which single students should be considered independent and thus have no claim on their parents' resources. However, criteria of independence that do not accord independent status at least in clear cases where parental responsibility has been drawn down in the past or has atrophied because a student has not needed to call on parental resources for some time would be inappropriate.

One way of simplifying the matter is to determine independence for the purpose of general student aid programs by rules that require only easy and relatively nonintrusive forms of verification. These rules should recognize the independence of single students only in the clearest cases. It would then be left to student aid officers to determine the validity of evidence rebutting the assumptions of these simple rules. They would, in effect, identify an additional class of independent students and could award aid to them from discretionary funds.

With this division of responsibility for determining independence, students might be determined independent for purposes of these programs if:

- They are over age 22 and have family responsibilities of their own, as evidenced by marriage and birth certificates.
- They are over age 25, as evidenced by birth certificates.
- They are orphans, as evidenced by death certificates.
- They have been fully self-supporting for three consecutive years immediately preceding their aid applications, as evidenced by IRS documents showing earnings of $3,000 a year or more.

Enhancing Program Coordination

One serious problem in student aid programs is that the various components do not adequately complement each other, and their administrative mechanisms have not been well coordinated.

- It is easy to find instances of prima facie unfairness in the relative treatment of students, because program rules and fund availabilities create anomalies among states, among colleges, and among students.
- Lack of any fundamental coordination reduces the benefits that can accrue from making any one program better and more simply administered; rather, it seems to impel efforts to complicate the individual programs by attempting to reduce inequities. Complexity then makes the programs vulnerable to abuse.
- The roles of parents and students themselves in financing education become more uncertain, and uncertainty gives rise to anxiety that financing for college will not be available.

What before-the-fact coordination requires, at a minimum, is a set of rules specifying that eligibility for one program begins only where eligibility for others leaves off. The expected parental contribution would first reduce BEOG eligibility. Then, if the parental contribution is not exhausted by this reduction, any excess over the maximum amount of BEOG eligibility would be applied to reducing state grant eligibility. This type of coordination also makes it possible to have a fair and consistent self-help expectation. Uniform self-help expectations can be introduced as expenses that neither federal or state grants are available to cover.

Federal financial incentives are also needed to counter the natural tendency of the states to prefer students choosing home-state institutions. In providing federal matching grants to encourage state spending for student aid, the federal formula should provide a special inducement for states to make their grants portable out-of-state, at least on a basis of reciprocity—that is, where another state also allows such portability.

The existing SSIG program provides an incentive for states to spend more on student aid, but this incentive is limited by the small size of federal appropriations for the program and by so-called maintenance-of-effort rules, which require that most state expenditures before enactment of the federal program be disregarded in calculating a state's matching funds.

Increasing Integrity and Simplicity

Vulnerability to abuse and excessive complexity of student aid programs are closely related. Proposed improvements in the way the programs operate should meet a double test. They should not only pass the test of effectiveness but should also be shown likely to reduce complexity and invitations to abuse.

A first principle—and a first set of steps to take—is to eliminate, wherever possible, unnecessary procedures that constitute occasions for abuse.

A second principle is that incentives to perform desirable actions and disincentives to perform undesirable ones can reduce both complexity and vulnerability to abuse.

A third principle is illustrated by the complexities and abuse inherent in systems for determining the student's eligibility for aid: subtlety in distinguishing the differing claims of students for aid through means tests must not be allowed to outrun practical and acceptable means of verifying those claims.

A fourth principle is that a premium should not be placed on student aid officers' facile cleverness in obtaining funds.

A fifth and final principle is that some abuses in the use of student aid funds can best be avoided if students are convinced that it is their own funds that are at risk, even if the funds come from public sources. Program rules should make it clear that what is wasted in paying for an inadequate program is the students' own money—an entitlement to grant aid that is being drawn down, earnings that represent their own efforts, and money from loans that will assuredly have to be repaid. To reinforce the sense that student aid funds belong to the students themselves, it would help to let students "bank" their grant entitlements for use later in life, to charge realistic interest rates on student loans, and to assure that CWS jobs demand as much effort as jobs elsewhere in the economy.

The Essential Commitments

A national commitment to equality of educational opportunity would recognize that:

- An opportunity to go to college is, for all those qualified and motivated to do so, a critical opportunity for a productive, autonomous, and socially responsible life.
- The full development of the intellectual capacities of our people, whether of great or modest talents, is vital to our future as a nation.
- Equality of opportunity for higher education is an indispensable part of any broader agenda for achieving equal opportunity in our society.

It is necessary, however, to be more specific about what equal opportunity for higher education entails.

- *Who should have such opportunities?* All those who are qualified for admission and wish to attend college should be financially able to do so.
- *What kinds of institutions should they be able to attend?* Most institutions should be financially accessible to students meeting their admissions standards, excluding no extensive class of institutions.
- *How much financial support should students be eligible for?* The student aid system should provide enough support to overcome financial obstacles but not so much as to attract students without strong educational motivation.
- *What should be expected of students themselves and of their families?* Student aid should make financing the costs of higher education manageable for all. But a student aid system that succeeds in doing so need not go so far as to eliminate the need for sacrifice, effort, and commitment on the part of the student and the student's family.

The measure of the success of the system should not be whether all groups participate equally in higher education. In a society in which both values and aspirations differ, and in which college attendance is not compulsory, there will be different rates and patterns of attendance. What should be achieved is a situation in which the decision whether or not to go to college can be made freely in all cases, because everyone would be able to attend college regardless of his or her financial circumstances.

The changing goals of student aid and the variety of interests at stake should not be allowed to divert efforts to build a student aid system designed to make good on a national commitment to equality of opportunity for higher education. Now is the time to reinforce, not weaken, the need-based character of the aid system if it is to serve well needy students, the colleges and universities they attend, and the national welfare. The issue is how best to combine the elements of the present aid system into a structure that meets the needs for coordination and equity.

Fair Practices in Higher Education:
Rights and Responsibilities of Students and Their Colleges in a Period of Intensified Competition for Enrollments
April 1979

Fair practice has been a basic and continuing theme of American higher education since the founding of Harvard in 1636. In recent times, higher education in the United States has made many contributions to ethical conduct by greatly expanding equality of opportunity in higher education; by maintaining the academic "value added" for its students even as it seems to have gone down substantially for many graduates of our high schools; by serving as a forum for discussions of many national issues such as civil rights, the war in Vietnam, and the physical environment; and by serving students in a manner that leaves most of them satisfied with the college they are attending, thereby providing a valuable model for other social institutions.

Yet we are concerned. We see certain signs of deterioration in important parts of academic life, in particular:

- A significant and apparently increasing amount of cheating by students in academic assignments
- A substantial misuse by students of public financial aid
- Theft and destruction by students of valuable property, most specifically library books and journals
- Inflation of grades by faculty members
- Competitive awarding of academic credits by some departments and by some institutions for insufficient and inadequate academic work
- Inflated and misleading advertising by some institutions in the search for students.

Most institutions of higher education, to a small or large degree, exhibit one or more of these destructive traits.

We are concerned about the prospective frantic search by colleges for scarce students in the 1980s and 1990s. Unless corrective actions are taken, such conditions are likely to lead some students to try to take even greater advantage of the situation and to make some colleges even more reluctant to insist on ethical conduct by students and even more likely to engage in improper conduct themselves. We are also concerned that these negative behavioral traits may indicate a larger and more deep-seated problem: a general loss of self-confidence and a sense of mutual trust, and a general decline in integrity of conduct on campus.

Institutional Rights and Student Responsibilities

Academic Programming

This is the portion of higher education most intimately concerned with teaching and learning; thus it is the core of the academic enterprise. Institutional rights and student responsibilities in this domain include:

1. Learning needs and desires should provide the rationale for enrolling in academic programs. Students should not manipulate programs to achieve other ends.
2. The learner should be informed. Catalogs and other institutionally disseminated literature on academic programs should be read.
3. The learner should take an active part in planning and executing his or her academic program within the context of stated requirements and existing institutional resources.
4. The learner should continually monitor his or her academic progress.
5. The learner should seek out available academic support services such as basic skills instruction, job placement, and advising as needed.
6. The learner should attend class and participate in other learning activities. Learners should also come to class prepared and should complete assignments on time.
7. The principle of academic honesty should be embraced.
8. The freedom of the academic community to inquire, publish, and teach should be respected.
9. The facilities and property of the academic community (for example, buildings, books, and computers) should also be respected.

Many students are not fully carrying out their responsibilities. The most serious breaches of responsibility, such as academic dishonesty, usually involve relatively small numbers of students. Cheating on tests and papers is an unfortunate exception that appears to involve a substantial minority of undergraduates. Students themselves are the principal victims of many of their lapses of responsibility—not being informed, passivity in academic planning, and not using available institutional services when needed.

Government traditionally has not been involved in this area because matters of institutional rights and student responsibility in academic affairs have been regarded as the prerogative of the higher education community. However, when student irresponsibility has moved into the realm of fraud and theft, governmental agencies have become more active.

There has been some activity by colleges aimed at improving the situation, but institutional efforts have been spotty. Colleges and their faculties have generally tended to be lax in punishing students for academic dishonesty, and most students have been unwilling to blow the whistle on peers who cheat.

Financial Aid and Tuition

For many students, financial aid and tuition are keys to college access and a source of growing influence in the world of higher education. For institutions, financial aid and tuition are essential for survival. Institutional rights and student responsibilities in this area include:

1. Students and potential students should be informed. They should be knowledgeable about the full cost of education, available financial aid programs and obligations,

refund policies, and the financial stability of their college or the colleges they are thinking of applying to. Toward this end, all students should read institutional statements on tuition and fees, and those students who want financial assistance should read institutional statements on that subject and consult the financial aid office.

2. The rationale for seeking financial aid should be to meet the costs of an education that could not be met, or could be met only with hardship, in the absence of such aid. Education should not be used as a vehicle for securing financial aid.

3. Students should read and fully comprehend contracts before signing them.

4. Tuition and financial aid reporting should be complete and accurate.

5. Tuition and financial aid obligations should be satisfied in a timely fashion.

Students have not completely fulfilled these responsibilities, and the failings have been the subject of heavy press coverage—particularly student loan defaults or other violations of tuition or financial aid responsibility. Student financial aid abuse of this type is a serious problem, but the relative number of students involved is small. The most common violation of responsibility among college students is failure to be informed about financial aid and tuition matters as well as signing forms without understanding the obligations they entail. This may be an even greater cause for default than deliberate dishonesty.

Admissions

Today the emphasis in admissions is on student rights; however, students also have certain basic responsibilities, and institutions are entitled to enjoy certain fundamental rights. These include:

1. Applicants and potential applicants should be knowledgeable about the available postsecondary opportunities at the colleges they are thinking of attending. Sources of information include the information an institution publishes about itself and comparative and evaluative guides published outside the colleges, visits to institutions, former students, state departments of education, and accrediting associations.

2. Applicants should honestly represent themselves in applying to a college.

Students need to consider available options more carefully, and while gross misrepresentation is the exception, many applicants neglect responsibility number 2 in small ways. It happens when a potential student writes a required admissions essay or conducts a campus visit in a manner designed to conform to projected institutional standards rather than to reflect his or her true feelings. It also happens when friends or relatives write an applicant's required admissions essays. The consequences can be quite damaging for the applicant who guesses wrong about the type of student an institution is looking for.

Student Rights and Institutional Responsibilities

Academic Programming

The basic rights and responsibilities associated with academic programming are as follows:

1. The emphasis in academic programming should be on quality.

2. Credit should be awarded only where it is due.
3. Clear and specific written documents describing policies for accepting credit from other institutions should be available.
4. Accurate information on the possible acceptability of an institution's credits elsewhere should be disclosed.
5. Academic evaluation should be fair and reasonable. Grades and evaluations should be meaningful, timely, and based wholly on academic considerations. Transcripts or records of grades should be properly maintained. Confidentiality and access to records should be guaranteed in accordance with the Family Educational Rights and Privacy Act of 1974.
6. Students should be informed regularly of their academic progress and should receive degrees after satisfying all stated academic requirements.
7. Adequate facilities and services to support academic programs should be provided.
8. Quality instruction should be offered. Faculty should have appropriate training, teach in areas of their expertise, keep up to date with their fields, meet scheduled classes, come to class prepared, be available to students outside of class, and in general should provide good teaching.
9. Institutional program requirements should be described in clear, specific, and accurate terms and should be available in written form. All requirements should be educationally meaningful.
10. Students should be notified of unusual features of academic programs that cannot be readily anticipated.
11. Requirements should not be unconditionally changed for students who have already enrolled in a program.
12. Courses that are offered should be comparable to their catalog descriptions.
13. All courses listed in the catalog should be offered periodically.
14. All academic programs should be continued until enrolled students making acceptable progress have had an opportunity to graduate. Program changes should be well planned and widely communicated and should incorporate an orderly transition from the old to the new.
15. The principle of academic honesty should be embraced.
16. Causes for dismissal should be published in clear and specific form; students should be dismissed only for appropriate cause and after due process.

There is no evidence of widespread abrogation of academic program responsibilities by colleges and universities, but there is some neglect even in a few well-respected institutions. Off-campus centers are a special case. They combine both innovative nontraditional programs and fly-by-night operations, representing vendorism at its best and worst.

Institutional Advertising

Advertising is the first contact many students have with a college and the only contact some students have before enrolling. Here student rights and institutional responsibilities are as follows:

1. Advertising should be accurate and reliable.
2. Advertising should be up to date.
3. Advertising should be complete—balanced and comprehensive.
4. Advertising should be understandable.

The college catalog is the best known and most maligned advertisement of all. Institutions face an unavoidable tension between using the catalog to define the relationship between themselves and their students and using it as an instrument to attract prospective students.

Financial Aid and Tuition

Student rights and institutional responsibilities in this area include:

1. Students and potential students should be informed of the full cost of education.
2. Students and potential students should be informed about the financial aid programs available to them, exemplary financial aid packages, the procedures for obtaining aid, and the criteria for awarding aid.
3. Accurate and up-to-date information about available financial aid should be offered.
4. Loan applicants should be informed of the source of their loans, loan repayment obligations and procedures, loan repayment schedules, consequences of not paying, and means of cancelling or deferring payments.
5. Fair and adequate refund policies should be employed, including offering refunds, having a written refund policy, publicly disseminating that policy, informing students how to get refunds, specifying a maximum time between receipt of a valid refund request and the actual refund, basing refunds on the amount of instruction received, and conforming to stated refund policies.
6. Fair and reasonable fees should be charged for infractions such as breaking laboratory equipment or losing a library book.
7. Tuition increases should be reasonable, and adequate notice of raises should be given.
8. Student tuition payments should be safeguarded, and records should be kept of the fees each student has paid.
9. Student loan defaults and other financial aid abuses should be discouraged.
10. Students should be informed about institutional financial instability if such a condition exists.

Intentionally abusive institutions are few in number. Some institutions, however, have been lax in providing complete financial information to students.

Admissions

In this area, student rights and institutional responsibilities include the following:

1. Written policies on recruitment and admissions should be available.
2. Students should be admitted on the basis of a publicly announced admissions policy.
3. A professional admissions staff should be employed, and salaries should not be based primarily on the number of students enrolled.
4. Prospective students should be given as complete and accurate a picture of an institution as possible. They should be encouraged to visit the campus and speak with faculty and students when possible.
5. Institutional services or benefits such as job placement or particular vocational programs should be clearly and specifically described.
6. Compensatory or support services should be available for students lacking the ability to complete institutional requirements at the time of admission.
7. Orientation should be offered to all newly enrolled students.

Many colleges are in serious need of students, and the students they are able to recruit are different from those of previous years—they are less able in basic skills, and a higher proportion of them are nontraditional students. In general, institutions are facing growing competition to attract such students and increasing diversity in what they must offer to meet such students' needs. This burden has caused some colleges to compromise their admissions responsibilities.

Recommendations for Students

If students are to protect their rights and take advantage of their opportunities, they must be better educated in consumer skills.

Recommendation 1: *Local schools and school districts should make consumer education available to students and their parents early enough to influence student curricular and life choices.*

Recommendation 2: *Broad-based Educational Information Centers, created by the Education Amendments of 1976 and currently being initiated on a small scale, should be fully funded to provide a complete range of information on educational alternatives, requirements, rights and responsibilities, and financial aid options; comparative data on institutions; guidance and counseling; and referral services to all people and schools desiring to use these services in every state.*

Recommendation 3: *The Fund for the Improvement of Postsecondary Education and other foundations with educational missions should support and evaluate alternative models of consumer education.*

In addition to the measures that we recommend schools, colleges, and other agencies adopt to improve student information, we believe students, as consumers, should take more of the initiative in becoming informed. To assist them, we offer the following checklist:

Questions Students Should Ask About a College

BEFORE ENROLLING

1. What are the entrance requirements?
2. What are the requirements for completing a course, program, or degree?
3. Who are the faculty?
4. What support services does this institution offer (for example, counseling, health care, compensatory education, job placement)?
5. What kind of learning environment is offered (for example, teaching methods, scope of programs, class size, transferability of credits, library, postgraduate activities of alumni?)
6. Are the types of equipment and facilities I need for my education available?
7. What are the total student costs of attendance, the types of financial aid available, the terms for receiving aid, the amount of financial aid that can be counted on and the circumstances in and extent to which tuition and fee refunds are available?
8. Are there a code of ethics, disciplinary policy, and grievance procedures that I can agree to comply with?

9.   Are there minimum standards of acceptable performance below which a student may be put on probation or expelled?

10. Is this institution equipped to serve my personal and academic needs?

AFTER ENROLLING

11. When and what types of orientation are available?

12. Are instruction, programs, staff, support services, facilities, grievance procedures, and institutional learning environment of the quality and quantity promised? Do they meet my needs?

13. Are faculty available outside of class?

14. Are evaluation and the awarding of credit meaningful, timely, and based wholly on academic criteria?

15. Are program changes made that could set back or impede my academic program?

16. Are tuition increases reasonable and announced in a timely fashion?

17. Am I conscientiously planning, monitoring, and carrying out my education?

18. Am I fulfilling my ethical responsibilities in a manner consistent with the institutional code of rights and responsibilities?

19. If attending a branch or off-campus center, is the program equivalent in quality to that of the institution's home campus?

Recommendations for Institutions

The Carnegie Council believes that, to fulfill its mission, higher education must be an ethical community. Emphasis should be placed on defining the rights and responsibilities of students and their colleges. Those listed previously provide a general model and convenient checklist by which students and colleges can evaluate their conduct. However, specific statements of rights and responsibilities must be geared to the character of an individual campus and the students who attend it.

Recommendation 4: *Every institution of higher education that has not already done so should produce a code of rights and responsibilities through the collaborative efforts of administrators, faculty, and students.*

Recommendation 5: *Colleges and universities should publish statements of the range of penalties that will be imposed for general classes of violations of their rights and firmly administer the penalties for infractions.* Institutions must not reward academic dishonesty. Penalties for willful dishonesty must be severe because truth is the stock in trade of the academic community.

Recommendation 6: *Institutions should develop equitable, easily navigable, and publicized grievance procedures.* Colleges and universities should consider appointing an institutionwide ombudsperson.

Recommendation 7: *Institutions should voluntarily embrace the principle of full and complete disclosure and provide students with comprehensive and accurate information on all pertinent aspects of institutional practice, including basic institutional identification and rules of governance; financial obligations; educational resources, process, and content; and indications of institutional effectiveness.*

College and university trustees should regularly review the state of institutional responsibility by asking the following questions about both on- and off-campus programs:

Trustee's Checklist of Basic Institutional Responsibilities

1. Does this institution have a realistic, equitable, and up-to-date code of rights and responsibilities?
2. Is institutional advertising and admissions literature, such as the college catalog, complete, accurate, up-to-date, understandable, and intended to serve as a contract between the institution and its students?
3. Are students given complete, accurate, and up-to-date information about the full cost of education, available financial aid, and the financial status of the institution?
4. Is chartered, approved, and accredited status accurately and completely described in institutional literature?
5. Are recruiting and admissions staff members professionals who admit only those students who are capable of benefiting from the institution's academic programs?
6. Are students provided with an orientation when they first enroll?
7. Are refund policies for tuition and other fees fair, accurate, and publicly disseminated?
8. Are institutional requirements educationally meaningful; described in clear, specific, and accurate form; and subject to change only with advance notice in a manner that will not impede progress of students who are already enrolled?
9. Are instructional programs, facilities, and equipment adequate, up-to-date, and accurately described in institutional publications?
10. Are evaluation (grading) and the awarding of credit fair, meaningful, timely, and based wholly on academic criteria?
11. Are student cheating and other forms of academic dishonesty actively discouraged by the institution?
12. Do faculty have a relatively low turnover rate and appropriate training?
13. Are students provided with services of the quality and quantity they have been promised, particularly with regard to job placement, compensatory education, courses of study, and counseling?
14. Are tuition increases reasonable and are students given adequate notice of them?
15. Does the institution periodically conduct a self-study of the state of rights and responsibilities on campus and issue annual reports in problem areas describing the ameliorative steps that have been taken and the results of these efforts?

Recommendations for Accrediting Associations

Accrediting associations are involved in issues of rights and responsibilities in two ways—through their traditional roles as voluntary, private membership organizations whose primary function is to decide whether institutions or programs have attained their stated purposes and to make recommendations for improvement; and, more recently, through federal and state requirements that institutions be accredited by recognized associations as a condition for participation in certain programs, particularly U.S. Office of Education student aid. The Council urges this practice be continued. At the same time, the Council is aware that there have been criticisms of accrediting associations for lax standards and unreliable performance. Accrediting associations are a diverse group. Some are doing very adequate jobs, and a number are not. In general, improvement is necessary.

Recommendation 8: *Regional accrediting associations should serve as the primary external actor in matters of institutional rights and responsibilities for accredited colleges.*

Recommendation 9: *Regional associations should (1) increase the thoroughness of institutional visits; (2) place greater emphasis upon reviewing ethical conduct, in particular by reviewing institutional advertising, policies for awarding credit, and catalogs as full disclosure statements intended to serve as a contract between the student and the college; (3) seek out eminently qualified people from around the country to serve on visiting teams; (4) consult with other professional associations and societies in developing academic program evaluation criteria and in identifying qualified people for visiting committees; (5) increase the number of trained full-time staff to assist visiting teams; (6) publish periodically a report on the status of all schools that are members or have applied for membership; and (7) embrace the principle of full disclosure by publishing accrediting team reports and publicly expose institutions engaging in bad practice.*

Recommendation 10: *All of the regional associations should make certain that the off-campus programs of their member institutions meet minimum standards appropriate to higher education and are comparable in quality to the standards expected of on-campus programs.* Off-campus programs should be evaluated regardless of where in the country they are located. The future of accredition depends on it.

As a check on responsibility, accrediting associations should address the following questions about institutions and themselves:

Basic Questions Accrediting Associations Should Ask

ABOUT COLLEGES AND UNIVERSITIES

1. Is the institution financially stable?
2. Is institutional advertising accurate and complete?
3. Are institutional recruiting practices fair?
4. Is institutional disclosure of necessary information to students and prospective students adequate?
5. Is the institutional catalog treated as a full and complete disclosure statement intended to serve as a contract between the students and the college?
6. Are institutional instructional programs and facilities adequate and appropriate in quality for an institution of higher education?
7. Are the institution's off-campus programs equal in quality to its on-campus programs?
8. Are institutional faculty and staff competent and appropriate in quality for an institution of higher education?
9. Are institutional record-keeping policies and practices adequate?
10. Are institutional tuition and fee refund policies fair and equitable?
11. Does the institution have a code of rights and responsibilities?
12. Does the institution discourage grade inflation, academic dishonesty, financial aid abuse, poor support services, and students' failure to take responsibility for their educations?
13. Does the institution accurately represent accredited or approved status?

ABOUT THEMSELVES

14.   Are institutional visits sufficiently frequent and thorough to permit comprehensive and up-to-date institutional evaluation?

15.   Are visiting teams composed of the best qualified people in the country?

16.   Does the association employ a sufficient number of trained, full-time staff members to assist each institutional visiting team?

17.   Does the association publish a report annually on the status of all schools that are members or have applied for membership?

18.   Does the association publish the final institutional evaluation reports produced following accrediting team visits and publicize institutions engaging in bad practice?

19.   Does the association have a fast, equitable, comprehensive, and well-publicized grievance mechanism for handling complaints by or about member institutions?

20.   Is ethical conduct (the state of rights and responsibilities on campus) a priority item on this association's agenda and a required part of the institutional self-study procedure?

Recommendations for the States

The Council recognizes that state agencies have an important role to play in the student-institutional relationship, beyond the roles of the institutions themselves and of the accrediting agencies. However, the comprehensiveness of existing state authorization statutes and regulations varies widely. As a consequence, some states have been more hospitable than others to irresponsible institutional and student practices. This variation has provided the primary rationale for federal intervention in this area.

To eliminate the now overlapping federal-state role, it is necessary for the states to fulfill their constitutionally assigned role and assume primary responsibility for education within their boundaries. Each state must set minimum standards for approving educational institutions.

Recommendation 11: *Each state that has not already done so should adopt standards comparable to those proposed in the Education Commission of the States' Model State Legislation for approval of postsecondary educational institutions and the authorization to grant degrees.*

Recommendation 12: *The states should accept the obligation for screening clearly inadequate programs offered by unaccredited colleges as part of their licensure and oversight responsibilities.* To date the state record is unsatisfactory, though by no means uniformly so.

Recommendations for the Federal Government

The federal government's role in education is tied to the spending and commerce powers granted by the U.S. Constitution. The federal government would have minimal influence on the relationship between students and colleges if institutions chose not to participate in federally funded aid programs. This indirect influence is reflected in the checkerboard pattern of policies and regulations and has resulted in poor communication among participating agencies, inadequate sharing of information about irresponsible institutions and students, a jumble of new regulations and reporting procedures, unequal demands upon institutions and students, and slow and inadequate enforcement of existing regulations.

Recommendation 13: *The federal government should (1) place more reliance upon state government, where regulation can be geared to the needs of the individual state and enforcement can be swifter, in matters of student and institutional rights, and should reserve for itself only those areas that touch directly upon its spending powers that are out of the purview of the states (such as collection of defaulted student loans); (2) make procedural compliance with existing laws and regulations easier for institutions and students by reducing, where possible, needless diversity in policies; (3) halt further "consumer" legislation until such time as the flood of new and existing regulations can be evaluated; and (4) eliminate procedural regulations that substantively infringe upon academic programming, such as the Veterans Administration 12-hour rule.*

The Office of Education's Division of Eligibility and Agency Evaluation, in particular, should subject petitions for recognition by accrediting associations to stricter scrutiny by establishing minimum submission requirements, visiting a larger sample of member institutions, reviewing visiting team reports more thoroughly, actively soliciting outside opinions on associations and their member schools, and appointing to its advisory committee the best qualified people in the country. To carry out the additional fieldwork responsibilities proposed, the division's professional staff will have to be increased. To ensure that the job can be done adequately, perhaps ten more professionals will be necessary.

With regard to student loan defaults and other forms of financial aid abuse, the Carnegie Council urges that the onus of antiabuse regulations be removed from institutions and placed squarely on the shoulders of abusive students, except as institutions encourage such abuse. The federal government should be more aggressive in trying to collect repayments and in bringing delinquent cases to court.

Recommendation 14: *The passage of legislation that would allow the Internal Revenue Service to turn over to the Veterans Administration and the Department of Health, Education, and Welfare the current addresses of loan defaulters, and state legislation that would allow the garnishment of the salaries of defaulters working for the state should be considered where it has not yet been adopted.*

Giving Youth a Better Chance:
Options for Education, Work, and Service
November 1979

Schooling, Employment, and Community Behavior: Inseparable Problems

We have become convinced that those who are concerned with the future of higher education must also give serious consideration to the severe labor market and school problems facing youth, especially minority group youth in inner cities and in some rural areas.

Rising youth unemployment has been arousing increasing concern in nearly all industrial democracies, and the prolongation of schooling has resulted in severe problems of adjustment for many young people who are held in school through a combination of parental and societal pressure and are not deriving much benefit from the experience.

We consider both the labor market and educational aspects of youth problems. It is those who have dropped out before completing high school and those who have graduated without having learned even the basic skills of reading and arithmetic that have the most difficult time in the job market. At the same time, the inadequacies of the schools are at least partly responsible for the fact that many youngsters drop out and many others learn very little.

Essential Facts

The "youth problem" in the United States is not going away. Yet our society has a better opportunity to deal effectively with it in the 1980s and the 1990s than it has had in the past two decades. Instead of growing explosively, as it did in the 1960s, the youth population will be declining throughout most of the period from now to 2000. This will make it possible to devote more resources to the solution of youth problems within a budget of stable or even declining expenditures for youth in toto.

What are the problems that are not going away of their own accord?

- Substantial dropout rates from high school: 23 percent overall, 35 percent for blacks, and 45 percent for Hispanics.
- Substantial numbers (estimated at 20 percent) of high school graduates have deficiencies in language and numerical skills.
- High school is an alienating experience for many young people.
- A substantial number of adults do not look back on their high school experience as rewarding.

- Nearly one-half of today's high school students do not consider the work in school to be hard enough.
- A general environment that would enable youth to make an effective transition into adulthood is deficient in many respects, including little early contact with the world of work and little opportunity for organized service to others.
- The transition into permanent jobs in the labor market is difficult for many youths.
- A sense of dependency is carried on too long; and, with it, a sense of rebellion against authority.
- Crime rates are high. More than 50 percent of all arrests are of youth under 25, and nearly 25 percent of those arrested are juveniles (under 18).
- Pockets of high and prolonged unemployment exist and will not be eradicated without special efforts. Nearly 50 percent of all unemployment is accounted for by persons 24 and younger, and some pockets of youth have unemployment rates of 60 percent and higher.
- Nearly 6 percent of youth seem to have opted out of education, the labor market, and other customary pursuits.
- The number of nonwhite youths will rise from 15.8 percent of the population aged 16 to 21 in 1980 to 18.7 percent in 1990 and then stabilize at about that proportion. This is an increase of nearly 20 percent in the share of the age cohort. Counting Hispanics, the minority portion of youth will be at least 25 percent and possibly as high as 30 percent in 2000.
- Those who fall behind are by no means all members of disadvantaged minority groups. The unemployment rate among low-income white youths is as high as among low-income black youths, and the school dropout rate of low-income white youths is even higher than that of low-income blacks. In terms of numbers, disadvantaged white youths far exceed disadvantaged minority youths.
- As those who are already advantaged advance, those who are less advantaged tend to fall farther behind, social cleavage widens, and social unrest accelerates. We are in danger of developing a permanent underclass, a self-perpetuating culture of poverty.
- Even among the most able, many young people fall behind in the race. We estimate that about 100,000 more young people would enter college each year if the percentage of most able (top quartile in academic ability) entrants from low-income and moderate-income families came up to that of the most affluent one-fourth of families. This loss of talent is costly to the nation.

As a society, we are spending a great deal more to help low-income youth enter college than we are spending to help low-income youth who are in high school, or who graduate from high school but do not enter college, or who drop out of school. We need to redress the balance.

The low level of expenditures on low-income high school youths reflects the fact that federal funds are heavily targeted toward prekindergarten, kindergarten, and elementary school children and not toward secondary school students. These priorities appear doubtful to us, in view of the serious problems of absenteeism and dropping out in grades 10, 11, and 12, and in view of deficits in basic skills.

Although we recommend certain increased expenditures, the problems call for more than just money. They call for mobilization within communities and for leadership on the part of employers and unions, as well as civic and school officials. National leadership and federal and state money can help, but in the end the problems will be solved, if at all, mostly in local communities.

Youth Unemployment

Youth unemployment has been exaggerated in the recent past because military personnel and college and high school students who are not in the labor force have been excluded from the base. For the age cohort as a whole, 6 percent are not in school (on a full-time basis) and not in the armed forces, but are in the labor force and yet are unemployed.

Americans tend to forget that more than 10 million young persons (under age 25), nearly 10 million adult women, and perhaps 5 million immigrants (legal and illegal) have been added to the labor force since 1960. Higher education has also absorbed 7.6 million additional young persons since 1960. The absorptive capacity of the labor market and of higher education over the past 20 years has been enormous; without it, what has been a difficult situation would have been an intolerable one.

Pockets of high unemployment among youth are concentrated in certain groups, particularly among black dropouts. Recent white dropouts also had a very high rate of unemployment, while single women fared considerably less well than men among the 1976 dropouts. The unemployment problem for youth is not one of massive denial of jobs across-the-board but of high incidence in specific categories.

We call attention to the 5.7 percent of the age cohort that is not in any other category (see Figure 1). Within this very miscellaneous category are discouraged workers who have withdrawn from jobseeking and alienated persons who have withdrawn from participation in organized society. They are not just out of school and out of the labor force; they are out of society. This group may constitute an even more severe problem than the unemployed—the latter at least are still trying to get a job.

The gravest problems are among the long-term unemployed (1.3 percent) and the out-of-society group (5.7 percent), which total about 7 percent of youth (16-21) or about 1.8 million persons, with 80 percent of this total in the out-of-society category.

The public attention directed at unemployment has obscured many other and more serious problems. Youth in America is not suffering from a single malady (unemployment), and no single patent medicine (full employment) will cure the many illnesses. We have instead a growth or a cancer in our body politic—causes not fully known, cure not fully known. But it creates great pain in the suffering of ruined lives, crime, drug addiction, lost hopes, social fears, reduced productivity, raised social expenditures, and disdain for authority. We need a full-participation society as much as we need a full-employment economy.

Fundamental Concerns

We concentrate our attention on the years from 16 to 21, when the problems of transition to adulthood are most intense. The most troublesome years are 16 to 17, when we are most likely to "lose the game" with and for some youth.

American society, based on industrial pursuits, creates very special difficulties for young persons. For youths, the transition from childhood to adulthood has at least four relatively new and troublesome aspects:

- The transition from school to work is very abrupt.
- The transition is also very long. We have greatly prolonged youth—the period from adolescence to adulthood. We have created what might be called compulsory youth: a substantial time between dependence and independence, a twilight zone of uncertainty and ambiguity of status.

Figure 1. Activity status of young people aged 16 to 21, 1978

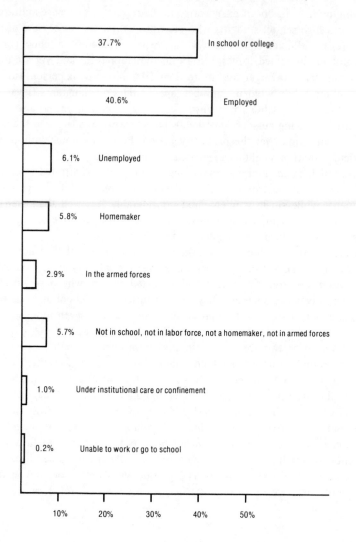

- No institution has a clear and fully accepted responsibility for following the welfare of persons through the stage of young adulthood. The influences of the family and the school have often declined by this time, and youths have not yet established their own families and their own more or less permanent job connections.
- Youths are often left largely to the guidance, companionship, and mercy of their peers and the electronic media.

Specifically, these are our major concerns: (1) reducing dropouts and absenteeism in high school, (2) improving basic skills of high school graduates, (3) giving high school students an opportunity to develop useful work habits, (4) reducing the alienating aspects of the high school experience, (5) easing the transition from high school to the labor market, (6) improving the paths into higher education, (7) improving the paths into military service, and (8) creating many more opportunities for other forms of service by youth.

We accept, for the purposes of this report, among other aspects of the environment, the following as "givens," whether we like them or not (and some of them we do not like):

- More one-parent families and more mothers at work
- The attractiveness of street life for some young people; the high returns for participation in the "subterranean" economy, in "off-the-books" activities; and the easy choice of full-time leisure
- The difficulty the schools and jobs have in competing with recreational and entertainment activities, even with the free and "adult" life of living on Aid to Families with Dependent Children
- The temporary, dead-end nature of many of the jobs in the unstructured labor market that provide most of the openings for young persons, the unattractive aspects of many of these jobs, and their comparatively low pay
- A standard minimum wage that applies also to youths, contrary to the situation in many other countries
- Continuing competition for youths in the labor market from women newly entering employment and from legal and illegal immigrants
- Heightened aspirations of youths for the types of jobs that they are willing to accept and a growing sense of the entitlements that society is thought to owe to them
- The continuing existence of some totally alienated young persons whom our recommendations will not reach
- The insolubility of some problems, which means that it is best to concentrate on problems that can be solved and on those that can be made more tolerable, even if not fully solved.

We emphasize that, just as there is no "youth problem" in the singular, there is also no single entity "youth." We have developed a typology to identify youth from various family backgrounds and personal circumstances:

I. *The Advantaged:* young persons from families in the top two-thirds of the income range and who finish high school

II. *The Financially Disadvantaged:* young persons from families in the bottom one-third of the income range who finish high school but, where doing so, may impose a financial hardship on their families and where attendance in college does impose such a hardship

III. *The Socially Deprived:* young persons who do not finish high school for reasons of social circumstances (family and community deprivations, and social prejudices)

IV. *The Personally Deprived:* young persons who do not finish high school for reasons of personal circumstances (mental, physical, or psychological disabilities)

V. *The Opt-outs:* young persons who do not choose to participate in established educational or economic institutions of society for reasons of personal choice or philosophical orientation

In this report we are most specifically concerned with the problems of youth in categories II (Financially Disadvantaged) and III (Socially Deprived), which account for about 38 percent of all youths, or about 8 million persons age 16 to 21.

Priority Recommendations

We have chosen to concentrate largely on recommendations for programs (1) that are open to all youth and not just to the more disadvantaged and deprived, although these latter may particularly benefit; (2) where administrative mechanisms are already in place to effectuate the program; (3) that are not highly vulnerable to error and abuse; (4) that have proven successful on trial in the United States or elsewhere; and (5) where the potential cost is reasonable. Our recommendations relate to social policy, but we emphasize that basic responsibility lies with the family and with the individual young person. Social policy can be greatly improved, but it cannot substitute for good environments in families and good decisions by youths.

We make the following recommendations:

1. Make age 16 the age of free choice to leave school, take a job, enter the military service, enter other forms of service, continue in school, enter college, or enter an apprenticeship. At age 21, young persons should be as fully independent as possible. Special help and the sense of dependency it fosters should not go on indefinitely.

HIGH SCHOOLS

2. Change the basic structure of high schools by making them smaller or by creating diversity within them or both; creating full-time specialty schools, particularly for grades 11 and 12; and creating part-time specialty schools—one or two days a week per student on a rotating basis—by providing one or two days a week for education-related work or service. We set forth several such models in Figure 2. We must find alternatives to the monolithic high school and its deadly weekly routine. We believe that instruction in basic skills and general knowledge can be concentrated without loss of achievement in three effectively used days per week.

3. Create work and service opportunities for students through the facilities of the high schools, making performance part of the student record. We also favor a renewed emphasis on student out-of-class activities.

4. Stop the tracking of students; all programs should be individualized programs.

5. Put most applied skill training in private shops, when not moved to the postsecondary level. The basic vocational (and academic) skills for the high school to concentrate on are the skills of literacy, numeracy, and good work habits.

6. Finance needy students through work-study programs and more effective efforts to place them in jobs.

7. Create job preparation and placement centers in the high schools that will follow students for their first two years after graduation or other termination.

8. Improve the capacity of secondary schools to teach basic skills by allocating more federal funds to them under the Elementary and Secondary Education Act.

9. Encourage earlier entry from high school into college and more programs combining the last year or two of high school with college.

10. Experiment with vouchers and greater freedom of choice, particularly among public schools. Bureaucratic controls have not assured quality; competition to survive may.

Figure 2. Illustrative models of alternative school plans at the secondary level

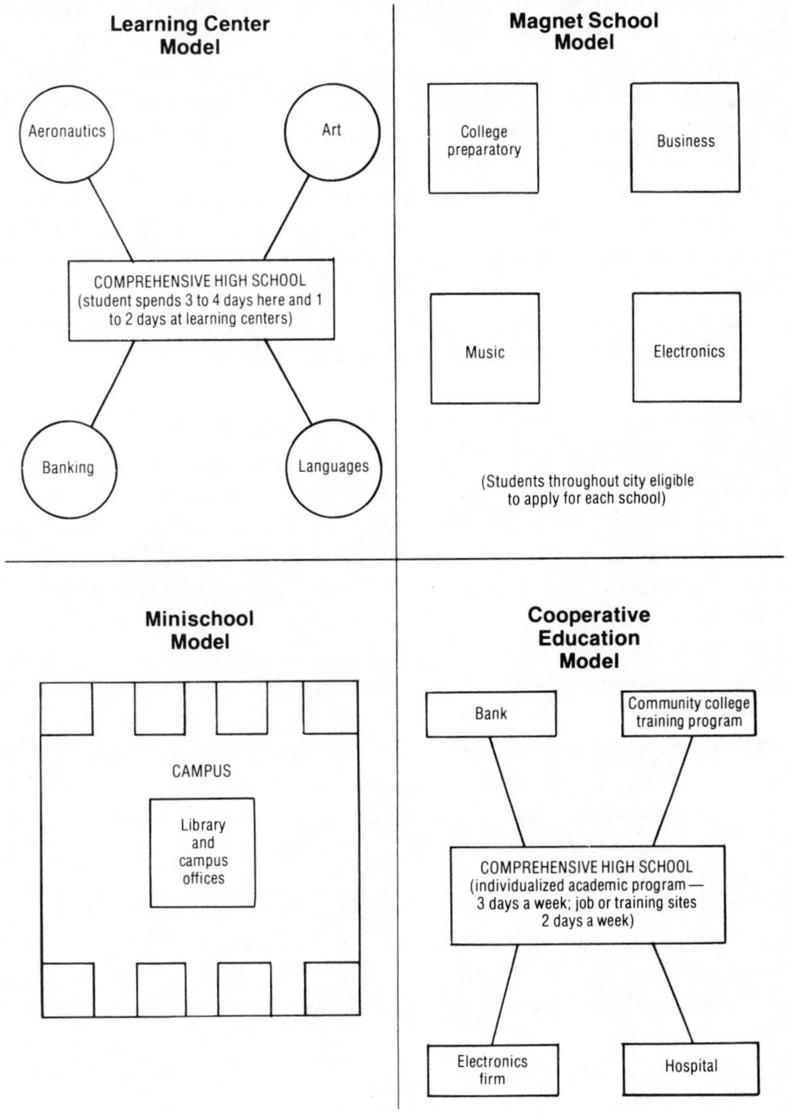

Learning Center Model

Aeronautics

Art

COMPREHENSIVE HIGH SCHOOL
(student spends 3 to 4 days here and 1 to 2 days at learning centers)

Banking

Languages

Magnet School Model

College preparatory

Business

Music

Electronics

(Students throughout city eligible to apply for each school)

Minischool Model

CAMPUS

Library and campus offices

Cooperative Education Model

Bank

Community college training program

COMPREHENSIVE HIGH SCHOOL
(individualized academic program — 3 days a week; job or training sites 2 days a week)

Electronics firm

Hospital

POSTSECONDARY

11. Concentrate most applied skill training at the postsecondary level and particularly in the community colleges.

12. Create programs in community colleges in which young persons can be prepared for jobs and placed in jobs on a part-time basis while attending college.

More broadly, the community college should take on a residual responsibility for youth. It would involve being available to all youths in the community to advise on academic and occupational opportunities, to offer job preparation classes, to make job placements, to work out individual combinations of employment and classroom instruction, to make referrals to Comprehensive Education and Training Act (CETA) employers as well as to sources of legal and medical advice, and to refer to and develop apprenticeship programs and service opportunities. Additional and specialized personnel will be required for this purpose. These might be known as youth service functions. Youths would be given an institutional base of operation.

13. Revise student aid programs to target them more toward low-income students.

14. Have all colleges create offices of community services to help students find off-campus service opportunities as part of their work-study assignments or on a volunteer basis.

15. Improve teacher training programs, including workplace experience for teachers.

16. Encourage colleges and universities to assist local schools in basic skills training.

LABOR MARKET

17. Eliminate special "protective" legislation in the employment of youth that restricts the work they can do as compared with adults.

18. Eliminate social security taxes for teenage youth and their employers, making it more profitable for the one to accept employment and the other to offer it.

19. Create nonprofit "job corporations" that will prepare and place students in jobs and handle their pay and fringe benefits—in effect, acting as contractors for them and making it easier for others to employ them.

20. Provide a system of retention bonuses for young persons who have suffered long-term unemployment or heavy turnover to encourage them to stay on jobs, as part of the CETA program and possibly after participation in prior CETA programs.

21. Augment current apprenticeship programs and create new ones, including civil service apprenticeships and military apprenticeships for 16 and 17 year olds and for persons 18 and over who are not eligible for service but who can be made eligible through such a program.

22. We do not recommend, at this time, a general program of wage subsidies for the employment of youth. Such programs have not proved very effective and appear too open to abuse and error. But we strongly favor training subsidies for employers who provide on-the-job training for disadvantaged youth or expand apprenticeship opportunities.

SERVICE

23. Create a multifaceted voluntary youth service, with initiative for most service projects coming from the local level and with educational benefits attached to the service program.

24. Create a National Educational Fund into which service credits and other contributions can be paid and then drawn upon later in life. We see a future in which students have a chance to earn the subsistence costs of their college education and some (but not always all) of their tuition; a future in which they are on a self-help basis.

25. Keep the draft voluntary. We see no current need for compulsory military service, and there are great problems in making it compulsory. We note that military policy, however it develops, will have a crucial impact on all youth policy.

COMMUNITY

26. Develop in every sizeable community a work-education council that will bring together school officials and representatives of employers, unions, and public agencies to coordinate programs for youth.

The proposals we advance should:

- Marginally aid the Advantaged youth.
- End the category of the Financially Disadvantaged youth by providing more opportunities for earnings, work-study grants, and student assistance, particularly in high school, since much has already been done at the college level.
- Substantially reduce the category of the Socially Deprived. Perhaps, over time, it can be cut in half. To wipe out this category entirely will take major renovations in living conditions in urban and rural slums, many improvements in the quality of family life, and the end of racial discrimination.
- Slightly affect, if at all, the Personally Deprived.
- Slightly affect, if at all, the numbers of the Opt-outs. There is an irreducible number of such youths in any society, and American culture as a whole seems to induce some expansion of this category.

Thus, slightly more than one-quarter of all youth would significantly benefit: the 20 percent who are Financially Disadvantaged and perhaps one-half (or 9 percent of the total) of the Socially Deprived. This amounts, currently, to 7.3 million persons. Problem groups would still remain, representing the impacts of the most intractable problems. However, potentially nearly all youth would be aided to some appreciable extent by the measures we support.

The net federal costs of our suggested programs range from $1.4 to $1.9 billion in 1980-81, depending on the severity of the current recession. If unemployment rises substantially in 1980, increased expenditures for youth programs will be needed. Several of our proposals, moreover, such as the work-study program and the comprehensive youth service program, call for gradually increasing expenditures during the 1980s, but these rising expenditures should be at least partially offset by reductions in the social costs associated with droupouts, juvenile delinquency, and school security measures, among others.

Against the costs of our proposals, we set greater equality of opportunity for all our youth; the liberation of talent now lost to society; a higher average level of basic skills; a smoother transition into the world of work; more certainty that most youths will have set before them one or more acceptable choices; the prospect that more youths will reach adulthood prepared to contribute constructively to the welfare of others; and a declaration that American society is concerned about its youth.

Should a depression come, we urge quick action on the following in particular: item 6, financing needy students in high school; item 13, targeting student financial aid in college more toward low-income students; item 21, creation of civil service and military apprenticeships; and item 23, creation of a multifaceted voluntary youth service.

The energy crisis adds to the importance of trying to hold students in high school in the afternoons, as compared with "tooling around," and to reduce absenteeism: item 2, breaking the deadly weekly routine; item 3, creating work and service opportunities; and item 9, creating opportunities to get an early start on college-credit studies.

We see, overall, a better future for most youth—even a much better future—for the next two decades than the past two, barring war and depression. The possibility, and we think the likelihood, of better social policies is one reason. The certainty of a deficit of youth—and the resultant competition to attract young persons by colleges, employers, the military, churches, and unions—is another reason. There should and can be more and better choices for youth; less segregation of youth from age, race from race, education from work and service, youth from employment, and opportunities for the poor from those for the rich; and less sense that youths are outsiders in relation to the rest of society—unwanted and often uncared for. These developments can help restore some of the largely lost challenge to youth that "you have the world before you."

A Note on the Special Problems of Young Women

The problems of young men and young women differ in significant respects and call for somewhat different policy emphases. Particularly important in this context is the problem of teenage pregnancies.

In spite of the pronounced drop in the birthrate since the late 1950s, teenage pregnancies continue to be a serious problem—not only for the individuals involved but for society as a whole. School policies can do much to determine whether the teenage mother is forced to terminate education abruptly as a result of her pregnancy or whether she is encouraged to complete her high school education.

The evidence that teenagers of both sexes who are not strongly motivated toward educational achievement are more likely to become involved in teenage pregnancies is especially important. Would the changes in school structure and school policies that we propose motivate more of these youngsters toward educational achievement and make them more wary of activities that interfere with educational progress?

Before leaving the question of sex differences, we need to refer to sexist attitudes toward school programs for young women that impede their educational achievement and ultimately their career options. It is very important to overcome the sex stereotypes that affect the interests and motivation of girls from early childhood onward. The secondary school experience is crucial in this context, because it is at this stage that girls may decide that it is not important to continue taking courses in mathematics and science, in which their performance tends, on the average, to be somewhat inferior to that of their fellow male students. Yet deficiency in mathematical training blocks a woman in college from majoring in many of the fields that lead to promising professional occupations. We believe that females should have opportunities equal to those of males to develop their highest skills.

The Importance of Being Sixteen: A New Age for Free Choice

Central to the proposals made in this report, whether they relate to schools, the labor market, or service opportunities, is the issue of the school-leaving age. We believe that compulsory schooling should not extend beyond the sixteenth birthday. The main reason for this recommendation is that many young people are held in school too long and would benefit from opportunities for experiences that would seem more challenging and closer to the "real world" than school, especially the big-city school.

Recommendation 1: *The legal age for the end of compulsory schooling should be no later than the sixteenth birthday. States with a higher school-leaving age should revise their legislation, but they may need to plan for gradual implementation so that opportunities* *for training, community service, and other activities for those who leave formal schooling at age 16 can be expanded.*

Options for the 16 year old. From their sixteenth birthday, or after completion of the school term following their sixteenth birthday, a wide variety of options should be available to youth.

Recommendation 2: *Beyond the sixteenth birthday, a young person should have the option of (1) additional secondary schooling and work options, (2) middle college and work options, (3) community college and work options, (4) apprenticeships, (5) work or training programs, or (6) youth service.*

Each of the options available to 16 and 17 year olds should lead to any of the options available at age 18 or older.

Whose responsibility? It is not our intention that a young person should be set adrift at age 16 or that the school should abdicate its responsibility.

Recommendation 3: *The responsibilities of secondary schools for school-leavers should not end at age 16. School districts should be required to ensure that those leaving school have acquired basic skills or are provided with opportunities for making up their deficiencies. School districts should also ensure that school-leavers are referred to appropriate education, training, work, or service programs and should follow the progress of school-leavers for at least two years after their departure from school.*

Education for Work and Work for Education

Work-experience programs. It is clear that many high school students—and junior high school students as well—are getting little out of school because they simply do not see the relevance to their future lives of what the school is attempting to teach them. We believe that school might become more meaningful to them if there were more options available for combinations of school and work experience.

We do not mean to suggest that every secondary school student should spend part of his or her time at work. The option should be there, but it should be entirely voluntary. Nor do we propose that all work available to high school students should be paid work. An opportunity to serve the community in a voluntary, unpaid capacity will attract many high school students and in some cases contribute far more to their personal development than a routine, paid job.

Recommendation 4: *School districts should develop plans to provide voluntary opportunities for combinations of work experience, community service, and education for all of their students, especially in the last two years of high school.*

A federal-state work-study program. The number of provisions of federal legislation that are available to provide financial support for work-experience programs at the high school level is substantial. Existing programs, however, are targeted on the disadvantaged or intended for vocational education students. We believe that there is a strong case for a more broadly based work-study program for high school students.

The program we propose should be developed and funded gradually, since many high schools will lack experience in administering it. We believe that the federal role should involve matching grants to the states on a three-to-one basis (75 percent federal funds) and that allocation to individual school districts should be a function of state governments. The agency employing the student would be expected to pay 20 percent of the wages, and the program would be confined to employment in public and nonprofit agencies.

To hold down the cost and also in recognition that high school students from middle- and upper-income families often have contacts that make it easier for them to find jobs than students from low-income families, we believe that the program should be income-tested initially. We suggest a standard of eligibility for students from families with incomes below the median, and funds in the first few years should be targeted to areas with high teenage unemployment rates.

Recommendation 5: *To meet the needs of students from lower-income and lower-middle-income families, who may have difficulty finding employment through normal labor market channels, a federal-state work-study program for secondary school students aged 16 to 19 should be established, modeled on the College Work-Study program. We recommend an initial federal appropriation of $300 million.*

The roadblocks. A serious obstacle in the development of work-experience programs is the difficulty of overcoming the aversion of employers to hiring young people. We believe that the formation of community work-education councils not only will build bridges between the schools and the labor market but will also develop more effective manpower and education programs for out-of-school youth and adults within communities.

Recommendation 6: *To carry out a broad-gauged work-experience program and to help meet employment needs of school dropouts and graduates, every school district should take the initiative in stimulating the development of a community work-education council if none exists. In addition, much more adequate placement and counseling services are a need that should be given high priority in all school districts.*

Year-round operation of schools. In many ways, a work-experience program could be more effectively developed in a school that operated year-round. Student vacation periods would be staggered, and thus there would not be a flood of students seeking work in the summer.

Recommendation 7: *School systems should seriously consider shifting to year-round operation where they are not now on such a schedule.*

Other extracurricular activities. Some communities will have greater difficulties than others in developing effective work-experience programs. Where there is a particularly heavy concentration of minority group youth, the difficulties are likely to be especially great. Particularly in such situations, but to some degree in all secondary schools, other nonacademic activity programs can be extremely important in accounting for favorable attitudes toward school and in keeping adolescents off the streets and out of trouble.

Recommendation 8: *Emphasis on nonacademic activities is essential in all secondary schools, especially in situations in which work-experience programs encounter difficulties.*

Vocational Education:
Change Everything, Including the Name

There are substantial doubts that vocational education is generally effective, especially at the secondary level. The chief problem with the effort to maintain funding for vocational education is that too much of the money goes to preserve the status quo. The time has come for fundamental changes in the status of vocational education, and these changes can be brought about without a massive new influx of funds. What is required is the more effective pooling of funds from a variety of sources, plus a more determined effort to develop alternatives to classroom vocational education.

More specifically, we believe that the following changes are needed:

1. Tracking of students in academic, general, and vocational programs at the high school level should cease. All students should be encouraged to participate in combinations of education, work experience, training, and service, though with varying emphases and with a more determined effort on the part of the school to develop an individualized program for each student.
2. Classroom vocational education at the high school level should be de-emphasized in favor of training conducted under employer auspices, apprenticeship, work-experience programs, cooperative education, and other programs that take the student into the community.
3. High school students should have opportunities to enroll in occupational courses at nearby community colleges and technical institutes. The problem of maintaining superior equipment and teachers who are familiar with advancing technology is too costly to be feasible in the typical school district, but it appears to be more manageable for community colleges and technical institutes.
4. Wherever feasible, states and localities should pool funds available from CETA, the public employment service, vocational education allocations, and the new high school work-study program that we have proposed to provide more effective combinations of education, training, and work-experience programs to students.

We believe that federal vocational education funds can become a more effective stimulator of change, but only through amendments to the legislation, reallocation of funding under the various provisions of the act, and more vigorous and imaginative leadership within the Office of Education in administering the legislation. We urge amending the Vocational Education Act to provide strong incentives for states to promote change. More specifically, we propose:

1. That current legislation be amended to provide for 75 percent (three-to-one) federal matching for (1) state programs aimed at encouraging the development of work-experience and cooperative education programs, (2) contracts for employer-oriented training, and (3) contracts with nearby postsecondary institutions to provide opportunities for occupational training for high school students.
2. That approximately one-half of the funds currently allocated by the federal government for basic vocational education grants and for program improvement and supportive services should be made subject to this new federal matching formula, and the proportion should be increased as time goes on.
3. That all terminology in the legislation that has the effect of confining programs to

"vocational" students be deleted, in keeping with the principle of eliminating tracking.

4. That the concept of special programs for the disadvantaged be eliminated except where they are specifically aimed at overcoming language handicaps. We do not believe that economically disadvantaged students should be segregated in special vocational education classes.

5. That no change be made in the minimum percentage of the federal allocation for postsecondary programs (15 percent). We believe that encouraging school districts to enter into contracts to provide opportunities for high school students to enroll in occupational programs in postsecondary institutions is a major necessity and that the funding for this purpose should come from the school districts.

Recommendation 9: *The federal Vocational Education Act should be renamed the Occupational Skills and Work-Study Act, and its provisions should be merged with those for the work-study program that we have recommended.*

The legislation should be amended to provide approximately $300 million of existing federal vocational education funds for 75 percent matching grants to the states to stimulate the development of programs that move skills training out of the high school classroom and into the workplace or community college.

Recommendation 10: *The Department of Labor and the Department of Health, Education, and Welfare should cooperate in developing policies for encouraging coordination of manpower and education programs for youth at the state and local levels and in seeking removal of legislative and administrative obstacles, such as differing eligibility conditions, to such coordination.*

A Fundamental Restructuring of Schools

The most far-reaching and controversial reform proposals in secondary education concern school structure. With the critical need to overcome the problems of the big-city school, the movement for alternative schools has gained momentum in the 1970s, and results of evaluations, indicating predominantly positive impacts on students, are beginning to be available.

A number of the more successful examples of alternative schools in large cities, especially magnet schools, have succeeded in attracting students of various racial and ethnic backgrounds from all parts of the city. The magnet schools are a series of specialty schools to which all students in the city are eligible to apply. They appear to have slowed the out-migration of white families that has left so many inner-city schools racially segregated. There are also schools, both public and private, that have outstanding records because of unique leadership, even though they are in slum locations. And there have been a few successful alternative school programs specifically designed to serve hard-core disadvantaged urban youth, which suggests that the appropriate combination of work orientation and intensified learning experience can overcome the drift of such students away from the schools and into patterns of juvenile delinquency.

In many of its reports on higher education, the Carnegie Council, and the Carnegie Commission before it, has emphasized the need to maintain and encourage diversity. The need is no less important at the secondary level. Some of our large cities have long had diversified schools. The challenge under present conditions is to promote diversity without encouraging segregation. With enough determination on the part of the community and school leadership, it can be done.

Recommendation 11: *School districts throughout the United States should develop local planning efforts, where they have not done so, aimed at determining whether magnet schools, alternative schools, or schools-within-schools are needed.*

Recommendation 12: *Plans for restructuring schools should ensure that racial integration will be encouraged, rather than jeopardized, through the development of new types of schools.*

Recommendation 13: *Boards of education and superintendents should give the principal of each school where change is to occur clear responsibility for planning and carrying out the change, in consultation with teachers, parents, and students.*

Recommendation 14: *Teachers' organizations should support innovation and play an active role in carrying it out.*

Recommendation 15: *Every school district should make certain that its secondary schools have programs, in cooperation with other community agencies, that encourage girls who become pregnant to complete their education.*

Toward Greater Equality of Opportunity for All Youth

Tuition tax credits. Undoubtedly the most widely discussed proposal for aid at the secondary level—in this case, aid to parents—in the last few years has been for tuition tax credits. Since relief would go only to parents of students in private schools, which charge tuition, and a large proportion of private school pupils are in Catholic parochial or other sectarian schools, this raises the issue of federal and state constitutional provisions for separation of state and church.

Recommendation 16: *The Council opposes tuition tax credits at the elementary and secondary level, just as we have opposed them at the postsecondary level, and for many of the same reasons. At the elementary and secondary level, they (1) may well be declared unconstitutional, (2) would help all parents with children in private schools regardless of need, and (3) might encourage a massive shift to private schools.*

Vouchers. Under various voucher plans, institutional subsidization of education would be discontinued and parents would be given vouchers equivalent to the estimated cost of educating a child in a public school, provided that the voucher was used for education in an approved school.

Most discussions of vouchers relate to plans that would facilitate free choice between public and private schools, but we believe that there is a case for at least some experiments designed to encourage choice between public schools. Such developments would not threaten the future of the public schools, as do proposals for voucher plans involving both public and private schools.

A serious obstacle to adoption of any voucher plan is the opposition of teachers' organizations, which view such plans as a threat to job security. Yet the present situation, in which it is often extremely difficult and costly for a school district to dismiss an incompetent teacher, is unsatisfactory. Moreover, diminishing student bodies and financial stringency are forcing layoffs of teachers and transfers of teachers within school districts.

Recommendation 17: *Small-scale experiments with voucher plans should be encouraged, especially experiments that are limited to public schools, but there should be no large-scale or statewide adoptions of voucher plans until the results of such experiments have been evaluated.*

Increasing resources. We have recommended adoption of a work-study program for secondary school students as one step toward greater equality of opportunity for all youth. We have also recommended shifting the allocation of a portion of vocational education funds so that they would be directed toward encouraging work experience for secondary school students. The other major need, as far as in-school youth are concerned, is allocation of additional resources to secondary schools, especially those that have large proportions of low-income students.

Recommendation 18: *The federal government should modify its policy of allocating meager funds to secondary schools under Title I of the Elementary and Secondary Act by increasing funding under the act specifically for the purpose of benefiting secondary schools. We suggest an initial increase for this purpose of $500 million in 1980-81.*

The Responsibilities of Postsecondary Education

Institutions of postsecondary education have an important stake in national policies aimed at overcoming the educational deficiencies of youth. Talent is lost to higher education when able young people leave school early. Colleges and universities, moreover, have had to devote increased resources in recent years to remedial courses aimed at overcoming deficiencies, especially in the use of the English language, of their entering students.

Institutions of higher education could make a greater contribution toward meeting the problems of youth than they are now making. The Boston program, in which each magnet high school is paired with a college or university in the area, is a model that could well be adopted in other areas.

Recommendation 19: *Colleges and universities in large metropolitan areas should seek opportunities to contribute to improving the quality of secondary school programs in their areas, preferably through joining in a communitywide pairing plan like the one in Boston.*

New and expanding roles for community colleges. Community colleges are playing a more important role in most. communities than other institutions of higher education in relation to the disadvantaged.

Recommendation 20: *Community colleges should (1) cooperate with CETA and school authorities in the development of training and work-experience programs, (2) experiment with admitting students at age 16 and with the development of middle colleges, (3) provide opportunities for high school students to participate in their occupational programs, and (4) develop more opportunities for cooperative education and apprenticeship for both secondary and postsecondary students.*

Comprehensive colleges should assume these responsibilities in communities that lack a community college.

The FIPSE program. In spring 1979, the Fund for the Improvement of Post-secondary Education (FIPSE) announced a program to fund projects that would apply the resources of institutions of postsecondary education to meeting the pressing needs of disadvantaged youth.

The program would have the immediate goal of identifying and learning about promising models emerging from postsecondary agencies as educational providers for CETA youth. We believe that the present experimental program will provide valuable guidance as to the types of projects that colleges and universities can carry out to aid disadvantaged youth.

Recommendation 21: *The annual appropriation for FIPSE should be increased from the $14 million included in the administration's fiscal year 1980 budget to $20 million in fiscal year 1981, under provisions that would allocate the additional $6 million to projects designed to serve disadvantaged youth.*

The Trio programs. An important link between secondary and postsecondary education in serving disadvantaged youth is provided by the so-called Trio programs or special programs for the disadvantaged—Talent Search, Upward Bound, and Educational Opportunity Centers. Under these programs, promising students from disadvantaged families are sought out and helped to prepare for college through summer seminars and other special programs.

Recommendation 22: *The federal government should continue to support the Trio programs and gradually increase their funding. We suggest an increase from $130 million in 1979-80 to $150 million (in constant 1979 dollars) in 1980-81.*

College students as a resource. College students can play an important part in programs for disadvantaged youth by serving as tutors, "big brothers," teachers' aides, assistants to organizers of community services, and in other ways.

Recommendation 23: *Especially on larger campuses, colleges and universities should coordinate participation of students in community service by establishing offices of community service.*

The training of teachers and administrators. The most important single contribution that universities and colleges can make to overcoming the problems of the schools is through radical changes in teacher training. There is widespread agreement that schools of education have not kept abreast of the changing problems of the schools, have not trained teachers to cope with the education of disadvantaged youngsters, and have not maintained influence on the teacher training that goes on in arts and sciences departments, where potential secondary school teachers get much of their higher education.

Recommendation 24: *The time has come for colleges and universities involved in teacher training to take decisive steps to reform that training to meet the changing needs of the schools in the 1980s. The president of the institution should take the lead in ensuring such changes if the school of education is resisting change.*

The Teacher Corps. The Teacher Corps is a Great Society program modeled after the

Peace Corps, in which a corps of teachers is trained to serve in urban or rural poverty areas. The positive results of the Teacher Corps program have been sufficiently impressive to warrant not only its continuation but also a gradual increase in funding for the program in the coming years.

Recommendation 25: *The federal government should continue to support the Teacher Corps, and the appropriation for the program should be increased from $37.5 million in 1979-80 to $40 million (in constant dollars) in 1980-81.*

The training of administrators. If there is one thing that emerges clearly from studies of problems in the schools, it is that the leadership of the principal is probably the most important single factor in explaining whether schools are meeting their problems successfully or not.

Recommendation 26: *Schools of education should give special attention to improving the training of school administrators, especially by giving preference to candidates for advanced degrees who have had varied types of teaching experience and by developing programs in school management in cooperation with schools of business or public administration.*

Training community coordinators. If work-education councils are to be effective, and if communities are to surmount the many obstacles to coordination of efforts, especially in large cities, trained community coordinators are needed. These persons should understand the economics and sociology of poverty, should know enough about industrial relations to work effectively with employer and union groups, and should know enough about problems of contemporary secondary schools to work effectively with school officials.

Recommendation 27: *Universities should develop interdisciplinary programs at the master's level for training community coordinators of programs for youth.*

The State Role in Financing Secondary Schools

The state role in the financing of secondary schools will continue to be important, and the state share in overall financing of the public schools is likely to increase due to the crisis in local school financing. We believe that there is a strong case for increased state support for the public schools and for particular attention to improving the quality of the secondary schools. At the same time, we urge that state aid not be given in such a way as to impair local control of the schools.

Recommendation 28: *The states should take advantage of declining enrollment growth by increasing state aid to local school districts, with particular attention to the needs of secondary schools. States that are below the national average in the percentage of personal income flowing to the public schools have a special need to review their school-financing policies.*

Better Paths into Labor Markets

Measures to increase labor market demand. One means of decreasing the cost of employing youths—and increasing their take-home pay—would be to exempt teenagers from social security coverage. Teenagers would not lose valuable benefits through exemption, because they would have the rest of their working lives to accumulate contributions toward retirement.

Recommendation 29: *Teenagers should be exempted from social security coverage.*

Involving the private sector. Ever since the Manpower Development and Training Act was adopted in 1962, there has been a program of federal subsidies to pay the costs of training incurred by employers who hire unemployed persons for on-the-job training. The provisions were gradually liberalized to allow employers partial wage subsidies, but the use of the program has been minimal.

Recommendation 30: *Federal government programs for training and employment of youth should place strong emphasis on efforts to involve private employers, especially through encouraging participation of employers in work-education councils and through provision of training subsidies, but wage subsidies should be limited to modest experimental programs.*

Apprenticeship. The chief feature that distinguishes apprenticeship from other forms of training is the existence of a contract between the apprentice, or his parent or legal guardian, and the employer. The apprentice agrees to work for the employer at a wage that begins at a rate well below the skilled journeyman's rate in the trade and gradually increases during training, while the employer provides instruction and practice leading to the acquisition of a recognized qualification as a skilled craftsman. When well conducted, apprenticeship programs have great advantages over most other types of vocational training available to young people.

To achieve substantial expansion of apprenticeship and continued progress in bringing women and minorities into apprenticeship programs, current efforts to increase the number of apprenticeable occupations must continue. In addition, we believe that the age for admission to apprenticeship programs should not exceed 16, a rigid requirement for high school graduation should be avoided, and apprenticeship opportunities should be made available in the last several years of high school.

Recommendation 31: *Federal and state programs to increase the number of apprenticeable occupations, to include more women and minorities in apprenticeship programs, to develop apprenticeship programs in the civil and military services, to seek the cooperation of community colleges in apprenticeship training, and to open up apprenticeship opportunities for secondary school students should continue.*

Preliminary training. Many young persons are now rejected for induction into the armed forces because of poor performance on tests or for other reasons. Even though we do not believe that the military draft should be resumed, opportunities for premilitary training should be expanded so that young people who fail to meet the standards for induction can overcome their deficiencies.

Recommendation 32: *The Department of Defense, in cooperation with the Department of Labor, should stimulate the development of premilitary training.*

Occupational orientation centers. In both Great Britain and Belgium, occupational assessment or orientation centers have been developed to assist young people who have not made a career choice to try out their work aptitudes and occupational preferences through a variety of tests and orientation programs. In the United States, occupational orientation is sometimes included in the skills centers that are funded through the CETA program and often located in community colleges, but it could be developed on a more generally available basis.

Recommendation 33: *CETA prime sponsors, schools, and community colleges should cooperate in making certain that opportunities for occupational orientation programs are available for both in-school and out-of-school youth.*

Regularizing odd jobs. Proposals for pilot programs designed to test various methods of stimulating the employment and training of youth deserve serious consideration for financial support from the federal government, foundations, or other sources. We select two of them for special consideration: (1) regularizing odd jobs and (2) job retention awards.

For many young people in large cities, odd jobs that provide little pay and no benefits are the only job opportunities available. A pilot program of contract service organizations that would offer full-time work to inner-city youth while providing homeowners and business firms with a regular means of contracting for odd jobs, including maintenance and repair, cleaning, painting, gardening, temporary office services, and others, should be established.

Recommendation 34: *The Department of Labor should encourage the development of a program that would provide full-time work to inner-city youth through contract service organizations that would regularize the odd-job labor market, using a combination of public and private funds.*

Job retention awards. A common complaint about many disadvantaged young people is that they do not stay on the job very long. The proposal for job retention awards is aimed at providing an incentive for young workers to stay on the job by providing taxfree cash awards to youths earning the minimum wage at three critical points during their first six months on the job. The awards would provide a lump-sum payment of $150 after 30 days, $300 after 90 days, and $450 after 180 days.

Recommendation 35: *The Department of Labor should provide support for pilot projects under which CETA prime sponsors would provide lump-sum payments to disadvantaged youth who stay on the job at several intervals during the first six months of employment.*

Protective legislation. Employment of young people is hampered by protective labor legislation, compulsory school attendance laws that require full-time attendance and interfere with the possibility of work-experience and cooperative education programs, and other types of legislation.

Recommendation 36: *The states should review protective legislation, compulsory attendance laws, and other legislation to remove unnecessary barriers to employment of youth.*

Toward increased flexibility. Certain federal regulations and funding formulas tend to limit the duration of training programs, which means that at best only certain entry-level skills can be provided. Limits on duration of training also tend to restrict the number of skills for which training can be provided.

Recommendation 37: *In the future development of training programs for out-of-school youth, greater emphasis should be placed on flexibility in the duration of programs and in the types of training provided.*

The Most Difficult Issue of All:
Policies for the Deprived

Even though our general view is that programs for youth should not be heavily targeted on the disadvantaged, it is clear that an exception needs to be made for the deprived, many of whom simply will not be reached by most manpower and educational programs. Programs for the deprived must be especially designed to reach the target group, must be intensive, must have low ratios of participants to teachers and other staff members, and must anticipate a significant attrition rate. They are almost certain to be more costly per participant than programs aimed at youths with less severe problems.

Recommendation 38: *Public and private agencies should cooperate in sponsoring and funding programs for the deprived, expanding program designs that have been successful, and discontinuing those that have failed or shown limited success.*

Recommendation 39: *In the event of a substantial rise in the unemployment rate in 1980, funds allocated to the Department of Labor for special youth programs should be augmented by $500 million, to be expended primarily on civil service apprenticeship programs at all levels of government and on public service employment.*

Recommendation 40: *Nevertheless, the long-run goal should be to increase the percentage of funds expended on in-school youth in CETA youth programs as success is achieved in reducing school dropout rates and unemployment rates of out-of-school youth.*

Youth Service: Voluntary for All

We favor the development of a comprehensive youth service on a gradual scale. It will take time to develop appropriate community projects, and political support for sudden authorization of a large-scale and therefore expensive comprehensive youth service is not likely to be forthcoming.

We propose that young people aged 16 to 24 be eligible for the service and that they should be expected to participate for a minimum of one year and a maximum of two years. However, we believe that 16 and 17 year olds should usually be involved in education, work-experience, and training programs in their own communities and that active recruitment for the comprehensive youth service should preferably begin at age 18. All young people should be counseled and urged to participate at some point from age 18 to age 24.

Recommendation 41: *We recommend establishment of a National Youth Service in which participation would be voluntary and all young people aged 16 to 24 would be eligible. Although a National Youth Service Foundation would be responsible for development of the program, projects would be initiated and administered on a decentralized basis.*

Local initiative and matching funds. We stress the importance of local initiative in the development of youth service programs. Rather than a national program with uniform requirements and regulations, we urge maximum flexibility at the local level. Moreover, although federal funds should be available for much of the financing, we believe that the program should operate principally through project proposals in local communities or, in some cases, by state agencies.

Recommendation 42: *One-half of the federal funds allocated for the program should call for 50 percent matching by the agency initiating the program. Such an agency would typically be a local community group, but it might also be a state agency or a consortium of institutions of higher education.*

    The initiating agency might seek a portion of the matching amount from state agencies or foundations.

Scope and funding. Compensation at the project level would be somewhat flexible, but in all cases of compensation below the minimum wage, the federal government would deposit the difference between actual compensation and the minimum wage on behalf of the participant in the National Education Fund proposed below.

    Military service would always be compensated at a somewhat higher level than civilian service, at least for the foreseeable future, in order to encourage an adequate flow of youth into the voluntary armed services. We envisage a gradual increase in the numbers involved in the civilian youth service to about one million by the end of the 1980s.

Recommendation 43: *We suggest an initial federal allocation of $600 million in 1980-81, which we estimate would accommodate 135,000 to 140,000 volunteers initially, including those already in ACTION and allowing for augmentation of funds through the matching provisions.*

A National Education Fund:
A Path to Self-Help

Linked with our proposal for a National Youth Service is a related proposal for a National Education Fund. The link would be in the form of educational credits that would be deposited in the National Education Fund on behalf of participating youths.

    Each person with deposits in the fund would have an individual account, with compound interest credited to each account at the maximum rate obtainable on long-term savings accounts. Withdrawals could be made only for educational purposes. However, there would be a right of withdrawal after five years, or in emergency situations, but only with the approval of special advisory committees. Only the individual's own contributions, with accumulated interest, could be withdrawn. Educational credits stemming from government contributions could not be withdrawn. Individual credits could also be freely withdrawn at age 55 for transfer to a retirement plan.

    Under our proposal, the federal government would match voluntary monthly pay deductions for those in the civilian portion of the National Youth Service on a one-to-one basis. There would also be stipulated federal credits unrelated to individual saving, and participants could also make additional voluntary unmatched contributions to the fund. Larger benefits would be provided for those opting for military service.

We believe that the policies relating to educational credits should be closely integrated with the Council's student aid policies. (See summary of *Next Steps for the 1980s in Student Financial Aid.*) A student completing civilian service and not eligible for student grants would be free to use his or her educational credits quite flexibly, although withdrawal from the fund would be permitted only for attendance at an approved educational institution, and the total amount withdrawn in any given year could not exceed the student's educational expenses. A student qualifying for student grants on the basis of family income would not lose his or her eligibility but could use the educational credits to meet the self-help requirements and also to avoid borrowing.

We believe that the National Education Fund should resemble the proposed National Student Loan Bank in that it should be a nonprofit private corporation chartered by the federal government. Although it might be set up as part of the National Student Loan Bank, under the same board of directors, we do not believe its establishment should be dependent on establishment of the National Student Loan Bank.

Recommendation 44: *We favor the establishment of a national Education Fund in which credits could be established for individual youths and adults from five sources: (1) voluntary savings by participants in youth service programs, (2) federal educational credits for youth service, (3) employer deposits on behalf of employees, (4) voluntary savings by employees up to age 55, and (5) contributions by parents on behalf of their children.*

Three Thousand Futures:
The Next Twenty Years for Higher Education
January 1980

During the next 20 years, enrollments may fall even as the total population continues to rise; real resources available to colleges and universities also may decline, even if the total Gross National Product (GNP) keeps increasing. Discussions of the future of higher education, however, are too often dominated by gloom and doom, even by a sense of panic. Our version of the future is, instead, that problems, even severe problems, lie ahead, but that there are reasonable solutions to most, if not all, of them; that it is better to plan to meet the future effectively than just to fear it as a new dark age. Becoming somewhat smaller is, we believe, compatible with becoming somewhat better.

Base Point: 1980

We start this analysis by taking a retrospective view of the 1970s. We challenge the conventional wisdom that the 1970s was a decade of disaster. Despite the "new depression" early in the decade and the OPEC crisis in the middle, and contrary to the impression left by many complaints and some cries of anguish, the 1970s were a good decade for higher education. But bad news was more likely to be featured than good news in the 1970s. An impression of higher education's threatened condition was created by (1) student unrest that shattered confidence on campus and support in the community; (2) the decline of male participation rates with the end of the military draft; (3) the first impact on the labor market of the new outpouring of college graduates, coincident with recurring recessions; and (4) the deep recession and dramatic rise in oil prices in 1974-75, which sent many colleges into financial deficits. These shocks were widely reported and deeply felt. What was not so evident was the underlying growth in enrollments and the sustained financial assistance, particularly by the states.

We note misconceptions about the 1970s for two reasons. First, they demonstrate a tendency of some academics to see only the worst aspects of higher education. Their views need to be discounted. Second, a presentation of the actualities shows that higher education enters the 1980s from a relatively high level of performance, not from a badly weakened situation, and is generally in a position of substantial strength as it faces the future.

So much has been happening to higher education in recent times that it is difficult to select a short list of the most important developments. However, we do advance the following (and incomplete) list:

- Increasing concentration of students in public institutions
- More and more regulation of both public and private institutions by governmental agencies

- More and more dependence on public sources of financial support
- Heavy concentration of students on large campuses of traditional form
- Substantial public confidence in higher education on a comparative basis
- Slowing and uncertain rates of enrollment growth
- An aging faculty
- More and more defensive reactions internally
- A new generation of students, with different values and attitudes
- More and more pressure to serve the student market.

Some of the drama of the next two decades will center around the efforts of many within the academic community, particularly faculty members, to hold onto what they value most from the past, and the necessity felt more strongly by administrators and trustees to adapt to the new realities of the student market.

A Judgment About Prospective Enrollments

The most dramatic feature of the next 20 years, as far as we now know, is the prospect of declining enrollments after more than three centuries of fairly steady increase (see Figure 1). We estimate a decline within a range of 5 to 15 percent for undergraduate enrollments. In setting forth our enrollment projections we do not wish to suggest that we have any illusions of certainty. We only wish to offer the variable weather view of the future that we hold as against alternative views ranging from disaster warnings to all-clear signs.

Our forecast starts with the 23 percent decline in 18-24 year olds projected by the U.S. Bureau of the Census by 1997. Factors that reduce the impact of this prospective decline upon college enrollments are:

- The 18-24-year age cohort accounts for only 80 percent of total full-time equivalent (FTE) enrollment. Adjusting for this reduces the prospective decline about 4 percent.
- The college participation of the over-25 age group will increase. This age group is growing, more of its members have been to college and are therefore inclined toward continued learning, and more of those who have not enrolled may do so, either for job advancement or to enhance nonvocational interests. Taken together, these changes could boost projected enrollments 9 percent.
- More participation by nonminority women can be expected, a change adding 4 percent to future enrollments. As is now the case in high school, a higher proportion of women than men may choose to go to college.
- Increased retention of students in college could boost enrollment 4 percent. The dropout rate for four-year colleges has declined from 50 to 40 percent recently, with "boredom" now cited as the most frequent reason for leaving.
- More of the population will be black. Among those in the same income range, a higher proportion of blacks than whites now go to college, and black participation in college probably will continue to increase. This could add 2 percent to total enrollment, if black participation matches that of whites.

Taken together, these factors entirely offset the projected decline. Adjusting for the impact of more part-time enrollment results in a 5 percent decline in FTE enrollment,

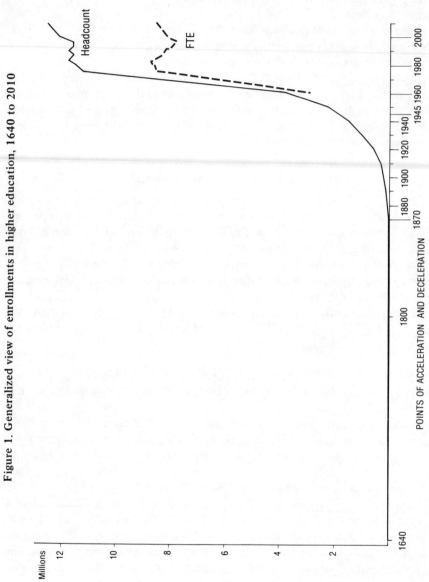

Figure 1. Generalized view of enrollments in higher education, 1640 to 2010

which could be deepened by a further decrease in college participation by 18-24-year-old males. This results in a projected overall national decline of 5 to 15 percent.

Military manpower policy and the incentives provided youths entering the job market are among the major uncertainties that can influence the college enrollment of young men, who now comprise 40 percent of attendees. The projected national decline could be reduced by three other factors not specifically incorporated in the Council's projections: (1) higher Hispanic student participation; (2) continued growth in foreign student enrollment; and (3) expansion of the number of 16- and 17-year-old high school students taking college courses.

The decline will not come, however, at an even pace. Undergraduate enrollments are likely to remain fairly even through the academic year starting in the fall of 1982, possibly rising some. Then we expect Slide I, from fall 1983 through the academic year starting in the fall of 1988 (followed by a possible rise in 1989 and 1990); and Slide II, from the fall of 1991 through the academic year starting in the fall of 1997. The first slide will carry enrollments down about 40 percent of the total decline, and the second slide—the remaining 60 percent—will be the more precipitous of the two. Colleges in general have about three more full academic years to prepare themselves for the onslaught of Slide I. Enrollments of 18 year olds will, of course, fluctuate much more than all enrollments, and some colleges heavily dependent upon them will be on a real roller coaster.

In a much more tentative way, we have tried to look ahead to the year 2010. We expect the future fertility rate to be higher than the 1.8 rate of the last few years. We use the maintenance rate (2.1) for the period 1997 to 2010 because the fertility rate might rise, and, more importantly, because rising levels of immigration are likely to have the same effect on enrollments. We do not expect that the United States, given its economic, political, and military positions in the world, and given the pressures for entry by aliens, will accept the possibility of a declining total population or a long-run decline in the college population.

If undergraduate enrollments should decline by 10 percent by 1997, we would expect them to rise to about 1979 levels by the year 2010. This will be the period when the grandchildren of the GIs start attending college, creating a new bulge.

The period from 2000 to 2010 will be a time of movement for other reasons than increasing enrollments. Faculty members recruited in the 1960s and 1970s—more than one-half of all faculty members—will be retiring during this period, which will create many opportunities for new hiring, including of women and minorities; lower the average age and average real salary levels of faculty members; and permit many adjustments to new fields of teaching and scholarship. The building space created in the 1960s and 1970s —one-half of all such space—will need to be remodeled or rebuilt. The conditions of the times are likely to draw into the leadership of higher education more persons interested in building institutions and undertaking innovations than was the case under the conditions of the prior two decades.

Graduate enrollments. We expect graduate enrollments to rise slightly between 1980 and 2000 in relation to undergraduate enrollments, despite the gloomy predictions about the value of the Ph.D. Too much has been made out of too little, in our judgment, based on prospects in too small a segment of the total. We have heard mostly about the less than 10 percent of graduate work that is in deep trouble (the academic Ph.D.) and less about the other more than 90 percent that has been moving along unimpaired or has even prospered. If graduate enrollments rise slightly relative to undergraduate enrollments, this would mean that they might (on the assumption of undergraduate declines in the range of 5 to 15 percent) remain roughly stable or fall roughly 10 percent. Our anticipations include:

- Possible continuing increases at the M.A. level and further increases in some advanced professional fields.
- A decline of 50 percent by 1990 in the number of Ph.D. candidates preparing for academic careers. (This group now accounts for only one-twelfth of total graduate enrollments.)

The important phenomenon at the graduate level is internal redistribution among fields and disciplines rather than any major overall rise or decline. Graduate education has become a volatile element within total enrollments; the plaything of the labor market, of changing public policies in supporting graduate fellowships, of shifting social and intellectual concerns. Consequently, we make no specific projections about graduate enrollments, only noting that we expect them, over the two decades as a whole, to rise somewhat compared to whatever may happen to undergraduate enrollments.

We end this discussion of potential enrollments with a caution. Earlier projections by the Carnegie Commission and the Carnegie Council have turned out to be on the high side. In comparison with most persons and groups looking ahead to the future of higher education, we are once again clearly at the optimistic end of the spectrum.

Implications of the demographic depression for students. Recent developments and the changes we project for the remainder of the century will give us a dramatically different composition of the national student body than we have had traditionally. In 1960, it was composed predominantly of young majority males attending full-time. By 2000, there will be more women than men, as many people over 21 as 21 and under, nearly as many part-time as full-time attendees, and one-quarter of all students will be members of minorities. Roughly one-half of the students in the classroom of 2000 would not be there if the composition of 1960 were continued. This is a fundamental change in higher education.

The demographic depression may cause difficulties for institutions, and for actual, and particularly for prospective, faculty members, but it may seem more like high prosperity for the students. They will seldom, if ever, have had it so good on campus. The difficulties of others can only redound to their advantage. This may well become their Golden Age.

A Disaggregative Approach to Enrollments

No demographic disease of epidemic proportions will sweep over all of higher education during the next 20 years. The demographic disease, rather, will be selective; some institutions will die from it; nearly all will be affected by it in one way or another; and all will need to take some precautions. But institutions must be looked at one at a time, case by case. Although we cannot make this examination (only the individual institutions can do that), we can indicate how an individual institution may be affected as part of the category within which it falls, by the region and locality where it is located, by its size and institutional identification, and by the presence of close competition.

Research universities, selective liberal arts colleges, and public community colleges are the least vulnerable categories of institutions. The best universities and liberal arts colleges, able to maintain their selectivity, may become better, while those not quite the best may become comparatively worse in the average, precollege caliber of their students. Community colleges, the fastest-growing segment of higher education in the past two decades, appeal to new categories of students, but are vulnerable to actions like Proposition 13 that affect local funding and to low retention rates.

Institutions of average or above average vulnerability include doctorate-granting universities with relatively modest research activities, whose academic Ph.D. programs will be hard hit, and the universities and colleges with multiple programs below the Ph.D. level. While there are wide variations within both groups, generally the public institutions have better-assured futures than the private ones.

The most vulnerable category, with enormous variations between individual institutions, includes the less-selective liberal arts colleges—many of which are located in the East and Midwest—and private two-year colleges, a declining group for some years.

The first group of institutions will be more concerned with internal adjustments than with total decline of enrollments; the second with both; and the third with total decline, including, in some instances, the possibility of mergers, extinction, or fundamental restructuring. Assuming that the first group loses less than the average in total enrollments and the second loses about the average or a little more, then heavy losses must be sustained within the third category. Only about 10 of the over 700 institutions in the more vulnerable categories are public; the remainder are private.

Viewed regionally, both the East and Midwest may lose about 10 percent in their comparative shares of college enrollment, while the South will gain 5 percent and the Southwest and West 10 percent or more. Some institutions in the South and West that are now in the second rank academically will make it into the first rank by the end of the century.

Private and public institutions are somewhat differently affected by these geographical variations. Nearly 60 percent of private FTE enrollment is in states rated as having "worse than average" or "much worse than average" enrollment prospects, but only about 40 percent of public enrollment is in such states.

At least 95 percent of all campuses underwent some significant change in the 1970s: they gained or lost enrollment, or opened or closed, or merged, or shifted to public control, or changed from one institutional category to another. Alteration of condition or status was almost universal; continuation of the status quo, almost non-existent. Each campus has had its own individual recent history and is likely to have its own individual future. Institutions of higher education have been riding off in all directions and will probably continue to do so: 3,000 different institutions face 3,000 different futures.

Implications of the demographic depression for faculty. The situation of faculty members has been deteriorating for at least the past five years and may continue to do so in important regards for another decade or more. The labor market consequences are most intense for young persons looking for their first jobs, junior faculty seeking tenure, temporary faculty kept in temporary status at college after college, and faculty members who would like to move from one institution to another but find no openings. Women and minorities were entering faculty status in significant but still insufficient numbers in the 1970s, and their prospects are diminished for most of the next two decades. Some faculty members with tenure now face dismissal; some colleges will close.

The fate of faculties is intimately tied to the fate of their current institutions, since so few faculty members will have the opportunity to move elsewhere. While students are likely to be advantaged, faculty members, by and large, can only be disadvantaged by the demographic depression. But the impacts will be quite varied, from some loss of real income to total loss of employment.

Anticipating the Next Two Decades

Looking ahead is not just a matter of curiosity. It is also a matter of effective adaptation—of trying to seize hold of the future and guide it, not just reacting to what will happen otherwise. We need to have some idea of where we would like to be 20 years from now in higher education if we are to guide our own future. At least the following contributions by higher education, it now appears, will be needed by the nation in 2000, and generally also in the years in between:

- Places to accommodate approximately the same number of students by 2010 as were enrolled in 1978
- Institutions representing at least the degree of diversity we have today
- Resources to impart higher levels of skill attainment than ever before
- Capabilities for more advanced scientific research
- Capabilities to educate a more active, better-informed, more humanely oriented citizenry
- Capabilities to offer greater equality of opportunity and the possibility of greater equality of earned income
- Abilities to provide ever more constructive evaluation for national self-renewal
- Capacities to provide more services to the surrounding community
- Capability to maintain a network of contact and communication.

Higher education needs a mood of anticipation and a sense of great purpose almost as much as it needs anything else: anticipation, at a minimum, of survival, but also anticipation of an even more useful future. American society might change drastically for better or worse over the next two decades, although we doubt this. Probably the least favorable situation for higher education would be a continuation of a national drift in no clear direction. We see, instead, possibilities for national and individual self-renewal within the context of present institutional arrangements as a result of:

- America's view of itself as a nation of progress, as on the cutting edge of civilization, as a power in the world. This view has been challenged recently, and we expect the nation to rise to the challenge. We may well experience a new burst of national vitality.
- The search for a way out of limited resources. New knowledge will be needed as never before to preserve and enhance the use of physical resources.
- The heightening of expectations of millions of Americans, particularly women, members of minority groups, and older persons. They want improved jobs, more fulfilling lives, and better health. Education is one route to each of these goals.

We expect that America will seek to maintain its place in a competitive world, that the search for an escape route from the current confines of fixed resources will go on, that Americans will not easily lower their individual expectations, and that the size of the American population will not be allowed to decline after 2000 almost regardless of fertility rates. Thus, we do not anticipate a fast or slow fade-out for American higher education. We expect it to continue to move forward in response to both national and individual aspirations.

Choices to Be Made

There is much that should be done, and much than can be accomplished. To maximize achievements, some hard choices must be made.

1. *Quality.* The quality of the academic product as measured by scores on tests taken before entering graduate work has deteriorated significantly, although the deterioration largely takes place prior to entry into college. We consider a desirable goal for the year 2000 to be a return to the academic quality level of 1960 in the achievement capacities of higher education graduates.

2. *Balance.* Between the sciences, the social sciences, the humanities, the creative and performing arts, and the professions, each institution should define and seek to achieve its own chosen balance and not just let ad hoc actions yield some unplanned result. Recently, more time has been spent on electives and less on general education. We see a great need for rethinking the undergraduate curriculum. Overall, we have two main concerns:

   (a) that the humanities are often being unduly neglected, and

   (b) that the creative and performing arts, given the new interests of students in the quality of their lives, may still be subject to further expansion.

3. *Integrity.* We are concerned over the deterioration of integrity on campuses; in particular, grade inflation, reduced academic requirements, low-quality off-campus programs, false promises by institutions, cheating, vandalism, and student defaults on loans. Higher education, which should set standards for other elements of society to emulate, now stands at the higher end of the range of "fraud, error, and abuse" in federal programs. The morality of this disturbs us. Each institution needs to examine its own conduct.

4. *Adaptations compatible with the academic standards and community character of each college.* Each institution will decide, and some have already decided, what adjustments will be made to the demographic depression. Main areas for adaptation are the following:

   - Admission. How far, if at all, will academic entrance requirements be reduced?

   - Recruitment. How much more effort will be put into recruitment?

   - Retention. What additional assistance will be given to students to encourage them to stay in college?

   - Programs. What new programs will be added? A corollary is: What old programs will be dropped?

   - New schedules. The labor market will make possible more "split-level weeks" because more people in the labor market are on a part-time basis and absenteeism has risen in some industries. This suggests a whole series of possible new schedules for higher education programs.

5. *Dynamism.* The effective "management of decline" is extraordinarily difficult. One tendency is to preserve the status quo in the short run, thus sometimes encouraging even further decline in the long run. There are ways to encourage dynamism:

   - Institutions can set a policy to reduce existing programs, perhaps by 1 to 3 percent a year, in order to start new programs.

   - The federal government can increase support for the Fund for Improvement of Post-Secondary Education (FIPSE).

   - State financing formulas can provide leeway for new endeavors.

- Private foundations can establish presidential discretionary endowment grants for innovation.
- Colleges can hold some percentage, for example, 10 percent, of their faculty positions in temporary or short-term appointments.
- Colleges can keep tenure ratios for faculty members at reasonable levels, for example, two-thirds of the total.

6. *Effective use of financial resources.* Two major ways to reduce costs are to lower the real levels of faculty salaries and to raise the student/faculty ratio. Either way has disadvantages. As between them, however, a judicious increase in ratios, by as much as an additional 10 percent, at least in large institutions, may be both preferable and more politic. We know of no novel ways to reduce costs, but we do urge consideration of more consortia, of more nearly year-round use of resources, of discontinuation of unnecessary Ph.D. programs—many of which should never have been started—and of policies by states that allow institutions to keep the results of their cost-saving efforts to use on new programs. None of these will save much money, but each has other advantages.

7. *Financing.* Higher education needs to reconcile itself to the unliklihood of any massive new federal programs. This places great emphasis on private support, which, over the long run, has been a falling component of support. The Carnegie Commission once suggested that it was reasonable to expect that tuition in public institutions be about one-third of instructional costs offset by tuition scholarships on the basis of need. The exception would be community colleges, which should have comparatively low tuition. The Council considers this to be a proposal worthy of consideration. Several states now approximate these levels. Tax policies should encourage private gifts to colleges. And states should consider all private gifts as over and above their own contributions.

8. *Leadership.* We believe that the future period requires even more able leadership than that just past. In particular, we see the necessity for longer terms of, say, 10 years normal minimum for presidents, because the problems are long-term and can be made worse by short-term presidents avoiding them or seeking short-term expedient solutions. We also see the need for more authority in the hands of the president, which means more active support from his or her board. We suggest:
- Better search methods
- More concentration by boards of trustees on looking for leaders rather than survival managers
- Procedures for an early informal review of a president with the understanding that following such a review the total term of office will be about 10 years
- Determination by boards to stand behind presidents who do well what the board has asked them to do.

   We are also concerned that the membership of boards of trustees be strengthened. Trustees, above all others, must assume the burden for the long-run and overall welfare of their institutions.

9. *Preservation of private colleges.* We have recommended state support of private institutions, particularly through tuition scholarships based on student need. We oppose bailouts because they reduce the sense of self-dependence, but we do favor assistance with mergers. We also oppose tax credits for tuition, both because such a program is very costly and because it is very regressive in its incidence. We also oppose takeovers of private institutions by public authorities, as a general policy,

because we believe the private sector should be continued under private governance. We favor experimentation with hybrid types that preserve the private character of institutions while making public funds available to them. The tuition scholarships that we support make the competition with public institutions more fair, based on the performance of the institution. Moreover, they can reduce the need for bailouts and help assure the autonomy of the private colleges.

10. *Basic research.* We have another major concern: the flow of young scholars into certain fields. This flow is prospectively not so much determined by the decline in enrollments, since the leading research universities will not be affected greatly, if at all. Rather it is determined by the low faculty retirement rates for the next 10 to 20 years. This will deny opportunities to the ablest potential young scientists, including women and minorities, to find university employment and may discourage them from getting the Ph.D. at all.

We have an overall concern about higher education that transcends individual aspects. This is what may happen to the internal life of the campus. This life consists of the many personal relations among individuals and groups on campus, and the spirit and tone of the campus. Decline of enrollments and increasing external controls can sadly affect it. We can only suggest that their potential effects be recognized early and that efforts be made, campus by campus and by higher education altogether, to offset them: to fight for community versus divisiveness, and for autonomy versus external domination.

The future holds many unknowns. It also holds a range of already known choices that can be made by decision-makers. Much of what needs to be done can only be achieved at the institutional level. A downward drift in quality, balance, integrity, dynamism, diversity, private initiative, and research capability is not only possible—it is quite likely. But it is not required by external events. It is a matter of choice, not just fate. The emphasis should be on "managing for excellence."

Courses of Action

Institutions. In addition to the choices that need to be made by institutions, discussed above, we believe that accreditation needs to be greatly improved as a backup to institutional efforts. This is necessary both to persuade government to accept higher-education-based accreditation and to police unfair competitive practices among accredited colleges and universities.

The states. The period ahead will be a state period in terms of new initiatives and responsibilities for the welfare of higher education, as the prior 20 years were a federal period in these terms. We have two great fears about state conduct. One is that some state financial planners will underestimate potential enrollments and will promise more in the way of savings than can be realized if higher education is not to be greatly harmed. We believe that the states generally should be prepared to maintain real per capita contributions to higher education at current levels. The other is that some educational and financial planners will see an opportunity to make higher education an agency of state government. Higher education performs as a largely autonomous segment of society much better than it would as just another government bureau.

We also advise states to:

• Prepare financing formulas that will encourage diversity and new initiatives, that make allowance for rising overhead costs per student as enrollments go down, and that permit institutions to keep the private funds they raise. On formulas, we specifically suggest that reductions be less than the reductions in student numbers, for example, a range of 0.6 to 0.8 reduction for each 1.0 decline in FTE.

- Introduce state equivalents of the Fund for Improvement of Postsecondary Education (FIPSE).
- Stop preaudit controls over expenditures, and emphasize instead postaudit measurements of managerial performance.
- Ease the possibility of transfers of funds within institutions, preferably through lump-sum appropriations.
- Provide for portability of state financial aid to students.
- Step in, as necessary, to assist mergers of institutions, which can be costly, and to help with close-outs—particularly the preservation of past records.

The states together, through regional associations and the Education Commission of the States nationally, may wish to:

- Encourage more sophisticated advance estimates of enrollments than many states now have. Bad data give rise to bad plans.
- Assist interstate consortia and cooperative use of facilities.

We are doubtful about state-mandated review of academic programs. We believe that such review is better conducted by the institutions themselves, by the accrediting agencies, and by the students making their choices; and we question the wisdom of such a great intrusion into academic affairs.

We recognize that states vary greatly in the prospective decline of their enrollments. There is more of a case to be made for full reliance on the student market where the decline is modest than where it is severe. Where it is severe, it may be better for the state to close, or better, merge campuses than to have them all deteriorate.

The federal government. In addition to providing financial aid to students, the federal government has a major role in maintaining the research capacity of higher education. We suggest:

- Continuation of the present level of support for research in colleges and universities at approximately 12 to 13 percent of total federal support of research and development (R&D), while raising total federal support of R&D to about 1.8 percent of the GNP, which it averaged in the 1960s.
- Establishment of a Fund for the Encouragement of Young Scientists. The fund would be used over a 20-year period to assist the flow of young scientists into faculty positions in selected fields in universities, either directly or through absorption of all or part of the costs of existing tenure positions. It would be administered by the National Science Foundation upon recommendations as to fields and means of distribution by the National Academy of Sciences and the National Academy of Engineering. We consider this to be a very important investment in the future.
- Encouragement, through appropriate tax policies, for industry and foundations to grant research funds to universities.
- Introduction of a policy to support research libraries and other research resources,

including computers, by including within overhead on research contracts a standard 5 percent allowance for this purpose. This policy should be adopted as a supplement rather than as an alternative to existing programs, particularly Title II, Part C of the Education Amendments of 1976, which should be fully funded at its 1979 authorization level of $20 million.

We suggest that the federal government also consider:

- Policies to reallocate funds for student financial assistance to target them more on lower-income students; to create a more viable loan program; to place more emphasis upon student self-help, including the College Work-Study program; and to assist the states with State Student Incentive Grants; all within existing total sums in constant dollars
- Gradual increases in the funds allocated to the Fund for the Improvement of Postsecondary Education.

We are disturbed not by the purposes of federal control over higher education, but by their execution. We particularly support the purposes of the affirmative action policy. We make four proposals:

- Regulations should be issued only after improved advance consultation with representatives of higher education.
- Regulations should not go beyond the purposes for which the money is appropriated.
- A "Regulatory Impact Statement" should be required in connection with each set of regulations.
- The zeal of bureaucrats pushing their own programs beyond the intent of the law and of lawyers trying in advance to cover every possibility of evasion and every potential case of litigation should be curbed.

The costs of these proposals are modest and are more than offset by prospective declines in costs because of lower enrollments. The consequence is that support of higher education will be a declining percentage of the GNP.

Higher Education and the World of the Future

We may underestimate the current ability of American higher education to adapt, survive, and advance. Much has been accomplished for individual Americans and for American society; yet there is still some unfinished business. We have not yet spread universal access to all populated parts of the nation, and we have a long way to go to make possible the participation of the ablest persons regardless of race, sex, and family income. These goals should be met by the year 2000.

We also have some new business, in particular: (1) introducing a more global perspective into higher education; (2) guiding the use of the new electronic technology; and (3) identifying the most productive areas for new research.

While we have a sense of great pride in what has been accomplished and great faith in the capacity of higher education for future contribution, we are still concerned that (1) the competition for students over the next two decades may be managed in ways that lead to a decline in academic quality, integrity of conduct, and the balance among fields; (2) in the absence of growth, institutions may lose their dynamism and flexibility; (3)

diversity among institutions may be reduced; (4) equality of results by regulation may gradually come to replace equality of opportunity; and (5) some of the effectiveness and creativity of students and scholars may be eroding.

Yet, despite these concerns, we believe that higher education will make essential contributions to the world of the future: to a more participative society of high quality, a society more universal in its concerns and more capable of self-renewal. Few other institutions have such capacity for the "improvement of the welfare of mankind around the world." The further cultivation of "man's unconquerable mind" may be the one best hope for a future greatly enhanced over the present we now know.

Supplements

The final report contains the following detailed technical supplements:

- Supplement A. Sources of Funds for Higher Education
- Supplement B. Carnegie Enrollment Projections
- Supplement C. The Labor Market and Higher Education
- Supplement D. Gainers and Losers Among Institutions of Higher Education
- Supplement E. Higher Education and Human Performance
- Supplement F. Equality of Opportunity and Equality of Earned Income
- Supplement G. Academic Schedules and the Split-level Week
- Supplement H. Faculty Development Present and Future
- Supplement I. Instructional Costs and Productivity, 1930-1977
- Supplement J. A Comparative Review of Scholarly, Scientific, and Technological Progress in the United States
- Supplement K. Smoothing Out the Flow of Young Scientists into Universities
- Supplement L. State Support of Higher Education

Part Three

Sponsored Research and Technical Reports

Adjusting to Changing Times

Presidents Confront Reality: From Edifice Complex to University Without Walls. By Lyman A. Glenny, John R. Shea, Janet H. Ruyle, and Kathryn H. Freschi. 1977.

In 1974, presidents of American colleges and universities were asked for their perceptions of change on their campuses that occurred as a result of enrollments and financing trends between 1968 and 1974, and for their expectations of change from 1974 to 1980.

The aggregation of responses of the individual presidents yields a basically optimistic set of views. Fewer see growth in total enrollments in the future (1974-1980) than saw them in the past (1968-1974), but fewer also see declines. Many expect to solve present enrollment difficulties by attracting adult, off-campus, and evening students. Funding problems do not dominate the views of administrators in our survey. Growth, not decline, remains the expectation. Presidents hope to tap alumni, corporations, foundations, and other private sources for more funds than in the past. Although they are aware of difficulties brought on by current conditions, most presidents express confidence in the ability of their institutions to modify curricular offerings, reallocate resources where needed, and otherwise plan and manage the resources available to them. No major changes are foreseen. Rather, recent changes are projected as meeting institutional and student needs of the future.

The Search for New Clientele

A major goal of the vast majority of institutions is to maintain or increase enrollments. While continuing to emphasize programs for traditional students, most presidents expect their institutions to recruit a wide range of nontraditional students as well—adults, part-time evening students, persons off-campus, and those principally interested in continuing education. Several difficulties, however, are clear:

- Few presidents see much expansion in personnel assigned to the function of recruitment and admissions.
- The untapped pool of adults may not be large enough to meet the enrollment aspirations of all institutions. Although a number of rather traditional, four-year institutions have been successful in attracting adults to selected programs, many colleges are in small towns and rural areas and thus are poorly situated to serve this new market. Moreover, the proportion of adults interested in degree programs as opposed to noncredit courses may not be very large.
- Continuing education services in four-year institutions in most states must be self-supporting. Altering this practice will not be easy. Yet, without full financing of adult programs, it may be difficult to attract large numbers of new students. If adult education is subsidized, some uneconomical programs may result. If self-

supporting, some colleges and universities will surely end up losing money in the unbridled competition for the same student groups.

- Many institutions may not be in a position to develop occupational and professional programs for young people, who have been shifting away from liberal arts to more vocationally oriented programs. Nor will it be easy to respond to the particular learning needs of adults. Adults have not, in the past, attended degree-credit programs in large numbers. Nor do they express much interest in traditional liberal arts programs. They typically seek learning experiences—at convenient times and places—that will help them solve everyday problems in their lives. Nevertheless, responses of the presidents imply that many institutions will seek to offer "old wine in new bottles." Moreover, those intent on building new curricula may not have the capital needed to do so, or will need to dig development money out of regular operating funds.

- For some areas of study (for example, business administration), the market for adult students appears destined to become glutted with new offerings.

- Oversupplies of trained persons will develop in several popular technical and quasi-professional areas. As happened in the case of people studying to become teachers and Ph.D.'s, students and the public may become disenchanted with higher education if the labor market is unable to absorb graduates into training-related occupations.

- Will the right people be available to teach in new programs, at new times and places? Presidents expect nontenured and part-time faculty to bear the brunt of reductions in staff. This pattern runs counter to traditions in staffing for part-time, adult students. Moreover, faculty are not easily shifted from one discipline to another, and there is little precedent (or money) for retaining them.

- Presidents anticipate more collective bargaining in the future. Indeed, they may well encourage collective bargaining by instituting teacher evaluation, higher promotion and tenure standards, and heavier workloads. While collective agreements may add to flexibility in some ways (for example, by favoring retraining and early retirement programs), such agreements are more likely to inhibit it in others (for example, restrictions on time and place of instruction, workload definitions and amounts, and rates of pay for moonlighting).

Securing Adequate Resources

In addition to the problem of securing funds for such special purposes as program development and faculty retraining, an equally serious matter involves rising unit costs and dwindling funds—and, consequently, declining services—as enrollments fall and wages and prices go up. Most presidents expect a higher level of funding from their traditional sources in 1980 than they received in 1974. Alumni, corporations, foundations, continuing education programs, and state governments are considered increasingly important. To meet rising costs and maintain and improve services, presidents face a number of problems:

- At the time of the survey (summer 1974), inflation was a serious problem. The market value of investment portfolios had declined. Endowment incomes had fallen. Several foundations had announced they were cutting back grants; others were quietly doing so. Special appeals for instructional funds are likely to fall on deaf ears if graduates continue to have difficulty finding employment in their chosen fields.

- For most states, revenues had fallen off as a consequence of an economic recession. More important in the long run, three-quarters of the states (including all of the large industrial ones) allocated a smaller share of their general revenues to higher education in 1973 than in immediately preceding years. At both state and national levels, budget analysts and political leaders assign low priority to higher education services.
- Some private colleges expect to "go public" in order to increase their funding base and ward off threats to their survival. But as enrollments drop in some public institutions, it is likely to become increasingly difficult to justify state support of private colleges, much less assumption of full responsibility for them.
- Some universities and a few colleges have long earned substantial amounts of money by offering evening courses on and off campus. This income has been used to support other, more costly, "regular" programs. With more institutions of all types offering continuing education programs, the profitability of such efforts may decline.

Flexibility, Responsiveness, and Efficiency

No matter what they do, some four-year institutions will be unable to ride out the storm of lower attendance rates and the underlying shift in the age distribution of the population. Other institutions may survive and maintain their vigor through internal efforts to remain flexible and efficient.

- Some presidents report that their institutions have taken actions to consolidate courses and programs and increase student-faculty ratios and faculty workloads. The majority, however, report little or no change in these areas.
- In general, presidents say that their institutions have not made extensive changes in the use of planning and management techniques. By 1980, however, many expect substantial change. These tools surely may help individual and collective decision making, but faith in their value may well exceed what can be achieved.
- Master plans, like other planning and management tools, are generally viewed positively by administrators. Will planning processes and documents, especially at system and state levels, continue to be a positive force in a period of reduced growth in enrollments and funding? The presidents reply affirmatively, but depression and competition lead almost inevitably to more state control over use of funds and to less flexibility.   '
- Administrators are naturally reluctant to forecast radical change in the structure and functioning of their institutions. Merger, consolidation, and consortium arrangements may help some institutions—especially in urban areas—provide services that otherwise would be out of their reach. Yet, fewer than one in ten presidents anticipate such action between now and 1980.

Stability in enrollments and funding is by no means bad. Many presidents anticipated the trends now affecting higher education and took steps to maintain the vitality of their institutions. Others have moved aggressively to reshape their programs to better fit the aspirations of individuals and the nation's emerging social priorities. Many public community colleges are rapidly restructuring their services to meet the needs of their constituencies. But others, such as nonselective private liberal arts colleges in rural areas, face great difficulties.

Despite the manifold problems presented by steady-state conditions, there is much room for optimism. A healthier, more diverse set of institutions and postsecondary educational services will surely emerge in the years ahead.

Challenges Past, Challenges Present: An Analysis of American Higher Education Since 1930. By David D. Henry. 1975.

The purpose of this interpretative essay is to highlight some of the changes that have taken place in higher education, to note some of the challenges and uncertainties, and to mark some of the responses in the years since the depression of the 1930s. Three main themes may be identified. The first is that adjustment to the social environment has been a prevailing characteristic of higher education. The second theme is that crisis and stress in higher education occur in periods of growth, intellectual ferment, and social excitement, as well as in periods of relative stability or of depression. The third theme is that the most troublesome times for higher education have been the years of public lack of confidence in its social significance.

Before the Crash

The period between the Civil War and World War I was comparatively prosperous. The belief grew that a college education would pay off in later life, and the need for credentialing came to be widely felt.

The remarkable growth of institutions after the Civil War and the numerous academic changes (particularly a new curriculum with scientific, professional, and technical subjects) were a response both to increasing complaints about the old colleges and to current social and economic changes. By 1910 the new way was established, although the stability between 1910 and 1930, apart from enrollment growth, was interrupted by World War I. The response to wartime demands was vigorous, imaginative, and united, making for new interaction with government, industry, and other segments of society and for greater public appreciation of the developing system.

Depression and Recovery

The effects of the depression of the 1930s on higher education were profound and lasting. The most serious impact was psychological. Academic people were hurt less than other segments of the population—in terms of finances, employment, and physical want—and institutions survived remarkably well. But the notion that security of employment was a built-in characteristic of academic life was severely jolted. Large numbers of college teachers were not released, but cutbacks in positions fell heavily upon the nontenure group—young instructors particularly. College teachers were also aware that many academic staff found places in newly created federal and state agencies, including emergency units that had posts requiring college degrees. Further, policy changes toward shorter-term appointments became disturbing, and the cutback in the modest savings of most academic families emphasized the inadequacy of pension arrangements.

Related to the disquiet of many faculty members was the feeling that collectively they did not have sufficient involvement in administrative decision making. Faculties were deprived of first-hand information about many institutional conditions and problems, and they often did not have a systematic way to make their views on pending issues known. Faculty involvement in educational decisions became common before 1930. But, with notable exceptions, this participation in governance did not reach into financial affairs or administrative organization.

Tuition was a matter of dispute then as now. Institutions felt that they could not afford the loss in income that would result from lowering charges. Students believed that they were being treated unfairly, since prices generally were falling, and their financial needs were increasing as employment and other forms of student assistance declined.

Although recovery started fairly quickly, the period of despair was long enough to encourage questionable recruiting practices and intensify competitiveness among institutions. The depression heightened the demand for external coordination, perceived as a means of eliminating waste and duplication and lowering costs. The first outcry for economy came from state government. Taking legislative concern over alleged high costs as a cue, state officers moved to tighten control over institutional budgets and expenditures.

Federal involvement. The most important theme of this period was the increasing support of higher education by the federal government. The Federal Emergency Relief Administration was created to help the states by providing for work-relief activity. In Minnesota, late in 1933, relief funds were used for students. The program was aimed at keeping students off the labor market and had immediate widespread acceptance, even by those who had been skeptical of federal action in the area of higher education.

The grants relieved the low enrollment problem in both public and private institutions. The tuition issue receded as a primary concern. Students were helped in meeting their personal financial requirements, and the work projects were useful. Federal student aid programs in the depression set the precedent for postwar educational benefits for veterans and the greatly expanded student aid programs of the 1960s and 1970s. It also opened a way for federal assistance to reach private institutions.

Student reactions. Students were not only thrown into the discomfiture of making ends meet and sharing in the general worries of their parents' generation, but felt that their future was uncertain and their aspirations destroyed. This uncertainty bred criticism of "the system." New student groups appeared and expressed interest in social problems. The range in point of view was wide, from criticism to proposals for action. Most criticisms centered on the external scene rather than educational institutions. The groups had enough common ground to be termed a student movement, but their chief common characteristics were their vitality and a "consciousness of kind" rather than militance.

Partial recovery. Enrollments returned to the familiar pattern of growth after only one biennium of decline. The 1935-36 resident college enrollment was 4.6 percent higher than the previous high in 1931-32. Education and general expenditures recovered nearly as rapidly, and the 1935-36 figure was within 1 percent of the 1931-32 peak amount. Expenses for these purposes had fully recovered by 1937-38, with a total more than 13 percent above 1931-32.

The recovery of faculty salaries was slower. Salaries paid to faculty in land-grant institutions during 1941-42 were still below the 1930-31 levels. Coupled with a rising cost of living, the slow recovery of faculty salaries proved one of the most lasting effects of the depression.

Impulses unfulfilled. There was little educational change in the 1930s that could be specifically attributed to the depression. The trends of the decade do not support the common assertion that reform or constructive innovation may result from cutbacks. The cutbacks were made without basic alternation in structure, and where traditional practices were disrupted, they were given priority in restoration.

World War II and Change

The World War II years were characterized by lack of government planning; delay as the nation debated policies and directions; initial wasteful confusion as plans were finally initiated almost on a trial and error basis; and tardy mobilization. Nearly every aspect of college and university administration became war related. From a peak enrollment of 1.5 million in 1939-40, civilian enrollments dropped 6 percent in 1941-42 and plummeted another 37.5 percent by 1943-44—the sharpest decline in the twentieth century. The upward trend was regained by 1945-46, when returning veterans helped boost the enrollment total more than 12 percent above the high in 1939-40.

Many faculty members left the campus for war-related employment or government service, both military and civilian. Vacancies had to be filled on short notice from a dwindling supply of teachers.

As fee income declined and costs increased, finances in general were threatened, although the burden did not fall equally on all institutions. Fortunately, with the help of government contracts and use of the colleges in military reserve programs, the overall financial decline halted by 1945-46.

A program evolves. The wartime program finally became defined by the fall of 1943. The regular instruction for nonmilitary students was supplemented by organized programs for army and navy enlisted and officer personnel.

The largest and one of the most impressive specially organized programs was the engineering, science, and management war-training unit. This program was instituted at the post-high school level to meet the shortage of technical workers, supervisors, and experts in fields essential to national defense. The courses were short and intensive, were offered at both the college and subcollege levels, and usually did not carry college credit, but some part-time evening students preferred them to traditional college work. Between 1940 and 1945, nearly 1.8 million men and women enrolled in such courses.

The colleges and universities reached into their communities in many other ways. First efforts went into activities that seemed naturally related to regular duties. First-aid classes, training for air-raid wardens, and centers for blood donations were organized quickly. Public forums, lectures, and conferences with subjects ranging from current affairs to postwar development also came naturally.

One important outgrowth of such activities, for both the community and the nation, was the inevitable emphasis on postwar planning. By the time the war ended, the public was far better informed about international relations and national concerns for the postwar world than it would have been otherwise.

This account does not deal with the research contributions of individual academic scientists, extensive and significant as such contributions were. As a result of their work, higher education came to be associated with war-related science activity. This was exceedingly effective and pointed the way to postwar use of academic staff and facilities in government-formulated research.

Veterans' Return

The enrollment of World War II veterans created the most rapid growth of colleges and universities in the history of higher education. The rate and the time period raised serious doubts as to whether the government had promised more than it could deliver. Failure of the institutions to respond could have had serious social consequences. That higher education was able to marshal resources for the task, whatever the shortcomings in its qualitative performance, is an outstanding record of ingenuity and dedication.

Two veterans' educational assistance acts made unprecedented federal expenditures in higher education possible. Public Law 346, passed in June 1944, the so-called GI Bill, provided education and training for all military personnel who had served a minimum of 90 days; and the earlier Public Law 16, passed in March 1943, expanded the vocational rehabilitation program for veterans with service-connected disabilities. The new concept of generous benefits for veterans generally (as contrasted with traditional benefits for the ill and the handicapped) was accepted.

At the time of the adoption of the legislation, no one anticipated the size of the response. The acceleration of veteran enrollments began in February 1946, when 125,000 new veterans registered. By fall, over a million crowded the campuses. There simply were not enough beds, teachers, classrooms, and laboratories; not enough equipment, libraries, offices, food service centers, and ordinary services. The results were overcrowding and inconveniences. Yet the experience came off with good spirit in nearly all quarters, with remarkable educational results, and few regrets on the part of the institutions or the veterans.

Housing was a major difficulty. The nation already had a housing shortage of immense proportions, occasioned by lack of construction and upkeep during the war years. The needs of the veterans on and off campus therefore made a bad situation worse. The federal government acted quickly with housing assistance.

A number of significant changes were occasioned by the veterans' return:

1. Higher education became a significant means to a national end for the policymakers.
2. The nonveteran youth of the nation were quick to note the new priority for higher education.
3. Those who were concerned with the enlargement of educational opportunity were given a national precedent for the value and feasibility of federal assistance.
4. Aid to students emerged, as it had in the depression, as an appropriate way for the federal government to be involved in higher education with a minimum of federal control.
5. The public image of the veteran as a good student, reliable, mature, and well motivated, carried over into the public evaluation of college students generally.
6. The new status of higher education broadened the appeal of academic careers for increasing numbers of highly qualified young people.
7. The off-campus sites temporarily acquired for surplus enrollments at a number of institutions served as beginnings for permanent new campuses in state systems, as foundations for new community colleges, and later as authorized permanent branches.
8. The tone of campus life changed. Undergraduate discipline systems were altered. The married student came to stay. In loco parentis did not disappear for another decade, but a breakthrough was made that kept widening with succeeding years. Student personnel work grew in importance. Exceptions to curricular rigidities that were granted to veterans made easier the adoption of permanent revisions in educational practice. Change was encouraged.

9.   Many other internal practices, policies, and services were initiated that would be-
     come permanent. The new flexibility in admissions would remain. Many previously
     experimental nontraditional arrangements had new acceptance and continued in
     force—correspondence instruction, short courses, tutorial clinics, and remedial
     courses. Student counseling expanded. Career preparation acquired new interest
     and influenced college curriculums as well as overall objectives of some institutions.

New Concepts and Emerging Goals

As higher education emerged from World War II, the academic community had the
feeling that colleges and universities had a new importance in national affairs. Academic
men of science had been heavily involved in harnessing atomic energy. Many faculty
members had served in important wartime posts for the government and for business,
industry, and civic affairs. The new mood induced new ideas.

The recommendations of the President's Commission on Higher Education, published under the general title *Higher Education for American Democracy,* gave focus to
discussions of the new situation. The main (and at the time startling) thrust of the report
was the elimination of all barriers to educational opportunity, so that "every citizen,
youth, and adult is enabled and encouraged to carry his education, formal and informal,
as far as his native capacities permit." The commission recommended doubling enrollments by 1960, development of community colleges, federal scholarships and fellowships, federal aid for general purposes and for physical plants in public institutions, and
legislation to prevent religious and racial discrimination.

The general goal of the report—to expand educational opportunity toward mass
higher education—was widely endorsed, although not without dissent. But the debate on
ways and means and appropriate limitations was widespread and centered on feasibility,
desirability of educating so many, the content of higher education for diverse groups,
and federal relationships.

Approximately a year after the final report of the President's Commission appeared, the Commission on Financing Higher Education was created by the Association
of American Universities. Both commissions tied their recommendations on economic
problems and sources of support to their concept of "diversity as the key to freedom"
and analyzed the functions of higher education in societal relationships.

On a number of issues the two commissions ran parallel, but on some they were
sharply divergent. The approach of the first commission was expansive and comprehensive in its social point of view; the approach of the second commission could be called
moderate, if not conservative, and was probably more realistic as to what might be
accomplished.

Uncertainty During Cold War

The uncertainty of higher education during the fifties was largely fallout from the Cold
War. The anti-Communist stance of the nation called for increased defense expenditures
and affected the economy. Inflation, partly caused by financing armaments and other
aids to allies, was on the rise. The partial mobilization raised questions about manpower
policy, including the probable continuation of selective service and the possibility of
universal military training. The debate affected student choice as to college attendance
and reduced the capability of institutions to anticipate future enrollment. The situation
seriously affected the morale of college and university personnel, not only through its
influence upon finance and mission, but in the harassment that came with the McCarthy

hearings; in unfair attacks on the loyalty of teachers, textbooks, and student groups; in loyalty oaths, with all their implications; and in vicious heresy-hunting.

In this setting, the subject most immediately troublesome to colleges and universities was the inability to plan for enrollments. As the veterans left the campuses, who would take their places? Veteran enrollment dropped from 1,122,738 in 1947 to 388,747 in 1951, and the downward trend would continue.

The uncertainty about enrollment was directly related to uncertainty about finance. In 1949-50 enrollments increased by 5 percent and institutional operating expenditures increased by 12.11 percent from their 1947-48 levels. In 1951-52 both enrollments and expenditures were down—enrollments by 13.8 percent and expenditures by 5.03 percent.

The search for operational funds could not ignore the shortage of physical plants and equipment, which had not kept up with enrollment growth and the increasing demand for varied service, including research. Wars, depression, and inflation had left huge deficits by any measure of adequacy. At no time did resources meet accumulated and new postcrisis needs. Further, as knowledge grew more complex, particularly in the sciences, costs increased beyond levels of historic growth.

Another result of the wartime atmosphere was the necessity of supporting the national goal of military preparedness and at the same time maintaining freedom of thought and expression in teaching and in the search for new knowledge. It was not Washington alone that threatened colleges and universities. The national scenario was imitated at state and community levels. The fear that political powers might strike the local campuses created uncertainty about the manner of organized resistance to the obvious violations of civil liberties and the accepted code of fair procedure.

New court decisions, legislation, and public attitudes make it difficult to understand in retrospect the impact of demagoguery that restrained even the president from speaking out against it as forcefully as he felt, the duress under which academic leaders operated, and to appreciate fully the doubt in the public mind as to the capability of educational institutions to cope with alleged Communist infiltration.

The student mood was one of withdrawal and acquiescence. Politics was characterized as "dirty business." Those who objected strenuously to the excesses risked considerable personal damage. Conforming or remaining silent seemed to be the best way out.

Increasing Enrollment and the Struggle for Resources

Before the end of the 1950s, educational ferment subsided and uncertainties faded in the preoccupation of universities—as early as 1956— with enrollment projections.

The increasing percentage of high school students who graduated and the increasing percentage of these that went on to college were principal factors in enrollment growth. Another important factor was demographic. Not only had the birthrate increased between 1940 and 1955, but infant mortality was lower. The increase in persons of college age would be greater than the past increase in relation to the number of births.

Enlarging capacity. Institutions grimly took stock of the requirements for new space, new equipment, and additional personnel. Underfinanced since 1930, administrators responsible for operations now anticipated an unprecedented scramble for resources. The first need would be for space. By 1956 the capital needs for a decade were estimated to be $13 billion, and some federal action would be required to prevent a massive denial of educational opportunity and a diminution of instructional quality.

Where would teachers come from? The question, which was of widespread concern in the late 1950s, applied first to the teachers needed at once in the elementary schools, but was relevant to faculties in the colleges. No general plan for supplying teachers had been seriously considered by 1955. Each institution seemed confident that it could raid another or that some solution would turn up. Improvement of faculty salaries was at the center of recruitment effectiveness.

Scramble for resources. From 1955 to 1965 the key question was whether student charges could be increased to sustain the proportion of institutional support that they had come to represent. Basic costs would rise to meet both inflation and the increased costs of extended services and facilities required for larger enrollments. That the proportion of educational income derived from student charges actually increased slightly, in both public and private sectors, is truly remarkable when one considers the dollar levels to which they rose. The increase in student financial aid—from gifts, institutional revenues, and state and federal programs—significantly contributed to this result, as did loan funds and work-study opportunities. Maintenance of at least the current proportion of educational expenditures supported by student charges was one of the incentives for institutional efforts.

The public interest in science and in an enlarged national capability in science, generated by Sputnik, also was a major factor in the rapid increase of federal assistance to students, graduate and undergraduate. An alternative to increased funding, of course, was to restrict educational opportunity. But the strong prevailing view was that the nation need not, would not, and could not afford to risk dividing up educational service instead of creating more.

Although the scramble for resources was productive, a huge deficit remained between need and reality. The steady increase in categorical assistance from the federal government pointed to the possibility of more such aid and the opening of new support channels from this source. Federal aid for higher education became the dominant theme on the agenda of academic planning.

Sputnik, Science, and Support

Before the 1960s, funds from the federal government to colleges and universities were for specific federal purposes and services—student aid, research, training programs for federal departments, participation in overseas activity, officer education for the military, the education of specialized personnel for other departments, and consultation with academic specialists. In spite of these and many other relationships over a period of more than 100 years, a federal policy to assist higher education fulfill its primary purposes was not legislated until 1965. Under law and precedent, higher education continued to be regarded as primarily a responsibility of the states.

Reasons for federal education policy. The tidal wave of students became a pressure point in this developing relationship. The data on capability versus enrollments indicated that even if former proportions of educational income could be sustained during the enrollment rise, substantially more help would be needed from the federal government.

Apprehensions and reservations about federal control, the question of public assistance for private institutions, the dangers of carrying mass higher education too far, and the intrusion of political forces beyond the formalities of government action faded when Sputnik, the first man-made satellite, orbited the earth in 1957. The reaction in all circles was consternation, sometimes close to panic. Questions flew as to why Russian scientific capability appeared to be superior to that of the United States, and they centered on American education.

In 1956 and early 1957, Congress and the administration were beginning to note the possible need for greater federal support for higher education in response to the prospective tidal wave of enrollment. But action was slow to develop. Without Sputnik, the National Defense Education Act of 1958, inadequate as it was as an aid to institutions, might not have been adopted—at least not at that time.

The law authorized diverse channels for federal assistance to higher education, most of which were later encompassed in the Higher Education Act of 1965. As with earlier programs, a defense tab linked the program to the traditional literal application of federal interests, but the effect of the legislation was a clear recognition that aiding students promotes the general welfare. The intent clearly was to use federal resources to strengthen higher education generally.

The most obvious response to Sputnik was the creation and rapid growth of the National Aeronautics and Space Administration. However, each of the major mission-oriented federal agencies continued to increase its funding of basic research as a proportion of overall allocations to research and development. Between 1963 and 1972, federal support of basic research at universities and colleges increased from $610 million to $1,409 million.

From about 1958, the education of highly trained manpower for university research and teaching and for research work in other areas also received national attention. As a result, large federal sums were made available for fellowships and traineeships, research assistantships, and training grants. Some institutional aid accompanied the grants. Loan funds and work-study opportunities for graduate students were established.

Changing federal policy. But the basic needs of higher education generally had not been met by policies that related federal support to national defense interests, and a challenge to the federal government as well as to other sources of support persisted. The major reason Congress had not undertaken sweeping new programs for colleges and universities was the absence of an integrated plan supported by all important elements of higher education. The doctrinaire debate over federal aid as well as over the appropriate means would go on as a consensus too slowly developed.

The significance of the failure to devise specific continuing policy was reflected in the years after 1968. In fact, the drastic changes in direction and funding contributed to a "new depression" in higher education.

Priority Lost

The chronicle of higher education in the decade 1958-1968 was one of unprecedented enrollment growth, expansion of programs, and increase in functions. But by about 1968, the cost trend induced by the growth period exceeded income prospects.

The downturn in the financial condition may be traced to a number of reasons. The unexpected acceleration in the general inflation rate magnified costs, and dollars bought less. Federal resources that had gone to institutional income declined as a proportion of educational expenditures; unsettled economic conditions affected income from endowments and gifts; and tuition income could not be significantly increased without diminishing returns or incurring political opposition or both.

There can be no doubt that this downturn stems from a loss of priority for higher education, which is in turn related to a lack of public confidence as to the importance of supporting higher education. Many of the contributing reasons for the shift in public

attitude may be identified; for example, public revulsion at the violence that characterized student protest from 1964 to 1970.

Economic insecurity looms large in recent public attitudes. Worry over inflation,
trends in living costs, and the level of government expenditures and taxes has induced a
mood of limited confidence in the immediate economic future. Apprehension that the
economic and political world may be unmanageable has encouraged resistance to public
expenditures except for military, welfare, and social service purposes. This resistance
leaves little room for discriminatory judgments about the long-term strength and stability
of institutions. Higher education is caught in a crisis of confidence in the economic
future.

The politics of higher education must be considered. During the early 1960s, gains
were the outcome of public faith in the inherent value of the enterprise. This faith was
given substance by public awareness of how higher education related to such highly publicized issues as national defense and the importance of science and technology in the
space age. Education potentially could contribute to the solution of problems that were
pressing social concerns—urban affairs, poverty, crime, race relations, industrial and
business expansion, professional needs, environmental control, and public management.

With the economic slowdown, complicated by inflation, competing demands for
public support became the subject of political action at all levels. Historically, higher
education has been dependent upon long-term public good will as contrasted with short-
term political action. In political activity, higher education has no interest group to fight
its battles, and it is not well organized to fight its own. Defense, welfare, transportation,
unemployment, crime prevention, health care, and other public services have been given
precedence in public concern.

Whether political inadequacy is a failure of the system or an inevitable condition
is a continuing question. That higher education has not been able to compete effectively
for public support at a time of limited resources is widely acknowledged and substan-
tiated by fiscal data.

Reflections for the Future

In looking at the stress, strain, and crisis in higher education from 1930 to 1970, three
elements stand out: the oscillations in growth and their consequences; the constancy
of change; and the significance of public evaluation and the nature of interaction with
the public.

Analyzing growth. When one charts the twentieth-century enrollment peaks by decades,
the graph line reflects continuous growth. This view obscures the tremendous oscillations
that occurred after World Wars I and II, after the depression, and in the 1950s. For institutions, the adjustments that had to be made in times of decline were as severe as meeting
the demands of the increase periods. All of these changes were unanticipated, and in each
one the momentum of the previous period was slowed. This braking of momentum
created deficits in resource acquisition and educational development that were never
completely overcome. The tendency to associate growth in higher education with good
times (public support and educational progress) and lack of growth with bad times
(constraint and stagnation) is superficial. Such a perspective overlooks the simple truth
that growth can be harmful if underfunded and can distort purposes if not perceptively
controlled.

To understand the period from 1930 to 1970, it is important to recognize that
the development of higher education was horizontal as well as vertical. Overall enroll-

ment increase was dramatic, but the cost increase of services and functions not directly related to instruction was equally if not more dramatic. The funds expended on student aid, project research, and new public services took on new dimensions, but they had little effect on support required for basic functions.

The term *affluence* is a misnomer as a description of the period. It is an error to apply the concept even to the 1960s. The cost per student calculated upon costs for basic operations did not increase significantly beyond the normal rate of inflation. But as the horizontal development progressed, it became apparent that a larger share of the national wealth would be required to underwrite the advance of higher education toward the goal of universal access.

Constancy of change. Although there has been a tendency to think of growth as the chief characteristic of higher education in the United States, the central and more compelling feature has really been continuous adaptation. But change must always be considered in terms of purposes and goals. The debate should be on how best to advance purpose rather than change; much confusion arises because we tend to debate change instead of purpose. To add to the difficulty, institutional goals change as they reflect conditions of social change and changing public conceptions.

Institutional adaptation must be supported by internal consensus as well as consensus among external constituencies that have interests at stake. Moreover, the diversity among institutions slows consensus-building. But the effort to find common ground among institutions of higher education as the basis for public interpretation of purpose, achievement, and potential must continue in the drive for higher public priority.

Higher education and the public. While higher education in the United States may be viewed as an instrument of society and therefore affected in many ways by the external environment—in character, purpose, strength, and structure—a complementary thesis must also be considered.

An influential force for constructive action has been the widespread belief that higher education or advanced learning, including research, is "the engine of social progress." Sometimes the belief has been a matter of faith and conviction; sometimes it has been based upon evidence of cause and effect. In either case, acceptance of the thesis has been the motivation for public policy in encouraging both institutions of higher education and the individual's pursuit of learning.

As a system, higher education has been less than ideally effective in communicating with the public. At every instance of crisis or stress, the general academic community has recognized the connection between public confidence and support, and considered briefly the ways and means of achieving public appreciation of goals, achievements, needs, and potential. Between those peaks of acute anxiety, however, the academic profession by and large has been indifferent, not even fully supportive of administrative efforts to build interpretative programs.

A new factor enters into the interpretation dilemma as the current demand for accountability demonstrates the need for information that will be intelligible to non-professional audiences. One response should be greater attention by scholars to higher education as an area of study.

How to improve communication is a large and complex subject. Past indifference and inertia cannot be overcome quickly. Responsibility centers in institutional action, although state, regional, and national agents have important roles in the process. The key requirement is that the effort be continuous, with high priority for action at all levels and in all institutions.

In the end, of course, the process is meaningless without substance. Program effectiveness and management efficiency must be at the heart of the effort.

Variables in an uncertain future. The future of higher education is tied to public confidence in its mission and social contributions and to its operational and managerial effectiveness in achieving these ends. The present depression in higher education is traceable in part to economic conditions, but the degree of cutback is traceable to a loss of confidence.

There will be unforseen climactic events that will affect the course of the nation, and with it the course of higher education. But the constants are there, too. New knowledge and advanced learning are essential to a civilized society, regardless of the variables. As long as the technological society exists, the centrality of higher education will remain. Further, as attention is turned increasingly to the creation and expansion of human services within society, higher education will be called upon to train those who staff the service components. Optimism derived from these constants is more than the residue of an old-fashioned faith. It is a realistic acknowledgment of where we are, and it can be grounds for confidence despite uncertainties.

Managing Multicampus Systems: Effective Administration in an Unsteady State. By Eugene C. Lee and Frank M. Bowen. 1975.

This is a study of the experiences of nine multicampus systems in coping with and planning for a period of limited growth, fiscal constraints, and possible retrenchment. The systems studied were the Universities of California, Illinois, Missouri, North Carolina, Texas, Wisconsin, the City and State Universities of New York, and the California State Universities and Colleges.* Information was gathered by reviewing pertinent documents and interviewing the systems' chief executive officers and their central administrative staffs.

Administrators in all nine multicampus systems are challenged by growth-inhibiting factors that emerged between 1970 and 1975 and are expected to continue through the 1980s. Shrinking financial support and stabilizing enrollment, the major inhibitions to physical growth, encompass a more complex set of variables. If a single factor, such as enrollment, is isolated, the appearance of a steady state may seem likely. But the isolation of one factor does not capture the current reality of multicampus governance.

On the contrary, these nine systems face an increasingly unsteady state of uneven and unpredictable distribution of students across campuses, with corresponding uncertainty about state and federal support. Differential enrollment and support—deliberately planned and otherwise—have always been a part of the multicampus scene, but by 1975 the problems these factors raise had dramatically increased in intensity. Constant or steady enrollment for the system as a whole almost always entails growth at one campus and decline at another. The result is generally imbalance, never steadiness, and often a turbulence described in at least one system as "street warfare."

Some important generalizations can be made however, drawing from the experience of the nine universities but completely applicable to none, concerning the directions in

---

*These same nine multicampus systems were studied by the authors in 1971. Their findings are presented in *The Multicampus University,* a report published by the Carnegie Commission.

which all multicampus systems must move. (The following generalizations are based on the information presented in six chapters of the report that deal in detail with the situations of each of the individual systems.)

Academic Planning and Program Review

Perhaps the major change across the nine multicampus systems is the dramatically increased emphasis on academic plans and planning procedures. They are now in the mainstream of governance and are the direct concern of chief executives and senior administrators. In 1970, such plans, when they existed, were largely compendia of campus aspirations—public relations statements rather than operational guidelines. Plans still present the public stance of the university, but they also function as working documents that explore options and alternatives among campuses on the basis of realistic demographic and fiscal projections, and they are subject to continuing analysis and revision.

In quantity and quality, the growth of academic program review matches the increased emphasis on planning. In 1970, the focus was limited to new programs, and the important questions were whether a new program was appropriate for a particular campus and whether the campus was academically ready to undertake it. The question of appropriateness has now become very specific, based on examination of student opportunities, similar programs at other system campuses, and supporting programs at the requesting campus. The question of readiness continues to focus on availability of faculty, library, and other appropriate resources. Now, as in the past, the question of where additional resources will come from looms large, but the possible answers are very often narrowed to one: new programs must be funded by reallocation from existing ones. Indeed, the fiscal impact of program change is universally the third critical question posed to proponents of new programs.

Central information systems now play a larger role, providing campuses with a wide range of comparable data about similar programs elsewhere in the system. Although conventional wisdom holds that such systems lead to centralized decisions, experience thus far points instead to more informed decisions on the campuses.

Routine or structured review of existing academic programs is new to most systems and a major change since 1970. Although reviews at the campus level may be undertaken by campus initiative, the emerging system role is to require campus program reviews. Periodic review—usually at five-year intervals—is often required of all programs.

Academic Budgeting

Operating budgets move academic program priorities from rhetoric to reality. Critical in times of growth, budgets are even more important today. In earlier years, continuing expansion meant flexibility, because the average cost of an additional student—a figure used to acquire funds—generally exceeded the actual marginal cost. Growth also meant self-correction, because enrollment increases in a following year caught up with errors in the budget period. Now, additional students are increasingly rare, and if enrollments decline, mechanical adherence to the old formulas could reduce funding below cost savings.

Although good reasons can be stated for changing the relationship, enrollment remains the critical factor in state funding. Both system and state budgetary agencies use enrollment formulas and guidelines of varying complexity. Although formulas may be changing, there is no indication that they will disappear (nor, we should add, that they are being mechanically applied). States have recognized that time is needed to adjust to enrollment changes, and systems have retained the flexibility to shift appropriated funds among campuses and programs to meet changing student demand.

We may expect—and hope—that budgetary procedures will continue to allow the maximum systemwide flexibility consistent with accountability for public funds. The authority of the multicampus system must permit it to encourage one campus to fund and staff programs differently from other campuses; the maintenance of such authority is a prime objective of system administrators.

The analytic capacity of state executive and legislative budgetary agencies is increasing. Although potentially beneficial, the immediate impact is mixed. The boundary between legitimate state fiscal concerns and educational prerogatives of multicampus systems should be defined more explicitly. In some instances, state probes seem unconstrained by an understanding of costs of response or the utility of such probes to senior state officials and budget officers. Staggered response deadlines, avoidance of duplicate inquiries, prior agreement on the precise reason for inquiry and the result desired, and costs and priority of requests should be among the minimal conditions of any state inquiry. Self-restraint on the part of governors, legislators, and their staffs is essential to avoid unnecessary and possibly harmful intervention in the internal management of academic affairs.

Similarly, procedures must be devised to separate educational policy from fiscal decisions wherever possible. The annual or biennial budget will remain the major vehicle for communicating state policy to higher education, but it should not become a catchall for policies which, however worthy, have only peripheral financial implications. For example, budget control language should not be used to mandate a particular organizational structure or staffing pattern within the multicampus system.

Strategies for Program Development

Between 1970 and 1975, systemwide academic activity had increased significantly in three related areas: nontraditional education, multicampus programs (including regional coordination), and innovative and experimental programs. Enrollment and resource constraints had been prime motivating factors for only one of these—multicampus programs. But all three have the potential to increase system effectiveness in a period of fiscal stringency and to enhance learning for the same (or lower) cost.

In 1975, nontraditional education—off-campus, degree-credit programs for part-time students—had become an important activity in only three systems, although it was being discussed in others. However, it holds the promise of permitting low-cost experimentation with new programs and new students without major and permanent resource commitments.

Multicampus academic programs have grown substantially in recent years, and much of this activity is clearly attributable to the need to stretch increasingly limited resources across a wider front. Regional coordination represents the most impressive recent effort in multicampus programs, an effort directly attributable to incentives to avoid unnecessary duplication among neighboring campuses. The role of central administration has been to stimulate development of regional arrangements rather than to manage them. Regional arrangements offer a practical halfway house between campus autonomy and centralized program direction, providing another example of how resource constraints can lead, not to centralization, but to deliberate strategies of decentralization.

Multicampus programs, regionally organized or otherwise, do not necessarily save money but do give students and faculty new program options. From this perspective, they are cost-effective. Such programs should be encouraged by central administrative leadership and by reform of systemwide and campus procedures that unnecessarily inhibit student and faculty mobility and development of joint programs.

Innovative instructional programs—new approaches and experiments in undergraduate education—are a major item on the agenda of systems (as opposed to campuses) in only two or three of the multicampus universities. The action is with faculty and students at the campuses, and this is as it should be. There remains a role for central administration, however, in serving as a catalyst to stimulate innovative activity, communicating experimental results throughout the entire system, providing funding, and—above all—ensuring effective evaluation.

Strategies for Faculty

The most obvious casualty of retrenchment is the faculty member who is laid off or fails to be reappointed because of enrollment cutbacks and resulting fiscal constraints. Less obvious but no less significant is the young Ph.D. who confronts an oversaturated job market and finds his professional career virtually terminated before it starts. For the institution, problems are more subtle. How can a "knowledge industry," as the modern university has been characterized, be made viable without continual introduction of new blood? How can a relatively static and aging faculty effectively deal with changing program emphases and new disciplinary demands? Experience of multicampus systems with such questions is limited, but consciousness is high that answers must be found if the institutions are to meet their responsibilities in the 1980s.

With specific reference to easing the personal trauma of retrenchment, the multicampus system has undoubted advantages. Campuses need adequate lead time to make program and personnel adjustments; time can be obtained by temporary transfers of positions from other campuses, by utilization of a systemwide pool of temporary positions, or by a combination of the two. However, the flexibility of the multicampus system is constrained externally by the need to maintain credibility with state officials who are concerned with imbalance in student-faculty ratios among campuses and internally by pressures from campuses for equity of treatment. Nevertheless, such flexibility is critical if multicampus systems are to operate as systems.

But even the greatest flexibility may not avoid layoffs. Indeed, deliberate program changes can require them. Preparation for possible retrenchment is necessary. The importance, for example, of an acceptable definition of fiscal emergency and of procedures for dealing with such an emergency cannot be overestimated.

Decisions concerning specific faculty are almost always campus matters. While some campus flexibility is permissible, policies and procedures governing these decisions must be generally uniform if systemwide equity is to be maintained and if the system is to withstand legal challenge. Conflicts between seniority and program balance must be resolved, and the outcome must certainly avoid development of a curriculum dominated by tenure considerations. Multicampus administrators, one step removed from the personal pressures of the moment, must monitor campus decisions closely in the interest of program balance.

In all layoff cases, the central administration staff can play a significant role in developing policies and programs concerning intercampus transfers, retraining, and relocation. In general, system policies should require that all campuses give good faith consideration to a person facing layoff from another campus within the system. Existing barriers to intercampus transfer should be eliminated, and procedures should be developed to facilitate it. Tenure, however, should be campus based, not systemwide. Regardless of the theoretical merits of systemwide tenure, we do not think that "mandatory mobility" can be practically implemented.

Many institutions recruited largely from a narrow age group in the 1960s and now have a relatively static and aging faculty. As a result, much greater attention must be given to faculty renewal. This is essentially an issue for departmental and campus resolution, but central administrations of multicampus systems should take the lead by reviewing the staffing patterns on each campus and establishing policies and guidelines.

We concur with the opinion of virtually all systemwide administrators that tenure quotas should not be set at either the system or the campus level. However, we distinguish between quotas, which state that only a fixed proportion of faculty can be advanced to tenure (no such plan exists in any of the nine university systems), and personnel plans that divide faculty positions into two groups, tenure track and temporary. The creation of a campus pool of temporary positions, from which a position can be assigned to a department facing a renewal problem, is an existing strategy that should be carefully considered by all systems as a matter of policy.

Variety in salary procedures and authority among campuses in most systems is as prevalent as it was when we first reported in 1971. In times of increasing concern over compensation brought about by collective bargaining, inflation, and budgetary cutbacks, it is doubtful that unintentional and unmonitored practices will, or should, be allowed to continue. The end result need not be centralization, but should be systemwide insistence that campuses have effective policies and practices that can stand public scrutiny.

Strategies for Students

Compared to other matters included in this study, systemwide activity in student affairs, here limited to admissions and transfers, remains relatively untouched by curtailment of growth. Problems of enrollment pleateaus and declines are largely campus- and program-specific, and there appears little that multicampus systems, as systems, can do about these internal imbalances. Students, unlike budgets, are not readily transferable from one campus to another, and—as with the faculty—forced mobility is simply not an effective strategy.

Declining enrollments can create pressures on campuses to lower requirements to attract students; larger enrollments mean greater budgetary and personnel resources. Unfortunate and unwarranted competition among campuses could be the result. To forestall this, systemwide monitoring and approval of campus undergraduate admission requirements will become essential. Unregulated enrollment competition should not become a substitute for the hard decisions of program and resource allocation that must be made.

These issues bring senior and community colleges into direct contact and possible conflict. Competition for students and programs requires continual review. Systemwide administrations must defend the activities of senior colleges where they are appropriate and curtail them where they are not.

The attraction of campuses, not the central assignment of students, will determine the enrollment future for most institutions. The raison d'etre for the multicampus system should be to increase the quality of campus programs in the face of tight resources and to attract students by promoting the qualities of diversity, specialization, and cooperation.

Systemwide informational programs can help students locate campuses and programs that are most appropriate to their needs and talents. In an era of resource and program constraints, specialized curricula will be concentrated on particular campuses. This, in turn, may lead to a need for selected systemwide programs that cut across specialties and draw upon the resources of the entire system. Central leadership in the recognition and implementation of such opportunities seems to be an essential response to the steady state.

Multicampus Systems in an Unsteady State

The record between 1970 and 1975 supports the theory that many important policy decisions involving public higher education within a state can be more effectively resolved by an educational institution than by arms of state government. The central administrations of multicampus systems may be one step removed from the internal administration of campuses, but they are university systems, not state agencies, and differences between the two are profound.

Nowhere are these differences more apparent than in the fact that, in the face of pressures to centralize, multicampus systems have been unusually sensitive to the values of individual campuses. Often, increased systemwide activity has focused on improving the quality of campus decision making, not on preempting judgments at the system-wide level.

Multicampus systems are in midstream. The expansionist dreams of the 1960s have been left behind and the harsh reality of the 1980s lies ahead. For the foreseeable future, creative use must be made of the unique organizational structure of multicampus administrations, which combines coordination and governance. Coordination implies continuing campus autonomy—the prerogative of the campuses to promote their own institutional style. Governance, on the other hand, implies that the central administration has direct operational responsibility and is accountable to the state for the sum of activity across campuses. The tension between campus and central responsibility cannot be resolved by abandoning either.

While the balance between centralization and campus authority will necessarily vary from system to system, an exemplary model would include the following:

- Continuing and conscious awareness that most decisions, most of the time, are better made at campuses than centrally
- Equal awareness that some decisions—often the hardest ones—must be made by the central administration and the governing board
- The best possible information—historical, current, and projected—about programs and needs, coupled with judicious use of such information for more informed decisions at both campus and systemwide levels
- Flexibility within the multicampus system to employ budgetary resources effectively among campuses—and at the campus level, among programs—to ensure diversity and specialization in a period of increasing fiscal constraints
- Equitable procedures for dealing with personnel retrenchment and positive programs of intercampus mobility to soften the impact of faculty layoffs
- Regional and systemwide academic programs that attract and engage the abilities of faculty and students beyond the horizons of a single campus
- Systemwide capacity—both technical and at the highest policy levels—for institutional self-analysis, evaluation, and change
- Ongoing efforts to mobilize energies of campus administrators, faculty, and students to seek solutions not only at their campuses but within the system as a whole.

Maintaining a balance between the system and the campuses will not be easy. Externally, state budgetary and coordinating agencies will be under pressure to intervene in system affairs. Internally, stability of staffing and—in some institutions—collective bargaining will harden traditional academic conservatism. Necessary flexibility at campus and system levels will be difficult to sustain, and controversy about which level should exercise it will abound. Nevertheless, a balance can be reached. Its achievement will define the success of multicampus systems in the unsteady state of the 1980s.

When Dreams and Heroes Died: A Portrait of Today's College Student. By Arthur Levine. 1980.

This volume is based upon several studies conducted under the auspices of the Carnegie Commission and the Carnegie Council, including national surveys of the undergraduates of 1969 and 1976, a 1978 survey of institutional and student changes since 1969, and visits in 1979 to 26 colleges and universities. In addition, extensive use was made of the Cooperative Institutional Research Program's annual studies of college freshmen.

The reality of the 1960s has already begun to fade. In the passing years, the students of the 1960s have grown larger than life, and their altruism and commitment to change have been exaggerated. Real events are dwarfed by the shadows of yesteryear. Nonetheless, there are differences between college students of today and their counterparts of the 1960s. By way of overview, three changes stand out.

1. The number of college students has increased substantially. In the autumn of 1969, 7,976,834 students were attending American colleges and universities. By 1979 the number was 11,669,429, a rise of 42 percent.
2. The composition of the student body has changed. High-achieving young people with wealthy, well-educated parents are, as in the 1960s, most likely to attend college. But the proportion of enrollment from traditionally underrepresented minority groups—blacks, women, and adults 25 and over, among others—has increased.
3. Student character has changed. Students today are more career oriented, better groomed, more concerned with material success, more concerned with self, and more practical than their counterparts in 1969-70.

The Making of a College Generation

The current generation of American college students came of age during a period of growing pessimism about the nation and its institutions. They entered adolescence between the time Lyndon Johnson's Great Society ended and Gerald Ford's promise to end the Watergate nightmare began. This was a period when national leaders and youth heroes were assassinated, when our cities were burned, when an unpopular war was being fought in Asia, when a Democratic convention was accompanied by rioting, when protesting students were killed by National Guardsmen, when intelligence agencies spied on citizens, when a president and a vice-president resigned from office for separate illegal activities, when some cabinet officers were fired for acts of conscience, and others were tried in the courts for crimes.

These events had a greater impact on this generation than they had for others. Part of the reason is that the protective and potentially moderating social institutions—the family and the schools—most intimately associated with the development of youthful optimism and trust waned in influence during this same period. The family acts less as an isolating protective cocoon today than it once did, and young people experience contact with the real world at an earlier age. The schools have changed in like manner. Where they once provided socialization for the adult world, they now provide an experience more akin to living in it. Young people today have more time for unplanned activities and live in less sheltered environments than their predecessors.

The children born in the late 1950s and early 1960s were the first generation born in the aftermath of home television. The full impact of television is unclear, but it is certain that in its very short history it has become one of the nation's principal baby-sitters, exposing the young to adult issues and problems even in their preschool years, a time once thought more appropriate for fairy tales.

For college students, young and old, all these changes—in society, the family, the schools, and the media—have added up to a sense that things are falling apart. To escape an inhospitable world, college students, like much of the rest of the country, are turning inward. For many, the one remaining refuge is "me." This emphasis on "me" is what differentiates periods of individual ascendancy like the present from periods of community ascendancy such as the early 1960s. The former are present oriented and hedonistic, emphasizing the primacy of duty to oneself; the latter are more future oriented, stressing the primacy of duty to others.

Politics: The Legacy of Vietnam and Watergate

According to today's students, Vietnam and Watergate were the events that most shaped their political and social views. For some (16 percent) who cited Vietnam and Watergate as significant, the result was positive. It encouraged them to consider careers in journalism or politics, engendered a renewed appreciation of ethics, or, when the perpetrators of Watergate were caught, made them think the system was indeed working. But for the majority (52 percent) the effect was negative. They reported being "turned off to politics." Between 1969 and 1978, the percentage of freshmen who considered it essential or very important to keep up with political affairs dropped from 51.4 to 36.6 percent. Student commitment to radical politics has decreased, too. Relative to 1969, fewer students classify themselves as left or right of center. Most say they're smack-dab in the middle.

This shift has been translated into more traditionally conservative stances on off-campus political issues. Today students are more likely to favor the death penalty, less coddling of criminals, alternatives to busing, and increased concern with majority rather than minority rights. Yet exactly the opposite has happened with respect to campus issues, where students are more apt to oppose censorship of student publications, bans on extremist speeches, institutional regulation of student behavior, and compulsory service for students. There is, however, no conflict between these positions. On campus issues, student opinions reflect an increasing interest in protecting their rights, and on the external issues, they reflect a lower level of concern for the welfare of others.

Along with these changes has come a decline in ideological politics of all types. Growing in their place, at a fast pace, is a very different style of political organization, more compatible with the current student mood: self-interest or "me-oriented" groups concerned with protecting or improving the lot of a single class of people, be they blacks, women, Latins, gays, Iranians, or New Yorkers.

The clamor of the 1960s has subsided, the relative quiet of the present has inspired a wave of nostalgia pieces about the activists of yesteryear and a sheaf of obituaries and explanations for the death of student protest. Reports of its demise are premature. It is true that relative to the 1960s the number and intensity of student protests has decreased. Three out of four institutions that were able to compare activity in 1969 and 1978 reported declines. However, the fact that one out of five undergraduates in 1976 had taken part in a demonstration is certainly very tangible proof that student unrest is far from dead.

There has, however, been a sharp shift in protest issues. The three most frequent causes for unrest in 1969 were the war in Vietnam, minority rights, and rules of student conduct. In 1978 they were student fees, institutional facilities, and faculty or staff hiring and firing. The emphasis changed from primarily off-campus issues to seemingly more "me-oriented" internal campus issues.

Changes in protest tactics have been dramatic. There has been a decline in all of the familiar tactics of the 1960s, including building takeovers, strikes, demonstrations, and the destruction of property. Instead, student protesters favor litigation and a variety of other peaceful endeavors. The 1970s witnessed the rise of two nationwide student lobbies—Public Interest Research Groups (PIRGS) and state student associations. PIRGS and student lobbies use a variety of tactics, including lobbying, litigation, media, community organizing, and demonstrations. These activities are more attuned to the current era, when students see less justification for violence, interruption of college classes, or even demonstrations on campus. They are also more practical, more individually oriented, more suitable to causes lacking in popular support, and less risky than the tactics of the 1960s.

Yesterday's omnipresent demand for student power has vanished, and what seemed a preoccupation with campus governance issues in the 1960s has become merely an auxiliary interest. Paradoxically, student attitudes about the role they should play in governance have changed very little over the two periods. Today's students want a slightly larger role in determining admissions policy and faculty appointment and promotion than their predecessors, but are willing to accept somewhat lesser roles in regulating degree requirements, course content, dormitory rules, and student discipline.

Part of the explanation for the change is that student participation in institutional governance has increased substantially since the 1960s. At the same time, an increasingly influential role for student government in establishing campus policy and operation has developed. This was the opinion of over one-third (36 percent) of American college presidents. In fact, five out of six presidents believe student government is at least as influential now as it was in 1969, if not more so.

Today there are more college students than steel workers, coal miners, automobile workers, needle workers, and farmers combined. This makes students not only one of the larger consumer groups, but also one of the potentially strongest voting blocks in the country. There was speculation that 18 year old suffrage would radically alter the face of national politics, but this has not happened. The vote was given to all 18 year olds, not just the third attending institutions of higher education. Even though college students gave a majority of their votes to Jimmy Carter in 1976, the majority of 18 year olds cast ballots for Gerald Ford. There is enormous diversity among young people, more powerful in politics than any shared youth culture. For this generation, national youth heroes are dead or unknown. College students, although as a whole more liberal politically than the general population, are quite politically divided themselves. And they vote in roughly the same low proportions as the general population.

Education: The Great Training Race

When undergraduates were asked what was most essential for them to get out of a college education in 1969, learning to get along with people and formulating values and goals for their lives were ranked first and second. Seven years later, these desires were outranked by getting a detailed grasp of a special field and obtaining training and skills for an occupation. Three-quarters of freshmen report that they are attending college in order to get a better job.

The single most obvious result of this emerging "vocomania" is that students' enrollment patterns have changed. Among subject areas, the big gainers are business, the health professions, biology (the gateway to medical school), agriculture, and other technical fields. Nearly a quarter of all freshmen intend to major in business, which is at the top of the heap; this represents nearly a 50 percent increase relative to 1969. The big losers have been the least occupationally useful fields—education, the humanities, and several of the social sciences.

Having chosen more career-oriented subjects, students are also spending more time studying them. The typical college curriculum is divided into three parts—the major, which has become increasingly career oriented; electives, which students can use to study any subjects they wish; and general education, which has traditionally been the least overtly vocational portion of an undergraduate education, emphasizing instead a broader range of skills and knowledge thought to be needed by all liberally educated people. Compared to the 1960s, students have cut short the amount of time they spend on general education and have used their electives to increase the number of courses in the major. Between 1967 and 1974, the proportion of credits students were taking in their area of concentration increased from 44 to 58 percent. At the same time, general education credits were reduced by more than a fifth. In a free marketplace without requirements the situation would be even more lopsided, since 41 percent of college students feel current degree requirements restrict them from taking as many courses in their major as they would like.

Increased vocationalism should probably not have been a surprise. Today's students are just turning the corner on a decade that brought unchecked inflation, three recessions, and intermittent crises of unemployment. Despite the objective reality of an improved marketplace in which students can sell their job skills today, the experiences of the recent past are still influencing higher education.

Competition is one obvious effect. The war of each against all generates a sense of desperation for many. Cheating and other forms of academic dishonesty have increased slightly since the 1960s. Pressure for grades is enormous. A majority of 1976 undergraduates said they were not doing as well as they would like academically; that they were under a great deal of pressure to get high grades; that it was possible to get good grades without understanding the material in their courses; and that their grades understated the true quality of their work. And one out of every three believed it to be difficult to get good grades and really learn something.

This comes at a time when the nation's campuses, like its high schools, are experiencing grade inflation. Between 1969 and 1976, the proportion of students with A and B grade point averages rose from 35 to 59 percent, and the proportion with averages of C or less declined from 25 to 13 percent. Nonetheless, three out of five college students believe their grades underrate the quality of the course work they produce. What makes the situation even more extraordinary is that today's college students are less well prepared than their predecessors in the 1960s. Undergraduate ability in reading, writing, and arithmetic has plummeted in recent years, as indicated by declining scores on the national college admissions examinations.

On the face of it, the poverty of undergraduate preparation, the race for jobs, the competitive atmosphere on campus, and the pressure for grades would seem to make college a dreadful experience for today's students. Not so. They are more satisfied with college than the students of the 1960s, who also were extremely satisfied. A majority of the undergraduates of the 1970s report being satisfied with college in general, with their majors, with their teaching, and even with the mechanics of grading.

The student of the 1970s is more traditional in academic values than the undergraduate of the last decade and is less interested in seeing things change. The demands of the 1960s for greater relevance, the abolition of grading requirements, and more attention to student emotional growth are less popular among students now. Fewer believe that less emphasis should be placed on specialized training in favor of a broad liberal education or that teaching effectiveness rather than research should be the primary criterion for faculty promotion. Concern with racism on campus is reduced, and fewer students believe special rules should govern minority programs.

This by no means implies a new age of tranquility in the academic kingdom. During campus visits, undergraduates were asked what advice they would give a high school senior planning to attend college. Consumer advice topped the list. Current economic, social, and demographic trends indicate that consumerism will very likely blossom in the next few years, perhaps reaching a peak in 1990, when demographic conditions will be worst for colleges and best for students. In other words, consumerism may well become the rallying cry of students for the next decade and the dominant theme governing college and university education.

Social Life

In the course of this research, students at 26 colleges across the country were asked what people at their schools did for fun. The situation was masterfully, if not originally or grammatically, captured by one student, not overly impressed with the question, who dismissed it, saying, "You know, we all do our own thing."

This is a socially liberal generation. A majority supports expanded roles for women, legalized abortion, and overturning prohibitions on homosexual relations. About half favor legalization of marijuana, liberalization of divorce laws, casual (as distinguished from promiscuous) sexual relationships, and living together before marriage. In fact, this generation is more liberal about such matters than the students of the 1960s were.

It would be a mistake, though, to equate this liberalism with a richer, better, or more vibrant social life. Just the opposite appears true. Current student liberalism is rooted in issues of personal freedom; that is, the rights of individuals to pursue their own lives without the encumbrance of external restrictions. The emphasis is upon "me," not "us." This tends to be a solitary perspective, not that of a group.

Factors that discourage social life include the rising proportions of part-time and older, working undergraduates; commuter students; and married students. Larger portions of the student body spend less time at college, have well-developed social lives before enrolling, and have other concerns outside of college that are of equal or greater importance to them.

All of this is not to say that college social life is dead. College social life today looks more like the 1960s than it looks different. Nonetheless, new activities are continually becoming fashionable, and old ones passé. With colleges and universities as with a kaleidoscope, the pieces remain the same, but their configuration is always changing. The qualities of diversity, individualism, escapism, and searching stand out more distinctly in today's configuration than they did ten years ago.

Diversity is apparent in the plethora of activities students enjoy and the conditions that prevent some of them from pursuing a campus social life. Students are more different from one another than before. They are a body of individuals with little sense of a shared collegiate culture; a group for which both drinking and praying are growth industries; a group with very liberal attitudes about personal freedoms. Even in the group activities they pursue, the self stands out. The increased competition of the classroom is the increased competition of the playing field. Escapism and searching are inseparably intertwined. The rationales students offer for participation in current health and religious movements confirm this.

Riding First Class on the Titanic

College students indicate that they are optimistic about their personal futures, but pessimistic about the future of the country. There is a sense among today's undergraduates of being passengers on a sinking ship, a Titanic if you will, called the United States or the world. And the current fatalism is fueling a spirit of hedonism. There is a growing belief among college students that, if they are doomed to ride on the Titanic, they should at least ride first class.

Going first class takes big bucks. Today's college students know it and are more interested in doing something about it than their predecessors; so say a majority of freshmen. This past decade witnessed a one-third increase in the proportion of first-year students for whom being well-off financially is an essential or very important objective.

The magic word in career choice today is "professional." Relative to the late 1960s, accounting, business, law, optometry, pharmacy, and most other professions that are not at the bottom of the job market are growing. Part of the allure of management or the professions, aside from money, is the glitter of status, personal recognition, and professional acclaim. The nonmaterial is less important to current students than it was to their counterparts in the 1960s. Freshmen now are much less interested in developing a philosophy of life. Perhaps if one believes that one is riding on a doomed ship, a philosophy of life becomes meaningless.

Undergraduates express a sense of being alone, which should not be confused with being lonely. Only three out of ten would describe themselves as such, and that represents a slight decrease over 1969. Students are proud of being able to withstand the accidents of fate independently, but at the same time they are sad that they have to do so.

Attitudes toward marriage and child-rearing are a good reflection of this. No more than a handful of the women participating in the campus interviews said marriage was their prime goal after college. Six out of ten college freshmen now say raising a family is very important or essential to them. A decade ago, seven out of ten felt this way. Having children was not a topic included in student group interviews conducted for this book, but it came up repeatedly. It was always brought up in the same way. When asked about future plans, a woman would occasionally say, almost as an afterthought, "I certainly don't want children." The idea of not having children wasn't particularly noteworthy. What stood out instead was the anger and vehemence of the women, most of whom seemed quite apolitical. Behind each statement was a feeling of being victimized—by men who will not share half the responsibility for raising children, by a society so horrid as to make it undesirable for mothers to bring their children into the world, and by the children themselves, who will halt their mothers' careers and put a serious crimp in their social lives. If college students have anything in common today, it is certainly a deep fear of becoming one of the victims. This is a theme that pervades their political, educational, and social lives.

A Retrospective

White males of upper- and middle-class background are culturally, if no longer numerically, the dominant campus group, a pattern broken only during major wars. And the reasons for attending college haven't changed very much, even if the preferences among them and the character of the colleges themselves have. Similarly, student activism existed in the earliest colleges and continues to the present. Then as now, activists comprised only a minority of undergraduates. The extracurricular life of students continues to supplement the academic life of the college. Fraternities, which date back to the eighteenth century, are alive and well today. And residential college life remains vibrant, though a bit worse for wear. In these ways, the post-1960s generation is precisely like all of the students who have come before them.

Times have changed, however. Our nation has gone through alternating periods that might be called wakeful and restful. Periods of waking are change oriented and reform minded; they are what were described earlier as times of community ascendancy. In this century, there have been three such periods—the progressive era (1904 to World War I), the Roosevelt/depression years (1932 to World War II), and the "1960s" (1957 to the Vietnam war). They tend to be times offering a sense of movement, excitement, adventure, and perhaps even magic. Their theme is promise, and their leaders are charismatic.

Periods of rest occurred after World War I, after World War II, and after the Vietnam war. These are times in which people are tired, having been asked, if necessary, to give their own lives, their families' lives, or their friends' lives to fight a war. People want a break. Thoughts and actions that were directed outward turn inward to concerns that may have been neglected—to getting one's life or the life of one's family in order. These are times that were referred to earlier as periods of individual ascendancy. The emphasis is on pragmatism. Such periods promise personal freedom, and their leaders are usually managers who can solve problems while allowing the public to rest.

Colleges, like all other social institutions, and students, like the rest of the population, follow these cycles. General student character varies from periods of community ascendancy to periods of individual ascendancy. In the current period of individual ascendancy, this generation is more like the students who came to higher education in the years immediately following World War I and World War II and their 1960s counterparts. The undergraduates of the 1960s similarly had a much greater resemblance to their progressive and New Deal era predecessors. This is not to say any of these college generations are exactly alike, but rather that they share certain broad commonalities.

Unique Aspects of the Post-1960s College Generation

The times. While the periods immediately following World Wars I and II brought the nation some rest, the 1970s were different. The anticipated rest never came or was continually interrupted. When people are denied rest, they become irritable, anxious, apathetic, and disoriented. One sees these characteristics today in both the country and its college students. The post-1960s college generation has endured restlessness for a longer period than any other group in this century. This may provide some explanation for the pervasive apathy among college students today, as well as the Titanic mentality.

Size. The post-1960s college generation is the largest ever to enter higher education. It is without a doubt more heterogeneous in background and experience than any of its predecessors. There is to this extent less of a shared collegiate culture than there was for previous generations.

Politics. Current undergraduates are more conservative politically and more liberal socially than in the 1960s. But students are in almost exactly the same place they were politically and socially in the 1960s relative to the adult population. This means that both students and the public have shifted to more conservative political attitudes and more liberal social opinions in the 1960s, but relative to one another there has been little change.

    Nonetheless, there are some very real differences that distinguish the post-1960s generation from its predecessors. Students today are more powerful politically both on and off campus than any other student generation has ever been. They are the first generation to have the vote and to live in a time when the principle of in loco parentis is moribund. Politically, student organizations are more powerful and effective than any of the groups that came before them. Ironically, as the base of student political power expands with increasing enrollment, so does the diversity that gives this generation less in common to work for. The focus on self, which divides students politically, will pass with time, but it seems quite likely that for the next decade diversity will increase with a concomitant decline in student political coherence and effectiveness.

Socialization. The family and the schools have had less influence in shaping the post-1960s college generation than its predecessors. And the media, particularly television and other nonprint forms, have contributed to the development of young people more than ever before. The future promises a continuation of this trend.

Longevity. The post-1960s college generation will live longer than the students who went to college before it. This means that they will probably need and perhaps even want new types of education—vocational instruction tied to a longer career, perhaps with more varied jobs comprising that career; knowledge and skills that will help them cope with a changing world; and postcollege study opportunities of all types.

A Recommendation

This generation is no better or worse than any other. And despite its similarities to others, it is different. Generational differences flow from generational needs. The post-1960s college generation has serious educational needs, including education that:

- Teaches people the skills of reading, writing, arithmetic, speaking, problem solving, lifelong learning, garbage sorting (the ability to identify the drivel, exaggerations, and untruths that we hear and read each day), and survival (how to cope with a rapidly changing environment)
- Emphasizes our common humanity and is concerned with our common problems
- Stresses values and ethics
- Prepares students for a career, not a specific job.

On Higher Education. By David Riesman. 1980

The Decline of Faculty Hegemony
and the Rise of Student Power

Between students and teachers, as between students and parents and other adults, an enormous variation in the degree of adult hegemony has existed through the ages and across cultures. For example, in some colleges in the United States, students have been almost totally subordinate to faculty assessments and have sought to internalize faculty values. However, we have now entered an era in the United States and in other Western industrial societies in which probably no more than 10 to 15 percent of students in post-secondary institutions enter willingly and wholeheartedly into such a regime of discipleship. Instead, two major phenomena have altered the relative power of the student estate vis-à-vis the faculty estate, vastly increasing the power of students.

One of these factors is loosely described by the term "the counterculture"—an ideological movement toward freedom from all restraints upon individual behavior—coupled with the creation of institutional forms to defend student rights. The counterculture, unlike, for instance, student protests against the Vietnam war, has not been an ephemeral movement, but rather one that has profoundly changed our whole society. Whereas in an earlier day it was an affair of the affluent, bitterly resented by stable working-class and middle-class students as well as their parents, like other movements in an egalitarian society the counterculture has been downwardly mobile, influencing the sexual and pharmacological behavior of once-resistant social-class cohorts.

The second factor is demographic. By the middle 1970s enrollments began to taper off and, among white males, actually to fall. All but a relatively small number of highly attractive and over-applied institutions discovered that it would not be possible to restore requirements that had been abandoned in the earlier era of protest. The main political strength within most institutions increasingly became that of the educational customer. In private as well as in public institutions, the faculty depended for personal and departmental survival on their attractiveness to students whose relative market power increased as their numbers began to decline.

I view neither a situation of total student subordination to faculty nor the reverse as idyllic. When student customers were plentiful, they were often mistreated and short-changed. Today, in an era of increased student hegemony, students are not always wise in the use of their greatly enhanced market power and short-change themselves. Like any other interest group, the student estate often does not grasp its own interests, and those who speak in its name are not always its friends. Yet at the same time faculty often become subordinated and victimized in a situation where market forces may dictate not only whole curricula but modes of individual instruction as well. The problem is made more difficult by the absence of suitable terms in which to describe the relation between students and academic institutions. Students are not only consumers; they are also producers of their own education—active agents who are not simply buying a service, but occupying a locale that makes possible the development of powers that depend in considerable part on their own capacities, wise choice, and degree of commitment; a locale that provides opportunities for stretching their individual powers of curiosity, intellectual

Note: This summary was prepared by the Carnegie Council staff on the basis of a preliminary manuscript and thus may not reflect the final organization but only suggest its contents.

excitement, and esthetic enjoyment, and hence increases their potential for a satisfying if not a self-satisfied life.

Inroads of the Counterculture

Among the student activists of the 1960s, there were very few who had unequivocally political and revolutionary aims, even though they might use slogans that had a revolutionary ring. They wanted freedom from the pressures they were under; their cry was "liberation," by which they meant personal liberation quite as much as cohort liberation. At the outset, the counterculture and political activism seemed to be allied: Both movements sought freedom from the constraints of university life, whether in the curriculum or in the extracurriculum. By the 1970s, especially in the nonelite colleges and universities, it had become clear that the counterculture, which promised liberation, had a much more potent impact and longer staying-power than activism, which promised hard work and repeated frustrations. Liberation—sexual, parietal, pharmacological—was attractive also to all but a handful of activists; and in the end the counterculture won out and has made its way throughout the society.

Many books have been written about the impact of the counterculture, the political protests, and the reforms in academic governance and curriculum during the 1960s and thereafter. I can only touch briefly here on some ways in which meritocracy was undermined as a result. Readers are familiar with the phenomenon of grade inflation, in which a C became, in effect, a failing grade. In addition to grade inflation, there came into being what might be termed the sanitized transcript, from which all failing grades were erased if students managed on repeated trials to pass a course; similarly, courses taken pass/no credit were simply eliminated if the student's performance did not meet the minimal requirement of a pass. However, by concealing the length of time taken for completion of a course, some information is withheld that may be relevant in some settings: We may want to know how fast a person learns as well as how much has eventually been learned.

One might also speak of diploma inflation as a result of the pressure to give course credit to remedial work, first demanded by and on behalf of underprepared blacks and then by other nonwhites similarly handicapped by family background and the inadequacies of previous schooling. It would have been better if, rather than condescending to these students and giving college-level credit for non-college-level work, one had asked them to take more time to get a baccalaureate, which would have been a more reliable indication of college-level performance. Some blacks demanded that they receive college-level credit for work physically done in postsecondary institutions, believing that it would be humiliating to do remedial noncredit work, and not seeing the humiliation involved in the concession of a regular grade for work that—the boundaries are concededly fuzzy—had not previously been regarded as college-level.

Meritocratic standards were not only fuzzy at the edges, but the whole structure of college credits based simply on time served had been built on tradition and tacit faculty norms. It did not take long for the very term "standards" to become a term of abuse, like "elitism," and since the rationale for grades and credits had been tacit, adversary attitudes within the faculty could, with varying degrees of difficulty, remove the legitimacy of prevailing conventions.

At the same time, the combination of political turmoil and countercultural flamboyance brought about a backlash against colleges and universities from legislators and influential constituents that succeeded in mandating increased teaching loads for faculty and increased accountability in terms of contact hours and systemwide managerial controls. These, in turn, led to further deprofessionalization at many institutions where the faculty felt under pressure not only from student customers, but from legislatures, state coordinating councils, and systemwide multicampus management. The faculty reaction to such monitoring was either sly resistance, as when supervision of a single thesis was registered as a course in order to meet the required number of hours, or the more open resistance of unionization. For many faculty, unionization was seen as protection not only against what they regarded as the arbitrariness of presidents, trustees, systemwide managers, and legislatures, but also against being completely subject to the whims of the student marketplace.

Impact of Demographic Decline

When the demographic curve began in the 1970s to make a dent on the euphoria of academic administrators, and they realized that there would be no vast increase in the proportion of high school graduates attending college, the belief grew that recruiting adults for evening or weekend or learning-at-a-distance programs would replace the youth cohort aged 18 to 24, which had previously been considered as the appropriate group for college attendance. In the funding formulae that had been set up in the immediate post-World War II period of expansion based on full-time equivalent (FTE) students, however, no thought had been given to the problems of additional expense imposed by adult students who could attend only part-time and perhaps take no more than a course every term, but who would cost as much to process and service as full-time students.

In the marketing scramble for students that has resulted, we have come full circle from the efforts of men like James Bryant Conant at Harvard to extend the reach of formerly regional universities to a nationwide clientele. In doing so, they invaded local catchbasins and forced local institutions to recruit more widely if they were to maintain or increase their share of the student market. This was when students were plentiful. Now, when students of all ages are eagerly sought for, every institution, at least within its geographic orbit, is in competition with almost every other.

Within institutions, one consequence of faculty efforts to conform to student tastes as enrollments drop is an excessive homogeneity of teaching styles. While this may appear to please the majority of students, there is no single all-purpose style that is satisfactory for all, and any one style is sure to be unsuitable for perhaps a substantial minority of students. Still another consequence is an increasing danger that student evaluations of faculty will be manipulated by individual faculty, faculty cliques, and student-faculty cadres as the dramatic fall in enrollments makes retention and the rare chance for tenure increasingly precarious. Like most of us, faculty almost invariably want to be liked, and whatever their personal tastes they must generally court the student vote, often with desperation. Students, like other Americans, tend to underestimate their influence where it is not associated with formal decision-making power; yet in many cases students do in fact help decide cases of retention or promotion through informal means as well as through formal evaluation procedures.

Some Hazards of Student Consumerism

It is an interesting question why students courted as they now are by colleges and thus possessing increased market power are on occasion so gullible about purchasing the important and useful tool of a college education. One reason is that many are insecure, and if a college goes after them hard they take it as a sign that they are really being courted. In spite of the deluge of promotional material they may have received, they prefer to believe that they have been selected, not that they are just one more body to be counted in a formula or for the student grants they can bring with them to help support a tuition-dependent private college. They have a vested interest in refusing to recognize their market power. Thus, even though not all apparent overselling results in a mismatch of student and institution, in a situation where so much fraud is possible it is natural that activists as well as state and federal officials want to intervene to protect the student consumer.

History is full of instances in which activists who have spoken in the name of a cohort have not always served the cohort optimally. Ralph Nader's attack on the Educational Testing Service (ETS) is one recent example. He is joined here by "revisionist" sociologists and historians who interpret the tests of the College Entrance Examination Board as an attempt to stratify students without knowledge of their history. In attacking the College Boards as culturally biased, those who speak in the name of blacks—whether blacks themselves or white radicals—have done a disservice to blacks. They have led not only to mismatching of blacks at high-pressure, predominantly white institutions, but they have made it appear that blacks get admitted to college on the basis of color and not on the basis of competence. The likeliest alternative to the tests may not only be recruitment identified solely by color and for "body count" to meet pressures for an appropriate number of disadvantaged students, but may also involve misleading blacks themselves as to where they might best pursue at least the first part of their postsecondary education.

The College Board was originally set up in order to avoid individual examinations by every single faculty member of a major institution and to avoid university attempts to accredit high schools. The nationalism of college attendance would not have been possible without the College Board, now joined by the American College Testing Program. By eliminating Greek and Latin as prerequisites, the College Board made all subjects equal; thus all high schools could enter the competition and, while this may have resulted in some dilution, it was the opposite of an effort to stratify.

One great advantage of the tests for all who are likely to be discriminated against is precisely their neutrality as far as high schools go. I have observed many cases where guidance counselors and headmasters sought to prevent the admission of students to selective colleges and would have succeeded if they had been the only source of information without evidence of the College Board's tests themselves.

There is further advantage in the Scholastic Achievement Tests (SATs) in comparison to the subject-matter tests, which were once the only ones used by the College Board; namely, that they free students from having to obey a particular division of labor in high school subjects. As tests of general intellectual ability without being completely content-free, the SATs help students who, for idiosyncratic reasons, have not wanted to subordinate themselves to particular teachers in their high schools, or who have been bored because of the slow pace of work or other less valorous reasons. The Graduate Record Examination (GRE) serves in the same way to free students from particular pedants and pressure groups in departments in liberal arts colleges—at many colleges, students do better in the GREs without having taken a particular subject than those who have majored in the subject.

Benefits of Student Power in Expanding the Curriculum

The new nonaffluent black and, more recently, Spanish-speaking students who sought admission to predominantly white universities in the 1960s and 1970s attempted to expand the curriculum to include black studies, ethnic studies, or an amalgam of "third-world" studies. Many wanted to have their presence recognized on campus in the regular curricular offerings, pointing out not incorrectly that there was already room for East Asian studies, Middle Eastern studies, and other area programs. Universities had expanded to include an enormous variety of subjects desired by some class of customers; why should these new customers not also be entitled to their share of the academic offerings?

Another area where student pressure has increased offerings that have enriched otherwise dehydrated curricula has been in the arts. It is difficult for traditional faculty and older alumni to grasp the fact that these can be serious subjects pursued in a determined and disciplined way, yet it is hard to find any students who work with greater ardor and zest, sometimes around the clock. Ironically, the very seriousness with which students pursue these subjects sometimes has led to objections from both faculty and some fellow students: namely, that their work is too professionalized, driving out amateur students and going too far to prepare them for immediate postbaccalaureate vocations. One cannot tell from content alone what is or is not a subject that is excessively professional. And what matters most for student consumers is to find a proper balance between work they can do in college that they can employ immediately on graduation and work that has a far longer horizon in time and place, adding to their curiosity and historical and cross-cultural knowledge.

Student Choice at Evangelical Colleges and Community Colleges

The one category of institution where the academic revolution of faculty hegemony made least headway, namely, the Protestant evangelical colleges, is still the arena in which students with greater or lesser willingness subordinate themselves to the authority—moral or spiritual, and not purely academic—of the institution and its faculty. These evangelical institutions differ very much from each other, though they are frequently stereotyped as academic and cultural backwaters by students and faculty at cosmopolitan institutions. In many curricular matters, these institutions are flexible—in part because they know what they are trying to do and hence are not threatened; in part because of collegial cohesiveness; and in some cases because the president and board of trustees exercise more authority over faculty than is true elsewhere where the academic revolution fully triumphed. For example, their flexibility in adapting innovations such as computer-assisted instruction or in meeting students' interests reflects the relative weakness of the departmentalism that hedges administrative leadership in major secular institutions.

Another of the virtues these institutions possess is that they serve as decompression chambers that make the passage from home to the larger world less traumatic for the shy and the provincial. All of the dozens of sects that established their own colleges were creating what might be thought of as halfway houses—even for the half of their students who do not stay through to the baccalaureate—that at once try to keep young people in the fold and attempt to make them sufficiently au courant with contemporary scientific knowledge and changing aesthetic conventions that they will not leave to attend secular colleges.

Although the evangelical colleges enroll but a small fraction of the postsecondary student body, they illustrate the limits of sovereignty based on students' market power in a dramatic way: They are, for the most part, tuition-dependent, and yet they retain nearly complete institutional authority.

In contrast, the public community colleges, recently the fastest growing segment of American postsecondary education, are by nature subject to consumer power. Their faculty have not lost hegemony because they never had it; but not only have they been subject to the authority of the administration, often headed by hard-driving and entrepreneurial presidents, but also to that of an increasingly far-flung network of students of all ages and virtually every conceivable interest, whom the faculty is hired to serve. The increasing market power of students makes traditional faculty at the multiversity resistant and resentful; they feel that they did not enter academic life to teach basketweaving (to use a common example) or to be part of an institution where basketweaving earns as many credits as physical chemistry. The community college, however, has never set such limits as to what is appropriate: defining its missions as service to the community, it exists to supply whatever is demanded, and to create demand by imaginative supply. Apart from its transfer students, who may have to meet certain minimal requirements at four-year institutions—a diminishing constraint as these four-year institutions become more and more eager for students—the community college has always offered students what many see as a virtue: namely, minimal commitment—the very opposite of the subordination demanded both by institutions that experienced the academic revolution and by those that maintained the combination of academic and religious authority of the evangelical colleges.

Burton Clark has described the community colleges as a way of convincing the lower socioeconomic strata that they can have a crack at higher education, while gently persuading them that they are not college material. Yet community college counselors and faculty often struggle in vain to retain students who approach the community college in an experimental and tentative way, but, having already learned to dislike school and to mistrust themselves as scholars, are ready to take flight at the first sign of difficulty or defeat.

Faculty Demoralization and Student Initiative

Like the evangelical colleges, community colleges are in a sense sui generis. Since the academic revolution scarcely touched them, the academic counterrevolution of student market power has had only marginal consequences for them. The feelings of victimization endemic for the faculty of most under-applied four-year institutions will develop in community colleges only as more and more faculty who are unable to get positions in four-year institutions gravitate toward them.

In contrast with the traditional careers of most community college faculty, a large proportion of the faculty of four-year colleges and universities began their careers with the aim of at least transmitting, if not advancing, their discipline. They do not enjoy regarding themselves as marketers of product lines, and they share the belief that too many concessions have been made to student sovereignty, to the disadvantage of the students and with the result of ruthless competition for student favor among faculty and departments. Concessions, once made, tend to become institutionalized; one reason it is now so difficult to reverse these concessions, apart from the investments as well as the benefits faculty have received from them, has to do with the democratization of internal governance that proceeded more or less at the same time. Apart from particular views expressed by, for example, junior faculty or activist students, the mere fact that the number of constituencies involved in making a decision is larger than in the 1950s inevitably means that even seemingly minor decisions take a great deal of time and may involve adversary and combative discussions that some faculty members find distasteful. Thus, scholarly and thoughtful individuals tend to withdraw from all levels of the decision-making process, and the achievement of curricular coherence becomes even less likely. We are living today in an era of political and pedagogic protectionism. The mood of the country is opposed to adventure and experiment except in foreign affairs, where a xenophobic recklessness is often manifest. For individuals who are still concerned with change, one result has been to internalize the desire for change—to seek to realize one's own potentialities as an individual, rather than as a member of a social or communal group. Even on campuses where most students are heavily oriented toward apparently vocationally useful courses there remains a flourishing interest in the arts and a turning away from sociology, planning, and urban studies toward psychology and non-curricular experiments in self-realization.

At its best, this inward turning has a certain monastic quality that is not isolating but seeks a few like-minded persons with whom to develop, for example, a work-sharing group. At its worst, the inward turn takes forms variously described as the new narcissism, me-ism, or heightened egocentrism. In either case, the world at large is given up as a lost cause, and the focus is on the self or on small groups.

Long before the present period of stasis and low morale in academia, I became convinced that students could do more to improve their own education than reformers of institutions could ever accomplish. I have followed the lead of Everett Hughes in dividing academic institutions into four categories. In the first, small in number but large in influence, students have to make an effort to avoid acquiring an education. These are the institutions where students are subordinate to faculty hegemony and have internalized faculty values. The second and far larger category—one that would include most major state universities, most private research universities, and those liberal arts colleges not included in the first group already mentioned—are institutions where the student has a fairly even chance of getting an education. The opportunities and facilities are there, and no obstacles to exploiting them exist, but one can get by without doing so. The third category includes the majority of institutions: namely, the unselective state and regional comprehensive colleges and universities and the almost entirely unselective private institutions. At these institutions, one has to make an effort to discover an education. At first glance, the peer culture appears wholly philistine and the faculty culture either philistine or indifferent or both. It is in such institutions that an honors program may rescue individual students, bringing them together with like-minded fellows they might not otherwise meet and with faculty intellectuals who would otherwise give up students as beyond redemption. The fourth category—of which I have yet to discover an example—is the residual one where, no matter what the effort of the student, it is impossible to get an education.

In colleges of the first type, where students have to work hard to avoid getting an education, they can still be passive. Student involvement in research is probably the easiest way a student can be turned from a passive consumer and absorber to an active agent, but a quite different way is through learning a foreign language and then making use of it, for example, in tutoring in bilingual schools or in travel abroad. A student exploring another culture who is fluent or becoming fluent in its language is no tourist. He or she is an active agent seeking to understand the ways of different peoples—an activity without which it seems to me impossible to have an adequate understanding of one's own country.

Some students have concluded that a vocational curriculum will not necessarily provide them with meaningful work; they know from summer and part-time jobs that they can make a living, and they look to college as supportive of interests that only in the rarest case will serve both as a vocation and as labor—this is one source, for example, of enrollments in the performing arts, not only among affluent students who can afford the risks, but among students in unselective colleges who can least afford the pleasures. In a way, their participation is a flight from the preoccupation with social relevance of the

1960s, an aspect of the turning inward already referred to, but it lacks the narcissistic implications that the latter often has when immediate gratification is sought rather than durable furniture for the mind and the artist's craft.

For that small minority of students who are self-starters, the new cultural freedoms that triumphed in the 1960s provide a way to explore both themselves and the greatly expanded curricular and extracurricular milieux, opportunities that are at once awesome and inspiring. If one follows the "little magazines" of poetry, photography, or criticism published today by undergraduates working together with faculty, one can find work of quite remarkable quality, often at a level of sophistication far beyond that of earlier student generations. Many of these students are not activist and therefore are regarded as apathetic by people who judge them from the vantage point of the activists of the late 1960s. But if one thinks of activity in less time-bound and ideological terms, these students are as active as any who have ever been in attendance at American colleges and universities.

But today many liberal arts colleges are filled with students for whom college is rarely a place for intellectual activity, but rather a way-station en route to medical school, law school, or other postbaccalaureate or professional work. These students are active in the sense of hard-working, but they are passive in the sense of not taking control of their own education apart from calculations as to what will best serve their postbaccalaureate vocational interests. It would be absurd to blame such students for running scared in the face of an uncertain occupational future. But it is also important to realize that, even if requirements are reimposed, they will simply go through the motions of fulfilling them. They will be passive in the sense that they will not be intellectually engaged with what they are studying. Such intellectual engagement has never been common among students in the United States, whose aims have always been, like that of most of those teaching them, either directly or covertly pragmatic and utilitarian. If one asks how we can inculcate the qualities of active responsiveness, alertness to the world, curiosity, and willingness to learn from all sources, whether approved or otherwise, I have few answers. But desirable outcomes do occur, and they are more likely at some institutions than at others.

If there must be a trade-off between faculty time spent in formal teaching and faculty time spent in advising students as to their college programs and their future careers, I believe the latter is of greater value. At most large institutions, faculty advising of students is at best an embarrassment and at worst a disgrace. My own general conclusion is that advising is the weakest link in the whole undergraduate process. Even though faculty advisors have had no special training in counseling, they can at least learn how to become switchboards to others who can be more helpful on specific problems.

Maintaining Diversity of Options
and Consistency of Standards

Because of the competitive market situation and its consequence for curricula and faculty attitudes, there are certain kinds of educational options that exist today only in small supply. An unusual student who seeks a coherent undergraduate curriculum has few places to choose from, and most of them are private. Among public institutions, the competition has led to a certain isomorphism as they compete by offering what their competitors offer, at least in name, rather than a specialty product that would limit their market. Furthermore, colleges that depend heavily on commuter students feel they must offer the fullest possible range of programs for students tied by residence, job, or marriage to particular localities. To offset this trend, the stronger and more attractive public universities could create voluntary islands of coherence as an option. A number of public institutions have created special colleges or programs emphasizing a core curriculum, but with varying degrees of success. Generally these have been residential universities where the costs for out-of-state students often approach those of the less costly institutions in the private sector. This is a severe limitation on nominal freedom of choice, especially in the light of the fact that, even for in-state students, most state universities offer relatively low tuition but cannot meet the costs of travel and subsistence, let alone those of foregone income.

States affect student choice by the amount of subsidy they provide for public institutions and, in a rare handful of states, by subsidy for private institutions. Similarly, the federal government has a decisive impact on the choices students make by means of its financial aid. Thus, the GI Bill of Rights after World War II, which paid students' tuitions wherever they went, allowed choice among not only private institutions of high selectivity but out-of-state institutions as well. In part because of institutions that abused the opportunity by raising their tuitions and otherwise deceiving veterans concerning available courses and facilities, later legislation has been much more restrictive, largely confining the Vietnam war veterans to public institutions.

When the Veteran's Administration had to decide after World War II which educational institutions were to be defined as entitled to the payment of veterans' tuition, it turned to the six regional accrediting associations that cover the country. These associations had fairly extensive experience visiting institutions to see whether they obeyed what were then fairly standard definitions of a college, such as possessing a library with a certain number of books, covering recognized arts and sciences subjects, and having some kind of procedure for the admission of students and approving their passage by stages to either the associate or the baccalaureate degree. As attacks on traditional post-secondary education mounted in the 1960s and as a number of new, nontraditional institutions began, these accrediting associations did not want to appear to stifle potentially valuable experiments. They made clear that their own mission was to be defined in terms of the mission of the institution itself. For example, they would attempt to discover whether a contract system of learning in comparison with the traditional graded pattern of examinations lived up to its own imperative to possess quality control.

Many federal officials dismissed the regional accrediting associations as private and voluntary organizations representing the interests of the academic, not-for-profit institutions and of necessity adversary to those of students. The opponents of reliance on accreditation to monitor abuses in the practices of colleges and universities, insofar as these affect students, noted that if accreditation was intended to see whether an institution lives up to the goals it has set for itself, in theory, at least, these goals could be lax and cursory, and accreditation could come to be virtually automatic.

To improve the performance of the regional associations, it would seem desirable to greatly expand the number of judicious faculty who could offer their services on visiting teams. Furthermore, a valuable use of a small amount of federal and perhaps also foundation support would be to strengthen the staffs of the accrediting associations so that the management of the whole process of accreditation could be improved by more careful selection of teams, workshops for the preparation of neophyte team members, and more careful scrutiny of those accreditation reports that might ordinarily lead to accreditation but perhaps raise questions requiring another visit to the institution.

State Licensing and Federal Intervention

The voluntary accrediting associations deal only with those postsecondary institutions we think of ordinarily as colleges or universities—institutions governed by boards of trustees or their equivalent, and run not for profit but for a presumed public purpose. States license schools of cosmetology, mortuary science, hairdressing, tavern keeping, and a host of other activities, and some states are lax when it comes to regulating such proprietary institutions. The vagaries of underenforcement of state licensing are compounded by the boundary-hopping institutions that, licensed and even given regional accreditation in one area, set up shop in other jurisdictions, often with no notice to local authorities.

I can offer no ready solution for the lacunae in this process of regulation. Up to this time, however, the dangers of further government regulation to already threatened academic standards seem to me to outweigh the benefits in preventing harm to particular students by fraudulent and boundary-hopping institutions. However, it is necessary to put aside those cases of fraud where the purchaser of educational credentials is not deceived; these are the instances of diploma mills, where the "student" is buying a credential. The fraud here is not on the buyer but is on other properly credentialed persons who are in competition with people possessing spurious degrees, and on the general public, which may also be deceived by such degrees. Clearly, state legislation and enforcement should put such enterprises out of business; if such enterprises do business across state lines, perhaps the post office can also act as an enforcement agency.

There is, admittedly, a gray area where external degree programs demand a certain amount of work by correspondence and perhaps a brief visit to the nearest branch of far-flung campuses and allow the doctorate to be "earned" on the basis of truly minimal performance. Even here, there is no fraud on the student consumer who knows what he or she is buying, often at quite large fees, in order to continue to work and reside full-time somewhere else while picking up a credential that will bring added income and status.

In 1976, the Fund for the Improvement of Postsecondary Education helped support the creation of the National Movement for Better Consumer Choice in Higher Education, one aim of which has been to increase the veracity and clarity of information in college catalogs. Its ideal has been a catalog certified by an independent auditor as containing accurate information on such matters as tuition throughout a four-year sequence (and refund policy in case of withdrawal), the kinds of programs offered by the college, rates of attrition, the jobs and postbaccalaureate education pursued by graduates, and other more or less "hard" data concerning the range of students' test scores so as to avoid gross mismatching of student and college.

But as an attempt to control fraudulent marketing practices and the mismatching of student and institution, the improvement of catalogs is a very limited remedy. The process of preparing audited catalogs may be useful to institutions, but it is not clear to what extent students and even guidance counselors will even look at them. For one thing, students do not read them. For another, most students choose institutions, in the minority of instances where there really are choices, on the basis of what students tell each other, or what alumni say, or what recruiters may say in private—and none of this can be monitored. Even at the most selective colleges, one often finds students who are attracted to the institution by its reputation or because their friends are going, regardless of the fact that, in the field of their particular interest, the institution may be deficient.

There is much more information available to students, counselors, parents, and others who have a hand in students' college choices than is currently made use of. Any federal effort to insist on more accurate information is likely to be successful only in the case of the grossest and most obvious frauds, where for example proprietary institutions promise sure-fire job placements when in fact their record in this respect is poor, or in helping protect foreign students from institutions eager to fill their underenrolled dormitories as well as classrooms. There may also be methods of controlling certain unethical practices that are becoming more common, such as using students as recruiters and paying them bounties. Auditing of the colleges' books would uncover such practices, and student complaints on the part of those recruited in this way might also come to the attention of federal agencies.

The Role of Government in Improving Counseling

It is convenient for activist student leaders and for those who speak on behalf of students to behave as if students are an oppressed cadre. But the argument of this volume is that, as valued customers in the vast majority of institutions that are increasingly underenrolled, students currently have the upper hand even where they do not have formal power. And when, as in the case of aggressive academic marketing, there are undoubted abuses, more government regulation will probably be less effective than government support for improved counseling. Considerable effort has gone into ways of improving the written information that colleges give to students and hence to improve the matching (which is now so often happenstance) between a particular student and a particular institution. But such efforts are probably fruitless for that growing cohort of students for whom the nearby community college appears optimal, not only in its negligible tuition, its easy opportunity for financial aid, and its closeness to home or work, but also in the minimal commitment it requires from the student. Some of these students are in metropolitan areas and have more choices than they realize among nearby community colleges, and often gain little information as to trade-offs between commuting a slightly longer distance to one institution and the superior programs it offers in the area of the student's interests.

It is extraordinarily difficult for people who have always assumed they would go to college, especially those from college-educated families, to imagine how forbidding the very title "college" or "university" can be to insecure prospective students. I have come across instances where students decide to attend the local public university but cannot find their way to their first class; they feel terribly stupid and are hesitant to ask where their class meets because they assume that "everyone" would know such facts. It is just such students, once given proper support, who could make optimal use of a local institution, their commitment deepening as their insecurities diminish. These considerations suggest the need for state, federal, local, and philanthropic efforts at upgrading counselors and lessening both the turnover that is common among them and their understandable frustrations of having to deal with too many students on too many issues of discipline as well as of guidance and advice, which is true at every level of education.

We need to experiment with what governments are able to do to assist counselors in school systems in increasing the sophistication of students and their families concerning the lifelong importance of educational questions, as well as in setting up more and better publicized centers, easily accessible to the bulk at least of the urban population, where students can get better advice. If we want to help students become more active producers of their own education, then we need not only to overcome the passivity that is so depressing in many of our elementary and secondary schools, but also to experiment much more than we have done with the Early College idea, in which students are removed from slack secondary schools to a college program. Students need to be persuaded that they have a choice, and shaken out of the assumption that some colleges are out of the question for them because they would not be able to get financial aid— an assumption that they do not check. Furthermore, students need diagnostic testing in order to individualize counseling and to give counselors more clues toward further inquiry concerning particular students. Here again, one needs to experiment with tests of noncognitive qualities in order to determine who can be counted on to perform up to and beyond the level of their measured achievement and who should take a chance on being stretched to that limit, although not taxed beyond it to the point where they will feel humiliated.

I cannot emphasize enough the importance of counseling community college students while in college to make clear to them the alternatives that still lie ahead, especially today when so many public and private colleges that once seemed formidable are underenrolled and eager, especially at the upper-division levels, to fill their ranks. This means that the transfer counselors at the community colleges must guard against the same kinds of senior college rapacity of which high school counselors must be wary. And receiving institutions must recognize that transfer students are freshmen twice, often even more uneasy and insecure than first-time freshman. For many students, the community college is a step up the ladder of academic and social mobility—indeed, often the only available door at the time in psychological if not financial terms. But many of these students go on to masters and doctoral study having gained extraordinary self-esteem from their double victory—first over the community college, and then over their baccalaureate institution.

Consumerism and Cynicism

Today, public preoccupation with consumerism in terms of consumer protection leads many students to run with rather than against the prevailing cycle. We are in an era of consumerism, accompanied by widespread cynicism about everything being a "sell," including, of course, college. There is a large element of truth in such a judgment, but like most cynicisms, it protects people from gullibility at the expense of depriving them of potential opportunity. Students need to learn some simple precautions about post-secondary education, especially about those programs that promise immediate vocational benefits; but for a large proportion of them, an increase of cynicism is hardly necessary—there's enough available already. Rather, we need to tap the residual sources of idealism that cynicism tends to cover over, sources of a desire to extend oneself in an era of seeming hedonism, and of the belief that one has some power over one's fate within the limitations imposed by time and circumstance, one's own qualities, the vocational outlook, and all the other variables that enter into a realistic assessment of choices that are, in spite of obstacles, still worthwhile.

Such a position contradicts the view that the value added by college to students' lives is, if not negligible, at least not measurable. In the aggregate, there may be little difference in terms of what colleges accomplish, but every teacher knows that, for individual students, a particular institution and one's trajectory within it makes a tremendous difference. Some colleges, and some programs within colleges, leave a stamp on people, for worse as well as for better, while others allow them to emerge much as they entered, their faculties unimpaired but not greatly altered.

I have come to think that, except for the most brilliant students, there is almost no college in America where an energetic student cannot find an education. But this avoids the question as to the degree of push one will get toward securing an education at one institution or another, or the degree of trauma and humiliation one may suffer at some of the more high-pressure places. These differences do not wash out. In some degree, however, they can be anticipated. That at least is my premise and my hope.

Academic Adaptations: Higher Education Prepares for the 1980s and 1990s. By Verne A. Stadtman. 1980.

This report relies upon information gathered in site visits by staff members of the Carnegie Council in 1979, Carnegie Commission and Council Surveys of students, faculty, and administrators in 1969 and 1975, and the Carnegie Council Survey of college presidents in 1978.

Colleges and universities are in some ways always new, changed constantly by forces of history and social developments. The major contextual factors that had an effect on higher education in 1969 were campus dissent and disruption related to both social and campus issues; an opening of the campuses to different types of students than had been admitted before; accommodations to individual differences among students through innovations in the programs and instructional technologies offered; great concern for the rising costs of operating increasingly expensive institutions; anticipation of continued enrollment growth for the ensuing decade; reasonably strong public confidence in higher education; and acceptance of the assumption of extensive authority in college and university affairs by the academic profession.

Problems of particular concern to higher education in the 1970s included shifts of power and authority, changed levels of financing, reduced enrollments, a reaching out for new clienteles, pressures to expand career education (often at the expense of liberal arts), shortages of jobs for new Ph.D.'s, the continued growth of collective bargaining, and the increasing influence of state and federal governments.

But colleges and universities are not isolated from the major events and trends of the times in which they exist, and many of their internal changes respond to the swirl of the world around them. Five events should be highlighted because they significantly altered the context in which colleges and universities operated during the decade. They are:

1. The lowering of the voting age, which made voters out of 98 percent of the national student body. Students cannot in the future be ignored as interested parties in the development of public as well as campus educational policy.

2. The Watergate scandal, which raised questions about the integrity of all social institutions. This concern translated into increased interests in the capacities of colleges and universities—from which leadership is presumed to come—to provide ethical and moral education.

3. With the end of the draft in 1973, the artificial demand for higher learning created by student exemptions ceased. The termination of the draft explains a significant portion of the decrease in enrollments, particularly as it was evident among white males, in the 1970s. Another consequence was that campus-centered dissent resulting from unpopular national defense and foreign policies abated.

4. The most serious depression to hit the country since World War II occurred in 1974-75. Coupled with continuing inflation, it posed severe problems for institutions forced to pay bigger bills with less revenue. Challenges to long-standing beliefs about the economic returns to education cast public doubt on the inevitable link between employment, success, and the college degree.

5. Federal support of research activities in colleges and universities began to decline after 1968. Although the nation's 133 doctorate-granting institutions were most directly affected by these reductions, all colleges ultimately felt the consequences in the form of a slowdown in knowledge production and curtailment of opportunities to apprentice prospective college teachers in research activities.

The realities and consequences of all of these trends—inside and beyond the campuses—have been felt in different ways by different kinds of institutions throughout American higher education.

Students

The astonishing growth in the capacity of institutions of higher education in the 1960s and 1970s was rationalized almost entirely on the basis of anticipated increases in the numbers of students seeking admission. And the student came. By fall 1979, 11 million of them were enrolled, an increase of more than one-third over the 8 million enrolled in 1969.

Part of this enrollment growth was caused by an increase in the birthrate after World War II. But this was only one of the reasons for enrollment growth. America's concerns for social justice and for extending the educational attainment of its populace fueled a movement to encourage colleges to open their doors to previously excluded groups in our society and to take affirmative action on behalf of equal treatment of women and members of racial minorities.

Until the women's movement gathered momentum in the 1960s and 1970s, the idea that women could combine education, careers, and parenting was not widely accepted. But once more, as the professions and other attractive occupational fields began to open up to women who had the appropriate preparation, colleges began to play a stronger role in helping them to broaden their opportunities.

The increase in the attendance of older women who are pursuing a delayed or interrupted education has been particularly impressive, almost doubling from 418,000 women over 35 years old in 1972 to 700,000 in 1976. And enrollment of older students has increased generally. Between 1972 and 1976, the enrollment of students over 25 increased from one-fourth of the total to about one-third. In 1978, more than three-fourths (78 percent) of the college presidents in the country reported that in the first five years of the 1980s they expected to emphasize recruitment of students in the older age groups.

The stage for this kind of emphasis was set in the 1960s and 1970s as colleges began to respond more sympathetically than in the past to the needs of students who could not attend classes full-time. The increased flexibility of college attendance patterns became a hallmark of higher education in the 1970s, and one of its most radical forms was made possible by the legitimization of the "stopout." Students were encouraged to stop out of college for a semester or more before receiving their degrees to spend time working, traveling, or engaging in some other constructive activity. In 1969, 17 percent of the undergraduates in American colleges and universities had stopped out; in 1976, the proportion had reached 26 percent.

Student ability. Presidents report that student quality is up because there are now more candidates for admission to choose from and because the students they enroll are better prepared than students in 1970. Presidents of the more selective institutions are particularly likely to see their students in these terms. Yet, the fact that there are large numbers of candidates for admission has another side that is frequently mentioned by the presidents of less-selective institutions: Some of the entering students lack the basic skills to succeed academically. The evidence supporting concern about a decline in student quality is impressive, particularly the decline in average scores of college entrance examinations. To make up for student deficiencies, 85 percent of American colleges and universities now offer compensatory or remedial education programs.

The trend toward seriousness. When asked to describe how students at their institutions were different in 1978 than they were in 1969-70, 24 percent of college presidents said they were "serious about their studies," and another 14 percent characterized them simply as "more serious." The top-ranked reason freshmen gave in 1978 for attending college was "to get a better job," and it was cited as important by at least 73 percent of the students at all institutions. And one way undergraduates demonstrate their career interests is by their choices of majors. Enrollment in majors with a professional or occupational orientation increased substantially between 1969 and 1976, while enrollment in the humanities, social sciences, and physical sciences all decreased.

Lifestyle. Students have become more independent in many ways. Student financial aid has diminished the dependence of students on their families. And students are no longer innocent; the culture that surrounds them is explicit on many subjects that were seldom discussed publicly by earlier generations. Moreover, colleges long ago abandoned even the pretense of exercising the kind of watchful care and supervision of students' personal lives that their custodial roles once obligated them to exercise.

The students of the 1970s are considerably more liberal in matters of lifestyle than previous generations. For example, an increasing percentage of entering freshmen believe that marijuana should be legalized (49.5 percent in 1978 vs. 25.6 percent in 1969) and divorce laws should be liberalized (48.6 percent in 1978 vs. 41.6 percent in 1969). In addition, 45.8 percent of the 1978 freshmen think people should live together before marriage, 48.6 percent believe sexual relations are all right if people like each other, and 53.7 percent believe abortion should be legalized.

With these trends toward freedom from conformity and control, where does their seriousness fit in? At least one place is beyond the surface manifestations of the new freedom to the huge moral and ethical burdens that go with its exercise. If students are considered serious, it is not just because their educational and career objectives are more serious than they once were, but also because they are assuming some enormous responsibilities for their own actions that previous college generations avoided, or at least shared with their families and their institutions.

The decline of political activism. The 1970s witnessed a dramatic decline in student protest. No one knows for sure why the change occurred, but speculation embraces such possibilities as the defusing of major issues with the end of the Vietnam war, the end of compulsory selective service, and progress in extending civil rights to members of minority groups, among others. It is also possible that students became distracted from political endeavors as they became increasingly aware that jobs for college graduates were becoming less plentiful and that their future careers might depend on academic efforts of the most serious kind.

Finally, students are becoming more conservative politically. The proportion of undergraduates regarding themselves as politically "left" or "liberal" dropped from 45 percent in 1969 to 35 percent in 1976, while those stating they were "moderately" or "strongly" conservative increased from 19 to 26 percent.

Student participation in governance. While students in the 1960s were preoccupied with external events and issues, students of the 1970s were more concerned with internal issues. And one of those issues is the extent to which students should have a voice in the governance of colleges and universities. About half of the presidents responding to the Carnegie Council survey indicated that a substantial minority of their students are interested in greater student participation in administrative and academic decision making, while about one-third indicated that student interest in participation had decreased.

One-third of the presidents indicated that the influence of student government had increased since 1969-70. In our visits to campuses, we found that there is considerable variation in student influence, but that in an era in which the user of educational services has a lot of say about how much, when, and how such services are to be provided, student preferences are receiving more serious attention.

Student satisfaction. In 1976, 72 percent of the nation's undergraduates reported that they were either "satisfied" or "very satisfied" with their colleges, an increase from 66 percent in 1969. One does not have to ignore the challenge of making college and university attendance more satisfying for the 28 percent of the students who did not find it so in 1976 to appreciate the achievement of colleges and universities these responses confirm. In order to satisfy nearly three-fourths of the nation's student body, our colleges have to be doing at least some things right.

Graduate students. In 1969 and again in 1976 graduate students were asked about their career expectations after completing their studies. In both years, teaching in elementary or secondary school, teaching or engaging in research at a college or university, or some form of professional activity dominated the choices made. But during the 1970s two important shifts occurred in the most frequently mentioned options. With the well-advertised decline in college enrollments and declining federal support for university research on the horizon, the percentage of graduate students expecting to work in colleges and universities decreased from 36.2 to 21.9 percent. The other direction of the shift in career expectations of graduate students leads into professional practice—those expecting to become employed professionals increased from 19.6 to 29.3 percent.

This general trend toward a decline in interest in academic careers is also indicated by shifts in the fields of study graduate students choose to devote themselves to. In the more academic fields, such as foreign languages, letters, mathematics, physical sciences, and the social sciences, enrollments have been declining. But there have been very substantial increases in enrollments in business and management, communications, public affairs and services, and the health professions.

Politically, graduate students appear to have drifted to the left at the very time that undergraduates were drifting to the middle-of-the-road and to the right. The shift probably results from the fact that many of the graduate students of 1975 were undergraduates during the 1960s and apparently brought their political commitments with them when they acquired their new status.

Whatever their political attitudes may be, graduate students are in remarkable agreement that their institutions are at least "fairly good" places for them to be. Over 90 percent expressed that view in both 1969 and 1976.

Concluding observations on students. Most of the information about students that has been collected and analyzed helps understanding their numbers, their socioeconomic status, their attitudes toward certain events and issues, their sexual characteristics, and their ethnic variety. All of these variables help in understanding some of the dynamics of educational policy and planning. They do little, however, to help us understand educational quality and the effectiveness of instructional strategies. We are coming to a point in the history of higher education when we have to pay more attention to helping everyone who gets into a classroom realize the best possible results from their learning potentials. Achieving that goal may require more studies of subtle differences and changes in the characteristics of students than we have so far been prepared to admit are relevant to higher educational policy.

The Faculty

The mood of American college and university faculty members has darkened during the 1970s for many reasons:

- The philosophical validity of the scientific method and the objectivity of academic inquiry began to be questioned in the 1960s.
- Harnessing nuclear energy, landing a man on the moon, and computerizing much of the daily lives of the members of industrial societies were tough acts to follow. They were also accompanied by potential hazards to the health and humanity of mankind.
- On the campuses, the student revolts of 1960s seemed at first to be directed at college and university leaders, but some faculty members were surprised to find that students considered them to be remote and uncaring. And faculty members who embraced the platforms of the student protesters were surprised by the antagonism of some of their colleagues.
- As faculty members began to take sides, they exposed the private life of the academic sector to view and criticism. The "real life" perspective was underscored by the growth of the movement to unionize college and university faculties because it emphasized bread-and-butter issues and deemphasized the faculty members' dedication and concern for the life of the mind and the enrichment of the national culture.
- Faculty members have found that the academic enterprise is no longer expanding and that, as a result, they are losing some of their bargaining power in negotiating with their current and potential employers.
- Faculty salaries have failed to keep up with the cost of living.
- Faculty members who happen to be women have an additional complaint. In all ranks, there continues to be a significant differential between the average salaries earned by men and those earned by women.

All of these factors notwithstanding, it would be a mistake to paint a picture of an unhappy professoriate. When asked in 1975 whether they would do it over again if they had the chance, 87 percent of American faculty members answered "definitely" or "probably" yes.

The growth of faculties. When enrollment increases, the size of college and university faculties also increases, and that situation prevailed throughout the 1970s. In 1969 there were 546,000 persons employed as either full-time or part-time faculty members, and by 1976 the number had increased to 781,000. These faculty increases did not, however, occur uniformly in institutions of higher education. The institutions that most frequently reported increases were those that include large numbers of new institutions and those that were particularly likely to experience enrollment growth. These were the two-year colleges, comprehensive colleges and universities, and some of the research and doctorate-granting universities. In the years ahead, most colleges and universities expect little or no change in the absolute numbers of instructional staff members.

Faculty responses to affirmative action. The 1970s were years of historic efforts in colleges and universities to redress some of the imbalances in the participation of women and members of minority groups in higher education, but the results have been modest. American academics disagree with many of the premises on which affirmative action is based and are defensive about the extent to which their institutions might be discriminatory in academic personnel matters. They are at least consenting, however, when it comes to the measures institutions might have to take to correct the present imbalance of opportunities that exist for women and minority groups.

Part-time faculty. Colleges and universities are finding part-time faculty members attractive. They teach only courses that need to be taught, and they involve no commitment by the institution to support the instructor's research. They are not part of the academic "ladder" and thus can be rewarded or discharged with none of the investment of time often spent in the periodic reviews involved in the hiring and promotion of regular faculty members. They require little office space and a minimum of staff support. And the percentage of part-time faculty members on the total instruction staff of colleges and universities has been increasing. In 1969 part-time staff members constituted an estimated 22 percent of the total of the instructional staff at the level of instructor and above, and by 1976 the percentage had risen to 31 percent.

Quality. Over two-thirds of college and university presidents said that the quality of their faculty has been enhanced. The truth is that there is an ample supply of qualified teachers and scholars in most fields, and thus colleges and universities have been revelling in a buyer's market. Despite the fact that there are more Ph.D.'s available for college teaching, the emphasis on teaching as opposed to research continues to be associated with the research or teaching orientation of the institutions that hire them. For example, interest in teaching remains strong at two-year colleges and liberal arts colleges and is fairly strong also at comprehensive colleges and universities, but is much lower in research universities.

   Wherever their teaching or research interests may lie, faculty members apparently are going to be more carefully evaluated when promotions are considered in the future. This is partly because the size of the pool of qualified applicants for academic positions is likely to exceed openings for several years, and partly because colleges and universities will feel that their financial resources are too limited to be invested in anything less than the best talent they can afford.

Representation in departments. One of the most difficult problems confronting academic deans at colleges and universities is matching institutional resources with student demand. Students' interests become known to institutional planners after the fact, and it may take several years for a college to reallocate its resources to take care of the changes when they occur. It is not simply a matter of adding faculty for a new high-interest field. More often, it is a matter of reassigning positions, as they become open, from less popular departments to those with the greatest demand.

Academic personnel policies in times of change. Colleges and universities are not likely to lay off faculty members in order to adjust to decreasing enrollments. For one thing, tenure policies make this very difficult. For another, there are less traumatic ways to accomplish some of these objectives.

   One hedge against having too many faculty members when enrollments begin to decline is to avoid hiring faculty members when enrollments are still rising. This inevitably means that the teaching load of the existing faculty will be increased, as is reflected in rising student to faculty ratios.

Encouraging some faculty members to take early retirement is a major change in academic personnel policy at some institutions, aimed less at staff reduction than at decreasing academic payroll costs. It reduces the number of staff members who are at the most senior levels, where they tend to be most expensive. Although only 14 percent of the nation's colleges and universities instituted such a policy between 1969 and 1978, 39 percent of them expect to have such policies in effect within the next five or six years.

In times of retrenchment, the difficulties that attend having a "tenured-in" faculty are so acute that some college officials are resolving to exert strong controls at the front end of the system, thus screening nominees for tenure with unprecedented care. Young faculty members in the 1980s may be in a double bind, where they not only have to compete strenuously for the few tenured positions that open up, but also must do so in accordance with much more severe promotion standards.

Faculty governance. How faculty members are hired, promoted, given tenure, and engaged in the day-to-day life of their institutions is governed largely by the way academic and administrative affairs are organized on the campuses. On relatively small campuses and at many two-year institutions, authority is concentrated at the top in the president, with institutionwide participation of faculty members being sporadic and largely advisory.

At large universities and colleges and at elite institutions, the faculties themselves are entrusted with authority over a broad range of matters in which they are considered to hold special professional competence. Among them are degree requirements, the shape of the curriculum, and policies for the appointment and promotion of academic personnel.

Overall, 58 percent of the presidents of American colleges and universities report that the general influence of faculty on campus policy and operations has increased since 1969. This increase should not, however, be interpreted to mean that the increased interest is expressed only through participation in the traditional faculty governance structures of the departments and senates. Some of it, at least, becomes apparent as a manifestation of the relatively recent introduction of faculty unionism.

Collective bargaining. In 1969-70, 7.5 percent of all colleges and universities had collective bargaining contracts in force. By 1978, the proportion had tripled. Thus far, faculty unionism is encountered mainly at public institutions—and particularly at relatively new institutions and at institutions that provide no other alternative for faculty participation in institutional decision making, especially two-year colleges. On the whole, however, faculty attitudes toward unionism tend to be positive. Even at universities where there are strong faculty governments and there is considerable hostility toward faculty bargaining, only 34 percent of the faculty agree that collective bargaining has no place in a college or university.

Despite faculty attitudes that are mostly favorable to collective bargaining on college and university campuses, I do not expect it to grow rapidly unless the day-to-day conditions of academic employment deteriorate badly under the pressures of enrollment decline and diminished financial resources.

Some concluding observations on the academic profession. Many academics develop a strong bond to the traditions and goals of their institutions. Such bonds are particularly close at those institutions where faculty members are deeply involved in the decision-

making processes of their colleges and come to regard themselves as agents of the institution's mission. But one of the consequences of recent developments in higher education is that tensions seem to be developing between the adherents of this professional
academic tradition and the marketplace orientation of colleges and universities. The
trends that contribute most to such tensions are:

1.   The increasing use of part-time faculty members. They not only are ineligible for
       some of the privileges of full-time academics, but also are not really expected to
       have strong feelings of membership in the campus community.
2.   The rapid growth of community colleges. Few faculty members have doctorates
       and the tradition of academic self-governance is weakest at community colleges,
       yet these institutions now serve more than one-third of all students enrolled.
3.   The increased awareness of opportunities for people to get postsecondary educa-
       tion at institutions other than colleges and universities tends to assign to traditional
       academics a more modest role than they once had in the total educational effort
       of the country.
4.   The deterioration of the job market in traditional institutions may force some
       academics into noncollegiate settings where their presence further blurs the dis-
       tinctions between faculties in the two sectors.
5.   The advent of faculty collective bargaining alters the relationship between academics
       and their institutions by making them less a part of the college or university's decision-
       making structure and to some extent more of an adversary manpower force.

Some of the tensions between the professional academic tradition and the emerging forces of the educational labor market are just becoming obvious as the 1970s end.
They will undoubtedly be increasingly important parts of academic life for many years
into the future.

Higher Education's Leadership

The trustees. There are about 47,000 trustees and regents in the United States, and they
serve on more than 2,300 boards serving more than 3,000 campuses. In general they are
expected to exercise such oversight and direction as may be necessary to make sure that
the purposes of an institution as perceived by the founders and defined by the purposes
of its endowment are properly served.

In 1978, when they were asked about the increase or decrease of power of various
constituencies since 1969-70, almost half of the college and university presidents said
the power of the governing boards had increased. In the Carnegie Council site visits, we
explored this matter more fully to determine the current ranking of constituencies that,
in the opinion of presidents, had the most power on the campuses in 1978. We found little
change since 1971, with governing boards ranked fourth in a field of eight groups that
included administrators other than presidents, individual faculty members, organized
faculty members, departments, student government, and individual students. The highest
ranking was given the presidents themselves.

Presidential leadership. On college and university campuses, the broadest perspectives
for viewing the general health and prospects of individual institutions are those of the
presidents. Most of them come to their positions with 25 to 30 years prior experience
as students, teachers, and administrators in higher education, and most hold doctorates.

One sobering thought for would-be reformers of colleges and universities is that the presidents they enlist in their cause today may have relatively little time in office to help them implement their proposals. Across the country, there were, on the average, 359 turnovers in college presidencies each year between 1974-75 and 1977-78—a turnover rate of about 13 percent a year, with an average (mean) term in office of 8.8 years.

Presidential authority. In the Carnegie Council's survey of college and university presidents in 1978, an effort was made to assess their estimates of their own authority within their institutions. They were asked if they had authority commensurate with the demands of their jobs. In both Comprehensive Universities and Colleges I and Research Universities I, more than 70 percent of the presidents say they have authority commensurate with their jobs, but even higher percentages of presidents in other institutions give the same answer.

Presidential concerns in 1978. They say it in many ways: "a chronic funding gap," "static or shrinking resource base," "costs cut to the bone," "inflation," "cash flow," and "$." However, it is said, it means *financing*, and it was the most frequent response of presidents in 1978 when we asked them: "Of all of the problems confronting your institution right now, which one is the greatest concern to you?" In all, more than 1,000 presidents, 45 percent of our respondents, gave answers that involved financing, and they outnumbered those who mentioned the second-ranking concern—decreasing enrollments— almost three to one.

The coming decline in the nation's college-age population has been well publicized for most of the past decade, and one might expect presidents to be more concerned about it than our survey results indicate. But for several reasons they are not:

- The decreases are not yet a reality on many campuses.
- Presidents have strategies in reserve for reaching out to new sources of students.
- Presidents believe they can survive comfortably with whatever share of the decreases may occur at their institutions.
- Presidents may hold to an optimistic view that whatever happens, the worst will affect other institutions and not their own.

In any event, of the presidents who see declining enrollments as their greatest problem, almost twice as many are in private institutions as in public ones.

"Improving the quality of education" is the third-ranking concern of the presidents in our survey. But those who give educational quality top level of importance cluster in two types of institutions:

- Liberal Arts Colleges I, which include many elite institutions and in which enrollment decreases are feared by a substantial number of presidents.
- Comprehensive Colleges and Universities, Liberal Arts Colleges II, and Two-Year Colleges, where open admissions policies are likely to prevail.

Concerns about governmental regulation and coordination and needs for new physical facilities are found most frequently among presidents of public institutions.

Institutional Change and Diversity

The title of the final Carnegie Council report, *Three Thousand Futures,* was chosen to reflect the fact that each college and university has its own future, and that general trends and prevailing practices need not affect all institutions in the same ways. This theme is repeated here in terms of the concept of diversity in higher education and the ways in which colleges and universities are adapting to prospects of falling enrollments and reduced resources.

The impulse of colleges and universities to emulate successful institutions is one of the reasons some observers fear for the future of diversity in American higher education. It also explains why much that is written about higher education takes the university model for granted as a norm rather than as one end of the institutional spectrum. But the prevailing direction of change in the 1970s was not toward university status per se. It was, instead, toward comprehensiveness. And the move toward comprehensiveness has not resulted from status seeking as much as it has from responses of colleges and universities to the decrease of their traditional sources of enrollments and to opportunities to render new types of services to new types of learners.

Literally, diversity is a condition of being different, and in higher education it can be found in several forms:

- *Programmatic diversity.* This involves the degree of comprehensiveness of an institution in its curricular offerings.
- *Procedural diversity.* This involves methods of instruction and modes of organizing the teaching function.
- *Systematic diversity.* This is found among institutions of different types, sizes, and controls.
- *Constituent diversity.* This diversity results from differences in the family backgrounds, abilities, preparation, values, and educational goals among students.
- *Prestige diversity.* This applies to colleges and universities that acquire a particular reputation for some kind of excellence.
- *Internal diversity.* This occurs when one institution seeks to serve more than one goal or mission, to provide education for special groups within the student constituency, or to utilize more than one approach or technique to achieve its educational objectives.
- *Institutional diversity.* This involves differentiation *among* colleges and universities and is especially associated with such factors as location, particular personnel and students, or a particular physical plant and environment.

Diversity is prized in American higher education because it (1) increases the range of choices available to learners; (2) makes higher education available to virtually everyone, despite differences among individuals; (3) matches education to the needs, goals, learning styles, speed, and abilities of individual students; (4) enables institutions to select their own missions; and (5) responds to the many pressures and needs of a complex society.

Threats to Diversity

Even in cases where the potential for diversity is formidable, it may not be fully realized. Among the threats to its full realization are inadequate systems of information, the demise of institutions, detailed coordination of higher education by central agencies, collective academic bargaining, and overzealous governmental regulation.

While the character of diversity in American higher education is constantly shifting, it will never disappear entirely. For one thing, the dimensions of diversity are, in the long run, determined not only by colleges and universities, but also by whatever one might call the total "system" or "resources" of higher learning, such as those provided by proprietary institutions, museums, private industry, and military establishments. Moreover, as institutions become more comprehensive, as they merge with one another, and as they add functions and programs, they become internally more diverse even though diversity among institutions may be diminished.

It is doubtful, however, that increased diversity within institutions balances out decreased diversity among institutions. Although there may be as much programmatic diversity within a few large comprehensive institutions or systems as there is among a greater number of colleges and universities of all sizes, the kind and quality of diversity is not the same. For example, within the larger institution or system there is less diversity of the sort that is linked to location, ambience, and traditions.

Some Concerns

Diversity of American higher education is not in any immediate danger of demise, but certain kinds of diversity may be diminished if current trends continue. But concerns for the strength of certain kinds of institutions seem to be particularly justified:

1. *Institutions that stand at the frontier of advanced learning and thought.* Doctorate-granting institutions already show signs of becoming a decreasing proportion of the nation's colleges and universities. The research functions of higher education have recently been undersupported and, if undernourished for too long in universities, they may be transferred to other types of institutions in our society.
2. *Institutions that enhance the abilities of certain types of students to learn.* In this regard, there is a decreasing availability of single-sex institutions and of institutions affiliated with religious denominations. There is no virtue in segregation of any kind for its own sake, but institutions for men, women, members of minorities, and adherents to certain beliefs do offer special intellectual challenges and special social support systems that encourage students to achieve nearer to the limits of their abilities.
3. *Small, experimenting, and developing institutions.* Of the 129 independent colleges and universities that closed between 1970 and 1978, 124 had less than 1,000 students. Smallness is not in itself a virtue, but many of these institutions have very special and important missions. For example, many seminaries, conservatories, and other specialized institutions are found among them. Other small institutions are new and possibly experimental. Some maintain high levels of quality in their personnel and programs.

There is now a special need for emphasis on:

1. Support and expansion of the research function of higher education
2. Adequate support and expansion of the Fund for the Improvement of Postsecondary Education (FIPSE), which has a good record of supporting innovation and constructive change in colleges and universities
3. Establishment of FIPSE-like agencies at the state level
4. The creation of new agencies and procedures for the support of small and developing institutions.

Adaptations to Decreasing Enrollments

Thus far, many more colleges and universities have lived with enrollment growth than have experienced decline. Enrollment has held steady, increased, or fluctuated but has "mostly increased" at more than three-fourths of American institutions of higher education in the past few years. The basic explanation of increasing enrollments has been the growth in the size of the college-age population of the country. But other factors were also involved, including certain institutional policy decisions that were made to attract and hold students. In particular, six factors have been important in enrollment growth at more than 50 percent of the nation's campuses.

Admissions and recruiting. The direct approach to increasing enrollments is to persuade more potential students to enroll, and that course has been adopted by more than 80 percent of the country's institutions of higher education. To direct this effort, 60 percent of all institutions increased the number of staff members engaged in admissions and recruitment activities by 10 percent between 1969-70 and 1977-78, and 36 percent of the institutions expect to do the same between 1977-78 and 1985-86. One consequence of the recent trends in admissions and recruitment is that prospective students are finding it easier to find a place in college. Half of the colleges and universities in the country now accept between 90 and 100 percent of freshman applicants.

Changes in admissions procedures in the 1970s show that colleges have responded to two trends. The first trend is toward greater flexibility in all programs and procedures in higher education. The second trend is toward preparing for future competition with other institutions for students. It involves the admission of new types of students and of students who only recently were on the margin of an institution's eligibility pool. The time when recruiting emphasis was almost entirely on high school graduates between the ages of 18 and 22 is long gone.

Not all of the efforts to seek out new types of students are designed to build enrollments per se. Not enough credit is given to colleges and universities whose concern for the "new" students reflects, first of all, a commitment to provide educational opportunities to members of ethnic and socioeconomic groups who have previously been denied them or who now have special needs for the education that colleges can provide. But the fact remains that recruiting students from expanded pools of prospects is often a matter not only of social conscience but also of minimizing losses of enrollment that are expected because lower birthrates of the 1960s failed to produce the numbers of prospective traditional students for the 1980s to which college recruiters have become accustomed.

Letting the world know. Public relations were once aimed principally at fund-raising targets and improving general goodwill. They are also the fourth most frequently given reason for increased enrollments. According to college and university officials, public relations contributed to enrollment increases at 83 percent of the country's institutions of higher education.

Increasing the options. One important way for colleges and universities to attract and keep students is to develop curricula and instructional modes that have strong student appeal. In our survey, 68 percent of college officials indicated that expanded high-demand program options—including new majors, work education, and the like—had caused some or substantial increase in their enrollments.

Modes of instruction. But the options colleges and universities make available to students are not restricted to courses and subjects. They also come in the form of different modes of instruction. It is not necessarily true that the "new instructional innovations" in higher education are all positively associated with enrollment increases. Even when they are—as is the case with large lecture classes at universities and the use of new electronic technologies at two-year colleges—the correlation can be as reliably explained by institutional accommodation to more students as by student preference for certain learning modes. The content of the curriculum is what students go to a college or university to obtain, and the relationship between the subjects taught and enrollment trends is clear. But students are not as aware as they should be of a full variety of instructional modes that are available.

Many colleges are therefore placing less emphasis on creating variety for their traditional undergraduate students and more on seeking out older students who can be served by instruction given off-campus or on evenings and weekends. It is in these efforts that I discern what may be the source of the most extensive transformation of the character of American higher education to result from the innovations of the 1970s.

The role of financial aid. Officials of American colleges and universities rank the availability of financial aid to students second, after increased recruitment activity, as the most frequent cause of enrollment increase in institutions of higher education. Student aid is important enough to an overwhelming majority of colleges and universities that they set aside some of their unrestricted revenues to provide scholarships or fee waivers to their needier students.

Student services. More than half of the colleges and universities indicated that improvement in student services was a cause of some or substantial increase in enrollments. Our questionnaire did not, unfortunately, probe for examples of what such services might be. Presumably they would include, residence halls, recreation facilities, cafeterias, libraries, and health services. Anything that would contribute to the comfort, welfare, and convenience of students probably constitutes an attraction. And two types of service that contribute to the retention of students once they enroll are advising and academic programs designed to help students overcome deficiencies in learning skills.

Factors in Decreasing Enrollments

When students start leaving colleges or universities—or even fail to try them—there are not always simple explanations. Students have their own reasons, and not all reasons apply to all institutions equally. In the Carnegie Council survey the five most frequently cited factors were: (1) decline in interest in liberal arts (64 percent); (2) end of the military draft (59 percent); (3) increase in the percentage of part-time students (59 percent); (4) high tuition (38 percent); and (5) increase in the percentage of transfer students relative to freshmen (34 percent).

Because of high proportions of institutions in all categories that cite the declining attraction of the liberal arts as a reason for enrollment decline, one must also suspect that disenchantment with the liberal arts may be translated into the assumption that there is a public disenchantment with traditional, academic higher education in general.

Although high tuition is regarded as a fairly high-ranking cause of enrollment decrease for all institutions, it is not so highly ranked at institutions that have actually experienced enrollment decreases since 1969-70. Moreover, it is much less frequently cited by officials of private institutions than by those at public colleges and universities.

The seventh-ranked cause of enrollment decreases, according to all respondents to the 1978 surveys, was a decline in retention rates. It was experienced at 29 percent of all colleges and universities. This is a case, however, where limiting judgments to those of officials at colleges and universities that have actually lost enrollments results in a much higher ranking for the factor as one contributing to enrollment decline. Among private institutions that actually lost enrollments, declining retention ranks as the number one factor in enrollment decline; officials of public institutions that lost enrollments rank declining retention rates second.

Increasing retention rates is something colleges and universities themselves can do something about, and the most frequently mentioned methods were:

1. Improving advising, counseling, and orientation programs, and closely monitoring student progress
2. Relaxing rules on student discipline and behavior and giving students more freedom on the campus
3. Making curricular changes, allowing for more individualized instruction and more flexible class scheduling
4. Instituting career-planning programs
5. Conducting exit interviews and following up on dropouts
6. Improving student activities and services.

Another factor in enrollment decline is the increased competition among colleges and universities for the students that are available. Across the country, 89 percent of the college and university presidents reported that they had experienced increased competition. No classification of college or universities seems exempt, and no single sector is a major source of competition for all others, but the competition is particularly threatening to small private institutions located in rural areas.

Modern competition takes several forms—competition in geographic convenience, competition in the comprehensiveness of offerings, and competition in price. One reason small private colleges feel competition so intensely is that they tend to be vulnerable on all counts.

Enrollment Decline and the New Consumerism

The term most frequently invoked to describe the current forces producing major changes in higher education is "consumerism." The term is hated by many writers about higher education because it seems to turn a noble enterprise into something crass and commercial. I personally do not object to the term as long as it is used to describe what I think it does—a condition in which those who seek out and pay for education are fewer in number than the opportunities for higher learning that institutions are prepared to open up to them.

Those who argue that the new consumerism shifts control and decision making to students are obviously right—at least in the long run. And, on balance, much that is good for students and for education can result from that shift. But there is a degree to which consumerism, including its least constructive consequences, is self-inflicted by colleges and universities when undesirable changes are made to encourage students to enroll and stay on campus and where policy makers try to anticipate rather than follow demand.

Prospects for the 1980s and 1990s

Asked to indicate what changes they would like to see at their institutions in the next decade, the presidents responding to the Council's 1978 surveys cast an impressively strong vote for improved quality. For example, 42 percent of them mentioned improved academic programs (the highest-ranked of all the goals mentioned). In addition, 29 percent wanted to have improved or expanded physical facilities, 15 percent would like to see the quality of the faculty improved, and 12 percent would like to see the quality of their institutions improved generally.

The second-ranked response to our question about desired changes for the coming decade was "increased endowment," and if this change were combined with the tenth-ranked "improved fund-raising," the desire for increased financial support from private sources would rise to the top in the ranking of desired changes. The third-ranked response was "improved and expanded physical facilities," while the fourth was "institutional goals defined."

Taken together, the presidents' desired changes give us reason for optimism. The changes preferred most frequently are defined in terms of things that improve the quality of colleges and universities, increase their independence, and render them of service to broader segments of society.

The final question in the Carnegie Council survey of college and university presidents was: "In your judgment, what are likely to be the most important issues facing American higher education between 1980 and the year 2000?" The ten most frequently mentioned issues ranged from "financing higher education," which was mentioned by 55 percent of the presidents, to "continuing education," which was mentioned by 7 percent of the presidents. In descending order of the frequency with which they were mentioned, the ten issues are:

1. Financing higher education
2. Redefining goals of higher education
3. Maintaining enrollments
4. Maintaining the autonomy of higher education
5. Strengthening the liberal arts
6. Preserving the private sector
7. Maintaining quality in higher education
8. Strengthening career education
9. Public confidence in higher education
10. Continuing education.

Forks in the Road

The presidents' agenda for the coming decades is not an easy one. The future of higher education depends in part on choices that have already been made by higher education decision makers. Some of them go a long way toward solving current problems, but others have long-term consequences that merit second thoughts. In choosing the forks in the road to explore briefly here, I have not assumed that any of them will necessarily be chosen by all kinds of institutions or even by most institutions of any one kind. I am only speculating on possible consequences if the roads are traveled too far by too many institutions without concern for where they might lead.

The increasing emphasis on specialization, particularly in career fields. Some colleges and universities obviously are well along this fork of the road and for good reasons. Specialization can be a valuable part of one's education, and much can be said for making the relationship between education and careers more explicit than it has in the past. My fear is that, if the greater emphasis on career preparation in colleges and universities is carried too far, too many college resources for what is often referred to as "liberal learning" may be jettisoned along the way.

The continuing trend toward comprehensiveness. Similar considerations relate to the tendency of small colleges to add functions and programs that change their basic mission and character. The threat to America's liberal arts colleges is not just impending bankruptcy and failure. They are also threatened by a loss of their distinctive character and function as they become larger and more comprehensive.

The development of new graduate-level, part-time, individualized programs. The specialized graduate programs that are now being designed and offered for part-time, usually fully employed students seeking specialized training in work-related fields not only meet a clear need, but also have provided the means for some institutions to increase both enrollments and revenues. But before this road is traveled by too many institutions, some consequences should be considered.

The first of these concerns the character of the degrees offered in these programs. Although many of these offerings involve studies in the evenings or on weekends for less than half a year, the degrees certifying their completion often are variants of traditional academic degrees. It is regrettable that pejorative distinctions may ultimately be made between degrees that carry essentially the same names but are awarded for different amounts and kinds of study. This problem probably deserves the attention of regional accrediting associations throughout the country.

A second consequence is that the profitable programs for older, part-time, employed learners may in time drive out the less profitable traditional programs of private liberal arts colleges.

A third concern is that the character of the academic profession gradually may be altered as colleges and universities offer more and more programs that rely heavily on adjunct, part-time instructors, hired from the community at large instead of from the academic ranks of the regular faculty.

The changing mission of community colleges. America's community colleges are still seeking out their basic mission. Originally conceived as institutions that could introduce young men and women to the general learning offered by colleges and universities in the first two years of instruction, they gradually acquired additional functions. They became institutions for the education of men and women for certain vocations and occupations. They became institutions that afforded a second chance to students who were unprepared for college or university at the end of their high school studies. And more recently they have been the colleges that produce education on demand in response to the needs and wishes of the communities they serve.

The troublesome aspect of the development is that the mission of these institutions has become increasingly difficult to discern. And related to that problem is the possibility that the original functions of these colleges may, in the future, be deemphasized or even disappear. The greatest problem posed by that possibility would be faced by students who need special help in overcoming educational deficiencies that were not removed during their high school years. In the absence of two-year transfer programs at community colleges, many students who have been especially dependent on community colleges may be stranded.

A suggestion. It is likely that the most threatened part of higher education in the United States in the 1980s and 1990s will be that part that is concerned primarily with liberal education. It is threatened, on the one hand, by the loss of institutions that have been traditionally committed to the mission of advancing liberal learning, and, on the other hand, by the competition of new programs that draw time, attention, and resources away from traditional liberal arts programs.

It now appears that the time is right to develop more middle colleges or transition colleges to perform these functions in a coordinated way. Ideally, the level of instruction offered should include that found in the last two years of high school and the first two years in college. If some of the current trends in higher education are to endure, the only way to protect them is to pull them together for development by special types of institutions.

Strategies for the 1980s and 1990s

In its final report, the Carnegie Council stressed that there are very few policies for meeting the conditions of the 1980s and 1990s that are appropriate for every institution. The Council report did contain a "checklist of imperatives" for colleges and universities that provides broad approaches for adapting to conditions of the next two decades (see summary of *Three Thousand Futures*). However, there are a few suggestions that might be made to particular types of institutions.

Universities

Maintaining support for research. The line between teaching and research is often vague. To some extent this ambiguity has benefited research activity in the past, because resources needed to advance research have been partially funded out of funding for instruction that increased along with growing enrollments. Now that enrollments are declining, some of that funding will be reduced or even disappear.

If support for research is to remain stable when enrollments go up and down, state legislators, educational policy makers, and the general public will have to become much better informed than they are now about the importance of such activity to the general intellectual health and productive capacity of our country. This may require a public relations effort of massive proportions.

Reducing the oversupply of doctorate holders. Because enrollments are going down, there are fewer positions open to new Ph.D.'s, and because higher percentages of faculties hold tenure, there will be even fewer openings in the future. What is the wisest course? Preparing people, at great cost to themselves, to institutions, and to society, for positions that may not exist? Or denying people opportunities to make the most of their talents and capacities? The resolution of this question involves the quality of education different institutions provide, the reasons they make the effort, and the integrity with which they select the students for their advanced programs. The message, as tired as it is, is that institutions will have to restrain some of their own ambitions—particularly when they lack resources of a quality that makes it possible to offer future academics doctorate programs that are of truly superior caliber.

Contributing to the education of teachers. Universities have a substantial share of the responsibility for training the teachers who work in the schools and the administrators who run them. We need to learn how to educate more students so that they will be "successful," not only in ways that are admired by academics, but also in ways that are recognized in the workplace, the home, and the community. And when we learn how that is done, we have to find ways to make the benefits available to larger proportions of young people than we have succeeded in reaching in the past.

Universities have a special role, as the centers of research in higher education, to study the differences in learning styles and abilities among individuals and to make the results of their studies available to practicing teachers. Improving the skills of pre-college students could be an important investment in the quality of college and university education in the coming decades.

Comprehensive Universities and Colleges

Many of these institutions are former teachers' colleges and continue to serve a teacher-training function. They, too, should be working with elementary and secondary schools for the improvement of learning skills of American youth. One possibility is that some of these institutions will overreact to the decreasing need for schoolteachers during the next decade and a half. Although some reduction in teacher-training activities is clearly in order, widespread abandonment of such programs would be ill-advised. A preferable strategy would be to use the 1980s and 1990s to concentrate on the improvement of the quality of teacher education and to train specialists in the instruction of students with exceptional learning styles or problems.

Liberal Arts Colleges

The strategies for most liberal arts colleges in the next decades are those with which most of them are all too familiar—conserving resources and recruiting as vigorously as possible. A few of them may be able to make alliances with other institutions to reduce expenses and share facilities. And some of them may be able to identify certain programs that merit special development and marketing.

Two-Year Colleges

Since survival is not a real problem for most of these institutions, the help they are most likely to need is in defining their role in higher education. Virtually all of their present functions are now shared with other institutions. Their most nearly unique function has been to provide educational opportunities for those who, for various reasons, have been unable to gain admission to four-year institutions or do not want to attend college too far away from home.

One new function recently suggested for community colleges is that of assuming residual responsibility for the youth in their communities. This is a totally new concept, and it remains to be seen whether it will be taken seriously. If it is, the United States may go further than any other industrialized country in institutionalizing its concern for giving youth a more productive role in society.

Too much of the discussion of the impending 20 years is phrased in terms of success and failure, but neither extreme represents the inevitable reality for most American colleges and universities. When the next two decades become a subject of history rather than conjecture, the interesting story will be how their efforts made a difference in the overall quality and character of American higher education.

Aspects of American Higher Education, 1969-1975. By Martin Trow. 1977.

In 1969, when the Carnegie Commission first began to gather information through broad national surveys of college teachers, graduate students, and undergraduates in a large sample of American colleges and universities, ferment and turbulence in higher education was at its height. The preceding few years had seen strikes, the occupation of buildings, and violent clashes between students and police on almost every major campus and on many of the smaller ones as well. By contrast, when the Carnegie Council sponsored comparable surveys in 1975, the emotional and political climate on campus had changed enormously. The war in southeast Asia had ended, and with it intense political ferment on the American campuses. In some areas of behavior and attitude, teachers and students did not change their views very much between 1969 and 1975. In other areas, they have become rather more liberal or permissive over these last few years, and in still others they have become more conservative.

In 1969, when undergraduate students were asked, "What is your overall evaluation of your college?" 66 percent said they were satisfied or very satisfied, and only 12 percent were dissatisfied or very dissatisfied. The rest were "on the fence." In 1975 comparable responses to that question were 71 percent satisfied and 9 percent dissatisfied. Almost exactly the same proportion of undergraduates in both 1969 and 1975 expressed themselves as satisfied with the quality of classroom instruction in their college. When presented with a similar statement, "I am basically satisfied with the education I am getting," graduate students showed a similar pattern of response—77 percent in 1969 and 70 percent in 1975 expressing their agreement either strongly or with reservations.

We cannot draw from these figures the conclusion that there are no grounds for dissatisfaction with American higher education. The appearance of the absence of discontent on American campuses today should not give us any great grounds for complacency, just as the misleading appearance of widespread discontent in 1969 should not have been the basis for some of the hasty innovations that were introduced at that time.

The Trend Toward Conservatism on Academic Issues

The area in which we find a distinct tendency toward more conservative positions than were held in 1969 is that of academic policy and practice. For example, a substantial majority of undergraduates in 1969 agreed, strongly or with reservations, that "Undergraduate education in America would be improved if grades were abolished." That proportion (59 percent in 1969) fell to 32 percent by 1975. Among faculty members, agreement with the same question fell from one-third (34 percent) to one-fifth (19 percent) in the same period. Similarly, agreement with the proposition that "Undergraduate education would be improved if all courses were elective" fell among undergraduates from 51 to 35 percent and among faculty from 21 to 13 percent between 1969 and 1975. Changes in attitudes toward academic work have not, on the whole, been very large, but they've been consistent on a number of different issues. For example, when students were asked what things are most important for them to get in college, they were slightly more likely in 1975 to say "training in skills for an occupation" and "a detailed grasp of a special field" than they were in 1969 and slightly less likely to answer "learning to get along with people" and "formulating the values and goals of my life." They were about as likely to reply "a well-rounded general education." Slightly more conservative, or at least more traditional, views are reflected in responses to the question "Would you agree or disagree that a professor's teaching inevitably reflects his political values?" In 1969 half the undergraduates agreed, strongly or with reservations, but by 1975 the proportion who agreed had fallen to 42 percent. Teachers' positive responses to a similar question fell from 40 to 30 percent over the same time period, also reflecting a more traditional belief in the possibilities of insulating academic work from personal political values.

Social Attitudes

If faculty and students have swung back moderately to more traditional academic attitudes and positions, on other, even more fundamental values, there has been remarkably little change on the college campuses between 1969 and 1975. For example, to the statement "I believe in a God who judges men," three-quarters of the undergraduates polled in 1969 agreed, strongly or with reservations; in 1975 the proportion was almost identical (76 percent). Again, to the question "Do you consider yourself deeply religious, moderately religious, largely indifferent, or basically opposed to religion?" the distribution among students and faculty has been almost unchanged since 1969. Among graduate students, the proportion calling themselves deeply or moderately religious has remained at a little over two-thirds; the proportion of faculty giving these two responses has fallen slightly from 69 to 63 percent.

The picture with respect to political values and identifications is similar. One can hardly find a six-year period in the political life of this country that has shown greater turbulence and swings of opinion and sentiment. And yet, here, too, our samples in American colleges and universities show a remarkable stability in their basic political identifications over this period of time. When we asked both students and faculty members, "How would you characterize yourself politically at the present time?" and offered them a five-point scale from "left" to "strongly conservative" along which they could locate themselves, the different groups (1) showed very similar distributions and (2) showed astonishing stability in their identifications from 1969 to 1975. If we combine the proportions of those who called themselves "left" and those who called themselves "liberal," we see that the proportion of undergraduates in these two categories together fell from 44 to 35 percent between 1969 and 1975; among graduate students, the proportion in these two categories was constant at about 41 percent over the two time periods. The stability in other categories of political self-identification was equally great; a very small percentage in any group at any time called themselves "moderately conservative"; and a little over a quarter, "middle of the road."

Race. Academic attitudes toward minorities have been remarkably ambivalent over the six-year period. About two out of five undergraduates polled, one-third of the graduate students, but only one-fourth of the faculty agreed that "any special academic program for black students should be administered and controlled by black people," and these proportions were almost identical in 1969 and 1975. By contrast, three-quarters of college and university teachers agreed that "any institution with a substantial number of black students should offer a program of Black Studies if they wish it," and the proportions on this issue rose slightly between 1969 and 1975. Studies are one thing; to accept racial criteria for administering them is quite another. But attitudes have shifted somewhat on the issues of special minority admissions and faculty appointments, reflecting a renewed strength of traditional academic values on these issues. For example, the proportion agreeing with the statement "The normal academic requirements should be relaxed in appointing members of minority groups to the faculty (here) (of my college)" is quite low in both time periods and among all groups; but, as low as it was, it fell sharply between 1969 and 1975, from 24 to 13 percent among undergraduates, from 19 to 14 percent among graduate students, and from 20 to 12 percent among the faculty members who were most directly concerned. Both the low levels of support for that position and the tendency for them to be going even lower are indications of the persistent strength of the academic value of universalism—that is, of emphasis on a person's work and achievement when one is making academic appointments rather than on his race or other personal characteristics.

On the broad question of education and integration, college students and teachers are distinctly more liberal than the general population. On the issue of whether "racial integration at the public elementary schools should be achieved even if it requires busing," polls have shown overwhelming opposition in the general population. But among college and university teachers, over one-third (38 percent) agree with that position, strongly or with reservations, although that proportion has declined somewhat from the 43 percent in agreement in 1969. Among undergraduates, who more closely reflect the attitudes of the general population, the proportions agreeing with that statement fell from 36 to 26 percent between 1969 and 1975, while among graduate students it remained relatively high, falling only slightly from 43 percent to 38 percent in that period.

Other issues. Part of the difficulty of capturing in a phrase or slogan the broad movement of sentiments and attitudes of college students and teachers over the past six years is that it has been inconsistent. We have already pointed to some areas where there has been little or no change since 1969, and others in which views have become somewhat more liberal or permissive. For example, views on campus toward the possession and use of marijuana have become much more permissive over the past six years, perhaps reflecting and perhaps in part causing the movement toward decriminalizing the possession of that drug. To the statement "Marijuana should be legalized," in 1969 only 30 percent of faculty, 36 percent of graduate students, and 46 percent of undergraduates replied that they agreed with or without reservations. By 1975 those proportions had risen to 50 percent among faculty, 56 percent among graduate students, and 55 percent among undergraduates.

But attitudes toward marijuana were not part of a general movement toward more liberal or permissive positions with respect to forms of crime or violence. For example, the proportion of undergraduates (the only group we asked) who supported the abolition of capital punishment fell from 60 to 36 percent between 1969 and 1975.

Attitudes toward women. Attitudes toward women on campus reflected, and perhaps led, changes in the attitudes toward women in the larger society. Whatever had been the case in earlier decades, by 1969 open expression of prejudice against women or doubts about their intellectual abilities and commitments were rare and unpopular on most campuses. When asked their views regarding the statement "The female graduate students in my department are not as dedicated as the males," only one college teacher in five expressed agreement, even with reservations, in 1969. Half of them expressed strong disagreement. Almost exactly the same proportions of graduate students held those views in that year. By 1975, the trend had gone even further; fewer than one in ten (8 percent) of faculty or graduate students agreed with that statement, while two-thirds of the teachers and three-quarters of the graduate students expressed strong disagreement.

Collective Bargaining and Faculty Characteristics

There has been much talk over the past few years about the rise of collective bargaining among college and university teachers, and even some tendencies in that direction. The attitudes of college and university teachers are on the whole favorable to the idea of collective bargaining, for others if not for themselves, and have become somewhat more favorable since 1969. For the statement "Collective bargaining by faculty members has no place in a college or university," the proportion agreeing, even with reservations, fell from 38 to 28 percent between 1969 and 1975; even in the big research universities, almost none of which have collective bargaining agreements for their teaching faculty, only about one-third would say that it has no place in higher education. Over three-quarters of college and university teachers believe, with or without reservations, that collective bargaining by faculty members "is likely to bring higher salaries and improved benefits"; only 5 percent disagree strongly with that statement. This surely expresses a disposition toward collective bargaining. Nevertheless, many faculty members—clearly still a majority—have some reservations. Moreover, these questions do not reveal what they believe they might lose with the advent of collective bargaining. Certainly most institutions of higher education have as yet shown no propensity to rush into collective bargaining.

Faculty members in 1975 were on average of higher rank and more likely to have tenure than in 1969. One half of all the college and university teachers in our sample held the rank of associate or full professor in 1975, as compared with 41 percent six years earlier. Proportions holding tenure had grown appreciably, from 49 percent in 1969 to 57 percent in 1975; in the universities, that proportion was up to about 60 percent from about 50 percent in 1969.

For all the talk in recent years about de-emphasizing research and re-emphasizing teaching, faculty in our 1975 sample showed a markedly greater inclination to write and publish than did faculty in 1969. In 1969 nearly three-quarters of all college and university teachers reported that they had never published or edited a book or monograph. By 1975 that figure was down to two-thirds. Two-thirds of all faculty members in 1969 had not published any kind of professional writing in the previous two years; in 1975 that figure was just one-half. And when asked whether their interest lay primarily in teaching or research, the great majority in 1975, as in 1969, still said "teaching," but the proportion who said "research" had risen from 15 to 25 percent, a very significant increase in that period.

There has been a sharp increase in the proportion of academics who perceive the need for publication. The proportion agreeing that "In my department it is very difficult for a person to achieve tenure if he does not publish" grew between 1969 and 1975 from 27 to 46 percent, and the proportion who strongly disagreed declined from nearly one-half to one-third of college and university teachers. It seems probable that it is just more difficult to gain tenure in a system that is no longer growing rapidly or at all, and that among all the criteria by which candidates for tenure are assessed, publication, as well as teaching and service, is being assessed more severely.

Student Finances

We can hardly review the state of higher education today without some reference to the effects of rising inflation, tuition, and living costs on the ability of students to finance their college careers. This has, however, been balanced, to some extent, by the extension of federal grants and loans. In the case of graduate students, however, there is considerable reason to believe that there are fewer graduate teaching and research assistantships than in 1969. In any event, one question asked in both 1969 and 1975 gives us some basis for assessing the judgment of the students themselves about their own financial situations.

Graduate students were asked in both 1969 and 1975, "How adequate are your finances to your present needs?" In 1969 just 24 percent of graduate students replied "inadequate" or "very inadequate"; by 1975 the proportion giving these responses was 30 percent. Only 5 percent in 1969 and 7 percent in 1975, however, said that their finances were "very inadequate" to their needs. A larger proportion of undergraduates expressed concern about their finances. When they were presented with the statement "My finances are adequate to my present needs," over one-third (36 percent) disagreed either strongly or with reservations in 1969; that proportion had risen to 45 percent in 1975.

But there is a broad subjective element in the assessment by students (as by anybody else) of their economic circumstances in relation to their own conception of their needs. For example, when presented with the statement "I am going deeply into debt to finance my graduate studies," fully a quarter of all graduate students in 1975 expressed agreement, and 11 percent expressed strong agreement, but nearly three-fourths reported that they hadn't borrowed anything from other than friends or family.

For all the discussion of student loans and federal support for those loans, they are, taken together, a relatively minor factor in the support of graduate students. Even if we include loans from family or friends together with government or bank loans and loans from their own institutions, only about 15 percent mention getting them at all, and only about 5 percent mention any of them as a primary source of their support while in graduate school. Similarly, the decline in the support of teaching research assistantships has been a relatively small factor overall. Seventeen percent mentioned them as a primary source of support in 1969, compared to 11 percent in 1975; and there was very little change in the proportion that mentioned fellowships and scholarships—about 8 percent in both years. The decline in assistantships may actually have greater educational consequences, both in the opportunities for graduate students to get experience teaching and to work closely with faculty members on research, and in the effects that fewer teaching assistants have on the education of undergraduates in the big universities that employ teaching assistants.

Effectiveness, Quality, and Integrity of Academic Programs

Changing Practices in Undergraduate Education. By Robert Blackburn,
Ellen Armstrong, Clifton Conrad, James Didham, and Thomas McKune. 1976.

This study systematically examines the extent and kind of curricular change in a random
sample of U.S. colleges and universities between 1967 and 1974. It deals with changing
degree requirements; the amount, structure, and content of general education; the major
in selected disciplines; and the number and use of electives. Phase I of the study involved
an analysis of college and university catalogs. Phase II used transcript analysis to examine
the programs of graduates of six arts and sciences departments at ten colleges and universities in 1967 and 1974. The principal goals in Phase II were to determine the extent
to which student course-taking agreed with the requirements stated in the official an-
nouncements of colleges and universities, and to ascertain whether there had been a
change since 1967 in the extent of student specialization.

Degree Requirements

While the number of hours required for both A.A. and B.A. (B.S.) degrees dropped
slightly between 1967 and 1974, the decrease was minor compared to the appreciable
shift away from breadth and toward specialization in the actual education received for
a four-year degree. The change toward specialization was greater for schools that appreciably increased the percentage of the degree that could be fulfilled by electives. However, even with no increase in elective choice, students in 1974 selected a higher fraction
of electives in their field of concentration than they did in 1967.

General Education

Amount. The proportion of a student's undergraduate program in general education
was about 22 percent less in 1974 than it was in 1967, a drop of about 12 credit hours
in four-year colleges and 5 credit hours in two-year colleges. The variation among institutions extended from complete elimination of all general education requirements to
an increase.

Structure. There was a move away from specific course requirements toward distribution
requirements, for which the student selects from among a more or less specified set of
course offerings. Furthermore, free choice increased substantially in those institutions
in which distribution requirements were previously the norm. The general education
curriculum in 1974 was much less structured than in 1967.

The increases and decreases in distribution requirements from institution to institution tended to offset one another overall. The absence of a net change is misleading, however, because the institutions that increased distribution requirements are the ones that previously had prescribed, not free, courses. Moreover, those institutions that decreased distribution requirements, in the main, moved toward more free courses, not toward a prescribed pattern. That is, an appreciable number of institutions changed the structure of general education, and the trend of this change was away from a fixed pattern.

Content. The number of classes required in each of the disciplinary areas—humanities, natural sciences, and the social sciences—declined. In 1974, the typical general education program required a higher percentage of humanities than natural sciences. On the average, the decrease in required course work was greatest in the humanities and least in the natural sciences. But although the absolute decreases differed for each disciplinary area, the percentage decreases were about the same.

Basics. The number of institutions requiring English, a foreign language, or mathematics as part of general education declined appreciably from 90 percent of the institutions surveyed to 72 percent for English, from 72 to 53 percent for a foreign language, and from 33 to 20 percent for mathematics. (Enrollments in these areas, however, were sometimes higher in 1974 because a few majors still required these subjects, especially the latter two.) In addition, the percentage of colleges and universities requiring physical education declined from 86 to 55 percent.

Public two-year colleges differed from the four-year colleges in several respects. Few required a foreign language or mathematics in either 1967 or 1974. They did, however, require English and physical education. Furthermore, not as many of these institutions have eliminated these requirements as have their four-year counterparts.

The Major

Amount. There was essentially no change in the number of courses individual majors required or in the fraction of the total degree requirements a major represented (about one-third). In both catalog statements and student behavior, regardless of whether an institution had otherwise changed its curriculum, little was altered in the amount of course work required or taken to complete a major. It was not possible to ascertain whether the requirements within majors remained specified or had been changed to give students more choice.

Disciplines. The natural sciences required the largest percentage of course work for the major in 1974 and had the lowest proportion of electives outside their area. Since general education is typically an institutional rather than a divisional requirement, the academic area that requires the most courses for its majors necessarily allows the fewest electives. Physics and biology students used about 37 percent of their courses in fulfilling major requirements in 1974. This was about 10 percentage points higher than for students in either the humanities or the social sciences. According to the transcript analyses, humanities students took the fewest courses in their majors, but the difference compared to social science majors was small.

Electives

Amount. The number of electives students may submit for a degree, after general education and major requirements have been met, increased appreciably by 37 to 52 percent. Electives now range from 26 to 41 percent of degree requirements.

Use. No matter how much the number of available elective courses increased from 1967 to 1974, a much greater share of elective time was spent in the division of the student's specialization than in either of the other two divisions, irrespective of disciplinary concentration. The overall course-taking pattern for the degree thus showed a significant increase in depth and a corresponding diminution of breadth. However, the elective courses were more likely to be taken in other departments within the major division than within the major department. If courses outside a student's major department but within his or her area of concentration can be called breadth, then the trend was for students to select breadth-within-depth rather than depth-within-depth. These trends toward depth were equally true for students who had no absolute increase in the number of electives in their program.

Discipline. When students elected courses outside their major division, the courses were more likely to be in the humanities or social sciences than in the natural sciences. With fewer general education science requirements and with a larger share of the increased elective time spent in the field of specialization, humanities and social science graduates took less natural science in 1974 than they did in 1967.

Institutions

While almost every college and university changed to some degree over the time period, and while there was great variation in the extent of change across institutions, private colleges changed more frequently, and to a more pronounced degree, than did public institutions. The less-selective private four-year colleges changed the most, and the public universities and community colleges changed the least, but no distinctive patterns emerged.

Implications

The final section of the report presents related findings on change by institutional type, extent and consequences of changes, direction of change, types of general education, the movement away from natural sciences, and two-year colleges. It concludes with observations of the faculty role in curriculum change; selected implications of the survey results for students, institutions, faculty, and society; and suggestions for further inquiry.

A Degree for College Teachers: The Doctor of Arts. By Paul L. Dressel and Magdala Thompson. 1978.

The Doctor of Arts (D.A.) degree, designed as preparation for college teaching, has been offered in at least 25 universities and in 21 different fields. Several institutions and departments, after a brief trial, have abandoned it, and there are many variations in programs for the degree. Nevertheless, it seems to have caught on, and further expansion is reasonably assured.

Ph.D. and D.A.—Contrasts and Comparisons

The development of the D.A. has been seriously hampered by insistence that it be equal in quality to the Ph.D., although different in character; equally demanding in admission, retention, and degree requirements; and equal with respect to time, course, and dissertation requirements. The meaning of these proposed requirements is at best ambiguous. How can one compare a D.D.S. and an M.D.? Dedicated to distinctive goals, these degrees necessarily differ in content and requirements.

D.A. programs can provide the following advantages:

- Broad coverage of a discipline or field relevant to undergraduate education, although it need not include advanced graduate courses in all topics that occur in the undergraduate curriculum
- Demonstration by the individual of a capability to achieve independent assimilation of new materials as a prelude to understanding how to direct undergraduate independent study
- A grasp of some of the most significant actual and possible interrelations of an area of study with other fields and with practical problems and concerns
- Mastery of research tools and methods of the discipline at a performance and demonstration level
- Demonstrated facility in use of research and evaluation tools and methods required to understand pedagogical research and engage in curricular and instructional experimentation
- A grasp of the nature and objectives of undergraduate education, of its diverse interpretations in various institutions, and of the differences between students in motivations, abilities, and goals
- Experience (internship) in college teaching, especially at the freshman and sophomore levels, where the greatest variety in student background and motivation is typically found
- Familiarity with the latest teaching technology and its most effective use.

In 1970, moral and financial support for the D.A. degree developed in swift succession. But the unfavorable employment picture for Ph.D.'s and diminished federal funding for graduate students, combined with enrollment declines and state moratoriums on the development of new degrees, slowed the growth of such programs. The fact that the D.A. programs survived these conditions and continued to grow and spread indicates both their merit and their need. The increase in programs has now slowed down considerably, but the number of students in the programs has greatly increased.

Diversity in the D.A.

No standard model or conception of the D.A. is yet apparent. Indeed, programs have developed in various patterns consonant with the intent to achieve acceptance of the degree on its own merits. This diversity makes it difficult to characterize the D.A. But diversity is essential because the typical D.A. candidate is not like the prospective Ph.D. Many of the D.A. students are mature individuals who have taken the task of teaching very seriously and have engaged in both the development of new courses in areas not previously studied and a continuing evaluation of their teaching and their instructional materials. A rigid, required D.A. program that takes no account of such rich and varied experience would make no sense.

Universities and faculties that espouse the D.A. degree should be cautious about permitting variations that may bring the degree into disrepute. Although it has been argued that former colleges of education could be the natural place to launch the D.A., initiating a new degree in institutions lacking experience with the doctorate can lead—and has led—to unsatisfactory practices and circumstances. These include:

- Mediocre or weak faculty with respect to scholarship
- Poor attitudes toward and misuse of the D.A. when faculty members hope for a Ph.D. and are forced to settle for a D.A.
- Futile attempts to define interdisciplinary approaches, thereby permitting a diffused program of unrelated blocks of credit from several disciplines
- Assignment of a block of credits and courses (possibly specified and required) in education, higher education, or psychology with little or no attempt to coordinate them and integrate them into the program as a whole
- Lack of staff, library resources, educational technology, and space to launch or support a program
- Lack of leadership and program review to assure that regulations and quality are upheld in planning individual programs
- Division of the program into a number of unrelated experiences including courses and seminars in the discipline, courses or seminars dealing with teaching and learning, research in the discipline, research on teaching, and internships
- Elimination of dissertation or thesis, leaving the program with no adequate and clearly defined culminating task
- Use of the D.A. degree as an alternative for Ph.D. candidates whose motivation and ability for research are lacking
- Acceptance of weak students to provide numbers justifying the existence of the program.

If they are to be respected, D.A. programs must not follow the pattern of secondary school teacher preparation, which requires a large block of education courses and credits that has little or no relation to the substantive disciplinary field in which teaching will be done. A department offering a D.A. must make a commitment to good teaching and take responsibility for and offer professional courses. This need not and should not prevent professors of education from participating in such courses and seminars.

Sound criteria for initiating a teaching-oriented doctorate must include, as a minimum:

1. There should be strong central administrative support and coordination from the office of the graduate dean.
2. There must be, at the least, a strong master's level program and some graduate professors who are also concerned with undergraduate instruction.
3. The institution must be one in which the quality of undergraduate education is a central and continuing concern of the administration.
4. A teaching doctorate should not be launched in an institution until there is a critical mass of key programs that can interact and cooperate.
5. There should be provision for individuals interested in interdisciplinary courses to develop programs on other than a departmental basis and also to have experience in the planning and teaching of such courses.

6. No program should be initiated without insistence that special efforts be made to provide a unified experience culminating in a planned and well-executed teaching role.

The issue of comparability of the D.A. and the Ph.D. is clearly less significant that defining the D.A. and gaining recognition of it on its own merits. A D.A. program should provide experiences that will enable its students to:

1. Acquire knowledge of a body of content in depth, including its structure and methodologies, and ability to present it effectively to undergraduates
2. Increase the quality of learning by emphasizing objectives that highlight the understanding and application of knowledge rather than the mere acquisition of facts
3. Define objectives and standards to be achieved by undergraduates and encourage the assumption of personal responsibility for their attainment
4. Broaden the conception of instruction to include techniques beyond the ubiquitous lecture and the recitation or question-answer approach
5. Develop sensitivity to student concerns and motivations and ability to interpret the discipline in such manner as to arouse student interest
6. Acquire professional knowledge and skills essential to effective communication of knowledge, including: knowledge of the principles of human learning and motivation; ability to apply them to the development and utilization of improved teaching procedures; awareness of and willingness to use a wide range of media for improving instruction and constructing more effective courses designed in reference to a total curriculum; and familiarity with the objectives of that curriculum
7. Recognize that for many undergraduates (including most majors) contact with a particular course or discipline will be of little consequence unless they acquire understanding of the significance and relevance of the materials to other areas of interest and to the problems and concerns of society, and unless they also acquire increased facility in broad behavioral objectives transcending particular courses and disciplines but essential to successful performance as a citizen and worker in society
8. Develop awareness of the learning process and of individual differences in interest and ability so that adaptations of assigned tasks and expectations can be made and students will become capable of continuing their learning beyond the confines of the classroom and campus
9. Develop evaluation feedback procedures whereby the teacher and each student are kept informed as to progress
10. Be sensitive to values and preconceptions implicit in the teacher's discipline and in the application of its principles and concepts to social and personal problems
11. Maintain continuing scholarly activity to keep abreast of new developments
12. Develop awareness of the relation of their discipline to other disciplines and to the current social scene and accept the obligation of communicating these relationships to students
13. Develop awareness of the role that each course plays in the undergraduate experience and a commitment to assist the student in integrating experiences in the course with other aspects of education.

To attain these goals, the prospective teacher certainly requires knowledge of a discipline or of the essential concepts, methodologies, and values of a group of related disciplines. But scholarship, in the sense of knowledge of content and of disciplinary structures and methodologies, is not enough; indeed, it may be subsidiary to other insights and competencies, because success as a teacher must be evaluated in reference to what students learn and apply as a result of being taught.

A graduate program that provides for all these outcomes must have:

1. Admission requirements that specify evidence of a deep interest and possibly some experience in teaching students, evidence of interest in communicating knowledge in ways that make a difference in the thought patterns and capabilities of students, and evidence of interest in interrelations of disciplines and of their applicability in understanding and resolving the problems of individuals and society

2. Systematic individual evaluation that is as much concerned with ability to communicate effectively with students as with substantive knowledge

3. Extradepartmental and interdisciplinary courses that require that the student relate his field of major study to other fields so as to enhance his insights into the significance of his major field and his ability to make it more meaningful to students of diverse interests and abilities

4. Graduate courses in which the professors are almost as concerned about the effectiveness of their own presentations as about the details and niceties of the materials presented

5. Graduate advisers who are in continuing contact with the candidates to assist them in interrelating and acquiring maximum benefit from their several experiences

6. Flexibility so that adjustments and waivers of aspects of the program will be made on the basis of the candidate's prior experience or individual interests and needs

7. Program definition in terms of attainment of the competencies required for successful college teaching rather than by credit quotas for the various elements of the program

8. The possibility of programs embracing two or more disciplines, viewed not in reference to their adequacy in providing mastery of the several disciplines, but rather as justified by the specification of unifying principles, problems, or themes and by the type of instruction and institutional program toward which the candidate is oriented

9. An internship that, depending on the prior experiences and ability of the individual, may move through several levels from observation of an unusually effective professor, assisting and consulting with such a person, developing and presenting (not solely by lecture) materials under the supervision of this professor, but culminating in full responsibility for preparing, teaching, and evaluating one or more courses involving students other than majors, thereby requiring the intern to be aware of the diversity in student backgrounds and goals that presents one of the most difficult teaching tasks

10. A thesis, dissertation, research, or evaluation effort, often related to the internship, that provides a demonstration of the prospective teacher's ability to interpret a disciplinary base to students in ways that facilitate broad behavioral learning rather than rote recall of facts.

Such a culminating experience would correct the danger inherent in a program that draws upon several fields of knowledge and can too readily result in a number of isolated experiences (disciplinary courses, professional courses, internship, and research) that are never integrated into a model of expected professional behavior.

The D.A. is here and here to stay. It is taking on an identifiable character and meets a need that Ph.D. programs have generally failed to serve.

Handbook on Undergraduate Curriculum. By Arthur Levine. 1978.

This handbook is intended to be a comprehensive reference bringing information to bear on educational decision making from the classroom level to the institutional level. Although it is too detailed and voluminous for adequate summarizing, an outline of its contents can be described in some detail.

Introduction

There is no such thing as *the* undergraduate curriculum in America. There are more than 3,000 colleges and universities in this country, and each has a curriculum that is in some ways unique. This would seem to make it impossible to discuss the subject, but, fortunately, American colleges and universities fall naturally into groups or clusters, and in these groups curricular similarities are found and differences are reduced to comprehensible levels. These groups are based on the 1970 typology of the Carnegie Commission *(A Classification of Institutions of Higher Education)*.

Faculty Characteristics

Teaching staffs at the nine types of institutions vary widely with respect to size, research credentials, research interest, concern with undergraduate academic problems, and quality of teaching performance.

Table 1 shows a 25-fold variation in faculty size between the largest type of institution and the smallest. The median department size varies 5-fold between the largest type and the smallest. The number of faculty and the size of departments decrease systematically by type among universities and four-year institutions, with Research Universities I the largest and baccalaureate-granting institutions the smallest. Two-Year Colleges employ more faculty than four-year liberal arts institutions.

Students at larger institutions have an opportunity to study with more faculty, but they do not rate their teaching as well as other undergraduates. Students are most satisfied with teaching and believe faculty to be most interested in their academic problems at smaller colleges—Liberal Arts Colleges I, Liberal Arts Colleges II, and Two-Year Colleges. Even so, the majority of undergraduates at all types of institutions rate their teaching satisfactory.

This situation exists despite wide variation in faculty interest in and training for teaching. With the exception of Liberal Arts Colleges I, whose mission is in great measure training students for graduate school, the interest of faculty in teaching over research increases progressively from type to type—from 46 percent in Research Universities I to 94 percent in Two-Year Colleges. Publication rates and percentage of faculty with Ph.D.'s vary in the same fashion. Teaching is rated quite highly, though not the best, at the institutions where faculty have the fewest Ph.D.'s, the highest rate of nonpublication, and the least interest in research.

Table 1. Characteristics of faculty at different institutions by Carnegie type

	Research Universities		Doctorate-Granting Universities		Comprehensive Universities and Colleges		Liberal Arts Colleges		Two-Year Colleges
	I	II	I	II	I	II	I	II	
Average number of FTE faculty	1,605	992	678	623	297	236	76	64	141
Median department size	21-25	16-20	16-20	11-15	11-15	11-15	6-7	4-5	6-7
Percentage of faculty with Ph.D.	66	63	64	57	48	45	57	38	10
Percentage of faculty more interested in teaching than research	46	56	61	68	82	86	82	91	94
Percentage of faculty without professional publications in last two years	18	23	28	36	52	58	53	69	82
Percentage of students believing "most faculty at my college are strongly interested in the academic problems of undergraduates"	38	44	52	44	53	57	81	70	65
Percentage of students satisfied with teaching at their college	65	64	71	65	68	69	85	76	76

Undergraduate Characteristics

The student bodies at the nine types of colleges and universities differ in size, sex, race, age, residential status, degree aspirations, high school achievement, parents' education, transfer rate, and competitiveness, as shown in Table 2. The largest university has 23 times the number of undergraduate students of the smallest college, and the average Research University II enrolls more than 15 times as many undergraduates as the average liberal arts college. Students at smaller colleges tend to be less competitive than their counterparts at larger universities. Other undergraduate characteristics seem less determined by institutional size than by college and university type.

The Two-Year College is a magnet for new or nontraditional students. It has the largest proportion of nonresidential students, older students, nonwhite students, and low academic achievers in terms of high school grade point average and degree aspirations. The counterparts for the traditional student are the most selective liberal arts college (Liberal Arts College I) and the most research-oriented university (Research University I). They enroll the largest proportion of young, white, high academic achievers whose fathers graduated from college. Interestingly, the major difference between the two types is that Research Universities I enroll the least women and Liberal Arts Colleges I enroll the most. This is so because selective liberal arts colleges are more likely than any other type of institution to be single sex colleges—particularly women's colleges.

Curriculum Characteristics

Tables 3, 4, and 5 deal with curriculum or curriculum-related concerns. Table 3 illustrates the range of subjects taught at the nine types of institutions. Subjects are divided into four areas: arts and science studies, professional studies, occupational/technical studies, and new subjects—those current topics that have only recently entered the undergraduate curriculum in substantial fashion. For three of the four areas, common or exemplary courses of study have been selected and the proportions of institutions of each type offering classes on the topic have been compared. This was not necessary for arts and science studies (consisting of subjects such as biology, psychology, and English), because nearly all of the colleges offer them in substantially the same form. With the exception of the arts and sciences, this table shows significant differences in subject matter emphasis between the nine types of colleges and universities. Professional studies are most common in doctorate-granting universities and least common in Liberal Arts Colleges I. Occupational/technical programs are found most frequently in two-year colleges and least frequently in Liberal Arts Colleges I and Research Universities I. New subjects are offered most often in Research Universities I and least often in Liberal Arts Colleges II.

Table 4 compares the number of courses offered and the ratio of courses to full-time equivalent faculty (a summary measure of full-time and part-time faculty) at the nine types of institutions. As might have been expected, the institutions with the most faculty and students offer the most courses—both undergraduate and graduate. Thus, the university with the most courses has nearly ten times as many as the institution with the fewest, which makes quite a difference for its students in terms of the diversity of courses available to them.

What is especially interesting in Table 4 is not this expected difference in the number of courses but the considerable differences between institutions in the ratio of courses to faculty members. Institutions with the largest number of courses—Research Universities I—have the lowest ratio of courses to faculty, while the four-year institutions with the smallest number of courses—Liberal Arts Colleges I and II—have the largest ratio.

Table 2. Characteristics of undergraduates at different institutions by Carnegie type

	Research Universities		Doctorate-Granting Universities		Comprehensive Universities and Colleges		Liberal Arts Colleges		Two-Year Colleges
	I	II	I	II	I	II	I	II	
Median number of FTE undergraduates	11,000 to 13,500	15,000 to 17,500	7,500 to 10,000	11,000	4,000 to 5,500	1,500 to 2,200	750 to 1,000	750 to 1,000	1,200 to 1,400
Percentage of women undergraduates	43	47	43	52	50	56	66	56	50
Percentage of nonwhite undergraduates	9	12	10	6	16	15	8	18	20
Percentage of undergraduates above 24 years of age	11	11	18	11	19	19	4	15	45
Median percentage of residential students	41-50	31-40	31-40	21-30	31-40	41-50	71-80	61-70	0
Percentage of students aspiring to a bachelor's degree or less	29	37	39	40	43	37	26	40	61
Percentage of students with A- average or better in high school	49	41	35	33	27	25	43	29	17
Percentage of students with C+ average or less in high school	9	12	15	14	20	17	8	20	31
Median fathers' education	college graduate	some college	some college	some college	high school graduate	high school graduate	college graduate	high school graduate	high school graduate
Percentage of students who attended more than one college	32	31	40	33	34	32	20	29	36
Percentage of faculty stating "students in my department are very competitive"	65	56	55	49	47	39	41	43	44

Table 3. Percentage of institutions offering undergraduate programs in selected subjects by Carnegie type

	Research Universities		Doctorate-Granting Universities		Comprehensive Universities and Colleges		Liberal Arts Colleges		Two-Year Colleges
	I	II	I	II	I	II	I	II	
Arts and Science	100	100	100	100	100	100	100	100	98
Professional Studies									
Business	66	77	91	95	91	83	46	94	93
Education	77	81	82	95	66	92	76	91	67
Engineering	91	73	77	50	37	13	5	6	55
Forestry	5	23	18	0	7	4	5	6	27
Health science	38	45	46	55	60	4	9	24	65
Home economics	14	50	45	60	40	29	5	9	32
Occupational Technical Studies									
Law enforcement	0	23	36	50	31	42	9	15	60
Medical technology	14	36	55	55	47	46	14	29	25
Secretarial science	0	18	18	20	24	46	5	21	73
Trade/technical	5	10	9	40	29	8	0	3	68
New Subjects									
Environmental studies	36	64	45	60	24	25	28	41	18
Ethnic studies	77	55	45	50	29	21	23	9	23
Urban studies	50	41	18	35	16	29	28	32	12
Women's studies	23	14	9	20	7	8	18	0	7

Table 4. Relationship between the average number of courses and faculty at different institutions by Carnegie type

	Research Universities		Doctorate-Granting Universities		Comprehensive Universities and Colleges		Liberal Arts Colleges		Two-Year Colleges
	I	II	I	II	I	II	I	II	
Number of courses offered									
Undergraduates	2,385	2,285	1,835	1,767	1,226	874	579	501	463
Graduate	2,132	1,754	1,043	916	298	108	12	3	0
Total	4,517	4,039	2,878	2,683	1,524	982	591	504	463
Course/faculty ratio									
Undergraduate	1.5	2.3	2.7	2.8	4.1	3.7	7.6	7.8	3.3
Graduate	1.3	1.8	1.5	1.5	1.0	.4	.2	.1	0
Total	2.8	4.1	4.2	4.3	5.1	4.1	7.8	7.9	3.3

For example, Research Universities I offer less than three courses per faculty member, while Liberal Arts Colleges I and II list nearly eight. Eight courses are a lot of subjects to teach, far more than most faculty are equipped to teach well. As a consequence, liberal arts faculty members may be required to broaden their teaching abilities significantly beyond their graduate training or else teach subjects in which they are not expert. At best, the difference in course/faculty ratios is the difference between having faculty who teach expert specialties and having faculty with broad expertise; at worst, it is the difference between myopic specialists and unqualified generalists.

Student perceptions of the academic ethos of the different colleges and universities are compared in Table 5. Students compare college with high school with increasing frequency as institutions (except Liberal Arts Colleges I) decrease in size, award less advanced degrees, and engage in less research. Impersonal treatment or being treated like a number in a book has exactly the opposite relationship (with three exceptions—Doctorate-Granting Universities II, Liberal Arts Colleges I, and Two-Year Colleges). Satisfaction with college and wasteful duplication of high school studies have no relationship to college similarity with high school or impersonal treatment. With the exception of Liberal Arts Colleges I, all institutions are comparable in satisfaction and duplication. This may be indicative either of a sorting process whereby students with differing college expectations and varying backgrounds choose institutions of varying types or of a process of adaptation whereby institutions mold themselves to the students they admit.

Part One: Undergraduate Curriculum Today

This section of the handbook consists of basic information about American college curricula and is primarily descriptive, dealing with normative practices, their history, strengths, weaknesses, and alternatives. Part One contains chapters entitled "General Education," "The Major or Concentration," "Basic and Advanced Skills and Knowledge," "Tests and Grades," "Education and Work," "Advising," "Credits and Degree," "Methods of Instruction," and "The Structure of Academic Time." These are the elements that make up the undergraduate curriculum. Together with the extracurriculum (the noncredit and nonclassroom activities available to students through recreational, social, and cultural activities sponsored by colleges or by college-related organizations) and the hidden curriculum (learning that is informally and sometimes inadvertently acquired by students in interactions with fellow students and faculty members and inferred from the rules and traditions of an institution), they constitute a college education. Every chapter in Part One discusses three points regarding each curriculum element: (1) its definition and history, (2) its current state, and (3) the popular criticisms and proposals arising out of the current state.

General Education

General education is the breadth component of the undergraduate curriculum and is usually defined on an institutionwide basis. It generally involves study in several subject areas and frequently aims to provide a common undergraduate experience for all students at a particular institution.

This chapter illustrates how the many different and occasionally conflicting definitions and purposes attributed to general education are largely a consequence of its historical evolution and notes that interest in this topic has recently increased. This interest has been premised in many institutions upon a desire to reinstitute the coherence felt to

Table 5. Academic ethos of different institutions by Carnegie type

	Research Universities		Doctorate-Granting Universities		Comprehensive Universities and Colleges		Liberal Arts Colleges		Two-Year Colleges
	I	II	I	II	I	II	I	II	
Percentage of undergraduates stating "my college is much like high school"	12	15	13	16	24	26	20	31	39
Percentage of undergraduates indicating "part of my undergraduate education was a wasteful repetition of high school"	37	40	38	42	40	41	22	37	36
Percentage of undergraduates satisfied with college	71	69	77	68	69	69	80	70	74
Percentage of undergraduates believing most students are treated like "numbers in a book"	65	60	50	59	45	36	9	18	33

be currently lacking in undergraduate education, to create common elements in a curriculum that has grown more individualized and diverse, and to provide moral training for young people in a time when moral scandals have rocked the nation.

The chapter discusses four of the most common philosophies of education upon which general education programs have been based; namely, perennialism, essentialism, progressivism, and reconstructionism. The amount of general education in the undergraduate program is also discussed. Three types of general education are described: core curricula, distribution requirements, and free electives (no required program). The most common components of general education programs—introductory disciplinary, advanced disciplinary, and interdisciplinary courses; freshman and senior seminars; and great books courses—are defined, and the content of general education, including advanced learning skills, field distribution requirements, and general understanding courses, is examined.

Certain aspects of general education have been regularly criticized. The following criticisms are examined in detail:

1. General education is a good idea in theory, but fails in practice.
2. General education programs are unpopular with students.
3. The student clientele of American colleges and universities is too heterogeneous to permit common general education programs.
4. General education is of little economic value to the student who is forced to study it.
5. General education programs are weak in educational and philosophical integrity.
6. General education is poorly timed.

The Major or Concentration

The major or concentration is the dominant and probably the most successful feature of undergraduate education today. It usually consists of a number of courses in one field or in two or more related fields and is the depth component of the curriculum. It is intended to provide students with a body of knowledge, methods of study, and practice appropriate to a subject or subject area.

In describing the style of the major, this chapter notes that most colleges (89 percent) have a major requirement, but the amount of the undergraduate curriculum devoted to the major varies by degree program and subject area. Also defined are types of majors, including disciplinary, interdisciplinary, field, joint, double, major-minor, and student-created majors as well as undergraduate programs with no major. The variety and number of majors in institutional categories and student and faculty relationships to the major are highlighted.

Finally, the validity of six common criticisms of the major is examined. These criticisms are:

1. Majors vary in quality and substance within as well as between schools.
2. Students spend too much time on the major.
3. Majors prepare students primarily for graduate school.
4. Liberal arts majors are at a disadvantage in the job market.
5. Majors and faculty specialization deleteriously dominate the undergraduate curriculum.
6. Neighboring colleges commonly duplicate most of each other's majors while failing to include other desirable fields in their curricula.

Basic and Advanced Skills and Knowledge

Basic skills are the abilities and *basic knowledge* is the information a student needs to embark on college study. Colleges differ in the kinds of skills and knowledge they regard as basic or entry-level. Proficiency in reading, writing, arithmetic, and study skills is considered essential for all college work; however, some colleges also require students to have advanced skills and knowledge in a foreign language, geometry, algebra, and English composition. Colleges also differ on the level of skills and knowledge within a subject they feel is necessary for undergraduate study.

Not all students enter college with the basic skills or knowledge necessary to function at their institution. The instruction provided to bring them up to required basic skills or knowledge levels is called compensatory education. The terms *remedial* and *developmental* education are frequently used as synonyms for *compensatory* education, but there are important differences. Remedial education implies improvement of student skills and knowledge for the purpose of entering a program for which the student was previously ineligible. Compensatory or developmental education emphasizes the building of new strengths and seeks to overcome deprivations associated with the home, family, and earlier study.

This chapter examines the state of basic and advanced skills and knowledge by presenting available data on student achievement in the areas of reading and writing, mathematics, natural science, social science, literature, and foreign language.

Nearly all colleges and universities offer one form or another of skills and knowledge education, and three types are defined. These are: (1) supplements to the traditional curriculum, (2) skills and knowledge courses, and (3) learning centers. Many colleges use combinations of all three. Finally, some current criticisms are explored, and proposals for improvement for those identified as valid are discussed. These criticisms are:

1. Declining scores on basic skills and knowledge tests by undergraduates are due to flaws in the tests rather than changes in student performance.
2. Skill declines are due to college open admissions practices, which permit unqualified students to attend institutions of higher education.
3. Compensatory education has a very low success rate.

Tests and Grades

Tests are the means of measuring student ability or attainment, and *grades* are the valuation of student performance. The characteristics and types of tests are identified in a discussion of the state of tests. This chapter is concerned chiefly with teacher-constructed examinations measuring achievement and not with standardized tests measuring aptitude.

The main types of teacher-constructed tests are defined. These include both course-based and non-course-based examinations. Non-course-based examinations assess the skills and knowledge accumulated in several courses rather than in any particular course.

The characteristics of grades are examined with reference to how grading systems differ from one another in purpose (formative versus summative evaluation), standards (absolute or relative), and audience (targeted at students or others). The various types of grading are described and evaluated.

The following criticisms of tests and grades are discussed:

1. Tests and grades yield little useful information and their use is detrimental to undergraduate education.

2. Nontraditional (nonletter or non-numerical) grades are a liability to students in applying to graduate and professional schools.

Education and Work

Education for work is alternately called vocational education, occupational education, and career education. The terms are not synonyms, but the differences between them are not obvious. Vocational education has traditionally been associated with schools rather than colleges and has developed a stereotypic connotation as low-level training. For this reason, neither of the terms *vocational* or *occupational* education are used in this volume; instead, college-level training in work subjects is called *professional/technical* education.

In 1969 and 1976, American undergraduates were asked by the Carnegie Commission (and Council) how important it was for them to get training and skills for an occupation from their college education. In 1969, 57 percent said it was essential, and in 1976, 67 percent responded in the same fashion.

The four types of education for work offered by colleges are (1) academic instruction, (2) work experiences (including internships, apprenticeships, cooperative education, and full- or part-time employment), (3) joint industry-higher education programs, and (4) vocational counseling. The appropriateness of education for work in an undergraduate program is also discussed.

Advising

Advising refers to counseling available to students or potential students that is directly or indirectly concerned with the undergraduate curriculum. The four principal types of advising are academic, vocational and career, personal, and special group (for example, minorities and women).

The sources of advising most frequently available to students include books and pamphlets, college orientation, faculty members, freshmen seminars, administrators, professional counselors and counseling centers, students, and team advising. Other forms of advising occasionally available to students include computers and other communication technology, alumni, community resource persons, and brokerage organizations.

The following major criticisms of advising are discussed:

1. There is too much advising in the American college; this serves only to coddle undergraduates and keep them dependent.
2. The quality of academic advising is generally poor.
3. Advising divides students into academic, vocational, and personal components and places emphasis largely on the academic, making complete student counseling difficult and in some cases impossible.

Credits and Degrees

The *credit* is a time-based, quantitative measure assigned to courses or course-equivalent learning. It is usually defined as 50 minutes of instruction per week for a term. As terms vary in length, credits are usually referred to as semester or quarter credits. *Unit* and *credit hour* are synonyms for *credit*.

The *degree* may be thought of as a grade or rank that colleges and universities confer upon students for their educational attainments. The bachelor's degree and the associate's degree are the two principal types awarded at the undergraduate level.

When students earn a predetermined number of credits, they are usually rewarded with degrees. It is important to note, however, that all undergraduate degrees are not credit based. The most common alternative requires that students complete a specified number of courses, each of equal weight, to earn a degree. For instance, Amherst College requires that students complete 32 semester courses in order to graduate with a bachelor of arts degree. The earliest degrees, doctoral degrees, were awarded at the University of Bologna in the early thirteenth century, but the credit system was not introduced until the 1870s.

There are currently almost 200 different associate degrees and 650 types of bachelor's degrees. The characteristics of the five principal degree programs (A.A., A.S., A.A.S., B.A., and B.S.) are discussed.

The following criticisms of degrees and credits are evaluated:

1.   The credit system is inappropriate for undergraduate education.
2.   Degrees have little meaning.
3.   The certification or degree-granting function of colleges undermines instruction.

Methods of Instruction

Teaching or *instruction* is defined as guidance or direction intended to cause learning. However, until recently, very little was known about learning. College and university instructors have all but ignored it and have concentrated instead on teaching. It is assumed by many educators that quality teaching, whatever that may be, yields quality learning.

Instruction is examined in terms of six primary teaching methods: (1) live courses, (2) mass media, (3) new technologies such as the computer, (4) independent study, (5) experimental education, and (6) libraries.

Live courses constitute by far the most common form of collegiate instruction. They are analysed in terms of the variation in size, duration, type of instructor, and teaching method. The evidence that exists about the impact of these characteristics on course effectiveness is presented.

The following criticisms of instructional methods are evaluated:

1.   The quality of undergraduate teaching is generally poor.
2.   Current undergraduate instruction does not adequately take account of student differences.

The Structure of Academic Time

The term *academic time* refers to college calendars and the number of years of study required for students to earn a degree. Bachelor of arts and bachelor of science degrees require four years of full-time study or the equivalent in 98.4 percent of American colleges and universities. Associate's degree programs almost uniformly last two years (in 99.6 percent of institutions). However, more and more curricular options are available that permit students to increase or decrease the amount of time spent in college.

Time-shortening practices include credit by examination, summer school attendance, course overloads, credit for experiential learning, college courses for high school students, early admission to college, early exit from high school, and compression of courses and programs. Time-lengthening practices include stopping out, noncredit remedial or compensatory education, repeating courses, part-time attendance, enrollment beyond the minimum number of credits needed for graduation, and college transfer.

Several time-variable practices are also discussed: progress by examination, self-paced instruction, competency-based education, and contract learning.

The four academic year calendars that dominate American higher education are the semester, the trimester, the 4-1-4 system, and the quarter system. Three others that are less prevalent are also discussed, namely, block, variable term length, and open entrance.

The following common criticisms of the structure of academic time are examined:

1. Time is an inappropriate commonality in undergraduate degrees.
2. Shortening the amount of time required to earn a college degree is infeasible at this time, since student aptitude test scores are declining nationally.
3. General education is weakened by time shortening.
4. Interruption or acceleration of the four-year course of studies results in poorer student performance.

Part Two: A Comparative and Historical
Perspective on Undergraduate Curriculum

A Comparison of Modern Philosophies of Higher Education

Philosophers have not always seen eye to eye on the purpose or form the undergraduate education should take. In the course of nearly three-and-one-half centuries of under-graduate education in this country, opinion about the purpose of college has evolved from consensus to a current state of wide disagreement.

This chapter describes, compares, and contrasts the visions of the university and the undergraduate curriculum of seven modern philosophers of education: John Cardinal Newman, John Dewey, Alfred North Whitehead, Thorstein Veblen, Abraham Flexner, Robert Hutchins, and Clark Kerr.

Proposals for Curriculum Change:
The Recent, the Radical, and the Rejected

This chapter presents the proposals of 21 contemporary authors or groups to change the undergraduate curriculum. These ideas differ from those in the preceding chapter in that they are not referred to as classics. Most are too new, too radical, or too recently rebuffed for this distinction. Their authors are Stephen Bailey, Daniel Bell, the Bressler Commission at Princeton, The Carnegie Foundation for the Advancement of Teaching, Arthur Chickering, K. Patricia Cross, Paulo Freire, Paul Goodman, Harold Hodgkinson, Sidney Phenix, Jean Piaget, Carl Rogers, E. F. Schumacher, B. F. Skinner, Harold Taylor, Alvin Toffler, and Robert Paul Wolfe. The authors disagree about what needs to be changed in undergraduate education, but all agree that significant changes are essential.

Curriculum Highlights of the Past: 1900-1964

Reform, innovation, and change have been characteristic of higher education in this country almost since its beginning. In fact, the second American college, William and Mary, adopted a reformed version of the classical curriculum of the first, Harvard. Since that time change in one form or another has been continuous. Yet there have been high-lights in curriculum change that are referred to regularly when people discuss under-graduate education. This chapter presents descriptions and life histories of 12 such high-lights of the twentieth century through 1964.

By the start of the twentieth century, the fundamental changes in higher education that had occurred during the nineteenth century—utilitarianism, research, graduate education, and populism, to name but a few—were assimilated and the modern American conception of undergraduate education had emerged. The period between the turn of the century and the start of World War I found the free elective curriculum waning in popularity. By the time of the war, the undergraduate program was similar to today's blend of free electives, breadth requirements, and concentration. It was also attacked on the same grounds as today's curriculum—for its lockstep approach, overspecialization, eclecticism, and general lack of integrity. The critics suggested four remedies, all called "liberal education." They were, more specifically, general education, collegiate education, experiential or life education, and honors and independent study. Between the end of World War I and the start of World War II, these remedies were most notably realized in the Contemporary Civilization program at Columbia University (1919), work-study at Antioch College (1921), the Honors program at Swarthmore College (1921), the Claremont cluster colleges (1925), the Experimental College at the University of Wisconsin (1927), the undergraduate college at the University of Chicago (1928), Bennington College (1932), the General College at the University of Minnesota (1932), and the Great Books program at St. John's College (1937).

During and after World War II, which made clear the common heritage and bonds among the American people, the curriculum change focused more specifically upon general education. With the end of the war, the national solidarity associated with a shared external enemy was threatened, and general education was viewed as a vehicle for reinforcement. Though many colleges wrote reports and adopted new curricula, the most influential and best-known curriculum was that adopted at Harvard as a result of a volume entitled *General Education in a Free Society* (1945).

Curriculum change acquired another theme in 1957 with the launching of Sputnik. Many viewed this space breakthrough as a Russian triumph over the intellectual and educational capacity of America. Curriculum reform in succeeding years emphasized intellectual excellence and acceleration of study. Oakland University (1959) in Rochester, Michigan, and New College (1964) in Sarasota, Florida, were founded in that spirit.

Current Curriculum Highlights: 1965 to the Present

The current era of curriculum reform is a by product of the 1964 Free Speech Movement at the University of California at Berkeley. As at Berkeley, the causes of campus unrest were frequently noncurricular, but the resulting soul searching brought to light student dissatisfaction with the post-Sputnik mentality and curriculum, which emphasized the needs of society but failed to consider the needs of the individual student. Experience with the civil rights movement and later with the war in Vietnam hastened the student rejection of post-Sputnik education.

The first curricular fruits of the new era were harvested in Berkeley within a year. They included Joseph Tussman's Experimental College Program, which was conceived before the Free Speech Movement but sought to overcome the educational problems that were criticized during the protest, and the autonomous Free University of Berkeley, a direct product of the student protest that was emulated on many campuses.

Student activism contributed directly or indirectly to other curricular changes of the late 1960s. The changes emphasized student-centered education and the adoption of new socially relevant courses. A concern for the whole student and affective learning was common. Major curriculum changes conceived or implemented during this period included the establishment of Simon's Rock (1965), the University of California at Santa Cruz (1965), Bensalem College at Fordham University (1967), a new curriculum at Brown University (1969), and Hampshire College (1970).

The nationwide student strike in reaction to the U.S. invasion of Cambodia and the shootings at Kent State and Jackson State universities in spring 1970 closed the 1960s era of campus unrest. Since that time, campus protests have continued, but their causes have more often been bread-and-butter issues such as rising tuition, faculty layoffs, and program cutbacks. The 1970s marked the end of visions of limitless growth for American colleges and universities, now faced with day-to-day realities of tight budgets and a ceiling or decline in student enrollments.

The impetus for change in the 1970s has come from administrators at institutions suffering from financing or enrollment declines, from public systems responding to perceived new needs, and from organizations not traditionally associated with higher education, such as brokerage organizations and proprietary schools. Some curriculum changes have been primarily procedural, concentrating on more efficient delivery systems and the measurement of educational outputs. Others have tried to attract or respond to a new variety of students—members of minority groups, the academically disadvantaged, adults, and the poor. Still others have involved the development of vocational curricula and community-based educational assistance centers. Some of the outstanding developments of the decade have involved the awarding of degrees by proprietary schools such as the Technical Career Institutes (1970), the creation of such nontraditional adult colleges as Metropolitan State University (1972), the development of competency-based curricula at Sterling College (1972), and the rise of brokerage organizations like the Capital Higher Education Service (1973).

A number of curriculum changes have traversed the moods of both the 1960s and 1970s. Flathead Valley Community College (1967) is an example of a college created in the 1960s but based on 1970s themes. Economic hardship reached the Flathead Valley in Montana before much of the rest of the country, so it developed a 1970s-style college before such colleges became fashionable. New College at the University of Alabama (1971) encompassed the moods of the 1960s and 1970s by adopting a curriculum that responded to the concerns of both periods.

The range of results from these curriculum changes has been wide. Some institutions and programs are flourishing; others are no longer in existence. The handbook describes these curriculum changes in chronological sequence, examines how each came into being, and observes how each has progressed.

Characteristics of Curriculum Change

Change implies something new and different. The degree of newness and differentness is relative; a change may be new and different only at the college at which it has been adopted. In fact, much of the prominent change in higher education might better be classified as renovation of older ideas than as innovation. Whether it is renovation or innovation, academic change exhibits several consistent patterns or characteristics in terms of strategy, stages, participants, and elements. This chapter reviews these characteristics, using as illustrations the institutions described in the previous two chapters.

Five different strategies are discussed: (1) the establishment of new colleges; (2) the development of innovative enclaves within existing colleges, (3) holistic change within existing colleges, (4) piecemeal change within existing colleges, and (5) peripheral change outside existing colleges.

The process of curriculum change involves four stages: (1) recognition of need, (2) planning and formulation of a solution, (3) initiation and implementation of the plan, and (4) institutionalization of the change. The making of educational policy involves and is actively influenced by many different participants, whose roles are examined.

A curriculum change can be described as successful if it achieves the purpose for which it was intended and continues without being prematurely cut down. Success or failure in curriculum change is the product of (1) the environment targeted for change, (2) the characteristics of the change, and (3) the process by which the change is introduced.

The Undergraduate Curriculum Around the World

In order to put the American undergraduate curriculum in perspective, this chapter looks at the character of undergraduate education in The People's Republic of China, France, the Federal Republic of Germany, Great Britain, Japan, Sweden, and the Union of Soviet Socialist Republics. All of these countries are facing or have faced the same two problems that confront the United States—increasing demands for access to higher education and the need for better articulation of the university with the needs of society. These problems have serious curriculum implications, and the seven countries have chosen to deal with them in a variety of different ways. In five of the seven—all but Great Britain and the Soviet Union—the result has been a major curriculum change in the past ten years.

A Chronological History of the Undergraduate Curriculum

This chapter provides a concluding overview and chronology of the history of undergraduate education from 532 B.C. to the present, divided into two sections: "Antecedents of American Higher Education" and "The American Experience." It is supplemented by Appendix A, a documentary history of 12 important events in the development of the American undergraduate curriculum. They are: (1) the making of Harvard College, 1642; (2) the founding of the University of Virginia, 1824; (3) the Yale Report of 1828; (4) the Morrill Land-Grant Act, 1862; (5) the creation of Cornell University, 1868; (6) the inauguration of Charles William Eliot as president of Harvard, 1869; (7) the establishment of The Johns Hopkins University, 1876; (8) the report of the Committee of Ten, 1893; (9) the launching of the Wisconsin Idea, 1904; (10) the Great Books curriculum at St. John's College, 1937; (11) the Harvard Redbook entitled *General Education in a Free Society*, 1945; and (12) the report of the President's Commission on Higher Education, 1947.

Curriculum: A History of the American Undergraduate Course of Study Since 1636. By Frederick Rudolph. 1977.

The curriculum is an arena in which the dimensions of American culture have been measured, a record of how the American people faced such matters as who were to be their leaders, whether the society was to be governed by an elite, and how far the concept of equality was to be carried in the provision of courses of study appropriate not just for the few but for the many.

The best way to misread or misunderstand a curriculum is from a catalog. Because the curriculum is a social artifact, the society itself is a more reliable source of curricular illumination. The traffic between the society and the curriculum may essentially have been all or mostly in one direction but, by any useful definition of culture, the traffic flows in both directions, the curriculum responding to the society and in turn shaping that society.

Curricular history is American history and, therefore, carries the burden of revealing the central purposes and driving directions of American society. As the curriculum has moved across time from being wholly prescribed to greatly elective, the loss of philosophic purpose has been repeatedly but unsuccessfully countered by structural devices designed to support some coherent, defensible general education. Yet perhaps there is really no curriculum, only an assumption of burdens and discrete programs for carrying them out: an accidental compromise between the only partially understood past and the unanticipated future.

The English College on the American Frontier

Going to college was one of the least likely things to happen to young men in the years before 1800 and for some years after, and it did not happen at all to young women. In its initial impulse the American college grew out of the tradition in European Calvinist communities of founding new colleges or reshaping old ones to "preserve the purity and continue the propagation of the faith."

But the curriculum could not exclusively be an instrument in the service of God or of Church and State, as the founders of Harvard and Yale had intended. Because they were colleges, the tools for fulfilling their purposes were the liberal arts and sciences, an inherited body of learning that had a life and purpose of its own. Whether they liked it or not, the colonial colleges were burdened with perpetuating the "learning and culture of Europe."

This purpose may have been gratuitous, but it was not allowed to be deflected, nor was it allowed to undermine the colleges' original purpose to qualify a governing elite for carrying forward the society that had created colleges in the first place as guarantees of their own permanence.

The curriculum of the English college on the American frontier was conditioned by poverty, its distance from England, the lack of concentrated centers of population, and the vast reaches of an unexplored and unsettled country. Students found themselves being taught as groups of freshmen or sophomores, whereas instruction at Oxford and Cambridge was an individual matter resting on the student-tutor relationship. The first and most noticeable casualty of these conditions was standards. In the colonies professional preparation for the practice of law and medicine fell out from under the sway of the colleges. Apprenticeship—cheaper, more practical, more informal—was substituted for the "theoretical and systematic education" traditionally offered by higher faculties in institutions of higher learning.

While remarkable stability was characteristic of the college course of study in the English colonies, the curriculum was responsive to European intellectual movements. The growth of mathematical studies in the curriculum was unavoidable once Newtownian physics made its way into the course of natural philosophy. The teaching of natural philosophy (physics) was transformed by the "New Learning." As first taught at Yale by Rector Abraham Pierson ("based on his own Harvard studies"), physics included a section on "angels," the kind of physics that required no mathematics to understand. At Harvard the breakthrough in physics toward a Newtonian orientation occurred under the tutelage of Charles Morton late in the seventeenth century, but in 1711 William and Mary College was the first college to establish a scientific professorship in America—a professorship of natural philosophy and mathematics.

Science was being organized into a number of discrete subjects, not just mathematics. Breaking loose from natural philosophy, from physics as it had long been taught, were such curricular departures as chemistry, geography, and natural history. And science was proposing a new way of looking at the world. The message that increasingly presented itself to the students of the colonial college was revolutionary: "The business of the mind (is) to discover things hitherto unknown."

One group of sciences—botany, chemistry, anatomy, and physiology—first appeared in those colleges that undertook to provide a medical course as well as a bachelor's course. The significance of these developments in drawing attention to the world at the expense of the sublime was not yet widely apparent, but the sciences had not only found their way into the curriculum—they were also speaking a new language, rearranging old priorities, and changing the definition of a college education.

In one sense the curriculum was a course in the learning and use of language. The proper use of the language of divinity was held in such high regard that at the time of the founding of Harvard the rules of Cambridge and Oxford called for the use of Latin in ordinary conversation. University authorities held their students to these rules with some difficulty, while similar rules in the American colleges failed.

The language and literature of the future—English—began to find support in an environment that was emancipating itself from the past. Oratory, history, and poetry were peripheral in the curriculum because they did not lend themselves to the old deductive logic and were, moreover, instruments of delight and emotion. Here were subjects and materials that went beyond the didactic to the esthetic and to a fuller definition and understanding of the human experience. The rise of such subjects was another measure of the decline of theological authority and of the shift to a concern with the nature of man.

In the meantime, while natural philosophy, which kept that Aristotelian label long after it might better have been called Newtonian physics, was spawning new subjects and encouraging mathematical studies, moral philosophy (ethics) was moving into an ascendancy over the curriculum as a whole. Developing into a kind of capstone course that was wonderfully reassuring in its insistence on the unity of knowledge and the benevolence of God, moral philosophy by the mid-eighteenth century had achieved dominance over logic, divinity, and metaphysics in the course of study.

This shift in emphasis and in the locus of moral guidance was accompanied by a recognition among the ruling elders of the New England colonies that they needed something more than the Bible to hold their communities together. The course in ethics became the place where an effort was made to find a substitute for a declining "divine coercive authority." If men could not be counted on to behave correctly because God said so, then reason and human nature—God's gifts to man—might be enlisted in the battle to bring them as near as possible to the side of the angels.

The route and methods by which ethics as a separate discipline elevated reason, surpassed theology, invited deist thought into the course of study, and generated a secular approach to moral questions were circuitous and complex, but the course was well on the way there by the end of the colonial period.

The scholastic tradition of syllogistic argumentation, with its presupposition that all truth could be demonstrated only by deduction rather than induction, became a clumsy device for discovering truth in an environment receptive to the New Learning. It had been an effective instrument for testing and mastering a prescribed course of study in a book-scarce environment that was friendly to the scholastic tradition, but it was absolutely useless as an instrument for the "advancement of free inquiry." Beginning in the 1760s the idea of the "man of letters" as a proper definition of the college graduate brought the study of belles lettres into the curriculum—oratory, history, poetry, literature. An emphasis on reason and observation, on rational moral behavior, replaced a reliance on divine law in the study of ethics. Professors replaced tutors, and tutors themselves became specialists. The syllogistic disputation and its reliance on deductive logic had all but disappeared.

The New American Curriculum

During the first half of the nineteenth century, higher education in the United States was not yet rationalized. Its character was disorderly, lacking in standards, without coherence. The colleges thought that they knew what had been holding society, fragile under the best of circumstances, together, but now everything was uncertain. Life in the United States looked like a free-for-all. Egalitarian impulses challenged the essentially elitist pretensions of the colleges. The agricultural-commercial world to which they had been attuned was undergoing strains that were moving it in the direction of a techno-logical-industrial order.

Progress was inescapable, and it undermined the traditional prestige of classical learning. The ancient languages and the classics did not lend themselves to egalitarianism: Their usefulness, while demonstrable, was limited to a narrow class. Graduates of the colleges, the liberally educated gentlemen, were themselves losing political influence to the rising West and the urban immigrant. Students appeared in the colleges whose sense of their own futures did not include careers in the traditional professions, but many more young men recognized a new path to status in the rise of wealthy self-made businessmen and did not appear in the colleges at all. Science, the very instrument of progress, made an insistent claim for attention, at the expense of the ancient languages.

Until the American Revolution, the colleges, for all of their difficult times and uncertainties, had not been defensive and nervous about their own legitimacy, but in the unsettled context of a dynamic new nation, they stumbled around in search of some secure identity. The absence of a system in the educational arrangements of the new republic was particularly apparent in college preparation. A student might arrive at college by a variety of roads—prepared by a resident tutor or by a local clergyman, in a private day school or a Latin grammar school, in the preparatory departments of the colleges themselves, or increasingly in multipurpose academies that provided a terminal general education as well as college preparation. This diversity of preparation was a chal-lenge to the college curriculum: It meant that the freshman year was often repetitive of secondary school and that colleges could not rely on any standards or any pattern of preparation.

The future of the American college, a definition of what should be going on there, was determined by Yale, for Harvard not only slipped away from the norm, whatever it was, but it would have been absolutely uncomfortable doing the same as all the others. In 1828 the Yale course of study may have been as stable a statement of values and purpose as could be found anywhere in the United States.

During the first three years, Yale students took courses mostly in Greek, Latin, and mathematics, but they also studied geography, history, science, astronomy, English grammar, and rhetoric. The senior year was a time for large questions and, to some ex-tent, a final process of refinement: moral philosophy and metaphysics, English com-position, and belles lettres. Each class experienced something special: Freshmen trans-lated from the Latin, sophomores and juniors were instructed in English composition; juniors received lecture demonstrations in experimental physics; seniors studied chem-istry, mineralogy, geology, and theoretical physics. Juniors and seniors debated; all classes declaimed, were instructed in rhetoric and oratory, and heard lectures from the professor of ancient languages.

This curriculum and the practices that supported it prompted an ill-conceived adolescent rebellion in 1825 by the students of Yale and induced the Connecticut legislature to write a report critical of the impracticality and unprogressive nature of the curriculum. The students appeared to be objecting to the style, the legislature to the content, but the Yale corporation took them both seriously, and asked the Yale faculty to prepare a report. The Yale Report, as it came to be known, provided a rationale for, and a focus for comprehending, a course of study that was wandering somewhere in the no-man's land between inflexibility and disintegration. Henceforth the American college curriculum could not be understood without reference to this first major effort to spell out both a philosophy and the particulars of an American system of higher education.

The report's summary view of the college course was a plea for quality. Conscious of the democratic pressures against a thorough education and the readiness with which a shallow education could be translated into social and economic mobility, Yale was uneasy about the prospects of a nation at the mercy of superficially educated demagogues and uncouth millionaires. Yale saw itself and the rest of the colleges as the ramparts of a free people. It could not and would not try to do everything. Conscious of its own failings, it would attempt to improve the quality of what it did the best way it knew how—by raising admissions standards.

In the defense of the ancient languages, those fundamental bastions with which the colleges had long identified themselves and their purposes, the report was uncompromising. A college education without the classics was not a college education. The ultimate strength of the classics was their superb effectiveness in strengthening and enlarging the mental facilities.

The emphasis of the report on the college as an environment for furnishing the mind with potentially useful and retrievable facts ran up against life itself. The curriculum embraced the uses of the past but withdrew from the uncertainties of the future. Trapped by the social and economic environment in which they had been reared, the authors of the Yale Report confronted the college course of study within a psychological framework that allowed them little room for imagination. Their respect for quality, for standards, for certain enduring definitions of human worth, was class bound. The Yale Report was an effort to apply the brakes to a country that was showing how to exploit everything and everybody but that had not yet learned how to harness human wisdom. It was not enough.

Most colleges in the decades before the Civil War found themselves drifting into certain practices intended to hold themselves and the curriculum together—electives, options, partial courses, parallel courses. Because survival was always on their minds, college authorities were not purists about the course of study. Since keeping knowledge out of the course of study was a sure way of keeping students out of the colleges, the simplest method, and the one most widely practiced, for accommodating new subjects was to welcome them, tuck them into the required course here and there, and make them optional when they piled up embarrassingly.

The practice of including peripheral lectures on the new subjects was another way of keeping abreast while falling behind, for falling behind clearly could not be avoided if the colleges insisted on holding on to the old course while adding on to it. At a time when depth in study and understanding was a common concern of the reformers, the vast majority of the colleges were edging toward greater superficiality and toward a confrontation that they were trying desperately to avoid—a confrontation with a whole set of inherited truths: A college course can contain everything a student needs to know; college authorities know best what that is; a student's special aptitudes and interests are a poor guide to what he should study; the mind is a set of muscles with inherent faculties that can be trained only by a demanding course in ancient languages and mathematics.

Electives overwhelmed the curriculum only after the curriculum collapsed of its own superficiality and its inability to sustain the interest of students.

Students everywhere soon learned what to do about the curriculum. As for its formal parts, most of them recognized the senior course in moral philosophy as a compensatory experience. It justified the curriculum and rationalized it, asserting that knowledge could be ordered, unified, and contained. By the nineteenth century the moral philosophy course had become a remarkable excursion into ethics. Politics, economics, sociology, law, government, history, esthetics, international law, and fine arts were territories into which the moral philosophers, usually the presidents, roamed.

The course was eminently utilitarian, and the students knew it. As a guide to ethical conduct, it served the happy purpose of bringing into harmony reason, intuition, and Christian orthodoxy. The moral philosophers were not social critics: They came down on the side of God, the United States, and the governing class. Moral philosophy lacked democratic pretension; it located virtue and wisdom not in the people but in an educated few fit to be their leaders.

The extracurriculum was an invention of necessity. The central institution of extracurricular life was the literary society. Making a temporary early appearance at Harvard in 1728 and a more lasting appearance at Yale in 1753, the literary society movement soon created a pair of rival societies at almost every American college. In their debates, orations, libraries, and literary exercises, they imparted a tremendous vitality to the intellectual life of the colleges. Lacking the restraints imposed on the classical curriculum by tradition and a narrow social purpose, they were in a position to welcome new subjects and interests into their libraries and their exercises—English literature, French literature, poetry, literary criticism, modern history, and creative writing. The functional student-centered college library first entered the American college as an extracurricular agency of the literary societies.

The societies existed with the approval of college authorities, who generally provided the space necessary for society activities and even arranged the hours of the regular course of study to accommodate those activities. The literary societies were testing grounds for those purposes of the colleges that could not be examined in the regular course of study—character, leadership, imagination, self-reliance—and therefore fulfilled in action what the senior course in moral philosophy could provide only in theory.

The literary societies' importance to what by mid-century had developed into the American system of higher education makes the term *extracurricular* a misnomer. This system consisted of the college chapel, the dying but still socially respectable and useful classical course of study, the capstone course in moral philosophy that was its great glory, and the extracurriculum with which the students took charge of their own education. At mid-century these four components were in as happy balance as they ever would be again. Henceforth all four would be on collision course.

Crisis and Redefinitions

The colleges were plagued by unpopularity and uncertainty of purpose into the 1870s and beyond. A developing rationale, even as the colleges headed unwittingly toward curricular chaos, made its appearance, however, not by some magic wand's stroke but because it could no longer be delayed.

The city and urban economic enterprise were alternatives to rural stagnation and farm life for hundreds of thousands of young Americans, and they were also alternatives to going to school and college; they provided environments in which life was recast and new opportunities seized. The transformation that took place in nineteenth-century America also found expression in the colleges as they stumbled toward clarifying how they were going to fit into the world of new technology, vast material gains, and broadened opportunities. Colleges geared to the need of village elites to flaunt their Latin and Greek required either a new rationale for the old curriculum or an altogether new curriculum. One or the other or some packaging of both would be necessary if the colleges were to be vital instruments of a democratic society.

Almost every new college in the developing West expressed the concern of its Eastern-educated founders for the future of a society that allowed itself to be taken over by barbarians. But the evidence suggests that, when the new self-made manufacturers, engineers, and merchants were ready to attach their names and fortunes to the development of schools of applied sciences, the classical colleges were standing in line with their hands out. Some of those colleges did what they could to avoid contamination—they affiliated, but they did not integrate.

The scientific schools did not open up the way for science in the classical colleges. Science, as studied in the classical colleges, was science as an instrument of human understanding and contemplation of the divine; while the science in the new scientific schools was science as an instrument of human arrogance and the exploitation of nature. The first of the scientific schools was developed from within the faculties of Yale and Harvard. Their students, for whom admissions standards were low and whose course of study was of three years' duration, were well aware of their second-class citizenship in the citadel of the arts.

The existence of these schools soon confronted the colleges with a major question of institutional integrity. Harvard solved the problem by giving the graduates of its scientific school a bachelor of science degree, beginning in 1851; the next year Yale created for the graduates of its scientific school the bachelor of philosophy. The adoption of these degrees provided an instrument for meeting the demand for a more practical course of study, for increasing enrollments and avoiding bankruptcy, and for maintaining the ingegrity of the B.A. degree.

But the example of the German university, with its traditions of research and subject-matter specialization, appealed to many American educators. Just how the concept of a higher faculty of scholars who created new knowledge and trained their successors could find a place in the American colleges was a baffling problem. The opening of Cornell University in 1868 at Ithaca, New York, was a particularly American answer. Cornell was revolutionary in design and influence—the first American university. Cornell's first president, Andrew D. White, spelled out his conviction that undergraduate education should be both special and general. He committed the university to generous access to fully developed programs of a vocational nature in a wide range of professions in which none was to be considered superior to any other. Cornell's readiness to extend formal training and professional recognition to such old occupations as farming, engineering, and business was accompanied by a desire to remedy the failure of the colleges to provide a general education of a nature that the public would support.

An appropriate balance between pure science and training in applied science was difficult to achieve. Students attracted to Cornell were so vocationally oriented that their pattern of course selections shoved Cornell more in the direction of an expanding technical curriculum than in the direction of a broadened range of opportunities in the liberal arts and sciences. At Harvard a different clientele used the elective system to shove Harvard in the opposite direction. In both cases, however, the lesson was clear: The shape of the curriculum, the growth of departments, the peculiar instructional mix of any particular institution was a measure of the degree of choice allowed to students and the responsiveness of the institution to those choices.

Cornell University was the first new institution of higher education in America since the founding of Harvard College to succeed in becoming a model for other institutions and a far-reaching influence on the curriculum.

It oriented the American university away from the dominant research interest that characterized the universities of Germany toward an emphasis on service to the material and moral aspirations of the middle class. This was an emphasis that the situation of American higher education required and that also explained Cornell's great popularity. Before identifying Cornell with research and scholarship, White identified it with an educational philosophy that helped poor but energetic young men and women to get rich. Thus, it enjoyed the almost unique experience of being selective in its admissions, and, after two years in operation, Cornell enrolled more than 250 freshmen, the largest first-year class thus far in American college history.

So persuasive to others was Cornell's success that the service function of the curriculum became a guiding motive in the development of the course of study in the great state universities and land-grant colleges founded under the Morrill Act of 1862. This act charged each state with using proceeds from the sale of the federal lands for the support of colleges of which "the leading object shall be, without excluding other scientific or classical studies, to teach such branches of learning as are related to agriculture and the mechanic arts."

Once a place like Cornell had demonstrated the existence of great popular approval for making career preparation a guiding purpose of its undergraduate curriculum, not only was the educational philosophy of the Morrill Act fully vindicated, but the college course of study itself was now fully wrested from the control of the classicists and henceforth at the mercy of the vocationalists. To a considerable extent, the history of the curriculum since the opening of Cornell has been a continuing struggle between the humanists, for whom Cornell's great success was a clear defeat, and the vocationalists, for whom Ithaca might properly be considered a shrine.

Cornell's one great weakness allowed a new institution in Baltimore, Johns Hopkins University, to become the first great American university dedicated to advanced learning and the production of scholars, and its success, like Cornell's, sent a creative impulse through institutions struggling to get out from under the grasp of collegiate traditions.

As a model of the research university, Johns Hopkins had much to convey—a spirit that could be carried anywhere and supported by vast philanthropies or by lonely scholars in their libraries; the concept of a *major* concentration in a cluster of related subjects constituting specialization, to which a broadening experience was added in a lesser cluster called a *minor*; and its young men with their Ph.D.'s and their enthusiasm for study and learning.

The decline of Johns Hopkins both as a center of production of scholars and as an influence after the 1890s was instructive evidence that scholarship and research could not easily be made the dominant purpose of an American university. Johns Hopkins, however, had paved the way for a successful assault on the undergraduate course of study; advanced work leading to the Ph.D. degree became one earmark of an American university; the degree itself became a necessary credential in the emerging profession of college and university teaching; the teachers proceeded to redesign the course of study according to educational philosophy as practiced in Baltimore.

Cornell's immediate success required of the old prestigious Eastern institutions soul searching of great intensity. While Yale hoped more or less to stand still, Harvard elected a new president, Charles W. Eliot, who in 1869 began a 40-year transformation of a provincial college into a national university.

One of Eliot's reforms was the use of electives, as an instrument for redefining Harvard. Eliot's sense of the appropriateness of the elective system for his purposes was unerring. He would not contaminate the classical with the technical or the technical with the classical, yet electives allowed Harvard to respect the individual talents, interest, and worth of every young man. The particular strength and peculiarity of Eliot's position was his recognition that the elective system would allow him to use the curriculum to fulfill that purpose as well as bring to the support of Harvard the resources necessary to carry it out. For a broadening of the elective system was an encouragement to students and professors to design a curriculum according to their interests, and there was no question in Eliot's mind what those interests would lead to—more applied science, more economic progress, more support from the manufacturing class, and enthusiastic students, enthusiastic professors, lively instruction, all moving toward a higher level of scholarship.

Eliot's design was not cynical. If it called for conquering Harvard College, it also called for raising the standards of admission at the professional schools to a level that required a B.A. for admission. The result was a strengthening of the college by giving it solid purpose and a new source of enrollment.

New degrees, new subjects, old courses redesigned—all proceeded from the movements that were receiving dramatic expression in Ithaca, Cambridge, and Baltimore. The old moral philosophy course became something of an anachronism in an environment that no longer addressed itself to the unity of knowledge but was so busy piling it up that to many observers only anarchy and disunity could be at the end of the road. On top of the change in the curriculum itself was added an accelerating change in the style of instruction and examining. The lecture became a characteristic substitute for the waning recitation method of instruction. The discussion-group approach to teaching moved into undergraduate instruction through teachers trained in the tradition of the German university seminar, in which the professor and a few students engaged in critical textual study and interpretation.

Two other areas of academic practice yielded to the pressure of change. The colonial college student was essentially ungraded and unexamined. At the high-water mark of the classical college, grading and examining were poisoned by the recitation system and made somewhat ridiculous by the extent to which public oral examinations were gestures in public relations and therefore not designed to show up student deficiencies.

In 1857 at Harvard the faculty and overseers decided that oral examinations had outlived their usefulness. They substituted written course examinations to be graded by the instructors and introduced the blue book to American academic practice. The significance of this departure for the course of study was far-reaching. The oral examinations had been a prop of the recitation system, which had been defended as the only way to prepare students for them; the argument was circular, but when one went, the other was bound to go also. Written course examinations freed instructors from an overemphasis on daily graded recitations and memorization; they changed what went on in class and what could go on in class; they helped to transform instructors from policemen to teachers. The practice of written course examinations was adopted at Yale in 1865. The rest of the colleges fell in line.

As for grading, Harvard removed a student's disciplinary record from the calculation of grades in 1869 and eight years later adopted a scale of 100, replacing it in 1883 with five letter grades—A through E. In 1895 letter grades were replaced by a new scale of rank by merit: "passed with distinction," "passed," and "failed." This search for the perfect grading system was a response to a changing curriculum and a changing climate of academic life. Examining and grading systems were barometers of curricular health and style and purpose.

In the East, literary societies were in decline, their place being taken by an invigorated curriculum and by extracurricular activities that would be less complementary to curricular purpose than they had been. Cornell and the developing state institutions were altogether free of the old religious commitment. The old moral philosophy course was passing away, and there was no capstone, no integrating experience, taking its place.

Disarray

In contrast to a century earlier, by 1900 the aspiring young men (and now women) who enrolled in the colleges (and now universities) greatly outnumbered those for whom the curriculum was a confirmation of social and economic status. Accelerating enrollments in higher education, moving 4.7 times as fast as population growth, represented a victory for the forces of reform: Colleges and universities were making themselves felt in the lives of a wider clientele. But diversity and democracy would exact a price in harmony, just as harmony had been bought at the cost of unpopularity, irrelevance, and a limited usefulness to an upper class.

One instrument of the new disharmony was a class of professionally trained academicians, professors with specialized training in a field of study that may not even have existed when they were born. The new breed of professors introduced into the classroom a seriousness, a respect for energetic inquiry, a concern for standards that were an inspiration to like-minded undergraduates, but the new academic style was so in awe of scholarly productivity that neglect of undergraduates became a corollary of professional purpose. Of course, the students knew how to turn the tables. It may have been only a coincidence that the professionalization of the faculties and the rise of football were simultaneous developments, but clearly, while both the professors and students had found for themselves thoroughly engrossing activities, these were activities that lacked the common purpose that held together the old course of study.

Yet for the curriculum as experienced by students, the professionalization of the professors also brought significant benefits. One of these certainly was the establishment of academic freedom and tenure as characteristic goals and expectations governing the college and university environment. These conditions, so supportive of the right of the professor to move into a world of ideas that might be contrary to the wishes of the governing authorities, were institutionalized in the formation of the Association of American University Professors in 1915, but before then the professors were demonstrating how academic freedom and security in their jobs could invigorate the course of study.

In a way that was not readily apparent, the colleges and universities were losing control over the course of study, not just to professors with new authority and students with elective freedom but to a burgeoning system of public high schools.

The rationalization of state systems of education, with the state university as ultimate arbiter, multiplied the number of high schools and required the abandonment the integral preparatory departments in the universities. This also meant, however, capitulation to the high schools. The certification system, which replaced the preparatory departments as the basic instrument of transfer from school to college, was the creation of the University of Michigan, which found itself in 1870 without any simple avenue to admission, neither a preparatory department nor a system of examinations. In the 1870s, under Michigan's leadership, the growing state universities of the Midwest worked out and adopted systems of accreditation whereby schools were certified as doing creditable college preparatory work or where their examinations were accepted as an adequate basis for admission.

The damage to the curriculum of all this maneuvering was in one sense only temporary. Once both the schools and universities arrived at a reasonably comfortable relationship, standards were moved ahead. The lasting damage to the traditional college and university curriculum occurred in the definition of subjects that were acceptable for college admission and that could be continued as course programs leading to college and university degrees. Here a battle shaped up between the private universities of the East and the old classical colleges on one side and the state universities and land-grant colleges on the other.

By 1900 the lack of articulation between a late-blooming high school system and an ancient but collapsing college course of study was so great that it was impossible to speak of *the* college curriculum. Measures to bring order out of confusion began as early as 1879 at a conference of New England colleges seeking agreement on uniform admissions requirements in English. Similar meetings in 1881 and 1882 on the classics and mathematics led to the beginnings of uniformity among the colleges and universities of New England and the formation of the New England Association of Colleges and Secondary Schools in 1885, the first of a number of similar regional organizations that developed out of school and college curricular disarray.

At the 1892 meeting of the National Education Association the appointment of a Committee on Secondary School Studies, known as the Committee of Ten, was in some ways an act of inspired exasperation. The Committee of Ten succeeded in defining a college preparatory course, but it did not define an American high school, and it did not tell college and university authorities on what grounds to admit students. Too many conflicting purposes were enmeshed in the admissions problem to allow for any clear solution. Each college and university chose the method or methods that it thought best served its purposes and allowed it to enroll a class.

The idea of a uniform universally recognized undergraduate course of study was dying along with the old curriculum. School and college associations of subject-matter teachers, even the creation in 1908 of the Carnegie Unit (one of four courses carried five days a week during the secondary school year), could temper but could not stem the disarray that had overtaken the college curriculum. Bewilderment overtook institutions displaced in less than two decades as standard bearers of higher education by universities that were brazen in their self-confidence and embarrassingly young in years.

For the colleges more was at stake than curricular strategies. In settling late in the nineteenth century on the concept of "the whole man" as an expression of their curricular purpose, the colleges selected a symbol around which they could rally their forces— a symbol that represented values that were conservative, antiprogressive, elitist, and nonmaterialistic. In rejecting the values of the new universities—specialization, power, materialism—the colleges confronted the twentieth century with the question as to whether both the college and the whole man possessed any survival value in a world that appeared to have settled on the great state and urban universities as the ultimate expression of the culture's intentions.

Liberal learning, however, was not dead. In its focus on the ideal, on human worth, on the intangibles of reflection and taste, it would have rough going in an age that was being defined by a raw materialism and widespread exploitation of both men and nature. In the colleges and universities, however, an aggressive vocationalism and a humorless pursuit of higher learning were not alone in giving new definition to the curriculum. Friends of the humanist tradition were not immobilized by the termination of Greek's long stranglehold on the course of study; to some extent they were liberated by it.

They discovered that the old values, the enduring questions, the challenges to judgment and morality, inhered in the new subjects quite as readily as they had in the old ones and that, relieved of the burden of the pietistic focus of an earlier day, they could move toward some accommodations with the intellectual focus of the new breed of professors without compromising their own values. Liberal education was a matter of style more than it was a matter of subjects, and, although it was appropriately uncomfortable with the new orientation, it had no difficulty in expressing itself through the modern languages, English literature, the fine arts, and philosophy. There utility, research, power, and service established no exclusive claims. Freed from the remnants of Puritan piety, the humanists edged toward an openness about taste and asserted a legitimacy for esthetics.

"Culture" became their special territory. Culture, not as anthropologists were coming to define it, but as "the higher and better things"—the enjoyments and understandings and appreciations that distinguished the liberally educated from the barbarian. Liberal culture was unwilling to bring science within its understanding or under its influence. At a time when the vocationalists and the scholars were making significant connections between the curriculum and the world, the humanists were giving new currency to the concept of the ivory tower.

Some colleges and universities managed to embrace utility, research, and culture and not to give themselves over to any one of the curricular styles that were available. No academic tool was more helpful in allowing an institution to do almost everything and anything than was the elective system, and no comparable device could have contained the energies that were seeking expression in the undergraduate curriculum.

An emerging profession of scholars used the elective system to free itself from a tradition of academic bookkeeping, class attendance, and examination by rote and to license the new professors as investigators, innovators, the advance agents of next year's truth. The consequences were new subjects, new depth, new skills, and new truth. For these advantages, for both student and professor, the elective system exacted a price. It did not destroy the unity of knowledge, but it made that ancient fiction more difficult to believe. To the extent that election roamed beyond the borders of the old curriculum, it expressed a loss of spiritual character and became a measure of secular power. In the interest of expansion, it lowered standards. It was expensive. In shifting the authority for defining a college education from society to the individual student, it allowed students to regard the college or university as an environment for establishing "prestige or connection," rather than as an environment fundamentally designed by the course of study. As they never could with the old curriculum, college and universities used the elective system to attract students on other than educational grounds.

Henceforth order and certainty in an institution of higher education would be less a function of the curriculum than of the bureaucracy that held it together. The last great statement of curricular uniformity and symmetry was the Yale Report of 1828; the first great statement of bureaucratic organization and symmetry was the University of Chicago. Chicago's founding president, William Rainey Harper, created an intricate administrative organization that moved from president down to heads of departments. It conveyed a sense of logic to the disorder that had befallen the curriculum. All that was needed to complete the design was a hierarchy of ranks that would facilitate the competitive movement of faculty, the measuring of departmental strength, and the clarification of academic procedure.

Imbedded in this structure were curricular innovations as well: The division of the year into four quarters, and each quarter into two six-week terms; the classification of courses as major and minors; the requirement that each student take one major and one minor a term. Harper's design offered to students, as pedagogical wisdom, an opportunity to avoid superficial learning by concentrating on no more than two or three subjects at a time. The four-quarter system made plant utilization more economical, and it allowed students to use their summer months profitably and to accelerate their education by a year or to take more than four years if necessary.

The University of Chicago was an immediate and resounding success because Harper, possessed of a mind that understood the organizing genius with which American industry had been rationalized in the years since the Civil War, provided a framework that allowed professors and students alike to go about their business with a maximum of individual freedom and a minimum of institutional coercion and discipline, as well as with a sense of certainty about how things were done and why. There was something close to genius and magic in the way in which Harper substituted bureaucratic organization for the course of study as the focus of institutional consensus. The curriculum at the University of Chicago was quite as chaotic as elsewhere, but it did not seem so, and that was an achievement not just for public relations but also for institutional sanity.

From the very beginning the contending styles of liberal culture, utility, and research were merged in the University of Chicago's sense of its own legitimacy. At Chicago culture and scholarship were regarded as "equipment for service," not as ends in themselves. Chicago confirmed a shift in purpose that had already been experienced elsewhere, from innoculating undergraduates with large doses of revealed religion and deductive truth to exposing them to methods and curricular experiences that forced on them some ultimate responsibility for the truths with which they had to live.

Remedies

In imposing the elective system on the American college, Eliot and others accomplished by indirection what they could not accomplish by persuasion: They broke down the hold of the classics, and they created universities. In many ways, however, the traditions of liberal learning and the purposes of the German university were incompatible. The elective system in the German university did not destroy the *gymnasium*, the institution to which was assigned the responsibility for providing students with a comprehensive introduction to the liberal arts and "a feeling of the basic unity of all knowledge"; instead, it built itself on the *gymnasium*. An altogether different result befell liberal learning as a consequence of mixing the elective system with the liberal arts college in the United States. Eliot and the Committee of Ten may have thought that they could reshape the American high school into a *gymnasium* or *lycée* and thus establish the liberal tradition as firmly in the secondary schools of the United States as in those of Germany and France, but they failed and at the same time left the college, the society's repository of liberal values and humane learning, crippled and confused.

Three new conditions placed limits on the extent to which the elective system could be brought under control: acceptance of the psychology of individual differences and interests; an accelerating increase in enrollment; and the expansion of the American high school as an instrument of social control and aspiration. All of these developments would have taken place, but not in the same way, without the elective system. Each of them strengthened its hold on the undergraduate curriculum because of the elective system.

Failure to bring the high schools under control meant, in the end, that the colleges and universities would have to offer, among other things, courses of study that were extensions of whatever was offered in the high schools. Because it possessed the authority of numbers and the powerful support of democratic mythology, the high school was able to use the principle of student electives and the psychology of individual differences to create high school programs that were in no way beholden to college and university authorities.

If the colleges were dependent for students on high schools that were indifferent to liberal learning and to curricular order, they were likewise dependent for professors on universities that were increasingly oriented to scholarly specialization and at the same time indifferent to liberal culture and a balanced course of study. There was no chance of recovery for the classics. Greek was gone, and Latin was on its way out. By 1915 fewer than 15 major colleges still required four years of Latin for the B.A. degree.

Remedies for curricular disorders defined the career of the course of study in the twentieth century. Once again attempts were made to see if any order, any coherence, any integrity could again be associated with the undergraduate curriculum. In the absence of any tradition of government licensing, supervision, and control, the first expressions of concern over the absence of common standards and practices came from the institutions themselves in their regional and national associations. In these efforts they were assisted by state and regional accrediting agencies and by the predicament that confronted the new philanthropic foundations when they began to give money away to the colleges and universities in the early years of the twentieth century.

The Carnegie Foundation's ambitious decision to provide every American college professor with a pension ran immediately into the question of what constituted a college. Officers and trustees of the foundation reduced the size of their problem at the outset by eliminating state institutions as well as private institutions with denominational affiliation and technical institutes that were not of college grade.

It found 45 colleges and published its list in June 1906. To make that magic list a college had to require 14 units of high school credit for admission, each unit signifying five recitations a week throughout the year in one subject. The "Carnegie Unit" had been born and, without so much as a word about the curriculum, the Foundation nonetheless narrowed the definition of a college and established standards by which the college course of study could be distinguished from the secondary school.

If the nineteenth-century benefactors supported the colleges and universities in what the institutions wanted to do, the great foundations in the twentieth century, with their enormous resources and their standardizing intentions, supported colleges and universities in what the foundations thought they ought to do.

Whether the most pressing problem confronting the colleges and universities was an absence of widely respected standards was arguable. Uniformity and coherence had fallen out of the course of study and somehow had to be brought back, but whether that could be done more through emphasis on form rather than content was about to become a permanent puzzle for college and university authorities and educational philosophers.

As early as 1885 David Starr Jordan, then president of Indiana University, had developed the idea of a major subject, an area of interest and concentration in which a student moved from elementary to advanced work during four years. Before the major would take hold, enthusiasm for the elective system would have to run its course. In addition, majors could not be developed out of thin air. They would have been impossible in the old colleges, where knowledge was elementary and the professors were generalists. A sufficient number of subject matter specialists would have to flow out of the graduate schools of arts and sciences into the colleges, a sufficient demand for new subjects and for study in depth would have to be delivered by the elective system, before the course of study was ready to offer itself over to the major subject system.

The triumph of concentration and distribution over election was facilitated by the adoption in most colleges and universities, by 1910, of the subject major. Major and minor areas of concentration were the first fruits of the elective system. Requiring a student to select one major, perhaps a minor, and to distribute some of his courses among four prescribed groups of courses after 1910 was essentially a matter of organizing an existing mass of courses into a systematic arrangement. The materials were already at hand. Concentration and distribution provided the curriculum with a rationale, which was something of an improvement on free election, which was only a license.

As early as 1910, 39 Harvard courses enrolled over 100 students, 14 over 200. A 1904 faculty report led to some modest remedies: In every large lecture course, a conference-quiz section was substituted for one lecture; sectioning by ability was rediscovered; and the awarding of the degree with distinction was adopted as an encouragement to students. By 1908 President Eliot could claim that a vast array of curricular devices had come to the aid of the lecture, not just conference-quiz sections: reserved reading shelves in the library, laboratory work in science, the problem approach to subject matter, fieldwork, theses, reports, the case method, source books, and seminars. Everywhere that they were tried—and they soon became standard practice—these new elements of the course of study encouraged students to take charge of their own education. To the extent that they were peripheral and the lecture central, however, they could not combat the injurious effect of the lecture system.

In redesigning the curriculum in ways intended to remedy the disarray, college and university authorities were burdened by a student body attracted to their campuses for reasons different from those that had motivated the small enrollments of the old colleges. Economic prosperity underwrote a degree of college attendance that, except for its fashionableness, was almost purposeless. The ethos of a commercial society supported college-going as an experience in social maturation and human relationships. The country lost its head over college athletics. In this environment, concentration and distribution, honors programs, and even the great humanist lecturers among the professors were rowing upstream.

An additional stimulus to curricular order and scholarly purposes was the appearance of a new examination rationale. Beginning in 1913 at Harvard the division of history, government, and economics adopted the practice of examining seniors in general or comprehensive examinations that covered material considered appropriate for the student's area of concentration, but not necessarily presented in his courses. In the 1920s, partly as a function of Harvard's commanding presence as a promulgator of academic standards, the comprehensive examination as an instrument for bringing coherence and design and some semblance of unity to the academic course made considerable headway.

As effective as all these devices were for bringing some order to the course of study, they avoided the question of whether knowledge itself could be brought under control and given some semblance of symmetry and unity. To the extent that the scientific method had been substituted for other once reliable sources of truth, truth and knowledge had become process rather than packages of inherited wisdom. And process gave every indication of turning out knowledge at a rate beyond the capacity of any individual to encompass or comprehend.

At the end of the first quarter of the twentieth century, the evidence was overwhelming that the American college was not going to disappear and that the American university would not be a transplanted English university or a transplanted German university. The curriculum was still a repository of conflicting purposes and contradictory educational philosophies, but a body of standard practices and expectations and a sophisticated bureaucracy imposed a semblance of rationality and sanity on a course of study that was sometimes beyond understanding. And in some measure the curriculum had been delivered from potential chaos.

The Last 50 Years

If in the nineteenth century the curriculum defined the market for higher learning, in the mid-twentieth century the market defined the curriculum. The result was not just a reversal of a restricted course and of limited enrollments. Another consequence was to make the curriculum particularly mercurial, quickly responsive to changing student tastes, foundation fads, and the day's events. Some institutions were more able than others to withstand the shifting moods and perceptions of the young. Relative curricular stability was a function of economics, geography, and history.

By 1976 concentration was in charge of the curriculum. If alternatives to the traditional major were to make any serious headway, some powerful practices would have to go. Colleges and universities would have to organize their faculties on some bureaucratic principle other than the department or greatly reduce faculty control over the curriculum or persuade graduate schools of arts and sciences to relax their indirect but inhibiting influence on efforts to reform the undergraduate course of study.

Every improvement in concentration, however, drew attention to the failure of the curriculum to support or define a general education. Dramatic experiments in general education, books and pamphlets explaining the need and extolling a plan, even a widespread wish that something might be done to compensate for the loss of unity and shared learning, did not succeed in changing the focus of the curriculum from the special to the general.

The worst failure occurred in the sciences. Scientific illiteracy became a characteristic of college-educated Americans sometime toward the middle of the twentieth century. The failure of the curriculum to achieve even the minimum goals of distribution required students to accept on faith concepts and ideas of no less importance than the now-discarded articles of faith that had supported both chapel and curriculum in the old college. General education had to make peace with specialization if it was to succeed in compensating for the narrowness that made specialization so dehumanizing, divisive, and incapable of providing any common ground or bond among educated people.

Until President James B. Conant of Harvard appointed a faculty committee on "the objectives of a general education in a free society" in 1943, college and university faculties were able to avoid the general education movement. Once the Harvard Committee had issued its report, however, the prestige of the country's oldest and most influential university was committed to the search for some way to provide a general education for the citizens of an atomistic, necessarily specialized, and unavoidably complex society. A landmark document, the Harvard Report of 1945 was an effort to put back into the curriculum certain qualities and values that fell out of it when history repudiated the Yale Report of 1828. It was an effort to confront the social and political forces of mid-century America and to write a prescription for sustaining the liberal tradition with a curriculum that recognized the legitimacy of individual interests and talents and at the same time established a common bond of general learning.

Harvard's "Red Book," as it was called, was an act of public service, a statesmanlike warning that the decline of a privileged class of broadly trained leaders and their displacement by a democracy of equal citizens had placed in jeopardy the capacity of modern societies, especially the United States, "to make decisions . . . with perspective and a sense of standards." In urging a revitalization of general education, Harvard proposed to democratize what had once been the education of a gentleman and an aristocrat and make it the education essential to the responsibilities of every citizen. The Harvard committee had expected to follow its report with the development of three divisional core courses as requirements in general education, but that aspiration fell victim to faculty power. Outside of those institutions that chose to be primarily identified with general education, the idea made little headway. The Harvard Report knew what was best for everyone, quite as much as a similar self-assurance (or wisdom) had found its way into the Yale Report. Both versions were subject to the same weaknesses. Whether they intended it or not, they proposed to use general education as a device for hurrying the aspiring middle class into the enjoyment of wealth and leisure that they did not yet possess.

The most unobtrusive curricular development of the twentieth century, in contrast, was the recognition of esthetic values and creativity as legitimate components of the course of study. Before the fine arts could become standard elements of the curriculum, either as experiences in enjoyment and creativity or as subjects of serious intellectual inquiry, colleges and universities had to release themselves from the inherited suspicion of the arts that a clerical past had imposed upon them. Defining the arts as essentially the province of women was another barrier not easily overcome. The rise of the arts, however, benefited from philanthropy that was prepared to acknowledge a vacuum in the curricular offerings of most institutions, a vacuum that became embarrassing as the country itself moved beyond the conquest of the continent to a greater sophistication and maturity.

Creativity presented the colleges and universities with problems different from those presented by programs in art history or the history of music, both of which, while clearly moving the curriculum into virtually unexplored esthetic territory, were nonetheless also bathed in the mystique of scientific research, specialization, and scholarship. Creativity called for different impulses, different environments, different measurements from those to which the colleges and universities on the whole were accustomed. Creative writing, drama, dance, and film made their way into the curriculum often obliquely and seldom without institutional condescension.

All the curricular experimentation, however, could not affect instruction by reducing the centrality of the lecture. Even as seminars and tutorials increased their role as alternatives to the lecture, especially in colleges and universities with highly selected student bodies, the lecture strengthened its position. Under the impact of new technology and numbers, closed-circuit television lifted the constraints that the size of lecture halls had placed on class size. Doubtful as it was as an encouragement to the kind of research experience or to the humanistic and moralistic orientation possible in small classes, the lecture survived. Yet there was something contrary about these authoritative 50-minute performances in a community of learning.

Alternatives to lectures, particularly such variations as those developed in the 1960s and 1970s—freshman seminars, independent study, and pass-fail courses—were more readily sustained in institutions composed almost entirely of competent, diligent students. Such institutions were surely few enough to assure a long life to the lecture and all of its faults as an instrument of learning.

As unsettling as it was to the serenity of college and university campuses, the student movement of the 1960s wrought no great transformation either in the curriculum or in the lecture system. The movement was not an attack on the curriculum or on instruction as such, but on an unpopular war that threatened students' lives and their respect for institutions, coupled with the fact that colleges and universities had become "detention centers" for hundreds of thousands of young men and women for whom society held out no meaningful employment as an alternative.

Curricular reform after World War II failed to dislodge the professors, reduce vocationalism, substitute general for specialized education, or create new institutions that were convincing models for the restructuring and redesigning of old institutions. Indeed, the old institutions were by now in the grasp of their own histories. More than models were necessary to move a college in new curricular directions.

Yet recent events so pushed and pulled the American student toward a vocational bias that we now witness the accelerating downgrading of those aspects of an undergraduate education that encourage imagination, judgment, decision, values. If the Great Depression taught students to be skeptical of specialized learning, that has not been the case in the 1970s, as students abandon a search for the knowledge that might make them interesting, even to themselves, and seek to achieve some kind of technical insurance against the future.

With the blessings of the U.S. Office of Education, the American high school is encouraged to embrace something called "career education"—a movement that promises its victims technical skills and "positive" attitudes toward work but neglects those educational experiences that might help to make them good, interesting, and wise men and women.

There may be one hopeful sign. We have all been frequently assured that we are moving into an era of a permanently unfavorable job market for college graduates. This message is generally delivered as bad news. It just may be good news. If there are not sufficient jobs available to justify an endless production of proficient technicians and if, as is quite apparent, we know not what else to do with the age group other than send it to college, perhaps we can stop making technicians and get back to the business of making human beings. The time may be at hand when a reevaluation of academic purpose and philosophy will encourage the curricular developments that will focus on the lives we lead, their quality, the enjoyment they give us, and the wisdom with which we lead them. If such a development does take place, human beings, as distinct from trained technicians, will not be at a disadvantage in the job market. And perhaps, once more, the idea of an educated person will have become a usable ideal.

Youth Education and Employment

Youth Education and Unemployment Problems: An International Perspective.
By Margaret S. Gordon with a chapter by Martin Trow. 1980.

Youth Unemployment in Western Industrial Countries

Youth unemployment, a problem of serious dimensions in the United States since at least the early 1960s, has spread to most other Western industrial countries. Policies adopted to alleviate the problem range from emphasizing vocational training to subsidizing employers who hire youth and creating public service jobs for young people. Activity is not confined to the labor market, however. Educational systems, particularly at the secondary level, are being reexamined, with special reference to seeking the appropriate mix between academic and vocational training.

Is the problem a short-term phenomenon that will soon go away or a long-term problem that will be plaguing Western societies for years to come? At least three hypotheses must be considered:

1. The problem is primarily cyclical—especially in Western Europe—and will disappear as economies recover.
2. The problem, resulting primarily from long-term structural changes in the labor market that are associated with advanced industrialization, is likely to persist for the foreseeable future.
3. The problem arises largely on the supply side of the labor market, resulting from the high birthrates in the years after World War II that led to the bulge in the number of teenagers entering the labor market in the 1960s and 1970s.

In the United States, the unemployment rate has been considerably higher for youth aged 16 to 19 throughout the postwar period than for youth in their early twenties, and thus the teenage problem arouses the most concern (see Figure 1). The teenage unemployment rate also has tended to rise over this period. The differential for those aged 20 to 24 has remained relatively constant, although their unemployment rate has shown a moderate upward trend.

The Cyclical Hypothesis

In the United States, youth unemployment becomes more serious in recessions, but the phenomenon is not cyclical in the sense that it disappears in periods of prosperity. The youth unemployment differential tends to behave countercyclically in recessions; layoffs cause adult unemployment rates to rise more sharply than teenage rates, but the adult rates then fall more rapidly in economic upswings. Although the problem is likely to

Figure 1. Percentage of civilian labor force unemployed, rate for adults aged 25 to 54 and rates for youthful age groups, United States, annual average, 1947 to 1976, and December 1977 (seasonally adjusted); and population growth in youthful age groups, actual, 1948 to 1976, and projected, 1977 to 1990

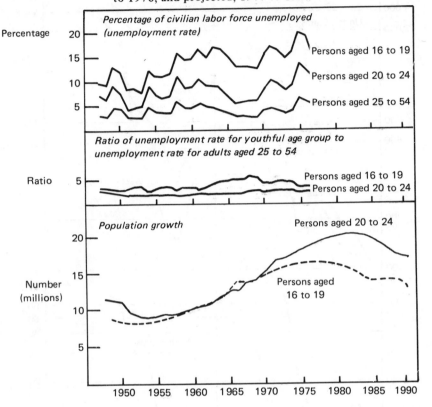

become less serious in the 1980s, when the size of the youthful population declines, it is unlikely to disappear.

Other Western countries, principally those that have experienced an especially sharp rise in the unemployment rate in the last few years, have also encountered a serious problem of youth unemployment (see Figure 2). A report of the Organization for Economic Cooperation and Development suggests that a youth unemployment problem will persist even after aggregate full employment is reached because of pressures on the demand side.

The Demand Hypothesis

Advancing industrialization imposes long-run structural changes on the labor market that impair employment opportunities for young people. The shift out of agriculture and the sluggishness of nonagricultural self-employment (small business) have greatly reduced family employment opportunities for youth. In the early decades of the present century, labor-management relations were far less formalized than they are today. Young people entered the labor force in unskilled jobs at low pay, often on a part-time or temporary basis. Although this pattern still exists, far more labor market rules and regulations now bar young people from certain types of jobs.

The decline in the relative importance of unskilled jobs in the course of industrialization has been a major factor on the demand side of the labor market. The rapidly

Figure 2. Number of unemployed aged 24 and younger, selected countries, 1967 to 1976

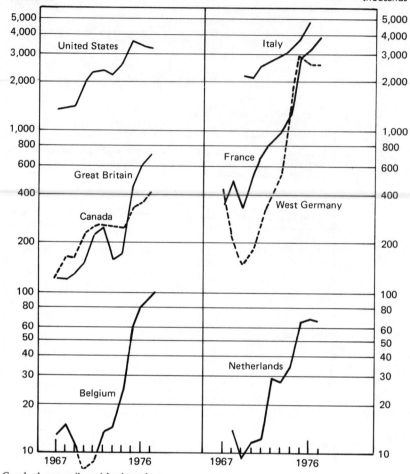

Note: Graphed on semilogarithmic scale.

growing trade and service sector does have many unskilled jobs that tend to replace diminishing unskilled openings in the secondary sector (manufacturing, construction, and utilities), but the industries in this sector are also affected to some extent by technological changes that reduce demand for the unskilled.

Technological developments have also altered the skill structure in many manufacturing industries. Mass production methods tend to increase the proportion of semiskilled workers in relation to both laborers and skilled workers. Also important is the rise in the ratio of nonproduction workers (often engineers) to production workers in technologically advanced industries, particularly in the U.S. aerospace industries.

Because of their inexperience and frequent lack of relevant training, employers cannot afford to hire young people entering the labor market at wages comparable to those paid to adult employees. But proposals to establish a reduced minimum, or subminimum, wage for youth have been strongly opposed by organized labor and have been defeated in Congress on several recent occasions. How much a subminimum wage would actually increase employment of young people is not very clear. One study indicates that the relative wages of teenagers would have to drop substantially to increase their employment appreciably.

In European countries where apprenticeship has played a more important role in training youth than in the United States, the demand for apprentices has declined appreciably in recent years. This has had a significant effect on youth unemployment, because apprenticeships tend to provide stable employment during those critical years when school leavers who do not go into apprenticeships are shopping around for acceptable jobs. Technological change has reduced the demand for apprentices in industries shifting to advanced technology and has led employers to seek young recruits with at least some upper secondary schooling for apprenticeships and other trainee positions. Another factor in the decline in the supply of apprenticeships has been a sharp increase in the compensation of apprentices.

In the United States, the geographical decentralization of industry on the demand side, along with increasing concentration of minority-group populations in inner cities on the supply side, has undoubtedly contributed to the exceedingly high unemployment rates among minority-group youth. The experience of a number of youth employment organizations tends to confirm the dual labor market theory that divides jobs into two categories—primary and secondary. Ghetto workers tend to be confined largely to secondary jobs, which are characterized by one or more of the following: low wages and few fringe benefits, debilitating production speeds, low status, unpleasant working conditions, unsympathetic supervision, inequitable industrial relations arrangements, few promotion opportunities, and unstable employment.

The Supply Hypothesis

That a rising youth unemployment problem is primarily attributable to a bulge in the teenage population seems plausible in view of the fact that most Western industrial countries—and a number of Eastern countries, as well—experienced high birthrates following World War II. Yet, while the birthrate remained high in the United States and Canada until the latter part of the 1950s, resulting in a bulge in the population aged 16 to 19 that lasted from the early 1960s to the mid-1970s, in some Western European countries a decline in the birthrate occurred after 1945, so that the bulge in the population aged 16 to 19 occurred in the early 1960s.

The bulge in the teenage population in many European countries did not cause a bulge in the teenage labor force. The rise in enrollment rates in upper secondary schools in Western Europe in the 1960s—a development that had occurred earlier in the United States and Canada—was so pronounced that teenage labor force participation rates declined sharply. Unlike the situation in the United States and Canada, secondary students in Western Europe do not usually seek part-time jobs. Thus, the bulge in the teenage labor force—as distinct from the teenage population—cannot be held responsible for teenage unemployment in most industrial countries before 1974. But in Great Britain, Sweden, and Germany there is apprehension about the current increase in the youthful population.

In the United States, distinguishing between white and nonwhite teenage unemployment rates casts additional doubt on the supply hypothesis. The unemployment differential for white teenagers rose very little in the 1960s except for males aged 16 to 17, but the nonwhite differential began to rise in the mid-1950s and rose much more sharply than the white differential in the 1960s.

However, other aspects of the supply hypothesis must be considered. Large numbers of married women have entered the labor force in recent decades and may be getting jobs that teenagers would have otherwise obtained. The labor force participation rate of women has risen substantially in Australia, Sweden, the United States, and Canada, and somewhat more moderately in Great Britain. It has remained relatively stable in France and has declined in Japan and Italy. It also declined slightly in Germany in the 1960s, but not recently.

A special analysis of U.S. decennial census data, however, showed that the number of occupations in which employment changes were relatively favorable for both women and teenagers and in which employment changes were relatively unfavorable for both women and teenagers far exceeded those in which trends for women and teenagers differed. Occupations in which the most spectacular gains were made by teenagers were low-paid, low-status service occupations, such as cooks, janitors, and cleaners. The part-time and often temporary character of many of these jobs undoubtedly contributed to the upward trend in teenage unemployment rates, especially for minority-group youth. Moreover, jobs of this type require very little training.

Illegal aliens compete for jobs with both youth and women. Recently arrived illegal immigrants often expect to remain only temporarily and are content to compete for secondary jobs. Foreign workers in Europe were hired when a shortage of native-born workers, including young people, existed, and many who have not returned to their homelands now hold jobs that might otherwise be available for youth. Particularly high unemployment rates are found among teenage children of foreign workers in some European countries.

College graduates in the United States have been getting lower-level white collar, blue collar, and service jobs in the 1970s that would have been obtained by high school graduates and dropouts in the 1960s. In other words, college graduates have been "bumping" young people with less education.

Certain additional aspects of youth unemployment are as follows:

1.   Although young people shift jobs relatively frequently in their first few years in the labor force—and this shifting helps to explain high youth unemployment rates— in 1976 less than 10 percent of unemployed persons aged 16 to 19 were out of work because of having left their last jobs. Nearly 70 percent were jobless because they were reentering the labor force or had never worked before.
2.   The search for a job by the youthful entrant or reentrant to the labor force does not usually last very long. However, when a recession deepens, these spells tend to lengthen. Moreover, young people are likely to have more frequent spells of unemployment and thus to be out of work for more weeks in any given year than adults.
3.   Unemployed youth include many students who are seeking part-time jobs. If all students aged 16 to 24 had been eliminated from the civilian labor force and from the unemployed, the national unemployment rate would have been reduced from 8.5 to 7.9 percent in 1975; however, the unemployment rate for all persons aged 16 to 24 would hardly have changed, because unemployment rates of students and nonstudents are about equal.
4.   Unemployment rates are inversely related to educational attainment in all the countries for which data are available, and are very high for high school dropouts.

Conclusions on Causes

The situation that seems to be common to nearly all industrial countries is the set of forces on the demand side of the labor market that impair job opportunities for youth. These forces will remain for a long time, and vigorous policies are needed if the youth unemployment problem is to be held within reasonable bounds. The long-run forces that have been decreasing the relative demand for young people in the labor market may well be intensified rather than reversed.

In the United States and Canada, the teenage population will be decreasing in the 1980s, and the population aged 20 to 24 will begin to decline around 1982-83. In the United States, the decline in the size of these youthful age groups is not likely to be off-set by the comparatively modest increase in labor force participation rates that is antici-pated, so that the overall supply of young people on the labor market will be decreasing. If manpower and related programs are not substantially changed, the unemployment rate will decline significantly for teenagers in general and moderately for adults aged 20 to 24. However, because the unemployment rates of inner-city blacks are so high, I foresee little improvement in that situation without much more far-reaching measures. Furthermore, because of higher birthrates in the black population, the percentage of blacks in the youthful population will rise throughout the coming decade.

In other countries the situation will vary considerably. A return to full employment would reduce youth unemployment rates substantially, but in Great Britain, Sweden, and Germany the current or impending increase in the youthful population may make reducing youth unemployment differentials difficult. In most Western European coun-tries, an increasing proportion of young people entering the labor market will be the children of foreign workers, who are likely to have differentially high unemployment rates. In addition, the adverse impact of long-run structural changes on the demand for young workers could well be intensified. Thus, few, if any, Western industrial countries can afford to be complacent about the prospect for the 1980s.

Policies to Combat Youth Unemployment

Unemployment policies in other countries that are especially worthy of consideration may be summarized as follows:

1. Denmark. Experimental residential programs for unemployed youth, which com-bine education, a choice of various types of work experience, and shared responsi-bility for providing residential services.
2. Great Britain.
    a. Community Industry, which operates a network of enterprises staffed by young people throughout the country. It provides goods and services that are of value to the community but that are not normally supplied by private enterprise.
    b. The Careers Service, which is entirely responsible for the placement of school leavers below the age of 18 and also usually handles those in older age groups for the first two years after they leave full-time education.
    c. A recently adopted comprehensive youth opportunities program for those under age 19, providing training, work experience, and educational options. Details of the actual projects are planned by local communities.
3. Japan. Training programs in industry that combine high school or postsecondary education and vocational training.
4. Sweden.
    a. Vocational guidance and career education in all schools, provided by specially trained full-time counselors for students beginning at about age 13.
    b. Selective labor market policies under the guidance of the National Labor Market Board, including extensive training programs, work relief, public service employment, moving allowances, and (recently) employer subsidies for hiring youth.

Educational Policies

Unlike labor market policies, which can be adopted rather quickly, educational policies evolve slowly. Moreover, the educational systems in a number of countries have bottlenecks that impede progress from one level of schooling to the next. This may exacerbate labor market problems by forcing ill-prepared youngsters onto the labor market.

At the heart of many of the difficulties involved in developing adequate manpower and educational policies for youth is the problem of achieving greater equality of opportunity in pursuing different paths from school to work. In the United States, students who go on to college can qualify for what is coming to be quite substantial student aid, but very little student aid is available at the secondary school level. Students who enroll in higher education usually qualify for aid in Western Europe, and a limited amount of student assistance is available at the secondary level in some European countries.

The most critical issues in educational policy relate especially to the secondary level and to the problem of improved preparation for the labor market of young people who are not going on to higher education. The most difficult problems at this level involve those students who have been "turned off" by school or who have not succeeded in acquiring basic literacy. Several developments deserve particular attention:

1. *Canada.* Cooperative education programs in most provinces alternate periods of study and work. They are intended for the less successful pupils in secondary schools.
2. *Denmark and Sweden.* Short courses for unemployed youth in upper secondary school.
3. *France.*
   a. The recent introduction of manual and technical training for all pupils in the core curriculum in the four years of secondary education.
   b. The introduction of entrance examinations for admission to institutions of higher education for candidates who have acquired an occupational qualification in secondary education.
4. *Great Britain.* The development of sixth-form colleges for the 16-19-year age group. These colleges have open admissions policies and, in many cases, academic and vocational options resembling those of community colleges in the United States.
5. *West Germany.* The upper secondary schools of North Rhine-Westphalia in which students can obtain both a vocational and an academic qualification, regardless of whether they are enrolled in primarily academic or primarily vocational programs.
6. *Poland.* The opportunities for graduates of both academic and vocational programs in secondary schools to be admitted to institutions of higher education.
7. *United States.* The gradual transformation of open-door community colleges from institutions in which the majority of students were recent high school graduates entering academic (transfer) programs to institutions with a far broader mix of youthful and adult students, with about as many students enrolled in occupational as in academic programs. The next stage may well be a more widespread and extensive merging of the occupational programs of high schools and community colleges.

The problems common to the secondary school systems of all Western industrial countries stem in part from the prolongation of schooling, which retains many students who in the earlier era would not have proceeded beyond the primary school stage and who in many cases do not thrive on an education program that is academically oriented.

In the next decade, extensive experimentation to provide a more stimulating school-work-training environment for such students is likely.

Comparative National Experiences

Youth education and unemployment are concerns of almost all industrial nations; they also present problems for the less-developed countries. The following reviews of youth problems are based on a series of essays prepared for the Carnegie Council by experts on youth in eight countries and one important developing area.

Great Britain
by Stuart Maclure

With the unemployment rate of 16 and 17 year olds running around 13 to 14 percent and that of 18 and 19 year olds about 10 percent in early 1977, British rates have been well below those of comparable age groups in the United States but above those in most other Western European countries. The youth unemployment problem is expected to be troublesome for some years to come. Britain experienced a rise in the birthrate from 1955 to 1964 (a second upward swing that occurred after the first sharp increase immediately following World War II, resulting in a bulge in the youthful population that will continue into the mid-1980s). The slow growth of the British economy and inflation are also grounds for pessimism about lowering both the overall unemployment rate and the high youth unemployment rate.

In Britain, as elsewhere, young people with poor educational qualifications are among minority groups under the age of 25, especially young West Indians. Nevertheless, the problem is much less severe than in the United States, because the minority-group population, though growing, is still a small proportion of the total.

Britain is one of the countries, along with West Germany and Sweden, in which legislation aimed at increasing job security of adult workers is viewed as discouraging the hiring of young people. Other policies have brought the wages of young people closer to those of adults, thereby further reducing employment opportunities for youth.

Youth unemployment has become a major political concern of the government. Substantial funds have been made available for special programs of job creation and industrial training for youth. In Britain, vocational training, largely in the form of apprenticeships, has traditionally been regarded as the responsibility of industry rather than of the schools. Unions have traditionally followed restrictionist policies regarding apprenticeship in order to hold down the supply of skilled workers. Some authorities complain that training is conducted on a narrow craft basis that is ill-suited to technological change. Although management tends to prefer policies that increase the supply of skilled workers, the employment of new apprentices falls off sharply in recessions when hiring is cut back, resulting in shortages of skilled workers shortly after recovery is under way.

The Industrial Training Act of 1964 set up training boards for each industry and provided payroll levies on employers to finance training programs organized by the boards. Progress was made under this legislation, especially in the engineering and construction industries, but the legislation was weakened in certain respects in 1973. However, the 1973 act established the Manpower Services Commission (MSC), which has employer, union, and public representatives, and has responsibility for manpower, employment, and training services. It also supervises the Training Services Agency, which has substantial funds to promote training.

Several policy developments are particularly deserving of comment.

Community Industry (CI). This agency operates a network of enterprises that provide various goods and services to communities that would not normally be supplied by private enterprise. Young people must be under 18 years of age and normally spend a year or more with the undertaking. They are paid wages and are expected to turn out work that meets the quality criteria of the users, who are mainly local authorities and community groups.

Youth employment subsidies. In 1975, the government announced a scheme under which employers that hired school leavers who had been previously employed for 6 weeks or less were to be paid £ 5 per week for the first 26 weeks, but school leavers could not be recruited to displace existing workers. A more flexible program followed in 1976, under which a subsidy of £ 10 a week was payable to employers hiring individuals under age 20 who had been continuously registered as unemployed for six months. More than 30,000 school leavers were hired under the first of these schemes, but under the second the number hired (10,000) fell considerably below that contemplated in the budgetary provision.

The Work Experience Program (WEP). Inaugurated in 1976, this program allocates funds for placing unemployed young workers aged 16 to 18 with private firms or local authorities for six months or more to gain experience. By March 1978, 60,000 young people had gone through the program, and about 40,000 could be accommodated at any given time. A followup survey of participants indicated that the majority of them had either been given permanent jobs by their WEP employers or had obtained other full-time jobs.

The Job Creation Program (JCP). This is a public service employment program designed to benefit communities by improving the environment or by contributing to the solution of social and community problems. Though not confined to youth, they are given priority. The authorization of projects is not the responsibility of local governmental bodies, but rather of lay committees representing local employers, union, and local authorities. By March 1977, the program had provided 75,000 jobs with an average duration of 31 weeks. A 1976 survey indicated that one-fifth of the participants had left to take a job during the program, while nearly half found work soon after completing it. The main criticism is the frequent absence of a significant training component.

The Careers Service. This agency is responsible for the placement of school leavers below the age of 18 and, in general, handles those in older age groups for the first two years after they leave full-time education. Administered locally, the service also offers guidance and referrals to manpower programs.

The Youth Opportunities Program. Because of the proliferation of separate youth programs, a MSC working party set up in 1976 recommended a comprehensive program for young people aged 16 to 18 who would receive uniform compensation for participating in a variety of work-experience or training programs. A number of existing programs would be merged in the new scheme. Only those who had been unemployed six weeks or more would be eligible, and a separate, temporary employment program was recommended for young people over age 19. The program for those aged 16 to 18 was funded to provide for a maximum of 234,000 young people a year, or about one-half of the commission's forecast of unemployment in this age group in 1978. Although the scope of the program did not satisfy some of the youth organizations, the cost of a fully comprehensive scheme was deemed prohibitive.

The provision for uniform compensation was intended to eliminate any element of financial advantage of one program over another, but the compensation rate is considerably more than the educational maintenance allowances offered to children from poor families who remain in school or college beyond the age of 16. This may cause difficulties when young people in a work-experience program later want to return to full-time education.

Issues in British education. Britain has taken decisive steps toward a more egalitarian educational system in the postwar period. The 1944 Education Act raised the minimum school-leaving age from 14 to 15 (increased to 16 in 1973), provided for the transfer of all students to secondary schools at age 11, and abolished all fees in the secondary schools. But two groups of secondary schools were maintained: (1) the grammar schools, which took roughly the top 25 percent in terms of IQ, and (2) the modern schools, which took all the rest. In the 1960s, however, rapid progress was made toward the establishment of comprehensive secondary schools open to all, and the Education Act of 1976 made the transition to such schools mandatory.

There has also been a trend toward more egalitarianism in postsecondary education in recent decades. The nonuniversity sector of higher education was developed between 1963 and 1972 and involved the expansion of both the colleges of education and the colleges of further education, along with the designation of some of the latter as "polytechnics," which offered an alternative to the universities for degree students. However, the attempt to encourage the development of professional training in the polytechnics has been only partially successful.

The rise in enrollment rates in British higher education has slowed down in the 1970s in part because of the less favorable job market for graduates. British higher education is also facing a leveling off or even a decline in enrollment because of the impending fall in the size of the college-age population. Although the movement for "recurrent education" has not gone as far in Britain as in Scandinavia or France, the British have made an important contribution to adult education through the Open University (OU), which has inspired similar programs in the United States and elsewhere. While those who enroll are likely to be in middle-class rather than working-class occupations, the enrollees have a much more working-class complexion in terms of father's occupation.

One of the prominent sociological phenomena in Britain is the shift from student activism in the 1960s to the relative quiet of the 1970s. At the same time, social mores have become more permissive. Meanwhile, the rise in juvenile crime has been more pronounced than the rise in crime throughout society, and many observers link the phenomenon to growing alienation of young people. Although statistics are unreliable, hard-drug use is currently increasing, and alcohol consumption has also risen markedly among both young people and adults.

Unemployment and the "Welfare State." The British case is pertinent to the frequent allegation that youth unemployment is at least partially attributable to the cash payments provided by the welfare state, which make subsistence easy. A young unemployed person in Great Britain can qualify for supplementary unemployment benefits paid on the basis of need without any qualifying period of employment. This has undoubtedly increased the incentive for young people to register as unemployed and may have encouraged waiting until an acceptable job turns up as well as an alternating pattern of work and unemployment. However, a survey conducted by the MSC showed that most unemployed young people were actively seeking jobs and that very few had refused a job offer. But the survey also showed that about half the employers believe that the motivation and basic education of young people has deteriorated over the past five years.

Changes in education and training for the 18-24-year age group are likely to be gradual and evolutionary. At the 16-19-year level, however, there are more signs of movement. It will not be possible in the long run to guarantee training or employment without extending it to all, but this raises basic questions about the relationship between education and manpower policies that are far from resolved. With more part-time education and more passage in and out of school and in and out of work experience, the case for a new and essentially more adventurous approach to recurrent education is strong. Yet this whole range of issues cannot be divorced from the urgent need to improve productivity in the British economy, and any design for improving the induction of young people from school into work must consider these issues.

West Germany
by Klaus von Dohnanyi

In an environment of rapid economic growth, the unemployment rate in West Germany was extraordinarily low from the mid-1950s to 1973-74. Nor was youth unemployment a problem, thanks in part to a traditional emphasis on apprenticeship as the predominant means of providing vocational education to the large proportion of German youth who leave school after completing compulsory education.

German unemployment rates seem very modest. Even at its peak in 1975, the overall German unemployment rate averaged only 3.7 percent, and the unemployment rate of those under 20 only 6.6 percent. The number of unemployed young people in West Germany is likely to increase, primarily because those born in the period of high birthrates—from about 1955 to 1963—are entering the labor market.

Measures to combat youth unemployment in the Federal Republic have been less extensive than those of many other industrial countries and have tended to center around vocational education in general and the apprenticeship system in particular. The government has emphasized macroeconomic policies aimed at restoring full employment rather than special measures aimed at youth. There have also been restrictions on the recruitment of foreign workers and refusals to renew expiring foreign labor contracts.

In apprenticeship programs, the youth or the parents enter into a contract with the training firm. The young people receive compensation from the firm, and the apprenticeship usually lasts for three years. Trainees are obliged to attend public vocational school for 6 to 12 hours a week, depending on their state of residence. There was an excess supply of apprenticeships from 1950 to 1967, but from 1967 to 1976 the total number of training positions declined somewhat. The factors in this decline include higher training costs and scientific developments, which have put more emphasis on theoretical education and less on practical skills. However, this trend was apparently reversed in 1977.

Limitations on admissions to universities have made the competition for apprenticeships more difficult for those with limited education, because graduates of secondary schools sometimes accept apprenticeship positions while waiting for possible later admission to universities. In doing so, they edge out applicants with less education.

In recent years, federal and state public agencies have created more training positions than are actually required for the training of junior staff, and firms engaged in training have agreed to add additional positions. These developments were evidently responsible for the 1977 reversal in the downward trend in the number of training positions.

The educational attainment of youth in West Germany has risen significantly since around 1960. University enrollment has also expanded rapidly, but not enough to accommodate the rising number of graduates of the *Gymnasien* (academic secondary schools) in the 1970s.

The educational system forces choices between educational streams at an early age, and shifting to a different stream later on is almost impossible. After the four-year primary school, a student chooses among three types of lower secondary schools: (1) the basic school *(Hauptschule)*, which leads directly to work or an apprenticeship; (2) a modern secondary or intermediate school *(Realschule)*, which leads to an intermediate degree and then to an upper technical school; and (3) the *Gymnasium*, which leads as a rule to the matriculation examination *(Abitur)* and then to the university and an academic or professional career. Those who do not choose the *Gymnasium* are essentially permanently blocked from a professional career, and many of those who do choose it encounter cutthroat competition for high grades that assure entry into the university.

Because the number of pupils choosing the *Gymnasium* and the *Realschule* increased sharply, there was a strong movement to increase the capacity of these schools, while the basic schools became repositories for less gifted and socially disadvantaged children, especially in urban areas. Meanwhile, in the 1960s, the need for expansion of vocational training tended to be neglected. As a result, a problem of unemployed teachers, lawyers, chemists, and engineers has developed, while jobs in trades and crafts go unfilled.

Many observers believe that the basic school must be upgraded. This would require making its educational standards at the lower secondary level comparable to those of the *Gymnasium*. This would allow the school types to merge, with comprehensive secondary schools replacing the three-level school system. However, this goal is opposed by well-to-do parents of *Gymnasium* students.

Concern over youth unemployment has resulted in several educational reforms.

The prolongation of schooling. There are proposals for a tenth compulsory school year, intended to reduce the supply of young people on the labor market. But the form that this tenth year should take has not been resolved; considerable support exists for a vocational, rather than a general, orientation, on the ground that youths of 15 or 16 generally show a high degree of "school-weariness" and could be kept in a general education program only reluctantly and without progress.

Student places at the universities. The federal government advocates increased admissions to universities. Expansion is viewed not only as a policy for the universities but also as part of a total educational strategy, because the *Gymnasium* graduates who are waiting to be admitted to universities are in job competition with other youth with less education.

Improving existing qualifications. In spite of the surplus of job seekers, some private firms have numerous vacancies that cannot be filled because of a dearth of qualified applicants. To help meet this problem, almost all of the states have adopted programs to encourage those who have dropped out of basic school to return to school for graduation. In addition, counseling services are being expanded, both within the schools and in the labor market.

Social Aspects. During the 1960s and early 1970s, youth in the Federal Republic, as in most industrial societies, developed a measure of independence, self-assurance, and joy of living that was unknown before. A changing system of values placed love, friendship, and comradeship in the foreground. Work and making a living became secondary. The rise of crime among youth in the Federal Republic has been relatively minor. Although alcohol consumption among youth has increased, per capita consumption of alcohol in the country has risen in general. The hard core of drug consumers among youths aged 14 to 24 is considered to be less than 0.5 percent of the population in this age group.

Problems may develop as the sons and daughters of foreign workers form a larger percentage of the young people entering the labor force. They are likely to be particularly susceptible to unemployment, and the dangers of radicalization under conditions of long-term unemployment, especially for those who have language difficulties and are socially isolated, are obvious.

Belgium
by Henri Janne

Throughout the 1960s and 1970s, the unemployment rate in Belgium was very low, but with the onset of the recession in 1974, it rose sharply, with a sharp increase in unemployment among the young. Youth unemployment in Belgium conforms to the familiar pattern of being heavily concentrated among those with relatively little educational attainment. On the whole, the measures adopted in Belgium to combat youth unemployment have not been extensive. Instead, general antirecession policies have been emphasized.

Centers for vocational readaptation. Belgium has long had a network of centers for retraining the unemployed, in which the subsistence costs of learners are covered by unemployment insurance. Gradually it became apparent that unemployed young people needed more individualized care and guidance than unemployed adults, and special centers for youth were created. These centers first test the skills and aspirations of the young and, if possible, adapt them to job opportunities. The second step consists of measures designed to increase motivation. If these measures prove insufficient the youngster proceeds to the third step, which determines the specific studies and training that the individual should undertake in a regular vocational center.

Probationary employment. This program was designed to encourage both public agencies and private firms to hire young people on a probationary basis. However, inadequate appropriations prevented public agencies from emphasizing the program, and private firms were reluctant to take on unneeded workers in a period of retrenchment. Therefore, in 1976 the government made the program compulsory under a law that required all private firms and public services employing more than 100 workers to hire probationers in numbers amounting to 1 percent of their total employment, with compensation amounting to something between unemployment insurance and normal pay. The probationers must be under 30 years of age, never have been employed before, and be holders of degrees awarded at the end of regular studies.

The effectiveness of this program is not yet clear, although the general impression is that results have not come up to expectations. The trade unions oppose it because they fear that it will result in illegally low compensation for the probationers.

Education and the social structure. Although the rise in educational attainment of young people in Belgium in the postwar period has been pronounced, the number of pupils who are held back because of lagging progress is shockingly large. For example, many in the 15-18-year age group, who should normally be in upper secondary schools, are actually enrolled in lower secondary schools, in which pupils are primarily in the 12-14-year age group. Moreover, the phenomenon of laggers actually begins in the first year of primary school, in which about one-fifth of the pupils are held back. Laggers consitute 40 percent of all pupils in the sixth grade.

Among the laggers in primary school, one-fourth in the first year and 43 percent in the sixth year are sons and daughters of unskilled workers. The percentages of laggers who are children of top professional and managerial workers are very small. In other words, the chances of falling behind are five times greater in the first year and four times greater in the sixth year for children of unskilled workers than for those whose fathers are at the top of the occupational ladder, in spite of efforts of the schools to promote as many pupils as possible. In the sixth year, the children of teachers do almost as well as the children of the top professional and managerial workers. These general relationships between social origins and progress in school continue at the lower secondary level.

University enrollment increased rapidly until the early stages of the recession, when poor employment prospects for university graduates appeared to discourage university enrollment but to stimulate enrollment in the nonuniversity sector of postsecondary education. After two years of economic recession, however, attitudes appear to have changed. Many young people prefer to enter the universities rather than register as unemployed, and the rate of increase in new enrollments has risen again. The universities seem to be performing a "parking" function, giving students a place to spend their time while waiting for an improvement in the employment situation. These findings cast considerable doubt on contentions that an adverse job market for college graduates will inevitably depress enrollment in higher education.

A survey conducted in 1969 showed that most young people tended to be satisfied with their relations with parents, and the great majority had confidence in the benefits of technical progress. On the other hand, attitudes toward school and the political system were decidedly negative. Although the family remains the strong point of integration, the price of family unity is permissiveness, which makes young people more aware of the authoritative orientation at school. However, the negative evaluation of the schools is moderated by the fact that dissatisfaction is strongest in the highest social classes and weakest in the lowest ones. For the lowest social categories, school is an avenue of upward mobility.

Youth in Belgium need "deschooling," which means, among other things, (1) individualization of training; (2) continuous, positive orientation and guidance through an optimal and flexible credit system; (3) alternatives to the classroom system, with provision for diversity of age and size of groups; (4) less instruction in classrooms and more through activities carried out where things happen and where knowledge is increased and skills are developed; (5) alternation of work and studies for the 14-15- and 18-19-year age groups, based on national standards of equitable earnings; and (6) recurrent education at all levels provided on the basis of paid educational leaves, by law or collective bargaining, for all types of studies, for self-improvement, or for community life.

In addition, youth need to be involved early and progressively in working life if opportunities for study become recurrent. Finally, unemployment of youth must be totally eliminated, and there should be more self-determination of cultural activities rather than passive consumption of commercial "choices."

Sweden
by Gösta Rehn

Sweden has managed to hold down its unemployment rate more successfully than most industrial countries in the 1970s. It averaged only about 1.6 percent in 1975 and 1976 but rose to around 2.5 percent in 1978. Part of Sweden's success in holding down its unemployment rate is attributable to the fact that, at any given time, the number of persons enrolled in Sweden's extensive labor market programs represents a larger percentage of the labor force than in most other countries. Sweden expands its labor market programs in recessions, and this cushions the rise in the unemployment rate.

There has been concern over a rising trend in youth unemployment, but youth unemployment rates in Sweden are low. The average for 1978 was 8 percent for the 16-19-year age group and 4 percent for the 20-24-year age group. Swedish data show the familiar relationship between educational attainment and unemployment in the youthful population. There has been particular concern about high unemployment among the 5 percent of each young cohort that drops out before completing compulsory school or that fails to obtain a school-leaving certificate because of excessive truancy. Another group with particularly high unemployment rates includes the children of foreign workers, who frequently lack adequate knowledge of Swedish. Their unemployment rate is about twice that of native Swedish youth.

Occasionally there has been a temporary surplus of university graduates in the 1970s, but these situations have been of short duration. Earlier expectations about easy access to jobs of high status, however, have had to be revised downward.

Youth unemployment has increased in Sweden for reasons similar to those in other countries: (1) the stagnant employment situation in manufacturing; (2) "no dismissal" policies; (3) the rapidly increasing supply of women in the labor market; and (4) the rise in wages of young workers, bringing their compensation closer to that of adults.

Sweden is well-known for its extensive "active labor market policies," which emphasize retraining the unemployed, moving allowances to help workers move from depressed areas to areas experiencing rapid economic growth, regional economic development, and countercyclical relief works and public service employment. Swedish economists and labor market officials have been pioneers in arguing that inflation in modern industrial countries can be held in check through labor market policies that are aimed not only at achieving reemployment of the unemployed but also at preventing or overcoming the shortages of skilled workers that develop under conditions of rapid economical growth.

Training programs. In principle, the training and retraining programs conducted by the Swedish Labor Market Board are not intended for persons under age 20, whose training and education are expected to occur within the school system, but exceptions have increased. The number of those aged 20 to 24 enrolled in such programs, however, has tended to be high from the start.

Most training under the auspices of the Labor Market Board is conducted at special or temporary centers maintained by the board. Courses are tuition-free, and trainees receive subsistence allowances that are above any unemployment benefits for which they might be eligible. Training at a center typically begins with eight weeks of general theoretical education. Vocational courses are held continuously throughout the year, and trainees can be admitted at any time. To encourage this, much of the training is individual with the teacher providing guidance rather than conducting a class.

Changes in vocational counseling. Counseling and guidance service has expanded considerably. Full-time officers for study and vocational orientation are being employed in all educational institutions. There is a debate in Sweden about whether counselors should try to steer young people toward further study immediately after compulsory school or should help in developing a recurrent education pattern. If those who seek work after compulsory school have difficulty in getting jobs, the employment service and vocational counselors help them to return to school even in the midst of a term. Thus, by encouraging certain courses to start continuously throughout the year, the secondary schools are encouraging a return to school.

Trainee positions. Apprenticeship has not been as important in Sweden as in some other Western European countries, but the rise in youth unemployment has led to much discussion of the need to expand the number of trainee positions. The laws against dismissals complicate the issue, because employers fear being tied to inexperienced trainees.

Local community councils. Local planning councils for youth are being established in all local government areas under mandatory legislation. The local school authorities lead these councils, which include representatives of the municipal authorities, the employment service, and employer and union organizations. The schools, in cooperation with these planning councils, also have responsibility for following, advising, and guiding all young people for two years after the end of compulsory school.

Employer subsidies. In addition to the training subsidies for existing employees, employers receive special subsidies for hiring and training teenagers. The young people are paid at rates provided for in collective agreements and must be kept on the job for at least three months. Each individual appointment of a young person must be approved by the trade union organization concerned. In practice, a majority of the young people hired under this program are kept on after their training.

Relief work. In 1975-76 the central government subsidy to municipalities for special work relief projects for youth was raised from 50 to 75 percent of payroll costs. As a result, the program expanded considerably.

Intensified labor market services. Employment services for youth are provided through the regular employment service. But an experiment with an enlarged employment service for youth in several cities was undertaken in 1975-76. It revealed that jobs were available for young people, but they were often of short duration and offered few prospects of promotions. Very few of the young people refused a job that was offered—contradicting the notion that much youth unemployment may be attributable to choosiness about jobs.

Perhaps 8 to 10 percent of the youths registering with the employment service are particularly difficult to place. They have often tried relief work and have been unable to cope with it; they are on the registers of the social welfare service; they frequently have alcohol or drug problems; they have a history of problems in school and often have not completed compulsory schooling. Joint efforts by the employment service and the social welfare service have suggested that offering these youngsters conventional relief work is insufficient. They also need access to adults who will be available both on and off the job. In addition, both their work and their free-time activities must be meaningful to them. Some small experiments to combine a rehabilitation program with relief work are being carried out.

Issues in Swedish education. Egalitarian reforms of the educational system have proceeded farther in Sweden than in most other countries of Western Europe. Since 1962 there have been no differentiated streams in the compulsory comprehensive schools for all children aged 7 to 16. In addition, grades are not repeated. Pupils needing extra support have access to remedial teaching.

In principle, school-leaving certificates entitle all pupils to go on to upper secondary school, but in practice the door is not quite so open. There are 23 different streams in the upper secondary schools, each having a different subject matter orientation, and some of them require completion of a special course in English or mathematics at the senior level of the comprehensive school or later. Moreover, admissions to some of the streams is limited by a shortage of places.

Since 1971-72, all pupils also attend a single, integrated type of upper secondary school. The percentage completing compulsory school and going on to upper secondary schools is high. In 1972, Sweden ranked behind the United States, Canada, and Japan in enrollment of 16 year olds (74 percent), but well above other Western European countries.

Although the comprehensive upper secondary schools were partly intended to overcome class distinctions in the types of programs pursued—and, along with this, in entrance to the university—a recent study shows that this goal has not yet been achieved. Decisions to continue in school, as well as the choice of subject in the upper secondary school, are strongly related to the father's education. Nevertheless, the increased scope of general subjects in the more practical streams has made it easier for large groups to go back to school later and continue their formal education.

The principle of recurrent education was explicitly established in the 1977 legislation on higher education reform. Eligibility for entrance to institutions of higher education has been extended to those who have at least a two-year upper secondary school certificate, as well as to persons who have reached the age of 25 and have had at least four years of work experience—provided that they are competent in Swedish and English and have a basic knowledge of the subject to be studied. However, entrance to all university and college studies is subject to quantitative limits.

Social and attitudinal aspects. Social and political reforms of the last few decades have produced one of Western Europe's most permissive societies. Among the formal expressions of this are the following: the abolition of physical punishment in schools (1959) and even in the home (1979), the prewar elimination of laws against contraception and the postwar introduction of sex education in schools, the gradual liberalization of abortion laws, and the elimination of restrictions on the purchase of alcohol (1955).

The most fundamental observation one can make about the behavior of the liberated postwar generations is that they have followed their parents' advice to prolong their education. The rapidly expanding facilities for further schooling have been extensively utilized by both teenagers and people in their early twenties.

On the political level, student unrest has subsided and the universities have returned to their traditional role, that is, as strongholds for conservative ideologies. Young workers also follow in their parents' footsteps in their allegiance to trade unions and political organizations, although rapid urbanization has meant membership difficulties for the latter. With adherence to trade unions becoming more a habit and an administrative arrangement than an expression of militancy in a class struggle, it is natural that the young display a growing passivity toward unions.

In the schools, particularly in the upper grades of compulsory schools (13-16 year olds), teachers complain about growing discipline problems. Efforts to improve the situation by making schools more interesting and relevant are under way through a reorganization of nonacademic activities. School life, it is thought, should be less isolated from the community and the world of work and should include not only academic teaching but also leisure-time activities. Opening school gates to representatives of voluntary organizations, business firms, and trade unions is part of the plan. At the pathological fringe, alienation among a minority of youth is clearly expressed in increased juvenile delinquency, alcoholism, and drug addiction.

On the whole, Sweden can be expected to continue its policy of antiauthoritarian and prodemocratic education in homes, schools, and preschool institutions, as well as democratization of life in workplaces. Perhaps the most interesting aspect of the Swedish experience is that, despite the strong emphasis on egalitarian policies and despite remarkable progress in raising the general level of educational attainment, socioeconomic status continues to be a crucial determinant of a young person's progress in the school system. How much difference the new university admissions policies will make remains to be seen, but they are clearly aimed at making the return to school easier for those with limited educational attainment.

Denmark
by K. Helveg Peterson

One of the reasons for the larger share of unemployment among young people in Denmark is the tendency for employers to take into account the family position of the employee when considering layoffs. Those who have families to care for are kept on at the expense of younger workers who have no families. Younger workers also suffer from lack of seniority when layoffs occur.

Most of the youthful unemployed have limited educational attainment. Experience has also shown that young people who have left school early are difficult to motivate for education later in life. Thus, the youth unemployment problem clearly cannot be solved by extending the school-leaving age or by offering continued educational training.

In line with the view that the unemployment situation is temporary, youth unemployment has been combated by keeping young people off the labor market until society can employ them. Most young people who take part in courses or enroll at a folk high school must sign a paper indicating that they are willing to interrupt their education if they are offered work.

Danish experiments. Denmark has carried out experiments involving work and education that have created motivation and interest among youth on a scale hitherto unknown. The Aabaek Continuation School, for example, is located on an old farm, and the students and teachers do all the necessary work connected with housekeeping and all the other functions carried on at the school, including farming, fishing, repairing furniture, building boats, and repairing automobiles. The training received by the students is closely associated with the practical work. Creating interest in education is quite easy when the education is directly motivated by work experience. The guiding principle is that the students must produce things that are necessary for survival. This creates a much different atmosphere from that at a school where the student follows a uniform curriculum. Many youngsters who have been quite incapable of adapting to a regular school flourish here, and the contact between the school and the community greatly helps the students find jobs in the neighborhood.

Three different schools in Tvind occupy a large campus. Included are a continuation school for those between the ages of 14 and 18, a traveling folk high school, and a teacher-training college. In all, the schools enroll about 1,000 students. As at Aabaek, the curriculum involves a combination of practical and theoretical work, and the types of occupational activities are very similar.

The traveling folk high school is a unique experiment. Started with one bus, the experiment has expanded, and the school now has about 70 buses. Groups of students travel all over the world to gather first-hand impressions and to acquire knowledge of each area by staying among the native residents.

The teacher-training college on this campus differs sharply from other such colleges. The program requires actual work experience for several years, along with visits to offices and factories. Only after this experience do the students prepare for the final examination, which resembles that in normal teacher training.

Although the experiments described above have been successful, their widespread application is hampered by lack of support from the central government and local authorities and by restrictive rules and regulations. Another serious obstacle is that experimental schools are not allowed to engage in production, lest they compete with existing industrial activities. The experiments that have engaged in production have done so on a limited scale. Problems also arise from the fact that funds available to combat unemployment come from various departments of the central government and from other types of institutions as well. Local boards representing the various administrative departments have been established, but this still results in a cumbersome working procedure.

One objection to these experiments is that they are residential institutions. Thus, only a limited number of young people can participate. Accordingly, there are proposals to establish centers all over the country where young people could work while living at home.

Poland
by Barbara Liberska

Though differing in manners and morals from their parents, Polish youth do not disagree with their parents' social goals or values, displaying instead a desire to live a peaceful and happy life in an accepted system of values. However, Polish youth of the 1970s have higher aspirations for education and work than their parents did.

The education system established in Poland after World War II was designed to eliminate inequalities of the past by following several principles: being large and flexible enough to provide educational opportunities for all who wish them, being so structured as to permit everyone to continue education to the highest level desired, adapting education to meet the economic needs of the country, and pursuing constant modernization. The result is a national school system that is uniform, free, and universal. Beyond compulsory education (after age 15) opportunities vary, but they are more readily available for some young people than for others; opportunities are especially inferior for rural youth.

In 1960, virtually all elementary school age children in Poland attended elementary school, but only 85 percent completed it; by 1974, this figure had grown to 90 percent. Among those completing elementary school, the percentage continuing to postcompulsory education has also steadily increased, reaching 94 percent by 1975. Those who complete compulsory education can continue education in a variety of general or vocational schools, enter a vocational training program, get a job while continuing to study part-time, remain dependent on their parents, or enter two-year compulsory military service (applicable to males only).

Among those going on to secondary school, the percentage proceeding to vocational schools has increased from 30 percent in 1960 to 55 percent in 1975, while the percentage going on to general secondary schools fell from 25 to 20 percent during the same period. The rise in enrollment in vocational schools has been in response to the growing need for skilled workers.

Those from general and vocational secondary schools who pass the final graduation examination are eligible for admission to all types of institutions of higher education. There are also postsecondary two-year schools that train general secondary school leavers for professional work. About 20 percent of those who enter institutions of higher education come from vocational schools.

Although enrollment in institutions of higher education has increased markedly, not all students who apply are admitted. The increased output from secondary education has not been matched by a corresponding increase in the capacity of institutions of higher education. Only 40 percent of the applicants were able to enter higher education between 1960 and 1975; about one-half of the applicants did not pass the entrance examinations.

Educational opportunities for workers. The movement toward expanding educational opportunities in Poland is augmented by a comprehensive system of education programs for working people. These programs are available at elementary, basic vocational, secondary, and higher education levels in evening and correspondence courses. Enrollment in these programs increased tremendously between 1960 and 1975. Workers are induced to participate through such incentives as additional paid holidays for study, shorter working hours, and free consultation time.

The participation of women has increased at all levels of education. Relatively more girls than boys enroll in general secondary schools, and in 1974 women constituted more than 50 percent of the students enrolled in higher education. Traditionally, women have studied economics and the humanities, but this pattern has changed, with more women studying technical and scientific subjects. Women now represent a majority of graduates in professions such as teaching, law, medicine, and economics.

Outside of the formal school system, industrial enterprises have programs of apprenticeship, on-the-job training, and professional improvement, and the military service provides numerous opportunities for vocational training and education. The Polish government has also emphasized the educational role of radio and television. The second television channel, established in 1970, devotes over 80 percent of its broadcasting time to education.

Also of special interest is the Voluntary Labor Corps. Young people enter camps for a specific period of time in which they live and work together, acquiring occupational qualifications while helping with construction work or harvesting. This program has grown, and in the 1970s some 30,000 youth were enrolled yearly.

At the beginning of the 1970s, the government established the Experts' Committee for the Development of a Report on the State of Education in Poland. The committee identified weaknesses in the Polish education system, including unequal opportunity in education for youth from lower socioeconomic backgrounds (especially rural youth); insufficient vocational guidance and school orientation programs; poor choice of post-compulsory vocational education by many students; insufficient postelementary schools in rural areas; high dropout rates and large numbers of students who require extra years to complete secondary school; too many youths quitting school after basic vocational school; and too few rural youth employed in agriculture because of the low standards of agricultural schools. Changes recommended by the committee included compulsory and universal education for 11 years (until age 18) in comprehensive schools; universal accessibility; curricula adjusted to national economic needs and to individual preferences; extensive education that can compete on a modern international basis; continuous education that can update skills as the economy progresses; and emphasis on extracurricular activities to help youth choose suitable occupations, along with some occupational training for all students in the last three years of compulsory education.

Between 1960 and 1970, when the baby boom generation was entering the labor force, Polish employment policy had to accommodate an increase in available workers that was twice as large as that of the 1950s. Three primary goals determined specific aspects of employment policy: (1) full employment, with distribution of manpower in accordance with the needs of the national economy; (2) full utilization of the educational attainment and professional qualifications of workers; and (3) constant upgrading and improvement of worker's qualifications.

Despite the large percentage of the 15-18-year age group in postcompulsory education or at work, a number of youth are still out of school and out of work. Efforts to encourage these youth to learn an occupation include information programs in elementary schools, in the youth press, and on radio and television; contacts with industrial enterprises; and activities of organizations such as the Voluntary Labor Corps.

Youth 18 and over are eligible for full-time jobs, and people in this age group enter full-time employment, go on to higher education, are recruited for military service, or seek additional vocational education or training, frequently signing training contracts with enterprises. The system under which many graduates of institutions of higher education enter employment is of special interest. In 1964 legislation was passed regulating their employment. The program operates through contracts by which students agree to work in an enterprise for a period of three years. The act applies to most studies except for some of the humanities and the arts. Labor exchange representatives in institutions of higher education establish contacts between prospective graduates and enterprises. As a rule, the demand for graduates is 20 percent higher than the number available, which increases the choices for graduates.

Students who do not use this contractual method are informed about prospective employment three months before completing studies by the labor exchange representative in their institution. Graduates who avoid entering work to which they have been assigned are obliged to return half of the cost of their education as well as the total amount of scholarship funds received.

After completing the three years of obligatory work, a graduate can go to any other enterprise, whether or not it is entitled to employ graduates of institutions of higher education. A graduate can also break a contract with the enterprise if the latter does not fulfill the terms of the contract. However, if the graduate breaks the contract without such a breach by the enterprise, the cost of his or her education must be repaid. A similar system of preliminary contracts, which are signed in the last year of study, has been introduced for vocational school graduates.

A problem that appears to be of particular concern in Poland is the failure to adequately match the particular training of graduates of institutions of higher education with the needs of the economy. Often the problem results from individuals choosing studies haphazardly or training for occupations for which they are unsuited. At the beginning of the 1970s, surveys of graduates indicated that about 25 percent were in jobs that were incompatible with their fields of studies.

The Polish case illustrates the fact that the problems of relations between education and work in a socialist society are very similar to those in capitalist societies. Despite the larger role of planning in the former, matching training and employment is difficult, and disparities of opportunity among socioeconomic strata are not easily overcome.

Japan
by Hidetoshi Kato

Japan has succeeded in maintaining a low overall unemployment rate of 2.0 percent in recent years, as well as a low youth unemployment rate. One reason for low youth unemployment is the intense pressure for young people to achieve a high level of education. The percentages of 16 and 17 year olds in Japan who were enrolled in school in 1970 were almost as high as those in the United States and Canada. Since the mid-1960s, when the percentage of junior high school graduates going on to senior high rose sharply, employers have referred to junior high school graduate workers as "golden eggs." To hire them, employers send recruiters to small rural junior high schools, where fewer graduates go on to senior high, to persuade the young people to come to their offices and factories. Japanese data show that the demand-to-supply ratio of workers aged 15 has been running around 6 to 1. Undoubtedly significant in this connection is the fact that these youth are usually hired for jobs in manufacturing, whereas senior high graduates are more likely to enter the trade and service sectors.

The greatest insecurity about employment in recent years has been among college and university graduates. In the past, when fewer than 10 percent of youths were enrolled in universities, there was an implicit, and often explicit, promise that graduates would be given stable managerial jobs in either the public or the private sector. By 1975, 31 percent of those entering the labor force were college or university graduates, and it was evident that demand for graduates had not met the increase in supply. Even graduates of such prestigious national universities as Tokyo or Kyoto encountered severe competition. Most graduates had to accept jobs that they considered relatively undesirable.

Actual unemployment among 20-24 year olds in Japan does not appear to be a serious problem. In 1975, the unemployment rate for this age group was about 1.5 times the national rate—a considerably lower ratio than that prevailing in most other industrial countries. Relative unemployment rates of those aged 15 to 19 are also low by international standards.

A decisive factor in the incredibly rapid industrialization of Japan over the past 100 years has been the consistent emphasis on education and the underlying philosophy that evaluation and recruitment of youth was to be based strictly on achievement rather than on social status. The traditions of intellectualism and an egalitarian examination system have been preserved—or at least have survived—throughout the modern history of Japan. The majority of Japanese people still firmly believe that higher education is the only path toward a good job, a stable income, and reputable social status. This belief continues despite the shift to a less favorable job market for graduates.

Competition in education starts very early. In addition to regular school, many Japanese parents send their children to private "supplementary schools" for two or three hours a day to get supplementary and more advanced curricula. Since junior high school is compulsory, every child is accepted by the local public school. However, many parents want their children to be accepted by a prestigious private school, which can be a starting point for successful higher education, which implies, eventually a successful career. In addition, many families are willing to pay even more money for private tutors at home. In a word, from primary school age on, Japanese children live in an extremely competitive world, and the only and absolute good for them is to be admitted by name universities.

In order to help meet the adverse employment situation for graduates of institutions of higher education, the School Education Law was amended in 1975 to give official recognition to professional schools as alternatives to postsecondary education and to provide partial government subsidies for such schools. The law established requirements for recognition as a professional school, distinguishing between professional high schools, which admitted junior high graduates and professional schools, which admitted senior high graduates. This development did not signify a shift in emphasis away from the regular educational system, but rather a shift from a monolithic educational philosophy to a pluralistic view. At the same time, employers now seem to be recruiting a better "manpower mix" of university graduates, high school graduates, and professional school graduates.

Full-time workers have a variety of opportunities to advance their education. For example, they may earn either senior high school or university credits through a public broadcasting system educational program that is conducted in conjunction with correspondence courses. To provide greater opportunities for adults to achieve a university education, the Ministry of Education has developed plans for a broadcasting university. It is to be an independent educational institution that utilizes the most sophisticated television technology and offers a degree course lasting a minimum of four years. The students will have a much wider choice of elective subjects than in the traditional universities, and the courses will be interdisciplinary.

Many companies have decided to establish their own training schools rather than recruit senior high school graduates. Junior high graduates are admitted to these schools through competitive examinations, and for three years they are full-time students in the equivalent of a regular senior high school. In addition to the same courses offered in the regular senior high school curriculum, they receive technical instruction on aspects of the companies' operations. These programs are highly regarded by both management and the students. Management views the programs as a reliable source of manpower trained specifically for the company's needs, while the students appreciate the guarantee of a job in a large company and the freedom from worry about tuition fees and other educational expenses. Students in these programs are also free of concern about the highly competitive entrance examinations that regular students face.

There is substantial discrimination against young women in employment in Japan. Employers usually do not want women, especially university graduates, because they often work for only three or four years and then quit when they get married. The number of independent and professional women working in different sectors has increased, but the status of women in the economy remains in great need of improvement.

The crowded generation. The baby boom generation following World War II was poorly accommodated by society in comparison with succeeding generations. This "crowded generation" experienced heavy psychological pressures from sheer density, and found itself in an extremely competitive environment both in school and in employment. The sense of overcrowdedness combined with democratic idealism to lead this generation to overall frustration and resentment. The violent campus unrest that took place in Japanese universities in 1968-1970 may have had its origin in the demographic, socio-psychological, and ideological characteristics of the students of the day.

Although the widely publicized generation gap of the 1960s seems to have become less serious in recent years, mass media affect young people today much more than they affected preceding age groups. The average number of hours young people spend watching television has been increasing. As in many other countries, the values transmitted by mass media often conflict with the values taught at home and in school.

The incidence of juvenile crime and delinquency has varied in recent years. Violent crimes such as burglary and rape have decreased significantly, but theft, especially of automobiles and motorcycles, has increased. Even so, juvenile crime and delinquency in Japan are relatively low compared with the situation in other industrial countries.

A recent cross-cultural study shows that Japanese youths are more work oriented than young people in other countries. They tend to view work as a means of developing themselves rather than a means of obtaining economic benefit. Young people today may be the children of affluence and are great spenders, but the work ethic has not disappeared.

The transition from youth to adulthood seems to have become extraordinarily complicated in Japan. Early sophistication has marked the young people of the past few decades, but many of them do not feel that they are adults yet. Because of the diffusion of higher education, many young people experience prolonged dependency upon their families and other socializing agents. In the past, when most young people began working in their late teens, their economic independence made them feel like adults.

Grave problems result from the intense competition to be admitted to the name universities. Yet the official recognition of professional schools has led to their increasing popularity, and many young people find them an attractive alternative. Thus, patterns of participation in higher education may change. At present, Japanese youth enjoy full employment, but this situation is unlikely to prevail 25 years from now. More social welfare measures must be taken to accommodate the demographics of the future, when society will be dominated by an old and middle-aged population.

Mexico and South Asia

The problems of transition from school to work in less-developed countries are not entirely dissimilar to those of the advanced countries, but they begin at a much earlier age. Instead of leaving school at age 15 or 16, youngsters tend to complete their schooling between ages 12 and 14, and the proportion who drop out of primary school or who never attend at all tends to be shockingly high in the countries included in this series. Sri Lanka is an exception to this pattern.

In the labor market, underemployment, rather than unemployment, tends to be the most serious problem, a situation that reflects in part the predominance of agriculture, where the work is highly seasonal. Nor are opportunities for young school leavers in cities significantly better. Lacking any specific training, and often even lacking literacy, youthful entrants to the labor force are largely confined to service occupations that tend to be casual, low paid, and dead-end.

Widespread poverty and rapid population growth complicate the efforts of governments to overcome these problems. Improving education and employment opportunities for young people cannot be separated from the far larger problems of accelerating economic growth and slowing population increases.

Mexico
by Alberto Hernández Medina and Carlos Muñoz Izquierdo

In spite of economic progress, inequality in the distribution of income in Mexico has tended to increase in recent decades. Disparities between the countryside and the city are enormous. In rural areas, for example, only about 9 percent of the age group attends the sixth grade, compared with 63 percent in urban areas. Nearly 40 percent of Mexico's population is in the agricultural sector, characterized by low productivity. The resulting emigration to urban areas has glutted urban job markets with uneducated, unskilled workers whose numbers increase faster than the ability of the growing industrial sector to absorb them.

The overall unemployment rate in Mexico in 1969 was relatively low (3.8 percent). Unemployment rates tend to be higher in the cities than in the rural areas, and, within the cities, unemployment rates are much higher for teenagers than for adults. Moreover, the underemployed population—including those who work only part of the year, underpaid workers, and those engaged in the informal labor market (odd jobs, street vending, and so forth)—is vast, averaging around 50 percent of the labor force in large cities.

Although there is an upward trend in educational attainment, the situation continues to be discouraging. The law requires young people to be educated until the age of 15, but many youths begin work at age 12 because their families simply cannot survive without the additional income. On the average, from 1959 to 1974, 77 percent of the relevant age group failed to complete primary education, and 88 percent failed to complete secondary school. Yet this average masks substantial change over the period. The enrollment rate of those aged 12 to 19, for example, rose from 23 percent in 1959 to 57 percent in 1975. Over this same period, on the average, about 3.5 percent of the relevant age group was enrolled in higher education, and only 0.8 percent graduated from institutions of higher education.

Because of the complexity of the youth unemployment problem, however, no substantial improvement is expected for at least 10 years. Structural changes are required, which cannot be accomplished overnight. Youth employment problems are grave and will continue to be serious, according to even the most optimistic observers, for some time to come.

South Asia
by Manzoor Ahmed

The combined population of South Asia—including Bangladesh, India, Pakistan, and Sri Lanka—was estimated at 771 million in 1975. These countries contain the world's largest concentration of poverty, with per capita income in 1975 ranging from $110 (U.S. dollars) to $150. The population in the 15-24-year age group in 1975 accounted for about 20 percent of the total population.

Conventional estimates of labor force participation, employment, and unemployment can be misleading when applied to South Asian economies, which are dominated by peasant agriculture. The data that are available show a higher incidence of unemployment among youths than among adults. The real dimensions of the employment situation of young people can only be properly interpreted by distinguishing between urban and rural youth and between the more educated and less educated groups.

In three of the countries, a large majority of young people in the labor force are illiterate or semiliterate, live in rural areas, and do their best to seek out a living from agriculture and other rural occupations. A relatively small minority with a considerable spread in educational attainment is employed in urban economic activities, and their occupational goals and life aspirations are tied to nonrural, modern economic activities. This picture also describes Sri Lanka, except that almost all of the rural youth in Sri Lanka are literate.

Though the total number of unemployed educated persons is relatively small compared with total youth employment, the unemployment rate tends to be higher among the educated than among illiterates, and higher at the middle level of education than at the bottom end. The phenomenon of unemployment among the educated in South Asia is interpreted in various ways, as a result of divergent normative and ideological points of view. Some look upon the problem as a waiting period between completion of education and job placement. According to this view, unemployed graduates eventually either find jobs that they desire or lower their sights and accept what is available. The remedy lies in measures that would reduce the waiting period and hasten the adjustment between both the number and expectations of job seekers and the number of jobs. The basic tools would be changes in the operations of the market mechanism—restricting the expansion of higher education and improving the flexibility of the labor market so that wages respond to the supply of labor.

Another view of unemployment among the educated emphasizes that the expectations created by the educational system and the knowledge imparted by it fail to prepare students for available work opportunities. Curricular reform toward a more "practical bias" in the school system is advocated, with a prominent role for informal education and easier access to education.

A third view is that the problem of unemployment among the educated is a symptom of more fundamental problems in the overall socioeconomic structure. Adherents of this view stress such problems as a production technology that perpetuates waste of human resources and dependence on industrial countries, the persistence of dual economies with sharp contrasts between urban and rural areas and modern and traditional sectors of the economy, and a political power structure that subsidizes unemployable university students but denies basic education to the masses.

Educational deficiencies. In the three large countries of the region, more than 90 percent of the population in the 15-24-year age group is not enrolled in educational institutions; over 50 percent of the youths are illiterate; 10 to 15 percent have a certain amount of secondary education; and the remainder have complete or incomplete primary education. In Sri Lanka, the literacy level of the youth population is around 90 percent, while nearly 50 percent have had some lower secondary education and about 14 percent have reached the eleventh grade or above. Secondary education is still very largely urban, and boys still make up the vast majority of secondary students.

The basic economic reasons for dropping out of primary education cannot be altered by any educational measure, but the opportunity cost of attending primary schools for the children of poor families could be reduced by introducing a part-time, variable-duration, flexible timetable.

The countries of the region recognize the need for literacy programs and adult education. Both India and Pakistan have literacy programs for adults, but so far the programs cover only a small fraction of the potential clientele. Proposals for reforming the secondary schools have tended to emphasize a more vocationally oriented education. However, since most students who enter these schools have only one purpose in mind— to qualify for the university—few students take up streams like fine arts and agriculture, or even the technical stream. Due to the problem of unemployment among university graduates, there have been many proposals for restricting entry into higher education.

Although there are a few training programs for out-of-school youths in South Asia, the total number of youths served by these programs is insignificant. There have also been some limited experiments with youth service programs, but logistical and management problems are often insurmountable, especially if the program is initiated and directed by the national government rather than by local groups.

All of the South Asian countries have encouraged small-scale and village industries as a means of creating employment opportunities at low capital cost and bringing the fruits of economic development to rural areas. India has had the largest and most diverse experience in this regard. While the number of people provided with employment by such programs is large, it pales in comparison with India's total labor force of over 200 million. Moreover, low productivity and low cash income still offer less than a living wage to most workers.

The opportunities for basic general education at the primary level can be widened and a larger population ensured a minimum level of educational achievement if the exclusive reliance on the conventional age-specific, full-time primary school is relaxed. A combined formal-informal strategy can be adopted that would (1) reduce the opportunity cost of participating in primary education for poor families, (2) involve local communities in enlarging primary education opportunities for their children, and (3) make primary education relevant to rural life and environment.

Functional literacy and education programs are needed for older youths and adults to complement the efforts to expand primary level education. These programs, however, need to be planned and implemented as part of larger economic improvement projects. The help of established voluntary organizations active in rural development and local voluntary groups is vital to implement them.

To resolve the conflict in secondary education between the main function of selecting and preparing students for higher education and the unsuccessful efforts to give it a vocational orientation, formal general education should be emphasized. The organizational and structural flexibility suggested for primary education must also be introduced at the secondary level on the same grounds of reducing opportunity costs, granting wider access, and mobilizing available resources for education.

The strategy for middle-level vocational and technical training should be to shift the main burden of skill development to employers and to strengthen the indigenous system of skill development in the traditional sector of the economy. The key to an effective program appears to be an intensive and fairly prolonged supervised work experience, provided at a low cost in a communal setting.

The most practical and feasible approach toward higher education development requires a two-pronged attack: first, restricting the growth of full-time, specialized, professional higher education through financial measures; and second, introducing structural and organizational changes that contribute to equal access, wider opportunities for general higher education, and improved professional preparation and career choices.

Postponed entry into higher education is suggested by the International Labor Organization. Students would be required to spend several years in productive work, and university selection would be based on work experience as well as on previous academic achievement; many students would find a university education unnecessary, and others would have clearer ideas about the type and level of higher education they needed.

Manpower policies must stop accepting existing patterns of employment and use human resources more effectively while removing gross socioeconomic inequities. Three specific actions are suggested as major ingredients of a positive manpower policy in South Asia.

First, the average wage of top-ranking public service jobs in South Asia is 15 to 20 times higher than that of the lowest ones. In contrast, the differential is around 5 to 1 in industrialized countries. Reducing wage differentials would decrease the demand for higher education generated by expectations of white collar jobs, help establish the dignity of labor, and attract young people to middle-level skills.

Second, formal educational qualifications should be systematically deemphasized as the criteria for recruitment in jobs.

Third, an important element of the positive manpower approach is close and systematic involvement of employers, in both public and private sectors, in establishing manpower development and utilization policies and programs. Incentives and disincentives through taxes and tax credits, licensing, and other regulatory measures can be used to encourage private sector employers to support skill development programs.

In South Asia, any real effort to improve the present prospects of youths must first attack rural poverty. It is impossible to meet the basic needs of the people of South

Asia by the end of this century without a highly egalitarian economic distribution policy and an economic development pattern that meets the basic needs of the poor and accepts the needs for changes in the pattern of production and investment.

There has been surprisingly little systematic effort in South Asia to increase labor intensity in agriculture. The myth that siphoning off the rural labor surplus to urban industries is the mainspring of economic development still exists in these countries. Similarly, modern, capital-intensive, high-technology industries create a relatively small amount of employment, use up large amounts of scarce capital, and often produce goods that do not satisfy the needs of the people. The policy guidelines for industrial development, therefore, should involve maximum use of the most abundant production factor, that is, labor.

Reflections on Youth Problems and Policies in the United States

by Martin Trow

In the European countries reported on in the essays sponsored by the Carnegie Council, rates of unemployment (and also of delinquency and crime) among youth are generally lower than in the United States, but the very high degree of concern of the authors and the panoply of programs and policies designed to meet the "problem" suggest other sources of worry. I suspect three such sources: first, the persistent trauma left by the widespread unemployment of the 1920s and 1930s; second, the claims of the Eastern "people's democracies" that they have provided at least full employment; and third, apprehension that the political discontent expressed by university students in the 1960s and since might spread among unemployed and working class youth, with grave danger to the survival of democratic societies.

The chief anxieties about youth in the United States include the following:

1. A concern about the high and rising rates of unemployment among all youth, and especially the fear that this might be permanent.
2. Anxiety about the very high figures reported for unemployment among young black men in inner-city slums. This is seen as a tragedy in itself, an immediate potential source of crime and delinquency and of more serious long-term problems.
3. There is more generalized concern that the traditional institutions of society that have helped youth in their transition to adulthood—the family, schools, churches, and youth groups—are not functioning as well as they have been. Instead, their place has been taken by a powerful youth culture that tends to prolong youthful attitudes of irresponsibility and hedonism.

The Secondary Labor Market

Governmental policy everywhere seems to be aimed at stable, secure, and well-paying jobs for young people either after completion of secondary or vocational education or after a period of study in postsecondary institutions. Discussions of youth in America, as abroad, view young people as in transition to the state of adulthood, and public policy is aimed at preparing youth for the primary labor market.

However, many young people do not enter the primary labor market directly after leaving school, but spend some time in the secondary market, where jobs are characterized by low pay and fringe benefits and little chance for advancement. These jobs in casual, unstructured work are the jobs where workers with employment disadvantages tend to work. But they are also the jobs in which youth find work, in part because of the relatively weak attachment of young people to the labor market and the consequent attractiveness of such jobs to them. This suggests that the focus of youth policies should not be exclusively or even primarily on the transition from school to work, but at least as much on the transition from the secondary to the primary labor market, which may occur from five to ten years after young people leave high school.

In the United States, many young people accomplish this transition without government aid. They enter and remain in the secondary market more or less voluntarily, seeing in their weak attachment to the job (and in its weak demands on them) a certain freedom—to remain in school or college, to drop in and out of school, or to try out different kinds of jobs and occupations in different parts of the country, and to enjoy the pleasures of the youth culture without responsibilities or deep commitments. At some point, often in their mid-twenties, these people come to want the better pay, job security, and opportunities for advancement available in the primary market. They then enter it, often at the same time taking on new family and financial responsibilities that tie them more securely to their primary market jobs.

Disadvantaged and deprived youth also enter the secondary market for its casualness, its weak job discipline and high turnover, the relative ease of getting and leaving such jobs, and the usefulness of these jobs in establishing eligibility for unemployment insurance and food stamps. Although employment in the secondary market is seen by advantaged youth to be temporary and interspersed with periods of schooling, travel, and the like, for deprived and disadvantaged youth it may not be temporary, but threatens to become permanent, and is more likely to be interspersed and supplemented by hustling and illegal activities than by schooling and travel.

The Hidden Economy

Another labor market resembles and indeed overlaps with the secondary labor market. It is the hidden economy—that part of the economy that is unregulated, untaxed, and untracked. In the United States, the illegal economy is substantial, especially in inner-city slum areas. It distorts our unemployment statistics for youth (as for adults), and thus affects the policies and programs for youth that are predicated on those data. But far more important, the economy of crime, like the larger hidden economy, is an important alternative both to legal employment, especially in the secondary labor market, and to public youth programs.

Cultural Unemployment

The European essays in the Carnegie Council series do not discuss the extent or significance of culturally determined unemployment. By this I mean the readiness of people, specifically young people, to remain unemployed rather than to accept work they consider demeaning and humiliating. The concept of cultural unemployment could be more broadly defined to include all attitudes and values that enter into employment patterns other than the rational calculus of gain and loss. Like the illegal economy, cultural unemployment gets analysts and commentators into the murky areas of attitudes, values, and preferences—forces and concepts that make many economists uneasy and governmental agencies even more so.

If we accept that some youth unemployment is voluntary, as it is among adults, it follows that such people are neither wholly in nor wholly out of the labor market, but "in" or "out" depending on the nature of the jobs available, their status and convenience, as well as their remuneration. But if some significant number of people who are counted as unemployed are so at least in part voluntarily, that certainly affects the meaning we have to attach to the concept of unemployment and to the so-called unemployment rates that result.

Unemployment rates are necessary for the conduct of public business. However, they do not provide a good basis for designing job and training programs for youth. They do not, for example, tell us how many people in any given area are, in fact, potential candidates for whatever youth programs the federal government may design for them.

Types of Youth and Policies for Youth

What characteristics of youth are relevant to the design of policies for them? Certainly there are important differences between age categories and in the level of education completed. Another is the financial resources available to young people, and that means in most cases their families' resources. The issue here is whether those resources are adequate to allow young people to realize their potential; that is, to find places in the world roughly commensurate with their own talents, energies, and aspirations.

Another characteristic of youth relevant to policies for them is whether their socialization and education up to the ages of 16 to 18 enables them to move toward and then accept and fulfill socially responsible adult roles in the society. Most people still believe that a person should be able to gain and hold a job when jobs are available and not be supported either by public welfare or through criminal activities. But even the most undemanding jobs require some motivation and ability to delay gratification, to plan ahead, and to get to work on time. Most jobs in modern society also demand minimum levels of competence in reading, writing, and arithmetic; the capacity to accept a certain measure of responsibility; and the ability to enter into and sustain personal relationships. In considering policies for youth, it may be useful to distinguish between young people whose early education and socialization have given them the motivation, skills, and personal qualities that will enable them to get and hold jobs, and those who are markedly deficient in any or all of these respects.

These variables generate a typology of youth with four categories, each with its own rather different characteristics (see Figure 3). Advantaged youth have both the

Figure 3. A typology of youth

		Early Education and Socialization	
		Adequate	*Inadequate*
Family Financial Resources	*Adequate*	The Advantaged	The Alienated
	Inadequate	The Disadvantaged	The Deprived

personal and financial resources to move toward adult roles that are roughly commensurate with their talents and ambitions. These are the people upon whom society most heavily depends, and no society can neglect the institutions and programs designed for them on the grounds that they can look after themselves. In the United States the institutions that have the major responsibility for preparing advantaged youth for adult roles are colleges and universities.

Alienated youth have not been deprived economically, but have difficulty in their transition to adult roles because of other problems relating to their earlier socialization, education, or both. They are alienated because they are psychologically and emotionally outside the society in which they live; their behavior is governed by their feeling apart from and often hostile to the dominant culture and social institutions. Some of these young people are in fact seeking and creating alternative socializing communities—in communes, in religious sects, or in political communities that embody distinctive philosophies and lifestyles. Others seek further education outside the traditional educational system, which many in this category have found punishing. Some are simply downwardly mobile for complicated reasons that involve their natural abilities and energies, their aspirations and values, and their family dynamics.

In many ways, disadvantaged youth present the most soluble problems for public policy. These young people have personal and academic skills, motivation, and in most cases family encouragement. They need financial aid, counseling, and in some cases publicly supported programs of employment to translate their potential into adult achievement. It is this group that provides the "new" students in postsecondary education, and whose members profit most from state scholarship programs and Basic Educational Opportunity Grants, low-cost loans, and inexpensive community and state colleges.

In the deprived category are to be found the young men and women who have the most severe problems of growth and maturation, who are at once most in need of help from public and private sources and least able to seek it out or profit from such help when it is offered. For these youth, a combination of poverty, inadequate education, and weak psychological resources results in a litany of human and social disaster: high rates of criminal activity, drug and alcohol addiction, chronic unemployment, physical and mental illness, dependence on public welfare, and institutionalization.

The problems of deprived youth are the object of many of the public policies and programs for youth, though few of them can be shown to have had much success with this group. This is partly because public agencies have not recognized important differences between disadvantaged and deprived youth. While the former need and can profit from additional resources for gaining skills and entry to adult jobs, deprived youth often have trouble using these resources. A combination of personality difficulties (including a low self-image and an inability to postpone gratification), cultural attitudes toward work, and a poor educational background make it difficult for deprived youth to get and hold legitimate jobs or gain educational credentials. In addition, their networks of friends and kin are not able to provide good leads to legitimate jobs or are actually recruiting them to the subterranean economy of hustling, petty theft, and the like.

Types of Secondary Labor Market Jobs

It may well be that the central problem of youth in other advanced industrial societies is their transition from school to the primary labor market. By contrast, the secondary labor market may play such an important role in the United States for all youth that the crucial problem here is not transition from school to the labor market, but rather from the secondary to the primary labor market. If that is the case, then we need to analyze more closely the variety of functions that the secondary labor market performs for different segments of youth. And to do this we need to look more closely at the characteristics of different jobs within the secondary market. One aspect is their usefulness or harmfulness in preparing people for better jobs in the primary market. At best, some jobs in the secondary market give young people responsibilities, experience in working with other people, experience in getting to work regularly and on time, the opportunity to use and care for tools, and other useful skills and habits. Many jobs held by young people in fast-food chains may in fact perform some of these functions. But other kinds of jobs in the secondary labor market teach attitudes and habits that are harmful to young peoples' future careers, often rewarding slack discipline with poor wages and insensitive supervision.

A second aspect of a secondary labor market job is whether it has links to the more secure, better-paying world of the primary labor market. If we combine these two dimensions in the fourfold table shown in Figure 4 we have a way of characterizing secondary labor market jobs that begins to help us analyze their functions for different types of youth.

Figure 4. A typology of secondary labor market jobs

		Work Experience as Preparation for Primary Labor Market Jobs	
		Good	*Poor*
		I	II
	Good	Informal apprenticeships "Bridge" jobs Nonunion construction	Marginal manufacturing Casual labor
Job-Provided Links to Primary Labor Market Jobs			
		III	IV
	Poor	Fast food chains	Criminal and quasicriminal activities: gambling, drugs, theft, etc.

Type I jobs provide good experience and training, and also help young people move into the primary market as they begin to take on adult roles and responsibilities. Much nonunion construction work offers this kind of experience, in which young people acquire a variety of skills that are useful in many other kinds of jobs as well as in the organized building trades. A traditional apprenticeship is designed precisely to be a Type I job, providing training in the skills and work habits necessary to become a journeyman, while also providing institutionalized channels for moving into regular long-term work careers. But while the formal apprenticeship is so close to the regular work career that it might well be considered part of the primary market, there are many informal apprenticeships, jobs in which young people are given an opportunity to learn a trade or craft while earning low pay and perhaps little or no fringe benefits.

Type II jobs are often jobs in marginal, fly-by-night firms, for example, machine shops that make toys, novelties, or souvenirs for a local market. Some kinds of casual labor are included here as well. Such jobs often put workers in touch with people doing similar work in bigger unionized firms. On the other hand, they may give young workers a poor experience in handling and caring for tools or in other aspects of work discipline.

Type III jobs may teach good work habits but are thought to be dead-end in the sense that they do not connect people up to better primary market jobs. Jobs in fast-food chains are predominantly staffed by 16-22 year olds, who perform all the tasks from operating the grill to running the cash register. But except for a tiny minority who make a career in fast-food operations, the jobs are simply a way of earning some cash through part-time work while going to school or on vacation.

Type IV jobs offer neither good work experience nor good connections to better legitimate jobs. Work in the illegal economy usually doesn't encourage movement to legal jobs, and for some youth, usually those with few or no family resources, these jobs become a trap, especially when they pay well enough to make available legitimate jobs look overdemanding and underpaid.

Joint Effects

The way in which youth use secondary labor market jobs is a function of characteristics both of the job and of the young people, their families, and other institutional resources available to them. If we look at our typologies of jobs and of youth together, we can see that school, family, friends, church, and job are alternative resources for helping young men and women become responsible and productive adults. The family is especially important, because it not only provides (or does not provide) resources of advice, money, job leads, and the like to its young adult members, but also shapes their characters in ways that determine whether they are able to take advantage of any of the resources available to them. If a young man or woman has the psychological and emotional capacity for dealing with the world—can establish personal relationships, postpone gratification, accept and discharge responsibility, and the like—then he or she may use any or all of these institutional resources in moving toward adult roles. For young persons who may not have many good leads for useful secondary labor market jobs, federal programs for youth employment play an important role. They are intended to supplement the private secondary job market and create a variety of supported or subsidized secondary labor market jobs that may be useful to young people. They are intended to be Type I or Type III jobs—that is, to provide good work experience and some links to the primary job market. On the whole, these jobs seem to be more successful in providing good work experience than in establishing links. In any event, the public programs for youth employment can be better understood as an effort to provide certain kinds of secondary labor market jobs for young people who are able to use them. And this helps us understand why they are much more successful in recruiting disadvantaged youth than deprived youth.

Just as publicly supported youth programs can be seen as an effort to supplement the various resources that help young people become adults, higher education can be seen in the same way. All of higher education is to some extent a preparation for adult jobs and careers. The qualities of mind, varieties of knowledge, and ways of speaking and writing that are the products of higher education are prerequisites for many kinds of upper-white-collar professional and administrative jobs in our society. Colleges also give students a circle of teachers and friends who can help at various stages in their adult careers. So a college or university education is rather like a Type I job in the secondary labor market: it is temporary and poorly paid, but provides good training for adult work and leads and links to adult jobs and careers.

The counseling and placement services of colleges and universities are especially noteworthy here as a special kind of resource for the transition to adult roles. The more skilled the job or career a young person is aiming for, the less likely it is that his or her network of family, friends, and neighbors will be able to give advice and introductions that would be helpful to gain the desired job or career. So, especially for students with modest backgrounds, college counseling placement services become increasingly useful.

The design of effective policies for youth requires much more detailed knowledge than we now have of how different kinds of youth do or do not make the transition to adult jobs and roles. For some advantaged youth, the dice are already so heavily loaded in their favor that no further public effort is needed (beyond its very considerable support for higher education). On the other hand, the dice are so heavily loaded against some deprived youth that we can scarcely imagine any public program having an appreciable effect. Deprived youth may well need more than additional resources; they may need, and at an earlier age than this essay is considering, a different kind of basic socialization, either in their own families or in a residential institution such as a boarding school. But there are many young people in between who have resources of character, intelligence, motivation, and networks of family and friends, but for whom additional help—a good secondary labor market job, a glimpse of a larger world and of broader opportunities—may have effects out of all proportion to the costs and effort involved.

On the whole, we suspect that in the United States most federally supported job programs thus far have had these generally benign effects for disadvantaged youth. But the problems of deprived youth in America remain largely unsolved, perhaps not even seriously attacked outside the system of criminal justice. Until we can see these problems as different in kind and not just in degree from those that disadvantaged youth face, as problems arising not only out of financial poverty but out of a poverty of personal and social resources, we can hardly begin to address them successfully.

Vocational Education and Training: Impact on Youth. By John T. Grasso and John R. Shea. 1979.

This report examines access to occupational education in high school and its impact on eventual educational attainment, postschool training, labor market success in the first few years out of school, and psychological well-being. The study is based on data from two cohorts in the National Longitudinal Surveys (NLS) of Labor Market Experience: 5,000 men who were 14 to 24 years of age when initially interviewed in the fall of 1966; and 5,000 young women who were the same age when first interviewed early in 1968. The study makes use of interview data through 1972 for women and through 1973 for men. Attention is restricted to (1) those who were in high school in the base year surveys and (2) men and women who were out of school and who had completed 10 to 15 years of school as of each survey year. The major variable of interest is high school curriculum (occupational, college preparatory, and general), by self-report of respondents.

Curriculum Assignment and Its Correlates

In the base year surveys, approximately 14 percent of the male and 20 percent of the female students in grades 10 to 12 were enrolled in occupational curricula. High school students in the NLS from occupational curricula differed from their counterparts in other programs in the following respects:

- College preparatory men and women, on the average, ranked noticeably higher in scholastic aptitude (SA) and socioeconomic origins (SEO) than did either occupational or general students. Differences between the latter groups were minor overall, except that black males in vocational programs displayed slightly higher academic aptitude than did their general counterparts.

- Although fewer blacks than whites chose (or were assigned to) an academic rather than a general program, within each third of the SA and SEO distributions blacks were more likely than whites to be college preparatory students. The fact that fewer blacks than whites were in academic programs is associated with the lower scholastic aptitude and social class background of black youth.

- Over four-fifths of college preparatory students in the base year surveys aspired to four or more years of college. Among the young men, nearly half the general students and a quarter of the vocational students wanted at least four years of college. Among the women, about one-third of the general and one-sixth of the occupational students held such high aspirations.

- Among male students, proportionately more blacks than whites in vocational programs aspired to four or more years of college. In other curriculum categories, more whites than blacks aspired to college. Among female students, blacks held about the same level of aspirations as whites, except that very few young white women in business and office programs wished to attend college.

- Occupational goals were consistent with educational aspirations, except that many young black men aspired to occupations that, in terms of typical educational requirements, ranked below their hoped-for educational attainment.

- The preferred occupations (at age 35) of female students were overwhelmingly sex stereotypic. Only 9 out of 297 occupational categories accounted for over two-thirds of expressed job preferences. Indeed, secretary, teacher, and "clerical and kindred" accounted for fully half the preferences. Except for black females, young men and women in occupational programs were somewhat more likely to want jobs for which preemployment preparation below the baccalaureate is sometimes available.

- Male students in vocational programs displayed less knowledge of occupations than did their general counterparts. Females in business and office studies, however, displayed more such information than did their peers from a general program. College preparatory students of both sexes were more likely to know about different occupations than were either occupational or general students.

Educational Attainment and Postschool Training

Aspirations and curriculum assignment are not always congruent. For example, some vocational students aspire to four or more years of college. Curriculum and goals can come into line through either revision of aspirations or movement between curricula. This pattern of change from year to year is not only important in its own right, but also must be understood in order to judge whether occupational programs enhance the likelihood that students will complete at least high school. The findings are as follows:

- Between the base year and first follow-up surveys, fewer than one in ten high school students moved from one major curriculum category to another. The net flow was away from general and college preparatory programs and toward occupational programs.

- Students who moved to occupational programs held aspirations in the base year that, on the average, were higher than those of occupational students in the base year but lower than those of students who stayed in college preparatory or even general programs from one year to the next.

- Remaining in a program two years in a row tended to raise the already high aspirations of college preparatory students but, in the case of male vocational students, to lower already relatively low aspirations.

- Regarding completion of high school, evidence is mixed as to the implications for males of being in a vocational rather than a general program. Controlling for SA, SEO, and other background variables, cross-sectional analysis for out-of-school youth seems to indicate that vocational studies enhance completion of high school. There is a positive correlation between having been most recently in a vocational program, rather than a general one, and highest year of school completed over the range from grade 10 through grade 12. However, tracing students from one year to the next suggests the opposite conclusion. That is, if anything, male students in a vocational program in 1966 were more likely to leave school by 1967 than were their general peers.

     Some students move to occupational programs as they progress through high school, and this fact may account for the mixed findings. Some vocational courses are offered only to seniors; others, to juniors and seniors only. Thus at any given time there are proportionately more seniors in occupational programs than juniors, and more juniors than sophomores. By itself, the net flow toward occupational studies results in a positive correlation between having been in an occupational program and highest year of school completed over the range from 10 to 12 years.

- With respect to females, the net flow toward occupational studies is less in evidence, and both the cross-sectional and longitudinal results indicate that women in a business and office curriculum are more likely than their general peers to complete at least 12 years of school.

- Having completed at least 10 years of school, students in vocational and business and office studies are less likely than are those in a general program to complete at least one year of college. Moreover, with the possible exception of students from the lowest third of the scholastic ability distribution, the net effect of pursuing an occupational program is a reduction in ultimate educational attainment of at least half a year.

- Path models indicate that between general and occupational students, the latter curriculum had a negative effect on educational attainment, apart from educational aspirations. For some students, low aspirations doubtless precede curriculum choice; for others, curriculum choice probably precedes clarification of educational goals. The addition of aspirations to a path model of educational attainment reduces the direct negative effect of curriculum on attainment by only about one-third. Among young black men, but not among white, differences in aspirations are largely independent of choice between a vocational and general program. Furthermore, for this group, the addition of aspirations to a path model has little or no effect on the negative relationship between vocational curriculum and attainment.

- Postschool training in company-sponsored programs, business colleges and technical institutes, apprenticeships, and the like is common. At the most recent follow-up surveys, about two-thirds of out-of-school young men with 10 to 15 years of schooling, and half the women, report having had some postschool training. Attesting to the opportunity afforded by postschool training, SA and SEO are less strongly related to having had some college *or* postschool training than to having completed one or more years of college. Among men, whites were more likely to have had such training than were blacks. However, perhaps because of manpower training programs and affirmative action efforts, the gap narrowed considerably between 1966 and 1971. Among women, racial differences in reported postschool training were slight.

Labor Market Outcomes

How effectively do various high school curricula prepare young people for later labor market experiences? This question was examined by analyzing the relationships between curriculum and several indicators of early labor market success, controlling for highest year of school completed, background characteristics (SA, SEO), and other variables conceivably associated with both curriculum and labor market outcomes, such as type of community of residence—rural, small town, or large city. The principal findings for respondents with exactly 12 years of school are as follows:

- Evidence is mixed as to whether a vocational program, in comparison with a general one, reduces the incidence or severity of unemployment. Unemployment rates at various survey dates are not consistently lower (or higher) for one curriculum group than for another. Analysis based on a measure of employment status as of the survey dates suggests that former students from occupational curricula are less likely to be jobless. However, analysis based on another measure (total number of spells of unemployment from 1966 to 1970) suggests that male high school graduates from vocational programs have had more total spells of unemployment than their general peers. Among white males at least, the average duration of the current spell of unemployment was shorter for vocational graduates, and fewer reported having had multiple spells over the entire period.

    Among employed young women with exactly 12 years of schooling, business and office students reported less unemployment than did general students, while college preparatory graduates were the most likely to have encountered joblessness.

- In terms of hourly rate of pay and annual earnings, only among female graduates is there clear evidence of an advantage to those who completed occupational programs in high school, and the positive effect is as large for young black women as for whites. Among young men, having been a vocational rather than a general student makes no difference.

- Postschool training may pay off somewhat more for former vocational than for general students. (Approximately equal proportions report training beyond high school.)

- Despite the fact that fewer young black than white men perceive that their postschool training has been useful in their current (or last) job, having had such training makes a positive contribution to early labor market success, and this effect is about as great for blacks as whites.

- Some vocational educators feel that occupational studies enhance the opportunity for self-employment, but there is no evidence in the NLS data to suggest that former vocational students are any more likely to be self-employed than are their general program counterparts.

- Job differences among high school graduates from the various curricula were minor, as measured by industry attachment, major occupational group, whether their occupation called for preemployment occupational preparation, and extent of job mobility.

Consideration of sample size rules out strong statements as to the implications of high school curriculum for the labor market success of high school dropouts and respondents with one to three years of college. Nevertheless, several observations can be made:

- Ignoring curriculum, "some college," as opposed to high school graduation only, makes a good deal of difference in pay, earnings, and occupational assignments, and the differences are sizeable for each race-sex group.

- Between dropping out of high school after grade 10 or 11 and completion of exactly 12 years, average differences in economic performance are, again, considerable. The one exception—and an important one—is that white males who left school early are not at a serious disadvantage, as judged by rate of pay, earnings, and especially their pattern of occupational assignments.

- Among whites, major differences in outcomes emerge for those with some college as compared to all those with less schooling. For blacks, the major differences are between high school dropouts and those who have completed at least high school.

- Employed women in the NLS overwhelmingly held sex-stereotypic jobs in 1972. Surprisingly, the sex composition of an occupation, as measured by the percentage that women represented of total 1970 employment in each occupation, made little or no difference for hourly rate of pay or earnings, especially among high school graduates. Among the high school dropouts, being in a "female job" depressed earnings somewhat, while among women with some college, the opposite was true.

- While fewer high school dropouts than graduates reported some postschool training, such training is positively related to labor market outcomes for both groups, and the effect of training is as great (if not greater) for dropouts as for graduates. This is true for men and women and for blacks as well as whites.

- Only for the young men is it possible to say anything about the relationship between high school curriculum and labor market outcomes for those with "some high school" or "some college." For rate of pay and earnings of males, having been in a vocational rather than a general program may make a slight positive contribution. Among females, occupational (largely business and office) students were unlikely either to drop out of high school or to obtain some college. This factor, plus relatively low labor force participation rates, led to an inadequate number of cases to permit comparison with the general track.

Psychological Outcomes

Regardless of the implications of curriculum for subsequent performance in the labor market, curriculum options are important because they enhance choice, respond to individual differences, and otherwise contribute to psychological well-being. Findings in this regard may be summarized as follows:

- College preparatory students express greater satisfaction with school than do either their occupational or general program counterparts. Few students in any program are "dissatisfied." Overall, black youngsters express greater satisfaction with school than do whites. Less satisfied with school are white males from occupational programs, but this is not due to their occupational studies.

- Vocational and office subjects are frequently cited when students are asked to name the subject they enjoyed the most. Very few youths disliked these subjects. The ratio of responses for subjects "enjoyed the most" to "disliked the most" is particularly high for occupational subjects, especially among students in occupational curricula and among those in the low third of the scholastic aptitude distribution. Black youngsters, however, were somewhat less likely than white to name a vocational course as their favorite.

- In terms of the perceived adequacy of their education in meeting their needs in the labor market, respondents from occupational programs were more likely than were their general peers to judge their schooling as adequate. However, this was not true of young black men. Women who have not completed college rate the adequacy of their preparation higher than do men.

- Black youths expressed less satisfaction with their jobs than did white. Black men perceived less progress in their work than did white, and felt their chances of reaching their occupational goals by age 30 were not as good, but had equally high desires to obtain more education.

Individuals with Special Needs

Vocational education is sometimes thought to be especially important for disadvantaged and handicapped youth. Inadequate sample cases prevent statements about the effects of curriculum on the labor market success of youth with health problems or those who grew up in homes where a language other than English was spoken. Nevertheless, in comparison with all graduates, these two "special needs" groups reported a higher mean hourly rate of pay. Related findings include:

- The age-earnings profile for young black male high school graduates is considerably flatter than it is for whites, giving some support to the dualist conception of the labor market. However, the actual change in rate of pay from 1966 to 1971 suggests that the black-white earnings gap for men narrowed somewhat in relative terms. The rapid gains in the earnings of young blacks entering the labor market may account for the apparent discrepancy between cross-sectional and longitudinal results.
- Young black men in the NLS were less likely than were their white counterparts with equivalent years of schooling to hold "good" jobs. And, while barriers between secondary and primary labor market jobs are not impenetrable, black youths —especially dropouts—made less progress than did whites in moving out of secondary and into primary jobs.
- Black male graduates from a general program were more likely than were those from an occupational curriculum to enter the primary sector or to escape the secondary. The opposite was true for white graduates.

Systemic Effects in the Labor Market and at Home

A relatively underexplored area of research has to do with the implications of high school curriculum for (1) do-it-yourself activity, (2) the level and nature of postschool training, and (3) difficult-to-measure, diffused effects on productivity. The NLS contains no information on the first topic, but provides limited evidence on the other two.

- Postschool training is common; men from vocational programs are as likely as their general peers to have received postschool training. However, the form is often different. Former general students are more likely to have received school-based training (e.g., in technical institutes); former vocational students more frequently report company training or "other vocational," a category that includes apprenticeship. It does not appear that postschool training duplicates skills developed in high school to any substantial degree.
- Both human capital theory and past research suggest that the kinds of occupational skills developed in schools may be socially rational, in the sense that (1) school-

based training is more cost-effective or (2) employers would not have sufficient incentives to develop skills in the workplace. In general, one would expect smaller firms to be less efficient than large firms in developing skills in the workplace.

This line of reasoning suggests that schools may tend to develop skills commonly found in smaller establishments. The findings indicate that black males from vocational programs were employed in industries with lower-than-average mean size of establishment. On the other hand, it is consistent with past research that having had some post-school training is positively associated with industry average size of establishment. These findings suggest that hourly rate of pay and earnings may capture only some of the social (economic) benefits that are derived from curricular experiences in the high school.

Conclusions and Recommendations

The research findings support the following recommendations:

- Educators and policymakers should judge the success of occupational training in high school on the basis of several indicators, not just training-related placement rates. These indicators include (1) congruence with career objectives, (2) differences in learning styles, (3) satisfaction of nonvocational purposes, (4) psychological well-being, (5) influence on eventual educational attainments, (6) economic benefits to the individual, (7) efficiency at the workplace, (8) ability to serve persons with special needs, and (9) overall cost-effectiveness.
- Educators and guidance personnel can improve career guidance by (1) increasing their efforts to inform students and parents of career opportunities and education and training options; (2) avoiding tracking, especially of young black men, into vocational rather than more general programs; and (3) being sensitive to the fact that sex-stereotypic vocational education for women may provide earnings in the first few years out of school that are at least as high as those in fields in which women are less concentrated.
- The allocation of federal and state funds for vocational education to areas with high concentrations of low-income or otherwise disadvantaged youth, or high drop-out rates, can be defended on purely fiscal grounds. In the case of young women, blacks who took business and office studies benefited as much as whites. We un-covered no evidence, however, indicating that vocational programs of the 1960s were especially beneficial for young black men in comparison with their general program counterparts.
- Post-high-school noncollegiate training warrants encouragement and support for at least three reasons. First, the influence of social class background and mental ability is much less potent when educational attainment is viewed broadly to include both collegiate and noncollegiate forms of training. Second, among the NLS men at least, blacks were less likely than were whites to have had any postschool training in 1966, but the relative gap closed considerably over the next five years, attesting perhaps to the success of equal opportunity efforts and manpower training programs. Finally, postschool training (1) was associated with clear economic benefits in terms of hourly rate of pay, (2) helped close (in relative but not ab-solute terms) the wage gap between white and black men, and (3) yielded benefits for both men and women at least as great for high school dropouts as for graduates.

Regarding access to and the impact of occupational education and training, there is a need for further research addressed to the following questions:

- What kinds of education and training experiences are most useful for young persons who are handicapped or disadvantaged in some way?
- In what way, if at all, do occupational studies influence acquisition of basic skills, such as reading and competency in mathematics? Does a "positive interaction" help to explain the economic advantage accruing to young women from business and office programs, compared to their general curriculum peers?
- Concerning curriculum for young men and their dropout rate from high school, can the divergent conclusions from cross-sectional and longitudinal analyses be resolved? Does experience with a vocational program influence the probability of dropping out? If so, what is the direction of the effect?
- Would a multivariate analysis of high school curriculum and employment of young women sustain the view that an occupational curriculum for female high school students reduces their subsequent unemployment?
- Why is it that young black men in the NLS in vocational programs had somewhat higher scholastic aptitude scores than did their general counterparts, and were more likely to aspire to four or more years of college, but actually attained less education?
- In the absence of public support for occupational training, would the volume and mix of occupational training provided through the marketplace be socially optimal? What benefits of publicly supported training, if any, are captured by employers and society at large?
- How important are nonmarket outcomes of vocational education? For example, what is the value of do-it-yourself activities facilitated by skills gained in school?

The Great Chinese Cultural Reversal: Education. By Clark Kerr. 1979.

This essay is part of the report of a study group that visited the People's Republic of China in April and May, 1978.* We were in China at a time when the political line on education, work, culture, and science was being fundamentally changed. The presentations made to us dealt heavily with the current transformations, and a central thrust of

---

*Members of the study group were: Clark Kerr, Chairman of the Study Group, and Chairman, Carnegie Council on Policy Studies in Higher Education; Catherine Kerr, community leader; John S. Service, Vice Chairman of the Study Group; Caroline Service; Stephen K. Bailey, Professor of Education and Social Policy, Harvard University, and President, National Academy of Education; Alfred Fitt, General Counsel, Congressional Budget Office of the United States; Harold Howe II, Vice President, Division of Education and Research, The Ford Foundation; Vernon E. Jordan, Jr., President, National Urban League, Inc.; James A. Perkins, Chairman of the Board, International Council for Educational Development, and Member, Carnegie Council on Policy Studies in Higher Education; Ruth Perkins; Alan Pifer, President, Carnegie Corporation of New York and of the Carnegie Foundation for the Advancement of Teaching, and Member, Carnegie Council on Policy Studies in Higher Education; Lois D. Rice, Vice President, College Entrance Examination Board, and Member, Carnegie Council on Policy Studies in Higher Education; Alice M. Rivlin, Director, Congressional Budget Office of the United States; Jerome M. Rosow, President, Work in America Institute, Inc.; Rosalyn

our questioning came to be how the policies of the Gang of Four, in effect from 1966 to 1976, were being changed. The most intense continuing debate within China is over educational policy, particularly over rules governing entrance into universities. An almost all-pervasive revocation of the policies of the four, a process of stabilizing the society and getting rid of the excesses, has been underway since the fall of 1976.

Modernization

The "Four Modernizations" in agriculture, industry, national defense, and science and technology are efforts to match the levels of modernization of the more advanced nations technologically "by the end of the century." These modernizations are the great new theme for national effort, and they place clear and direct demands on policies and practices in education and science. Modernization of science (and education related to it) is central to the success of the other three.

If modernization is to be successful, China must create vast numbers of skilled personnel as rapidly as possible, and it is making great new efforts to find and develop talent throughout Chinese society. It is not possible to be both for modernization and against meritocracy, but it is possible to avoid development of a "new class" with special privileges for its members and their children. The real issue is not whether a meritocracy is being developed—it is, but whether or not this meritocracy will evolve into a privileged "new class."

Contradictions and Tensions

Mao not only understood contradictions, he made use of them and even approved of them. Current contradictions in China include:

- "Red" versus "expert," with the current emphasis on the expert and thus on meritocracy
- Modernization versus egalitarianism, with the current emphasis upon modernization but not without an ongoing tug of war
- Rural versus urban, with the current emphasis on urban and industrial development
- Discipline versus constant mass participation, with the current emphasis upon discipline
- Trained intellect versus political spirit, with the current emphasis on the training of the intellect
- The blooming of a "hundred flowers" versus the single correct line, with the current emphasis on a carefully and cautiously chosen "hundred flowers"

Rosow, artist; John R. Shea, Senior Fellow, Carnegie Council on Policy Studies in Higher Education; Nadine C. Shea; Willard Wirtz, Chairman, National Manpower Institute; Jane Q. Wirtz, Member of the Board of Directors, Goodwill Industries of America; Daniel Yankelovich, President, Yankelovich, Skelly and White, Inc., and Member of the Executive Committee, Work in America Institute, Inc.; Hasmieg Yankelovich; Mitchell Sviridoff, Vice-President, Division of National Affairs, The Ford Foundation, was an original member of the group but, to our regret, could not participate at the last moment, because of a serious illness in his family.

The essay summarized here was originally published as part of *Observations on the Relations Between Education and Work in the People's Republic of China: Report of a Study Group, 1978* (Clark Kerr, Chairman). The extended study group report also includes general observations by members of the study group; a background paper on education in China by John Shea; reports on specific visits by John Shea, with additional comments by other members of the study group; the itinerary for the study group; written questions addressed to the Ministry of Education and to the State Bureau of Labor; policy documentation; and a selected bibliography.

- Bureaucrats versus "the people," with the bureaucrats again in an enhanced position
- Academic versus revolutionary (social justice in admissions, creation of the "new man," politics triumphant) models of education, with the present emphasis almost totally on the academic model
- Hard work versus revolutionary politics, with hard work and "promote production" the current themes.

We met no open supporters of the Gang of Four, and we heard strong denunciations of the four and their supporters, both publicly and privately, by people who really seemed to mean it. But the gang had its supporters. And the policies of the gang still stand as alternatives for anyone unhappy for any reason—for example, not getting admitted to a university—with the Moderates.

Tensions are endemic in any society undergoing rapid change and perhaps particularly in one that has repudiated so much of its history. Everything before 1949 was repudiated by the successful revolutionaries; everything in the Liu period of 1952 to 1966 except the Great Leap Forward (1958-1960) was repudiated by the supporters of the Cultural Revolution; and everything under the Gang of Four from 1966 to 1976 has been repudiated by the now triumphant Moderates. There must be fears now that there will be new repudiations in the future, and this may help to explain why some of the new policies seem to be followed with a sense of caution.

We felt, however, that the current line does have mass support; that it appeals to widespread desires for the fruits of modernization; and that it finds strong justification in the fear of Russia and the determination of the Chinese people never to be subject again to foreign invasion or domination. It has behind it, then, both an internal and an external logic. The policies of the four, also, seemed to us to have been divisive and counterproductive in a number of areas affecting education, such as the heavy emphasis upon class heritage in judging people and the rejection of discipline and scholarship. But no one can surely know that the gang or its successor, in some form or another, has been defeated forever. This is the greatest internal issue for China: whether or not there may not once again be an episode of repudiation of the recent past.

The great mystery for us was what role Mao really played in the decade 1966-1976. In the end, he did condemn the gang, but he also hated bureaucracy, distrusted intellectuals, and loved revolutionary change. When we asked what the Gang of Four had done from 1966 to 1976, we got strong condemnation, but when we asked what Mao had done beginning in 1966 with his sponsorship of the Cultural Revolution, we got either strong support or a guarded and somewhat equivocal defense. In any event, the blaming it on the Gang of Four version of history does give the current leadership a chance to start anew, to blame past failures on the gang, to justify current policies to rectify the errors of the recent past, and above all to save the reputation of Mao as the central deity in their pantheon. We reached no firm judgment on the true role of Mao during this period, on his real policies toward education, culture, and science. We left China as we entered it—puzzled about Mao and Maoism.

New Policies

Education. China is a nation almost frantically engaged in the great task of education—in the schools, factories, and communes, and over radio and television; and the emphasis is on the "back to the basics"—once again "one must study." The several new policies include:

- Literacy is now at the 70 percent level and rising. The policy is to provide as soon as possible eight years of education in rural areas and ten in urban areas. Postsecondary education is being expanded rapidly. Facilities, however, seem to be rather meager by U.S. standards. The student/teacher ratios are very high (except in the universities, where they are almost unbelievably low), and the instructional methodology is still based on memorization and recitation.
- The new emphasis is on "hard" subjects, particularly mathematics but also science in general. English is widely taught, as fast as teachers can be trained, as a means of access to Western technology. Arabic numerals are in universal use, and the first steps are being made toward transition to the Latin alphabet. But there is still substantial although reduced emphasis upon political ideology.
- "Key" schools and universities across the country are receiving special support to provide models of academic excellence.
- Discipline seems to have been fully restored in the classroom; the teachers teach and the students study. This may be less true at the university level.
- Theory is once again elevated over practice in many subjects.
- Talent is sought. Class heritage is largely ignored in practice and almost totally in policy on the ground that all young people are children of the revolution. Once again, after a ten-year hiatus, the best students go to "key" schools and universities; the most talented in many areas attend special programs in children's palaces. Examinations, increasingly national in scope, are being heavily emphasized.
- The length of educational programs is being increased.
- Graduate work is being reinstituted.
- Research is being reintroduced both in the universities and in the institutes of the Chinese Academy of Science. A new Academy of Social Sciences has just been created.
- Scholars are being sent abroad to scientific meetings; lecturers are being brought in from foreign countries; and Western scientific books and journals are being acquired and made available for study as fast as possible.

Education and work. Formerly there was a policy of "half-study, half-work" which apparently in some places meant, we were told, "half-politics, half-work." The current policy is:

- To teach attitudes favorable to the dignity of all useful work and to working hard.
- To have students visit factories and communes to see people at work, including their parents; and to have shops and gardens inside the schools wherever possible.
- To have students work 15 percent of the time in the school or in an outside factory or agricultural commune. "Work" now includes mental as well as manual labor. (This is an enormous and fundamental change, for one original purpose of the work policy was to elevate the status of manual labor and to denigrate mental labor.)
- To have many students (perhaps 70 to 80 percent) engaged in employment between secondary and higher education; about 20 to 30 percent of those admitted now

go directly to college from middle school (the rough equivalent of the U.S. high school).

- To operate substantial educational programs in factories and communes to enable workers to improve their general knowledge and upgrade their technical skills.

We were not impressed with the work projects we saw in schools (except for technical and agricultural schools). They seemed to be more for show than of basic importance. Nonetheless, we were impressed with the efforts to orient students toward work and to give them some working experience outside the school.

Education on and off the job. We saw an all-out effort at training on and off the job in apprenticeship programs; part-time and full-time schools in the factories; evening schools; three-day schools, where students can attend school three days and then work three days while another group goes to school three days; radio and television programs; and correspondence courses.

These "nontraditional" approaches to education cost less than the more traditional ones; find talent that was not found earlier in the schools; create a greater sense of equality of opportunity; provide a safety valve for disappointed expectations of persons who missed out on university careers; and get faster results in actual production. They do tend to impart less basic knowledge and to be more narrowly specialized in content. But China needs many more skilled workers, technicians and middle managers, and "nontraditional" programs are a good way to get them.

Cultural activities. Under the Gang of Four, science, scholarship, and artistic activity were controlled at best and decimated at worst. Everything foreign was suspect, as was anything classical within Chinese culture, and anything current that did not have a revolutionary theme. The current emphasis is "back to 1966" (but as yet no farther), and this has meant an immense opening of opportunity for expansion of intellectual and cultural activity.

Science. Science is now a great key to modernization. Scientists must be trained as fast as possible, research activity restored as fast as possible, and foreign developments absorbed as fast as possible.

Accomplishments and Problems

We were impressed with the following accomplishments:

- The achievement of building national pride and unity
- The spread of literacy
- The universal availability and relatively equitable distribution of food and minimal housing and clothing
- The access to medical services on a mass basis through clinics in factories, communes, and neighborhoods and the heavy emphasis on personal health care education.
- The excellent care of children, including in childcare centers that seem to be almost universally available
- The effort to give security to old persons and to provide them with useful tasks in a "caring society"

- The achievement of a much higher status for women than was traditional in Chinese society
- The decentralization of welfare activities into local communities and individual families
- The control of population increase
- The absence of shack towns around the cities (requiring, of course, strict control over the movements of people)
- The excellent care taken of the land and the productivity of the countryside
- The general sense of high expectations for the future and pride in past accomplishments.

We noted these problems:

- The small number of trained persons and the enormous task of developing them.
- The inefficiency of the factories, but not of the craft workshops.
- The gravity of damage done during the "lost decade" to university teaching activities and all research activities.
- The difficult situation for youth. Many have been "sent down" to the countryside and have little chance of getting back. All know they must serve somewhere in accordance with the plans of the state, but where they will serve is uncertain. They are given little free choice, although their wishes and the needs of their parents are taken into account when making assignments. There have been many reports of dissatisfaction among them.
- Making centralization work in education and other areas of society.
- Achieving modernization by the year 2000. This is an enormous task for a 20-year period, given the base from which China starts and the fact that other nations do not stand still.

The biggest issues we see ahead are:

- Can China really be modernized by 2000?
- Will the pendulum swing again? Can there be a stable synthesis between the contrasting approaches in education and politics?
- Can higher education and the research establishment carry the burden to be placed upon them by all-out modernization efforts?
- Will the new meritocracy turn into a "new class"?
- To what extent can equality of opportunity be increased, particularly for those in rural areas, and the comparative equality of income be maintained?
- Can youth be given more freedom of choice while still being assured of a place to serve?

Notations

1. The elapsed time of customary schooling in China is longer than it seems—5 to 7 years in rural areas and small towns and 10 in metropolitan areas versus 12 in the United States. But due to a number of factors, the number of school days for metropolitan areas is much the same in the two countries, but for rural areas is at least 30 percent less in China.
2. The Chinese written language is a great handicap to them. It takes so long to learn that it takes away time from other subjects.

3. Morality, particularly "serve the people," is taught directly and emphatically. "Moral conduct" includes trusting the government, including its current leaders— a definition of moral conduct painful to American ears.

4. Much is said and written about equality in China. There are no extremes of wealth and poverty. However, there is no simple contrast between equality in China and inequality in the United States. We saw a society more egalitarian in principle but more hierarchical in practice than the United States.

5. The educational system seemed comparatively strong in math and science, very strong in the creative and performing arts (with a high ideological content) and physical education, and very weak in the social sciences and humanities.

6. We were very confused about their system of planning; about how they integrate their economic plan, their manpower plan, their educational plan, and their actual placement of school graduates. We were just told at the local level that they get their plan from above and that sometimes they were consulted about it in advance.

7. There is still much confusion about administrative structure, but in the schools and in places of work, administrative authority is being greatly increased.

8. The old professors kept their tenure during the 1966-1976 period; the newer professors keep their tenure now—after 1976. Politics may be in command; but not over tenure.

9. The Chinese school system is based on the theory of environmental determination: the environment makes the child and the state will make the environment. Certainly, the Chinese system, from an American point of view, is authoritarian, but it is also humane in its treatment of young children and particularly of the less advantaged among them. It seemed much less humane to us in its treatment of youth; but then our system also greatly lacks elements of humanity in the treatment of youth. There is an inherent problem in the transition from youth to adulthood in any industrial society.

10. We concluded that much of what is said about the Gang of Four is true. Their path did lead to disaster. They challenged most fundamentally the sense of continuity and orderliness of the Chinese people.

11. China seems to be a society in a stage of development that needs—or at least makes good use of—its enemies: the four at home, the Russians abroad.

12. We noted how well schools can work with good teachers but poor equipment and facilities. We noted also how the best students are encouraged to assist the teachers and to help other students. We were impressed by the orderly character of the classrooms, but we found them to be characterized by rote learning.

What the United States Might Learn

The two systems are so different that little, if anything, can be transferred directly from one to the other except technology and finished products. Our hosts, however, showed interest particularly in our two-year colleges, our system of college entrance examinations, and our support of scientific research.

We were impressed with at least two elements of their system:

- The effort to make early contact between the world of work and the world of education; although we were not impressed with the work projects in the schools that we saw.

- The assurance of a place for useful activity for every youth; although we could never find acceptable the compulsory aspects of their system and the lack of choice within it. We provide more freedom of choice but a clearly inadequate total supply of choices. The puzzle is how to provide their assurance with our choice.

Educational Leaves for Employees: European Experience for American Consideration. By Konrad von Moltke and Norbert Schneevoigt. 1977.

For the purposes of this study we define educational leave as the opportunity for dependent employees to participate in education or training during working hours without complete loss of pay and without loss of employment rights. We examine opportunities for educational leave in Europe without regard to the legal basis on which they exist. Current policies in Europe meet all the criteria of educational leave as we define it here. Elements of educational leave policies exist in all countries, and in some they are more advanced than in others. (This volume includes chapters analyzing the specific policies and problems of educational leave in Germany, Sweden, Italy, Austria, Belgium, the Netherlands, Norway, and the United Kingdom.)

Although the nature of the educational experience depends to a significant extent on content, we do not believe that a satisfactory distinction can be made between vocational and other forms of education. Considerations of content certainly do not determine whether opportunities for educational leave exist. Educational leave requires continuation not only of pay but also of job security. The necessity of job security implies a limit to the duration of educational leave that is often shorter than may be educationally desirable. Although job security is inherent in our definition, we include in our overall consideration programs that provide educational opportunities for the unemployed and that are available only to persons who have resigned their previous position. In societies with strong programs of social security, it may, indeed, be argued that while security in a specific job cannot be guaranteed, all the social and economic effects of continued employment can be safeguarded, thus fulfilling the intention behind the requirement for employment security in educational leave.

Educational Leave Effects

It is useful to consider not so much educational leave policies as the educational leave effects of a variety of educational, social, or economic policies. Our approach to the question of educational leave simply asks what opportunities actually exist that have the effect, whether originally intended or not, of enabling employees to pursue study during working hours without full loss of pay.

The actual rates of participation lie between 5 and 10 percent of the labor force, with probably more than 8 percent involved in every country. No more accurate assessment of the orders of magnitude is possible at present.

Voluntary adult education. The greater part of ongoing voluntary adult education activities in most countries fails to qualify as educational leave because it takes place outside company time and has no effect on an employee's status. But a significant number of those presently engaged in adult education will tend to pursue their studies within the framework of an educational leave policy if this is possible.

Training financed by industry. In most industrialized countries, between 5 and 10 percent of the workforce is currently exposed every year to some kind of vocationally related training provided at the expense and request of their employers.

Trade union training. Nearly all countries have policies providing for training of trade union officials on company time, with the cost of courses borne by the trade unions or even by public funds. This, in effect, constitutes a right to educational leave for a selected group of workers.

In-service training for civil servants. Previous studies disregard the very substantial rights to educational leave that have already been realized in the public sector.

Labor market training schemes. There are generally two types of policies for labor market intervention: those designed to adapt the employed to new or changing conditions or to provide protection against unemployment and those designed to help the unemployed find new positions or to facilitate greater job mobility. The former are essentially an extension of in-service training. The latter programs do not fulfill the requirement that job security be maintained. They are all geared to facilitating the return of unemployed persons to the workforce; hence a significant number of the participants are able to engage in these programs while receiving remuneration from public authorities, with assurance of further employment. In most cases, however, job security is achieved in general terms, not in regard to a specific position.

Educational leave effects within the military. Military establishments in most Western countries have developed very extensive educational programs for their personnel.

The European Debate on Educational Leave

Labor market policies and in-service training in industry. There is virtually unanimous agreement in all countries on the need for an active labor market policy that includes the possibility of retraining grants to individuals or to industry. This is part of the normal policy of social support that a modern industrial society must offer its citizens. These labor market policies provide a large proportion of presently identifiable educational leave effects in European countries. Common to all countries is the priority attached to maintaining an adequate program of labor market interventions. These are considered to be educational policies only in a secondary sense, a fact reflected in administrative responsibility and the allocation of resources. As a rule, the Ministry of Labor is responsible for the program. The principal exception is Italy, where regional educational authorities have recently taken over this responsibility from the Ministry of Labor.

Labor market policies, together with the in-service training programs of industry—which are, in turn, often partially subsidized through the labor market policies—provide a broad base of intervention relative to changing conditions of work. There is a full range of programs with educational leave effects outside the purview of the traditional institutions of education and beyond the ken of most educational authorities. In discussing educational leave programs, employers and trade unions have tended to view these activities as privileged and not subject to reconsideration in the light of a more comprehensive policy of educational leave.

Employer and trade union arguments. While details of national policymaking vary, there is virtually no variation from country to country in the attitudes and arguments of employers and trade unions for and against educational leave.

Employers' organizations typically favor educational leave in principle, but distinguish between leave benefiting the enterprise and that benefiting the individual. The enterprise is to be responsible for the former, while the individual must develop the resources and motivation for the latter. Typically, reference is made to the responsibilities of the individual in a democratic society and to the principles of liberal policies in a free market. Such a view is based on an analysis of the role of industry in modern societies that differs fundamentally from that used by the trade unions. The neat compartmentalization assumes a much less pervasive influence by industry on the lives of its employees and on the development of society than the employees themselves feel. Almost inevitably, employers' organizations tend to emphasize the cost factor and the limited ability of the economy in general and of industry in particular to carry the burden of additional expenses for social or educational policies.

The employers' emphasis on the lack of economic resources is generally viewed by the trade unions as self-serving, and thus far no adequate analysis exists that could counter this political response and provide a basis for reaching a defensible description of the actual possibilities. It is virtually impossible to project the cost of policy initiatives in adult education in Europe.

The arguments put forward by the trade unions, across national boundaries, represent the obverse of the reasoning adopted by the employers. They emphasize the need for collective action to overcome the isolation and alienation of the worker; they stress the desirability of having articulate citizens in a democratic society, of making adult education available to underprivileged groups, and of maintaining the workforce at a high level of mobility. These arguments must be seen in the context of a strong class consciousness, often combined with an ideological view of society and the intention of initiating fundamental change.

The area of agreement between employers and trade unions is restricted to the complex of established measures oriented toward the labor market—state intervention and the in-service training of industry. The common ground on all other issues is so minimal that agreement can be reached only through political decision making or through the victory of one point of view over the other in contract negotiations.

In all European countries, educational authorities have been less involved in the educational leave debate than might have been expected. Their coinage is still the relatively much more vague concept of recurrent education, and they have yet to realize the significance of institutionalized education that exists beyond the institutions under their control—in the form of the internal training of industry and the activities of the labor market authorities. Insofar as educators have been involved in the debate on educational leave to date, that involvement has mostly occurred within the framework of adult education rather than with reference to vocational training or the institutions of front-load education.

Education or training. One of the central issues in the debate on educational leave in all European countries is the relationship between vocational and general education. Insofar as educational leave is vocationally oriented, employers are significantly more willing to provide special financial support directly or indirectly, through payroll levies or special tax funds; other cases, they argue, are primarily social and should be considered the responsibility of the community at large.

A satisfactory distinction between vocational and general education is not possible in abstract terms. It is impossible to define the effect of a course in terms of its content alone; context is equally determinant in relation both to what is learned and to how it affects the participant's working life. Context encompasses all the elements of time, place, and group that characterize a given educational experience.

The right to education. The constitutions of European countries all provide that the citizen has the right to full development of his personality and the state has the responsibility of providing equal access to education. Traditionally, this constitutional obligation has been interpreted as applying only to the institutions of initial schooling. Increasingly, however, the question of whether it extends to all forms of education, including adult education in general and educational leave in particular, is raised.

Permanent Education, Recurrent Education, Educational Leave

Permanent education and recurrent education have become accepted and reasonably well-defined concepts in Europe since they first obtained currency in the late 1960s. Educational leave would seem to be one of the major policy initiatives aimed at realizing the ideas behind the postulate of recurrent education.

It is impossible to prepare an individual for a working life of 40 or more years during 10 years of his youth, a few years of adolescence, and the first years of adult life. Advocates of recurrent education generally relate this observation to the requirements of the modern labor market, the developments of technology, and a notion of the obsolescence of knowledge. The idea that those who have received education should and need to continue to learn after leaving school or university is part and parcel of the idea of education itself. What is new in the idea of recurrent education is the notion that the process of continuing education requires purposive, institutional intervention in later life. There are essentially four arguments used to justify purposive intervention; they are discussed below.

Progress of knowledge and changes in technology. Although this is probably the most frequently cited reason for permanent education, it also has the most limited application: only those who have received fairly extensive initial training are likely to be affected by the development of new knowledge and new technology in such a way as to require fundamental updating of their education during working life.

Changes in working life. For the vast majority of the working population, the effects of new knowledge are felt most directly as they impinge upon their place of work. Two arguments are generally advanced in this context. First, the labor market is not static; entire professions disappear and the character of many occupations is transformed several times over during a single working life. Provision must therefore be made to allow people to adjust to these changes. Second, with advances in knowledge and technology, the labor market requires larger numbers of increasingly highly trained people. During the last few years, however, a number of studies have explored the developing structure of the labor market and labor qualifications in Europe and have come to the unexpected conclusion that future demand will be greatest for unqualified labor. This conclusion has led to a vigorous debate about the size and character of the growing service sector of the economy and the question of whether the relevant studies are not biased toward the production sector, which is decreasing in size.

Changes in community life. Community life has been subject to major changes during the 60 years since World War I. The average citizen must master an increasing number of skills if he is to remain minimally effective in such a society, and particularly in a democratic one. Literacy alone is not enough; numeracy, articulateness, and some basic analytic skills have become part of the minimal educational requirements of all citizens, regardless of the demands of the labor market. The argument that those citizens who have not had the opportunity to acquire such skills in their initial phase of education should be given the opportunity to acquire them and that those who have received more extensive education should be able to maintain what they have learned in an active and contemporary form is powerful.

Equality of opportunity. The argument that recurrent education can provide greater equality of educational opportunity continues to be advanced. It holds that a system of recurrent education will allow those who failed to profit from their initial encounter with education to recover lost ground in later life. It also holds that voluntary adult education and retraining is now utilized by a privileged group; a system of recurrent education will permit other groups in society easy access to these social benefits.

The problem is that, if adult education is already available to the educationally privileged, providing it for the less privileged will only remove a further relative disadvantage; it will not be a source of relative advancement. Both versions of this argument indicate the difficulty of ascertaining the relevance of recurrent education to equality of educational opportunity. As a working hypothesis, we assume that educational leave policies can have positive impact in terms of equality of educational opportunity only if they are selectively designed to benefit educationally disadvantaged groups and if opportunities for adult education do not already exist.

These arguments apply equally to educational leave. Permanent and recurrent education are generally viewed as ends in themselves; educational leave policies are, however, instrumental—as all implemented policies ultimately must be. This begs the question of what ends an educational leave policy is specifically designed to achieve. While the four major goals listed above certainly provide a broad frame of reference for educational leave policy, they are generally reduced to more immediate concerns. Among these, the most important are the political impulse and the concern for mobility.

Some advocates of educational leave, however—educators and trade unionists for the most part—emphasize political objectives. In its most sophisticated form, this conception of educational leave aims at a personal emancipation and political enlightenment of the participants that would enable them to participate in political life in such a way as to change the very conditions that produced the narrow perspectives they formerly had.

Problems in Educational Leave Policies

Educational leaves and the labor market. There is some debate over the extent to which persons who have once entered employment can perceive educational experiences apart from the pressing day-to-day reality of their work. Can practices acquired on the job rather than through formal education subsequently be changed through the processes of formal education? For many employees the conditions of work constitute one of the prime determinants of their lives. It is therefore important to determine whether educational leave is viewed by participants as work or nonwork. If educational leave is viewed as work, participants' attitudes will be those they maintain toward work—in many instances, a grudging acquiescence rather than the active participation desirable for successful adult education. If educational leave is viewed as nonwork, its scope and effectiveness is likely to be limited to areas outside the environment of work.

There is a self-reinforcing relationship between initial education, work, and further education that is almost impossible to alter by educational means alone: persons who have succeeded in initial education have access to more attractive jobs; they in turn are more willing to participate in further education, and their opportunities to do so are better. Thus educational leave and work appear inextricably linked.

Educational leave should be viewed not as a means of achieving a policy of recurrent education but as part of a number of interlocking social and economic policies, the crux of which must be to change the conditions of work—the leading variable in adult life.

Education has always been expected to deal with matters of importance beyond the immediate present; but the evidence suggests that the more immediate the concerns in educational leave, the greater the likelihood of achieving identifiable goals. This may be attributed in part to a testing error. Short-term effects can be tested with existing methods, whereas long-term changes are hardly ascertainable and can never be attributed to given causes. Nevertheless, the difficulties go deeper: the concept of recurrent education implies that there are no long-term goals of education other than the very general one of learning to learn. The underlying image of a person's development is that it is fragmented and that there are probably very few matters of content of long-term significance. This approach to the current problems of education certainly increases the role of adult education while also stripping it of its traditional, cultural, long-term goals. Given the assumption that education will recur periodically, should a student be expected to learn anything that reaches beyond the next anticipated phase of education—particularly since one assumes that all learning will be subject to change?

Andragogy. Since the 1920s, the term *andragogy* in European discussions of adult education has referred to a "pedagogy for adults." In dealing with adults, it is necessary to accept that there are increasingly irreversible conditions of age, experience, and social life. At the very least, the input required to achieve change increases when dealing with adults as long as they are employed.

The critical issue is whether educational leave is conceived of as an instrument of change or simply one of adjustment. European experience to date shows that educational leave effects can indeed be a means of making certain adjustments to changing conditions, most often in relation to changing technology and shifts in employment.

Andragogy is not only a method of dealing with adults; it also defines questions of content and teachers; who can teach what to adults? Adult education in Europe was not originally aimed at allowing adults to complete formal educational requirements, but has been related to democratization and to the building of a more broadly based culture, particularly as part of the process of rebuilding after the two world wars. Remedial and vocational adult education have been grafted on to an established system. While this has brought enormous growth, it has also brought fundamental change. The much more short-term, utilitarian aspects of the newer elements of the adult education system conflict with the traditional approach. There is a certain danger in the assumption that all adult education is equivalent so long as adults are participating. Not only does the content of adult education differ widely; the adults do also.

Adult education: the market approach versus the program approach. The European situation indicates two possible avenues for developing education for adults. In France a market system has been created, albeit with the employers rather than the employees/students as the consumers. In Sweden and Germany, where a vigorous but uncoordinated adult education sector existed, there has been stronger emphasis on systematizing and supplementing the institutional offerings through regulations and subsidies, and providing students with the means of access—in other words, on a more programmatic approach. Either approach has difficulties: if a market mechanism is to be employed, the problem of regulation has rapidly to be faced; if a more programmatic approach is adopted, the dangers of "schooling" are particularly acute, since any systematization carries with it the danger of eliminating vital variety.

The time frame of educational leave. In Europe, the problems encountered in expanding adult education are interlocking, and this makes them particularly intractable. One issue that underlies all others concerns the timing of educational leave. Every country has been trying to find an acceptable compromise between what is educationally necessary, educationally desirable, and economically feasible. Difficulties arise because there are no satisfactory measures for what is educationally necessary or economically feasible.

Two basic patterns exist for bridging this gap: provision of regular but limited annual periods of leave with nearly full salary maintenance, and provision of occasional lengthy or unlimited periods of leave, generally involving a fairly substantial financial sacrifice on the part of the beneficiary. The former is by far the most widespread provision. It appears to be satisfactory for achieving limited ends, such as teaching specific skills, but it is open to serious objections as a means of achieving long-term effects.

In an attempt to confront the problems raised by lack of time, a theory has been developed that educational leave is meant only to provide a "motivational trigger." The idea is that educational leave should attract persons back into the process of education. There are elements of this theory in the educational leave policies of all of the countries studied, and it constitutes a major consideration in educational leave in Europe at the present time.

The alternative form of providing educational leave is through occasional entitlements for long periods of absence (sabbaticals, study leaves, and so forth). This is very rare in Europe. Sweden has the only program that provides long-term leave with job security and financial support.

Unions and educational leave policies. One of the most striking common features among European countries is the role of the trade unions both in initiating and sustaining the debate on educational leave and in the final implementation of policies. There are a number of reasons for the special role of the unions in the development of educational leave policies. First, regardless of who provides the legal basis or financing, educational leave policies can be viewed as a fringe benefit and a cost factor in the employment policies of industry. In all such matters, the unions have a major, institutionally secured voice. Furthermore, the class structure of society remains relatively strong in Europe, and the unions are the only effective spokesman for those groups that are not at present benefiting from some form of educational leave effects. The unions view educational leave as a means of extending their efforts to educate their members to be effective participants in the increasingly complex decision-making processes in industry.

In all countries, the unions have been the first to raise the issue of educational leave in contract negotiations with the employers. In every instance, the employers have resisted implementing such a proposal, and legislation has been introduced only as a means of resolving fundamental issues that could not be settled at the negotiating table.

Access to educational leave. Studies have shown a direct correlation between the length of initial education and the likelihood of participation in adult education. It is frequently argued that persons who have experienced success in education will be more likely to return to education at a later stage. Moreover, those with higher levels of education are exposed more directly to the effects of changes in knowledge and technology and will be more easily able to recognize the necessity and benefit of participating in further education. Finally, persons with higher levels of education will be in occupations that allow greater flexibility in the disposition of one's time: the right to leave without pay or compensatory time off for extra hours worked is generally not accorded to blue-collar workers or to white-collar workers of low status.

The flaw in this view is that it is based entirely on the educational aspects of the problem. There is an even stronger correlation between occupational status and participation in further education. In other words, for persons with short initial education, the higher they rank in the employment hierarchy, the more they tend to participate in further education. Even lengthy initial education seems not to ensure high levels of participation if the employment status is low. Motivation for educational leave thus appears to derive at least as strongly from occupational status as from prior learning.

Given this structure of educational leave effects, the debate in three of the four countries has centered on two issues: (1) whether to create a broad policy framework for this disparate set of educational leave effects and (2) how to reach those groups most obviously failing to benefit from the existing possibilities. The two issues are to some extent divergent: a broad framework would tend to create new opportunities for those who already have opportunities, while attempts to reach groups previously failing to benefit from educational leave opportunities will have to be fragmentary, aimed at specific target populations and designed to exclude those already benefiting most. Obviously, these two initiatives can be combined by making special provision for underprivileged groups within the framework of a broad structural policy.

The prospects of achieving greater equality of educational opportunity through educational leave policies do not appear to be very promising in countries with highly selective systems of education. The experience of early and decisive selection linked to stratified social hierarchies and relatively low levels of geographic mobility makes it almost impossible to reintroduce persons with low levels of education to the educational process at a later stage.

Financing educational leave. Schemes for financing educational leave are so diverse that no generalization is possible. It is also impossible to make any definite statement on the distribution of financial burdens between the three principal parties—the state, the employers, and the employees. Insofar as one can view tax exemption of educational expenses as a state contribution, more than 50 percent of the funding for educational leave is provided by the state. Employees probably contribute no more than 5 to 10 percent (through travel expenses and earnings foregone), with the remainder coming from the employers.

More important than who contributes to the costs of educational leave is the financing mechanism that is chosen. This will have a direct influence on two subsidiary issues: the ease or difficulty of exercising the right to educational leave, and who ultimately decides who will participate in what forms of educational leave.

From the beneficiary's point of view, the critical issue is the amount of nonrecoverable expense or loss of income involved, and it is probably immaterial whether the contribution takes the form of direct expense (as for course costs) or earnings foregone. When a contribution from the participant is required, a contribution of time probably presents the smallest motivational obstacle, although limits probably exist as to the proportions of the necessary time that a participant can be expected to contribute. At some point an educational leave policy comes to resemble a subsidy to voluntary adult education rather than a particularly attractive benefit.

From the employer's point of view, the critical issue is whether he distributes funds directly (to the employee or to the institution offering the course) or whether an intermediary is established. The more direct the form of disbursement, the greater the likelihood that the employer will also be able to influence the utilization of resources.

From the state's point of view, the critical issue is its ability to control, or at least influence, the flow of funds and thereby the priorities of the program.

The particular scheme that is chosen reflects the attempt to balance these three sets of priorities—beneficiary's, employer's, and state's—within the political setting of the various countries. These priorities are not irreconcilable, at least at the theoretical level, although in practice there are large areas of conflict—about the extent, for instance, to which the unions are to be recognized as fully representative of individual employees' interests. At the heart of the compromise that is ultimately achieved lies the question of who decides who will participate in educational leave.

Relationship to existing institutions of education. Despite the often-expressed hope that recurrent education—educational leave in particular—will provide impetus for change and the reform of existing educational institutions, there is no evidence to show that this has actually been happening.

With the exception of Sweden, vocational education has not been integrated into the institutions of secondary and higher education, which are most often identified with initial education. Thus the impact of educational leave policies has not occurred where one would most often look for it. The major exceptions are the systems of adult education in France and Germany, which are being subjected to change, probably because they are not yet firmly set in structure and procedure in either country.

In assessing the effects of educational leave policies on existing institutions, we must also consider their effects on industry. Industry is to some extent already an educational institution, although opinions differ widely on whether this is beneficial or not. Certainly the impact of the conditions of work on an individual are as important—if not more important—as the impact of education. As efforts are made to integrate work and retraining and work and educational leave more closely, the place of work could also become the site of education. This has happened only in the narrowest sense; where retraining involves job-induction activities, these have often been conducted at the place of work itself. But the thrust of educational leave is much broader than simply conducting retraining at the place of work; it raises issues that have thus far been avoided about the place of work and its effects on the employee. In this sense, change has occurred no more in industry than in the regular institutions of education, although it must be contemplated as a possible consequence, in some respects even as a necessary condition, of a successful educational leave program.

Is educational leave an educational policy? In the context of the compartmentalized political relationships that characterize virtually all European countries, policy issues dealing with educational leave always have three elements: an educational, a labor market, and a social policy element. Each of these can be, and has been, treated in relative isolation. However, implemented educational leave effects in Europe have thus far occurred principally in the context of labor market policy and not of educational policy.

Thus whether or not educational leave policies are educational policies depends on who defines and implements them. Thus far, only very few educational leave policies designed with the typical concerns of the educational system in mind have been implemented. The reasons for the educational systems' relative lack of success in developing viable responses to the challenges they are faced with are manifold. In part they lie within the systems themselves; in part they are external. A contributing factor to the lack of success is distaste for the messy business of industry and labor. Educational leave policies are of necessity social and labor market policies. Until educational authorities learn the necessary skills of negotiation, compromise, and political maneuver, educational leave policy will remain primarily an instrument of social and labor market policy rather than educational policy.

Disseminating information on educational leave. Individual beneficiaries are unable to exercise their rights except as a member of some group; as an employee of a specific firm or as a member of a union, a club, or an association. Even where educational leave is an individual right, the complexities of the societies involved make collective organization a precondition to the exercise of that right. The flow of information thus becomes a process of at least two stages: the individual deals with a group, the group with an intermediary organization, which ultimately leads to direct contact with the source of information. Seen in this light, the distinction between educational leave as an individual right as opposed to a collective one becomes much less important than one might assume; with few exceptions, the exercise of the individual right requires some form of collective support.

The flow of information itself is also usually a two-step process: first it is necessary to inform people that information exists; then it is necessary to provide counseling to assist in obtaining and interpreting this information. The provision of counseling alone is probably not sufficient. Methods currently in use for information dissemination range from the totally unsystematic to highly financed, systematic efforts. Efforts using informal channels of communication trusted by the workers and designed to reach as close as possible to the place of work offer greatest promise of success.

Conclusion. The absence of an accepted definition of educational leave corresponds to the absence of educational leave policies. Even within the theoretical frame of reference we have developed, there remain many practical and fundamental problems to be resolved; with the single exception of the developing situation in Sweden, it is certainly premature to speak of educational leave policies in Europe.

The prospects for educational leave depend heavily on the overall economic situation and specifically the availability of resources for an extension of education. It would be rash to venture any prediction of the future development of educational leave in Europe. Clearly no further progress toward the realization of educational leave policies is to be expected, unless the potential of educational leave as a means of purposive change to the benefit of participants and society has been made clear to both the decision makers and the potential participants in such programs.

A desirable educational leave policy should rest on two indispensable premises: (1) it must be oriented toward the diverse needs and conditions of adult students and should rely on their voluntary cooperation in the educational process, and (2) it must not only serve fairly short-term economic and social purposes but must also contain elements that are clearly educational in the sense that they transcend the individual, the immediate, and the specific to include questions relating to the character and future of our society and its history and means of expression and achieving change.

The future development of educational leave policies clearly hinges on the clarification of the difficult questions connected with this "educational" element of such policies. We are confronted with the apparently unbridled development of modern societies and the increasing inability of individuals to experience themselves as effective members of these societies. These are clearly issues education must address itself to, and the context for such a venture could very well be educational leave. In this sense, educational leave policies have an important contribution to make to the further development of Western democratic societies. There are few institutions still capable of providing an embracing view of our societies. In spite of their dedication to specialization, educational institutions still have this possibility, particularly when dealing with adult populations. But participants must be removed from the continuing pressures of adult life if they are to be receptive to what education still has to offer them. Only a leave of absence can allow adults to step back and take a fresh look at their position in life and to review some of the otherwise suppressed difficulties.

This development is more easily described than achieved, especially since many adults have never acquired the capacity to translate personal experience into broad social and political terms or to analyze the context in which they exist. To realize this objective, however, a structured educational experience is required. Such a goal could not be achieved within a week or two of educational leave because in most cases it is not realized even in years of initial schooling.

Experience and theoretical reflection show that the work role is the pivotal factor in the self-perception, attitudes, and behavior of adults. What is important is that the experience offered through educational leave ultimately transcends the confines of this work role. So far as these considerations enter into the further development of educational leave policy, clearly they would have to lead to a new round of intensive rethinking and reform throughout the educational system.

Education for Employment: Knowledge for Action. By the National Academy of Education Task Force on Education and Employment. Clark Kerr, Chairman. 1979.

Our task has been to examine the relationship between the acquisition and use of knowledge and skills—including attitudes and sensibilities—that contribute to the performance of useful tasks and the amount and quality of work activities (both paid and unpaid). The topics we have selected for examination and our conclusions are informed by the following values:

- Each member of society should be able to choose from a reasonable set of opportunities: (1) curricular emphases in the schools; (2) college, work, or other postsecondary channels to adulthood; and (3) work, service, leisure, and continuing or recurrent education during one's potentially productive years.
- Education and training institutions should perform their functions effectively and efficiently.
- The amount and kind of education and training should be responsive to the needs of the labor market as well as to individual desires and social needs.

- Schools and colleges should serve to strengthen the capacity and inclination of individuals to perform an array of important non-market-oriented work within families and the larger community.

Where We Stand: Principal Findings

1.   The composition of the labor force and the kinds of work people are paid to perform will change considerably over the next decade or so, but demographic trends suggest some easing in the years ahead of the serious employment problems faced by many young people.

The baby boom of the 1940s will continue to be felt in the age structure of the work force. Men and women 25 to 44 years of age will account for practically all of the increase of nearly 20 million workers expected over the next 10 years. The number of young people seeking work, which accelerated so rapidly from 1965 to 1974, will increase slightly between 1978 and 1980 and thereafter decline slightly. What this means, of course, is that youths entering the labor market in the 1980s will not face such stiff competition for jobs from their peers.

The occupational structure will continue to shift toward services as opposed to production activities. Of the 58 million openings expected for entrants and reentrants to the civilian labor force, 34 million are expected in white collar work, 11 million in service occupations and 12.5 million in blue collar categories. As many as seven of every ten openings will be to replace persons leaving the labor force by choice or because of death or retirement. The dominant role of attrition points to continuity in the kinds of work people will be paid to perform.

2.   The economic value of a college degree has doubtless fallen for new graduates somewhat since the mid-1960s. Problems of adjustment in the supply of and demand for highly educated manpower will continue, but the worst adjustment problems are probably over.

The period from 1964 to 1969 was unusual in that a decrease took place in the ratio of college to high school graduates in the labor force. A very sharp turnaround, however, began in 1969. The number of persons in the workforce with a high school education increased from only 38.4 to 39.8 million between 1969 and 1976. The number with four or more years of college shot up from 12.6 to 16.5 million. In part, this turnaround reflects the influence of the military draft in the earlier period and the lesser likelihood in recent years of college students going on to graduate school. Looking ahead through the 1980s, it is conceivable that, as a smaller cohort of college graduates enters the labor market, the average rate of return on a college education for new graduates, which is still substantial, will increase somewhat in comparison with the corresponding cohort of the early and mid-1970s.

3.   Although individuals adjust quite quickly to changing opportunities, our ability to forecast changes in labor supply and demand, especially at a disaggregated level, is in need of improvement.

Projections of the Bureau of Labor Statistics indicate that demand conditions for those who will graduate over the next 10 years should be no worse, and probably will be better, than for youths who entered the job market since the late 1960s. Assuming a continuation in past trends in the percentage of college graduates in various occupations, some 12.1 million openings are forecast for persons receiving baccalaureate or higher degrees. This number is about 1 million lower than the number of college-educated persons likely to enter or reenter the work force. The projected oversupply prior to adjustments is especially great for (1) Ph.D.-level manpower, especially in the liberal arts, because of the reduced need for college faculty; (2) baccalaureate holders, especially men, in nontechnical specialties; and (3) teachers in many areas because of steady or declining enrollments in the schools.

Sharp changes in government policy are difficult to forecast and result in violent pulsations in the labor market. But such changes are not the only reason forecasts go astray. Most projections are simply based on extrapolations of the past, with little or no attention to adjustment processes and to their implications until hindsight becomes possible—and even then the agencies have been slow to detect and report on important turning points. The costs to individuals and society of a failure to develop greater sophistication in forecasting labor market developments, especially in fields and occupations where training is long, costly, and specialized, is great.

4.   While broad trends are generally predictable and favorable, there are several groups of persons who face special problems in the job market: inner-city youths (especially Hispanics and blacks) not in school and without work; women reentering the work force; and older persons nearing retirement or with special employment needs stemming from disability or displacement.

We fear that large numbers of young people—especially minority youths with less than a high school education—will have great difficulty moving from relatively unstructured, often rather casual "youth jobs" to more secure career positions. Certainly, the sheer size of the present youth cohort points to the probability that many young people will find the process of work establishment a long and painful one.

What is needed to ease this problem is a series of improvements in schooling, counseling, and especially job placement and encouragement to employers to develop more good jobs and to invest in those members of the work force who are now "outsiders" to preferred employment.

5.   Additional years of schooling, for most people, have real and long-lasting effects on their economic well-being and on several noneconomic aspects of their lives.

Research consistently demonstrates a positive relationship between highest year of school completed and success in the labor market, as measured by occupational status, earnings, and employment stability—not for each individual, but on the average. Native ability, what happens at home and in one's neighborhood, and other factors— including experiences in school—doubtless influence how much education people obtain, but plenty of room is left for personal effort, aspirations, and other influences.

Even though more young people with high school diplomas and college degrees have chosen (or have only been able to find) work in occupations that in the past have not employed large numbers of people with as much education, evidence points to beneficial effects of schooling outside the employment relationship. A number of studies reveal a positive association between years of school completed and physical condition, effective parenting, contribution through voluntary service, and adaptation to external forces and new opportunities. At the same time, measured job satisfaction is largely unrelated to educational attainments, probably because better-educated persons expect more.

6.   Recent declines in test scores are attributable, in part, to greater equality of opportunity in access to higher education. But a change in the composition of test takers is only one factor, and questions have arisen as to curriculum content, seriousness of purpose, and the way students spend their time, both in and outside of school. The implications of declining test scores for worklife are not entirely clear.

Contrary to popular belief, students may be spending less time on school work now than 20 or 30 years ago. More time is taken for parent conferences, and changes have occurred in the course and program options students exercise. Specialty courses have to some extent replaced more traditional academic courses. This raises the question of whether standardized tests are measuring as well as in the past what students are asked to learn. The answer is not completely clear. Scholastic Aptitude Test (SAT) scores are more strongly correlated with grades than in the past and still predict very well successful completion of the freshman year of college. At the same time, the relevance of test score declines for "life beyond school" is less clear. Surely, for most jobs, basic competency in verbal and mathematical areas is very important, especially for movement to higher rungs on promotion ladders.

7.   *Research on the effects of schooling indicates that doubling school resources does not double learning. Nevertheless, more schooling helps, and extreme pessimism as to the effects of schooling on later achievements is unfounded.*

The importance of time actually spent in and out of school studying what a curriculum offers can be seen in the rather consistent, positive relationship between number of years of school completed and labor market and other achievements. Most research on "school effects" has ignored this point. The question generally posed has been whether, controlling for highest year of school completed, existing variation in school resources has made much difference. This ignores the time question as well as the effects of early schooling on highest year of school completed. One thing large-scale surveys do reveal, however, is that crude measures of the environment outside the school (for example, highest year of school completed by father and mother) correlate strongly with both the amount of schooling and later attainments. Little is known, however, about the interactive effects of schooling and home life.

8.   *Major curricular options in the high school respond to individual differences in aptitudes and interests by widening choices. Vocational courses tend to be psychologically congenial for many youths and have a modest positive impact on the earnings of young women who do not go on to college.*

Most high school students either like or feel neutral about practical subject-matter courses, but negative feelings are common in academic areas. Students in the three major curriculum categories—academic, vocational, and general—differ from one another in several ways. College preparatory students (about 40 percent of the total) stand out from their peers on measures of mental ability and socioeconomic background. Among the remainder, girls in vocational studies rank higher than their general peers, while boys in vocational areas rank lower. Curriculum choice coincides with educational aspirations, which are, on the whole, high among secondary school students.

Large portions of students from all three curriculum categories acquire experience and training in a variety of postsecondary alternatives to college: business colleges and technical institutes, company programs, and military service and apprenticeships.

9.   *Work-education programs vary enormously in purpose, organization, and clientele served. This variation may explain the uncertain consequences of such programs in general. Program quality and choice of work assignment seem to be important determinants of the longer-term consequences of having participated in a work-education program.*

Advocates of work-education programs emphasize career exploration, discovery of one's aptitudes and interests, feelings of contribution, and acquisition of useful skills. With respect to longer-term consequences, the average effects are modest at best. While anecdotal evidence is frequently cited, we have found no careful studies demonstrating that work-education programs are especially beneficial to women and minority men. They probably are, but evidence one way or the other is lacking.

10.   The services of paid guidance personnel constitute a small but important part of a larger set of formal and informal influences that guide young people (and adults) as they make career development decisions at many points in their lives.

Numerous studies reveal that when it comes to educational and occupational decisions, parents and friends, books, and often teachers are a preferred source of information and advice compared with guidance counselors. Guidance counselors are, however, important in several areas, including course scheduling, providing information about careers, financial aid, and choice of college.

11.   Advances in career development theory, expanded options, and certain technological developments point to the desirability of comprehensive systems of career guidance that encourage maximum self-direction.

A recognition of differences in individuals' motivation and need and the information requirements implied by expanding options in the postsecondary years have led to a rethinking of the functions of guidance personnel. Comprehensive systems are being developed—using the curriculum from the elementary grades onward, print and non-print (computer) materials on occupational and educational options, career centers, work-experience programs, and other resources—to assist people in making choices.

12.   There is probably a need for more career development services and improvement of those which exist, yet empirical evidence on the comparative utility of alternative guidance services is lacking.

The influence of some guidance activities can be assessed: for example, whether career awareness activities lead to greater occupational information. Complex and longer-term outcomes (for example, motivation, acquisition of basic skills, and job satisfaction), however, are more difficult to determine and have been investigated only rarely.

13.   Increasing numbers of adults—including persons nearing retirement—are participating in adult, recurrent, or lifelong education. Issues such as benefits and costs, individual and social needs, and public finance are just beginning to be addressed.

Increasing productivity, better health and longer lives, and the changing age composition of the population suggest that adult learning will continue to grow at least moderately in the years ahead. At least three approaches to additional public financing of lifelong learning are under consideration: tax credits, modification in student financial aid programs, and categorical support for programs or clients. Each can be expected to vary in impact and cost. Relatively little is known about the implications of tuition assistance and other forms of public support in either real or financial terms. Issues of equity, purpose, and benefits are involved in each.

14.   A careful, wide-range review is needed of the effectiveness and impact of federal programs related to education, work, and service.

Since the early 1960s, many new programs and a great deal of money have been directed toward improving the relationship between education and employment. We have concluded, in general, that an all-out effort is needed to acquire more knowledge and stimulate more action in eight specific areas: (1) developing basic skills; (2) improving the quality of work-education programs by improving teaching, involving parents, making greater use of performance examinations to monitor progress, and including opportunities for students to leave school temporarily for work or service; (3) developing more comprehensive and systematic guidance and counseling services for youths and adults; (4) involving parents, everyday citizens, and community leaders in the work of schools, and fostering productive relationships between the worlds of work and formal education; (5) finding ways to finance and encourage recurrent education in areas of substantial benefit to individuals and to the larger society; (6) focusing greater attention on the education and employment needs of groups all too often treated as "outsiders"—for example, out-of-school urban youths with little education or work experience; (7) determination of which government programs are working well, which are not, and what can be done at federal, state, and local levels to improve the relationship between education and employment; and (8) identification of the probable nature of human resource, employment, and educational problems likely to emerge in the 1980s and 1990s.

Recommendations for Educators

The richness of the environment outside schools and colleges, and evidence that extra-school experiences are often preeminent in influencing what people derive from schooling, argue for educators to broaden their concept of their role. The Task Force recommends: *that educators seek to enhance the joint contribution of schools and families by working closely with parents on developing the reasoning and other basic skills of their children, especially in the preschool and early grades; work with community leaders and employers in development of curricula and quality work-education programs; and work with state and other agencies—including the media—to improve career guidance and related services.*

Elementary and secondary schools. Little attention has been paid in recent years to the purposes and performance of secondary schools, the task of which is to foster the development of each young person's potential. The Task Force recommends: *that local school officials and teachers (1) continue to emphasize basic skills; (2) establish performance goals whenever possible; (3) provide high-quality options to traditional curricula (such as carefully conceived experiential learning opportunities); (4) avoid unnecessary compartmentalization of programs and invidious status distinctions among them; (5) seek better use of student time; (6) reduce sex stereotypes and other sources of bias; (7) employ trained guidance personnel in guidance activities; and (8) keep all students as close to the "mainstream" as possible.*

Colleges and universities. Colleges and universities can enhance the relationship between education and work in a number of ways. They not only develop manpower but are important employers and users of talent as well. The Task Force recommends: *that college and university officials (1) examine their own actions to see if they contribute to imbalances between supply and demand in labor markets; (2) where appropriate, respond to indicators of imbalance; (3) work cooperatively with secondary schools to delineate functions, reduce overlap, and assure program continuity; (4) seek to assure as much learning value as possible from College Work-Study assignments, field experiences, and internships; and (5) indicate to students, especially those firmly committed to the liberal arts or teaching, how to combine subject matter interests with the development of marketable skills.*

Adult learning needs. Demographic and other trends suggest that increasing numbers of adults will be returning to school—either full or part time—in the years ahead. All educational institutions with interest and ability to respond should examine, if they have not done so already, how they might meet such needs. Professional schools and research universities should continue their efforts to provide continuing education for lawyers, engineers, physicians, and others who desire it. Schools of business administration can provide continuing education to middle-level managers. Community colleges, vocational/technical schools, and some high schools are in a position to assist women reentering the labor force, craft workers being groomed for supervisory positions, and the like. The Task Force recommends: *that school and college officials (1) work closely with mayors and governors to respond to the needs of adults in developing employment skills; (2) adjust calendars and adapt programs to adult clientele; (3) assist employers and professional and employee associations in solving such problems as obsolescence; (4) adjust personnel policies to make better use of practitioners in training roles; and (5) coordinate their efforts with other education and training institutions to minimize unnecessary duplication of effort.*

Systemwide Matters. Several problem areas call for increased cooperation and coordination of effort between higher education and the schools and between state officials and local education agencies. Occupational licensure has expanded over the years, causing a "closing off" of certain pathways to selected occupations. Reform of professional credential requirements has been facilitated by one nontraditional alternative—degrees via examinations.

Additional areas of concern call for state/local or state/institution cooperation. One such area is guidance and counseling, where the extensiveness of the labor market and economies in the development and utilization of educational and occupational information make collaborative arrangements highly desirable. Another area of concern is staff development. Here colleges and universities, teacher training centers, local districts, and employers can all benefit from joint action. Another area in which state/local cooperation would be fruitful involves developing closer links between education and the business and industry community. The Task Force recommends: *that schools and colleges work closely with state officials (1) to develop comprehensive career guidance systems serviceable to youths and adults; (2) to assure that pre-service and in-service training of administrators, teachers, and staff specialists is responsive to the realities of the labor market and to the emerging new competencies of educators; and (3) to develop nontraditional alternatives to the acquisition of credentials in the trades and professions.*

Work-education programs. Cooperative education—which both develops skills and tests career interests—and other kinds of work-education programs are an important component of the general educational system. Work-education programs differ enormously in purpose, clientele, quality, and effectiveness. Further, some programs of this type are offered (or taken) for the wrong reasons—to avoid discipline problems in the classroom, to avoid unpopular subject matter, to avoid homework, and so forth. Despite these problems, the Task Force believes that work and work experience for students can be educative and therefore recommends: *that schools and colleges (1) clearly define the purposes of work-education programs; (2) carefully select (and encourage) students to participate who can profit therefrom; (3) devote resources necessary to assure high quality; and (4) carefully link experiential learning to work in classrooms and laboratories.*

Recommendations for Employers and Employee Organizations

Responding to labor market realities. Long-range corporate planning to meet human resource and production needs is increasingly important, not only because of changing demographics but also as a result of technological change, shifts in world markets, and affirmative action goals. In large enterprises, including government agencies, upgrading possibilities, motivation, and the transferability of knowledge and skill from one job to another are importantly interrelated.

For all of these reasons, the Task Force recommends: *that employers carefully plan short- and long-term responses to changes in the availability of persons entering or reentering the work force, and give special attention to restructuring jobs, adding flexibility where possible to encourage job sharing, part-time, and intermittent work, and developing ways to help those with little work experience become productive on the job.*

Cooperation with schools and colleges. We are convinced (1) that employers, schools, and all who wish to learn about work have overlapping interests and (2) that by working together more can be accomplished than by working apart. Therefore, the Task Force recommends: *that employers, employee organizations, and educators work together in ways that are mutually beneficial to learners. Employers should articulate more clearly the qualities they seek in the graduates of schools and colleges, and assist schools and colleges by providing part-time student job opportunities, faculty-staff development programs (for instance in the summer), and assistance with student guidance. Educators should work to see that learners acquire and practice skills of value in employment.*

Meeting employment needs of youths. The magnitude of youth unemployment is apparent; causes and solutions are somewhat less clear, except that the size of the youth cohort itself and protracted recessions in 1970-71 and 1974-76 are importantly implicated. Inadequate socialization—not wholly the responsibility of schools and colleges —is also a factor. We suspect that unrealistically high occupational and wage expectations are not an important factor in the persistent, high differential between youth and adult unemployment rates. Preferences for part-time and temporary work, however, probably are—at least for youths still in school.

The Task Force recommends: *that employers and employee organizations (1) work closely with educators through Community Education-Work Councils and with employment and training officials to assist in developing job opportunities and carefully designed work-education programs to encourage close ties between work in school and work outside and (2) support efforts to test the feasibility of federal-state payment of the nonwage, social security costs of employing youths in general (see recommendations to government policy makers).*

Facilitating maximum freedom of individual choice. Morale problems, job dissatisfaction, reduced productivity, and other problems can be lessened by recurrent opportunities to extend established skills and learn new ones. Thus, the Task Force recommends: *that employers and employee organizations reevaluate their policies and strive to develop greater flexibility in hiring policies, work schedules, vacation periods, job security rules, and in tuition and other fringe benefits, so as to facilitate continuing and recurrent education of their employees.*

Education and training at work. Companies provide a substantial amount of organized instruction, especially those with large numbers of employees. The Task Force recommends: *that employers and employee associations work together to develop greater lifelong learning opportunities at work. Two areas deserve special attention: (1) the needs* of scientists, engineers, and teachers who often suffer because of technological obsolescence and (2) the need to maintain, extend, or redirect the careers of workers on layoff so that they are prepared to take on new or old roles in better economic times.

Recommendations for Government Policy Makers

Problems of youths in the labor market. Unemployment among out-of-school youths, expecially in urban poverty areas, is a serious problem, especially when the economy is operating at less than full capacity. It will be difficult to reduce the nation's unemployment rate to 4.5 or 5.5 percent unless a way is found to narrow the gap between youth and adult unemployment rates.

Regardless of causes of youth unemployment, its reduction almost surely depends on several actions. Most important is the creation of jobs through general expansion in the economy and specifically targeted public service jobs. Rather than advocating a youth minimum wage, we would suggest experiments wherein government revenues are used to pay social security taxes for those under age 21. Such an approach would maintain the integrity of the minimum wage but at the same time recognize the employment needs of youths whose productivity is low or uncertain.

The Task Force recommends: *that the federal government undertake a series of experiments in selected states and localities to ascertain the effect of subsidizing a portion of the nonwage costs associated with employing persons under 21 years of age.*

Manpower forecasting. An absence of timely and reliable forecasts of trends in the labor market is costly to society and to individuals. Better forecasting models would reduce such costs. One means of improvement would be to concentrate on occupations where forecasts have validity and margins of error are relatively small. Another is to eschew straight-line extrapolation of past trends. A third is to build adjustments into forecasting models. The Task Force recommends: *that the federal government develop models to forecast manpower supply and demand, including probable adjustments to imbalances, and that special attention be given to occupations calling for costly and lengthy training.*

Support for information, research, innovation, and reform. The federal government has a special role in research, which is costly and affects people in many diverse parts of the nation. Dissemination of the information resulting from research should be an important by-product of federal support, but all too often the appropriate channels of communication have not been fully utilized.

The Task Force recommends: *that the federal government continue to support (1) the establishment of Educational Opportunity and Educational Information Centers, (2) career education reforms, (3) strengthening of guidance and counseling, (4) development of occupational information systems for states and regions, (5) reforms to enable educational institutions to be more responsive to adults, and (6) experiments in lifelong learning.*

Review of federal programs. The 1970s witnessed a substantial increase in the relative importance of income transfers from the federal treasury to individuals and to state and local units of government. In part, this reflects decisions to decentralize the administration of programs to units of state and local government. It also reflects growth in social security, unemployment compensation, and other payments to individuals.

Without questioning the wisdom of recent developments, but recognizing the important interrelationships involving levels of government and types of spending, the

Task Force recommends: *that a thorough-going review be conducted as to the real and fiscal effects of the existing array of federal programs related to education and employment.*

State policy toward education and employment. States can assist in a reduction in overall unemployment, while enhancing productivity, by providing start-up training to businesses expanding or relocating in a state. The states have a very important role to play in the development of career information systems, since employment and education agencies have both interest and expertise in this area. Another important policy arena for states involves delineation of functions—for example, the role of institutions providing various developmental or basic skills training for adults. State policies can also make a difference in efficient use of community resources by encouraging joint use of expensive facilities. States also have a role in encouraging program articulation between levels of the school system and in helping schools and colleges to expand or improve their services. And since higher education produces much of the manpower eventually employed in elementary and secondary schools, some degree of coordination in this area is an important function of state government. The Task Force recommends: *that state officials carefully review policies and programs related to education and employment and, where indicated, make adjustments to improve the coordination, effectiveness, and efficiency of state activities.*

Occupational licensure. The number of occupations licensed in one or more states has increased dramatically since World War II, with both good and bad results. Reciprocity from state to state is a problem; different state requirements interfere with interstate mobility. Many occupations are licensed when alternative means of social control are more appropriate or efficient. Federal and state policies on health care and childcare have become intertwined with occupational licensure issues. Although members of a trade or profession often stand to benefit by restricting the number of persons who can enter their occupation, there are times when the benefits of licensure probably exceed the costs. The capacity of governments to distinguish such instances from others, however, is not well developed. To improve the licensure process, the Task Force recommends: *that state officials reform their occupational licensure procedures by adding laypeople to licensure boards, conducting their business in public, having an independent agency examine the likely impact of actions contemplated, and developing alternative, nontraditional routes to credentials.*

Recommendations for Students, Parents, and the General Public

Career guidance and choice. Guidance systems are being designed for maximum self-direction, but there remains an orientation in many guidance services toward averages, norms, and past trends. For this reason alone, individuals and families need practice in making decisions for themselves. The Task Force recommends: *that young people be given assistance in exploring interests and aptitudes, in clarifying values, in learning how to use community resources, and in developing habits conducive to finding and progressing in congenial work.*

Choice of curriculum and extracurricular activities. In junior and senior high schools, students, with the help of their parents, must make a number of important choices of what courses to take and what extracurricular activities to pursue. A broad base of general skills is always helpful—and sometimes essential—in guiding a young person toward realistic education and employment goals. The abilities to think, to express oneself in writing, and to perform mathematical operations are fundamentally important because they are needed in nearly all dimensions of life and because they serve to keep later options open. The Task Force recommends: *that parent-teacher organizations and community groups sponsor study groups and workshops to assist students and parents (1) to see what can be learned through various elements of the school curriculum and through various extracurricular activities; (2) to clarify goals and values; and (3) to design plans that take account of each youngster's aptitudes, interests, and circumstances.*

Whether to attend college. College is only one of several channels into adult life and work. Others include training in the military service, full-time employment, apprenticeship, or attending a company school, technical institute, or business college. In addition, it is increasingly possible to work, travel, or engage in public service and return to school at a later time. Many young people need a period away from school, especially if their career plans and lifestyle needs are unclear.

The Task Force recommends: *that parents, guidance personnel, community groups, and young people (1) pay close attention to unfolding developments in the labor market that affect youths; (2) use the resources of schools, libraries, and career guidance centers to keep abreast of education and employment options; and (3) consider the many reasons why one may wish to pursue one or more of the many channels to adulthood.*

College field of study. Because of constantly changing conditions in the job market for new college graduates, it is important for college and university personnel and for college students to be as sensitive as possible to student needs and the needs of the labor market. The Task Force recommends: *that the services of career planning and placement offices be made available to college students and that students pursue opportunities to gain work experience and to explore aptitudes and interests and, if attracted to the liberal arts and to teaching, be especially aware of the job market, but if opportunities are limited or if one's commitment is not strong, to examine other opportunities that combine personal interests with labor market realities.*

Adult learning needs. Over the next decade or two, many adults will be moving into new jobs or new career areas, and others will be returning to the workforce after an extensive absence while raising children. Support systems exist to assist some adults who seek training, retraining, and assistance in finding suitable employment. However, relatively few people take advantage of such aid.

The Task Force recommends: *(1) that adults returning to work following an absence from the labor force assess their aptitudes and interests in terms of labor market realities and assist local government agencies, such as the public library, the schools, and community groups, to develop community-oriented counseling and guidance resources for adults; and (2) that adults now at work take advantage of learning opportunities offered at work and in their communities.*

Recommendations for the Research Community

Policy-oriented inquiry should be sensitive to issues, timely, and both comprehensive in its implications and disaggregative in its understanding. Listed below are the most important gaps in knowledge which, if closed, would contribute significantly to public policy and private decision making.

Knowledge gaps. Within the domain of *labor market trends and adjustments,* the Task Force believes that answers to the following questions are especially important:

1.   What education and employment problems are likely to emerge in the 1980s and

1990s in response to demographic trends, energy problems, and other social and technological developments?

2.   What adjustments take place in response to supply/demand imbalances in labor markets for college-trained people?

3.   What becomes of recent college graduates who are unable to obtain work in professional, managerial, or technical sales areas? How are employers responding? Do graduates continue to pursue careers requiring a college education? Which ones are successful, and why?

4.   What factors influence supply/demand imbalances in the labor market? How do educational institutions, government policies and programs, and employer practices affect supply/demand imbalances?

5.   Are students responding to market conditions in their choice of field of study and whether to attend graduate school? Are there qualitative changes in the academic units of college and universities that reflect student response to the labor market?

6.   What kinds of students are most adaptable to changing labor market conditions, and what are the pecuniary and nonpecuniary factors that influence choice of fields of study and occupation?

To promote *informed decision making* for policy makers and for students and their families, the Task Force believes that the following questions deserve attention:

1.   What aspects of the school experience enable people to adapt quickly, to maintain better health, to be more effective parents, and to engage in volunteer, cooperative behavior?

2.   What are the implications, if any, of declining test scores for working life?

3.   How and to what extent does schooling, in conjunction with home and neighborhood, influence the amount of education people eventually obtain?

4.   How do extracurricular activities affect students who pursue them? Is the amount of time spent in these activities as important as the quality of the time spent? How do parents and other family members influence what a child learns?

In the years ahead, policy deliberations, especially at the federal level, will almost certainly involve comparisons of the effectiveness (and net cost) of the options open to young people once they leave high school. This necessarily calls for a better understanding of the implications of *interruptions in schooling, public service jobs, vocational and manpower training, student aid programs, and occupational licensure.*

1.   Which elements of the high school curriculum are most useful to young people, especially those who do not plan to attend college? In particular, what knowledge and skills add to values not measured in the marketplace (for example, do-it-yourself activity)? How do newer elements of curricula, such as unpaid work experience and activities such as Outward Bound, affect students?

2.   Do early work experiences influence goals, aspirations, and subsequent educational attainment? Are the effects more salient for girls than for boys, for lower-class than middle-class youngsters?

3.   How does the "social ecology" of the school influence the nature and purposes of work-education programs at the secondary level?

4.   What are the implications of work-education at the postsecondary level for lost earnings, length of schooling, and economic returns?

5.   What combinations and sequences of schooling, further training, and jobs are useful and beneficial? What factors influence access to preferred channels?

6.   What are the individual and social consequences of skill development, both on and off the job, in terms of productivity and sharing of knowledge and skill at the workplace?

7.   Under what conditions is occupational licensure beneficial? How does it affect incentives for additional education and training? Can means be developed to permit persons to obtain credentials in nontraditional ways?

In order to assist people to make more *informed choices* and to respond to their own needs, the Task Force believes that the following questions need answers:

1.   Where are the important "choice points" in the human life cycle, and what channels of guidance are most effective at these points?

2.   What information and advice is most helpful to college students in the liberal arts and to graduate students, whose options in the past were largely restricted to college teaching?

3.   Are guidance activities responsive to the common and distinctive needs of minorities, women, reentrants to the work force, gifted youngsters, and persons with physical or mental impairments? Do guidance counselors dampen high aspirations if standardized test scores are low? Is appropriate consideration given to experience, motivation, and individual talents?

4.   How effective are modern career guidance systems in terms of acquisition of basic skills and long-term outcomes?

5.   Would support and expansion of free-standing, community-based career guidance services help satisfy the career development needs of both youths and adults?

The Task Force believes that the nation's policy on *lifelong learning* will continue to evolve in the years ahead. We therefore urge research and experimentation addressed to the following questions:

1.   What personal and institutional motivations and available programs and financial arrangements influence adults to pursue additional education and training of various types?

2.   What individual and social benefits are derived from various types of adult learning? Here we urge experimentation with parent education, and programs for the elderly and youths with uncertain goals.

3.   What can be done to prevent or retard obsolescence among people employed in highly technical fields who have been out of school for several years to ensure maximum utilization of their potential?

4.   How can colleges, universities, and other employers use the talents of young people who are unable to secure jobs as teachers?

The consequences of learning. Although much is known about the impact of formal schooling on some dimensions of life—most notably personal economic well-being—less well understood, but potentially very important in the years ahead, are effects on the quality of life and on useful non-market-oriented activities. The mechanisms through which early influences are felt later in life—post-school training, self-study, income—are not altogether clear, nor do we understand why different persons are affected in different ways. The Task Force recommends: *that scholars and research organizations study (1) the multiple effects of schooling and work; (2) the influence of particular sequences of school and nonschool experiences; and (3) the durability of outcomes.*

Learning outside school. Given the very imperfect understanding that now exists concerning the way in which environmental factors influence the development of attributes important in employment, the Task Force recommends: *that scholars devote special attention (1) to the influence of qualitative dimensions of work and schooling, (2) to the separate (and joint) effects of forces outside school and the workplace, such as family, peers, and leisure-time activities, and (3) to the influence of employer policies and practices regarding training, work assignments, and promotions.*

Methods and processes. Research to date has not been as helpful to decision makers as it might have been. The Task Force recommends: *that researchers and sponsors of research put greater emphasis on (1) understanding individual differences in the effects of programs and experiences; (2) longitudinal research on the influence of psychological variables and the long-term consequences of earlier experience; (3) the contributions of several disciplines to policy-related research; and (4) exchange programs whereby researchers become familiar with policy formulation and policy makers articulate their information needs to the research community.*

Achieving Social Justice

The Pursuit of Fairness in Admissions to Higher Education.
By Winton H. Manning. 1977.*

This essay examines the policy issues that are at the root of the *Bakke* case from the standpoint of education rather than the law. The central issue is whether racial or ethnic minority status may be explicitly considered in the process of admitting students to higher education, and, concomitantly, whether universities should adopt policies that grant preferential treatment to applicants on this basis. At the heart of this problem lies the question of how equality of opportunity should be pursued. Is equality of opportunity to be defined in terms of individual merit, so that rewards are attained only by those who earn them through individual efforts, or must one go further and take into account the effects of poverty, prejudice, and discrimination with which racial and ethnic minorities have been burdened? This is an issue of group versus individual equity, and the search for a solution to the problem in the long run depends upon how one resolves the issue of choice among competing values. This essay examines these value choices from the perspective of educational policy and experience, particularly as reflected in the functioning of the nation's graduate and professional schools.

The Admissions Process and Consideration of Race

Admissions to college or graduate school can be conceived in two ways: contest and sponsored admission. Contest admission involves a system in which admission is a prize attained by the applicant's own efforts. By contrast, in sponsored admission, individuals do not win matriculation, but rather are inducted into an educational program that leads to a professional career, following selection by competent sponsors or judges. At the graduate and professional level the predominant mode is that of sponsored admission, for which the objective is making the optimal use of the human resources of talent that are available to the institution.

Opposition to sponsored admission beguiles some persons because they confuse the exercise of responsible judgment by those experienced in educational selection with notions of privilege, secrecy, and arbitrariness, which are as much an enemy of sponsored admission as of contest admission. But the *Bakke* case understandably evoked concern as to the limits on discretionary choice.

Two arguments for improving quality—the benefits to the intellectual environment flowing from diversity in a student body and the educational requirements necessary if excellence in professional service programs is to be attained—are generally regarded

*Originally published as part of the volume entitled *Selective Admissions in Higher Education*.

as the most persuasive for regarding race as relevant to admissions policies at graduate and professional schools. Other rationales include provision of minority leadership and the remediation of educational disadvantage. Two more controversial arguments spring mainly from technical questions arising from the use of tests, namely, alleged cultural bias of tests and their insufficiency in measuring a broad spectrum of talents and potential. Finally, two essentially political arguments are sometimes offered for considering race in admissions, namely reparations (giving preferential treatment based on past injustice) and accommodation to political stress.

Educational Due Process in Admissions

Despite the broad discretion legitimately accorded to the institution in its choice among applicants, there are nevertheless limits to that freedom. A primary consideration that ought to govern the admissions policies of colleges and universities is the development and application of the concept of educational due process.

Addressing the issue of due process in admissions, Gellhorn and Hornby make the following recommendations:*

1. At a minimum, state-supported graduate and professional schools should articulate ascertainable standards or criteria for admissions. Once developed, these standards should be disseminated to the field of applicants and then applied in a uniform and impartial manner.
2. The standards or criteria for use in selecting matriculants must be validated—that is, reliably shown to measure qualities relevant to legitimate educational objectives of the graduate or professional program.
3. Whatever criteria are used, universities should routinely allow applicants the procedural opportunity to demonstrate that those particular criteria are inappropriate for assessing their attributes.
4. Upon request, a rejected applicant should be given a statement of the reason(s) for his rejection.
5. Where rejection relies on information not submitted by the applicant, he should be given access to this information and an opportunity to explain or contradict it.

To these recommendations it would seem to be reasonable to add two others, aimed at providing educational due process:

6. Standards or criteria for use in selecting matriculants should represent a reasonably broad array of those qualities shown to be relevant; that is, assuring sufficiency in standards employed rather than relying on one or two attributes, such as academic competence as reflected in test scores and grades alone.
7. An institution may employ different or overlapping standards in two or more phases; that is, the institution may choose to identify first a pool of minimally qualified candidates, relying primarily upon assessments of academic competence to determine admissibility. In a second stage assessment, the institution may utilize other characteristics, including personal attributes, life experience, and other traits that commend themselves for consideration in the selection process.

---

*"Constitutional Limitations on Admissions Procedures and Standards—Beyond Affirmative Action," *Virginia Law Review*, 1974, *60*, 975-1011.

Implementation of due process policies in admissions coupled with broader dissemination of information about programs and admission requirements would be of particular help to minority students, who are often enrolled in undergraduate schools and colleges that are comparatively lacking in information about graduate and professional education.

A Two-Stage Model of the Admissions Process

Selective graduate and professional schools, like many selective colleges, not only have many more applicants than they can admit but may have an excess of qualified applicants. Accordingly, they make an effort, first, to eliminate from consideration those applicants who do not meet some minimal standard of admissibility, and second, to address the task of selection of a class of students from the still large pool of qualified applicants.

A decision about admissibility is concerned with the question: Does the applicant possess the requisite prior education and minimum intellectual ability and aptitude necessary to pursue a sustained program of academic study offered by the institution? Decisions concerning admissibility ordinarily focus on academic competencies rather than personal attributes and accomplishments of a nonacademic character.

In recent years, graduate and professional schools have been caught up in an "inflationary" spiral, in which minimal standards have been successively inflated. This has had a particularly unfortunate effect upon educationally disadvantaged students, because when minimal standards are set at arbitrarily high levels they screen out very high proportions of them and are perceived as arbitrary and unreasonable barriers.

Once a decision on admissibility has been reached, the second stage of the admissions process—selection—can begin. This decision is concerned with the question: Given that these applicants are admissible, what subgroup of them will best advance the educational philosophy and objectives of the institution, the profession, and society?

At this stage in the admissions process, the full range of the value preferences of the institution come into play, including whether racial or ethnic membership may be considered in selection. From the standpoint of education and professions the answer to that question should be yes. Race *is* relevant because it represents not mere skin color, but the consequences of the minority racial experience in America.

Admittedly, there are ways in which the use of race—indeed of nearly any human characteristic—could defeat the aims of responsible admissions policy; what we are arguing for here is the relevance of race to selection decisions within a complex, sequentially ordered process, whose fairness must be judged in terms of the impact of the entire system rather than dealt with as an abstract component.

Special Programs and Decision Strategies

Given the fairly wide range of competence of students deemed admissible, some students may need additional academic assistance. This may be true even though these students are, in fact, minimally qualified. It is understandable that many students in need of such academic assistance are disadvantaged students whose previous preparation has been hampered by lack of educational opportunity. However, the development of special programs to assist such students is not incompatible with adherence to a minimal standards model, *if* the institution carefully evaluates their progress and assures uniform standards of performance and output for all students.

Much of the concern aroused by the *Bakke* case arises from admission procedures that appear to employ racial quotas. A quota is at work when an applicant is not permitted to compete for all the places in an entire class. The use of quotas represents an educationally undesirable decision strategy and is potentially iniquitous and demeaning.

On the other hand, the incorporation of race as one factor in a weighting system in which it is considered at the final stage of selection with respect to balancing the mix of a class is educationally desirable. What actually happens when a weighting model is employed is that wherever the selection cut-off might be drawn, there are large numbers of candidates whose combined selection indices differ only slightly. Hence, final consideration of the pool of all candidates can include such factors as geographic distributions, career aspirations, sex, ethnic or racial status, and so forth.

Conclusion

The courts should intrude no further into the educational process, of which admissions is an integral part, than is absolutely necessary in order to assure that constitutional principles are guaranteed. From an educational policy standpoint, ethnic and racial status *is* relevant to the fulfillment of the educational objectives of graduate and professional schools. Sensitive, responsive, and fair admissions policies can be devised and implemented that do take special factors such as race into account, and do so in ways that are conducive to the attainment of important educational goals.

The Status of Selective Admissions. By Warren W. Willingham, Hunter M. Breland, and Associates. 1977.*

The purpose of this report is to provide an overview of selective admissions in several institutional settings, to describe briefly the general nature of special admission programs for underrepresented groups of students, to report available statistics on admission of minority and majority students, and to describe strengths and weaknesses of measures used in selecting students. Five major institutional settings in which selective admissions occur are treated: selective undergraduate colleges, graduate schools of arts and sciences, law schools, medical schools, and graduate management schools.

The process by which institutions select students is complex and varies from situation to situation. To a considerable degree, this is the case because selective admissions serve several purposes, and these purposes vary somewhat from institution to institution. In selecting students the interest is not only to enroll the most competent but to serve other institutional responsibilities as well (for example, to supply graduates in different fields).

As a result, academic ability as measured by grades and test scores is a major basis for selecting students, but it is by no means the only consideration. Many other aspects of the student's experience and personal qualities come into play, including race and other background variables. Use of such variables as a basis for admissions gives rise to the controversial social issues represented in the *Bakke* case.

Admissions and Enrollment Data

Two types of data are of interest. The first and most popular consists of the proportions of persons from different groups that are represented in the enrollments and degree

*Originally published as part of the volume entitled *Selective Admissions in Higher Education.*

awards of institutions in different categories. A second shows the rates of acceptance of individuals classified by ethnic groups and by evidence of academic promise. Both kinds of data—particularly the second—are difficult to obtain. Several organizations have conducted surveys of enrollments by ethnic status, but there are many problems of comparability across surveys and of interpretation.

At the undergraduate level, there appears to have been an increase in minority freshman enrollments in four-year institutions from about 11 percent in 1967 to about 14 percent in 1976. This gain in minority enrollment in four-year institutions has not been matched in two-year institutions.

Despite limitations in available data, it is clear that minority enrollments in graduate and professional schools are somewhat less than in undergraduate four-year institutions. The data in Table 1 are based upon different surveys and therefore are not strictly comparable (for example, the medical school enrollment includes a larger proportion of blacks in traditionally black schools than is the case for law school enrollment). But there is a notable consistency across these types of institutions with respect to both the extent of minority representation and the increase from 1969 to 1976. For the three minority groups shown, total representation in each institutional setting was about 5 percent in 1969 and some 8 to 9 percent in 1976.

Table 1. Summary comparison of graduate, law, and medical school enrollment representations (in percentages) of blacks, Spanish-surnamed persons, and American Indians for 1969 and 1976

Group	Graduate schools	Law schools	Medical schools
	1969		
Blacks	4.0	3.8	4.2
Spanish-surnamed	1.1	1.0	0.5
American-Indian	0.3	0.1	0.1
Total	5.4	4.9	4.8
	1976		
Blacks	6.4	5.4	6.7
Spanish-surnamed	1.5	2.3	2.1
American Indian	0.4	0.3	0.3
Total	8.3	8.0	9.1

Note: Total representation of these minorities in 1976 was about 12 percent for undergraduate schools and 5 percent for graduate management schools.

However, important variations within institutions lie behind generally similar increases in different types of institutions. For example, the data for graduate schools include substantial representation of blacks in the field of education, where admission is less selective. In law and medicine, on the other hand, admission has become extremely competitive in recent years. The somewhat effective efforts to increase minority enrollment in these highly prized fields are probably due in part to extensive special aid and recruitment programs organized or facilitated by national organizations in these professional areas.

Another important fact not revealed by Table 1 is that recent increases in minority representation occurred largely in the early part of the 1969-1976 time period. The leveling of minority enrollments in the last two or three years may be related to the truly dramatic increase in the numbers and representation of women in higher education.

Between 1968 and 1976, the proportion of women in entering law classes increased from 12 to 28 percent. Thus, while minorities have gained some in representation, women have gained much more. Two factors seem to be involved. There are larger numbers of women applicants, and women fare well in acquiring traditional academic credentials such as grades and scores on admissions tests.

Data concerning acceptance rates have only recently become available and in only two of the settings investigated. In the spring of 1977, the Law School Admission Council compiled extensive data on over 76,000 students who applied to accredited law schools to start classes in the fall of 1976. Of 4,299 blacks who applied for 1976, 39 percent were offered admission by an accredited law school, while 45 percent of Chicanos and 59 percent of whites applying were offered admission. The highest acceptance rate for any group was 60 percent for women applicants.

Although these gross figures may seem discriminatory, a closer look at acceptance rates within groups with similar academic credentials tells a different story. Acceptance rates of blacks and Chicanos with average undergraduate grades and average Law School Admission Test (LSAT) scores were considerably higher than acceptance rates for other applicants with comparable credentials. From these data it is clear that affirmative action was being practiced by the law schools, but it is also clear that many members of minorities who applied presented academic credentials that were not competitive with those presented by other applicants. Both undergraduate grades and LSAT scores were low on the the average for minority applicants to law schools in 1976. Therefore, even if test score considerations were waived for minorities, the problem of low undergraduate grades remains.

Acceptance rate data are also available for medical schools. Of 42,303 applicants to medical schools for 1975-76, 36 percent were accepted. Of 2,288 blacks who applied, 41 percent were accepted; of Chicano applicants, 52 percent were accepted. For other groups, 43 percent of American Indians, 32 percent of Orientals, 42 percent of mainland Puerto Ricans, 36 percent of Commonwealth Puerto Ricans, 32 percent of Cubans, and 37 percent of whites were accepted. Medical school data concerning acceptance rates for students at particular levels of grade point average (GPA) and test scores present a picture of affirmative action generally similar to that of the law school data described above.

Use and Limitations of Selection Measures

Both grades and test scores, the traditional measures of academic competence, have weaknesses as selection measures, but the strengths of these traditional variables clearly outweigh their weaknesses. Grades give the most direct evidence of capability and motivation for academic achievement, though they incorporate many potential inequities owing to wide fluctuations in grading standards. Admission tests measure a limited type of talent but reflect important general abilities and competence developed through the educational process, and serve as a useful standard that offsets some of the weaknesses of grades.

The previous GPA tends to be a somewhat better predictor than admissions tests at the undergraduate level, and the opposite is true at the graduate level, but in each case both measures make a useful contribution. Evidence also shows the traditional measures to be more accurate than other information available. Even moderately valid measures can be useful in more selective programs because predictors are more effective when a small proportion of applicants is selected. Moreover, as long as moderately valid predictors are equally valid for all subpopulations, they make a positive contribution to fair decision making.

There is little evidence to suggest that the validity of tests and grades does not extend to minority groups. Studies indicate that grades and admission test scores tend to predict that minorities will perform slightly better in subsequent academic work than they actually do perform which is the reverse of what one would expect if these measures were biased against them.

Because of limitations in predictive accuracy and because there are other important considerations in selecting applicants, experienced admissions officers and measurement specialists have always counseled against undue reliance on the quantified, readily available indicators of scholastic ability. Nevertheless, the traditional measures do receive heavy emphasis in practical use. This suggests the need for giving more attention to other selection measures that take account of a broader range of talent and the achievements of students in and out of school that contribute to their educational goals.

It is also evident that many personal qualities and characteristics of students that may be relevant in selection cannot be adequately evaluated except through the subjective judgment of the experienced faculty and staff of educational institutions. Better methods of incorporating such judgment in the admissions process are needed so that significant personal and institutional values are not lost. Some feel that, at times, litigation tends to force use of rigid procedures that may create only an illusion of fairness and might lead to a mechanistic process shortsighted in its social values and effectiveness. It is necessary, however, to guard against inequities that can easily result from ambiguous policy and loose procedure. It would seem especially useful to work toward a more systematic and open process—an educational due process encouraging use of all relevant information and subjective judgments that are sound in principle and fair in application.

High Skills and New Knowledge

Area Health Education Centers: The Pioneering Years, 1972-1978.
By Charles E. Odegaard. 1979.*

In *Higher Education and the Nation's Health,* the Carnegie Commission declared that Americans deserved and should expect better health care and that better health care was a high national priority. To serve all the people everywhere, the Commission believed it necessary to increase the geographic dispersion of health training centers and recommended that a university health science center be located in every metropolitan area with a population of 350,000 or more. In addition, it recommended developing area health education centers (AHECs) in communities with populations below 350,000.

AHECs would be affiliated with university health science centers, providing facilities for patient care; educational programs for house officers and M.D. candidates who could rotate through an AHEC from a health science center; clinical experience for allied health students; and continuing educational programs for health manpower. The nucleus of an AHEC usually would be a community hospital, which would be visited regularly by the health science center faculty.

In essence, the Carnegie Commission advocated some decentralization of medical education away from university health centers and into AHECs with more emphasis on primary care. This decentralization of medical education would reduce pressure in many communities for additional medical schools. The Commission believed that the decentralization of residency training also would help to correct maldistribution of physicians not only geographical, but also in terms of specialties. The need for better geographical and specialty distribution of physicians was reiterated in congressional hearings in 1971, and AHECs as described by the Carnegie Commission were specifically mentioned as a promising way to meet this double need. The legislation passed by Congress in 1971 authorized grants or contracts to train or retrain health personnel in facilities located in areas designated by the Secretary of Health, Education, and Welfare (HEW) and selected to improve the distribution of health personnel by area or by specialty group.

The Carnegie Commission emphasized that, although adequate health care education is a prerequisite to adequate health care delivery, it by no means guarantees it. We can, however, review the educational process as it has changed in accordance with the AHEC concept to see if the change increases the likelihood that a higher proportion of physicians or other health care providers will show interest in and willingness to consider serving neglected rural and inner-city populations.

*This report also included a detailed history of the legislation and administrative regulations developed for AHECs, as well as descriptions of each of the 11 AHECs. *Eleven Area Health Education Centers: The View from the Grass Roots* is available from the University of Washington Press, Seattle, Washington.

General Conclusions

The existence of significant regional differences within the United States was heavily underscored by my experiences with the 11 AHEC projects (in North Carolina, South Carolina, California, Illinois, North Dakota, West Virginia, Maine, Minnesota, Missouri, Texas, and New Mexico). However desirable and broadly applicable the strategic goal of the AHEC concept itself may be, the federal government can easily preclude the possibility of ultimate nationwide achievement of this goal by prescribing tactics that may have been successfully applied in some regions but are not adaptable to the peculiarities of others.

My review of the 11 original AHECs leads unquestionably to the conclusion that beneficial results can flow from them in the attitudes of present and future health care providers toward practice in cities and rural areas that are not close to existing university health science centers. None of these 11 projects, at least from 1972 to 1978, has had actual experience with efforts to develop educational interventions in inner-city areas.

University Health Science Centers

The matter of commitment. The first question to be asked about any university health science center considering or being considered for an AHEC program is how much commitment its academic administrators and faculties have to undertaking educational outreach. For some decades, university health science centers have been subject to centripetal forces that have built up large centralized facilities. Implicit in the AHEC concept, however, is a flow of effort away from the university health science center toward developing clinical educational opportunities in more remote locations, with the facilities and professional groups there collaborating with the faculties of the university centers under the supervision of the university centers. The effective establishment of an AHEC program represents such a departure from accustomed practices that a conscious commitment on the part of university centers to the desirability and importance of educational outreach is required.

One reason for undertaking outreach activities may be that more space is needed for clinical instruction, particularly in medicine. The need is occasioned by a decision to expand the size of a medical school to accommodate larger student enrollment. As the costs of building clinical facilities skyrocket, it becomes increasingly difficult to obtain the large funds required to expand. Therefore, existing community facilities, even if at some distance, become more attractive.

However, even if clinical facilities could be enlarged, the patterns of patient referral to an existing university health science center may not provide a larger inflow of patients. Schools vary greatly in the size of their catchment area for patients and in the degree to which they can reasonably expect to increase patient inflow to their facilities. The use of existing facilities elsewhere and, thus, access to more patients for a portion of the clinical instruction given to students may be necessary.

Until recently, university centers have concentrated a large part of their efforts on training specialists and subspecialists to the exclusion of developing replacements for general practitioners and more general kinds of specialists who, in years past, found it desirable to refer patients with complex and difficult problems to the university hospitals. The new breed of physicians who were trained as superspecialists have now largely replaced the older generation. This new breed now encourages more community hospitals to acquire advanced medical technology and to develop the sophisticated teams for special care that were previously found only in university hospitals. They thus see fewer reasons to refer their patients to university centers and increasingly regard themselves as competitors with the university centers.

Another source of pressure on the university to look beyond its own hospitals has been the criticism that university hospitals have not been producing the primary care physicians needed to serve the needs of patients suffering from chronic or "ordinary" ailments. Clinical students and residents need to be exposed to the more diverse patient care situations found in community hospitals, clinics, and physicians' offices, where primary and secondary care patients are more readily seen.

Interest of a university health science center in outreach service can be stimulated by political pressure, particularly on public university centers. Such pressure consists of complaints to state officials about underserved communities. A positive version of this situation can be the realization by a university center that a favorable reaction to its funding requests may be induced by its efforts to help meet community health care needs of areas removed from the immediate university environment. The majority of the original 11 AHEC projects have, indeed, experienced a happy response to their outreach efforts in the form of the assumption of funding for their outreach activities, at levels well above those obtained from the federal government, by state and local government and institutional and private sources.

Establishing an AHEC program in a university health center. Given the tendency for clinical departments to be strong feudalities within a medical school and the need for their positive endorsement and participation in an effective AHEC program, it is advisable to have a medical AHEC committee that directly involves the medical school dean and the department chairmen in policy discussions on the school's activities in the AHEC program.

Because interaction between physicians and other health professionals is required in any health care delivery situation and because improvement in delivery is dependent on the availability of adequately trained professionals of various types, AHEC programs should look beyond physician education alone to include efforts on behalf of other health providers. The 1976 legislation provided that AHEC contracts should include participation by at least two other health-professions schools or programs (including schools of dentistry). This is a reasonable provision. The experience of the original AHECs demonstrates the beneficial effect of efforts to improve the level of training and availability of nurses and allied health providers through opportunities to decentralize the education of the university's students in these fields.

The 1978 Request for Proposal for an AHEC issued by HEW requires as a condition for a contract that there shall be an AHEC program advisory committee composed of senior representatives of each of the health-professions schools and programs that are actively participating in the program, such that membership will include individuals with training and experience in at least medicine (or osteopathy), dentistry, nursing, and allied health; and, in addition, at least one representative of each AHEC established by the university. It would be reasonable for any institution endeavoring to develop an AHEC program to have such an advisory committee to assess its activities and also to meet the new federal requirement that this committee meet with the AHEC project director at least quarterly to review progress and problems and to plan for further development of the program.

A program planned for a single AHEC area may involve a first year for planning, a second year for development, a third and fourth year for operations with expanding federal support, to be followed by a fifth and sixth (final) year of declining federal support, with the expectation that funding by the contracting institution will be augmented in these later years. The net effect of these stipulations is to make it clear that any institution receiving an AHEC contract is presumed to be developing a long-range program and will explore other sources of funding. Such sources might include state, county, or local governments, other educational institutions in the area engaged in health provider education, health provider institutions, and private sources. As the medical school and its confreres in health education turn toward these sources, they cannot avoid entering a fiscal and political arena. If an AHEC program is of any consequence in an institution, it must be a major educational venture whose policies, procedures, and means of support demand attention at the level of presidents, deans of health science schools, department chairmen, and many faculty members.

Area Health Education Centers

Regional diversity. Embedded in the AHEC concept is the notion of an area or region that can be served in various ways by a central agency or facility. In many parts of the country, demography lends itself readily to this concept because an outlying region becomes dependent on one city for economic, professional, health, social, educational, cultural, and transportation services. Such urban centers are natural locations for AHECs. North Carolina has such centers, but there are also sections of North Carolina without obvious population centers within a convenient range. In such areas, centers have had to be developed by linking hospitals in different communities into a consortium.

Minnesota's demography, by contrast, does not lend itself well to regional organization. The Twin Cities area is a large metropolis with a surrounding service area. Duluth, St. Cloud, and Rochester are urban centers and potential centers for regional AHECs, but for various reasons the University of Minnesota has not been able to turn them into AHECs. Large parts of the state, however, are sprinkled with small towns and have no regional structures around centers that could readily serve as AHECs.

The development of AHECs also can be hindered by cultural diversity. Regional attitudes and antipathies and local loyalties and jealousies are significant influences on AHEC development.

Professional differences. The attitudes of practicing physicians in potential area centers can substantially affect the development of an AHEC program. In some communities, physicians are willing and even eager to have residency programs in a variety of medical specialties and, as the need for more primary physicians has become evident, to see family practice and general internal medicine residencies established. But many residents will wish to practice in or near the area of their residency, and they become business competitors of their teachers. This aspect of the residency program may be perceived as a disadvantage by local physicians. The final decision is likely to turn upon the assessment of the market by the practicing group. If the critical mass of physicians in the area perceive the catchment area for patients to be sufficiently large that they feel secure in their practices and do not fear too much competition from newcomers in their own specialties, they are likely to favor the introduction or increase of residents in specialty training in the area.

The level of commitment attained by the practicing physicians and medical schools in a community being considered as a center for an AHEC has much to do with determining the feasibility of an actual program. A Senate committee report in 1974 indicates that Congress has endeavored to ensure the full commitment of medical schools by instituting a number of requirements for the recipients of AHEC contracts. But Congress has gone too far in writing prescriptions for AHEC programs and should not go further in interfering with local adjustments that may make progress possible in many potential centers for AHEC programs.

The content of an AHEC program can be affected from one area to another by variations in issues that arise in interprofessional relationships. The resolution of such issues may go well beyond the powers of any single university health science center. An instance of this is growing conflict between the medical profession and the nursing profession over the definition of the role of the nurse-practitioner. Until these conflicts are resolved, and until there is a resolution of the conflict within the nursing profession over the levels at which nurse-practitioners should be trained, it will be difficult for educational institutions to determine the types of training programs to be offered, and for health care to be made available in localities in which direct treatment by physicians is not easily accessible.

Relationship among educational institutions. Contracting university health science centers have developed new kinds of relationships with other educational institutions in the AHEC area. Activities in nursing and allied health have led to most of the increased contacts between the contracting university health science centers and educational institutions. Technical institutes, community colleges, or private colleges may sponsor one- or two-year certificates or A.D. or R.N. programs. Four-year institutions, public and private, may offer baccalaureate degrees in nursing and certain allied health fields.

Faculty status in AHECs. In recent decades the faculties of most health science schools have become heavily involved in research, while most community hospitals and their attending staffs are not funded, equipped, or staffed for a commitment to research comparable to that usually found at university centers, although the AHEC experience has shown that practitioners with talent for teaching can be found in these communities. The university health science centers with experience in AHEC programs have generally recognized that the criteria for appointments to the faculty at AHEC centers will differ in some degree from those used for faculty at the university center. Primarily, there is less emphasis on research experience for AHEC faculty.

In endeavoring to decentralize part of the educational process by developing instruction of health professionals in remote areas, most of the AHEC projects have also recognized the need to help develop support for instruction embodied in learning resources, books, journals, and, increasingly, audiovisual learning materials. Such materials are also an important adjunct to efforts to make continuing education available to health providers in the area. In some cases, the result has been the establishment of learning resource networks.

As a result, in some AHEC areas the scholarly minded health professional now has access to a substantial body of learning resources. It seems likely that this improved access will lead both to better education of health professionals and to better care of patients in the area.

The AHECs. The 11 original AHECs adjusted to their particular local situations through diverse structural patterns in their subcontract relations. In many AHEC areas reliance upon a principal subcontract with a hospital or a consortium of hospitals proved feasible, but in other areas it has not. The law authorizing AHECs now provides that a medical school wishing to develop an AHEC program must work through a single legal entity within the area, one of whose principal functions is the operation of the center, which, in turn, has responsibility to provide for or conduct all the educational activities that make up the AHEC program. The diverse experiences of the original pioneering AHECs reveal, however, that there are areas in the United States in need of improvement in the availability of health care, but in which it is difficult to find or create an organized legal entity capable of providing for or conducting AHEC functions. In some cases the contracting universities have achieved beneficial educational results in AHEC areas by working not through a single entity, but with several—other hospitals, junior colleges, four-year colleges, another university, or even a branch of the contracting university health science center established as an entity within the AHEC area. It is unfortunate that the federal regulations are so rigid that, if enforced, federal assistance would be denied to university health science centers simply because the prescribed federal model for the organization of an AHEC does not fit the sentiments and institutional attitudes within the area.

Although the prescribed AHEC organizational form is too rigid, the requirement in the 1976 law that each AHEC have an advisory board, of which at least 75 percent of the members are health service providers and consumers from the area served by the center, is prudent. While this advisory board should not be administratively responsible for conducting actual programs, its review of the AHEC program should serve as an antidote to overly narrow professional and institutional leadership and to the possible confinement of AHEC programs to the major community or communities within an AHEC area to the neglect of outlying towns and more rural areas.

Phases in development of AHEC projects. The original AHEC projects were instituted in 1972. Because the AHEC concept was then new, proposals for the projects were hastily drafted by the university health science centers and hastily reviewed by the federal authorities responsible for determing the final award of contracts. The lack of federal control and review resulting from the excessive turnover in administrative personnel associated with the changing structure of HEW—from central to regional and back to central federal responsibility—left each AHEC project in those years relatively free to find its own way.

The hazard now is that the newer AHECs, to obtain federal assistance, must conform to many specific requirements, despite the great diversity among areas in the United States. They also have a shortened time span for federal financial assistance within which to plan, develop, and operate an AHEC program, and the program is expected to continue operation without further federal assistance after the sixth year.

I fear that the federal program as now defined calls for a rigid cookie cutter model to be achieved in a relatively short period of time, and that under these terms a successful ongoing AHEC program can be launched only in restricted cases where highly favorable circumstances for such a program exist both at the university health science center and in the defined AHEC area. I hope that the federal government will realize this, and that HEW will be given flexibility to consider proposals for experimental AHEC programs in areas with inherently difficult situations requiring time and ingenious programming to achieve progress.

AHEC contracts or grants? The decision by HEW to support AHECs through contracts with university health science centers seems to have been generally acceptable. In my visits to the AHECs, some mention of proceeding on a grant rather than contract basis was made, though certain project directors argued forcibly that the contract procedure was distinctly preferable for an AHEC program. It provides the basis for a business-like relationship between the university and entities in the AHEC area that serve as subcontractors. Questions as to performance can be related to specific work statements, and an atmosphere of accountability for services rendered is engendered.

The principal complaint among the AHEC project directors and their staffs was not the contract form of relationship to the federal government, but the time spent in and frustrations associated with negotiations with the federal officials in the annual review of the contracts for program modifications and budget agreements. Frequent reorganizations within HEW also contributed to the problem.

Conclusion

My visits to the 11 contracting university health science centers and to their AHEC areas have convinced me of the soundness of the Carnegie Commission's recommendations for development of AHECs, both for instruction of medical students and residents and for continuing the education of established practitioners. The AHEC concept provides a needed antidote to the imbalance in educational outcomes that has dominated university health science centers in the post-World War II years. Changes in the learning environment indicate that AHECs will contribute to better distribution of health providers, both geographically and by specialty, and to the regular upgrading of the knowledge and skill of health practitioners. However, additional innovations in actual delivery systems also may be needed to bring health providers to neglected populations in particularly difficult circumstances. I reach this general conclusion despite the fact that there are varying degrees of success and failure among the 11 pioneering projects. Their efforts offer promises of beneficial results as well as useful lessons for other institutions initiating AHEC programs.

There can be no question that federal interest in the Carnegie Commission recommendations and willingness to provide funds to initiate AHEC programs was of strategic importance in the launching of the AHEC projects. Yet, in the six years from 1972 to 1978, the total federal funding for the 11 projects came to slightly over $81 million—an average of only $1,360,000 per project per year. When one considers the beneficial changes in the 11 states and the nonfederal financing that has been generated in support of the programs of most of the projects, the return on federal dollars spent has been substantial.

The revision of the federal program associated with the change in the authorizing legislation in 1976 may make the prospect of federal contracts for AHECs less attractive to university health science centers. Helpful as federal funds might be, if they are not available or are available only under unworkable terms, the need for readjustment in the output of types of health professionals to bring them into better adaptation to health care service needs is great enough that, as a matter of professional concern, university health science centers should endeavor to find other ways of supporting AHEC-type changes in the system. Indeed, the level of dissatisfaction with health care delivery is so great that, if universities do not find ways to remedy educational defects related to these problems, they are likely to find themselves under increasing pressure to change. The health care of the American people would greatly benefit if many more university health science centers pursued the goals of the pioneer AHECs, and so would the status of professional health providers and educators.

Quantitative Policy Analysis Models of Demand and Supply in Higher Education. Technical reports for a project directed by Roy Radner and Charlotte V. Kuh. 1978.*

Enrollment and Cost Effects of Financial Aid Plans for Higher Education

by Joseph Hurd

Although many student aid policy recommendations have been made, until recently the facts needed to choose among them have been crude or nonexistent. One wants to know how, and by how much, a change in the cost of attending a college or university will change enrollment demand. And one wants to know how much the new enrollments will add to the cost of an aid plan. Without estimates of what might be called *enrollment effects*, it is difficult to choose between contending aid proposals where the intention of the proposal is to change the relationship between higher education attendance and family income.

We have chosen to define equality of opportunity as follows: For students of a given level of academic ability, attendance at institutions of higher education (IHE) shall be the same regardless of family income. To be sure, we cannot directly quantify academic ability. Instead, we use Scholastic Aptitude Test (SAT) scores as a measure of it.

We have developed a model of sufficient generality to estimate the enrollment effects of alternative policy changes on the cost of the policy plan under consideration. Our model is such that enrollment effects and plan costs (of policy plans that typically base changes in tuition levels or student grants on family income) can be calculated so that the impact of the plan on various income groups or academic ability levels can be isolated.

We have used our model to analyze the impact on enrollment of five different policy plans for student aid in United States higher education: two versions of the proposals of the Carnegie Council, a proposal by the Committee for Economic Development (CED), and two variants of our own Equal Opportunity plan. We have calculated the cost of each plan for a typical year (1976), had the students taken advantage of the proposed aid. We have not calculated student response to work-study aid or to student loans, although we are quite certain that these two programs also have an effect on enrollment.

There are several criteria by which we can rank the plans. All propose aid by need rather than by merit. Carnegie Plan I would grant substantial aid ($1,600) to students with family incomes of less than $7,600 and a decreasing proportion of that amount as income rises to the no-aid cutoff point of $12,900. Instructional costs of up to $1,500 would be covered or partially covered by the same income-aid formula. Regardless of income, $750 would be granted to students attending a private university or college, although the total private subsidy and instructional cost granted could not exceed $1,500.

Carnegie Plan II would grant aid in exactly the same manner and amounts as would Carnegie Plan I, except that the $750 grant to students attending a private college or university would be eliminated.

The CED plan is similar to Carnegie Plan II in terms of aid, although it makes no provision for aid to cover instructional costs. However, it does propose to increase public college and university tuition to meet half the cost of instruction.

---

*Originally published as six separate technical reports.

The Equal Opportunity plans we propose are based on granting aid so that the "net burden of cost" (cost adjusted by grants and divided by family income) does not change as income rises to the income norm. Above that income level no aid is proposed. Equal Opportunity Plan I would grant aid by this procedure to students having a family income of less than $12,900. Equal Opportunity Plan II would grant aid to students having a family income of less than $22,000.

We estimate the cost in direct aid of the plans in 1976, had they been funded for at least the previous six years, to be: Carnegie Plan I, $7.9 billion; Equal Opportunity Plan II, $6.7 billion; Carnegie Plan II, $6.3 billion; Equal Opportunity Plan I, $2.9 billion; and the CED plan, $2.5 billion. Adding the induced cost of the plans (the subsidy provided by the IHE as a result of tuition being less than the average cost of instruction), the total costs would be: Carnegie Plan I, $9.0 billion; Equal Opportunity Plan II, $7.3 billion; Carnegie Plan II, $7.3 billion; Equal Opportunity Plan I, $3.2 billion; and the CED plan, $2.7 billion. All amounts are in 1974 dollars.

The Carnegie plans would increase FTE enrollments by about 13 percent, the Equal Opportunity Plan II by about 6 percent, the Equal Opportunity Plan I by about 4 percent, and the CED plan by less than 4 percent.

The plans would not be equally easy to administer and implement. With the most difficult task of obtaining funds completed, the Carnegie plans could be administered through existing college and university aid offices. The CED plan, on the other hand, would require national direction or legislation to require the state-controlled colleges and universities to raise their tuitions at the proper time and by the required amounts. The Equal Opportunity plans would require regulation of some type to prevent unwarranted tuition increases, which otherwise would be partially covered by grants.

Let us remind ourselves that all the plans induce increases in the demand for higher education. We have implicitly assumed that there would be a sufficiently large supply of places so that this increased demand could be satisfied without either increasing instructional cost per student or rationing places. In cases where the implementation of a plan would induce greater demand than could be accommodated, actual attendance would be less than we have predicted. This means that our cost estimates should be considered an upper limit; we do not expect the plans to cost more than our estimates, and in some cases they may cost less.

It is hardly conceivable that in the near future the people of the United States will turn away from college and university education as a means of enriching their lives and enhancing their economic opportunities. As long as higher education is perceived as necessary to attain prestige and pecuniary reward, public policies will be needed to achieve social and economic justice. While it is not a perfect tool, this analysis is a step toward understanding and evaluating the efficacy of policy proposals.

Market Conditions and Tenure in U.S. Higher Education, 1955-1973

by Roy Radner and Charlotte V. Kuh

The argument most frequently given for the existence and extension of tenure is that of academic freedom, yet tenure has economic as well as political implications. The question addressed here is how, as an economic variable, tenure has changed as conditions in the academic labor market have changed and how it may change in the future.

Tenure is, however, but one aspect of adjustment in academic labor markets. Salaries, workloads, attrition, retirement, and the age structure of faculty are other aspects of adjustment that would have to be considered in a complete model of the academic labor market.

We look at tenure as one aspect of adjustment in a market where faculty/student ratios and salaries adjust slowly and are constrained to be more or less equal within ranks and across fields. From the point of view of the faculty member, tenure provides security of employment. If alternative occupations carry with them some nonzero chance of unemployment, a tenured job in academia will be more attractive because of its security of employment than a nontenured job that in all other respects offers similar characteristics. Clearly, if a tenured job also means a promotion in rank and salary, lifetime income will also be higher the earlier an individual is promoted to tenure. In the presence of constraints on salaries, tenure can act as a "compensating differential" that enables academic employers to compete for qualified persons even though they pay lower salaries than nonacademic employers. Within academia, differences in chances of obtaining tenure may allow those fields with greatest growth or greatest nonacademic competition can compete, even though salaries are constrained to be equal across fields and within ranks.

Although tenure may be used as a competitive weapon, it is a two-edged sword. From the point of view of the academic employer, tenure acts as a constraint on labor force adjustment in the face of changing enrollment demand. In particular, when enrollment becomes stable it limits the institution to two main sources of attrition, which can create places for new hires: retirement and nonrenewal of contracts for nontenured faculty.

Tenure also has implications for the age structure of the faculty. The younger are those that are given tenure, the longer is the tenure commitment of the institution. The result of failure to plan for a decline in demand following a period of growth is a lengthy commitment to a young but aging faculty.

Our statistical model estimates the tenure rate, which we define as the chance that a nontenured faculty member will be granted tenure in any given year. The tenure rate is dependent upon conditions specific to that year and on the time that has elapsed since the faculty member obtained the Ph.D. degree. Time since the Ph.D. is presumably correlated with the accumulation of those things upon which the decision to grant tenure is based: publications, teaching experience, reputation, and so forth. This age effect, however, is modified by market conditions for which the date effect is a proxy. For example, simply by virtue of being nontenured and available in the expanding academic market of the early 1960s, we would think that a faculty member would have a greater chance of being given tenure than if he had been nontenured in the early 1950s, at the same age.

The model reveals that the tenure rate did indeed increase during the period of rapid growth in academia from 1960 to 1968 in all types of institutions and in all fields within these institutions. After 1968, the tenure rate continued to increase in public institutions, but more slowly. However, in private institutions, the tenure rate remained constant or declined between 1968 and 1972. Thus it would appear that tenure rate did, indeed, behave as an economic variable in the sense that higher tenure rates occurred at the same time as the rapid increase in employment in academia. In private institutions, which were relatively harder hit by the declining rate of increase in enrollments in the late 1960s, we see quite rapid downward adjustment of tenure rates at the same time.

Market Conditions and Tenure for Ph.D.'s in U.S. Higher Education: Results from the 1975 Carnegie Faculty Survey and a Comparison with Results from the 1973 ACE Survey

by Charlotte V. Kuh

This technical report describes the results of the tenure rate estimation model (see above), using data obtained from the 1975 Survey of Teaching Faculty sponsored by the Carnegie

Council. Qualitatively, the results are similar to those found using data from the 1973 ACE Survey for the years that are covered by both surveys. There was a rapid fall in the median time to tenure during the 1960s, when there was the most rapid increase in enrollments. Quantitatively, however, the median times to tenure estimated from the 1975 data are lower than those estimated from the 1973 data for the earlier years (1950-1968). The most important specific results were:

1. For all types and control of institutions, median times to tenure fell rapidly from 1961 until the late 1960s. Thereafter, they rose slowly through 1973 for universities and private colleges and leveled off for public colleges. Generally, the median time to tenure is longer in private than in public institutions. This same pattern is found in broad fields. We also find that the median time to tenure is longer in the physical and biological sciences than in the humanities and social sciences.

2. We investigated possible explanations for the lower median times to tenure for earlier years that were estimated for the 1975 Survey. It appears that the differences result from systematic differences of the incidence of tenure for the older cohorts. At any age, the older cohorts in the 1975 sample are more likely to be tenured than the older cohorts in the 1973 sample. We think that this may be due to selective attrition of nontenured older faculty.

U.S. Doctorate Faculty After the Boom: Demographic Projections to 2000

by Luis Fernandez

The academic labor market during the next quarter century promises to be chronically depressed. All indicators point to a slowing down and eventual contraction in total enrollments at four-year institutions. From the historical record of the academic labor market, the current disequilibrium can be expected to lead to an increased flow of experienced faculty to nonacademic employment and to a fall in the rates of promotion to tenure.

Our projections are based on the observation that, conditional on age and years of experience in academia, the proportion of faculty who received tenure or who left academia in a given year is stable over time. Hence knowing the number of faculty at each age in a given year allows us to predict quite accurately the number of each age in the subsequent year. However, the accuracy can be considerably improved by also controlling for the type of institution each faculty member is employed at and whether he is working full-time or part-time. To avoid unnecessary complications, in this paper we have chosen to restrict our attention to full-time doctorate faculty at four-year institutions.

The projections reveal fairly robust patterns in the evolution of the age structure of doctorate faculty and the creation of new junior faculty positions.

•   Under all of our projections, the level of hiring increases during the 1970s and then declines during the 1980s, bottoming out in 1985-86. The most optimistic projection of doctorate hiring for 1976 to 1995 is 155,000 people, or an average of 7,750 people a year. Earlier projections indicated that between 1976 and 1990 there would be 568,000 new doctorates conferred.

•   Although changes in the rate of retirement and out-migration and changes in the faculty/student ratio have sizable *percentage* impacts on the number of new junior faculty positions available, since the level of hiring is going to be very low during the rest of this century, *absolute* changes are small. Increases in nontenured quit rates lead to modest increases in hiring, but have very little impact on the tenure ratio or the age distribution: such action reveals itself to be simply a "revolving door" policy. Increasing the tenured quit rate is much more effective for keeping the tenure ratio low. Unfortunately, it is not clear how institutions can change their quit rates without encouraging the most gifted faculty to leave first.

- Early retirement turns out to be disappointing. At most 1,000 new junior faculty positions are created in any year by early retirement of the senior faculty. In addition, because early retirement has a rapid impact on hiring, in order to have the most effective countercyclical impact it seems best to *delay* its implementation until 1990. Other policies must be relied on to smooth hiring in the 1980s.
- There is a continuous aging of faculty in every projection. By 1995 the median age of the doctorate faculty will increase by 8 to 11 years over its value of 41.7 in 1975. The percentage of faculty over the age of 50 will increase from the current 24.6 percent to between 51.2 and 57.8 percent. Even when early retirement is assumed to have been instituted, the percentage of faculty in 1995 over the age of 50 is projected to be almost double its current level.

Our projections also shed light on several other important questions:

- In order for tenure quotas to be superior to early retirement programs for halting the rise in the tenure ratio, it appears they have to be very low quotas. If such low promotion rates imply actually forcing junior faculty to change employers every few years, this could succeed in clearing the market of the best young talent. Yet, early retirement appears to be a weak policy either for insuring faculty vitality or for improving the job market for new doctorates who wish to work in academia.
- If affirmative action programs are successful, one should observe the same rates of hiring, promotion, and termination for women and minorities as one observes for white males. Our projections indicate that, despite the low rate of hires projected for the next two decades, if women are treated equally with men, then the fraction of women in academia could be trebled by the end of the century. Furthermore, if the current rate of increase in the fraction of doctorates awarded to women continues unabated, nontenured faculty will have almost equal numbers of men and women by the year 2000.

Field Disaggregated Analysis and Projections of Graduate Enrollment and Higher Degree Production

by Christoph von Rothkirch

Since the end of the 1960s, when the booming growth of higher education in general and its graduate sector in particular was reduced to moderate annual increases or even decreases, much effort has been made to analyze these dynamics and find reliable projections of likely future developments. The threat of growing unemployment among Ph.D.'s, in particular, has caused researchers in universities and other agencies to develop models for analyzing, forecasting, and evaluating policy for the academic labor market.

Nearly all of the existing models of graduate higher education are too crude with respect to their level of aggregation. They neglect that student enrollment and degree completion behavior is considerably different in distinct academic fields.

Disaggregation with respect to academic fields is especially necessary if a model is used for the evaluation of policies and the analysis of policy impacts. Present conditions, as well as likely future developments in the academic labor market, are not the same in all fields. Therefore, market adjustment policies based only on global analyses might improve one part of the market but impair another.

The methods used in this analysis are trend comparison and extrapolation. No hypotheses about graduate student behavior are presumed. The results, however, not only indicate that behavior-explaining models must be constructed on a field-disaggregated level, but also yield plausible rationales concerning the factors influencing student decisions. While the majority of B.A. graduates still enroll in graduate or professional schools, more and more of those who enroll do not aspire to the doctorate and are content with a lower-level degree.

This shift clearly indicates the students' responsiveness to changing job possibilities and prospects. Since the beginning of the 1970s traditionally academic fields, such as English, foreign languages, mathematics, and social sciences, as well as research-oriented fields, such as engineering and the physical sciences, experienced a steady and strong decrease of shares of graduate enrollment. In contrast, graduate enrollment in professionally oriented fields, such as architecture, business administration, computer science, and public administration, increased continuously above the average.

If these trends last in the near future, higher degree production in the 1980s will be considerably different from traditional patterns. The share of Ph.D. production in engineering, mathematics, physical sciences, arts, letters, and social sciences, which totalled more than one-half of all Ph.D.'s awarded before 1971, will decrease to less than one-third in 1983 and thereafter.

The field-disaggregated analysis of graduate enrollment and higher degree production, however, shows also that the economically based hypothesis of market responsiveness cannot explain all recent changes. In agriculture, biological sciences, and education, for example, graduate enrollment as well as higher degrees awarded are still increasing, in spite of bad job prospects in those fields inside and outside academia. This development indicates that there are also noneconomic factors, such as concern for the physical and social environment, that influence educational and career decisions.

Preserving a Lost Generation: Policies to Assure a Steady Flow of Young Scholars until the Year 2000

by Roy Radner and Charlotte V. Kuh

If no radical changes occur over the next ten years in the aggregate relationships among college-age cohort sizes, rates of college-going, and ratios of doctoral faculty to students, the mid-1980s and mid-1990s will see precipitous, but probably temporary, declines in the demand for new Ph.D. faculty. Without the implementation of policies designed to offset such cyclical fluctuations, the evolution of the academic age structure will mirror this history of changes in the size of student cohorts, and will have serious consequences for academic research and teaching. It is in both the national interest and the interest of individual institutions to assure a moderate but steady flow of young doctorate scholars into academia, and the initatives for suitable programs should come from both levels. On the national level, we recommend that steps be taken immediately to lay the groundwork for a Junior Scholars Program that would go into effect in the mid-1980s.

This program should be self-liquidating, in the sense that it should provide no more research positions than can be turned into teaching positions after the demographic troughs have been passed. On the institutional level, we recommend that early retirement programs be introduced to fit projected changes in age structure and teaching demand. At both levels, in order for these programs to assure smooth, demographically generated fluctuations in the hiring of young doctoral scholars, the timing of implementation should be an important consideration in the planning process. This report spells out these recommendations in more detail, and outlines the consequences, in terms of faculty demography and program costs, of these and alternative programs.

Adequacy of Governance

Legislative Issues in Faculty Collective Bargaining. By David E. Feller and Matthew W. Finkin. 1977.*

The focus of this study is on legislation governing collective bargaining for faculty in institutions of higher education. In the private sector, the applicable statute, at least for institutions having a certain minimum impact upon interstate commerce, is the National Labor Relations Act (NLRA). State public institutions of higher education are not subject to the national legislation but constitute a subvariety of public employment governed by state legislation.

Although we are concerned with public, rather than private, institutions of higher education, we shall try to avoid the vast range of issues that are peculiar to public employment generally but have no special significance for higher education. This means that many, although not all, of the considerations we urge would be applicable to special legislation dealing with collective bargaining for faculty in institutions of higher education in the private sector.

The fundamental theme of this study is that one aspect of the employment relationship particular to faculty in institutions of higher learning requires separate treatment in any legislation establishing a system of collective bargaining, particularly for public employees. That aspect, or characteristic, is embodied in systems of academic self-governance.

In mature institutions of higher education the basic assumption, in the absence of collective bargaining, is contrary to that in other employment. Faculty play a large and often dispositive role in the formulation and implementation of educational policy and in decisions on the selection and retention of faculty members. Thus decisions on what programs of instruction to offer, what students to admit to them, whom to recruit or retain to teach them, or even whether to terminate a program altogether, which in industry would be viewed as the archetypical management prerogatives of deciding what to produce, how, and with what labor, are customarily made by the faculty, or only after extensive consultation with it.

The reasons for such faculty participation are closely interrelated. First, decisions of this kind require a high degree of professional expertise. This assumes, rightly, that those most familiar with both the academic discipline and the needs of the institution should participate in the decision-making process. Second, the successful conduct of an academic enterprise requires the active cooperation of the faculty. Finally, the participation of the faculty is one safeguard for academic freedom.

The difference between the more usual employer-employee relationship and the relationship between administration and faculty in higher education has led some to conclude that collective bargaining is incompatible with the academic world and that

*Originally published as part of the volume entitled *Faculty Bargaining in Public Higher Education.*

its introduction would lead to the demise of academic government. We disagree. First, although faculty members perform many functions that in the usual employment relationship would be regarded as managerial, they also remain employees. For example, they are paid salaries, are concerned with pensions and fringe benefits, want adequate working conditions, and need places to park their cars. In most institutions of higher education, these subjects are not collegially governed by the faculty. The absence of collective bargaining thus means the absence of any organized voice for faculty on these nonacademic but important matters.

The second reason collective bargaining is not inconsistent with academic government is empirical. The experience of the past few years suggests strongly that, given the appropriate statutory environment, and sometimes even in the absence of that environment, collective bargaining and the traditional form of academic governance can coexist.

Our three most important conclusions are as follows. First, the most significant factor in adjusting faculty collective bargaining to higher education lies in the proper definition of the bargaining unit. It is crucial that the unit for the selection of collective bargaining representatives be as congruent as is reasonably possible with the constituency of the existing system of faculty government. The central problem here is to achieve an accommodation between this quintessential principle and the public employer's interest in a manageable structure for the actual bargaining. Second, any attempt to limit the scope of bargaining in order to provide separate compartments for academic government and the issues subject to collective bargaining is essentially unworkable, and the scope of bargaining should be sufficiently broad to allow the bargaining agent to achieve an accommodation with institutional government. Third, the statute must make it clear that internal faculty governing agencies are not labor or employee organizations. Finally, if the statute is otherwise constructed so as to foster the maintenance of institutions of faculty government, no additional provision need or should be made for some special form of collective bargaining election ballot or for student involvement in the bargaining process.

Definition of "Labor Organization" or "Employee Organization"

Most state laws follow the NLRA's prohibition on company unionism, which makes it unfair labor practice for an employer to dominate, interfere in, or support a labor organization. The goal is to assure that employees will be represented by an organization of their own choosing. Moreover, the federal definition of a labor organization includes any organization of any kind that exists for the purpose in whole or in part of dealing with the employer. A latent danger is that a university administration will be prohibited from participating in or supporting duly established faculty governing bodies by a more mechanical reading of similar language in a state law. Accordingly, prudence suggests that the definition of an employee organization preclude such a reading. On the other hand, it is of critical importance that the senate structure be considered in making unit determinations for faculty bargaining.

Recommended provision 1. An "employee organization" is any organization of any kind in which employees participate and that exists for the purpose in whole or in part of collective bargaining with the public employer; provided that, except for the purpose of determining the history of employee representation in a unit determination, any committee, council, senate, or other such body in any institution of higher education in which faculty participate in whole or in part and that serves as part of the internal governing structure of such institution shall not be deemed an employee organization.

Recommended provision 2. A "supervisor" is any individual having authority, in the interest of the employer, to hire, transfer, suspend, lay off, recall, promote, discharge, assign, reward, or discipline other employees, or responsibly to direct them, or to adjust their grievances, or effectively to recommend such action if in connection with the foregoing the exercise of such authority is not of a merely routine or clerical nature, but requires the use of independent judgment; provided that in an institution of higher education, any chairman, director, coordinator, principal investigator, or other leader of an academic unit, component, or program who performs any of the above duties primarily in the interest of members of the academic unit, component, or program or who supervises any persons not included in the bargaining unit shall not be deemed a supervisor for that reason.

Definition of "Managerial Employee"

Although not mentioned in the NLRA itself, managerial employees have, like supervisors, been excluded from representation rights under the NLRA by judicial decision. Regardless of whether a state statute attempts to codify such exclusion or to allow managerial personnel to form separate bargaining units, there is a danger that members of the faculty, or members of faculty committees, who exercise discretion in the conduct of the educational enterprise may fall within the definition of managerial employees. Again, the importance of maintaining the integrity of the core faculty for unit purposes suggests that some legislative provision may be needed.

Recommended provision 3. "Managerial employee" means any employee having significant discretionary responsibilities for formulating or administering policies and programs on behalf of the public employer; provided that in an institution of higher education no employee or group of employees shall be deemed to be managerial employees because the employee or group of employees participates in decisions with respect to courses, curriculum, personnel, or other matters of educational policy.

Determination of an Appropriate Bargaining Unit

The statute should distinguish between the determination of an appropriate bargaining unit, really the election district for which the would-be bargaining agents must compete, and the actual bargaining structure that may eventually develop. Thus it should reject the notion that some perfect or most appropriate unit exists. That approach would require the board to visualize the bargaining process in advance, weigh the pros and cons of various bargaining structures, and decide which is the most preferred. The result, usually coupled with a policy that favors more comprehensive bargaining units, makes organizing more difficult and, more important, simply lumps diverse groups together. Thus the bargaining agent would have to accommodate more competing interests than its internal political processes can reasonably withstand. The educational impact of such homogenization may be devastating. Accordingly, a better policy, attuned to achieving a workable adjustment of bargaining and faculty government, is to make the faculty governance constituency the unit for the bargaining election and to make it clear that the unit so defined is not the only one in which bargaining can take place.

The following recommendation contains two significant elements for higher education. It lists the criteria commonly used in state unit determination provisions but includes, as one element, the structure of academic government. This provides some flexibility. For those systems that exhibit a high degree of centralized control and whose campuses are, essentially, branches of a unitarily governed institution, this recommendation would permit the labor board to find a single unit appropriate. On the other hand, in institutions where each campus exercises substantial autonomy in academic decision making, it would permit separate campus units.

The second major element is the prohibition of inclusion by the Public Employment Relations Board of faculty and nonfaculty in a single unit, whatever the geographic determination, except where a majority of both groups desire such a broader unit.

Finally, by specifying that a unit can be found to be appropriate even if another unit might also be appropriate, the recommended provision makes it clear that the statute does not mandate a particular bargaining structure, but allows the parties, within the limits of the permissibly appropriate units, to create their own structure.

Recommended provision 4. In determining an appropriate unit, the Public Employment Relations Board shall consider the community of interest of employees, including occupational community of interest, the commonality of terms and conditions of employment, common supervision, degree of interchange, geographic separation, extent of organization, and history of representation in the division or subdivision of the employer involved, and, in any institution of higher education, the structure of academic government; provided that in any state college or university no unit shall include both faculty and nonfaculty (as defined by the institution's governance structure) unless a majority of each group, voting separately, approves representation in such a broader unit; and provided that no unit shall include both professional and nonprofessional employees unless a majority of such professional employees vote for inclusion in such unit. The board may determine a unit to be appropriate in a particular case even though some other unit might also be appropriate.

Bargaining Structure

As a concomitant of the above, the statute should make plain that combinations of various bargaining units can cluster for bargaining purposes or, alternatively, that the public employer can require joint bargaining on issues of statewide impact or engage in pattern bargaining if the labor organizations refuse to form a coalition. In this way management can rationalize its bargaining structure, avoiding whipsawing or leapfrogging, while each representative retains a duty solely to its local constituency. Moreover, accommodations made between bargaining representatives can be made at arms length and not by submerging interests within all-inclusive units.

Recommended provision 5. It shall not be an unfair labor practice:

1. for a public employer and a labor organization representing employees in two or more bargaining units to agree to merge such units into a single unit for the purpose of collective bargaining, if the employees involved could appropriately have been included within a single bargaining unit
2. for a public employer (a) to demand joint bargaining by two or more employee organizations with respect to matters that have customarily been provided on a uniform basis among the employees represented by such labor organizations, or (b) if joint bargaining is not agreed to by those employee organizations or no agreement is reached acceptable to all parties, to conclude an agreement as to such matters with the organization or organizations that represent the largest number of employees and to refuse to bargain further with any other organizations as to such matters unless that other organization agrees to accept the terms so negotiated

3.   for two or more employee organizations to demand joint bargaining with a public employer with respect to matters that have customarily been provided on a uniform basis among the employees represented by such employee organizations.

Scope of Bargaining

At the outset we reject the "forbidden-permitted" approach as unsupportable on both doctrinal and practical grounds. Doctrinally, it holds that the public employer cannot agree to terms of a collective agreement that limits its power to exercise governmental authority; thus it fails to perceive that the governmental employer retains the ability to control the terms of the bargain subject only to whatever impasse provisions the state wishes to make. Practically, this approach ultimately rests on the assumption that public employee unions will have too much power unless their scope of bargaining is narrowed. We do not believe that recent experience necessarily bears out this judgment; nor do we believe that unions bargain tenaciously on controversial issues of social policy, about which their members will invariably have many views.

The exemption of policy matters, including the faculty role in their formulation, from the range of permissible bargaining places faculty government on a decidedly weak foundation. Logically, if such matters are management prerogatives, then those faculty who formulate policy should be excluded from the unit as managerial personnel, but this would produce ludicrous divisions within the faculty. Further, the exemption of such matters from the scope of bargaining ignores the fact that such decisions affect faculty in the most direct fashion and that greater security for a faculty voice in institutional affairs may be one of the factors militating toward collective bargaining. Finally, such restrictions produce unworkable distinctions between the bargainable and the forbidden.

However, we do not believe the "mandatory-permissive" distinction is an entirely satisfactory alternative. It does limit the matters upon which the employer is forbidden to take unilateral action without first bargaining, but it injects into the bargaining process itself a set of legalistic distinctions that serve no useful purpose so long as the public employer is free to reject proposals that it believes it should as a matter of policy. In the public sector the distinction can, and indeed has, led to extensive litigation that has no observable purpose and occupies time and attention better spent resolving the underlying dispute.

Because of these considerations, the following proposal deals separately with the conduct of bargaining and unilateral action.

Recommended provision 6: scope of bargaining. For purposes of this Act, to bargain collectively is the performance of the mutual obligation of the public employer and the collective representative to meet, upon request, at reasonable times and confer in good faith with respect to any matter affecting or arising out of the employment relationship, or the negotiation of an agreement or any question arising thereunder, and the execution of a written contract incorporating any agreement reached if requested by either party; but such obligation does not compel either party to agree to a proposal or require the making of a concession.

Recommended provision 7: management rights.

1.   Any right a public employer might otherwise have to take action of any kind shall not be affected or limited by the obligation to bargain collectively except as provided herein.

2. Before changing any existing policy or practice directly affecting the wages, hours, or terms and conditions of employment (including those governing employee participation in the exercise of the employer's rights) of employees represented by an exclusive bargaining representative, a public employer shall first propose such change to the bargaining representative. If agreement is not reached, the public employer may institute such proposed change after bargaining to impasse or, if the provisions for the resolution of bargaining impasses provided in this Act are invoked by the bargaining representative, after final disposition under such provisions.
3. A public employer may, by agreement with a collective bargaining representative, limit or modify any of the rights otherwise preserved by this Section. An exclusive bargaining representative may, in conjunction with such agreement, limit or modify its right to bargain with respect to the subject matter of such agreement.

Subsection 3 therefore provides that the employer's right to take action may be limited by agreement and that the collective bargaining representative may, in conjunction therewith, agree to waive its right to bargain. On other matters, such as faculty disciplinary procedures, the parties may agree merely to a modification of existing policy but leave the subject open to further negotiations. On still others the parties may see no present need for change and simply rely on the statutory status quo. Accordingly, subsection 3 speaks of "agreement with a collective bargaining representative" rather than a "provision of a collective bargaining agreement."

To be sure, the parties will doubtless settle kindred issues simultaneously and embody the agreement on them in a single instrument. It can, but need not, be a comprehensive collective bargaining agreement as commonly employed in industry. It could not, in the structure proposed, however, either waive the right of the employer to take action, after bargaining, on matters not covered by agreement or waive the right of the union to bargain on such matters.

These provisions have added relevance in light of the proposals on bargaining structure made earlier. Centralized coalition or pattern bargaining on economic issues may well occur against the employer's perceived need to make a single, timely submission to the legislature. Before or after those issues are resolved, other representatives of the public employer may be dealing with bargaining agents on wholly unrelated items. There should be no need to compel trade-offs between them at the highest centralized level of bargaining in order to reach a single "wrap-up" agreement.

Union Security

An acceptable union security provision would be particularly useful in higher education to the extent it conduces toward greater faculty participation in the bargaining organization. However, we have also suggested that, as a matter of sound policy, faculty bargaining agents should accommodate dissenting faculty who oppose unionization on grounds of conscience; dismissal of faculty for refusal to support the bargaining agent seems far too harsh a sanction for an enterprise that prizes tolerance of personal opinion or eccentricity. Thus the real question is what kind of union security device should be adopted.

We believe, on balance, it is preferable to allow the public employer and the bargaining agent to work out, by agreement, the terms and conditions of the agency shop, as in private employment—subject to certain conditions, including a conscientious objector provision.

Recommended provision 8. Nothing in this statute, or any other statute of this state, shall preclude a public employer from making an agreement with a labor organization (not established, maintained, or assisted by any unfair labor practice) providing for the deduction from the wages of employees, and the payment to the labor organization, of amounts no greater than the periodic dues, initiation fees, and assessments uniformly required as a condition of acquiring or retaining membership if (1) such labor organization is the representative of the employees, as provided in this statute, (2) membership in such labor organization is available to any employee from whose wages such deductions are made on the same terms and conditions generally applicable to other members, and (3) provision is made for the exemption of any employee from such deductions on the grounds of conscientious objection to the payment of dues or fees to any labor organization, which exemption may be conditioned upon the payment by the exempted employee to any nonreligious charity or charities of amounts no greater than the deductions that would otherwise be made.

State Experience in Collective Bargaining. By Joseph W. Garbarino. 1977.*

This analysis is concerned with the adminstrative aspects of new bargaining arrangements in four-year colleges and universities and discusses five of the most important problems relative to academic unionism that have arisen in the seven states studied.

Bargaining Structure and the Identity of the Employer

In five of the seven states the governor's office has a direct influence on the bargaining process. In four of the states an agency of executive office functions as the employer and conducts negotiations. This represents perhaps the most important single administrative change that faculty bargaining has introduced into higher education. Although the potential for direct intervention into the academic substance of bargaining by the governor's office clearly exists, this development has not created major problems in relations between the executive branch and the central headquarters of the systems. This seems to be the result of the narrow scope of the bargaining—with the states' interests being financial rather than educational.

   The trend in the states will be toward identifying the governor as the employer in order to bring the coordination of pay policy for state employers into a single office. Where institutions remain as the employer of record, and are therefore the negotiators, close coordination between the governor's office and the bargainers will probably develop, thereby reducing the differences between the two approaches.

   The two extremes of current practice are exemplified by New York and Massachusetts. In New York, the governor's office negotiates directly with the faculty union of the State University of New York, whereas in Massachusetts the administration of each institution negotiates with its campus faculty union. Despite its dangers, the New York approach seems to provide the best combination of bargaining arrangements likely to be obtained by higher education. The state functions as the employer/negotiator but appears to have had little independent influence on the academic content of the contracts. The

*Originally published as part of the volume entitled *Faculty Bargaining in Public Higher Education.*

economic provisions of the contract settlement itself have not come into effect until the legislature has provided funds, the governor has supported the resulting agreement, and the funding problem has been handled independently of the general budget for the institution. It is also a sound principle to link the responsibility for negotiations and financing within the governor's office.

Students and the Bargaining Process

Students are interested in the effect of bargaining on their participation in governance and in the potential detrimental results of bargaining on their interests. The usual student response is to protect their role in traditional governance structures and also to try to achieve participation in faculty bargaining, although there is very little experience as of 1977 with direct student participation.

In general, the protection of students' interests should be the concern of the administration. Usually students will find that most decisions affecting their welfare are made as part of the general budgetary process, away from the bargaining table. In addition, student participation in faculty bargaining is likely to make reaching an agreement between the principals more difficult and to contribute to factionalism and instability in the internal affairs of faculty unions.

Student governments or other student organizations are likely to develop a form of bilateral bargaining with administrators to protect their interests. It would be a serious mistake to give these arrangements formal status in law and thereby encourage the growth of formal student representation in negotiations.

Administrative Issues

Collective bargaining by faculty is highly concentrated in large multi-institutional systems. Although conflicts arise between central administrations and the state agencies that usually control the bargaining, the greatest concern with the results of bargaining is found internally in its effects on the relations between central and campus administrations. Although a good deal of coordination and consultation between the central offices and the separate campuses is typical, local administrations feel that bargaining has contributed to a shift of authority and initiative in a wide variety of matters to the central administrations of the systems. Bargaining by system headquarters is a powerful reinforcement of the existing tendencies toward centralization and exerts pressure toward a uniform policy on issues covered. In order to maintain campus diversity and independence, experiments with two-tier bargaining—with local administrators and unions bargaining on a noneconomic basis—ought to be encouraged.

The three issues arising out of internal administrative problems are unions of graduate students, unions of middle management, and the agency shop issue. In institutions with substantial graduate programs, the question of dealing with graduate student unions may arise, whether or not the faculties unionize. Where there are unions of faculty on campus, the question of whether the organized students and faculty should be in separate unions or combined arises. Their inclusion in the same bargaining units is undesirable because of differences in bargaining agenda, and in many cases employed students and faculty have an employer-employee relationship.

The question of middle management unions raises some of the same issues, but the more important question is one of the managerial role. The university may well evolve into a collection of organized groups facing a shrinking cadre of top management across the bargaining table. This problem may be insoluble without support from legislation limiting rights of supervisors in the bargaining process.

Finally, there is the question of the agency shop, requiring the compulsory payment of a service fee to the union. The principal problem is the relation of tenure and academic freedom to the agency shop when the payment of the service fee is made a condition of employment. University administrators will probably adopt the most common employer strategy on this issue, that of waiting for the union to achieve high levels (75 percent or more) of voluntary membership before granting the union or agency shop.

Financial Resources

The Costs of Higher Education: How Much Do Colleges and Universities
Spend per Student and How Much Should They Spend?
By Howard R. Bowen. 1980.

How much does it cost to educate students in America's colleges and universities? What
are the factors determining these costs? And how much, from the point of view of the
public interest, should it cost in the 1980s and beyond? These are the questions addressed in this study.

The scope of the study is limited to institutional costs for the education of students. It excludes costs for organized research, organized public service, auxiliary enterprises, and teaching hospitals. It also omits costs associated with the attendance of
students, costs such as personal expenses, transportation, books and supplies, and forgone
income. It would have been interesting and desirable to inquire into all these costs, but,
in view of the difficult statistical and conceptual problems, it was decided to limit the
study to the educational costs of institutions. These include the costs of instruction
and departmental research, student financial aid paid from institutional funds, student
services, and a pro rata share of academic support, institutional support, plant operation
and maintenance, and mandatory transfers.

The unit in which costs are measured is a standardized *student unit*. The number of
student units in any college or university (or in any group of institutions or in the whole
higher educational system) is the number of full-time equivalent (FTE) students weighted
according to the academic level of the students. Different weights are assigned to lower
division, upper division, graduate, and professional students, reflecting the different
educational costs for the several academic levels. As a result of the weighting procedure,
the number of student units exceeds the number of FTE students in all but the two-
year colleges.

Given the definition of a student unit, it was possible to calculate unit costs and
thus to study long-term cost trends, to compare costs among institutions or groups of
institutions, to study factors influencing cost, to study the effect of institutional differences in cost upon educational outcomes, and ultimately to reach some tentative
answers to the question of how much higher education should cost in the 1980s and
beyond.

Basic Concepts and Principles

A theme running through the entire study is that costs are determined by revenues.
Viewing the matter from the standpoint of the whole higher educational system, average
cost per student unit is determined by the amount of money society chooses to spend
relative to the mission or workload assigned to or adopted by the institutions in the
system. The amount of funding will be influenced by the prevailing concept of what
higher education should be like, by public attitudes about the importance of higher
education, and by the competition of other uses for public and private funds. These social

concepts, attitudes, and values fluctuate over time and bring about significant and in-
exorable changes in available funds, and therefore in unit costs, of higher education.
The same phenomenon, when looked at from the standpoint of a single institution, is
that unit costs are determined by the amount of money the institution can raise—relative
to its mission or workload. And the single-minded objective of virtually all institutions
is to maximize unit cost. Indeed, the success of educational leaders is often judged by
their ability to raise money from all conceivable sources so that unit cost can be as high
as possible.

As background for later discussions, four misconceptions should be considered.
First, not all costs are in the form of money payments. A balanced cash budget is not
always the hallmark of financial soundness. A hidden cost in many institutions is the
deterioration of assets when insufficient provision is made for their maintenance. Everyone is familiar with deferred maintenance of buildings and equipment, but educators and
boards are less attentive to the depreciation and obsolescence of buildings and equipment when there are inadequate reserves for replacement and to the depletion of in-
ventories. And they are sometimes even less cognizant of the decline in intangible assets
that are vastly more important in the life of a college than physical things. The intangibles include the ability to retain and recruit qualified faculty and staff, the capacity to
retain and recruit qualified students, ties to sources of appropriations and gifts, and the
ongoing internal organization of the institution with its definition of roles, its communication systems, its customs and traditions, and above all its morale. These are the stuff
of which colleges and universities are made; deferred maintenance of these intangible
assets is a cost. When it persists over time and is of significant magnitude, it is a devastating cost.

Second, another misconception is the equating of low cost with efficiency. Efficiency is properly defined as a ratio between benefits and costs. For example, efficiency
is increased when cost is cut without a proportional loss in benefits. But there is no gain
in efficiency if when cost is reduced benefits are cut more than proportionately.

Third, high cost in colleges and universities is often excused on the ground that
higher education is a "labor-intensive industry." The concept of labor intensiveness is
ambiguous and probably not very important in determining cost behavior. In any case,
higher education is not especially labor intensive.

Finally, a fourth misconception is that higher education is destined always to be
subject to increasing cost over time. Higher education shares with health care, churches,
and many other fields the characteristics of a "professional industry." Cost reduction in
such fields tends to be sluggish, but improved efficiency in them is not impossible. In
fact, higher educational costs per unit (in constant dollars) have been stable or slowly
falling over long periods of time—one such period being the 1970s. The effect of these
cost trends on educational quality or performance may, however, be adverse.

Long-Term Trends and Their Implications

An intensive investigation of unit costs over the years from 1929-30 to 1977-78 revealed
that cost per student unit (in constant dollars) declined slowly during the period 1929-30
to 1949-50 and again in the 1970s, but that it rose rapidly in the period from 1949-50
to 1969-70. The last period, often called the "golden years," was an exceptional episode in the history of American higher education. The nation recognized the need not
only to expand but also to improve the higher educational system. The decline in unit
cost over periods before and after the golden years reflected in part the dramatic ex-

pansion of the low-cost *public* sector of higher education relative to the high-cost *private* sector. The overall cost reduction was due in part to a structural change in the system. This change has been largely completed, and further cost reduction from this source is likely to be less pronounced in the future.

The stability of costs during the decades of the 1930s, 1940s, and 1970s was due also to the sluggishness in the rise of staff compensation. From 1929-30 to 1949-50, faculty and administrative compensation (in constant dollars) was about stable, increasing at the rate of only 0.29 percent a year, and from 1969-70 to 1977-78 it was also nearly stable, decreasing slowly by -0.53 percent a year. An intervening period of handsome pay raises occurred in the golden years, when the average annual increases were 3.13 percent. Except during the 1950s and 1960s, faculty and administrative compensation failed by a wide margin to keep pace with pay in the rest of the economy, though it did almost keep pace with inflation. Data on the compensation of general service staff are scarce. Such evidence as is available suggests that in 1977-78 it was below that for comparable work in private business. The flat trend in compensation during the 1970s suggests that there may be deferred maintenance of the intangible asset "ability to retain and recruit qualified faculty and staff." Though there has so far been no flight from academic employment, there are signs, if the present gap in compensation between higher education and other industries widens, that recruitment and retention of qualified people will become progressively more difficult and that educational quality will deteriorate.

Over the past two decades, substantial costs have been imposed on higher education through social pressure and governmental mandate. These are labeled "socially imposed costs." Examples are costs connected with occupational safety and health, provision for the handicapped, increasingly rigorous building codes, employee fringe benefits, collective bargaining, affirmative action, the Buckley amendment, women's athletics, environmental requirements, local contributions in lieu of taxes, demands for innumerable statistical reports, broadened participation in institutional decision making, and dozens of others. The objectives of most of these demands are laudable, but they do involve costs. Estimates of the amounts are not very reliable, but they may be as much as 7 to 8 percent of total institutional budgets. These socially imposed costs do not necessarily increase overall institutional costs by the same amount unless funding sources are willing to increase revenues accordingly. To the extent that funds are not increased, as is often alleged to be the case, then the effect is to force rearrangement of internal budgets to absorb the socially imposed costs. In that event, total unit costs do not rise, but the quality of education may suffer.

As one way of judging the position of American higher educational systems in 1979-80, an attempt was made to estimate the cost of restoring the system to the level of performance it attained in 1969-70. The year 1969-70 was a turning point between the golden years and the more austere 1970s. It marked the culmination of the undoubted advancement of American higher education during the 1950s and 1960s. Since 1969-70 the system has probably slipped in several ways: the institutions became larger and less personal; academic schedules were modified to shorten the time that students were in contact with faculty; faculty effectiveness declined in subtle ways; the percentage of students from disadvantaged backgrounds increased and colleges and universities were not able to adjust to serving simultaneously the needs of both its traditional and its newer clienteles; the proportion of part-time and nonresidential students increased, and many such students could not make full use of the traditional facilities and services that had been designed primarily for full-time residential students; and, finally, the increasing vocational interests of students combined with the market orientation of institutions led to the weakening of the liberal ideal in higher education and to lowering of academic standards. The decline in quality or performance was not intentional, it was not due to neglect, and it was not the result of bad management; rather it was due to the inability of the higher educational system to adjust in a mere decade or two to the unprecedented responsibilities flowing from the vastly increased number and diversity of students. Though money alone would not automatically restore the higher educational system to the level of performance it achieved in the critical year 1969-70, additional funds would be necessary. The estimated increase in funds needed in 1979-80 merely to restore the 1969-70 level of staff, salaries, and maintenance would be of the order of $4 billion, an increase of about 10 or 11 percent over the actual educational expenditures in that year. However, to make a dent in the qualitative problems, funds beyond the estimated $4 billion would be required. The evident conclusion is that in the 1980s and beyond the nation should increase the funding of higher education. One way would be to convert any quantitative savings from declining enrollments into qualitative improvement of education.

Cost Differences Among Institutions and Their Implications

When the unit costs of institutions are compared, the most significant finding is the amazing differences in total cost of education per student unit. Some of the differences can of course be attributed to statistical anomalies and to subtle differences that are not recognized in the classifications of institutions. Yet, no matter how much care goes into the statistics and into the classifications, substantial cost differences persist. The facts can be explained only by the revenue theory of cost, namely, that institutions raise all the money they can and spend it all. The differences among institutions in the way they allocate their resources internally are also remarkable. On the basis of the data, one is hard put to identify a pattern of allocation that could be called normal.

One of the purposes of this study was to compare patterns of expenditure of more affluent and less affluent institutions. It was hoped to gain some insights into cost requirements by learning what more affluent institutions can afford that less affluent institutions must do without. The results were less than those hoped for because of the wide variance among institutions in the internal allocation of funds and the resulting low correlations between institutional affluence and allocations to various purposes. Nevertheless, by comparing the expenditure patterns of the least affluent quintile of institutions with the most affluent quintile, some interesting conclusions emerge. On the average, well-to-do institutions spend more for everything than financially poor institutions, but on a percentage basis they spend less on direct instruction and physical plant and more on student financial aid, nonacademic staff, and goods and services purchased from outside vendors, and they accumulate more endowment. The obvious implication is that colleges and universities, like families, spend more on nonessentials as they become more affluent. This is known as raising the standard of living.

Another approach to the effects of affluence was an inquiry into the relationship of affluence to outcomes. Do rich institutions produce greater educational results than financially poor institutions and, if so, how much greater? Data on educational outcomes for individual institutions are extremely scarce and difficult to interpret, so this investigation was far from definitive. However, as a result of the generous cooperation of several scholars and institutions, it was possible to correlate or compare costs per student unit with various outcome indicators. The correlations were in some cases significant and positive (though not impressively high) and in other cases nonexistent. The conclusion from this exercise was that the relationship between institutional affluence and outcomes is tenuous and uncertain. Even when the correlations were significant and positive, regression analysis suggested that the impact of affluence on outcomes was very small. For example, a doubling of expenditures per student unit would in most instances yield only a 5 to 15 percent increase in indexes of outcomes. In any event, the variance among institutions was so great that at any level of outcomes there would be institutions with vastly different expenditures per student. The conclusion, on the basis of incomplete evidence, was that unit cost and outcomes are not closely related and that there are many factors other than money that determine institutional outcomes.

The relationship between institutional size and cost has been frequently studied, usually with ambiguous results. This matter was investigated again in the present study with what may be more definitive conclusions. It is clear from most previous studies as well as the present one that there is no significant relationship between size and unit cost except possibly that costs tend to be high in tiny institutions of a few hundred students (though in my judgment, even this finding is questionable). The reason for the lack of correlation between size and cost is that cost is determined by the amount of money institutions can raise. If they achieve economies of scale, they simply spend the savings through internal reallocations and overall costs are not reduced. But at the same time it is abundantly clear that particular unit costs of institutions decline with increasing size. This is true for the simple reason that many facilities and services can only be acquired in large increments, and that they can be used more intensively in a large institution than in a small one. Examples of such facilities are pipe organs, rare books, electron microscopes, computers, professors of exotic specialties, and many others. When institutional size grows, the pipe organ can be used by more students and cost per unit declines. But the saving will not show up as a reduction in overall cost per unit unless revenues decline by a corresponding amount. In considering the relation of size and cost, it is essential to think of diseconomies of scale as well as economies of scale. The diseconomies are mainly in the form of adverse effects on educational quality. That the diseconomies tend to be intangible does not necessarily render them less significant than economies of scale.

What Should Higher Education Cost?

The variance among institutions with respect to cost and resource allocation was found to be so great and the relationship between cost and outcomes so tenuous that the study of institutions did not yield much guidance on the question of what higher education should cost. The variance, however, seemed much wider than it should be—particularly the variance on the low side of the median. It was judged that perhaps one-third of all institutions in the United States—public as well as private, large as well as small—are operating with less money than is needed for a minimally adequate education. The cost of bringing them up to a minimal standard was estimated to be on the order of $3 billion.

In connection with the longitudinal study of costs, it has been estimated that to bring the whole higher educational system in 1979-80 up to the level of performance it achieved in 1969-70 would cost about $4 billion. Adding to this an amount for overall qualitative improvement plus the $3 billion needed to raise the less affluent institutions to a minimal level would make the total 1979-80 deficit as much as $10 billion, an amount equal to perhaps 25 percent of actual educational expenditures.

The argument that higher education needs more money because it has slipped in quality over the decade of the 1970s and because the least affluent third of the institutions have less money than they need to reach a minimal standard may well be dismissed as useless in the 1980s. The competition for public and philanthropic funds may be so keen that higher education will do well to keep up with inflation, let alone receive a 25 percent increase in constant dollar funds. However, American higher education may be facing a decline in enrollments in the 1980s. It is possible that any savings from this source could be redirected from provision for numbers to improvement of quality.

But it would be improper to couch the conclusions of this study solely in terms of financial needs. By far the most significant finding is that the relationship between cost and educational outcomes is tenuous. The correlations are low and the regression functions indicate that increments of money yield relatively small increases in outcomes. Furthermore, institutions with about the same financial resources apparently produce quite different educational results. So it must be evident that there is more to excellence in education than money and that it behooves institutions to learn to be more efficient in converting resources into educational benefits.

Foundations and Higher Education: Grant Making from Golden Years Through Steady State. By Earl F. Cheit and Theodore E. Lobman. 1980.

The Diminishing Influence of Private Foundations

Foundations are among the shapers of American higher education. Their initiatives have pioneered in the area of educational opportunity for blacks; have produced standards for courses, credit, and admissions; have developed and implemented the concept of faculty pension funds; and have been highly influential in the development of student financial aid, libraries, and adult education. Foundations conceived of the educational experiment, and foundation-supported experiments have yielded such educational developments as honors courses and international exchanges. By providing small-scale support for new ideas, foundations have promoted change. They have nourished research universities in their infancy. Entirely new, full-status disciplines, including anthropology and micro-biology, have evolved from foundation grants. Foundations have helped enable academics to escape from subservience to patronage; until the foundation grants of the 1920s, the only faculty members who could pursue research were independently wealthy.

These accomplishments are particularly remarkable in view of the relatively small sums that have been involved. But these small sums produced leverage that resulted in educational effects of disproportionate size.

Despite this illustrious background, today's foundations are not confident about their current role. In the past few years, several large foundations have completed extensive reviews of their programs, reconsidering their roles not only in education but in all fields. Where higher education is concerned, reassessment yields three major questions:

1.   What are foundations doing in higher education now?
2.   Where does higher education grant making seem to be heading?
3.   Can foundations have an important role in higher education in the future?

Critics disagree over whether decline in foundation influence is due to limited resources, limited vision, changed circumstances, competition from other fields, or some combination of these factors, but the decline is not disputed. The declining real value of the foundations' incomes, combined with exceptional cost inflation in higher education, has dramatically intensified competition for grants and put great pressure on foundation leaders concerned with the effectiveness of their diminishing contributions. The former vacuum is now crowded with institutions, achievements, and expectations, many of which are the product of public expenditures that dwarf the foundation contribution.

Government-supported foundations are of growing importance in higher education. Through a variety of support mechanisms, including four major government foundations —the National Science Foundation, the Fund for the Improvement of Postsecondary Education, the National Endowment for the Arts, and the National Endowment for the Humanities—the government is allegedly doing most of the things foundation grants once did, and more.

When foundations are analyzed today, the main issue is not whether they give leadership to higher education, but what important role, if any, they can play in the future.

Conflicting Criticisms of Foundations

The influence of foundations on higher education has been criticized on various contradictory grounds. The most frequent criticism is that foundations play it safe, that they are unwilling to make risky or even innovative grants. Yet college presidents are increasingly critical of foundations for their alleged infatuation with innovation and their failure to support what is proven and good. Such inconsistencies arise because information about foundations is limited, and there has been a very small comparative base for judgment.

Many more foundations now exist than before World War II, and it is far more difficult to keep track of their activities. Grant-making activities are to higher education what theoretical research is to the solution of practical problems: their contribution to higher education is unpredictable before the fact and undecipherable until long after. Foundation expenditures are not only smaller in relative terms; they are also more diffuse—almost camouflaged in the large-scale dynamics of higher education. Finally, the foundation tradition of privateness has hindered efforts to persuade many foundations to write more about themselves. In order to study current activities of foundations, one must rely on the grant descriptions in annual reports, which actually reflect aspirations, not effects. One can find out about general areas where foundations are making grants, but rarely what they are actually accomplishing.

The Grant Classification System

From time to time we read accounts of grants made by private philanthropic foundations to restore a local campus building, to add a new course to the curriculum of a nearby college, to enable faculty members at the university to do research, or to give general support to a higher education association in Washington, D.C. These are typical of the various kinds of grants foundations make for higher education purposes.

If we look behind the immediate objective of these grants to their underlying purpose, we see that the grant to restore a building helps *sustain* the college to continue doing what it has been doing. The grant to add a new course to the curriculum helps to *develop* the institution—to change it or help it do something new. A research grant *employs* the resources of the university; whereas a grant to a higher education association is one whose purpose is the *general strengthening* of higher education. These four categories—(1) sustaining, (2) developing, (3) employing, and (4) general strengthening— form the basis of the classification system used in this study.

The Foundations Studied

The United States has more than 28,000 grant-making foundations. The total number of foundations making grants for higher education, though obviously fewer than 28,000, is too great to permit studying them individually. Thus, our first task was to select an appropriate sample of foundations and apply our classification system to their grant-making activities.

Our aim was to analyze the experience of three kinds of grant-making foundations —community, corporate, and those usually referred to as "general purpose" foundations. Operating foundations were excluded. Two of these three categories reflect the foundations' source of funds, which in turn influences their work. Community foundations are created by many donors, and corporate foundations by business firms. General purpose foundations are usually created by individuals or families.

Because "general purpose" is such an important category, we sought to have the study sample include foundations of different sizes to determine the differences in grant making, if any, due to this characteristic. Although it is customary to refer to large, medium, and small foundations, there are no established definitions of these categories. The sample includes general purpose foundations with total grants in a range from less than $500,000 to more than $220 million.

The study sample includes a good representation of large foundations and of their interests, particularly in research. Because the sample is dominated by large foundations, much of the analysis applies only to that special group. It is this group, however, that is in the position to offer leadership to other foundations.

Compared with other summaries of foundation giving, these data are unique in two ways. First, unlike other sources, all grants affecting higher education are included in the analysis. Second, the data are unique in that they quantify foundation attention to certain issues as well as to conventional purposes, such as endowment, buildings, student aid, and research.

Purposes and Recipients of Grants

Development grants to institutions of higher education account for 37.3 percent of the total sample expenditures in 1974. Grants for the employment of individual institutions for research and public services and grants for general strengthening activities that affect more than one campus each accounted for about one-quarter of all grants made by the sample foundations in 1974. The support provided for sustenance of existing activities on campus amounts to about 10 percent of all grants made by the sample foundations.

The allocation of foundation grants for the years 1970 and 1974 is shown in Table 1, which gives the percentage of total grants devoted to each of the four major grant types in the classification system.

Changing emphasis, 1970 to 1974. Between 1970 and 1974, foundations moved from support of research toward support of development. Although total foundation grants for higher education in the sample were larger in 1974 than in 1970, the funds available for research and public service—employment, under our classification—dropped by almost $14 million. The dollar value of grants for employment declined from 31.6 percent to 25.3 percent of total foundation grants. At the same time, development grants increased from $67 million to about $88 million, or from 28.9 to 37.3 percent.

The other overall shifts are away from general strengthening and toward sustenance. The proportion of the sample total for sustenance rose slightly in the four-year period,

Table 1. Distribution of grants among grant types, 1970 and 1974

Grant type	Amount (thousands)		Percentage of total dollars		Average grant size (thousands)	
	1970	*1974*	*1970*	*1974*	*1970*	*1974*
Sustenance	$20,916	$ 24,113	9.0%	10.2%	$ 78	$ 50
Development	67,092	88,196	28.9	37.3	149	125
Employment	73,482	59,759	31.6	25.3	137	108
General strengthening	70,832	64,239	30.5	27.2	164	121
Total	$232,321	$236,308	100.0%	100.0%		
AVERAGE, ALL TYPES					$138	$104

Note: Columns may not always add exactly to totals because of rounding.

while the proportion for general strengthening fell slightly. The distribution of sustenance grants is fairly similar for the two years studied; about 75 percent go for current operations, plant, and equipment. The remainder are shared by a variety of sustenance purposes. The importance of the development grants is revealed by their average size—$125,000 in 1974. In contrast, sustenance grants average less than one-half that amount. The changes in grant making between 1970 and 1974 are substantial, but our data do not tell whether this is a one-time shift or part of a continuing trend.

The average size for all four types of grants dropped considerably between 1970 and 1974, from $138,000 to $104,000. Because these figures include authorizations, it is not possible to determine if the declining average is due to smaller yearly payments per grant or fewer years of grant life. In either case, the smaller average size suggests a policy of seeking greater budget flexibility.

These findings tend to confirm the conventional belief that foundations are attracted by something new. That development is the highest foundation priority in higher education is not surprising; but sustenance activities, at 10 percent, were somewhat larger than we expected. The most striking shift in priorities between 1970 and 1974 is the decline in employment grants—a dismaying finding for advocates of the research and public service missions of higher education.

Diversity within the trends. A close examination of the sample of grants reveals that foundation interests are highly diverse. The range of grant-making interests is remarkable, and it is important to emphasize two points. First, virtually every conceivable aspect of higher education operations has had at least some grant support from the foundations in our study sample. One may argue about the appropriate ratio of grants in one area versus another, but it is clear that foundation grants reach almost all aspects of higher education. Second, although foundation grant making did shift emphasis, as we have noted, a strong commitment was maintained to each of the four grant types.

Who Receives Foundation Grants?

Not only does foundation grant making cover virtually every aspect of higher education operations, it goes to all types of institutions. Using the classification of institutions of higher education developed by the Carnegie Commission in 1973 and other categories to analyze types of grantees in the sample, it was possible to determine how successful different types of institutions are in attracting grants.

Research universities have a special claim on higher education grants. Among the types of grantees examined in our study, research universities received more than one-third of the total grants. Next in importance is the unclassified category of colleges—mostly foreign institutions—followed by liberal arts colleges, with 12 percent for "highly selective" and "other" combined. Grants in the two categories of organizations other than colleges and universities totalled more than 10 percent in 1974, while foundation-administered higher education activities accounted for 1.5 percent of the grants in the sample.

The striking decline in employment grants noted earlier is revealed in a marked decline in support for research universities—from 48 to 37 percent between 1970 and 1974. Most other types of colleges gained at the expense of the research universities.

Public versus private institutions. The majority of foundation grants for higher education go to private institutions—twice the amount that is granted to public institutions. Despite other changes in grant making, this two-to-one ratio remained about the same from 1970 to 1974.

The patterns of grant making to public and private institutions are quite different. Not surprisingly, the public institutions receive very little sustenance; this is probably assumed to be the state's responsibility. As was the case for the entire sample, development support increased at the expense of employment for both public and private grantees. Compared with private schools, a much larger share of foundation support of public institutions went for employment. This is because the support for public institutions is even more concentrated at research universities than it is for private institutions; there are very few public liberal arts colleges.

Foundation funding of research institutions favors the private universities by a wide margin. Much of the difference is in sustenance, of which the foundations provide very little to public institutions. Private research universities also receive more than twice as much development money as public universities. And most significant for those concerned specifically with research, foundation employment for private research institutions exceeded that for public research institutions by about 50 percent in 1974, although the difference narrowed considerably from 1970.

Support for different academic disciplines. When grants are classified by academic discipline, a very uneven picture emerges. Contrary to popular belief, grants for the humanities exceeded those for the social sciences, and humanities grants increased fourfold between the two sample years. However, because smaller and family foundations are underrepresented in our sample, foundation interest in the humanities may be overstated. Grants for the social sciences were relatively low compared with other areas. The life and physical sciences received the most funding among those grants in our sample that could be identified with a single area; the professions were a close second.

Support for research. People concerned about the research mission of higher education will find little to cheer in these data. As we have already seen, research funding declined between 1970 and 1974. The reduction in research funding resulted in a large decline in support for research universities, over 40 percent of whose support is for employment purposes (it was over 50 percent in 1970). This decline in research funding by the foundations we studied appears to be a conscious policy choice—not an accidental result of the period chosen for study—although the reasons are not entirely clear.

Within the research category, applied activities attracted twice the support given basic research. This stands in marked contrast to 1970, when basic research accounted for under half of research funding. Between 1970 and 1974, changing grant-making policies most affected (1) research universities among all institutions, (2) research funding among all grant purposes, and (3) basic research among all research missions. The combined effect on the research universities is considerable.

Special Characteristics of Grantees and Grants

The commitment of foundations to institutions that serve a special group of students is modest. About 10 percent of the grants in the sample went to institutions serving specific groups in the population, and this proportion increased only slightly between 1970 and 1974. In 1974, black institutions received the major share of the expenditures for these institutions.

A growing number of foundation grants were designated for several specific higher education concerns. The largest amount went to increasing access to higher education, but a number of grants supported nontraditional education, particularly higher education in nontraditional locations. Grants for the creation of nontraditional alternatives on existing campuses, however, declined between 1970 and 1974, although the amounts for nontraditional students and nontraditional locations increased.

The support for interdisciplinary activities, primarily in curriculum, declined during the period. Foundations paid little attention to the problems that institutions face in accommodating reduced rates of growth (or no growth). Only one grant in 1974 dealt explicitly with the problem of institutional contraction.

Different Types of Foundations

Grant making differs markedly by type of foundation. General purpose foundations give low priority to sustenance activities, high priority to development, with remaining priorities divided equally between employment and general strengthening of higher education. Corporate foundations accord lower priority to employment and give far more to sustenance. Community foundations give the highest proportion of sustenance grants and the lowest of general strengthening grants. This is largely because much of community-foundation higher education expenditures are nondiscretionary bequests in the form of relatively unrestricted aid for specified campuses in the community.

Thus we see several patterns of foundation grant-making policy: General purpose foundations have a strong preference for development grants; community foundations favor both development and sustenance grants; and corporate foundations favor general strengthening of higher education. However, individual foundations within each of these categories do not necessarily follow the overall pattern. When individual general purpose foundations are analyzed, for example, sharp variations in policy are found, even within the limited area of higher education. Whatever the differences among foundations, the grant policies of individual foundations seem generally stable. The relative share of each grant type was about the same in each of the two years studied.

Foundation Reports

Only 14 percent of the 2,818 foundations listed in the 1977 *Foundation Directory* published annual reports, and 26 percent of these are either community or company-sponsored foundations. In analyzing the annual reports considered for use in this study, we learned that their flaws are similar to those of corporate annual reports: the poor ones are vague, inflated, self-congratulatory, and incomplete. We prepared a checklist of 22 kinds of information that would be included in a good annual report, listed under five headings: (1) identification of grantee; (2) amount and form of payment; (3) statement of grant purposes, intended activities, and expected outcomes; (4) general statement of the foundation's policies; and (5) the usefulness of the annual report format.

Each of the higher education sections of the 1974 annual reports in the study was tested for the elements in our checklist. Inasmuch as these reports had already been screened for usefulness in our study, it should be clear that our ratings pertain to some of the best reports available, not a random selection. The bottom of our list would rank near the top of the total foundation sector.

Reports that contained 17 or more of the items on the checklist (or 16, with "outstanding" in one of them) were ranked "excellent." Those in the 12 to 16 range were ranked "good," and the remaining reports, whose scores were 8 to 11, were ranked "fair." Most of the foundations in the sample met at least 16 of the 22 criteria, with about a quarter ranking as excellent. Even relative to our select group, however, about a quarter ranked only as fair.

What Are Foundations Doing in Higher Education?

The dominant characteristic of foundation grants to higher education is the wide range of interests they reflect. Almost every conceivable aspect of higher education receives some attention in grant making. While diversity is evident, a single "foundation agenda" in higher education is not. There is a foundation sector, unified by its fairly homogeneous group of decision makers, a shared approach to problems, and a loosely defined network of individuals and information on which many foundations draw to make decisions. But the great number and geographical dispersion of foundations—together with a deep tradition of privateness, independent action, and to some extent, competition—guarantee diversity among them and make generalizations about their overall policies or effects hazardous.

Among the great variety of items that interest foundations, development, that is, the improvement of institutions by change, is the most important. This warrants the inference that the tradition of supporting innovation, which was established in the early part of this century, is being observed by the majority of the foundations in our sample.

Short-term, project-based seed money dominates the foundation approach to higher education. For many years now, foundations have recognized the decline of their dollar importance to higher education and have apparently sought to compensate for this diminishing leverage—hence the continued interest in seed money. Because foundations show a preference for innovation and for ideas that can be replicated elsewhere, they also incline toward the support of projects that have a relatively short life span and that presumably have the ability to command operating funds after the startup period if they are successful. In short, they want their budgets to have as much annual flexibility as possible.

Where Is Higher Education Grant Making Headed?

From our grant data, our study of reports, and our less systematic observation of foundations in the years since 1974, we would cite three trends in higher education grant making.

1.   *Higher education an important but declining priority*. Although higher education remains an important priority for the foundation sector, support has not kept pace with inflation and, as a result, total foundation grants are a declining share of total higher education expenditures. Our sample data show a decline in real terms in

the 1974 grants compared with 1970. For our sample of foundations, the ratio of higher education grants to total grants declined from over 50 percent in 1970 to under 40 percent in 1974.

The reasons for this decline in foundation concern for higher education are not obvious. Of course, competition for grants is keener because demands on foundations are growing from many sources. But a more subtle reason may be the transitional state of higher education and the lack of clarity about a foundation role. In the late 1960s, foundations responded to proposals that promised major reform and lasting benefit if only startup costs could be covered. The yield was thin. Faced with this disappointment, foundation officers were not encouraged to do more.

2. *Trying to do more with less.* With their leverage weakened and with public funds dominating a much larger higher education field, foundations have difficulty responding to new conditions faced by higher education. Their skill in finding ways to do more with less will be put to a severe test.

One way foundations have sought to do more with less is in helping institutions broaden their base of support for programs. Some foundations are trying to involve corporations, because corporations are generally more disposed than many foundations to make grants for sustenance. Another obvious way to do more with less is through joint action, thereby bringing more funds to bear on particular problems.

The once highly regarded demonstration project has lost its cachet. Most foundations seem to feel that, if money is to be spent, the project must do more than simply demonstrate what can be done. Project designers are asked to show not only whether success can be shared but also how it can be shared.

Another way to do more with less is to influence federal policy. Foundations in 1979 feel freer of governmental threat than at any time in the past decade. Foundation leaders emphasize their freedom, and it seems likely they will use it to examine government policies. They have certainly done so in the case of higher education policy. The most significant analyses and criticisms of government activities in this field have been foundation supported.

Along with the tendency of foundations to make smaller grants, there is a contrasting tendency to "wholesale" grants—to make large grants to other agencies that will redistribute them. This helps keep foundations' operating costs down and enables them to reach more institutions and avoid difficult (often political) decisions. There is increased grant making to so-called umbrella organizations (associations working with several institutions at one time) in an effort to spread the value of grants over more organizations. There is also more effort to evaluate and disseminate results. While evaluation is not yet a highly developed field, more of it is being done.

3. *Increasing professionalism and bureaucracy in grant making.* Among the professionally managed foundations, there are important signs of far greater sensitivity in grant making, reflecting the new conditions in both higher education and foundations. Nor only are foundation officers concerned about identifying the foundation role; many are also sharing those concerns with the public and with potential grantees.

There is evidence that foundations are trying to work toward a "steady state." For example, program officers tell us they usually require applicants to demonstrate how pilot projects, if successful, can be funded in the long term. Financial condition is rarely taken for granted in proposal reviews.

Professionalism and the desire to be responsive also invite bureaucracy. Foundations wanting a fair and comprehensive program must rely on more documentation, outside advisory committees, and in some cases more extensive internal evaluations. This inevitably adds formality to the decision process, which, paradoxically, can reduce responsiveness. Finally, professionalism may imply less money for unusual ideas: reliance on networks of expert information rather than on instinct probably increases the conventionality of approved requests.

Can Foundations Play an Important Role in the Future of Higher Education?

If foundations are to have an important future role, they must take several steps:

- *Developing a strategy.* A program strategy has many advantages for both foundation and grant seeker. It provides a reference for internal consistency; it gives both foundation staff and board a reference for evaluating impact. A strategy sets goals and provides for a longer-term commitment to them, if evaluation shows it is warranted. The development of a strategy also requires continuing review and evaluation of grants to determine the effectiveness of individual choices and to reassess the utility of the strategy.

- *Encouraging and strengthening inner direction.* The internal sense of direction and priorities of many institutions has become unclear or hard to articulate. Inner direction is needed today, when market and patron forces are ascending and shaping institutions. The federal policy of funding students (but not institutions) has accelerated the growing strength of market forces, while newer forms of federal and state regulation have increased patron control. Neither federal nor state policy offers comparable strength to inner direction.

  All but a few favored colleges and universities are trying to respond to increased market and patron forces while trying to assert appropriate inner direction. Foundations can be helpful in this process—not as a bulwark against market and patron forces, but to facilitate the development of a coherent curriculum and a sense of institutional priorities.

  Institutions need help providing leadership to make themselves qualitatively strong at times of reduced quantitative growth. That help could be expected from academic research. But thus far colleges and universities have been better at discovering and teaching methods of decision making than in applying them to their own circumstances.

- *Selectivity and recognizing superior achievement.* The major goals of government involvement in higher education are to insure access and equality of opportunity. Private philanthropic funds have been (and can be) directed much more selectively at qualitative goals rather than at access and equality. Government foundations today, especially the Fund for Improvement of Postsecondary Education, are pressured to make grants to all parts of the country and all types of endeavors. Private philanthropic foundations do not face the same intensity of pressures and can again be more selective.

  The goal of advancing superior achievement in all academic areas can provide support for students who have moved through special opportunity programs and are now ready for advanced training. This is an example of an area in which foundations are now active. There are opportunities for grants for merit in community colleges as well as in research universities, in public institutions as well as private, in student aid as well as in research.

Several factors support the view that foundations can play an important role in the future of higher education.

- *Public funds insufficient.* It is unlikely that public funds could perform all of the functions now being performed by private funds. Among these functions are those best handled by foundations: maintenance of institutional flexibility, diversity, and autonomy; serving as an outside aid, critic, and stimulator of government itself; providing some stability in response to shifting government policy; rewarding merit; providing excellence in public institutions; and providing leverage in raising additional funds through broader citizen support.
- *Foundation funds are growing.* One main consequence of the so-called tax rebellion is a reduction in funds available for higher education. This is reflected in a reduced growth rate rather than an absolute reduction, but funds are no longer keeping pace with the consumer price index and thus represent an absolute reduction in real support. At the same time, foundation funds, particularly those of corporate and community foundations, are growing. While the rate of foundation growth is not enough to change the overall size of the foundation functions in higher education, it is probably enough to stabilize them, if foundations elect to do so.

  Another hopeful sign is the likely probating of major industrial fortunes made during and after World War II. If the federal tax provisions avoid greater disincentive to create such foundations, higher education and the nonprofit sector as a whole can look forward to new sources of support.

  Corporate philanthropy is also a growth area. The growth of corporate profits, greater pressure from major corporate leaders to increase giving, and the growing perception by corporations of the need for a social policy can be expected to improve both the size and thoughtfulness of corporate giving in the future.
- *Institutions the main concern of foundations.* Institutional health—vitality and the ability to meet goals—is not the top priority of federal funds for higher education. Federal programs serve important public purposes of student access and opportunity and, to a lesser extent, institutional research capacity and various forms of specific public service. Institutional welfare, however, is generally assumed to be a by-product or the responsibility of the states. The states assume primary responsibility for planning and funding colleges and universities, but they do so in the interest of a variety of state goals, not primarily for institutional health.

  Foundations have by no means made institutions their only priority, but institutional health is clearly a higher foundation priority than it is with any other organized funder. At a time of increased pressure, complexity, and control, that foundation role is more important today than ever.
- *Higher education remains important.* A final reason for predicting an important higher education role for foundations is the continued importance of higher education itself. The long-term outlook for higher education is one of stability and continued importance to the nation. The growing complexity and interdependence of all of society's institutions will focus attention on the importance of higher education, and it will again become that classic object of foundation interest, a target of opportunity.

The Venture Capital of Higher Education: The Private and Public Sources of Discretionary Funds. By Martin Kramer. 1980.

Until well into this century, American higher education depended for its support primarily on gifts, endowments, tuition, and fees. It was a diverse system of support, reflecting the distinct educational premises of many different groups and individual founders. The institutions of the system, public as well as private, exercised and valued a remarkable degree of autonomy—from governments, from peer institutions, and from parents and students. They were free to respond with their own programs to new goals and problems.

The role of private support declined in the 1950s and 1960s, but American higher education did not lose those desirable characteristics that private support had fostered. What seems to have happened is that the rapid growth of the system in these decades had two effects that cancelled each other out. On the one hand, the financial role of government increased greatly, causing a relative decline in the private role. On the other hand, the expansion of the system proceeded so rapidly that public funds "behaved" more like private funds than before or since those years, thus aiding institutional autonomy.

The Postponed Crisis

The end of the era of growth in the 1970s changed this state of affairs. By itself, the end of growth meant an end to autonomy in allocating slack funds, since there tended to be few such funds or none. In addition, rapid inflation meant that the money the legislature appropriated for the coming year would almost certainly be too little, and could hardly ever be too much. Formulas began to hurt rather than help. Real overhead costs increased as the requirements of facility maintenance, central services, and administration caught up with the greater scale of expanded institutions; and new faculty positions were increasingly unavailable to adjust the size of departments to match relative enrollments.

The end of the era of growth has thus left us with a situation in which private resources cover a smaller proportion of total institutional outlays than they did before the era began. Concurrently, public funds have become much more important and have lost, or are rapidly losing, much of the flexibility they had while growth was occurring. Accordingly, it is now, and not during the period of rapid growth, that the diversity, autonomy, and adaptability of the system may diminish, and now that steps need to be taken to preserve these distinctive qualities of the American system.

The creative health of institutions. The topic of this essay is finance, but the concern is not so much with the financial health as with the creative health of institutions; it is with the margin of financing that makes possible robust health over and above sheer survival. Such a margin has usually been provided by private funds and by public funds used on similar terms.

Public and private institutions have different tasks in securing their creative health. The survival of public institutions is seldom threatened, even in bad times, but they need to find resources—either private funds or public funds usable as though they were private—that will allow them to adapt, take risks, and give operational expression to autonomously developed ideas about what they should strive to accomplish. Otherwise they run the risk of becoming publicly owned utilities, unable to make the creative contribution that society expects of them. Private institutions, on the other hand, are finding that the costs of survival are preempting more and more of the private resources on which they depend.

The urgency of new financial resources. The present situation must be regarded as extremely serious. The net constant dollar return on endowment funds has fallen precipitously because of inflation and the no-win securities markets of the 1970s. And marginal costs are rising. If colleges and universities survive the drop in enrollments that is in the demographic cards for the 1980s, they will typically have to spread relatively fixed costs over fewer students. Any constant level of endowment or current gifts per student will cover a smaller share of costs per student.

Another factor is the age of faculty and facilities. Older faculty cost more. Older buildings and laboratory equipment are expensive in a different sense: theirs is the cost of obsolescence. The costs of the aging of these investments will be immense, and the charge on institutions' current discretionary resources, whether through replacement or supplementation of older investments, will be more than can be sustained in any obvious way.

When inflation is eventually conquered and a survey is made of the damage it has done, college and university endowments will be among the more conspicuous disaster areas. Individuals and corporate donors who have recovered from the inflationary years will hear urgent appeals for help, and they will be genuine.

Who will be able and willing to give? Where can higher levels of discretionary resources be expected to come from? Wealthy individuals and the foundations they create will continue to be major contributors, but they are obviously affected by the same factors that have brought about the shrinkage of institutional endowments. The churches will no doubt continue to do what they can, especially when the private institutions they have sponsored are threatened. However, alumni and corporations would seem to be the main hope. They have been battered by inflation and energy prices along with everyone else, but they make their gifts mainly from approximately current earnings, which tend most nearly to keep pace with inflation and stand to benefit most immediately and directly from a revival of productivity in the economy.

Initiative and Private Resources

Until quite recently, the history of American higher education was one of increasing distance between the providers of funds and the initiators of new programs of education and scholarship. This distance has been a major factor in the evolution of a distinctive American academic style in the conduct of college and university affairs. The American academic style is most clearly represented in the kind of leadership expected of the presidents of institutions. On the one hand, they are expected to be entrepreneurs, seeking the financial and scholarly resources that will make excellence possible and organizing these resources into distinctive and effective programs of teaching and research. On the other hand, American academic leaders are expected to be protective of the institution and to buffer its values and academic assets against the damage that could be caused by an often indifferent, sometimes short-sighted, and occasionally hostile world. Academic leaders are not considered successful unless they can perform both the entrepreneurial and protective functions.

The American academic style and public funding. The American academic style has many virtues. It is extraordinarily creative. It can accept innovations and resist fads. It is highly conducive to academic freedom. It adapts well to specific circumstances, asking what can be done in a particular institution to enhance the education of its particular students and the productivity of its particular faculty. It works well with government when government offers opportunities and incentives congenial to the entrepreneurial spirit.

It is not so good, however, at adapting rapidly and smoothly when general performance standards are imposed from without, when entrepreneurial approaches are consistently impeded, or when its own deliberative organization is effectively overruled. It then responds with an exaggeration of the protective aspects of the style, and its creative and responsive qualities may become dormant or atrophy. This is exactly what has tended to happen as the consequences of greater dependence on public funds have become clearer. The traditional distance separating the providers of funds from the day-to-day conduct of academic business have begun to contract, since the purposes of public programs are increasingly incompatible with the notion of such distance.

The principle of public benefaction now seems to be that the funds themselves are the instrument of the public purpose; that is, they are intended as levers of control. If this is really the position of the public providers of funds, then the painfully won distance between the source of funding and the conduct of academic affairs is not just abbreviated; it is more or less annihilated. In that event, we can hardly expect the traditions built on the assumption of such distance to serve very well. Whether public benefaction must be on a basis so inconsistent with the American academic style remains to be seen.

Accountability to the Future

A concept basic to an understanding of how public and private support differ is accountability. Accountability for public funds is, in practice, overwhelmingly a present accountability. Governments tend to want to see the results of their expenditures right away— buildings built, utility bills paid, faculty compensated, and students supported by aid. Many of the needs addressed by government are immediate, and requiring accountability for higher education expenditures in similarly immediate terms helps to make government allocative choices more comparable. Moreover, there is an avoidance of commitments binding on successor lawmakers in present accountability, which is viewed as valuable in a democracy.

Accountability to the past is most conspicuous in endowments and dedicated funds. The purposes of such gifts can be narrow and the conditions imposed on expenditures very restrictive. For the following reasons, however, institutions seldom find their hands seriously tied:

1. The law of trusts limits the conditions a donor can impose.
2. Donors can usually be persuaded to see that flexibility will be needed in the future use of a fund.
3. Endowments for specific purposes can often give the institution discretionary funds by substituting endowment funds for the unrestricted funds the institution would have spent to achieve these purposes, freeing the unrestricted funds for other uses.
4. When an endowment imposes a new mission on an institution, it will often be a quite acceptable one, increasing the balance and scope of the institution's programs.
5. An institution can usually afford to reject an entirely inappropriate private gift without threatening its own survival.

Accountability to the future is the kind of accountability that usually characterizes alumni giving. Alumni do not expect to have a right to scrutinize current institutional outlays in detail, nor are their gifts usually conditional, although they are sometimes designated for particular purposes. But whether alumni will continue to give, and at what levels, depends on how well the institution appears to be doing.

On balance, colleges and universities probably prefer accountability to the future to either accountability to the past or accountability to the present. Next most desirable is fiduciary accountability to the past, because of the great flexibility it carries in practice. Least desirable is present accountability, because it verges on accountability for day-to-day actions and because it can be the vehicle for direct control.

If a future-oriented accountability (or an accountability to the past, which is largely indistinguishable) is a reason why some kinds of private support have been so valuable a force in shaping American higher education, then it is not privateness per se that is important. Government support can, in principle, be future-oriented. But for that to be the case, there has to be wide public understanding of the highly future-oriented goals of higher education and of the need for autonomy in the pursuit of them. What the public and legislators need to understand is not that all funds for higher education should be given to academics to be used at their absolute discretion. The point is rather that there really is an area in which academic judgments, individual and corporate, are likely to be better in the long run than the judgment of government officials, however sophisticated.

Fat Years and Lean Years

A shift in accountability for state funds toward accountability to the present has almost certainly occurred, although documenting the shift in state accountability in a rigorous way does not appear possible. Three phenomena tend to complicate an assessment of any shift in the terms of accountability:

1. *The ambiguity of formula funding.* Formula funding systems were rarely adopted initially with accountability considerations much in mind, but the idea tends to develop that the factors in the formula represent the purposes for which the funds are to be spent. Such interpretation makes a formula an obvious tool for control.
2. *The ambivalence of governance structures.* This refers to the frequent merger of executive and oversight functions in governing and coordinating boards.
3. *Informal relationships in the accountability process.* Some of the relationships that develop in the accountability process strongly favor accountability to the future, while others create an exacting accountability to the present.

The public as benefactor. In the era of growth, what would have been mere logrolling in projects to construct highways or prisons became, in the case of higher education, a gratifying opportunity for state political leaders to participate in a flowering of science and scholarship. Constituents were clearly demanding more college places, and this meant that very large outlays would have to be made. Other states were being lavish in attempting to create universities of national and international reputation; why not the legislator's own state?

What resulted were spending decisions far more like those of private donors than those of state legislators in dealing with routine state services. Absent was the demand for immediate results, other than the obvious ones of accommodating students and injecting money into local economies. Absent, too, was the demand that means be clearly justified by ends. The end of expansion inevitably altered the view state political leaders had of their relationship to institutions.

Funding mechanics, in forward and in reverse. The end of growth and the professionalization of resource allocation have affected the impersonal mechanisms regulating the flow of funds and the way these mechanisms operate. The era of growth often generated funding surpluses, in the special sense that they made funds available to institutions in excess of the outlays to which they were committed by the receipt of funding or by previous commitments. Funding formulas were mainly enrollment-driven; that is, with growing enrollments the same formula would produce a larger dollar amount each year. The recipient institution was obligated to accommodate the added students, but the typical formula did not say how they were to be accommodated or that the amount spent on each should be the full amount of the increment in funding produced. Such discretion allowed extraordinary freedom to shape the institution and its character. There was further leeway in the fact that the incremental dollar amount produced by each new enrollment was constant and was usually intended to cover average costs. The marginal cost of accommodating an additional student would almost certainly be less than average cost, since many fixed expenses would be spread over a larger number of students. Thus, average-cost formulas produced surpluses for new academic activities or services, but did so less and less as growth slowed in the 1970s.

In the era of growth, it was often not possible to provide exactly the same amount of instructional or other resources to the added students because buildings could not be built or instructors hired quickly enough. Outlays were inevitably delayed, and this temporary startup efficiency created additional surpluses. The slowing or cessation of growth put an end to surpluses generated in this way.

Making room for academic autonomy in modern government. The most refractory case of commitments levied on the present by the past is that of academic facilities. Most institutions of higher education do not account for depreciation or in any other regular way allow facilities investments to be written off. But if an orderly accounting were made for obsolescence and maladaptation, and if the public budget process provided for such depreciation, there would be funds for needed renovation and replacement. The point is that growth and creativity are not inevitably yoked together. They seem to be only because accounting and budget procedures for higher education have not developed the appropriate techniques for dealing with the distinctive nature of academic creativity.

Another fallacy is that rationality and professionalism in the allocation of public resources is inevitably the enemy of academic autonomy and creativity. Indeed, there is a need for just such qualities in developing methods of framing alternatives in budgets so that decision makers will recognize that creativity is at stake. If this could be done, formulas would no longer operate mindlessly to produce boom followed by bust, and would recognize the continuing need of institutions for resources to allocate to new ventures.

Restoring Financial Autonomy

The prospects for more private support. Continued growth in philanthropic giving to higher education depends on the likelihood of and weight assigned to a number of positive and negative trends. On the positive side, the economy could return to a path of strong growth in the 1980s. Such a benign trend would be occurring as the members of the large college classes of the 1960s reach a fairly high point in their lifetime earning trajectories, a point at which they might begin to be concerned with the quality of the higher education experiences their children will have. On the negative side, inflation could continue without much real growth. If individuals were then to feel that their own security and autonomy were threatened by economic conditions, it could be exceedingly difficult to persuade them to give more to support the security and autonomy of colleges and universities.

An agenda for the states. In the area of state action there are also positive and negative trends. On the positive side, the shrinkage of college-age cohorts now in prospect means that greatly augmented state appropriations are not inevitable and that states will have a chance to experiment with new funding devices. Part of what they save by reducing amounts in accordance with enrollment-based formulas can be allocated to project and incentive grants more consistent with institutional autonomy.

On the negative side, legislators are eager to use savings of any kind for costly programs in other areas or for taxpayer relief. It is hard to tell state legislators that funding mechanisms should be altered precisely when they start operating in favor of the state treasury rather than against it. And it is hard to expect state legislators to abandon use of the kinds of controls, increasingly subtle, that the professional budget analysts provide them for purposes that are benign and activist in intent.

A federal role. Since 1972 a political consensus has developed that federal support for higher education should primarily take the form of student aid and research grants. It can be argued that such federal assistance is, in principle, more supportive of the autonomy of colleges and universities than general institutional aid and certainly more supportive than aid based on enrollment-driven formulas. Student aid, in theory, embraces both the autonomous and service functions, since some of the costs of each are included in the tuition charges to be defrayed by student aid. Federal support for research also has great potential for supporting the autonomous functions. Indeed, it has supported them in the past, although the trend of changing accountability standards seems to be in the direction of eroding this support. The most helpful development would be for Congress explicitly to convert indirect-cost allowances into payments that include indirect costs but also include an additional percentage allowance representing a part of the costs attributable to the distinctive way in which universities provide an environment for research.

A challenge program. It is unrealistic to expect any one source of funds to take action that would restore the balance between discretionary and nondiscretionary funds. Yet all sources could be expected to do something. It perhaps makes sense, therefore, to envision the kind of action that might right the balance as somewhat in the nature of the challenge grant programs used in institutional fund raising. If alumni, corporations, and federal and state governments could each count on the other parties to do their share, each could quite properly see its own action as having leverage to correct the imbalance by an amount exceeding its separate contribution. To illustrate roughly, the following set of actions would eventually correct the imbalance of $1.5 billion projected for 1980-81:

	Discretionary funds provided (in millions of dollars)
State government. Channeling 25 percent of savings attributable to an average 10 percent enrollment decline in the 1980s into non-formula-based funding mechanisms supportive of autonomy	$400
Federal government. Funding indirect costs in research grant programs at rates 5 percentage points higher than audited costs would dictate	300
Philanthropy. Additional current funds and endowment income derived from gifts of alumni, other individuals, and corporations	800

An increase in private funding should be accompanied by an effort by public authorities to recognize the implications of the role they have created for themselves and to match the private effort. The public still wants excellence in its institutions, and it, like private donors, must accept the fact that if it wants colleges and universities to do work of excellence, considerable institutional autonomy in the use of funds is entailed. What is difficult is to persuade the parties involved that the problem is real and not an artifact of special pleading. Only then are constructive changes in the financial support of higher education likely to take place.

Purposes and Performance

Investment in Learning: The Individual and Social Value of American
Higher Education. By Howard R. Bowen with the collaboration of
Peter Clecak, Jacqueline Powers Doud, and Gordon K. Douglass. 1977.

Are our colleges and universities worth what they cost? For generations, the American
people have thought so. Recently, however, they have become more skeptical toward
higher education and other social institutions as well. Many argue that the huge and
costly enterprise of higher education is overextended, that the value of its outcomes does
not justify the amount of resources employed, and that public subsidies should be curtailed. There are insistent calls for "accountability," meaning intelligible reporting of
specific outcomes as well as formal accounting for expenditures.

Current knowledge of the consequences of higher education is substantial and is
found in a vast literature derived mainly from research and scholarship in psychology,
sociology, education, philosophy, social criticism, and economics. This volume gathers
the scattered knowledge, interprets and evaluates it, raises methodological questions,
and provides analysis where empirical data are weak, in order to judge whether American
higher education is worth what it costs and to suggest policies that may flow from the
conclusions.

Part One: The Setting

Chapter 1 describes the functions of the higher educational system, introduces the
idea of the efficiency of higher education as a ratio between outcomes produced and
resources employed, and considers methodological issues relating to the study of outcomes. Chapter 2 examines the goals or intended outcomes of higher education and
concludes with a catalog of specific goals. This catalog is regarded as a list of hypotheses
about the outcomes of higher education. The remainder of the book investigates the
degree to which each goal is in fact achieved.

Part Two: Consequences for Individuals

Part Two is concerned with the impacts of higher education on students as individuals.
These impacts are achieved not only through formal academic teaching but also through
the many extracurricular influences of colleges and universities. Chapter 3 reviews knowledge about the cognitive or intellectual development of students. Chapter 4 concerns
their emotional and moral development or affective growth. Chapters 5 and 6 review
their growth in practical competence—the development of valuable traits for citizenship,
economic productivity, family life, consumer behavior, leisure, and health. Chapter 7
surveys the impact of higher education on students regarded as whole persons and includes the views of students and alumni about the worth of their education. Chapter 8
considers the range of differences between colleges and universities in their impact
on students.

Part Three: Consequences for Society

Part Three is concerned with the direct and indirect consequences of higher education for society at large. Chapter 9 deals with the impacts upon society produced by the changes in individual students through education. Chapter 10 summarizes the societal impacts of research and public service. Chapter 11 is devoted to the impact of higher education on social equality and inequality. Chapter 12 examines the findings of economists concerning the monetary returns from investments in higher education. Chapter 13 weighs the views on college outcomes of social observers ranging from Ivan Illich to James Coleman.

Part Four: Conclusions

Outcomes as Changes in Individuals

Specific effects. The primary purpose of higher education is to change people in desirable ways. These changes may, in turn, have profound effects on the economy and the society and even on the course of history. But in the first instance, the objective is to modify the traits and behavior patterns of individual human beings. This is not to imply that higher education tries to fit every student into the same mold; rather it is a source of opportunities to which individual students will respond in different ways according to their talents, interests, and aspirations.

College education significantly raises the level of knowledge, the intellectual disposition, and the cognitive powers of its students. It produces a large increase in substantive knowledge; moderate increases in verbal skills, intellectual tolerance, esthetic sensibility, and lifelong cognitive development; and small increases in mathematical skills, rationality, and creativity. These generalizations are based primarily upon studies describing changes in students from the freshman to the senior years or comparing college-educated people with others.

College education also helps students find their personal identity and make lifetime choices congruent with this identity. It moderately increases their psychological well-being as well as their understanding, human sympathy, and tolerance toward other ethnic and national groups and toward people who hold differing opinions. It may have a small impact on refinement of taste, conduct, and manner. And it produces a moderate decrease in religious interest and observance. College increases relativism, tolerance, and flexibility in the area of personal morality. It also appears to narrow the traditional differences between the sexes: masculine traits decrease for men and increase for women; and feminine traits increase for men and decrease for women.

Higher education greatly enhances the practical competence of its students as citizens, workers, family members, and consumers. It also influences their leisure activities, their health, and their general ability to cope with life's problems. Perhaps the main influence of college on practical competence is that it helps students develop skills and traits of general applicability such as verbal facility, substantive knowledge, rational approach to problems, intellectual tolerance, future orientation, adaptability, and self-confidence.

The gains in practical competence associated with higher education may be summarized as follows: citizenship—moderate; economic productivity—moderate; family life—large; consumer behavior—small; leisure—small; and health—moderate.

Personality structure. Cutting across these specific effects of college on its students are important changes in personality structure. The most distinctive and important one is the liberation of the personality. As compared with others, college-educated people on the average are more open-minded toward new ideas, more curious, more adventurous in confronting new questions and problems, and more open to experience. They are likely to be more rational in their approach to issues. They are more aware of a diversity of opinions and outlooks, of the legitimacy of disagreement, and of the uncertain and contingent nature of truth. They are more tolerant of ambiguity and relativity, and more willing to think in terms of probabilities rather than certainties. They are less swayed by tradition and convention. They are less authoritarian, less prejudiced, and less dogmatic. At the same time, they are more independent and autonomous in their views, more self-confident, and more ready to disagree. They are more cosmopolitan. This liberation, so evident in ways of thinking and in general outlook, carries over into liberalism in religion, personal morals, and social views.

Second, researchers in the field of personality development find that students become more independent and self-sufficient during the college years. Seniors are more self-confident, assertive, and autonomous than freshmen. They are more ready to express impulses, more spontaneous, more venturesome, more self-confident, and more poised. They are less sociable, less gregarious, and less extroverted. They have less need for active and intense emotional expression and self-indulgence. They are more resourceful, organized, motivated, fully involved, and persistent. Their emotional and psychological stability increases.

Finally, college influences the values and interests of its students. They become more interested in ideas—in general education, as distinguished from specific vocational education. They become more concerned with self-expression and other intrinsic returns from careers, as distinguished from returns in the form of income and security. They develop interests in esthetic experience and awareness; in sensitivity to inner feelings and experiences; in tolerance toward persons and groups of different ethnic, religious, national, and socioeconomic backgrounds; in political and community affairs; and in the careful rearing and education of children. On the other hand, college education appears to reduce interest in formal religious observance. Its effect on altruism leading to kindness, sympathy, unselfishness, friendliness, and sociability appears to be more positive toward groups of persons in the abstract than toward fellow human beings as individuals.

The whole person. For two reasons, these average changes tend to understate the total impact of higher education. First, the changes observed for the various dimensions of cognitive, affective, and practical development obscure significant changes for individual students regarded as whole human beings. Each individual draws different consequences from college. Some gain a great deal along particular dimensions, while others lose ground or remain unchanged along the same dimensions. As a result, the average change on each dimension considered separately will tend to be small, but the change in students as whole persons may be very great as they shore up particular weaknesses, avoid those areas in which they have achieved adequate development, and pursue their particular interests. Time and energy prevents any student from achieving large gains on every single dimension. Selection is inevitable, and different students make different choices as to the dimensions on which to concentrate.

The worth of changes in individuals. What is the worth of the changes in individuals wrought by higher education? One may argue that whatever is being spent on higher education is a measure of its worth. This approach, however, begs the question because the purpose of the present study is to judge whether the American people are spending too much, too little, or the right amount for higher education. Nevertheless, that the American people devote $85 billion of resources each year to higher education is some evidence that they value it highly.

A second approach is to find out the reactions of the clients to their own college education. Numerous studies conducted over many years have consistently shown that two-thirds or more of students and alumni hold favorable attitudes toward their college educations—toward the academic programs to which they were exposed or toward their overall college experience, including the direct satisfactions associated with attendance.

A third approach is to consider the possible increases in the capital value of human beings resulting from higher education. These estimates can only be rough guesses, but they may give some idea of orders of magnitude. Without going into detail, we may reasonably estimate the value of a college-age person at $400,000 to $700,000 in 1977 dollars. Given this value, assume that through higher education students achieve a 10 percent overall "improvement" in the realization of their human potentialities and in their capacities as workers, citizens, family members, and consumers. This improvement would be over and above any improvement achieved by comparable persons who did not attend college. The addition to their value would then be 10 percent of $400,000 to $700,000, or $40,000 to $70,000. This amount would equal or exceed the cost per student of four years of higher education, which is about $40,000 (including institutional costs plus forgone income and incidental costs borne by students).

A fourth approach to estimating the value of college education is to draw upon the findings of Denison regarding the sources of the growth in U.S. national income over the period 1929-1969.* Denison estimated how much potential annual national income grew over this period and also estimated what percent of this growth was due to education. A rough estimate is that the national income in 1969 ascribable to higher education would be approximately $20 billion, while over the same time period the average annual cost of higher education, including institutional instructional costs, forgone income, and incidental expenses, was about $11 or $12 billion. On this basis, the instructional activities of higher education have handsomely paid their way in the past.

A fifth approach is to estimate the "rate of return" on investments in higher education. The investments are the sum of the costs of operating colleges and universities, the forgone income of students, and the incidental costs of college attendance. The return consists of the stream of increased earnings enjoyed by students as a result of attending college. The rate of return is the annual increment in earnings as a percentage of the investment after allowance for depreciation of the investment. The great majority of estimates have been of the order of 8 to 15 percent. This percentage is in the same range as the rate of return on investments in physical capital with comparable degrees of risk. If investments in higher education produce rates of return comparable to those derived from physical assets, when the return includes only money earnings, then the total returns on higher education, including all the nonmonetary benefits, must be substantially higher than those earned by physical capital.

The clear inference from these exceedingly rough estimates is that higher education probably pays off in monetary returns alone and that the many nonmonetary returns are a handsome bonus that makes higher education a high-return industry. However, the calculations of monetary returns must be taken with reservations. They are only rough

*Denison, E. F. *Accounting for United States Economic Growth, 1929-1969.* Washington, D.C.: Brookings Institution, 1974.

guesses based on inadequate data, heroic assumptions, and past experience that may not be duplicated in the future.

Consumer satisfactions. Higher education is, in part, a consumer good that may be valued for its own sake. The experience of attending college is rewarding for many students. Most alumni report that they gained lasting personal benefits from college. Considering that four years of college are about 5 percent of an average lifetime, its contributions to the quality of life are far from trivial.

Outcomes As Changes in Society

One effect of higher education upon society is exerted through the change it produces in its students, who eventually become members of society. When well-educated, cultivated persons are received into society, their presence will almost inevitably modify the general social environment. They may influence the prevailing patterns of interests, values, attitudes, and behavior. This may happen even if the educated persons are passive toward others and intend no influence over them. But if the educated persons take on professional and leadership roles, as they are likely to do, the influence may be magnified.

A second effect of higher education on society is achieved through research and public service. Basic research in the natural sciences as conducted in higher education produces a high return on the investment. Its return alone probably compensates for the expenditures on all research and public service activities. Research in the social studies and related disciplines fosters new social perspectives, provides the data to monitor the performance of our society, and has many applications to practical decision making in both public and private affairs. It also provides knowledge of value for its own sake.

The varied activities of colleges and universities in the areas of scholarship, philosophical and religious inquiry, social criticism, public policy analysis, and cultivation of the fine arts are all enormously valuable in preserving the cultural heritage and advancing civilization—but there is no way of placing dollar values on the outcomes of these functions.

The direct public services rendered by higher education also contribute substantially to societal welfare. These include health care, libraries and museums, dramatic and musical performances, recreational facilities and programs, consulting in a wide range of fields, and maintaining a standby pool of knowledge and expertise to be drawn upon when needed. In addition, all the activities of higher education—instruction as well as research and public service—are sources of national prestige and national military power. They also are sources of enjoyment and satisfaction to the general public, who find interest and pride in living in a world of advancing knowledge and dramatic scientific breakthroughs.

Third, higher education may contribute to the quest for human equality. This, however, is a potential, not an actual, effect. Since higher education in the past has served mainly the privileged classes—those privileged by virtue of income, social status, and (to some extent) native ability—it probably has not had a leveling effect. Indeed, the range of differences in educational level among the American people today may be at an all-time high. If, in the future, higher education in its many forms could be extended steadily to more people, the incomes and social status of the less-educated might rise, and progress toward human equality might be achieved.

The Consequences of Higher Education

A tidy dollar comparison of costs and benefits is conspicuously absent from the above summary. There is no bottom line, but the sum of the benefits exceeds the total cost by a factor of three or more. The monetary returns alone, in the form of enhanced earnings of workers and improved technology, are probably sufficient to offset all the costs. But over and above the monetary returns are the personal development and life enrichment of millions of people, the preservation of the cultural heritage, the advancement of knowledge and the arts, a major contribution to national prestige and power, and the direct satisfactions derived from college attendance and from living in a society where knowledge and the arts flourish. These nonmonetary benefits surely are far greater than the monetary benefits—so much greater, in fact, that individual and social decisions about the future of higher education should be made primarily on the basis of nonmonetary considerations and only secondarily on the basis of monetary factors.

The Current Debate

America's enthusiasm for education has derived from a deep faith in education as the foundation of a workable democratic society and from the belief that every individual should have the chance, and even the obligation, for personal fulfillment through learning. It has been reinforced solidly by the desire of submerged groups to get ahead and by the economic need for trained manpower.

At each stage in the past development of higher education, there have been those who believed that the three Rs are enough, that only an elite minority of people were educable beyond a few years of school, or that the nation could not afford additional education. Today, many believe that education has been overdone, and it is alleged that a large proportion of our people are uneducable, that there are not enough jobs for educated people, or that the nation cannot afford the heavy costs. Yet, it is quite clear that the enormous growth of colleges and universities has taken us only partway toward the long-held ideal of education for every person up to the limit of his potentialities. Total enrollments could conceivably double over the next generation if the nation chose to offer incentives and learning opportunities relevant to the needs of new clienteles.

The question to be faced, then, is whether the historic development of higher education should be resumed, whether the amount of higher education should be stabilized at about its present level, or whether it should be cut back. The conclusion that the total return from higher education today is several times greater than the total cost does not necessarily imply that it would pay the nation to expand the higher educational system. Expansion can be justified only if successive increments of cost will produce equal or greater increments of benefit. The limit of economical expansion is reached at the point where incremental cost and incremental benefit are equal.

A Moral Imperative and Some Practical Considerations

In terms of incremental analysis, would growth in the number of educated people significantly increase economic productivity or enhance the quality of life? Would expansion of research and public service speed up technological progress or enrich the culture? Some believe the answers may be "no" or "not much." And their viewpoint is supported by the fact that some countries having relatively small higher educational establishments —such as Britain or Switzerland—manage nevertheless to achieve visibly advanced economies and high cultures. It is indeed possible that provision of college education to an increasing proportion of the American people or the expansion of research and public service might contribute little to the growth of the economy or the enhancement of the culture. However, these negative assessments of the potential economic and cultural impacts of expanded higher education greatly underrate the possibilities of incremental advantage. But the future of higher education should not and need not rest on guesses about such possibilities. It should be decided on moral grounds based on the following propositions:

1. That higher education contributes to the cognitive and affective qualities and the practical competence of people as individuals and is therefore conducive to their full development as whole human beings.
2. That higher education enhances the quality of social life in many ways.
3. That the number of persons who could benefit from higher education greatly exceeds the number who now partake of it, especially if innovative programs suited to diverse clienteles were available.
4. Given these three propositions, a moral imperative follows. It is that, on moral (not economic) grounds, each person should have the opportunity, and the obligation as well, to develop fully his or her unique personal powers.

The proposal to push ahead with the expansion of higher education raises important practical considerations. The expansion of higher education might increase the supply of people aspiring to technical, professional, and managerial jobs beyond the capacity of the economy to employ them. It is often argued that such expansion would lead to unemployment and discontent, and at worst to social upheaval. This argument raises a serious moral issue, implying as it does that a large part of the population with the potential for personal development through higher education should be held down deliberately to lives of relative ignorance. Such an outcome would be indefensible. The argument also is questionable from the economic standpoint. It assumes that the economy offers a more or less fixed inventory of jobs to which the labor force must adjust. On the contrary, there is a mutual adjustment process between the jobs the economy provides and the jobs the workers want. The economy can and does adjust to the workers available. For example, in the past, as the number of people presenting themselves for manual work has decreased and the number seeking white-collar work has increased, the economy has adjusted its technology and its product mix to accommodate the labor supply.

Granting that expansion of higher education is desirable, will students actually attend in ever-increasing numbers? Judging from past experience, the numbers will depend on the terms on which higher education is offered. These terms include tuition and fees, student aid, the quality and variety of programs, the convenience of time and place, arrangements for released time from work, the state of the labor market, the general level of economic prosperity, and, not least, the accepted ideology of college attendance. One thing is certain: If the earnings from jobs traditionally reserved for college graduates decline, the incentive to attend will be weakened and the need for public subsidy will increase.

Though higher education may be clothed with a pervasive moral imperative, it does not have unlimited claims on resources. There are important competing values. In extending higher education, therefore, the higher education community is heavily obliged to be efficient in the use of resources. Some of the resources needed for expansion will have to be bought with improved efficiency in existing operations. The higher education establishment is not well equipped for the tasks that lie ahead, the new conceptions, new forms, and new methods are needed. At best, the cost of extending higher education will be high.

The next two decades will be an ideal period in which to press ahead toward opening higher education to an increasing proportion of the population. First, well-known demographic trends will tend to reduce traditional enrollments and make room for population groups not previously represented. Second, the relatively heavy unemployment of the recent past, which may persist into the future, could be ameliorated if more people—especially uneducated youth, among whom unemployment rates are severe—could fill idle time by learning. Third, in meeting the twin problems of natural resource depletion and pollution, the nation will be forced to reduce the relative share of the Gross National Product (GNP) derived from goods-producing industries and to increase the share from service-producing industries. Higher education happens to be a service industry of great value that makes minimal claims on scarce natural resources and generates little environmental pollution.

A Possible Future for Higher Education

An exploration of outcomes suggests that the historic growth of higher education in the United States has been beneficial and, further, that future returns may be reaped through widening it to include more people and deepening it to intensify personal development of those already included. In the future, however, the potential incremental returns will be mainly in the fulfillment of individual lives and the building of a humane civilization rather than in raising the earnings and status of individuals and augmenting the GNP.

Since the regular work of the world will still need to be done, people will require training for a wide range of conventional jobs. To meet the special needs of the future, however, great cadres of scientists, engineers, physicians, other health workers, social scientists, teachers, social workers, humanists, and other vocationally trained persons will be needed to help find ways to conserve resources, clean up the environment, restore the cities, overcome racial injustice, improve health, eradicate poverty, and achieve economic stability. There will be no shortage of work to be done if the nation is dedicated to solving these problems and building a better—not necessarily more opulent—life.

The activities of research and public service would be intensified and not curtailed, as is so often proposed. Higher education would give increasing attention to the advancement of basic knowledge, to the preservation of the cultural heritage, to the exploration of means and values in a contemporary setting, to the analysis and evaluation of public policies and societal trends, and to the cultivation of the arts.

Open access and strong encouragement would be given to all the people to achieve education commensurate with their capacities. This would be done on the premise that learning is essential both to personal fulfillment and to cultural advancement. The extension of education in this way would not mean that everyone would graduate from a conventional college at age twenty-one but rather that each person would be given the genuine opportunity and encouragement to develop himself during his whole lifetime. To this end, the educational system would adjust and diversify its programs so that it could accommodate persons of varying backgrounds, interests, talents, and ages. Such education would provide an array of programs suited to a large majority of people. These programs would be available at convenient times and places. They would be supplied at low cost to the students, and thus they would allow for appropriate financial aid and released time from work. The educational system would be flexible in admissions requirements and in prerequisites. It would recognize learning from all sources, and it would include both degree and nondegree programs. It would meet vocational as well as personal needs, but its underlying emphasis would be on liberal learning—redefined to fit twenty-first-century conditions and needs. Over several generations it would expect to draw millions of disadvantaged persons into the mainstream of American society. The overriding purpose of higher education would change from that of preparing people to fill particular slots in the economy and adding to the GNP to that of helping them achieve personal fulfillment and building a civilization compatible with the nature of human beings and the limitations of the environment. Vocational education would continue to be an essential function, but it would be combined in a symbiotic relationship with liberal education.

This suggests that the nation embark on an educational adventure that has never before been attempted in human history—an adventure designed to banish ignorance as far as it can be banished, and to maximize human life.

Expanding the International Dimension of Higher Education.
By Barbara B. Burn. 1980.

Introduction: Global Education*

One question confronting American higher education and the American people at the beginning of the 1980s is whether the opportunities for expanding and improving international education that were lost in the 1960s should now be recovered. In the judgment of many, including the Carnegie Council, the answer is yes, for several reasons:

- The proper concern of education is the whole world, not just a part of it.
- Knowledge respects no national boundaries. Intellectuals of all nations contribute to the scope of human knowledge and understanding.
- The ability of educated people to use what they know in the advancement of any human enterprise is greatly enlarged by the acquisition of knowledge and skills that enable them to function effectively in more than one country or culture.
- One of the central problems of all nations has become the use of nonrenewable resources.
- In many other matters—including the prevention of nuclear war and the arrest of inflation—international cooperation becomes increasingly crucial. Such cooperation cannot be effective unless substantial numbers of men and women in all countries have a good understanding of the people and conditions in other parts of the world.
- Nations in which the global perspectives of large parts of the populations are well developed have an international advantage. More of their people are likely to understand the international implications of events and policies at home, and more of their people who have occasion to visit or conduct business abroad will have the capacity to make themselves and their country understood by others.
- It is inconceivable that any country that aspires to international leadership can exercise that role if its people are undereducated in international affairs.

It is now essential that the United States reverse the erosive trends in international education that have been with us for the past decade. More specifically, we need to:

1. Give more attention to global perspectives and languages in the development of the curriculum.

*The introduction to this volume was written by Clark Kerr and reflects the consensus of the Carnegie Council as evidenced in several discussions of international education.

2.   Continue to encourage students in other countries to study in the United States. Their presence in our classrooms contributes to world stability, peace, and mutual understanding.
3.   Take steps to prevent exploitation of foreign students by institutions that seek only to bolster their own enrollments.
4.   Take steps also to prevent foreign student exploitation of educational opportunities in the United States as a means simply of gaining entry to the country.
5.   Devise better federal government mechanisms for the improvement and encouragement of international education. Although international education is not the responsibility solely of the federal government, there is a great need for federal leadership and effective national programs.
6.   Develop the experts and library resources needed for international education programs without concern for enrollment levels of such programs.
7.   Recognize the importance of international scholarship not only for serving the national interest but also as a means of meeting long-term needs for intellectual competence in understanding various cultures in the world around us.

Global Perspectives in the Curriculum

As a first step away from a fractional view of humanity, colleges and universities should make provision for students who want to combine studies in an academic or occupational specialty with a foreign language and studies of some other part of the world. There is something to be said for the argument that all Americans need to be bilingual and that colleges and high schools share the responsibility for achieving that goal. However, foreign-language instruction has declined in popularity and importance in both schools and colleges.

Among the reasons frequently cited for this decline is the fact that English is now the leading world language and Americans therefore expect to be able to speak and be understood in their own tongue wherever they go. This argument overlooks the fact that students of a foreign language acquire more than communication skills. They also acquire insights into the cultures of other countries and broaden their perspectives on their own daily lives. One suggestion we have for colleges and universities is that they make these values more explicit. Students should be taught about foreign cultures and institutions at the same time they learn the languages themselves. To facilitate and improve such instruction, teachers of foreign languages in the United States might be asked to receive part of their training at colleges in other countries.

Colleges and universities with formal study-abroad programs obviously have a responsibility to make sure that the students who participate in them are properly prepared, not only in the language but also in aspects of the general culture and the level of academic instruction to be encountered in the countries they visit. Most students should be carefully and thoroughly counseled before they leave the United States so that they know what to expect and will understand their limitations and opportunities as learners in another land. Consideration should also be given to greater use of students who have spent time in other countries as resources for instruction after they return.

An increased familiarity with the people and cultures of other countries is becoming a valuable asset of any well-educated person. International components should be included in the general education programs of both secondary schools and colleges. Language instruction should begin in American schools as early as educationally possible, and evaluations of competence should be substituted for the amount of time spent in a foreign-language class as a means of determining a student's readiness to advance to higher levels.

The Role of the Federal Government

The federal government should make firm commitments to support programs that stimulate international scholarship, foreign-language studies, exchange of students and faculty members between nations, and cultivation of intellectual, technical, and creative resources on the nation's campuses that will facilitate American assistance and participation in cooperative efforts in other parts of the world. One way for the federal government to demonstrate the seriousness of its concerns for international education would be to strengthen current programs and take advantage of opportunities that already exist. We encourage the federal government to:

- Provide for the use of funds for international education and for financial aid generally to support study abroad.
- Pursue the mandate of the International Communication Agency to acquaint Americans with other cultures and peoples in ways that include college students among target groups.
- Maintain sufficient funding for National Defense Education Act Title VI centers to make possible the implementation of Section 603, which is intended to increase American students' understanding of the cultures of other nations.
- Double the level of funding for undergraduate international studies administered by the Office of Education and increase the time period for grants.
- Continue federal funding of programs to increase the expertise of study-abroad administrators. A major goal should be to strengthen study abroad as a priority activity of colleges and universities.
- Financially support a full revival of the Fulbright exchange program.
- Provide financial support on a long-term basis for other major exchanges, including those with the USSR, Eastern Europe, and the People's Republic of China.
- Increase the federal funding of Title VI area and international studies centers and programs from the $9.4 million provided in 1978-79 to $12 million in 1980-81.
- Create a national center to collect, on a continuing basis, data on area specialists by country or region, language, and discipline.
- Fund foreign affairs research at the level of $10 to $15 million annually. A new federal agency should be established to administer these funds and, to be effective, should be as independent as possible and should award grants on a peer-review basis.

Protecting Basic Resources

A fully mature effort to introduce and sustain international perspectives on a college or university campus requires the development of certain basic services and resources. Among them are adequate counseling and advising services for foreign students and for American students contemplating study abroad; experts on different countries and geographic regions; personnel to maintain liaison with government agencies, other institutions, consortia, and associations and businesses that have international interests; and library resources to support strong international study programs. It is unrealistic and undesirable for every institution to create all of these resources or to cover every possible country or area, much less every international issue, in depth. But every institution should have sufficient resources to reflect multinational interests and concerns in general. Beyond that, some colleges and universities should also attempt to develop depth in one or several country, area, or international interest fields. Through cooperative arrangements with other institutions and consortia, colleges and universities should also make the faculty members and specialized library resources of neighboring institutions available to their own students.

The need for specialists and for specialized knowledge in the international field is not constantly the same. It is felt unevenly and shifts with the sometimes erratic flow of history. Anticipating such needs requires that the sources of training and study about other countries and international issues exist somewhere on a sustained basis and that they do not appear and disappear solely in response to enrollment demands.

There is much more involved in international education than the national interest alone. Modern men and women need to be aware of their place and potential in the context of an international environment. Higher education is a central component of knowledge systems, and knowledge systems are now international. We need a new vision for higher education that goes beyond the land-grant or even urban-grant tradition. A new role for higher education may be emerging: the cultivation of thought about the future of world society.

International Education in Perspective

Since World War II, international education has tended to react to shifting currents in international relations. In the early postwar period, the Fulbright program was the intellectual counterpart to the Marshall Plan, launching an international exchange of scholars that paralleled the massive economic cooperation undertaken by the United States and Europe. The cold war brought with it a greater emphasis on the training of foreign-language and area studies specialists. In the 1960s, the need for greater understanding between nations stimulated increased interest in international education. In that period, the primary goal of international education was to help the foreign aid program lead the developing nations toward prosperity and democracy, using America as a model. The most recent phase in international education reflects a new awareness of the interdependence of nations. Issues that were formerly regarded as domestic have become international.

In order to prepare Americans to live in an increasingly interrelated world, international education must involve a major transformation of the entire educational system. Where higher education is concerned, this implies that virtually the entire curriculum must be transformed so that it can serve as a vehicle for increased knowledge about other countries and greater recognition of the transnational character of most issues.

International studies have traditionally comprised mainly the study of foreign countries and regions—commonly referred to as area studies—and international relations. *International relations* focuses on the interactions and interrelationships between governments and other organizations, public and private, as well as individuals, and typically is taught in political science departments. *Area studies,* in contrast, tend to be interdisciplinary, involving such fields as political science, history, literature, sociology, and the foreign language of the region or country concerned.

However, international studies, including international relations and area studies, are only one part of international education. International education also includes comparative, transnational, and so-called global studies, which focus more on issues and problems than on specific areas. Although international and global studies should be complementary, all too often they are viewed as competitive in terms of objectives, institutional priorities, and funding.

Higher education has already been "internationalized" to some extent. Social science and humanities departments offer courses dealing with other cultures and international issues. Considerable progress has been made in this area. For international education to be effective, however, not only should more courses be offered on other countries (especially non-Western countries) and on international topics, but the entire curriculum should be permeated by an international outlook.

International Education at the Undergraduate Level

The Schools

International education is a low priority in elementary and secondary education. Parents, teachers, and school administrators are not yet persuaded that contemporary social conditions compel greater emphasis on international education. The decline in foreign-language requirements for admission to colleges and universities has taken its toll on foreign-language enrollments in the schools, which have proceeded to drop their own foreign-language requirements. Moreover, the fact that foreign languages often are not taught very well deters students from enrolling in them. Finally, the foreign-language programs that do exist tend to neglect teaching about other cultures.

One effective way of strengthening international education—the establishment of international schools—is in its infancy in the United States; only a handful of such schools currently exist. Other means for strengthening international education, especially foreign-language teaching in the schools, are the magnet school system and the introduction of the International Baccalaureate. In the magnet school system, a selected school emphasizes a particular teaching method or a certain curricular theme and enrolls students from a wider area than the local district. The International Baccalaureate, a program for able high school students, requires an emphasis on foreign-language study as well as international studies in literature and history.

Higher Education

International studies have made impressive progress in the past 20 years, though they still have a long way to go. The base for undergraduate international studies may now sufficiently meet the current level of demand. What is urgently needed is a major expansion in the demand. More students should be attracted to international studies, and an international component should be included in courses that have not traditionally been part of international studies programs. To accomplish this, more faculty trained in international studies or in international aspects of their disciplines are needed. In addition, existing faculty should have many more opportunities to revitalize their international expertise. Among the ways in which this may be accomplished are the following:

1. Offering more seminars like those sponsored by the National Endowment for the Humanities, which extend the international education expertise of existing faculty.
2. Federal funding for the preparation of new curricular materials and special seminars to retrain teachers to teach new curricula.
3. Because overseas experience offers a unique opportunity to increase faculty competence in international education, opportunities to teach and do research abroad should be increased significantly.
4. Colleges and universities should support international education by providing released-time and professional-growth grants to selected faculty members specifically in order to expand their international experience and expertise.

In general, undergraduate international studies have suffered a decline. However, there is growing interest in international studies on the part of students in professional schools as well as those preparing for graduate work in business and law or for graduate programs combining international and professional studies. The reluctance of colleges and universities to recognize international education as a professional priority, together with their failure to emphasize any teaching and research that does not center on a particular discipline, may be the most intractable obstacle to the strengthening of international education.

Two relatively recent developments give cause for optimism about the future of international education. The International Communication Agency has a new mandate to increase the American people's knowledge and understanding of other countries, and the National Endowment for the Humanities is increasing its support for international education through its fellowship programs.

Foreign-Language Study

Registrations in foreign-language courses in colleges and universities dropped nearly 19 percent between 1968 and 1977, from about 15 percent of all degree-credit students to 9 percent. Foreign-language enrollments in public secondary schools dropped from 4.75 million in 1968 to 4 million in 1974. Indeed, nearly one-fifth of these schools offer no foreign language at all.

Many reasons are proffered for this decline: poor teaching, especially at the high school level; the dropping of foreign languages as a degree requirement; the decrease in Europe's influence on the United States; American parochialism—the assumption that, if English is a leading world language, then English speakers need speak no language but their own; and finally, the declining number of jobs, especially teaching jobs, for people who specialize in foreign languages.

The solution to the problem of poor teaching may be found in the development of specific goals together with the recognition that real proficiency in a language cannot be achieved in one or two years of study. Other solutions include a national policy endorsing the principle that every pupil should have an opportunity to learn a foreign language. And foreign-language instruction should be geared to realistic, competency-based learning outcomes that permit (1) better articulation between language programs in secondary and postsecondary education and (2) more effective instructional methods and strategies.

The dropping of foreign-language requirements for admission to or graduation from college is widely recognized as a major problem. The recent trend toward restoring distribution requirements should benefit foreign languages, and this, in turn, should increase foreign-language study in secondary schools and eventually generate new openings for teachers of foreign languages. Because foreign-language instruction is offered primarily by high schools as part of their general education curriculum, it is in the high schools that efforts to improve language teaching should be concentrated.

International Student Exchanges

Foreign Students in the United States

The number of foreign students in American colleges and universities has increased dramatically from 53,100 in 1960-61 to an estimated 250,000 in 1978-79. However, relative to the total number of students in higher education, they have remained below 2 percent since 1960. Although the United States enrolls more foreign students than any other developed nation, it ranks twenty-first in terms of the percentage of students coming from other countries.

The majority of foreign students are undergraduates, and the greatest recent increase has occurred in the community colleges: from 10 percent of all foreign students in 1970-71 to 15 percent in 1975-76. But the foreign student population in the United States is clustered; close to half are at the major research universities. Among the fields in which foreign students were enrolled in 1976-77 are engineering (24.1 percent), business and management (17 percent), the natural and life sciences (11.3 percent), social sciences (10.3 percent), humanities (7.1 percent), and agriculture (6 percent).

The geographic origins of foreign students have changed significantly since the mid-1960s. The greatest change is the dramatic increase in students from OPEC countries—from 14,090 in 1971-72 to 52,040 in 1976-77, or close to one-fifth of all foreign students in the United States.

In the past few years, a number of colleges and universities have made a more deliberate effort to use foreign students as an international education resource in formal academic programs as well as informal activities. Foreign students help orient American students who are about to study in their countries; tutor American students in their languages; and advise and participate in cross-cultural workshops designed to analyze intercultural values and attitudes and to identify and eliminate cultural stereotyping.

Essential to the success of cross-cultural programs are committed and professionally trained staff members to evaluate, advise, and follow up on foreign students. However, declining enrollments have spurred some institutions and agencies to undertake active recruitment of foreign students for income purposes without paying sufficient attention to the students' educational qualifications or the institution's capacity to meet their academic needs. Foreign students should be recruited in a responsible manner and should be viewed as a positive resource for international education. Every effort should be made to make sure foreign students have a beneficial sojourn in the United States; that mismatches between students' educational goals and the institutions in which they enroll are avoided; and that the students gain a wide acquaintance with American life and values.

American Students Abroad

An increasing number of students go abroad for independent study, to serve as interns, or to participate in practical training programs. However, at the graduate level, there has probably been a decline in overseas study and research as funding for them has diminished. The contribution of study abroad to personal growth and academic motivation and achievement is widely acknowledged. But as long as only 1 percent of all college and university students study abroad annually, the constituency will remain insufficient to stimulate significant institutional or national support.

Overseas study is not without problems. "Island" or "ghetto" programs—which transport American students abroad, use American faculty, and have the students living and studying with each other rather than with native students—do little to facilitate the direct contact with the foreign culture and society that is such an essential ingredient of study abroad. Other deterrents to overseas study are its rising cost, the decline in foreign-language study in the United States, and the concomitant reduction in student motivation and capacity for overseas study and restriction of foreigners working abroad. The increasing concern of some American institutions with filling their own classrooms and dormitories, hence discouraging their students from studying abroad, is another, more subtle, obstacle.

The paucity of scholarship aid for undergraduate study abroad is another deterrent, although students at some institutions are able to use federal aid for this purpose. Colleges and universities could help alleviate this problem by ensuring that students who are eligible for Basic Educational Opportunity Grants can avail themselves of this aid when studying abroad. Work-study funding should also be available for study abroad.

At many institutions, study abroad is not recognized as a legitimate academic experience meriting institutional financial support along with other academic programs. All too often, study-abroad programs are expected to be self-financing. Some colleges and universities even operate such programs as a source of revenue.

The administration of overseas study is deficient in several respects. Advisers and their students may lack the knowledge to select among the vast number of available programs. As a result, many students go abroad inadequately prepared for the experience. Moreover, few colleges or universities have follow-up programs in which the student's overseas experience is reinforced and integrated into his or her ongoing activities so that it can have a "multiplier effect" on other students and on the intellectual climate of the institution. Study abroad and foreign student programs are rarely integrated so that they complement each other. Another problem area is the matter of accreditation. Regional accrediting associations do not evaluate overseas study programs.

A long-term trend in international student exchanges is the shift from free to organized student mobility. Colleges and universities enter into agreements with foreign institutions for reciprocal exchange of students. One reason for this is that in many countries limits have been placed on foreign-student admissions. Also, institutions have had difficulty accommodating all qualified students and have become increasingly reluctant to subsidize students from other countries. Student mobility has caused the system to close up—that is, the increase in openings for foreign students has not kept pace with demand—as students who are unable to gain admission to their home institutions have sought admission abroad, putting new pressures on other educational systems.

The trend toward reciprocity may make it even more difficult for the individual American student to be admitted independently at an institution abroad, thus further limiting free mobility. However, in the long run it will not only lead to equitable exchanges but will also provide more opportunities to study abroad for students attending institutions with reciprocal exchange agreements.

International Faculty Exchanges

There were few institutionalized programs of reciprocal faculty exchange until after World War II, when both private and public institutions entered the field. At the core of two-way exchanges was the Fulbright program, which was created with funds made available through the renegotiation of outstanding European debts to the United States. The Fulbright program was originally focused on a handful of countries, largely in Western Europe. Today it has direct links with over 120 nations. The 500 to 550 American faculty who go abroad on Fulbrights each year therefore are spread out much more thinly than they once were. Although the number of exchanges has remained fairly constant, the intensity of American faculty contacts abroad has diminished in many important areas.

Two-thirds of the American faculty members abroad on Fulbrights are engaged in lecturing rather than research. However, far more Fulbright-sponsored foreign professors conduct research than lecture at American institutions. As a consequence of the teaching/research imbalance in the Fulbright program, it is far more likely that a student at a major institution abroad will hear an American lecturer than that an American student will hear a foreign lecturer. This imbalance may be attributed in good measure to language problems. The overwhelming majority of Americans who lecture abroad do so in English.

One means of reducing financial problems has been to fund the Fulbright program on a more truly bilateral basis (although there are more than twice as many foreign Fulbright recipients coming to the United States as there are American recipients going abroad). Much has been done to stretch the available funds; yet stipends for practically all American scholars abroad are now so low as to impose genuine hardship on many participants unless they secure supplementary funding. As a result, many distinguished faculty do not even bother to apply. Perhaps the time has come for funding to be shared equally by the United States and other nations, at least those in the developed world.

Another problem for faculty exchanges is the imbalance within the various exchanges.

There are at least five types of asymmetry. First, there is a persisting asymmetry in the types of American institutions hosting foreign scholars and teachers. There is a far greater concentration of visiting scholars at a small number of research universities than is probably healthy. The same conditions prevail for American scholars going abroad, resulting in massive exposure to American teacher-scholars at a few major institutions, and no contact at all at many other institutions.

A second asymmetry exists among the types of American institutions that send scholars abroad. While 71 percent of the faculty at major research institutions travel abroad at some point in their career, only 29 percent of community college faculty do.

A third asymmetry exists among American faculty members participating in exchanges. International scholarly and pedagogical exchanges are dominated by the fields of medicine and engineering.

A fourth asymmetry involves the dramatic differences in the degree of contact with specific foreign countries. The United Kingdom, France, Canada, and Germany claim fully three-fifths of all visits by American scholars abroad.

The fifth asymmetry involves organization. Given the centralized control prevailing in many foreign countries, American institutions are placed under pressure to operate in a more centralized fashion than they otherwise would. Paradoxically, such centralization, so important for the establishment of contact, takes a heavy toll in terms of local support. As a result, U.S. exchange organizations lack the strong, localized constituencies that are essential to their existence over the long term.

These problems can be addressed by the following action-oriented proposals.

1. The Fulbright program should be revitalized and funded to a degree that will enable it to meet its responsibilities and attract the best potential participants. Other major exchanges should be placed on a secure footing by the provision of federal and other support on a long-term basis.

2. The Board of Foreign Scholarships and other agencies concerned with scholarly exchanges should review the allocation of exchange resources and establish priorities by location and discipline.

3. All exchanges should insist on a high degree of reciprocity.

4. With respect to organization, the administrators of the Fulbright program and other major exchanges should make a greater effort to foster direct, unmediated contact between individual scholars and institutions.

5. The major programs, including the Fulbright program, should permit joint applications by scholars in two or more countries. This would foster both collaborative research and collaborative teaching.

The Role of American Universities in Development Assistance

While the United States has a long tradition of assistance to other nations, only since World War II have American universities served as a major resource in this area. In 1973, departing from its cold war emphasis on higher education and economic infrastructure, American technical assistance took some new directions. The AID policy launched that year called for concentration on "the poorest of the poor," that is, the 40 or 50 countries with annual per capita incomes under $150 in 1969 dollars. The new policy reflected disenchantment with AID's earlier emphasis on major projects such as building dams and roads and the failure of technical assistance to improve the living conditions of the poor majorities in less developed countries (LDCs).

Since 1975, there has been growing recognition that there are major differences between the LDCs. Many LDCs, especially the middle-income countries, now need less infrastructural support and more scientific and technological development. The assistance they need is not so much unilateral aid as a collaborative relationship.

Title XII of the Foreign Assistance Act of 1975 is aimed toward a collaborative relationship between American agricultural colleges and universities and the LDCs in solving the world's agricultural and hunger problems. The international projects of American colleges and universities should not be an isolated activity of the faculty members involved; rather, they should be part of a commitment that is central to the aims of the institution and in keeping with its administrative structure.

Advanced Training and Research

The federal government launched an effort to support foreign languages and other critical subjects under the Sputnik-prompted National Defense Education Act (NDEA) of 1958. Title VI of NDEA authorized programs for foreign-language and area studies in order to increase the national pool of specialists in foreign languages, area studies, and world affairs and to update the knowledge of existing specialists; to provide new knowledge about other nations—expecially non-Western ones—through research and development; and to develop improved curricula and instructional materials. Overall, Title VI has produced an impressive pool of area and international specialists and provided international education to many thousands of undergraduates. It has also strengthened foreign-language study, especially in the less commonly taught languages.

Because of the spiraling costs of foreign-area library collections, and because these are crucial to area research, a major effort is needed at the national level to sustain them. Such collections have grown impressively in the past 20 years with foundation and federal support. But with the termination of substantial foundation funding and the erosion of federal money, the maintenance of these collections is threatened. Area studies collections are particularly vulnerable to budget cuts by universities because of their high unit costs and low rate of use. The time is long past when a single institution could collect everything. Increased cooperation among major repositories will be essential in the future for the acquisition, processing, and servicing of foreign materials, especially because of the decentralized structure of the library system in the United States. Support for foreign-affairs-related research should include both substantial subsidies to collections designated as national or regional repositories and national leadership in support of a system for sharing the costs of and access to major collections.

The maintenance of a strong private sector capability in advanced foreign affairs research is needed. Continuing basic research cannot be carried out by the federal intelligence establishment, because its research is dominated by short-term deadlines and the immediate demands stemming from current intelligence issues. It must therefore draw upon the research carried on in universities—their intellectual and analytical capital —for both substance and perspective.

Basic research must be undertaken not just in universities but also in private research firms and at overseas centers for advanced research. Diverse in their origins, facilities, and programs, these centers share a commitment to scholarship on other countries and cultures, scholarship that feeds into international studies at all levels of American education.

The fundamental issue of how much international and area studies are enough has long defied solution. With the diminution of both foundation and governmental funding, this issue has grown increasingly acute, especially since job opportunities in higher education for area specialists have diminished considerably. Prospects for retaining the present level of expertise at the major research universities are relatively good. However, graduate international programs at second-tier institutions face an uncertain future unless international studies are given the greater priority they now require. In view of shrinking enrollments and diminishing financial support, these graduate programs may have difficulty even holding their own. The net effect is a further decline in job opportunities in higher education for international and area studies graduates. An exception is such graduates who also have advanced degrees from professional schools.

The federal government's demand for foreign-language, international, and area specialists is unlikely to grow appreciably unless filling more government positions with these specialists, especially those with foreign-language skills, becomes a matter of policy. An increase in the demand of American business for the graduates of advanced training programs in foreign languages and international studies is also unlikely. Corporations operating abroad want people with this academic background, but only if it augments professional training in business or related fields.

In the long run, the most effective approach to strengthening the international expertise of American business would probably be to provide more foreign-language and international training to business school students. This involves building into the curricula of these schools courses that focus on international studies and the international aspects of business.

Future Directions

There is considerable support for the following general proposals on the future of international and area studies centers and programs:

1. A network of first-rate international and area studies centers is needed; this requires substantial federal support in order to (a) train faculty and researches for the higher education system, (b) produce the "thin stream" of highly qualified specialists required by federal agencies concerned with international affairs, and (c) provide international expertise for business and other professions involved in international activities.

2. The nation's international research needs mandate the continuing support of a number of high-quality centers so that new information and ideas about other countries and international issues can be generated on a sustained basis, not as a shifting response to the foreign-policy preoccupations of the moment.

3. The outstanding area studies centers that now exist should serve as a national resource so that existing specialists can revitalize and enhance their competence through postdoctoral research and related activities at these centers.

4. The center network should encompass all countries and their languages. It should also include comparative studies on problems of worldwide interest.

5. Related to the preceding function—and meriting greater priority—are (a) intercenter cooperation on problems spanning two or more major regions of the world and (b) collaboration between centers and professional schools.

6. In addition to the system of major national centers, a regional network of second-tier centers and programs should be dispersed throughout the country. Their outreach programs should include undergraduates within their own institutions as well as a range of organizations in the wider community.

7. Because much of the research on other countries and cultures is now carried out by scholars from those countries, international and area studies centers in the United States should build bridges to centers in other countries through scholarly exchange and cooperative research.

While the anticipated demand for specialists in international and area studies is not expected to increase and may even diminish in the coming decade, this should not be allowed to determine the appropriate level of federal and other funding for the field. The employment situation for area studies Ph.D.s in the United States may require greater emphasis on postdoctoral support, professional school programs (including professional international studies), and terminal M.A.s. But a basic core of training and research must be maintained irrespective of the employment prospects of graduates and of the immediate relevance and applicability of the research.

In short, market demand for people trained in international and area studies is only one of a number of pertinent considerations. If the demand does not assure these people employment, it may be that the factors affecting the demand, rather than the supply, need alteration. Market demand should increase to correspond to the actual needs of the United States for international expertise. To this end, public understanding of these needs should be enchanced, and the centers for advanced training and research should play an active role in this effort.

Organizing for International Education

Institutions can strengthen their international education programs in the following ways:

1. Using foreign students as a teaching resource
2. Involving faculty with experience in development assistance in international studies programs
3. Using experts in international studies for the predeparture orientation of faculty who are about to participate in development assistance programs
4. Increasing the collaboration between international education programs and professional schools, with the twofold goal of internationalizing curricula in the latter and encouraging area studies majors to obtain professional as well as international training
5. Finding ways of incorporating overseas experience into academic counseling
6. Making greater use of international studies faculty and graduate students to develop links with institutions of higher education in appropriate regions.

The pluralism and complexity of higher education in the United States can be bewildering to people in other countries. It also means that there is no single voice speaking for American higher education to institutions and agencies abroad. A clearinghouse for communication between higher education institutions in the United States and abroad is needed. Such an organization would facilitate interinstitutional contacts, attempt to meet the information needs of foreign agencies and organizations seeking to place students in U.S. colleges and universities, and facilitate access by foreign institutions to the appropriate U.S. institutions for purposes of technical assistance, program development, colloborative research, staff development, and the like. In the view of experienced observers, it should be established outside of the federal government.

The future offers mixed promises. While much is happening in international education, it falls far short of national needs. The pluralism and diversity of the American scene have made possible a variety of initiatives, but unless international education is raised to the level of a national commitment, it will continue to be peripheral to many colleges and universities and will be a victim of competition at the campus level and among national organizations. For international education to become a major priority enlisting coordinated support at all levels, institutional and national leadership must recognize and articulate this priority and match rhetoric with resources.

Part Four

Supplements

Supplements

Members of the Carnegie Commission, 1967-1973*

Eric Ashby
The Master
Clare College
Cambridge, England

Ralph M. Besse
Partner
Squire, Sanders & Dempsey,
*   Counsellors at Law*

Joseph P. Cosand
Professor of Education and Director
Center for Higher Education
University of Michigan

William Friday
President
University of North Carolina

The Honorable Patricia Roberts Harris
Partner
Fried, Frank, Harris, Shriver &
*   Kampelman, Attorneys*

David D. Henry
President Emeritus
Distinguished Professor of Higher
*   Education*
University of Illinois

Theodore M. Hesburgh, C.S.C.
President
University of Notre Dame

Stanley J. Heywood
President
Eastern Montana College

Carl Kaysen
Director
Institute for Advanced Study at Princeton

Kenneth Keniston
Professor of Psychology
School of Medicine
Yale University

Katharine E. McBride
President Emeritus
Bryn Mawr College

James A. Perkins
Chairman of the Board
International Council for
*   Educational Development*

Clifton W. Phalen
Chairman of the Executive Committee
Marine Midland Banks, Inc.

Nathan M. Pusey
President
The Andrew W. Mellon Foundation

David Riesman
Henry Ford II Professor of Social Sciences
Harvard University

The Honorable William W. Scranton

Norton Simon

Kenneth Tollett
Distinguished Professor of
*   Higher Education*
Howard University

Clark Kerr
Chairman

*This list gives titles held at the time the members served.

Members of the Carnegie Council, 1973-1979*

William G. Bowen, 1974-1977
President
Princeton University

Ernest L. Boyer, 1974-1977
Chancellor
State University of New York

Nolen M. Ellison
President
Cuyahoga Community College

Nell P. Eurich
Senior Consultant
International Council for
Educational Development

Daniel J. Evans
President
The Evergreen State College

E. K. Fretwell, Jr.
Chancellor
The University of North Carolina
at Charlotte

Philip R. Lee, 1976-1977
Professor of Social Medicine and Director
Health Policy Program
University of California, San Francisco

Margaret L. A. MacVicar
Associate Professor of Physical Science
Massachusetts Institute of Technology

Frank Newman
President
University of Rhode Island

Robert M. O'Neil
Vice President
Indiana University at Bloomington

Rosemary Park
Professor of Education, Emeritus
University of California, Los Angeles

James A. Perkins
Chairman of the Board
International Council for Educational
Development

Alan Pifer
President
The Carnegie Foundation for the
Advancement of Teaching

Joseph B. Platt
President
Claremont University Center

Lois D. Rice
Vice President
College Entrance Examination Board

William M. Roth

Stephen H. Spurr
Professor
LBJ School of Public Affairs
University of Texas at Austin

Pauline Tompkins, 1973-1976
President
Cedar Crest College

William Van Alstyne, 1973-1976
Professor of Law
Duke University

Clifton R. Wharton, Jr., 1973-1975
President
Michigan State University

Clark Kerr
Chairperson and Director

*This list gives titles held at the time the members served.

Dates and Locations of Carnegie Commission Meetings, 1967-1973

Dates	*Location*
June 1-2, 1967	New York, New York
September 22-23, 1967	Washington, D.C.
November 16-17, 1967	New York, New York
January 19-20, 1968	Chicago, Illinois
March 15-16, 1968	Atlanta, Georgia
April 19-20, 1968	New York, New York
June 21-22, 1968	New York, New York
September 13-14, 1968	New York, New York
November 15-16, 1968	Chapel Hill, North Carolina
January 24-25, 1969	Washington, D.C.
March 14-15, 1969	New York, New York
June 18-21, 1969	Berkeley, California
December 4-6, 1969	Washington, D.C.
February 20-21, 1970	Boston, Massachusetts
April 17-18, 1970	St. Louis, Missouri
June 26-27, 1970	Urbana, Illinois
October 2-3, 1970	Boulder, Colorado
November 6-7, 1970	Detroit, Michigan
December 4-5, 1970	New York, New York
January 15-16, 1971	New Orleans, Louisiana
February 19-20, 1971	Houston, Texas
April 16-17, 1971	Miami Beach, Florida
June 24-26, 1971	Vancouver, British Columbia, and Seattle, Washington
October 8-9, 1971	Philadelphia, Pennsylvania
November 5-6, 1971	Oberlin, Ohio
December 2-4, 1971	Los Angeles, California
February 3-5, 1972	San Juan, Puerto Rico
April 13-15, 1972	Nashville, Tennessee
June 22-24, 1972	Minneapolis, Minnesota
October 5-7, 1972	Iowa City, Iowa
December 6-8, 1972	Honolulu, Hawaii
March 1-3, 1973	Albuquerque, New Mexico
May 24-25, 1973	Princeton, New Jersey

Dates and Locations of Carnegie Council Meetings, 1973-1979

Dates	*Location*
December 17, 1973	New York, New York
April 1, 1974	New York, New York
April 15, 1974	Claremont, California
May 29, 1974	New York, New York
October 8-9, 1974	Berkeley, California
January 9-11, 1975	Berkeley, California
February 6-7, 1975	Berkeley, California
April 14, 1975*	Salt Lake City, Utah
May 5-7, 1975	Princeton, New Jersey
June 18-19, 1975	New York, New York
October 10-11, 1975	Washington, D.C.
November 19, 1975*	New York, New York
January 8-9, 1976	Tampa, Florida
February 5-6, 1976	Berkeley, California
March 25-26, 1976	Berkeley, California
April 12, 1976*	Ann Arbor, Michigan
June 14-15, 1976	Albany, New York
October 21-23, 1976	Toronto, Canada
January 6-8, 1977	Berkeley, California
February 17-19, 1977	Tempe, Arizona
April 17, 1977	Nashville, Tennessee
June 15-17, 1977	Fairbanks and Anchorage, Alaska
September 7-8, 1977	New York, New York
November 16-17, 1977	New York, New York
January 11-13, 1978	LaJolla and San Diego, California
April 15-16, 1978	Wellesley, Massachusetts
June 14-16, 1978[†]	Notre Dame, Indiana
October 10-11, 1978	Washington, D.C.
November 15-16, 1978	New York, New York
February 8-11, 1979	Ajijic, Mexico
April 24-25, 1979*	Berkeley, California
June 20-22, 1979	Missoula, Montana
October 4-6, 1979	West Greenwich, Rhode Island

*Joint meeting with the Board of Trustees of The Carnegie Foundation for the Advancement of Teaching.

[†] Joint meeting with members of Carnegie Commission.

Members of the Carnegie Commission Staff, 1967-1973*

Terry Y. Allen, *Assistant Editor*
Gloria Copeland, *Executive Assistant*
Florence Eisemann, *Senior Administrative Assistant*
Marian L. Gade, *Postgraduate Researcher*
Margaret S. Gordon, *Associate Director*
Maureen I. Kawaoka, *Administrative Secretary*
Virginia B. Smith, *Associate Director*
Verne A. Stadtman, *Associate Director and Editor*
Wendy Walton, *Secretary*

*This list includes all persons who served during one-half or more of the life of the Commission on either a full-time or part-time basis, with their last titles.

Members of the Carnegie Council Staff, 1974-1979*

Charlotte Alhadeff, *Research Specialist*
Robert O. Berdahl, *Senior Fellow* (1974-1976)
Nancy A. Blumenstock, *Editor*
William Carmichael, *Research Assistant*
Earl F. Cheit, *Associate Director* (1974-1975)
C. E. Christian, *Research Fellow*
Florence Eisemann, *Administrative Assistant*
Sandra Elman, *Research Assistant*
Marian L. Gade, *Postgraduate Researcher*
Margaret S. Gordon, *Associate Director*
Ruth Goto, *Postgraduate Researcher*
Sura Johnson, *Survey Coordinator*
Barbara Jordan, *Secretary* (1974-1975)
Maureen Kawaoka, *Administrative Secretary*
Martin Kramer, *Senior Fellow*
Arthur Levine, *Senior Fellow*
Sandra Loris, *Secretary*
Jeanne M. Marengo, *Secretary* (1973-1978)
Lillian North, *Secretary*
Thomas Phalen, *Research Assistant*
Nanette Sand, *Librarian*
Karen Seriguchi, *Editorial Assistant* (1973-1976)
John R. Shea, *Senior Fellow*
Verne A. Stadtman, *Associate Director and Editor*
Katrine Stephenson, *Office Manager*
Rachel Volberg, *Research Assistant*
Claudia White, *Secretary*
Scott C. Wren, *Research Associate*
Sylvia Zuck, *Secretary*

*This list includes all persons who served half-time or more for two years or more of the Council's existence or who served for the last six months of the Council's term, with their last titles.

Members of the Carnegie Commission's Technical Advisory Committee, 1967-1973

Frederick E. Balderston, 1969-1973
Chairman
Center for Research
  in Management Sciences
University of California, Berkeley

David Blackwell, 1969-1973
Professor
Department of Statistics
University of California, Berkeley

Lewis Butler, 1971-1973
Planning Coordinator, Health
  Policy Program and Adjunct
  Professor
School of Medicine
University of California, San Francisco

Earl F. Cheit, 1970-1973
Professor
Schools of Business Administration
University of California, Berkeley

Charles Hitch, 1967-1969
President of the University of California

Eugene C. Lee, 1970-1973
Director
Institute of Governmental Studies
University of California, Berkeley

Seymour Martin Lipset, 1972-1973
Fellow
Center for Advanced Studies
  in the Behavioral Sciences
Stanford, California

T. R. McConnell, 1967-1973
Professor Emeritus
School of Education
University of California, Berkeley

Joseph Pechman, 1970-1971
then Visiting Professor
Department of Economics
University of California, Berkeley

Roy Radner
Professor
Department of Economics and Statistics
University of California, Berkeley

David Riesman, 1968-1969
then Fellow
Center for Advanced Studies
  in the Behavioral Sciences
Stanford, California

George Shultz, 1968-1969
then Fellow
Center for Advanced Studies
  in the Behavioral Sciences
Stanford, California

Neil J. Smelser
University Professor of Sociology
University of California, Berkeley

Martin Trow
Professor
Department of Sociology
University of California, Berkeley

Lloyd Ulman, 1968-1973
Director
Institute of Industrial Relations
University of California, Berkeley

Members of the Carnegie Council's Technical Advisory Committee, 1974-1979

Frederick E. Balderston
Chairman
Center for Research
    in Management Sciences
University of California, Berkeley

Earl F. Cheit
Dean
Schools of Business Administration
University of California, Berkeley

Lyman Glenny
Professor
School of Education
University of California, Berkeley

Charlotte V. Kuh
Professor
Graduate School of Education
Harvard University

Eugene C. Lee
Director
Institute of Governmental Studies
University of California, Berkeley

Lewis Mayhew
Professor
School of Education
Stanford University

T. R. McConnell
Professor Emeritus
School of Education
University of California, Berkeley

Roy Radner
Professor
Department of Economics
University of California, Berkeley

Neil J. Smelser
Professor
Department of Sociology
University of California, Berkeley

Martin Trow
Professor
Graduate School of Public Policy
University of California, Berkeley

Publications of the Carnegie Commission

Policy Reports

Quality and Equality: New Levels of Federal Responsibility for Higher Education, December 1968; *Revised Recommendations*, June 1970

A Chance to Learn: An Action Agenda for Equal Opportunity in Higher Education, March 1970

The Open-Door Colleges: Policies for Community Colleges, June 1970

Higher Education and the Nation's Health: Policies for Medical and Dental Education, October 1970

Less Time, More Options: Education Beyond the High School, January 1971

From Isolation to Mainstream: Problems of Colleges Founded for Negroes, February 1971

The Capitol and the Campus: State Responsibility for Postsecondary Education, April 1971

Dissent and Disruption: Proposals for Consideration by the Campus, June 1971

New Students and New Places: Policies for the Future Growth and Development of American Higher Education, October 1971

Institutional Aid: Federal Support to Colleges and Universities, February 1972

The Fourth Revolution: Instructional Technology in Higher Education, June 1972

The More Effective Use of Resources: An Imperative for Higher Education, June 1972

Reform on Campus: Changing Students, Changing Academic Programs, June 1972

The Campus and the City: Maximizing Assets and Reducing Programs, December 1972

College Graduates and Jobs: Adjusting to a New Labor Market Situation, April 1973

Governance of Higher Education: Six Priority Problems, April 1973

The Purposes and the Performance of Higher Education in the United States: Approaching the Year 2000, June 1973

Higher Education: Who Pays? Who Benefits? Who Should Pay?, July 1973

Continuity and Discontinuity: Higher Education and the Schools, August 1973

Opportunities for Women in Higher Education: Their Current Participation, Prospects for the Future, and Recommendations for Action, September 1973

Toward a Learning Society: Alternative Channels to Life, Work, and Service, October 1973

Priorities for Action: Final Report of the Carnegie Commission on Higher Education, October 1973

Sponsored Studies

Howard R. Bowen, *The Finance of Higher Education*, August 1968

William G. Bowen, *The Economics of the Major Private Universities*, August 1968

Ronald A. Wolk, *Alternative Methods of Federal Funding for Higher Education*, December 1968

Dale M. Heckman and Warren Bryan Martin, *Inventory of Current Research on Higher Education, 1968,* December 1968

E. Alden Dunham, *Colleges of the Forgotten Americans: A Profile of State Colleges and Regional Universities,* November 1969

Andrew M. Greeley, *From Backwater to Mainstream: A Profile of Catholic Higher Education,* November 1969

Heinz Eulau and Harold Quinley, *State Officials and Higher Education: A Survey of the Opinions and Expectations of Policy Makers in Nine States,* May 1970

Stephen H. Spurr, *Academic Degree Structures: Innovative Approaches–Principles of Reform in Degree Structures in the United States,* May 1970

Dwight R. Ladd, *Change in Educational Policy: Self-Studies in Selected Colleges and Universities,* July 1970

Lewis B. Mayhew, *Graduate and Professional Education, 1980: A Survey of Institutional Plans,* August 1970

Oscar Handlin and Mary F. Handlin, *The American College and American Culture: Socialization as a Function of Higher Education,* September 1970

Joe L. Spaeth and Andrew M. Greeley, *Recent Alumni and Higher Education: A Survey of College Graduates,* September 1970

Irwin T. Sanders and Jennifer C. Ward, *Bridges to Understanding: International Programs of American Colleges and Universities,* December 1970

Barbara B. Burn, with chapters by Clark Kerr, Philip Altback, and James A Perkins, *Higher Education in Nine Countries: A Comparative Study of Colleges and Universities Abroad,* February 1971

Rashi Fein and Gerald I. Weber, *Financing Medical Education: An Analysis of Alternative Policies and Mechanisms,* February 1971

Earl F. Cheit, *The New Depression in Higher Education: A Study of Financial Aid Conditions at 41 Colleges and Universities,* February 1971

Leland L. Medsker and Dale Tillery, *Breaking the Access Barriers: A Profile of Two-Year Colleges,* March 1971

Frank Bowles and Frank A. DeCosta, *Between Two Worlds: A Profile of Negro Higher Education,* April 1971

Eric Ashby, *Any Person, Any Study: An Essay on American Higher Education,* April 1971

Morris T. Keeton, *Models and Mavericks: A Profile of the Private Liberal Arts Colleges,* May 1971

Robert W. Hartman, *Credit for College: Public Policy for Student Loans,* June 1971

Howard R. Bowen and Gordon K. Douglass, *Efficiency in Liberal Education: A Study of Comparative Instructional Costs for Different Ways of Organizing Teaching-Learning in a Liberal Arts College,* September 1971

Eugene C. Lee and Frank M. Bowen, *The Multicampus University: A Study of Academic Governance,* September 1971

Harold L. Hodgkinson, *Institutions in Transition: A Profile of Change in Higher Education* (incorporating the 1970 statistical report), September 1971

Stephen B. Withey et al., *A Degree and What Else? Correlates and Consequences of a College Education,* October 1971

Joseph Ben-David, *American Higher Education: Directions Old and New,* December 1971

Alexander W. Astin and Calvin B. T. Lee, *The Invisible Colleges: A Profile of Small, Private Colleges with Limited Resources,* January 1972

Harold Orlans, *The Nonprofit Research Institute: Its Origin, Operation, Problems, and Prospects,* March 1972

Edgar H. Schein, *Professional Education: Some New Directions,* March 1972

C. Robert Pace, *Education and Evangelism: A Profile of Protestant Colleges,* June 1972

Dael Wolfle, *The Home of Science: The Role of the University,* June 1972

Seymour E. Harris, *A Statistical Portrait of Higher Education,* June 1972

Roger E. Levien, *The Emerging Technology: Instructional Uses of the Computer in Higher Education,* November 1972

C. Arnold Anderson, Mary Jean Bowman, and Vincent Tinto, *Where Colleges Are and Who Attends: Effects of Accessibility on College Attendance,* November 1972

Herbert L. Packer and Thomas Ehrlich, *New Directions in Legal Education,* November 1972 [abridged paperback edition, April 1973]

James A. Perkins, Ed., *The University as an Organization,* February 1973

Richard J. Storr, *The Beginning of the Future: A Historical Approach to Graduate Education in the Arts and Sciences,* June 1973

David Riesman and Verne A. Stadtman, Eds., *Academic Transformation: Seventeen Institutions Under Pressure,* June 1973

George Nash et al., *The University and the City: Eight Cases of Involvement,* June 1973

Jack Morrison, *The Rise of the Arts on the American Campus,* July 1973

Alexander M. Mood, *The Future of Higher Education: Some Speculations and Suggestions,* September 1973

Carl Kaysen, Ed., *Content and Context: Essays on College Education,* October 1973

Alain Touraine, *The Academic System in American Society,* November 1973

Michael D. Cohen and James G. March, *Leadership and Ambiguity: The American College President,* November 1973

Stephen Steinberg, *The Academic Melting Pot: Catholics and Jews in Higher Education,* November 1973

Edward Gross and Paul V. Grambsch, *Changes in University Organization, 1964-1971,* May 1974.

Everett C. Hughes, Barrie Thorne, Agostino M. DeBaggis, Arnold Gurin, and David

Williams, *Education for the Professions of Medicine, Law, Theology, and Social Welfare,* November 1973

Margaret S. Gordon, Ed., *Higher Education and the Labor Market,* January 1974

Saul D. Feldman, *Escape from the Doll's House: Women in Graduate and Professional School Education,* January 1974

Richard A. Lester, *Antibias Regulation of Universities: Faculty Problems and their Solutions,* July 1974

Harland G. Bloland and Sue M. Bloland, *American Learned Societies in Transition: The Impact of Dissent and Recession,* September 1974

Paul Taubman and Terence Wales, *Higher Education and Earnings: College as an Investment and a Screening Device,* November 1974

Thomas Juster, Ed., *Education, Income, and Human Behavior,* December 1974

Seymour Martin Lipset and David Riesman, *Education and Politics at Harvard,* May 1975

Everett Carll Ladd, Jr., and Seymour Martin Lipset, *The Divided Academy: Professors and Politics,* May 1975

Earl F. Cheit, *The Useful Arts and the Liberal Tradition,* June 1975

Joseph W. Garbarino in association with Bill Aussieker, *Faculty Bargaining: Change and Conflict,* June 1975

Martin Trow, Ed., *Teachers and Students: Aspects of American Higher Education,* July 1975

Florence Howe, Ed., *Women and the Power to Change,* July 1975

John Fralick Rockart and Michael S. Scott Morton, *Computers and the Learning Process in Higher Education,* July 1975

Roy Radner and Leonard S. Miller with the collaboration of Douglas L. Adkins and Frederick E. Balderston, *Demand and Supply in United States Higher Education,* November 1975

Allan M. Cartter, *The Ph.D. and the Academic Labor Market,* March 1976

Joseph Ben-David, *Centers of Learning: Britain, France, Germany, United States,* May 1977

Richard B. Freeman, *Black Elite: The New Market for Highly Educated Black Americans,* May 1977

Technical Reports

Harold Hodgkinson, *Institutions in Transition: A Study of Change in Higher Education,* June 1970

June A. O'Neill, *Resource Use in Higher Education: Trends in Output and Inputs, 1930-1967,* July 1971

Mark S. Blumberg, *Trends and Projections of Physicians in the United States, 1967-2002,* July 1971

Richard E. Peterson and John A. Bilorusky, *May 1970: The Campus Aftermath of Cambodia and Kent State,* October 1971

Paul Taubman and Terence Wales, *Mental Ability and Higher Educational Attainment in the 20th Century,* June 1972

Richard E. Peterson, *American College and University Enrollment Trends in 1971,* June 1972

Alexander M. Mood et al., *Papers on Efficiency in the Management of Higher Education,* August 1972

Ann Heiss, *An Inventory of Academic Innovation and Reform,* March 1973

Earl F. Cheit, *The New Depression in Higher Education: Two Years Later,* April 1973

Richard S. Eckaus, *Estimating the Returns to Education: A Disaggregated Approach,* April 1973

June A. O'Neill, *Sources of Funds to Colleges and Universities,* May 1973

Everett Carll Ladd, Jr., and Seymour Martin Lipset, *Professors, Unions, and American Higher Education,* May 1973

Carnegie Commission on Higher Education, *A Classification of Institutions of Higher Education,* November 1973

Margaret A. Fay and Jeff A. Weintraub, *Political Ideologies of Graduate Students: Crystallization, Consistency, and Contextual Effects,* February 1974

Thomas J. Karwin, *Flying a Learning Center: Design and Costs of an Off-Campus Space for Learning,* February 1974

C. Robert Pace, *The Demise of Diversity? A Comparative Profile of Eight Types of Institutions,* March 1974

Carnegie Commission on Higher Education, *Tuition: A Supplemental Statement on the Report of the Carnegie Commission on Higher Education on 'Who Pays? Who Benefits? Who Should Pay?,'* April 1974

Michio Nagai, *An Owl Before Dusk,* October 1975

Leonard S. Miller and Roy Radner, *Demand and Supply in United States Higher Education: A Technical Supplement,* November 1975

Douglas L. Adkins, *The Great American Degree Machine: An Economic Analysis of the Human Resource Output of Higher Education,* November 1975

Reprints

Theodore W. Schultz, "Resources for Higher Education: An Economist's View," reprinted from *Journal of Political Economy,* vol. 76, no. 3, May/June 1968

Clark Kerr, "Industrial Relations and University Relations," reprinted from *Proceedings of the 21st Annual Winter Meeting of the Industrial Relations Research Association,* pp. 15-25

Clark Kerr, "New Challenges to the College and University," reprinted from *Agenda for the Nation,* Kermit Gordon, Ed., Brookings Institution, Washington D.C., 1968

Clark Kerr, "Presidential Discontent," reprinted from *Perspectives on Campus Tensions: Papers Prepared for the Special Committee on Campus Tensions,* David C. Nichols, Ed., American Council on Education, Washington, D.C., September 1970

Harold Hodgkinson, "Student Protest—An Institutional and National Profile," reprinted from *The Record,* vol. 71, no. 4, May 1970

Kenneth Keniston, "What's Bugging the Students?" reprinted from the *Educational Record,* vol. 51, no. 2, Spring 1970

Seymour M. Lipset, "The Politics of Academia," reprinted from *Perspectives on Campus Tensions: Papers Prepared for the Special Committee on Campus Tensions,* David C. Nichols, Ed., American Council on Education, Washington, D.C., September 1970

Seymour M. Lipset and Everett C. Ladd, Jr., ". . . And What Professors Think," reprinted from *Psychology Today,* vol. 4, no. 6, November 1970

Roy Radner and Leonard S. Miller, "Demand and Supply in U.S. Higher Education: A Progress Report," reprinted from *American Economic Review,* vol. 60, no. 2, May 1970

Kenneth Keniston and Michael Lerner, "The Unholy Alliance Against the Campus," reprinted from *New York Times Magazine,* November 8, 1970

Neil Timm, "A New Method of Measuring States' Higher Education Burden," reprinted from *Journal of Higher Education,* vol. 42, no. 1, January 1971

Joseph W. Garbarino, "Precarious Professors: New Patterns of Representation," reprinted from *Industrial Relations,* vol. 10, no. 1, February 1971

Earl F. Cheit, "Regent Watching," reprinted from *AGB Reports,* vol. 13, no. 6, March 1971

Seymour M. Lipset and Everett C. Ladd, Jr., "Jewish Academics in the United States: Their Achievements, Culture and Politics," reprinted from *American Jewish Year Book, 1971*

Seymour M. Lipset and Everett C. Ladd, Jr., "The Divided Professoriate," reprinted from *Change,* vol. 3, no. 3, May 1971

Seymour M. Lipset and Everett C. Ladd, Jr., "The Politics of American Political Scientists," reprinted from *PS,* vol. 4, no. 2, Spring 1971

Allan M. Cartter, "Scientific Manpower for 1970-1985," reprinted from *Science,* vol. 172, no. 3979, April 9, 1971

Seymour M. Lipset and Everett C. Ladd, Jr., "American Social Scientists and the Growth of Campus Political Activism in the 1960s" reprinted from *Social Sciences Information,* vol. 10, no. 2, April 1971

James A. Perkins, "International Programs of U.S. Colleges and Universities: Priorities for the Seventies," reprinted from *Occasional Paper No. 1,* International Council for Educational Development, July 1971

Mark S. Blumberg, "Accelerated Programs of Medical Education," reprinted from *Journal of Medical Education,* vol. 46, no. 8, August 1971

Seymour M. Lipset and Everett C. Ladd, Jr., "College Generations—from the 1930s to the 1960s," reprinted from *The Public Interest,* no. 25, Summer 1971

Virginia B. Smith, "More For Less: Higher Education's New Priority," reprinted from *Universal Higher Education: Costs and Benefits,* American Council on Education, Washington, D.C., 1971

Joseph W. Garbarino, "Faculty Unionism: From Theory to Practice," reprinted from *Industrial Relations,* vol. 11, no. 1, February 1972

Seymour M. Lipset, "Academia and Politics in America," reprinted from *Imagination and Precision in the Social Sciences,* Thomas J. Nossiter, Ed., Faber and Faber, London, 1972

Everett C. Ladd, Jr., and Seymour M. Lipset, "Politics of Academic Natural Scientists and Engineers," reprinted from *Science,* vol. 176, no. 4039, June 9, 1972

Seymour M. Lipset and Richard B. Dobson, "The Intellectual as Critic and Rebel: With Special Reference to the United States and the Soviet Union," reprinted from *Daedalus,* vol. 101, no. 3, Summer 1972

Seymour M. Lipset and Everett C. Ladd, Jr., "The Politics of American Sociologists," reprinted from *American Journal of Sociology,* vol. 78, no. 1, July 1972

Martin Trow, "The Distribution of Academic Tenure in American Higher Education," reprinted from *The Tenure Debate,* Bardwell Smith, Ed., Jossey-Bass, San Francisco, 1972

Alan Pifer, "The Nature and Origins of the Carnegie Commission on Higher Education," based on a speech delivered to the Pennsylvania Association of Colleges and Universities on October 16, 1972, and reprinted by permission of The Carnegie Foundation for the Advancement of Teaching

Earl F. Cheit, "Coming of Middle Age in Higher Education," based on an address to the Joint Session of the American Association of State Colleges and Universities and the National Association of State Universities and Land-Grant Colleges in Washington, D.C., on November 13, 1972, and reprinted by permission of the National Association of State Universities and Land-Grant Colleges

Bill Aussieker and Joseph W. Garbarino, "Measuring Faculty Unionism: Quantity and Quality," reprinted from *Industrial Relations,* vol. 12, no. 2, May 1973

Publications of the Carnegie Council

Policy Reports

The Federal Role in Postsecondary Education: Unfinished Business, 1975-1980, April 1975

More Than Survival: Prospects for Higher Education in a Period of Uncertainty, Carnegie Foundation for the Advancement of Teaching, April 1975

Low or No Tuition: The Feasibility of a National Policy for the First Two Years of College, May 1975

Making Affirmative Action Work in Higher Education: An Analysis of Institutional and Federal Policies with Recommendations, August 1975

The States and Higher Education: A Proud Past and a Vital Future, Carnegie Foundation for the Advancement of Teaching, May 1976

Progress and Problems in Medical and Dental Education: Federal Support Versus Federal Control, September 1976

Federal Reorganization: Education and Scholarship, April 1977

Faculty Bargaining in Public Higher Education: A Report and Two Essays, May 1977

Selective Admissions in Higher Education: Comment and Recommendations and Two Reports, October 1977

The States and Private Higher Education: Problems and Policies in a New Era, December 1977

Missions of the College Curriculum: A Contemporary Review with Suggestions. Carnegie Foundation for the Advancement of Teaching, December 1977

Next Steps for the 1980s in Student Financial Aid: A Fourth Alternative, March 1979

Fair Practices in Higher Education: Rights and Responsibilities of Students and Their Colleges in a Period of Intensified Competition for Enrollments, April 1979

Giving Youth a Better Chance: Options for Education, Work, and Service, November 1979

Three Thousand Futures: The Next Twenty Years for Higher Education, January 1980

Sponsored Research Reports

Eugene C. Lee and Frank M. Bowen, *Managing Multicampus Systems: Effective Administration in an Unsteady State,* November 1975

David D. Henry, *Challenges Past, Challenges Present: An Analysis of American Higher Education Since 1930,* November 1975

Lyman A. Glenny, John R. Shea, Janet H. Ruyle, Kathryn H. Freschi, *Presidents Confront Reality: From Edifice Complex to University Without Walls,* January 1976

Konrad von Moltke and Norbert Schneevoigt, *Educational Leaves for Employees: European Experience for American Consideration,* May 1977

Howard R. Bowen, *Investment in Learning: The Individual and Social Value of American Higher Education,* November 1977

Frederick Rudolph, *Curriculum: A History of the American Undergraduate Course of Study Since 1636,* December 1977

Arthur Levine, *Handbook on Undergraduate Curriculum,* May 1978

National Academy of Education Task Force on Education and Employment, *Education for Employment: Knowledge for Action,* March 1979

Barbara B. Burn, *Expanding the International Dimension of Higher Education,* March 1980

Arthur Levine, *When Dreams and Heroes Died: A Portrait of Today's College Student,* forthcoming

Verne A. Stadtman, *Academic Adaptations: Higher Education Prepares for the 1980s and 1990s,* forthcoming

David Riesman, *On Higher Education,* forthcoming

Howard R. Bowen, *Costs of Higher Education: An Inquiry into the Educational Expenditures of American Colleges and Universities,* forthcoming

Technical Reports

Robert Blackburn, Ellen Armstrong, Clifton Conrad, James Didham, Thomas McKune, *Changing Practices in Undergraduate Education,* June 1976

The States and Higher Education: A Proud Past and A Vital Future, Supplement to a Commentary of The Carnegie Foundation for the Advancement of Teaching, June 1976

Carnegie Council on Policy Studies in Higher Education, *A Classification of Institutions of Higher Education: Revised Edition,* December 1976

Martin Trow, *Aspects of American Higher Education, 1969-1975,* January 1977

Paul L. Dressel and Mary Magdala Thompson, *A Degree for College Teachers: The Doctor of Arts,* February 1978

Joseph Hurd, *Enrollment and Cost Effect of Financial Aid Plans for Higher Education* (Technical Report 1), June 1978

Roy Radner and Charlotte V. Kuh, *Market Conditions and Tenure in U.S. Higher Education 1955-1973* (Technical Report 2), July 1978

Charlotte V. Kuh, *Market Conditions and Tenure for Ph.D.'s in U.S. Higher Education: Results from the 1975 Carnegie Faculty Survey and Comparison with Results from the 1973 ACE Survey* (Technical Report 3), July 1978

Martin Trow, *Carnegie Council National Surveys 1975-1976: Aspects of American Higher Education* (Vol. 1), unpublished

Carnegie Council on Policy Studies in Higher Education, *Carnegie Council National Surveys 1975-1976: Faculty Marginals* (Vol. 2), September 1978

Carnegie Council on Policy Studies in Higher Education, *Carnegie Council National Surveys 1975-1976: Undergraduate Marginals* (Vol. 3), September 1978

Carnegie Council on Policy Studies in Higher Education, *Carnegie Council National Surveys 1975-1976: Graduate Student Marginals* (Vol. 4), September 1978

Luis Fernandez, *U.S. Faculty After the Boom: Demographic Projections to 2000* (Technical Report 4), October 1978

Christoph von Rothkirch, *Field Disaggregated Analysis and Projections of Graduate Enrollment and Higher Degree Production* (Technical Report 5), October 1978

Roy Radner and Charlotte V. Kuh, *Preserving a Lost Generation: Policies to Assure a Steady Flow of Young Scholars Until the Year 2000* (Final Technical Report), October 1978

Clark Kerr, Chairman, *Observations on the Relations Between Education and Work in the People's Republic of China: Report of a Study Group, 1978,* February 1979

Hidetoshi Kato, *Education and Youth Employment in Japan,* February 1979

Alberto Hernández Medina, Carlos Muñoz Izquierdo, Manzoor Ahmed, *Education and Youth Employment in Less Developed Countries: Mexico and South Asia,* February 1979

Klaus von Dohnanyi, *Education and Youth Employment in the Federal Republic of Germany,* March 1979

Henri Janne, *Education and Youth Employment in Belgium,* May 1979

Stuart Maclure, *Education and Youth Employment in Great Britain,* May 1979

Barbara Liberska, *Education and Youth Employment in Poland,* June 1979

John T. Grasso and John R. Shea, *Vocational Education and Training: Impact on Youth,* June 1979

Charles E. Odegaard, *Area Health Education Centers: The Pioneering Years, 1972-1978,* December 1979

Margaret S. Gordon with a chapter by Martin Trow, *Youth Education and Unemployment Problems: An International Perspective,* January 1980

Charles E. Odegaard, *Eleven Area Health Education Centers: The View from the Grass Roots,* January 1980

Earl F. Cheit and Theodore E. Lobman, *Foundations and Higher Education: Grant Making from Golden Years Through Steady State,* March 1980

Martin Kramer, *The Venture Capital of Higher Education: The Private and Public Sources of Discretionary Funds,* May 1980

Gösta Rehn, K. Helveg Petersen, *Education and Youth Employment in Sweden and Denmark,* forthcoming

Special Report

Scott C. Wren, *The College Student and Higher Education Policy: What Stake and What Purpose?,* October 1975

Notes on Dissemination and Availability of Reports

The reports of the Carnegie Commission and the Carnegie Council were intended to assist persons engaged in the making of educational policy and to inform higher education scholars. They were sent as promptly and directly as possible to certain officials in the national and state governments, to presidents of all colleges and universities in the United States, to the principal officers of certain educational and civic organizations, to executives of major foundations, and to certain other individuals designated by the chairman or by the Commission or Council. All reports were sent by special arrangement to over 160 major libraries that agreed to serve as publicly available depositories for the Carnegie reports in the United States and abroad. Policy reports were also sent routinely to education writers throughout the country. In most instances, policy reports were released at press conferences that provided an opportunity for reporters to clarify information and conclusions.

Sponsored research and technical reports often concerned subjects of limited, specialized interest to scholars and practitioners in higher education. These were normally sent, therefore, to a somewhat smaller group than the one receiving policy reports. For example, college and university presidents often were not included automatically in the mailing lists for these reports. In general, therefore, policy reports were distributed automatically to an average of 5,000 persons; research reports were distributed to about 1,000 persons. Some of the technical reports were circulated to fewer than 500.

The policy and research reports were published under special agreements between the Commission and Council and commercial publishers. In the case of the Commission, an agreement was made with McGraw-Hill Book Company in New York. The publisher for the Council was Jossey-Bass Inc. in San Francisco. These companies produced the publications in the Carnegie series and made them available to the general public and to specialists who wished to acquire them after the initial distribution. Technical reports were produced by the editorial staff of the Carnegie Commission and Council in cooperation with various printers.

Many of the policy and research reports continue to be available from McGraw-Hill Book Company or Jossey-Bass Inc. at the present time, although some titles are out of print. Technical reports and reprints that were distributed only through the offices of the Commission or the Council are no longer available.*

*A very limited supply of the essays in the Council's series on youth in other countries is available through the Institute of Industrial Relations at the University of California, Berkeley, California 94720. Copies of *Observations on the Relations Between Education and Work in the People's Republic in China* and an abbreviated reprint of *Three Thousand Futures* are available from Clark Kerr at the Center for Studies in Higher Education, University of California, Berkeley, California 94720. Copies of *The College Student and Higher Education Policy* are available through the National Student Educational Fund, 2000 P Street N.W., Suite 305, Washington, D.C. 20036.

Domestic Depositories of Carnegie Commission and Carnegie Council Publications

Alderman Library
University of Virginia
Charlottesville, Virginia

American Council on Education
Washington, D.C.

Brown University Library
Providence, Rhode Island

Bryn Mawr College
Bryn Mawr, Pennsylvania

Case Western Reserve University
Cleveland, Ohio

Clark University
Worcester, Massachusetts

Columbia University
New York, New York

Cornell University Medical Library
New York, New York

Duke University
Durham, North Carolina

Eastern Montana College
Billings, Montana

Educational Testing Service
Berkeley, California

Education Library
Ohio State University Libraries
Columbus, Ohio

Education Library
University of Rochester
Rochester, New York

Education-Psychology Library
University of Oregon
Eugene, Oregon

Emory University
Atlanta, Georgia

General Administration Library
University of North Carolina
Chapel Hill, North Carolina

Georgetown University Main Library
Washington, D.C.

Gutman Library
Harvard University
Cambridge, Massachusetts

Harvard College Library
Cambridge, Massachusetts

Hillman Library
University of Pittsburgh
Pittsburgh, Pennsylvania

Howard-Tilton Library
Tulane University
New Orleans, Louisiana

Howard University
Washington, D.C.

Humanities Library
Massachusetts Institute of Technology
Cambridge, Massachusetts

Indiana University Library
Bloomington, Indiana

Joint University Libraries
Nashville, Tennessee

Michigan State University
East Lansing, Michigan

Moffitt Undergraduate Library
University of California, Berkeley
Berkeley, California

M. S. Eisenhower Library
Johns Hopkins University
Baltimore, Maryland

Mullen Library
Catholic University of America
Washington, D.C.

National Institute of Education
Department of Health, Education,
   and Welfare
Washington, D.C.

New York Public Library
New York, New York

New York University
New York, New York

Northwestern University Library
Evanston, Illinois

Pattee Library
Pennsylvania State University
University Park, Pennsylvania

Princeton University Library
Princeton, New Jersey

Purdue University Libraries
West Lafayette, Indiana

R. A. Milliken Memorial Library
California Institute of Technology
Pasadena, California

School of Education Library
University of Pennsylvania
Philadelphia, Pennsylvania

Southern Regional Education Board
Atlanta, Georgia

Stanford University
Stanford, California

Sterling Memorial Library
Yale University
New Haven, Connecticut

Syracuse University
Syracuse, New York

Teachers College
Columbia University
New York, New York 10027

The University Library
State University of New York at Albany
Albany, New York

University of Alaska
College, Alaska

University of Chicago Library
Chicago, Illinois

University of Colorado Libraries
Boulder, Colorado

University of Hawaii Library
Honolulu, Hawaii

University of Illinois
Chicago, Illinois

University of Illinois Library
Urbana, Illinois

University of Iowa Libraries
Iowa City, Iowa

University of Kansas Libraries
Lawrence, Kansas

University of Maryland
College Park, Maryland

University of Michigan
Ann Arbor, Michigan

University of Missouri
Columbia, Missouri

University of Nebraska Libraries
Lincoln, Nebraska

University of Notre Dame Memorial
   Library
Notre Dame, Indiana

University of Scranton
Scranton, Pennsylvania

University of Southern California
Los Angeles, California

University of Washington Libraries
Seattle, Washington

University of Wisconsin
Madison, Wisconsin

Washington University Libraries
St. Louis, Missouri

Western Interstate Commission for Higher
   Education
Boulder, Colorado

Wilson Library
University of Minnesota
Minneapolis, Minnesota

Wilson Library
University of North Carolina
   at Chapel Hill
Chapel Hill, North Carolina

Foreign Depositories of Carnegie Commission and Carnegie Council Publications

American University in Cairo Library
Cairo, Egypt

American University of Beirut
Beirut, Lebanon

Baillieu Library
University of Melbourne
Parkville, Victoria, Australia

Albrecht Bayer, AKA Auslandsamt
Ruprecht-Karl-Universität
Heidelberg, West Germany

Biblioteca Universitaria Alessandrina
Rome, Italy

Bibliothèque Publique et Universitaire
de Genève
Geneva, Switzerland

Bodleian Library
Oxford University
Oxford, England

The British Library
London, England

Deutsches Bibel-Archiv
Hamburg, West Germany

Education Library
Kyoto University
Kyoto, Japan

Freie Universität Berlin
Berlin, West Germany

Institute of Education
University of London
London, England

Instituto Bibliotecologico
Universidad de Buenos Aires
Buenos Aires, Argentina

Jewish National and University Library
Jerusalem, Israel

Johann Wolfgang Goethe-Universität
Frankfurt
Frankfurt am Main, West Germany

J. W. Jagger Library
University of Cape Town
Rondebosch, South Africa

Karachi University
Karachi, Pakistan

Jan Kluczynski, Director
Institute of Science Policy and
Higher Education
Warsaw, Poland

McLennan Library
McGill University Libraries
Montreal, Canada

Main Library
University of British Columbia
Vancouver, Canada

Dr. Alberto Martinelli
28 Via Fontana
20122 Milan, Italy

The Minister's Secretariat
The Ministry of Education
Tokyo, Japan

Norsk-Pedagogis Studiesamling
Oslo, Norway

Old College
University of Edinburgh
Edinburgh, Scotland

Ontario Institute for Studies in Education
Toronto, Ontario, Canada

Organization for Economic Cooperation
and Development
Paris, France

Pedagoji Enstitüsü
Istanbul University Library
Laleli, Istanbul, Turkey

Peking University
Peking, Hopei, People's Republic of China

Professor Jan Szezepanski
Vice Chairman
Polish Academy of Science
Warsaw, Poland

Slovenska Pedagogicka Kniznica
Bratislava, Czechoslovakia

Stockholm Universitets Bibliotek
Stockholm, Sweden

Tata Institute of Social Sciences
Deonar, Bombay, India

United Nations Educational,
Scientific and Cultural Organization
Institute for Education
Hamburg, Germany

United Nations Educational,
Scientific and Cultural Organization
Library
Paris, France

Universidad Federal do Rio de Janeiro
Rio de Janeiro, Brazil

Universidad Nacional Autónoma de
México
Ciudad Universitaria, Mexico

Universidad Nacional de Colombia
Bogota, Colombia

Universita Karlova
Prague, Czechoslovakia

Universitätsbibliothek
Bonn, West Germany

Université Libre de Bruxelles
Brussels, Belgium

Universiteit van Amsterdam
Amsterdam, The Netherlands

University Library
Budapest, Hungary

University of Bombay
Bombay, India

University of Calcutta
Calcutta, India

University of Canterbury
Christchurch, New Zealand

University of Indonesia
Jakarta, Indonesia

University of Madras
Madras, India

University of Teheran
Teheran, Iran

University of Tokyo Library
Tokyo, Japan

University of West Indies Library
Kingston, Jamaica

University Library
Cambridge University
Cambridge, England

University of Lancaster
Bailrigg, Lancaster, England

University of Nairobi
Nairobi, Kenya

University of Puerto Rico
Riod Piedras, Puerto Rico

University of Singapore
Singapore

University of Sydney Library
Sydney, Australia

University of Toronto
Toronto, Ontario, Canada

Zentralbibliothek Zürich
Zürich, Switzerland

Index